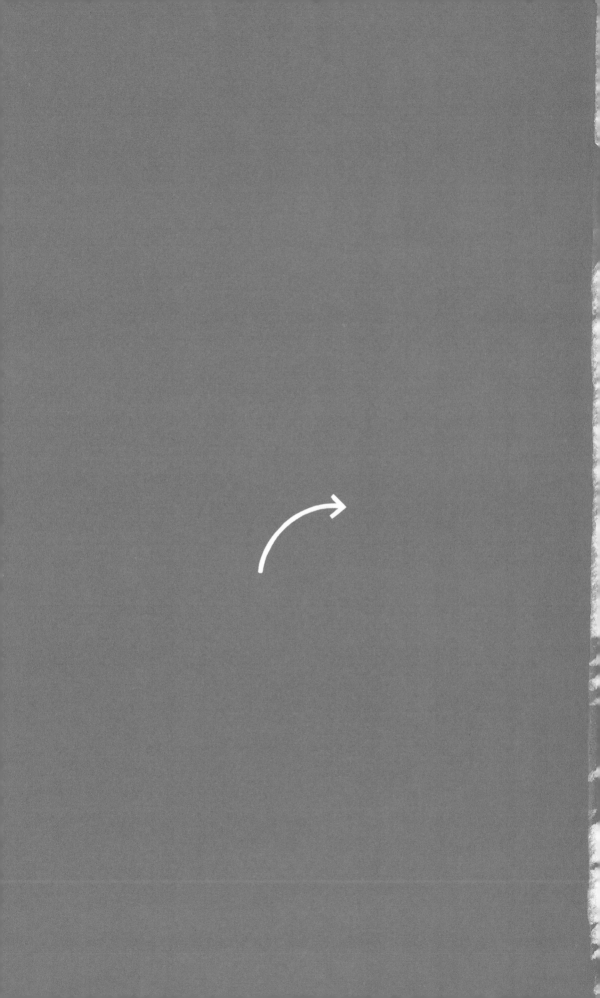

Lateral Cooking

→ One dish leads to another

Lateral Cooking

Niki Segnit

Foreword by Yotam Ottolenghi

Design & illustration by A Practice for Everyday Life

BLOOMSBURY PUBLISHING

NEW YORK · LONDON · OXFORD · NEW DELHI · SYDNEY

"*The New Yorker* magazine ran an interview with a cove called Lemuel Benedict—now that *is* a proper New York name. He took a monster hangover to The Waldorf and ordered hot buttered toast, crisp bacon, two poached eggs and a hooker of hollandaise. The chef was intrigued, substituted English muffin for toast, Canadian bacon (back) for crisp (streaky) and there you are: A legend was born. This is how cooks make food: They see something, taste something, and then tinker with it."
—A.A. GILL, BREAKFAST AT THE WOLSELEY

"When we try to pick out anything by itself, we find it hitched to everything else in the universe."
—JOHN MUIR, MY FIRST SUMMER IN THE SIERRA

Foreword

There is only a handful of books that end up becoming handbooks in my ideal sense of the word: a bound companion I keep on hand, always ready for use; an undisputed, dependable voice of authority on a subject close to my heart. *The Flavor Thesaurus*, Niki Segnit's first book, is my handbook for pairing flavors.

I received my copy from a friend in 2010. After a quick run-through and an initial feeling of awe at the chutzpah of the endeavor, I sat down and read. I read it cover-to-cover and could not believe my luck. Someone had just handed me the equivalent of the Rubik's cube solution booklet I had as a child—only this one held the solution for every kitchen puzzle imaginable!

As a chef and a food writer, my job is to endlessly test flavor combinations. I do this in my head, I do this in saucepans and roasting pans; I do this in soup bowls and glass tumblers; and I do it on the tip of my tongue. *The Flavor Thesaurus* is, really, the only tool that allows me to test some of my assumptions without having to turn on the oven. Will aniseed work with pineapple? Let me ask Niki. Should I add parsnip to my fish stew? I'll just flick through my little handbook here.

Yet what I find immensely gratifying is not the few minutes shaved off aimless straying on the way to a dish, but the sense of encouragement and reassurance that I am on the right track, that my thoughts are reasonable and well-grounded. In her writing, Niki Segnit brings together a towering edifice of cooks, food writers, and experts to inspire the utmost confidence. And even as she presents their weightier points, she makes absolutely sure no one falls asleep. Chuckling away while reading a book about food is not something that happens to me very often; it's a regular occurrence with either of Segnit's books on my lap.

Here's a wonderful example from *Lateral Cooking*: "Broth is a stock with benefits—the ingredients that create it are eaten rather than discarded. *Pot au feu* is a good basic example. It's a 'poem of the French soul,' according to Daniel Boulud, and one that takes a good while to compose. Marlene Dietrich liked to make it in the lulls between scenes. It doesn't, however, require a lot of attention, so there'll be plenty of time to run your lines and pluck your eyebrows." Who wouldn't be seduced by the Boulud-Dietrich-Segnit trio?

The point I am making is serious, though. What is so compelling about the world of Niki Segnit is the way she takes her phenomenal body of work—based, no doubt, on long days spent in reading rooms with heaps of scholarly texts—and then deftly weaves in personal stories and anecdotes. Humor is an essential element, as is the sensuality of eating, lest anyone get the wrong impression about *this* particular thesaurus.

Her distinctively relaxed style, combined with a clever, schematic way of breaking down a vast subject into palatable—though not always bite-sized—pieces is carried through with great panache to *Lateral Cooking*. In the same way as our food experiences were deconstructed in her first book, giving us clarity of the crystally kind and lots of "a-ha" moments, her second book examines our food activities and shows how magically interconnected they all are. By exposing the relatedness of one cooking technique to another, and of one dish to the next, it uncovers the very syntax of cooking.

As a food writer, I have to admit that I am pretty jealous of this achievement. It shows a depth of understanding and a degree of insight that I probably couldn't ever master. But what I am far more resentful of is the fact that Segnit has managed to fulfill one of my deepest, nerdiest fantasies. When writing recipes, I find it almost impossible to accept the moment at which I need to stop testing. It simply kills me every time I'm forced to lay to rest all the variations that haven't been tried, the potential masterpieces that will have eluded me if I don't explore one final option. It's the culinary equivalent of FOMO, the Fear of Missing Out that epitomizes the angst of our age.

Lateral Cooking is devoid of any such anxieties because it is a cookbook full of open-ended recipes. On top of the official version, Segnit offers a bunch of "Leeways," to use her term. These keep the recipes alive; they grant us freedom to experiment, given confidence by the rich toolkit Segnit generously equips us with. So a simple loaf of bread, for example, can have a third of the flour in it replaced with the same weight of warm apple purée—which, when baked, fills the room "with the aroma of apple fritters." Who on earth would be happy with a boring old standard loaf after reading this? And if apples, why not quinces? Or apricots? Or even zucchini?

It takes a person with a particular kind of knowledge to open up a whole load of roads-not-taken for those of us who are keen on going on a journey of exploration: knowing how to write whimsically, cleverly, confidently, and yet modestly; knowing how to cook; knowing how to inform and not bore; knowing how to entertain and tickle; knowing how to enchant and enrapture the imagination. These are the writer's qualities that have brought about another handbook— one for imaginative cooking.

YOTAM OTTOLENGHI

Learning to Cook Sideways

My maternal grandmother cooked everything from scratch and by heart—that is, with an assessing eye, an experienced touch, and absolutely no recourse to written instruction whatsoever. What would she have made of the shelves in my kitchen? There's Anna, Claudia, Delia, Fuchsia, Madhur, Marcella, Nigel, Nigella, and Yotam. There's *The Fruit Book, The Vegetable Book, The Mustard Book, The Yogurt Book,* and *The River Cottage Meat Book.* There's *How to Cook, How to Eat, What to Eat,* and *What to Eat Now.* And yet for years the size of my library was inversely proportional to my confidence in cooking from it. I could cook something a dozen times and still have to dig out the recipe. When I did, I conformed to the image of the Stepford cook: obedient to the point of OCD. If a recipe called for one teaspoon of water, I would lean level with the tap and fill a teaspoon precisely to the brim, discarding it and starting again if the spoon overflowed and left me millimetrically shy of the measure.

In my defense, my grandmother's culinary horizons were narrower than my own. Her repertoire comprised, perhaps, a few dozen classic British dishes, seasonally adapted. What lurked beneath the crust of her crumble depended on what fruit was available: rhubarb stalks from under their upended bucket, or apples from any of the six varieties she grew in her tiny back garden. Over the course of my childhood and adolescence, Indian, Thai, and Chinese food were added to the melting pot of British cuisine, or at least British culinary competence, on top of the French, Italian, and Spanish classics mastered by my mother's generation. Now keen cooks can buy Japanese nori and sushi rolling mats in their local supermarket. Hawaiian *poke* is the big thing this year, apparently. Compared to my gran's homely roll-call of toad in the hole, shepherd's pie, and jam roly-poly, the vastness of today's international repertoire surely inhibits its committal to memory. And in any case, would it be worth it, when you can look up anything online?

My short answer is yes. My long answer is this book.

Lateral Cooking grew out of the experiments with flavor combinations that informed my first book, *The Flavor Thesaurus.* Simply stated, testing whether one ingredient complemented another often called either for the adaptation of a classic dish or the creation of a new one. Putting these borrowed and original recipes to the service of one flavor combination after another, I began to get a feel for the basic formulae that underpinned them. I put them through, essentially, a process of reverse engineering—adapting or inventing a dish, then stripping it down until I had the starting point for all the other flavor combinations I wanted to try.

↓

As my folder of starting points grew stout, I began to write down quantities for different dishes and portion sizes, and opportunities for leeway—that is, workable substitutions when certain ingredients weren't available, or interesting variations I'd either come across in my reading or thought up myself. Eventually I realized not only that I was referring to my tattered manila folder more than any of the cookbooks on my shelf, but also that I was beginning not to refer to the folder either. I was learning to cook by a combination of memory and instinct, like my grandmother.

Bread, for example. In the old days I'd select a book from my shelf, depending on what sort of instruction suited my mood. Homey yet bracingly strict? Traditionalist? Modernist? Terroir-fixated ethico-sensualist? No wonder I never quite figured out what the common denominators were. I was too busy worrying about the provenance of my sorghum flour, or whether a Gruyère and walnut fougasse hatched in a walled garden in Wales could possibly taste the same baked in a dodgy old oven off the Euston Road in London. But after identifying a standard starting point for bread—and bread has one of the most standard—I had, within a couple of loaves, weaned myself from reference to the method. A few more, and the proportions of flour, water, yeast, salt, and sugar were committed to memory. At the same time, I became accustomed to the feeling of dough on the fingers, its demands for more flour or water, and the point when the gluten has stretched and you feel the consistency change, subtly but unmistakably, like the day summer shades into autumn.

↓

The basis of *Lateral Cooking*, then, is a set of starting points, which, once you're familiar with them, will prove almost infinitely adaptable, according to whatever is in your fridge, in season, on offer at the market, or you feel like making. With any luck, the starting points will help you become the kind of cook I've always wanted to be— the kind that can tug down a bowl and get cracking on a dish whose precise quantities and combination of ingredients might vary each time I made it. An instinctive cook, in short.

With such memorability in mind, I have erred on the side of simplicity in the starting-point recipes. There will be fancier ways to make a loaf, or a stock, or a mayonnaise, and I make no claims that my methods represent any sort of ideal. What they do represent, I hope, is a set of basic preparations that it's up to you to elaborate, to particularize, to make your own. Each of them has been rigorously tested, but part of the point of *Lateral Cooking* is to encourage experiment, and experiments, as the post-Stepford cook in me is happier to accept, can and will go wrong. All I can say is that an openness to error is a prerequisite of the freer approach to cooking that I hope the book might inspire.

My work on *The Flavor Thesaurus* has left me with a permanently flavor-orientated cast of mind, which leads to the second major element of *Lateral Cooking*—a range of flavoring options for each of its starting points. So many classic dishes are, at heart, flavor variations on a common theme that it seemed natural to progress from the basic method to the adjustments in flavor that turn a béchamel, for example, into a Mornay sauce or a soubise. In addition to the classics, I've also grouped more loosely related flavor variations together. For instance, following the starting point for *fesenjan*, the Persian stew typically made with crushed walnuts and pomegranate molasses, you'll find other nut-based stews like korma, African *mafe*, Georgian *satsivi*, and Peruvian *aji de gallina*, all of which have ingredients in common and similar methods. Try a few of these lovely stews, and you'll soon be squirreling through your kitchen cupboards for nuts to create your own take on them.

Then there are the more obscure, non-traditional, and even counter-intuitive suggestions. For these I've trawled the ideas of chefs and food writers, past and present, as well as devising a few of my own. Granted, sometimes only vanilla will do, but no lover of ice cream should rest until they've tried the olive oil variety that I first sampled in Ronda, or the sweet and sour cream-cheese ice cream devised by Alain Ducasse. The Japanese flavor their ice cream with sesame. My current favorite is lemon, made by a method so simple it requires neither a custard base nor any churning.

As to original flavoring ideas, I hope the fun I've had departing from the classics demonstrates how a grounding in the basic principles can free you up to follow your own chains of association. Researching custard, for example, I came across a Greek dish, *galaktoboureko*, which, despite sounding like something from the Death Star canteen, turned out to be a very homey hybrid of a napoleon and baklava— more specifically, a lemon- (or vanilla-, or cinnamon-) flavored custard, sandwiched between layers of phyllo pastry, drizzled with a sugar syrup flavored with orange, brandy, or ouzo, and finished with a shake of confectioners' sugar. I had some phyllo pastry, and some pastis that could stand in for ouzo. But which flavor to try for the custard? Vanilla was too vanilla. Lemon sounded nice. But then my mind turned to coconut. I have had a thing about coconut tarts since, aged seven, I first read Clement Freud's *Grimble* ("The tart... was the best thing he had eaten since the corned beef and apricot jam sandwich"), and begged my mother to make me one. The idea of crunchy flakes of phyllo against a trembling coconut-flavored custard reawakened that early yearning. What if I set off the creamy sweetness with a sharp lime-flavored syrup? Or warmed it with cinnamon? Or spiced rum? I was straying a long way from Greece, but not so far from the essence of the original that the results failed simultaneously to honor it and to embody something new. (I went with the coconut and lime. It was out of this world: galaktically good.)

I always find it frustrating when I follow a recipe that sounds terrific on paper, only to find its supposedly dominant flavors smothered by something stronger. Likewise, I've bought far too many flavored chocolate bars, in snazzy wrappers with prices to match, that amount to little more than chocolate with a curious aftertaste. All the flavoring options in *Lateral Cooking* have been tried and tested—both for their deliciousness and, (slightly) less subjectively, to ensure the flavor in question is detectable in the finished dish. Today's cooks have a stupendous variety of inexpensive aromatics at their disposal—so if you're going to use them, I say do it conspicuously.

↓

The idea that the individual starting points might lie on a continuum, linking one with the next, came to me as I started to put the contents of my manila folder into order. Organizing the starting points like this, I felt, would make learning to cook by heart that much easier, especially if I could, wherever possible, keep quantities and methods consistent. Take the nuts continuum, for example. Marzipan can be nothing more than a mixture of equal weights of ground almonds and sugar with just enough egg white to bring them together. Macaroons, the next point on the continuum, simply call for more egg white, which is beaten with the sugar before the ground almonds are folded in; as with marzipan, equal weights of sugar and ground almonds are used. Use the whole egg, rather than just the white, and you have the batter for Santiago cake (add whole oranges and baking powder to make Claudia Roden's famous variation on it). Add the same weight of butter as sugar and almonds for frangipane—and so on, through the linked sequence of nut dishes, to end at the Persian nut stew *fesenjan*.

In my steady transformation from recipe-dependent to ingredient-led cook, I've found that I've become less wasteful, since I have more ideas for cooking whatever is to hand. Furthermore, developing an understanding of the *relationship* between recipes has made me more resourceful in the kitchen. If you're planning to serve fresh popovers with scrambled eggs for lunch, make some extra batter, add a little water, and you're halfway to Crêpes Suzette for supper. Or loosen the batter with milk to make *crespelle*, which can be stuffed with ricotta and spinach for a meat-free Monday supper. If you're whipping up a chocolate tart for a dinner party, and have some ganache left over, you could divide it into batches, flavor one with cardamom and one with *poire* eau-de-vie, or whatever flavoring strikes your fancy, then roll into truffles. Or, add more cream to make a versatile chocolate sauce. It never hurts to have a jug of chocolate sauce in the fridge.

Catch on to the family relationship between dishes, both in terms of ingredients and techniques, and you realize how certain preparations you'd thought were outside your experience are, in fact, reassuringly similar to dishes you've made a dozen times before. How could I have shied from trying my own tortillas when I routinely made chapatis? Once I'd started building on my chapati experience to make my own tortillas, an ancillary benefit of expanded *technique* became apparent— in this case, getting better at rolling. Soon I could roll fresh tagliatelle for two faster by hand than it took me to locate, dust, assemble, use, dismantle, and wash up my pasta machine. It's a question of confidence, ultimately. Nail the daily loaf and brioche feels like less of a challenge.

None of this is to cock a snook at recipes. I still get lost in cookbooks, old and new, and tear recipes out of magazines and paste them in my scrapbook. It's just that now I can't read a recipe without wondering whether, at base, it boils down to one of the starting points collected in this book. If it doesn't, I make a note. I have some exploring to do.

↓

SOME GENERAL ADVICE FOR THE LATERAL COOK

The first thing I would say is: Cook. A lot. The Internet in its abysmal depths makes it easy, and all too tempting, to subsume yourself in theory. But there's no replacement for practice, and plenty of it. Creating your own version of a dish is a case of trial and error—you'll need to make it several times to get it right. Make notes along the way. Too often I've soldiered on, confident I'll remember the ingredients I used to tweak a dish one way or another, only to find myself racking my brains the following day. Last year, the precise makeup of my improvised and much-lauded Christmas fruitcake went unrecorded, and this year's wasn't half as good, haunted as it was by the Cake of Christmas Past.

The second: Practice self-forgiveness. Once in a while your first attempt at a dish will turn out brilliantly, but more often, bracing yourself as you remove your chocolate Genoise from the oven, you'll be faced with the stark reality of human imperfection. And this is as it should be. That first mutant crêpe died so its successors could live. Experiencing the process of cooking a dish is an indispensable part of understanding it, and, naturally, you can't adapt something to your own tastes until you know what it is you're adapting.

Third: Blame your tools. Variations in cookware, utensils, appliances, room temperature, and the side of bed you got out of can all have unpredictable effects on your cooking. Ovens are notoriously capricious. There's a good article on Slate.com called "Ignore Your Oven Dial" that I recommend you read. The best you can do, it would seem, is to use an oven thermometer to check how accurately the temperature knob accords with reality. Accept that domestic-oven controls are approximate and you'll start to rely more on your senses to judge whether something is cooked.

↓

The book is divided into twelve chapters, or continuums. Each one begins with a short essay about the dishes the continuum comprises, and how those dishes are connected. The rest of the chapter is divided between "starting points"—giving a basic recipe for each dish and a "Leeway" section detailing possible adaptations and substitutions— and "Flavors & Variations," describing the many directions a dish can be taken in, and hopefully providing some inspiration for your own experiments. Where useful, there's also a pictorial section for further stimulus.

I have tried to make clear distinctions between "authentic" recipes and various in-the-vein-of approximations, but I fully accept some instances may be arguable. Even for the simplest of dishes there are squabbles, if not to say armed confrontations, over what constitutes the real thing. Note also that the starting-point recipes are not conventionally laid out. For example, oven temperatures and directions for preparing pans are not given at the outset—so it's essential that you read the recipes through at least once before starting to cook.

Once you get to know the starting points—or your personalized versions of them—you can use them to "read" the recipes in other cookbooks and magazines. For example, with the starting point for custard in mind, you can judge pretty accurately whether other versions are likely to be too sweet or too rich for your taste.

Likewise, you might use the tips in the Leeway sections of this book to adapt comparable recipes you find elsewhere. I'm not promising that it will always work; nor should the results be attributed to the originator of the recipe in question. But if you're short of a stipulated egg, or a carton of buttermilk, the wriggle room laid out in the Leeways may prove helpful, if only to save you from the hell of the online cooking forum, where the most innocent, practical question can quickly devolve into a vicious and dogmatic scrap.

Some of the given Flavors & Variations are entirely consistent with the starting points. Others deviate, to a degree, in their ingredients, proportions, or methods, and are included more to demonstrate how departures from the starting point can achieve a similar end. Where a starting point is split between two or more preparations, such as flatbreads and crackers, some of the Flavors & Variations will be for one preparation or the other: It will be clear from the context which is which. That said, the vast majority of starting-point flavorings will be applicable to all the preparations. Further, in many of the continuums, flavors categorized under one starting point can be applied pretty freely to the others.

Where, in the name of clarity, I've picked an example flavor for a starting point—strawberry in the case of sorbet, for instance—note that the Flavors & Variations will apply to sorbets in general, rather than strawberry in particular. In most instances the Leeway will likewise apply to the general principle rather than any specified flavor.

Please exercise common sense when it comes to hygiene and the risk of food poisoning. Keep your hands and equipment clean at all times. Familiarize yourself with the ingredients that need to be cooked through before serving. If you're unsure what constitutes "cooked," a digital thermometer, and the temperature guides it invariably comes with, will prove very handy. Learn which ingredients need to be kept refrigerated, and cool cooked foods as quickly as possible, especially in the case of rice, meat, seafood, eggs, and dairy products.

↓

SOME NOTES ON MEASURES AND INGREDIENTS

VOLUME VERSUS WEIGHT This book is an adaptation of the U.K. metric edition. The translation into American measurements has not been literal, the main objective being to keep the starting points memorable, and their reiterations in the Flavors & Variations sections as clear as possible. It's been an interesting exercise. Europeans are sometimes sniffy about the American measurement system, especially as the received wisdom has taken hold that everything, especially baking ingredients, needs to be weighed to the last milligram. I'm not so sure that's true, at least in domestic kitchens. Americans have been baking with volume measurements for generations, and have no shortage of great bakers, or excellent baking books reliant on the cup. That said, if you're aiming at greater improvisation in the kitchen, partly by committing recipes to memory, weight ratios often do have an advantage over volume. Pound cake is the classic example: It calls for equal weights of each ingredient. Which is a cake-walk to remember compared to 1⅔ cups of flour, scant 1 cup of butter, 1 cup of sugar, and 3–4 eggs. For this reason, and because there are a fair number of cooks in the States who work with both systems, I refer to these weight-based rules when I think they'll be useful or interesting.

BAKING SODA Not interchangeable with baking powder. Baking soda needs acidic ingredients (buttermilk, brown sugar, molasses) to activate it. Use too much in a cake or bread and it will create a soapy or metallic taste. Baking powder, for its part, is a mixture of baking soda and an acidic activator.

BUTTER Use unsalted so you can salt to taste. Salted is fine if you're only using a few tablespoons in a bread dough or a batter.

COOKING OIL I often call for a bland oil, by which I mean peanut, corn, grapeseed, canola, or vegetable. Sunflower too, although I know that for health reasons many people prefer not to heat it.

EGGS Assume either large or extra large, unless one or the other is stated. A large egg in the U.S. weighs about 57g, extra large 64g.

MIREPOIX A fancy name for the mixture of diced onion, carrot, and celery used as a base in many recipes.

OVEN TEMPERATURES I use a fan oven (also called a fan-assisted or convection oven). If you have a conventional oven you will need to increase the oven temperatures given in the recipes by about 25°F.

SEASONING For the most part I don't mention when and if to add black pepper—that's up to you. As for salt, the levels I recommend are to my taste, which you may find on the low side. This book would be considerably saltier if my husband had written it.

↓

DEEP-FRYING WITHOUT A DEEP FRYER

Use a pan no more than one third full of oil: Oils with a high smoke point, such as peanut, corn, or canola oil, are particularly good for deep-frying. Lard is another option. Some cooks like to use a wok, but only do this if yours is stable on the burner. If your pan has a handle, keep it pointing toward the center of the stovetop, where it's less likely to be knocked. Keep any children or pets well out of the way, and never leave hot oil unattended. Have the lid of the pan close at hand to cover the pan immediately if it catches fire. If not the lid, use a baking sheet or a kitchen fire extinguisher. Never throw water on an oil fire.

Heat the oil over a medium heat, uncovered. Check the temperature with a deep-fry thermometer: You're aiming for 350–375°F. If you don't have a thermometer, use a cube of dry-ish bread, which should turn golden brown in 10–15 seconds. Alternatively, if you're frying battered ingredients, a drop of batter should sink, then immediately rise to the surface and start to sizzle and color. Wet food will make the hot oil splutter, so dry it as best you can before frying. Be careful not to drop ingredients into the oil, as it will splash; use tongs or a strainer to lower them in instead. Fry in batches to avoid crowding the pan and lowering the temperature of the oil. In between batches, bring the oil back to optimum heat and skim off any debris. If the oil starts to smoke at any stage, remove it from the heat immediately and let it cool.

Once the ingredients are cooked, remove them to a tray or plate lined with paper towels to soak up excess fat. If necessary, keep them warm in a low oven until you're ready to serve. When you're finished with the oil, let it cool completely before straining it into a jug, then funnel it back into the bottle; discard your deep-frying oil if it starts to taste rancid or takes on any unwanted flavors.

Bread

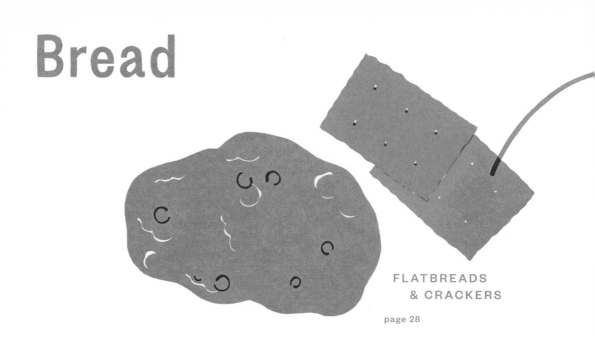

**FLATBREADS
& CRACKERS**

page 28

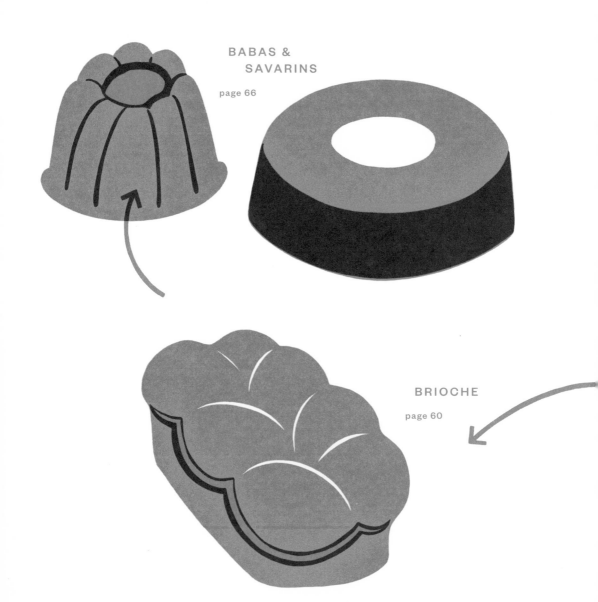

**BABAS &
SAVARINS**

page 66

BRIOCHE

page 60

Toward the end of a month-long road trip from Louisiana to Nevada, I started to miss my kitchen. I could be found trailing around vast grocery stores, deterred from buying steak or fish or vegetables for want of anywhere to cook them, with so few items in my shopping cart that I became convinced the store detective was tailing me. Most often I would end up buying canisters of dried herbs or interesting spice mixes. This, of course, created its own set of problems at the airport. Plump, transparent packets of brownish-green plant matter are not designed to smooth your passage through security.

My notebooks were as crammed as my suitcase. Scribbled sketches and descriptions, some legible, of ideas collected en route: twenty-layer lasagne, barrel-fermented cocktails, kimchi *croque monsieur*, a *tres leches* cake I'd eaten in the Sonoran Desert and was itching to adapt. And what did I do with this spirit of culinary adventurism on my return home to London? Make bread. Not green olive and amaranth seed *dampfnudel*. Just ordinary brown bread, plain and good and familiar.

For I had opened the front door of my flat to find a strange smell. My mind riffled through its olfactory index cards and came up with Essaouira, a windswept, salt-caked city on the Atlantic Coast of Morocco where they make backgammon sets and pen-holders and other sundry tourist tat from thuya, a local wood famous for its pungency. Something was clearly wrong.

Usually when unoccupied for a few days the flat developed a cold, bland aroma, like refrigerated pastry. Not a street bazaar in North Africa. There had been a leak from the flat above and the smell was coming from water-swollen floorboards. I rolled up my sleeves, fetched down a bowl, and made bread. In this respect, at least, real estate agents are right. There is nothing so redolent of warmth, shelter, and comfort as the smell of browning flour and yeast. It did more than mask the reek of rotting floorboards; it reestablished our residence.

I made a lot of bread during the months it took to sort out the insurance, by which time the habit was ingrained to the extent that I've hardly bought a loaf since. A direct result of unforeseeable water damage, my breadmaking habit can thus be considered an act of God. Yeast-leavened bread is one of the easiest recipes to learn by heart—four basic ingredients combined in more-or-less standard proportions and by a simple method. It is also highly amenable to experimentation.

As to the method, you will within a few loaves have a feel for the right texture and know how to recognize the moment when the dough is sufficiently worked. That's not to say I have it down pat. My hands lack the strength the master baker needs to pull and twist and truly dominate the dough. In my case, it's a pretty even match. Perfect or not, my homemade efforts are consistently good, and far cheaper than the loaves in the local fancy bakery. Of the hundreds I have made, only one tasted terrible (because I used truffle oil—I know, I know). And a few have fallen short of the ideal rise. My father-in-law's six-year-old sachet of instant dry yeast can take the rap for one of these, but the others were mostly the result of using water that was too hot for the yeast. Nonetheless, toasted and spread generously with smoked salmon pâté, even the dinkiest slices can look rather elegant, and you can always tell your guests you custom-baked the loaf for canapés.

Once you develop the breadmaking habit, the experimental phase will soon follow. There are so many ways of adapting the basic recipe: replacing the water with beer, milk, hard cider, wine, or fruit juice; using different combinations of flours; adding nuts, seeds, or dried fruit. Starting with small quantities of dough is a good idea when experimenting with more outlandish flavors. Bread proportions are easy to scale, and it can be enjoyable to knead a small amount with one hand—so much so that one day I lost myself and made fourteen small mounds of dough, leaving them to rise on every available surface in the kitchen. Returning about an hour later, it was like walking into a breast-implant showroom.

To make a simple loaf, use 4 cups white bread flour, 1¼ cups warm water, 2 tsp instant yeast, and 1 tsp salt. To this you might add oil, or a little butter, and 1–2 tbsp of sugar to enrich and develop the flavor. Understand that this is in no way *my* recipe. It's very much the standard, and is therefore worth committing to memory. This proportion of flour to liquid applies to all but one of the starting points on the bread continuum, making it easier to gauge the practical differences made by the tweaks and variations in ingredients along the way, and to help develop an understanding of what might happen when you make a change. It won't be long before you can make a huge range of breads by heart.

F L A T B R E A D S And so to the first starting point on the bread continuum: unleavened flatbreads and crackers. Making this sort of dough is a simple matter of adding enough warm water to flour to make a unified mass that feels nice to knead. You don't really need a recipe at all, but it's not a bad idea to follow the basic bread proportions above, leaving out the yeast. It may be that you need to add a little extra liquid to bring all the flour into the dough, especially when using whole wheat flour, say for chapatis. Brown flour is thirstier than white. Begin with our starting point, adding the liquid in small increments until your dough hits the sweet spot of springy firmness between dry and sticky.
A water spritzer will be your friend here. If you overshoot on the liquid, add more flour. Once it feels right, knead for a few minutes, then let rest (covered or wrapped) at room temperature for half an hour before rolling out. Seasoned chapati-wallahs can turn a ball of dough into a disk ready for the pan without a rolling pin, using the sort of glancing slaps of the hands with which the rest of us might rid our palms of excess flour.

This most basic of recipes—flour, salt, and water—comes in a surprising number of variations. Chapati dough is made with atta, a soft whole wheat flour that is also used to make flaky parathas and puffed puris. You can try all three of these breads—distinguished by their different finishing techniques—with just one batch of dough (see pages 29 and 34). Made with maida, a soft white flour, the same dough yields a bread called luchi and a sweetened version of the same, which can be rolled extra-thin to make the pancakes served with Peking duck. Tortillas are made in a similar way, either with wheat flour or a treated cornmeal called masa harina, and sometimes a little lard. It's worth noting that both cornmeal and masa harina make for a considerably stickier dough.

CRACKERS Several varieties of cracker share the starting point with flatbreads, but the dough is rolled, cut, and then baked, rather than being cooked on the stovetop. Jewish matzo crackers are made with white flour, and olive oil is added to the dough in such quantities that you'll need to ease up on the water a bit. Like soda crackers, matzo are pricked all over with a fork, to prevent them from buckling in the dry heat of the oven. You'll also find oatcakes and charcoal crackers in the Flavors & Variations section, alongside the Japanese buckwheat noodles *ni-hachi* soba. Pasta dough, that is the sort without egg, can be made with an identical mixture of flour, oil, and warm water. The difference is in the length of the knead—about 10 minutes, before its 30-minute rest at room temperature.

The addition of just a small amount of a chemical leavening agent— i.e. baking soda or baking powder—to the same ingredients can make a disproportionate difference. This extremely versatile starting point is next on the continuum. The finished leavened bread will have a more honeycombed, spongy texture, as in a slightly puffier flatbread, or something more suited to a classic cheese sandwich.

SODA BREAD If it *is* a sliceable bread you're after, but time is of the essence, a soda bread is hard to beat. As Elizabeth David observes, this quick bread calls for a light hand and no patience—the opposite of the qualities demanded by its yeast-risen equivalent. "Everybody who cooks, in however limited a way, should know how to make a loaf of soda bread," she says. Apply the general flour-to-liquid ratio, working with 2 cups all-purpose flour and ⅔ cup buttermilk (or any of the similarly acidic liquid alternatives listed under Leeway), ½ tsp salt, and ½ tsp baking soda. As with unleavened and yeast breads, a little fat and sugar can be added. If I need a loaf in a hurry, I make a soda bread with atta, the very fine whole wheat flour used for chapatis, and add an egg. It may not be quite what you might find on an Irish farmhouse table, but it's my favorite of the many versions of soda bread I've tried. In Ireland, the sweetened soda bread called Spotted Dog is made with dried fruit. A Tennessean might well be tempted to call it a biscuit with benefits.

Biscuits are made from the same starting point as soda bread, but here the butter is mandatory. Rub in 2–3 tbsp per 2 cups flour. For fruited biscuits (a.k.a. scones), it is standard to add 2–4 tbsp sugar, and common to throw in a handful of dried fruit and some vanilla extract. In the U.K., both the plain and the sweet biscuits are known as scones, and are served with jam and cream. As an ingénue in Atlanta, I kept seeing roadside ads for biscuits and gravy that conjured images of chocolate cookies floating in beefy broth. Each to their own, I thought, until a native Georgian ordered me a plate of biscuits smothered in thick, peppery gravy and I quickly saw the point.

My mother makes her biscuits with baking powder. When I first tasted the kind made with baking soda I wasn't convinced. Soda can have a distinctly unappetizing, alkaline, metallic/soapy character. Add too much, and it can give your baked treat a whiff of a fresh-fish market being scrubbed down with bleach at the close of business. Used judiciously, however, it can lend your biscuits a crisp clarity of flavor that makes the most wonderful contrast to the fatty indulgence of clotted cream or butter. A hint of soda is notably compatible with cured foods, as in the pairing, native to the Deep South, of biscuits with country ham, or the unbeatable Irish combination of soda bread and smoked salmon.

The same dough is used to make cobbler—a fruit compote (or a meat stew) paved with what might be described as shallow biscuits that is baked in the oven. It's a shortcut to the ample satisfactions of a pie. This starting point not only furnishes a quick bread, but a quick pastry; where pie pastries need to be rested in the fridge before cooking, biscuit dough is best used as soon as it is mixed. You don't even need to roll it out. Simply place spoonfuls on top of whatever it is you're cobbling, and bake.

YEAST-RISEN A yeasted loaf, on the other hand, is by necessity a slow business. Even made with instant yeast, which only requires one rise, and with a nice warm corner ready for the rise to take place, it will still be a good hour and a half until your bread is baked. And most people would agree it's best left for a few hours after it emerges from the oven. The advantage of making bread regularly, as I have since my ceiling nearly caved in, is that you soon get the hang of how to fit it into your schedule. It might never be quick. But you can make it convenient. Very little of the process is hands-on. Our starting point requires 12–15 minutes of your time, then a break for an hour or so (during which you can wring out your paperbacks and wash down your walls with mold-remover), then a few more minutes of activity before the bread has a second rise (or proves) and then heads into the oven for approximately half an hour.

If it suits you better, you can always slow the process by letting the dough rise in the fridge. Most seasoned breadmakers concur that a stately rise improves the flavor. One Friday evening, I mixed up a basic dough in between applying layers of eyeliner, then left it to rise while I went to the pub. The next morning, opening the fridge to fetch bacon and butter for breakfast, I found two beautiful loaves plump in their pans and ready for the oven, as if prepped by culinary elves, even if my husband spoiled the magic by reminding me that I'd shaped the dough and put it in the pans before falling into bed.

I must have had one wine too many, as my original plan had been to make one loaf and use the remaining dough for pizzas and a tray of *fatayer*, a triangular Arab pie filled with lamb, spinach, or cheese. This basic bread dough is amazingly versatile. It can be shaped into rings and risen, then boiled and baked to make bagels. Knead in a little extra oil to make focaccia: Roll it into a rectangle, let it rise, pucker it all over like a chesterfield sofa, add your preferred toppings, and bake. Breadsticks (grissini), bread soup bowls, and even pies can all be made using the same dough. It's almost always worth making a large amount if you have space to store it. Start with 8 cups of flour and work from there.

If you've never made your own croissants, try taking some spare dough and laminating it. Lamination, or layering, is the process used to turn plain old pastry dough into multileaved puff. The process is as simple as laying a rectangle of cold butter over the dough, then rolling and folding it several times. Once the lamination is done, the dough is rolled out before being cut into triangles that can be rolled up into the classic crescent shape, or rectangles that can be folded into *pains au chocolat* or *pains au raisin*.

Before moving along the continuum, it's worth noting that there are two important alternative approaches to yeast-risen bread. The first is the sponge method. This involves making a batter using the yeast, warm water, and some of the flour, and leaving it, if possible overnight, to bubble into a tasty mulch before the rest of the ingredients are added, and the dough is risen and baked in the usual way. You'll find details of the sponge method on page 46. If time is no object, it's definitely the way to go, because the slower fermentation creates a greater depth of flavor.

If time is *really* no object—if you're prepared to wait the days it takes for natural yeasts to grow—you should consider making a starter, or "mother," for sourdough bread. Sourdough starter is made by mixing up flour and water. Regularly "feeding" it with fresh flour and water will, with luck, generate a naturally yeasted, highly flavored batter that will eventually be strong enough to leaven a loaf. Making bread this way is an undertaking, but an enjoyable one, and once you've caught the breadmaking bug it's next to inevitable you'll be tempted to make sourdough. I've had mixed results over the years. More than once I have found my mother too weak to leaven a loaf; even when it works,

I can find the sourness excessive, as if I've added too much ascorbic acid powder. In *Tartine Bread*, surfer-baker Chad Robertson lays out his technique (extending to over twenty-six pages) for a sourdough loaf that is at once highly flavorful and not particularly sour, which is the way I think it should be. So much of the artisanal sourdough you find in hipster bakeries is confrontationally sour, like your woebegone friend who thinks it's a hoot to be negative about everything.

B
U
N
S

A small tweak takes us from yeast-risen bread to buns—fruited buns, hot dog buns, and burger buns. These soft, fluffy breads use mildly enriched dough, made by replacing some or all of the water with milk, adding an egg, and a little butter and sugar too. Throw in a handful of raisins and pumpkin-pie spice if you want to make tea cakes. An unsurprising consequence of adding another liquid ingredient (egg) is that the dough can be quite sticky. You'll be glad of a dough hook attachment for your electric mixer, or at the very least some plastic gloves if you're mixing by hand.

B
R
I
O
C
H
E

In *The Art of French Baking*, Ginette Mathiot gives a recipe for "poor man's brioche," which on close inspection differs little from our starting point for buns. Bona-fide brioche dough is nothing but bun dough with a lot more egg and a lot more butter. As you might imagine, the quantities of egg and butter render the usual binding agents, milk or water, mostly redundant. Nonetheless, the quantities are consistent with our starting point for yeast-risen bread. Our brioche calls for 5 eggs. The content of an extra large egg is about 3¼ tbsp, so 5 eggs makes almost a cup. Add to this the ¼ cup or so water or milk used to activate the yeast, and there it is again: the standard 1¼ cups of liquid to 4 cups flour. The result is a kneadable dough. To this, however, you need to work in the butter. The standard amount is half a stick of butter for every cup of flour, the same as for shortcrust pastry. (Your dough can, in fact, be used as a pastry—roll it out to make a tart shell, or wrap it around sausages for saucisson brioche.) So for a dough containing 4 cups of flour, you'll have to incorporate 2 sticks of butter. For this reason, most recipes recommend making brioche in a stand mixer, or failing that, either using a hand-held electric mixer fitted with dough hooks or a food processor. Failing *that*, there'll be nothing for it other than to do it the hard way. Roll your sleeves up, put on some mood music, and work until the butter becomes one with the dough. Even if you don't enjoy the sensation, take heart from the fact that your hands will be soft for a few days.

As any pastrymaker will know, butter prevents the gluten strands in flour from lengthening, which is the desired effect when making shortcrust, and very much not the desired effect when making bread. Furthermore, butter is no friend to yeast, and neither is egg. It's for these reasons that, among breads, brioche is the trickiest. The most common problem is that it fails to rise much, or as quickly as you expected (even though the generous quantity of egg will have some leavening effect). The most common solution is patience. Making brioche can easily take three times longer than you have been led to expect.

The large amount of egg white in brioche also makes it vulnerable to drying out during the baking process. Some *briochiers* avoid this by replacing an egg white or two with yolk. Even so, it should be noted that homemade brioche does not enjoy the same shelf-life as the supermarket variety. Make sure there's room in the freezer for any brioche not consumed within 48 hours, or put stale remainders to good use as French toast; in bread pudding; or simply sliced and toasted, then drizzled with syrup and served with cream. Use a rum syrup and you'll have something approaching a low-rise rum baba.

B A B A S   Babas and savarins are the next starting point along the
&   continuum. Take a bite before pouring on the syrup and you'll note
&   that the bun is quite dry. Its destiny, however, is to be so soused in
s   rum that it becomes, in effect, an after-dinner drink with a dessert
A   in it. According to Elena Molokhovets, it was traditional to give babas
v   three rises, but most modern recipes stipulate two, and some, as in
A   this book, only one rise. There are even versions that dispense with
R   yeast in favor of baking powder, like the baba in *The Art of French*
I   *Baking*. The baba mixture in our starting point is at the wetter end
N   of the spectrum—instead of replacing most of the water or milk with
s   eggs, as in brioche, I use them in addition: ⅔ cup milk and 3 eggs for
s   2 cups flour. The result is closer to a thick batter than a dough.

According to culinary historian Richard Foss, the French flavored their babas with brandy until 1835, when a Parisian pâtisserie switched allegiance to rum, thereby bringing the idea to the attention of chefs. It was, however, the ring mold, invented in 1844, that won the rum baba its continental fame. Alain Ducasse serves his baba in the alternative classic shape, akin to a stout-stalked, small-capped porcini mushroom, presented on a gleaming silver dish. The waiter splits the baba from cap to foot and offers a choice of six premium rums, giving tasting notes for each, before finishing off the dish with Chantilly cream.

In contrast to the neat rum used by Ducasse, most recipes call for (a more economical) sugar syrup laced with rum. Elena Molokhovets says this should be "sweet but watery." I'm not so keen. The classic rum baba is too close to the proverbial cake left out in the rain. I prefer the denser sweetness of gulab jamun and baklava, each bite exuding a sweetness as sticky as a romantic novel. For this reason, I make my rum syrup with a 3:2 sugar-to-water ratio, as opposed to the standard parity. Many recipes recommend cooking the rum with the sugar syrup. Unless you're about to operate heavy machinery or treat a subdural hematoma, this is a terrible idea. To cook the rum is to drive off its flavor molecules, leaving the good stuff tasting cheap and the cheap stuff tasting like bad vanilla flavoring. If you do want to restrict the amount of alcohol in your syrup, far better to add a teeny amount of raw rum to a sugar syrup flavored with a vanilla bean. Alcohol content can also be reduced by replacing the rum with liqueur, most of which contain about half the ABV. Crème de cacao and Kahlúa are excellent candidates if you plan to garnish your baba with cream. If fruit is involved, try Amaretto. You might alternatively consult a cocktail book like *Death & Co*, or, for nonalcoholic inspiration, the syrup Flavors & Variations section on pages [434-8].

In some recipes the baba itself is embellished. Russian babkas are often flavored with lemon zest or almond. Currants, soaked in more rum, or kirsch, are popular too, and may be augmented with grated citrus zest and diced candied peel, like a miniaturized panettone. Obviously, whatever cake flavoring you choose should complement the flavor of your syrup, and vice versa.

You may have noted that the mixtures along the continuum have been getting steadily wetter, from unleavened bread, dry enough to roll very thinly, through yeasted bread and tacky bun dough to buttery brioche and batter-like baba. As a rule, they get richer, too. At the heart is the same basic idea: 1¼ cups liquid to 4 cups flour, which makes them pretty easy to commit to memory. Ruined floorboards or no, you'll soon be able to fetch a bowl, grab the ingredients, and get on with it. The reward is in the eating, and the sharing. Good fresh bread is irresistible to all but the stoniest-hearted devotee of low carbs.

Flatbreads & Crackers

A versatile starting point that can be used to make a dough for all sorts of flatbreads, including chapatis and tortillas. Make a few batches, and you'll see why people in India and Mexico bother to make their own. Don't feel restricted to their cuisine of origin. Fresh flatbreads are excellent with thick soups, bean stews, and for quesadilla-style sandwiches. The same dough can be boiled to make noodles (see buckwheat, page [30]) and baked for crackers.

For 8 (7-in) round flatbreads, or 16 (3-in) round crackers

INGREDIENTS
2 cups all-purpose flour [A] [B]
1 tsp salt
⅔ cup warm water [C] [D]
1–2 tbsp fat—optional

1. Sift the flour and salt into a bowl, make a well in the center, and add the warm water. Mix to a dough using a spoon, your hand, or both. Add a little more flour or water as necessary to create a soft dough that's not too sticky.
   The water needs to be warm to make the dough more sticky and cohesive. For a richer, more supple dough, 1–2 tbsp oil or melted butter or lard can be added to the water. Or rub *solid* fat into the flour until it's all but vanished, then add the water.

2. Knead the dough for 1–2 minutes until smooth.

3. Cover the kneaded dough with a clean dish towel and let it rest for 30 minutes. If making crackers, wrap in plastic wrap and leave in the fridge for 30 minutes to firm up, so the dough can be rolled out and cut into defined shapes.

   FOR FLATBREADS
   Divide the dough into 8 evenly sized pieces, then roll into balls. With a rolling pin, roll out each ball to a rough circle, about ⅛ in thick. Cook the breads on a hot, unoiled skillet or griddle pan until brown and spotted on one side. Then flip and aim for the same on the other. Keep the cooked breads wrapped up warm while you finish the rest.
   You can use flour when rolling out, but it could make the bread a bit dry. A lightly oiled surface is preferable. Turn the circle like a steering wheel every now and then, and flip it over a couple of times, too. Keep any unused dough covered to prevent it from drying out. To optimize the

cooked bread's flavor, brush it with a little melted butter or ghee while hot, and give it a modest sprinkle of salt. The bread is best eaten soon after it's cooked. Raw dough can be stored in the fridge for a few days.

FOR CRACKERS

Roll out the chilled dough to ⅛-in thickness, then cut into crackers using a knife, pizza wheel, or cookie cutter. Transfer to a greased baking sheet and prick with a fork, or dock with a dough docker or skewer. Bake at 400°F for 8–10 minutes until the crackers have golden patches. Cool on a rack and keep in an airtight tin.

LEEWAY

A Atta or whole wheat flour will make a chapati. Note that whole wheat flours tend to need a little more liquid to make a good soft dough; start with ⅔ cup and add more as necessary. Use white flour to make South African roti or Indian luchi. For crisp puris, which are also made with white flour, proceed as opposite, before deep-frying the rolled-out breads one at a time. The dough will puff up, so be prepared to keep it submerged with tongs.

B This dough is hospitable to add-ins like grated carrot or chopped herbs.

C Use warm juice in place of the water. Some, like carrot, will give the dough a mild flavor and a vibrant color. Remember to roll out on a lightly oiled, as opposed to floured, surface. (In the case of my beet flatbread, this looked not unlike calamine lotion rubbed on bad sunburn.)

D Use cold water, but you might need a little more of it.

BARLEY

How medieval English peasants loathed their brown, coarse barley bread, even more so when supplemented with beans. Imagine the ragged churls, to bed on a heavy stomach, dreaming of soft bread made with wheat. If only they could try a slice of processed white loaf, compressible to a pellet of claggy, dense paste, and see where that desire has left us. As wheat strains became more adaptable to poor climates and capable of returning higher yields of easy-to-harvest grain, barley fell from favor. That said, in some places it remains one of a few viable crops—parts of Scandinavia, for example. In Norway, it's traditional to celebrate a child's baptism with a barley flatbread, some of which is put aside for *their* grandchild's ceremony. Barley is now enjoying something of a comeback, precisely for the reasons it was once shunned: its strong flavor and lack of gluten, as well as more contemporary desiderata like being notably low on the glycemic index. You can make flatbreads with barley flour alone, but using about 25 percent wheat flour will make the dough easier to roll out and the finished breads more tender. Compared to using wheat flour alone, more warm water may be required to bring the dough together, but start with ⅔ cup and add in small increments until a soft dough forms.

BUCKWHEAT

The flatbreads starting point can be used to make noodles, including Japanese *ni-hachi* soba. *Ni-hachi* means "twice 8": Centuries ago a bowl cost 16 mon, the currency of Japan before the yen took over in 1870. As it happens, 2 and 8 also represent the weight ratio of wheat flour to buckwheat. Artisan soba are made with buckwheat flour alone, but for the inexperienced this dough is tricky to fashion into noodles that will cook without breaking up. By contrast, the gluten in wheat flour helps *ni-hachi* dough cohere. I use hot water to accelerate its activation, although this isn't authentic. Use 1½ cups buckwheat flour, ½ cup all-purpose flour, and ⅔ cup hot water. Make up the dough as for flatbreads. Note how the instant you add liquid to the flour the fragrance of buckwheat rises like the ghost of the grain: dry and nutty, with a tang that recalls sourdough. Once the dough has come together, knead it for about 10 minutes, then roll it out as thinly as possible into a rectangle. Dust very lightly but thoroughly with buckwheat flour, then fold in the short ends so they touch. Dust the surface and fold in again. Cut into noodles about ⅛ in wide. Cook immediately in boiling salted water, green tea, or broth for 1–2 minutes. A simple way to eat your practice noodles is with a few dashes of soy sauce and toasted sesame oil and some thinly sliced scallions, though you can use them in any recipe that calls for fresh soba or, according to Shizuo Tsuji, for udon. Noodles can also be made with wheat flour alone, like pasta, but using semolina flour or cornstarch to dust the layers.

CHARCOAL

In a paper published in the *British Medical Journal* in 1862, Thomas Skinner M.D. noted that the problem with charcoal, "a most invaluable medicine," was the near-impossibility of administering it. Charcoal crackers, he said, were one possible solution, if only patients could be encouraged to take more than a nibble. Around this time the London baker J.L. Bragg solved the problem by making a cracker with fine stone-ground charcoal. The company bearing his name continues to make them today, using activated charcoal derived from coconut husks. Activated charcoal is still the main treatment for patients who arrive in the ER suffering from poisoning, especially of unknown or mixed origin. Usually administered as a soft drink or slurry, it absorbs toxins and has an emetic effect on most patients. Good to know if your unpasteurized Camembert is a bit on the ripe side. Make your own charcoal crackers, as long as you don't mind your kitchen looking like you've taken up action painting with blackboard paint. Rub 2 tbsp butter into the flour and salt at step [1], then mix in 4 tbsp fine activated charcoal (available from online sources) before adding the liquid and proceeding from step [2] to finish the crackers.

CHICKPEA, SPINACH & NIGELLA

Missi roti is an unleavened flatbread popular in Rajasthan and the Punjab that combines chickpea and whole wheat flours, and usually something green for flavoring—maybe some spinach, cilantro leaves, or scallions, or all three. Pomegranate or ajwain seeds (a thyme-flavored aromatic native to India and Pakistan) provide an optional sharp or bitter dimension. Ajwain seeds are sometimes labeled lovage on their Indian packaging, but be prepared for them to taste of thyme, with hints of anise and oregano, rather than the distinct celery flavor of what we call lovage. I like my *missi* roti with spinach and nigella seeds. The cooked rounds of bread are so fibrous you'd think they were woven rather than kneaded. Use 50/50 chickpea flour and whole wheat flour, then mix with the salt and 2 handfuls of frozen chopped spinach, thawed and squeezed, and 1 tsp nigella seeds. Bring the dough together using warm water as per the method for flatbreads, but hold some back, because the spinach will yield its own moisture. Cook in a hot nonstick skillet (or *tawa*) until brown and spotted, turning and brushing with ghee or butter once or twice. Brush the just-cooked bread with some more ghee or butter and give it a little sprinkle of sea salt to maximize the flavors. Eat your *missi* roti while it's still warm. I like mine with good-quality cottage cheese and a tickle of lime pickle.

CHINESE PANCAKES

Making your own Peking duck and pancakes is borderline eccentric—like, say, making your own car. If you insist, for the authentic Chinese-restaurant experience, make sure you provide at least one pancake less than each diner would like. James Martin gives a recipe that makes a wetter flatbread dough and requires boiling rather than warm water: 1¾ cups white bread flour to ¾ cup boiling water. No need to rest the dough. Simply divide it into 16 balls of equal size. Roll out into rounds as thin as possible, cook as per the flatbreads method, and keep warm until needed. Serve in a bamboo steamer.

CINNAMON

I was relishing a plate of hot eggplant fries at Moro's tapas offspring, Morito, in London, when I spied a piece of flatbread masquerading as a napkin at the bottom of our bread basket. I wrapped it around a bundle of fries and took a bite. The bread was flavored with cinnamon, just enough to be noticeable. That we flagged down the waitress and ordered another basket with such urgency was only a matter of due diligence; we needed to verify the compatibility of cinnamon flatbread with salt-cod *croquetas*, harissa, and a racy sheep's cheese with honeycomb. The hint of warm spice wreathed the *bacalao* and cheese like aromatic smoke from a campfire. For something similar, use our starting point to make a dough with a mix of whole wheat and white flours. When cooked, brush the bread with a little butter, then shake over some cinnamon. How much? Somewhere between a rumor and a whisper. If you start to hear jingle bells, you've overshot.

COCONUT

Pol roti is a very popular Sri Lankan flatbread made with a mixture of grated coconut and wheat flour. Grating fresh coconut gives juicing passion fruit a run for its money when it comes to Sisyphean kitchen tasks. Live a little by using a food processor, or, better still, buy a pouch of frozen grated coconut from your local Indian or Thai supermarket. The rest is a breeze. It's a lovely dough to roll, cooperative and smooth. Savory *pol* roti might contain sliced onion, shredded curry leaves, or fresh or dried chili. These usually accompany curries, or are served for breakfast with a piquant onion, fish flake, and chili sambol called *lunu miris*. Plain *pol* roti are eaten with butter and jam, or *kithul,* a maple-syrup-like extract of *Caryota urens*, a tree also known as the toddy, jaggery, or wine palm. Mix 1 cup all-purpose flour with 1 cup grated coconut, ½ tsp salt, and 4–5 tbsp warm water or coconut water, then make as per the method for flatbreads (less liquid is needed to bring the dough together because the grated coconut is so moist).

CORN

A single scoop of masa harina and I understood why in Mexico, unlike so many countries, corn has not been entirely trounced by wheat. A freshly made corn tortilla is sweet, with a yielding texture that makes transcendent sense of your tostada or enchilada. By comparison, store-bought tortillas have the mouthfeel of wet cardboard. Masa takes a good deal more water than wheat: 2 cups masa harina to 1½ cups warm water. Make as per the starting point until you reach the finishing directions for flatbreads, then cook your tortillas on a *medium* heat for about 15 seconds on one side. Flip, and cook for 30–45 seconds until the tortilla is speckled brown. Flip once more, and cook until the same effect is achieved: Cook on too low a heat and your tortilla will dry out; too high and it'll blister. Collect the finished tortillas in a basket, wrap in a clean dish towel, and let rest for 10 minutes.

MATZO

At Passover Seder it's traditional to refer to matzo as "the bread of our affliction." Whatever happened to the seven-layer cake of salvation, wonders Kugel in *Hope: A Tragedy*, by Shalom Auslander. To make matzo crackers, follow our starting point, using all-purpose flour. Make the well, as at step 1, but *before* adding the water, pour in 3 tbsp olive oil, then add just enough warm water to make the dough soft but not too sticky. Let rest, unless you're making your matzo for Passover, in which case the dough must be made and cooked within 18 minutes, to forestall any fermentation. Divide the dough into 12 equal pieces and roll out each one until it's nearly see-through. Sprinkle with salt, prick all over with a fork (or apply a dough docker), then bake on a preheated baking sheet at 475°F for about 3 minutes; turn over and give it 1–2 minutes more. Let cool on a rack while you bake the rest.

MILLET

Waverley Root was a bit dismissive of millet: It was a primitive food for primitive cultures. Although millet is among the hardiest of cereal crops, the Romans tossed it aside for barley as soon as they could. According to *The Oxford Companion to Food*, millet can range from "thoroughly palatable to bitter and unpleasant." In India, a species called finger millet, or *ragi*, is used to make roti. Follow the starting point for flatbreads, although note that you may need a little more water to bring the dough together. *Ragi* has a striking fragrance—the sort of dusty, mingled aroma familiar from the spice aisle of an Indian grocery. When I rolled the pinky-gray dough into a passable flatbread and transferred it to the pan, it looked like Iggy Pop's tongue, circa 1972.

OATCAKES

A Methodist's cookie. Top a plain oatcake with squeezy-cheese cross-eyes and a lolling tongue made of ham and it would still be dead serious. Oatcakes even *look* like sackcloth. Still, they are very easy to make, especially if you've committed the starting-point proportions to memory: 2 cups Scottish oat meal to just ½ cup hot water (with 1–2 tbsp fat melted into it), and 1 tsp salt. Use medium-ground oat meal, or a mix of 70 percent medium oat meal and 30 percent coarse or pinhead if you want something more fibrous. It takes all of 2 minutes to mix the dough, warm and heavy in the hands, recalling horse-feeds made up in winter. Once mixed, let the oat meal expand and cohere for a few minutes, then roll out and cut rounds as per the method for crackers, baking 20 minutes. Easy enough to make a big batch of dough, divide it, and try a few flavor variants. Add boldly flavored whole seeds, like caraway or cumin, to serve with stinky cheese, or add diced mixed candied peel and mustard, to serve with Cheddar cheese. Marcus Wareing makes a pumpkin seed and thyme oatcake, which he suggests pairs well with Camembert or goat's cheese.

POTATO PARATHAS

Carb-coupling—as terrifying to the dieter as double denim is to the fashionista. An English "chip butty" (a sandwich of fries) will do it, as will a Spanish *bocadillo de tortilla* (potato-omelet sandwich) or an Indian potato paratha, even if the last has the mildly redeeming feature of being made with whole wheat bread. The basis of a potato paratha is the chapati, as outlined at ^ under Leeway, but once the rounds are rolled, about 1 tbsp potato curry is spooned into the middle. The sides of the chapati are then drawn up around the curry, and the whole thing is re-rolled into as flat a disk as can be managed without splitting it. It's now ready to cook on the griddle pan, as per the method for flatbreads. Some cooks find it easier to place the filling on a roti and then seal it with another on top, which has the advantage of accommodating more filling. To make the potato curry, warm some vegetable oil in a pan. Add 1 tsp cumin seeds and wait until they start to pop before stirring in half an onion, finely chopped. When the onion has softened a little, add chopped green chili to taste. Sprinkle in 2 tsp garam masala and stir, then quickly add a heaped cup of mashed potato. When it's all well mixed, taste for seasoning, add ¼ tsp amchoor (mango powder) for an optional lick of sourness, and stir in some chopped cilantro, if you like. Common alternatives to the potato filling are keema (spiced ground lamb with peas), a thick dal, or vegetable curry.

REFRIED BEAN PUPUSAS

In El Salvador and Honduras, they take tortillas a stage further to make *pupusas*. Divide your corn tortilla dough (page ³²) into portions the size of golf balls. Take one and press your thumb into it, making an indentation large enough to hold 1 tbsp refried beans. Fill, then work the surrounding dough, gently easing and stretching it to cover the filling. Roll (or press) the ball out until it's about ¼ in thick. The filling will be less likely to protrude if the dough is not too dry. Cook your *pupusas* on a griddle pan, over a medium heat, for 1–2 minutes each side, until they develop brown sunspots. Expect something like a thin quesadilla, but with crisper edges. It's notable how sweet the masa dough tastes next to the salty, cumin-scented beans. Other fillings include grated cheese or *chicharrones* (meaty pork crackling). A mixture of these with beans is not considered beyond the pale. *Pupusas* are traditionally accompanied by a spicy, fermented pickle called *crudito*, made with cabbage, carrot, onion, and chili.

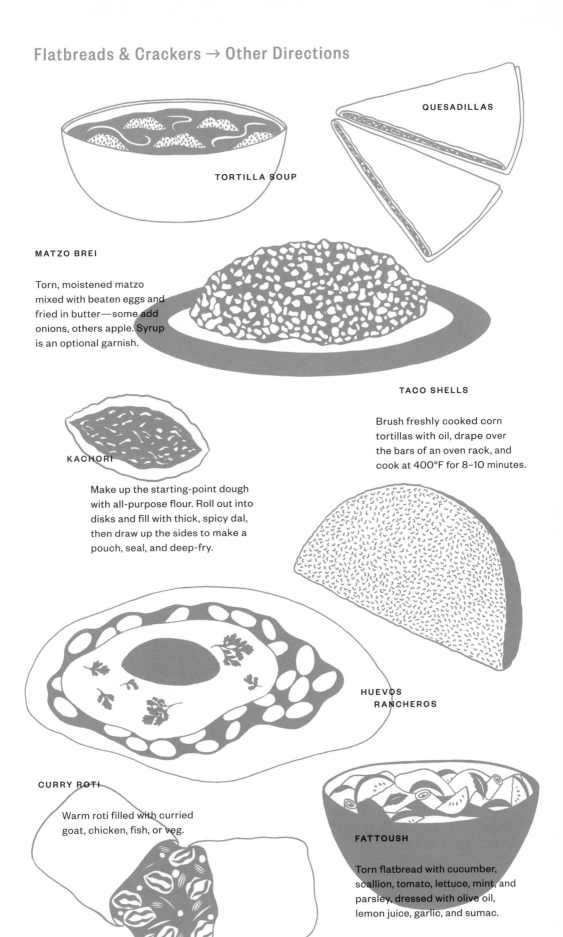

QUESADILLAS

TORTILLA SOUP

MATZO BREI

Torn, moistened matzo mixed with beaten eggs and fried in butter—some add onions, others apple. Syrup is an optional garnish.

TACO SHELLS

Brush freshly cooked corn tortillas with oil, drape over the bars of an oven rack, and cook at 400°F for 8–10 minutes.

KACHORI

Make up the starting-point dough with all-purpose flour. Roll out into disks and fill with thick, spicy dal, then draw up the sides to make a pouch, seal, and deep-fry.

HUEVOS RANCHEROS

CURRY ROTI

Warm roti filled with curried goat, chicken, fish, or veg.

FATTOUSH

Torn flatbread with cucumber, scallion, tomato, lettuce, mint, and parsley, dressed with olive oil, lemon juice, garlic, and sumac.

Soda Bread, Biscuits & Cobbler

A small step on from the starting point for flatbreads and crackers: still calls for 2 cups flour to ⅔ cup liquid (cold, in this instance), but with the addition of a chemical leavener, meaning the dough can be shaped into a loaf like Irish soda bread. The same dough, slightly enriched with butter, can be used for biscuits, or to top cooked fruit or stew to make a cobbler. A minor variation on this dough is used for the oyster crackers that are traditionally served with chowder (page [232]).

For 6 biscuits, 1 small round loaf, or enough cobbles for a 9-in dish

INGREDIENTS
2 cups all-purpose flour [A] [B]
½ tsp baking soda [C] [D]
½ tsp salt
2 tbsp butter for biscuits or cobbler—optional for soda bread [E]
1–3 tbsp sugar for biscuits or cobbler—optional for soda bread
⅔–1 cup buttermilk [F] [G] [H] [I] [J]

1   Sift the flour, baking soda, and salt into a bowl. Stir to give it a good mix.

2   Rub in the butter (if using) until all but vanished. Stir in the sugar (if using). Make a well in the center and add ⅔ cup of the buttermilk. Mix to a dough using a spoon, your hand, or both. Add a little more flour or buttermilk as necessary to create a dough that's soft but not too sticky.
    That said, some cooks like their cobbler dough on the sticky side, to be dropped from a spoon onto the fruit before cooking.

3   Flour your hands and transfer the dough to a lightly floured surface. Gently shape (rather than knead) until you have a cohesive dough.

    FOR SODA BREAD
    Fashion the dough into a low-ish dome and immediately place on a greased baking sheet, prick it all over with a toothpick or skewer, and cut a deep, wide cross into the top. Bake at 400°F for 25–30 minutes or until a skewer inserted into the center comes out clean. Transfer to a rack and let cool a little before using. Eat within a day or two.

FOR BISCUITS

Roll out the dough to a thickness of ¾ in and cut into squares, triangles, or rounds. Transfer the biscuits to a lightly greased baking sheet, then brush the tops with egg or yolk for a shiny effect, or sprinkle them with flour for matte. Bake toward the top of a 400°F oven for 15 minutes, checking now and then to ensure they don't brown too much.

The sensible thing to do is cut your rolled-out square into small squares or triangles with a knife—this way you can use all of the dough. Some cooks make their biscuits by fashioning the dough into a round and then cutting it into wedges. If this offends your sense of tradition, cut the rolled-out dough into 2½-in rounds. You'll need to push the scraps together to make the sixth one. Push the cutter straight down. Don't twist, or your biscuits won't rise as high.

FOR COBBLER

If you intend to drop spoonfuls directly onto whatever is being cobbled, you need only follow the method to step [2]. Otherwise, follow the instructions to the end of step [3], then roll out the dough to about ½ in thick. Press out circles of about 2-in diameter and lay them on top of the fruit or stew.

Cobbler topping can be baked for 30–45 minutes at 325–350°F. If what is underneath needs longer, add the topping later in the cooking time.

LEEWAY

[A] Use at least half whole wheat flour for soda bread. Bread flour can be used, but all-purpose is better. Atta (fine whole wheat chapati flour) makes excellent soda bread, although it's less rustic than the traditional Irish loaf.

[B] It's not recommended to replace all the wheat flour with flour made from gluten-free grains, but you can use up to half the amount. It's traditional to add about ⅓ cup rolled oats to the flour for soda bread, in which case you'll probably need to up the amount of buttermilk a little.

[C] If you like to taste the soda, use ¾ tsp baking soda.

[D] Use 2 tsp baking powder in place of the ½ tsp baking soda. In this case you won't need the acidity provided by buttermilk—you can use ordinary milk instead.

[E] James Villas, author of an entire book dedicated to biscuits, says that you can substitute heavy cream for the butter.

[F] If you need a bit more liquid but have no more buttermilk, it's fine to add some milk or water.

[G] Make your own buttermilk substitute: Pour 1 tbsp lemon juice into a measuring cup, add enough milk to measure ⅔ cup, and leave for 10 minutes to curdle. Alternatively, whisk 1 tsp cream of tartar into ⅔ cup milk. Again, leave for 10–15 minutes for the magic to happen. →

H Use plain yogurt thinned with water instead of the buttermilk.

I Some cooks make their soda bread with water and vinegar
—⅔ cup water to 2 tsp vinegar—in place of the buttermilk.
It's a shade rougher in texture, but still good.

J Some recipes for soda bread call for the addition of an egg,
whisked into the buttermilk. The finished loaf will be bigger
than its eggless counterpart, the crumb less dense, and
the crust chewier.

ANCHOVY & THYME

A mid-nineteenth-century recipe for cobbler, recounted by Mark McWilliams in *The Story Behind the Dish*, suggests lining the sides of a pot-pie dish with pastry, before adding the fruit and fitting a pastry lid. Once cooked, the cobbler was inverted onto a dish to create a deep, rather homely tart. An elaborate way of avoiding a soggy bottom (a gag so popular on *The Great British Baking Show* that it had its own dressing room). Contemporary cobblers use biscuit dough rather than pastry, and dispense with lining the dish, in favor of a simple topping on baked fruit or, sometimes, a savory stew: the quickest pie there is. In one variant, the cook need only space out spoonfuls of a rather wet dough over the surface, like dumplings. Anchovy and thyme is an apt flavor variation for a beef and carrot filling. Finely chop 8–10 anchovies and stir them into the flour with the liquid along with 1 tsp dried or 2 tsp chopped fresh thyme. Reduce the salt to ¼ tsp.

CELERY, ONION & HERB

Michel Roux Jr.'s highly aromatic take on soda bread includes chopped onion and celery and celery seed, all sweated in butter, then added to the flour and baking soda, once some butter has been rubbed into them. An improvised buttermilk of milk and lemon juice is used to start to bring the dough together, before plenty of chopped mint, parsley, and lovage or celery leaves are stirred in. The dough is made with double our starting-point quantities and baked in a 9 x 5 x 3-in (8-cup) loaf pan at 400°F for 40–50 minutes. It tastes deliciously savory, strangely like a Cornish pasty, by which I mean the proper beef-and-turnip sort, not chicken and chorizo or squid rogan josh.

CORN-CHOC CHIP

One wintry afternoon, I made up a batch of biscuits using a mixture of cornmeal and wheat flour, and added dark chocolate chips. When the biscuits had cooled sufficiently, I sat at the kitchen table and tried one with my eyes closed. It reminded me of something. I couldn't think what. Then it hit me. I'd reinvented the "chocolate cornflake wheel," the slender disks of chocolate-covered cereal, cut into six segments, that were sold in supermarkets in my youth, until higher-margin chocolate treats like brownies and cupcakes displaced them. Follow the method for biscuits, substituting fine cornmeal for half of the flour and adding as many chocolate chips as fancy or frugality dictates. Tend toward the top end of the sugar quantity suggested in our starting point.

ONION

If, writes the restaurateur Stephen Bull, he were to be "forever denied, as retribution for some imaginary transgression," a single favorite thing to eat, it would have to be the scone. "Never mind… a grey-legged partridge or a caramelized scallop, the removal of the humble scone from my diet would be a dreadful punishment. I'm not sure why this should be; the scone is, in baking terms, one of the lower invertebrates, hardly a sophisticated confection." Bull gives a recipe for a dough made with cheese and sun-dried tomato—ideal, he suggests, for a cobbler or a biscuit to serve with scrambled eggs and bacon. I also like his onion biscuit recipe, especially because he suggests serving it with poached eggs and an onion sauce, which would make an excellent vegetarian brunch if you replaced the duck or bacon fat with butter. Cook ½ large onion, finely chopped, in 2 tbsp duck or bacon fat until lightly browned. Set aside, and then, in the same pan, cook 2 tbsp thinly sliced leeks for about 5 minutes. Rub 4 tbsp butter into scant 2 cups all-purpose flour, sifted with ½ tsp each of baking soda and salt. Stir in the onion, leek, and 3 tbsp grated Parmesan. Mix in as much of scant 1 cup plain yogurt as is needed to make a dough that's sticky but not wet. Transfer to a floured surface and knead for a few seconds. Roll out to a thickness of ¾ in, and cut out 2-in rounds. Bake on a lightly greased baking sheet at 400°F for about 15 minutes. Serve the biscuits cut in half with a poached egg on top, plus an onion purée made with 1 cup thinly sliced onions cooked in a covered saucepan over a medium heat with 2 tbsp butter and a pinch of salt until meltingly soft; blend the onion with just over ½ cup hot milk, adding some cream if, in Bull's words, "you're reckless."

PARSNIP, PARMESAN & SAGE

Parsnip and Parmesan is a signature Delia Smith combination. Her roast parsnips in Parmesan have become such a Christmas staple in the U.K. that she has since created a quick-to-make loaf in the soda-bread vein. Smith suggests serving the latter with tomato soup, or alongside a plate of washed-rind cheese with apple and celery, but I like it with fried eggs, sausage, and bacon for breakfast. Grate the parsnip and dice the cheese the night before, then all you have to do in the morning is to mix the dough and slip it into the oven before digging out the skillet. The following adapts Smith's flavors to our starting point for soda bread. Use all-purpose flour, sifting it into a bowl with ½ tsp salt and 2 tsp baking powder (no soda). Add 1½ cups grated parsnip and stir to coat it evenly with flour. Add scant ½ cup Parmesan, cut into ¼-in dice, and a heaped tbsp finely chopped fresh sage. Mix to a dough with 5 tbsp milk and 1 extra large beaten egg. (Less liquid is used than in our starting point, due to the wetness of the grated parsnip, and the egg.) Bank on 35–40 minutes in a 400°F oven, about 10 minutes longer than the unflavored bread. When it's ready, a skewer inserted into the center should come out clean.

PESTO

Supermarket pesto can have a cut-grass quality that isn't altogether pleasant on pasta. It's a cut above, however, used in biscuit dough. Add 2 tbsp pesto to our starting point for biscuits, and use only ½ cup buttermilk. Opt for square or triangular biscuits, rather than fussing over rounds, and you can be eating them inside 20 minutes, split in half, still warm, and with a finger's depth of cold, white, creamy goat's cheese.

RAISIN

This lightly sweetened, fruity version of Irish soda bread—known as Spotted Dog—is a good alternative to cake if you're watching your sugar consumption. Butter a slice and, if you're pining for jam, try crushing a few ripe raspberries on top. Neither soda bread nor biscuits keep too well, but they'll still be good for toasting after a few days, and will last longer if you include some sugar and fat in the dough. Add 1 tbsp sugar and a handful of raisins to the flour mix in our starting point. Beat in an egg with the liquid if you want softer, cakier results. Caraway seeds are a common addition to Irish-American soda bread: Throw in 1–2 tbsp seeds, along with the sugar and raisins.

SEMOLINA

Harcha are Moroccan flatbreads-cum-cakes, a bit like English muffins. They're made with semolina flour, a little sugar, warm milk, and butter, and cooked like pancakes. In a bowl, mix 2 cups semolina flour with 1–3 tbsp sugar, ¼ tsp salt, and 1 tsp baking powder. Melt ½ cup butter with ½ cup milk, and mix this into the dry ingredients. Give the dry ingredients a minute or two to absorb the milk and butter, then knead into a smooth (and notably greasy) dough. Roll out to a thickness of roughly ¼ in, press out circles, and cook on a medium-hot griddle pan until browned on the underside, then flip and brown the other side. Eat warm, split in half and spread with honey and cream cheese. In place of milk, some cooks use buttermilk or leftover mint tea; I once tried using freshly brewed mint tea, but it wasn't apparent in the finished *harcha*.

SWEET POTATO & PECAN

Thomas Jefferson was a gourmet. He was the first man in America to grow fennel, and he adored the fine wines of Burgundy. His recipe for sweet potato biscuits has been adopted and adapted by The City Tavern, a historical re-enactment restaurant in Philadelphia, where they bake them every day. They are rich, nutty, and fruity, with hints of spice and creaminess. If a biscuit could be *premier cru*, these would make the grade. The following is a slight adaptation of their adaptation. Rub ½ cup butter into 2½ cups all-purpose flour, then stir in ½ cup packed light brown sugar, ½ tsp each of ground ginger, allspice, and cinnamon, and 1 tbsp baking powder. Make a well in the center and rub in a cup of cold mashed sweet potato with ½ cup heavy cream and ¼ cup chopped pecans. Roll out the dough 1¼ in thick and cut out 2-in rounds. Bake ¾ in apart on a lightly greased baking sheet at 350°F for 25–30 minutes (i.e. in a slightly cooler oven and for a longer time than in our starting point for biscuits).

TREACLE

If beer is liquid bread, then bitter, malted Irish treacle loaf is sliceable Guinness, especially with a generous head of ivory whipped butter, deep enough to leave a blob on your nose. Follow the starting point for soda bread, adding 1 tbsp sugar to the all-purpose flour. Add just ½ cup buttermilk, with 3 tbsp molasses stirred into it, at step 2.

YOGURT & NIGELLA SEED

Naan is the classic scapegoat for curry-gluttony. Clutching at their stomach after a tableful of poppadoms, bhajis, *and* pakoras, dal (for health purposes), tikkas, thalis, and bhunas, someone is bound to say, "We shouldn't have ordered the naan." But who can resist that characteristic fragrance of nigella seeds? You can make a very good, quick approximation using our starting point for soda bread, even if classic naan is usually yeast-leavened. Use a 50/50 mix of warmed plain yogurt and milk for the liquid, 2 tsp baking powder rather than baking soda, and ¼ tsp nigella seeds to the 2 cups all-purpose flour. If you have time, give it a 5-minute knead and a 15-minute rest at room temperature. Roll the dough out to the shape of a very old man's ear and sprinkle a few seeds over the top before cooking on a griddle pan, or, so the bread develops a charred edge, on the barbecue—the rolled-out dough can be laid directly on the grill. Flip once. Just remember not to leave any rolled-out uncooked dough near the heat, or it will turn to goo. For something akin to a Peshwari naan, blend ½ cup dried shredded coconut, ⅓ cup golden raisins, and ½ cup sliced almonds or pistachios to a rough paste, and spread a small amount between two rolled-out rounds of dough. Seal the edges, then roll out again, trying not to break the surface, and cook.

BOSTON BAKED BEANS ON TOAST

page 248

DUBLIN CODDLE WITH SODA BREAD

Bacon, sausages, onion, and potatoes, very slowly simmered in water or hard cider, garnished with parsley, and with a big hunk of soda bread on the side.

CRUMBS USED FOR BROWN-BREAD ICE CREAM

page 492

SODA BREAD, OYSTERS & A PINT OF GUINNESS

SAVORY BREAD PUDDING

(Detectable soda flavor is not so nice in a sweet version.)

CROUTONS

Break stale bread into pieces, toss in oil, and toast in a 400°F oven until crisp, then use on soups and salads.

CRACKERS FOR CHEESE

Slice old soda bread thinly, brush with oil, and bake at 400°F for 10 minutes.

SODA BREAD

... for smoked salmon, or eaten warm with butter and jam.

IRISH STEW WITH SODA-BREAD COBBLES

Yeast-Risen Bread

This starting point involves the same ratio of liquid to flour as the previous two, but yeast is used in place of the chemical leavening agent in quick breads. A yeasted dough is extremely versatile. It can be used to make loaves, rolls, pizza bases, flatbreads, grissini, bagels, and, with the addition of extra fat, focaccia and croissants. Make a large batch of dough and you'll have a cooling rack like a Thanksgiving festival. If you're not in a hurry, the sponge method outlined below at [I] under Leeway will result in a better flavor.

For a medium-size round loaf, or 12–14 rolls [A]

INGREDIENTS
4 cups bread flour [B]
2 tsp instant yeast [C] [D]
1 tsp salt [E]
1–2 tbsp sugar—optional [F]
1–2 tbsp butter or oil—optional [G]
1¼ cups warm water [H]
Milk or beaten egg for brushing—optional

[1] Measure the flour into a large bowl. Stir in the yeast, salt, and (if using) sugar. If using fat, either rub 1–2 tbsp diced butter into the flour until it's all but vanished, or add 1–2 tbsp of oil to the warm water poured in at the next step.
Fat helps the bread keep longer. Even in such small amounts, butter also improves the flavor.

[2] Make a well in the center and add the warm water. Mix it all to a dough using a spoon, your hand, or both. Add more flour or water as necessary to create a dough that's soft but not sticky.

[3] Knead the dough for 8–10 minutes until smooth.
Add any chopped nuts, dried fruit, or diced candied peel toward the end of kneading. Some cooks might add these at step [5], briefly kneading them in to distribute them evenly.

[4] Transfer the dough to a large, lightly oiled bowl and find a nice warm spot for it. Cover the bowl with a clean dish towel, or an oiled shower cap or piece of plastic wrap. Let the dough rise until double in size. How long this will take depends on the warmth of its environment. Start checking after 40 minutes.

5 When it has risen, deflate the puffed dough with your fingers.
At this point you can put the dough in a large freezer bag (it will slowly expand) and leave it in the fridge for later use—it can be kept for 7 days.

6 Fashion the dough into the desired shape(s) and transfer to a lightly greased baking sheet.

7 Give the dough its second rise in a warm place, covered. Again, you are waiting for it *almost* to double in size. Start checking at 30 minutes for a round loaf, 20 minutes for rolls.
Don't let the bread rise too much, or it will deflate in the oven. It's better to under- than over-rise.

8 Dust with flour. Or gently brush with milk or beaten egg.
The latter will give you glossiness, and can act as an adhesive for seeds. Slash the top of your loaf, if you like.
The slash could be a cross, a leaflike stalk and veins, or whatever takes your fancy. The effect is not only decorative, but gives the bread the freedom to expand. Use a razor blade unless you have a very sharp knife.

9 Bake a loaf for 20 minutes at 425°F, then lower the temperature to 350°F and bake for 10–20 minutes longer. Rolls will need just 12–15 minutes at 425°F. The finished bread should sound hollow when tapped on the base.
If you're baking the bread in a pan, you may want to unmold it after its 30–40 minutes are up, and give it a further 5 minutes in the oven, placed directly on the rack, for a crisper crust.

10 Transfer the bread to a wire rack to cool.

LEEWAY

A These amounts will also make 4–6 pizza bases. To make 2–3 rolls—a good quantity for flavor-testing—use 1 cup flour, ¼ tsp salt, ½ tsp instant yeast, and 5 tbsp water. For a 9 x 5 x 3-in (8-cup) loaf pan, use 3⅓ cups flour, ¾ tsp salt, 1½ tsp instant yeast, and 1 cup water. The dough should reach about rim-height at step ⁷.

B Whole wheat and spelt flours will yield well-risen yeast bread. Some of the wheat flour can be replaced with rye or buckwheat flour, or fine cornmeal, but only up to about 30 percent, as their lower gluten levels will result in less of a rise.

C Bread made with instant yeast can be baked after only one rise, so you can skip steps ⁴ and ⁵ if you're in a hurry. However, two rises, as outlined here, will give the bread a better flavor. →

D   For yeasts that need activating, add 1 cake compressed fresh or 1 tbsp active dry to ½ cup warm water with 1 tsp sugar. Leave for 15 minutes to froth up, then add at step 2 with the remaining warm water.

E   This amount of salt is on the modest side. Many recipes call for 2 tsp.

F   Add a little sugar to the dough, if you like—say 1–2 tbsp for taste. Use maple syrup, honey, or any other sugar that takes your fancy. Molasses and barley malt syrup are often used in whole wheat breads.

G   Fat is both optional and exchangeable. Use butter, lard, olive or sunflower oil, or the flavored oil left over from a jar of sun-dried tomatoes.

H   Keep your liquid options open: Use apple juice, beer, or hard cider. Milk gives a soft, very white-crumbed bread; the water used to boil potatoes gives a delicious crisp texture to the crust.

I   The sponge method inarguably makes finer-tasting bread. To apply it to our starting point, mix 1½ tsp instant yeast with half (2 cups) of the flour and about two thirds of the warm water. Cover and leave for at least 4 hours, and up to 24. Then add the rest of the flour—with butter rubbed in, if you like—and salt. Mix to a dough. You may need more than the remaining amount of warm water. Then pick up the method from step 3. Note that because the bread is given a longer rise, it needs less yeast.

Yeast-Risen Bread → Flavors & Variations

APPLE

Nestled among the half-timbered houses of Beuvron-en-Auge, in Normandy, France, there's a bakery called Au Bon Pain—no relation to the American chain—that sells a *pain au cidre* made with the local staples of apple chunks and hard cider. In its recipe for apple bread, *The Modern Practical Bread Baker* suggests replacing one third of the flour with warm apple purée, and using only enough warm water to bring the dough together. I gave it a whirl. Once it had risen, I baked the dough into rolls, which filled the room with the aroma of apple fritters when I opened the oven door. Sadly, they didn't taste much like apple fritters, but they did have a mildly sweet, bun-like crumb inside a delicious crunchy crust.

BAGELS

Hive off a bit of your yeast-risen dough to see how simple it is to make bagels. I say simple. The hard bit is making them look round and seamless, more like a bangle than a bike lock. If you're using the sponge method for the dough (see opposite), so much the better for flavor, but don't worry if not. After all, the bagel is foremost a textural matter, a workout for the jaw. My New Yorker cousin always has one for breakfast, and he can talk all day. When the dough has risen once, deflate and divide into 14 equal pieces. Roll into balls, make a hole in each one, and spin on your finger to make a ring. Or, roll each piece into a 6-in snake and join the ends firmly to make a ring. Poach in plenty of boiling salted water, no more than 2 or 3 at a time, for a minute on each side. Remove and drain on clean dish towels. Transfer to a lightly greased baking sheet, brush with beaten egg, and sprinkle with seeds if you like, then bake at 400°F for 20–25 minutes.

BATH OLIVERS

"The biscuits [crackers] are particularly nice, but so simple that they seem as if they were made only with flour, butter and water; but that there is some secret connected with the making has been proved by the attempts to produce them made by the uninitiated, that have only resulted in unworthy imitations of the real article. The Oliver is peculiarly crisp, and is good for either dessert or with cheese, it is stated to be the only biscuit that is fermented, and on that account is good for invalids suffering from acidity on the stomach, for which yeast is a corrective." Pause before you throw away your antacids. Dr. William Oliver, Bath-based inventor of the eponymous biscuit, also believed that the city's water could cure infertility, epilepsy, and piles. The entry above, from an 1874 edition of *The Food Journal*, goes on to explain that Bath Olivers are always gratefully received as a gift by aristocrats. In *Brideshead Revisited*, Sebastian and Charles learn to appreciate wine ("It is a little, shy wine like a gazelle"/"Like a flute by still water") by working their way steadily through the cellars at

Brideshead, cleansing their palates between swigs of fifty-year-old vintages with Bath Olivers. The following is adapted from *The Domestic Dictionary* of 1842. Melt 6 tbsp butter in scant 1 cup warm milk, then stir it into 4 cups bread flour, 1 tsp instant yeast, and 1 tsp salt. Knead only until the dough is smooth, then wrap it in a clean dish towel (or plastic wrap) and leave it somewhere warm for 15 minutes. Roll and fold the dough several times, as if making rough puff pastry (page 574), then roll out to about ⅛ in thick. Dock the dough (i.e. poke it all over with a skewer or knitting needle) and cut out large circles. Bake on a lightly greased baking sheet in a 275°F oven for 20 minutes. The results will taste better than the manufactured kind, which are made with palm oil (the Flytes would *not* have approved). If you've never tried a Bath Oliver, imagine a sugarless Petit Beurre cookie.

CHERRY & HAZELNUT

Fruit and nut is a classic combination in breads destined for the cheeseboard. Raisin and walnut is the first among equals. The upscale bakery chain Maison Kayser sells a pretty pistachio and dried apricot variation. Hazelnut and dried cherry is equally happy with a goat's cheese, a sprightly Gorgonzola, or a fruity Comté. A mid-brown dough is ideal (50/50 white and whole wheat flour), but you may take it a few notches darker or lighter as you see fit. Consider adding 1–2 tbsp of barley malt extract or molasses, particularly if you like fruitcake with cheese. Add the nuts and dried fruit toward the end of kneading at step 3 and distribute them evenly: ⅓ cup toasted hazelnuts and 3 tbsp dried cherries is a good place to start for 4 cups flour.

CHESTNUT

Chestnut bread is a taste you might possibly acquire if you lived two hundred miles from the nearest village and had just polished off the last of the scrawny goats that eke out an existence on your barren mountain. Alexandre Dumas wrote that bread made with chestnut flour "is always of bad quality, heavy and difficult to digest." Xenophon of Athens, historian and student of Socrates, described it as "headachey." Mixing chestnut flour with flour from another grain is the best way to try it for the first time. In his focaccia recipe, Giorgio Locatelli suggests that 10 percent of the bread flour might be replaced with chestnut flour (or chickpea flour, or toasted rice flour). Before chestnut trees were all but wiped out in the U.S. by sweet chestnut blight, the Cherokees made bread with a mix of chestnut purée and cornmeal. The chestnuts were dried and smoked over fires in little stone structures that would look rustic and cute to anyone who hadn't seen *The Blair Witch Project*.

CORIANDER SEED & FENNEL

Much as I enjoy twirling with my arms stretched out, whenever I'm halfway up a mountainside and it's been four hours since breakfast, I feel less like Julie Andrews, and more like Alfred Wainwright with a stone in his boot. By the time I'd hobbled into the Punch Bowl Inn at Crosthwaite, in England's Lake District, I was too hungry for an aperitif. Too hungry to speak. Too hungry to read the menu. Salvation came in the form of a bread basket, filled with slices of a darkish loaf riddled with coriander seed and fennel. Hunger is not only the best sauce. It makes a damn fine butter, too. Intent on making something similar at home, I mixed 2⅓ cups rye flour and 2 cups whole wheat flour with the yeast and salt, plus 1 tbsp unsweetened cocoa powder, and 1 tbsp each of lightly crushed fennel and coriander seeds. Then, with the warm water, I added 1 tbsp molasses. I'd only had a stroll up nearby Primrose Hill, but my loaf tasted pretty good.

CROISSANTS

Make croissants at least once, if only to relish the smell of them baking. They're almost as good on the nose as in the mouth. Almost. The intense, salty butteriness is so much more noticeable in homemade. Croissants are the lobsters of the bread basket: the crack of the claw-like end piece and the soft flesh inside. Abjure jam and serve them with a little paper dipping cup of melted butter. It's worth noting here that there's really no need to get up at 5 A.M. to bake your croissants. Simply cook them a day or two before you plan to serve, then cool, wrap well, and keep in something airtight at room temperature. When you're ready to serve, unwrap and reheat at 350°F for 5–10 minutes. They'll still taste (and smell) heavenly. Make a yeast-risen bread dough with 4 cups flour, following the method to the end of step 5 Leave the dough in the fridge while you roll out 2 sticks of butter into a rectangle about ½ in thick. Retrieve the dough, and roll it out into a rectangle just big enough to encase the butter. Lay the butter in the center and fold the dough around the butter until entirely enclosed. Flip your butter-dough parcel over and roll it out into as big a rectangle as possible, then fold and turn as you would rough puff pastry (page 574), chilling the dough for a short spell in the fridge or freezer whenever it's getting too warm, and again once all four turns are complete. When the folded and turned dough has chilled for at least 30 minutes, divide it into two roughly equal pieces. Roll out each into a rectangle about 10 in wide and as long as possible. Cut the dough into isosceles triangles, about 4 in at their base and 10 in high. This amount will yield 20–24 triangles, depending on how thick or thin you've rolled it out. In each case, snip a ½-in nick into the dough halfway along the base, and pull the base points apart slightly as you roll the dough up toward the pointy end of the triangle. Curl the two ends toward each other to form a crescent. Transfer to a parchment-lined baking sheet, glaze with beaten egg, and let rise a final time. Bake for 20–25 minutes at 400°F.

CUMIN OR CARAWAY

Elizabeth David writes that cumin is "particularly successful" in rye bread, although caraway and the seldom-seen dill seed meet with her approval, too. Cumin-flavored breads are found in northern Europe and the Middle East, and French *pain au cumin* is a lovely counterpoint to Munster, Époisses, or Vacherin cheese. The cumin in *pain au cumin* may actually be cumin or caraway: Either way, the cheese pairings work wonderfully. Munster, from the Vosges region, is sticky, often itself described as spicy, and seems to bring out the best in both seeds, even more so when accompanied by a glass of spicy Gewürztraminer.

FOCACCIA

For a picnic lunch in Rome, hit one of the bakeries in the Trastevere to buy mattresses of focaccia (artichoke leaf and Parmesan, or squash blossom with mozzarella and anchovy, or just plain sea salt). Buy a bag of fresh peaches or figs from a market stall and, stopping at the *enoteca* for a bottle of something light and white, head for the Villa Doria Pamphili, taking in the fabulous views of the city as you labor uphill. Eat your lunch by the lake, watching the turtles basking in the shallow water like stepping stones. Take a postprandial nap on any leftover bread. Focaccia might look like more effort than an ordinary loaf, but it isn't. Make as per the starting point, using half bread flour and half 00 if your larder allows. At step 2, knead 3 tbsp olive oil into the dough. Continue to knead on an oiled, not floured, surface. At this stage you may pine for a mixer with a dough hook, but after its rise the dough will be a pleasure to touch—silky and elastic. Continue as per the method. At step 6, fashion the dough into a rectangle roughly 12 x 8 in. Transfer it to a lightly oiled baking sheet, slip into a plastic-bag tent, and let rise until it's puffed up nicely. Finally, poke it all over with your index finger, as if you were a rather insistent person making a point, then brush with a mix of 2 tbsp olive oil and 1 tbsp water. Sprinkle with sea salt and bake at 400°F for 20–25 minutes. Additional ingredients like rosemary, sun-dried tomatoes, olives, or sliced onion can be scattered over the top before baking.

LEMON

When, after you've made the lemonade, life continues to give you lemons, make lemon bread. Richard Bertinet suggests serving lemon rolls in summer with salad or smoked salmon. Adapt our starting point by adding the grated zest of 2 lemons toward the end of kneading.

PAIN AU VIN & AUX HERBES

Red wine and thyme cures all ills. Adapt the starting point by using 1¼ cups warm red wine instead of the water at step 2. Add 4 tsp sugar, plus either the leaves picked off a couple of bushy sprigs of thyme, or about 1 heaped tsp dried thyme. A grated small red onion added to the dough at its second knead will make it even tastier.

POTATO

The discovery that potato has a miraculous effect on bread dough can be credited to a grain shortage, according to Elizabeth David. She notes that potato bread makes particularly good toast, and I agree. It's worth slicing fairly thickly, as the sweet, springy bread takes on a crumpet-like character by the time it pops up. Use mashed potato and its cooking water for the best result. As with potato gnocchi, it's wise to use dry, starchy potatoes, boiling them in their skins before drying, peeling, and mashing. Adapt our starting point by rubbing ¾ cup mash into 3 cups bread flour. Sprinkle in the salt, noting that if the potato water was salted, you'll need to reduce the salt to ½–¾ tsp. Make a well, and add 2 tsp instant yeast and *up to* 1 cup warm potato-cooking water. The Grain Store in London makes a potato and rye bread using 1½ cups mash, 1¼ cups white bread flour, and ¾ cup rye flour, with just 4 tbsp water to allow for the moisture in the potatoes. You'll have to add flour as you knead, because the dough gets wetter the more it is worked. The bread is served toasted, spread with seaweed butter and scattered with herb leaves.

RYE

I asked Karl Ove Knausgård for his crispbread recipe, but by the twenty-sixth page he still hadn't got around to measuring the flour, and I needed to get on. Surprisingly, crispbread dough is not dissimilar to our yeast-risen dough, but since it's rye you're using, you'll need more water. Try 4 cups rye flour, about 1½ cups warm water (or whatever it takes to make a workable dough), half the quantity of yeast (whichever sort you use), and 2 tsp salt. No need for embellishment, although you might add a little molasses to the mix, and a few pinches of caraway seeds or aniseed sprinkled over the dough as you roll it out. Give the dough an hour to ferment (or leave it in the fridge overnight or while you're at work). Don't expect much of a rise. Roll it out thinly. It's up to you whether your crispbreads are big or small, round or rectangular, but if you're aiming for large and round, press a ½-in hole out of the center, to help keep them fairly flat as they cook. For the same reason, no matter what shape and size you're making, dock the dough with a dough docker, skewer, or knitting needle before it goes into the oven. Bake on a lightly floured baking sheet for about 15 minutes at 400°F until crisp and dry. The finished crispbread will keep for at least two weeks in an airtight container. For an easier-to-roll dough, or if you're after a rye sandwich loaf, mix the rye flour with whole wheat flour. Best to use no more than 50 percent rye flour; the closer you approach that limit, the more your bread will take on the darkness and complexity of a mid-period Ingmar Bergman movie. Andrew Whitley warns that if you simply substitute rye for wheat in a recipe using baker's yeast, you can "expect a brick." For all its textural difficulties, rye is hospitable to several interesting flavor blends. Nigel Slater adds grated Parmesan and chopped walnuts during the second knead of a loaf made with rye, whole wheat spelt, and white wheat flours. Dan Lepard gives a recipe for black-pepper rye bread brought together with warm black coffee.

SAUERKRAUT

Add vinegar to a yeasted bread dough for a faux-sourdough effect, or give it a similar tang with citric acid, sour cream, or sauerkraut. This sauerkraut bread makes a great pastrami sandwich, or anything Reubenesque for that matter. Mix half a 28-oz jar of well-squeezed sauerkraut with 2 cups bread flour, 1 tbsp sugar, 1½ tsp salt, 4 tbsp plain yogurt, 1 tbsp caraway seeds, 1½ tsp instant yeast, and ¾ cup hand-hot water, followed by as much spelt flour as you need to make the dough kneadable—up to about 2 cups. Then follow the method from step 3 onward, giving the dough its first rise in a bowl, and a second in a 9 x 5 x 3-in (8-cup) loaf pan, before baking for 15 minutes at 400°F, and then 40 minutes at 350°F.

SPELT

Spelt was once the most commonly used grain in Europe, and the kind available today is biologically identical to the variety that was eaten in Roman times. It's a member of the *Triticum* family, which also includes newer additions like *Triticum aestivum*, bread wheat, and *Triticum turgidum* var. *durum*, the primary pasta and couscous cultivar. Spelt contains more protein, minerals, and vitamins than its younger relatives, and its fans are convinced it has a better flavor, too. But its nutritious double hull, hard as a centurion's helmet, caused its fall from favor in the nineteenth century: It's tough work to harvest and mill spelt. Possibly one of the grain's greatest fans, the twelfth-century German abbess Hildegard of Bingen (canonized, not before time, in 2012) ate spelt toast or spelt porridge as the first meal of the day, sometimes with a cup of spelt coffee. (She also advocated beer, wine, and a nap at midday, and should by rights have a chain of holistic health spas named after her.) Use 4½ cups of spelt flour instead of 4 cups of bread flour in the starting point but watch the rise. It may be faster than with standard wheat flour.

WHOLE WHEAT

In *A Little Dinner Before the Play*, Agnes Jekyll, sister-in-law of the more famous Gertrude, recalls a "certain *maigre* luncheon on a sunny Friday of an early summer." Her small party ate newly laid eggs scrambled with young asparagus and pink-fleshed trout with tiny potatoes and crisp lettuce. "A wholemeal loaf and milk scones were there, with homemade cream cheese; the first fruits of the bee-hive also, tasting of the scent of lime trees in blossom, and the last fruits of the dairy in golden butter. Woodland strawberries, harbingers of the summer, in leaf-lined baskets, gave out their fugitive aroma, and finally a brown jug of coffee freshly roasted and ground, hot and fragrant beyond all previous experience, brought its valedictory blessing to a perfect meal." And you went to Subway for a tuna sandwich. For a whole wheat loaf like Jekyll's, substitute whole wheat flour for the white bread flour in our starting point, and be prepared to use more warm water than the specified amount.

Yeast-Risen Bread → Other Directions

CALZONE

Roll and stretch dough into a rough circle, place filling on one half, fold over the other half, and seal with water. Bake at 425°F for 10–15 minutes.

FATAYER

Roll out ¼-in-thick circles and fill with lamb, spinach, or cheese. Fold in dough on three sides, seal with water, and bake at 425°F for 10–15 minutes.

AS A BOWL FOR SOUP

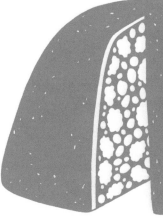

STEAMED CILANTRO BUNS (YUTANGZA)

Roll out circles of dough, brush with melted butter, and spoon on chopped cilantro. Fold edges to center and roll into a bun. Brush with melted butter, let rise, and then steam, half-covered, for 20 minutes.

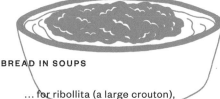

BREAD IN SOUPS

… for ribollita (a large crouton), pappa al pomodoro (torn into pieces), pancotto (cooked to a soft mash), and gazpacho (ground into crumbs).

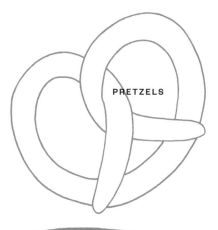

SUMMER PUDDING

Bread is used to line a pudding basin before it's filled with berries. An English classic.

PRETZELS

BREAD SAUCE

Bread is also used in sauces like tarator (page 304) and in some nut stews, such as *aji de gallina* (page 312) and *romesco de peix* (page 315).

MIGAS DE PASTOR

"Shepherd's bread crumbs"— mixed with garlic, paprika, chopped serrano ham, and olive oil. Many other variations, including sweet versions.

Buns

The optional butter and sugar in our yeast-risen bread are standard for buns. The dough is further enriched with milk, in place of water, plus an egg. This starting point covers burger and hot dog buns, tea cakes, and fruited breads.

For 8–10 buns, or a medium-size round fruit bread [A]

INGREDIENTS
4 tbsp butter
4 cups bread flour [B]
2 tsp instant yeast [C][D]
1–4 tbsp sugar [E]
½ tsp salt [F]
1¼ cups warm milk
1 egg [G]
For tea cakes or fruited bread: 2 tsp pumpkin-pie spice and ½ cup raisins

1   In a large bowl, rub the butter into the flour until it has all but vanished, then stir in the yeast, sugar, salt, and (if using) pumpkin-pie spice.

2   Make a well in the center and pour in the warm milk and the beaten egg. Mix it all to a dough using a spoon, your hand, or both. It'll be stickier than plain bread dough.

3   Transfer the dough to a lightly floured surface and knead for about 8–10 minutes until smooth. Add raisins (if using) toward the end.
    If you don't like handling sticky dough, use a mixer with a dough hook.

4   Transfer the kneaded dough to a large, lightly oiled bowl and find a warm spot for it. Cover the bowl with a clean dish towel, or a piece of plastic wrap, and let rise until double in size. Start checking after 40 minutes.

5   When it has doubled in size, deflate the dough with your fingers.
    At this point you can put it in a large freezer bag and leave it in the fridge for later use—it can be kept for a week.

6   Fashion into rounds for tea cakes or burger buns, torpedo shapes for hot dog buns, or a round loaf. Transfer to a lightly greased baking sheet.

7 Give the dough its second rise, covered. Start to check after 20 minutes for buns, 30 for a loaf. You're after an approximate doubling in size.
A tented plastic shopping bag can be used for a cover.

8 Bake at 400°F. Buns will need 12–18 minutes, a loaf about 35 minutes.
Brush burger and hot dog buns with beaten egg and sprinkle with sesame seeds before baking, if you like.

9 Remove from the sheet and transfer to a wire rack to cool.
Warm tea cakes or fruit bread can be brushed with heated, strained apricot jam to glaze them.

LEEWAY

A For a loaf baked in a 9 x 5 x 3-in (8-cup) loaf pan, use 3⅓ cups flour, 2 tbsp butter, 1½ tsp yeast, 2 tbsp sugar, 1 cup warm milk, 1 egg minus 2 tsp of the white, plus pumpkin-pie spice and raisins as required.

B Replace some or all of the white flour in tea cakes or fruit bread with whole wheat flour, or some rye flour. You may need a little extra milk to bring the dough together. (Such substitutions might not be appropriate in burger and hot dog buns.)

C Bread made with instant yeast can be baked after one rise, so you can skip steps 4 and 5 if you're in a hurry. Two rises give a better flavor.

D For yeasts that need activating, add 1 cake compressed fresh or 1 tbsp active dry to ½ cup warm milk with 1 tsp sugar. Leave for 15 minutes to froth up, then add at step 2, with the remaining warm milk.

E Use any sort of sugar.

F The amount of salt stipulated here will be okay for any buns, but you may wish to add another ½ tsp to the mix if you're not after particularly sweet results.

G The egg can be omitted. Or use 1 or 2 yolks in place of a whole egg for a softer texture (whites have a drying effect).

CHALLAH

The braided, enriched Jewish bread called challah is a godsend for the dairy-intolerant. It's made with water rather than milk, and oil rather than butter. A little more egg is required than in our starting point, and honey often takes the place of sugar. It's often said that challah is the very best bread for French toast or bread pudding. Maybe so, but that presupposes the existence of leftovers, an unlikely state of affairs if you've ever tried challah toasted. My first loaf was gone before the day was out. Make as per the starting point, omitting the butter and sugar, and using 2 tbsp honey dissolved in 1 cup warm water in place of the milk. Add an extra yolk with the egg. At step 6, divide the dough into three equal portions and roll into snakes (you may need to shake a veil of flour over the portions to make this manageable). Transfer to a lightly oiled baking sheet and braid the snakes together, starting in the middle and working your way out to the ends. Let rise, then brush with beaten egg, sprinkle with poppy or sesame seeds, and bake at 350°F for about 40 minutes. Cool on a wire rack. In Jewish tradition, the Sabbath meal usually begins with two loaves of challah, representing the double portions of manna that fell from heaven during the Israelites' forty years in the desert.

DILL & COTTAGE CHEESE

In the 1960 Pillsbury Bake-Off, a Mrs. Leona Schnuelle of Nebraska won the rather handsome first prize of $25,000 for her "dilly bread." Schnuelle used cottage cheese in place of the whey her mother had used to make bread on the family farm, and dill seed because a previous winner had used sesame seeds in her entry. She was onto a winner, she realized, when she caught the first whiff of the bread in the oven. As an alternative to dill, M.F.K. Fisher suggests making this enriched bread with chives, parsley (fresh or dried), or tarragon, which she says would go well with cold roast chicken on a picnic. The following is a slight adaptation of the original. Make up half of our starting-point quantity with 1½ tbsp butter, 2 cups bread flour, 1 tsp instant yeast, 2 tbsp sugar, and ½ tsp salt. When you come to add the warm milk and egg, follow by 1 cup cottage cheese, 1 tbsp grated onion, 2 tsp dill seed, and ¼ tsp baking soda. Give the dough its second rise in a lightly greased 8-in springform pan and bake at 340°F for 40 minutes. Brush the finished bread with melted butter and scatter over sea salt.

GINGER

Ginger buns: not a saucy gangster's moll, but a fixture of Jewish bakeries in Amsterdam. The recipe adapts our starting point by including the egg in the liquid, so only 1 cup milk is needed. (This is crucial, because the dough must be rolled out, and it would otherwise be too wet.) Make the dough as per the method, omitting the sugar if you prefer. After the first rise, roll it into two rectangles of about 12 x 6 in, then cut each of these into 6 smaller rectangles of 6 x 2 in. Mix together finely diced candied ginger (about 6 pieces), 3 tbsp melted butter, and 4 tbsp sugar. Spread this filling lengthwise along the middle of each rectangle, then roll it into a long tube and seal with a little water and some pinching. Using your hands, roll the tubes over some sugar, deploying the same technique you once used to make Play-Doh snakes. Once they're about 9 in long, curl each one into a coil and transfer to a lightly greased baking sheet. Paint with ginger syrup (from the jar of candied ginger) and let rise until they're doubled in size, then bake at 350°F for 15–20 minutes.

LARDY CAKE

The traditional British lardy cake may have a reputation for being an indulgence, but in fact most recipes call for a lot less sugar and fat than the average cookie or cupcake. There are many regional variations, but most involve layering a yeast-risen dough with lard, sugar, and dried fruit: As Charles Campion notes, lardy cake is the cousin of a croissant. (Incidentally, in his recipe, Campion uses butter, not lard.) Some lardy cake recipes stipulate a plain dough, as per the starting point for yeast-risen bread, but I prefer bun dough in my loose adaptation of Elizabeth David's recipe for Northumberland lardy cake. Follow the starting point for buns, making up half the given quantity, using an egg yolk in place of the egg, and no butter. Once you have deflated the dough at step 5, roll it out into a rectangle, mentally dividing it lengthwise into thirds: Over two of the thirds, scatter 2 tbsp lard, cut into pea-size pieces, 3 tbsp dried currants, and 2 tbsp sugar, patting down lightly. Fold the unadorned third over the middle adorned third, then fold the remaining adorned third over that, so you have a three-story stack. Roll the stack out into a rectangle again, and repeat with the same quantities of lard, currants, and sugar, this time aiming for a square to fit into a greased 8-in pan. Let rise for about an hour, then bake at 400°F for 30–35 minutes.

PUMPKIN

The Brazilians eat a bun-like pumpkin bread called *pão de abóbora* or *pão de jerimum*. Follow the starting point, increasing the sugar to ½ cup and using 4 tbsp vegetable oil in place of the butter. For a conventionally sweet bun, add 1 tbsp pumpkin-pie spice to the flour; for a savory version, leave out the sugar altogether and use a little chopped sage. Mix the yeast and salt into the flour, incorporate the oil and half the warm milk plus 1 cup pumpkin or butternut squash purée. Then add as much of the remaining warm milk as needed to produce a dough that's soft but not sticky. Continue from step 3 of the method.

ROSEMARY

Easter aesthetes may prefer to shun chocolate eggs full of M&M's for the sweet Tuscan bread known as *pan di ramerino*. It's a bun-like bread made with water and oil rather than milk and butter. At step 2, soften a rosemary stalk and ⅔ cup dried currants in 4 tbsp olive oil, remove from the heat, then discard the rosemary and stir in ¼ cup sugar. Set aside while you measure 1¼ cups warm water and add it to the flour, yeast, and salt. Scrape in the currants with their oil, then add the beaten egg and mix to a dough. Pick up the method from step ³, to make 10 buns. If you're wondering what the Easter connection might be, rosemary is for remembrance.

SESAME

Tahinov gata are tahini-flavored Armenian rolls that deserve a place alongside *pain au chocolat* or almond croissants. Make up a dough as per our starting point for buns, but use double the amount of butter—melted, rather than softened—and add it with the milk and egg. After the first rise, divide the dough into 8 balls. Roll out each one to an 8-in round, spread with 1–2 tbsp tahini, and sprinkle over 4 tsp light brown sugar. A further sprinkle of ground cinnamon is optional. Roll up each one like a tiny Armenian carpet, then simultaneously stretch and twist it like a piece of rope. Coil each into the shape of a snail shell, and tuck the ends in. Transfer to a lightly greased baking sheet and let them rise for 30 minutes, before gently brushing the tops with beaten egg yolk and baking them at 375°F for 35 minutes. I have also made these rolls with yeast-risen bread (i.e. non-enriched) dough (page ⁴⁴), and they are still fabulous. The tahini is luscious and rich, and the sugar elevates it to special-treat status, demanding an accompanying cup of your favorite coffee. Nutella, smooth or crunchy peanut butter, or marzipan can be used in place of tahini. Or take a cue from the snail shape and use moss-green snail butter—that is, butter mashed with minced parsley and garlic (hold the sugar).

SPIRAL BUNS

Chelsea buns, glazed spirals of dough containing lemon zest, currants, sugar, and butter, were invented at the Bun House in Pimlico Road, London, in the early eighteenth century. They were an immediate craze. Some prefer to split and butter their buns, as you would a tea cake, but I think that misses the point: A Chelsea bun must be unwound, length by edible length, like a licorice wheel. The dough contains brioche-like levels of butter, and is rolled into rectangles before being folded a few times, like puff pastry, then rolled up. Or you can adapt our starting point for a simpler, sparer sort of spiral bun. Once the dough has had its first rise, deflate it and roll it out to an 18 × 12-in rectangle. Excepting a ¾-in margin, dot the dough with 6 tbsp unsalted butter, cut into pea-size pieces, and ½ cup dried currants, then sprinkle over 6 tbsp brown sugar. Roll the dough up from a long edge, so it looks like a bolster, then trim off the ends and cut across into 12 equal slices. Transfer these to a greased baking sheet, spacing them about 1 in apart, then let rise in a plastic-bag tent until roughly doubled in size. As the buns expand during rising and baking (15–20 minutes at 425°F), they should join up, creating the desired square-ish shape. Remove from the oven and immediately glaze with a mixture of 2 tbsp sugar dissolved in 1 tbsp hot milk. Leave for 5 minutes, then separate the buns. The painter Arthur Lett-Haines felt the standard-size Chelsea bun was "rather large and bucolic," so made his buns petit-four-size and decorated them with Angostura-flavored royal icing and poppy seeds.

STOLLEN

The shape of this classic German Christmas cake is supposed to suggest the swaddled baby Jesus, at least if it's the sort of stollen with marzipan in the middle. Commercial bakers have taken to selling it at Christmas in the U.K., but are invariably Scrooge-like with the marzipan, whereas home bakers can control the crucial marzipan-to-bun-dough ratio. When sliced, my first attempt at stollen looked like a fried egg. Not bad, but too much marzipan in one place. Andrew Whitley gets around the problem by laying a sheet of marzipan over the dough and rolling it up, roulade-style, so the marzipan is more evenly distributed. Classic stollen is made as per our starting point. Here I use half the quantities, i.e. 2 cups flour and, rather than ½ egg, just the yolk. You can add raisins (brandy- or rum-soaked, if you like), diced candied peel, grated citrus zest, and baking spices to taste—a little cardamom is good. After the first rise, punch down the dough and roll it out into a rectangle about 10 x 6 in. Lay a 9-in-long cylinder of approximately ⅔ cup marzipan (page 280) along the length of the dough, placing it in the center. Fold the ½ in of dough at each end up and over the marzipan, then fold over the long sides, allowing a decent overlap. Transfer to a lightly greased baking sheet, seam-side down, and let rise. Once the stollen is about twice its original size, bake at 375°F for 20 minutes. Remove and sprinkle with confectioners' sugar, or top with a confectioners' sugar and lemon juice glaze. Delia Smith likes her stollen toasted.

Brioche

Brioche is a mildly sweet, golden bread often eaten for breakfast with milky coffee or hot chocolate. Most of the milk used to make the buns in the previous starting point is replaced by beaten egg. This makes for a pretty sticky dough—and then you start adding the butter. Lots of it. It's both an ordeal and an experience to make by hand, so a food-mixer alternative is given at [A] under Leeway.

For 2 loaves, or a 9-bun "flower" in a 10-in round pan [B]

INGREDIENTS
1 tbsp instant yeast [C]
4 cups bread flour [D]
1 tsp salt
2–4 tbsp sugar
4 tbsp warm milk or water
5 large eggs [E]
2 sticks unsalted butter, softened [F] [G]

[1] Measure the yeast, flour, salt, and sugar into a large bowl. Give it a mix.

[2] Make a well in the center and pour in the milk or water and beaten eggs, then mix to a dough. Transfer the mixture to a lightly floured surface and knead for 8–10 minutes until smooth.

[3] Divide the butter into four equal portions and knead it into the dough, portion by portion. With each addition of butter, you'll go through a sticky phase, but fear not: Keep going and the dough will become smooth and stretchy again. The whole process might take as long as 30 minutes.

[4] Find a nice warm spot and cover the bowl with lightly oiled plastic wrap. Leave for 1–2 hours. Don't expect it to rise like bread dough—it contains too much butter for that. [H]

[5] Deflate the puffed dough with your fingers. Knead for a minute, then cover and let rise in the fridge for 4–16 hours.
If the dough hasn't quite doubled in size, take it out and let it complete its rise somewhere cozier. If you're planning to shape your brioche into balls or braided loaves, it may ultimately need a further short stint in the fridge to firm up.

6 Shape the dough. For loaves, use 2 buttered 8½ x 4½ x 2½-in (6-cup) loaf pans; for a "flower," divide into 9 balls and place in a round pan. Let rise, covered, somewhere warm until doubled.

7 Glaze the top of the brioche with egg yolk, and bake at 375°F for 20–25 minutes. Buns should be checked after 12 minutes.

8 Wrap the finished brioche tightly in foil, or a plastic food bag, and use within 2–3 days. If you doubt you'll get through it in that time, wrap and freeze it.

LEEWAY

A The process is pretty much the same using an electric mixer. Mix up the dough and knead with a dough hook for 7 minutes until smooth and elastic, then add the butter 2 tbsp at a time, allowing it to become incorporated before adding more. When all the butter is mixed in, and the dough is shiny and smooth, pick up from step 4.

B Half this quantity will do for a classic 9-in brioche mold. At step 6, tear off roughly a fifth of the dough. Roll both the large and small pieces into balls, and make a depression in the larger piece in which the smaller can nestle. Give the dough its third rise and continue. Glaze with egg yolk and bake for 30–35 minutes.

C Use 2 packages of active dry yeast or 1¼ cakes of compressed fresh yeast in place of instant; some recipes call for them in preference. Activate either in the warm milk or water with 1 tsp sugar, leaving it for 15 minutes to froth, and add at step 2 with the eggs.

D Some cooks use all-purpose flour, or 00, in place of white bread flour.

E If you only have 4 eggs, use 7 tbsp warm milk.

F Regrettably, melting the butter and adding it from the outset doesn't work. Many have tried and failed.

G Halve the butter amount for a lean brioche. For a rich brioche use double the butter quantity, although this is not advisable if you're making the dough by hand—it will be too sticky to manage.

H Brioche is quite a fussy dough, and doesn't always rise as fast as the recipe suggests. Patience will be your friend here. Note that some people are uncomfortable leaving a butter-and-egg-enriched dough sitting around at room temperature for 4 or maybe 5 hours. I'm not, but it's your call.

BRIE

Who put the Brie in brioche? Alexandre Dumas, in his *Dictionary of Cuisine* (1873), claims that it was once common to make brioche with the cheese, although the food scholar Darra Goldstein dismisses this as "fakelore." Which is not to say that it's a bad idea: Several cooks have experimented with it. Cheesemaker-turned-baker Peter Reinhart notes that while adding grated cheese to a dough might add some flavor and softness, it has a tendency to disappear in the finished article. His recommendation is to roll the dough around the cheese. Try encasing small triangles of Brie into *fatayer*-like dough shapes (page 53). *Pane al formaggio* is an Italian cheese brioche, not unlike a panettone enriched with grated Parmesan and studded with pieces of pecorino in place of the raisins, or in addition to them.

CHOCOLATE & SICHUAN PEPPER

Brioche rolls with chocolate chips are so popular that even discount grocery stores sell them. Should a surfeit of them have dulled your palate, try the chocolate and Sichuan pepper brioche devised by the Parisian pâtissier Gontran Cherrier. If buttery bread, chocolate, and the lemony, sub-Novocaine tingle of the pepper aren't stimulation enough, Cherrier recommends trying it with foie gras or strawberry jam (drop the "or"—I'll have both). The addition of cocoa powder makes the dough even trickier than that for regular brioche, so making this by hand is not advised. In place of bread flour, Cherrier uses 4½ cups all-purpose flour. Use active dry yeast and activate it in 5 tbsp warm milk with 1 tsp of sugar. Put 4 tbsp sugar in a bowl with the flour, 4 tbsp sifted unsweetened cocoa powder, 2 tsp salt, 1 tsp crushed Sichuan pepper, and ½ cup semisweet chocolate chips. Add the yeast mixture and stir it in, followed by 6 eggs. Then work in 2 sticks butter in four installments, as per our starting point. Let rise twice at room temperature, the first time for about an hour, the second for about 45 minutes, before transferring to two 8½ x 4½ x 2½-in (6-cup) loaf pans. Let rise a final time, then bake your brioche loaves for about 35 minutes at 350°F.

ORANGE-FLOWER WATER

A very common flavoring in brioche-type cakes. In his fascinating book *The Taste of Bread*, Raymond Calvel describes the Provençal Christmas bread, *pompe des rois*, the ring-shaped *fouace de Rodez* from Aveyron, and *mouna*. Indigenous to Algeria, but now found in southern France and beyond, *mouna* is a gorgeous, orange-flower-scented boule of brioche, studded with crystal sugar, and often enhanced with candied orange peel and Cointreau; in Oran, one of four Christian dioceses in the country, it's traditionally eaten at Easter. To make a simple floral-scented brioche, replace 1 of the eggs with 3 tbsp orange-flower water, beating it into the other 4 eggs.

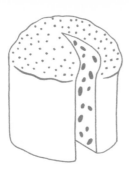

PANETTONE

The French look down on Milanese panettone, considering it the perfumed poseur of the brioche family. The fussy extracts get in the way of the natural flavorings: eggs, butter, and fermentation. Lord knows what they'd make of one flashy recipe for panettone I came across, which adds ground coriander, fennel, and pine nuts to the mix. (I'd often wondered what you might eat off those Versace tea plates you see in Bloomingdale's, and now I know.) According to *Fenaroli's Handbook of Flavor Ingredients*, authentic Milanese panettone is made with wheat flour, natural yeast, butter, sugar, whole eggs, yolks, raisins, citron, orange peel, candied fruit, salt, milk, and powdered dry malt, enhanced with a blended aromatic essence, concentrated so as not to interfere with the leavening process. Fenaroli suggests equal parts orange, citron, and mandarin oil, with a lesser amount of bergamot and vanilla. You can make something not dissimilar at home, and given the splendor of the results, the whole process is delightfully simple. The basic principle is to cross-breed a cake mix with a yeasted-dough sponge. Measure out ⅔ cup dried currants. Transfer a quarter of them to a small pan, cover with Marsala, and warm them. Stir in the grated zest of 1 orange, 1 lemon, and 2 mandarins, and let soak. Mix the rest of the currants with ⅓ cup diced mixed candied peel and toss in a little flour. Set aside. Make a yeast sponge with 1¼ cups bread flour, 1½ tsp instant yeast, 1 tsp sugar, and ½ cup warm water. Let rise until doubled in size. Once it's getting close, cream ⅔ cup soft butter with 6 tbsp sugar. Mix in 2 eggs and 4 yolks (at room temperature). The eggs may curdle if you're mixing by hand, but don't worry—it won't affect the finished product. Add 7 tbsp hand-hot milk, 2 tbsp Marsala, 1 tsp orange extract, ½ tsp salt, and the yeast sponge and mix thoroughly. Add 2 cups flour and mix, followed by as much of up to 2 cups more flour as needed to make a soft dough. Pick up from step 4 of the method, noting that the dough will probably need at least 2 hours to double in size. Deflate the dough, then knead in your soaked and floured fruits for only as long as it takes to distribute them evenly. Transfer to an 8-in springform pan that has been fitted with a tall collar of parchment paper, and let rise until it has attained proper panettone height: This might take 2½ hours, it might take 4. Brush with egg white and, if you like, sprinkle with crystal sugar. Bake at 425°F for 10 minutes, then 350°F for 30–40 minutes. You may want to tent the top with foil after the first 15–20 minutes to arrest browning. If you're not fussed about currants and mixed peel, note that the Lombardy pasticceria Scarpato makes a panettone that replaces them with pieces of marrons glacés. Pandoro is another option. It has no other bits in it, and although it contains a hint of citron oil, the dominant flavor is butter. A slice with Marsala ice cream and a few dots of good balsamic is a winning alternative to the British plum pudding at Christmas.

PRALINE

The name Pralus, from Roanne near Lyon, in France, will be familiar to anyone with expensive tastes in confectionery, but before they made their name in chocolate, the brand was famous for the sublime "Praluline" brioche invented by Auguste Pralus himself. The bun is flavored with Valencian almonds and Piedmont hazelnuts cooked in pink rose sugar, cracked, then added to the dough and sprinkled over the top of the brioche. The result looks like something Mariah Carey might feed to her unicorns for tea. (Pink pralines can be bought from online sources.) Add 3 oz pralines, roughly crushed, to the dough just before you shape it. A hand-fashioned round will be perfectly authentic, but you can aim for a neater brioche shape if you prefer. Give it an egg wash, and sprinkle over a further 1 oz of the crushed pralines. Let rise and bake as described in the starting point.

SAUSAGE

Baking *saucisson* in brioche is pretty popular in France. Definitely a cut above pigs in blankets, especially in Lyon, where a local variant contains a quantity of truffles and garlic. In Majorca, *ensaïmada* is made with a brioche-like dough, but with lard in place of butter (*saïm* is Mallorquín for lard). The results are quite visually distinct: Rather than a taut up-do like a Picasso bust of Marie-Thérèse Walter, *ensaïmada* dough is folded and rolled into a loose coil like a fire hose. Most *ensaïmadas* are liberally dusted with confectioners' sugar, but some are taken in a savory direction with pieces of *sobrassada*, the soft, spreadable Balearic cousin of chorizo. Thanks to Spanish colonization, the bread has a second home in the Philippines. *Ensaymada* is a bit chubbier than its Old World antecedent, and might be covered with grated cheese, or filled with *ube* (purple yam) or *monggo* (mung-bean paste).

SWEET CORN

As eaten at The Grain Store in London's King's Cross: A slice of fermented corn brioche, toasted and served with tapioca cooked in squid ink to look like caviar and sour cream with dill. I couldn't detect much of a fermented tang from the corn, but corn and butter are such happy bedfellows, who cares? Keep the amount of salt very low and you could pass this off as a cake. Simmer the kernels cut from 1 ear of sweet corn in ½ cup milk for 2 minutes. Drain, retaining 2 tbsp of the milk to use in the dough. Follow our starting point, halving the quantities—in the case of egg, use 2 whole eggs plus 1 yolk. Add the cooked sweet corn kernels to the dough toward the end of kneading. The rises will take a great deal longer than usual. Transfer the dough to an 8½ x 4½ x 2½-in (6-cup) loaf pan for its second rise.

Brioche → Other Directions

BURGER BUNS

TARTE TROPÉZIENNE

A layer cake made with rum or orange-flower water brioche, filled with whipped cream, pastry cream, and/or buttercream.

BRIOCHE FRUIT TART

Use like puff pastry in a tarte Tatin: Cook fruit in butter and sugar until caramelized, cover with a circle of brioche dough, and bake at 350°F for 30 minutes.

SWEET BREAD PUDDING

PAN DE MUERTO

A lean brioche flavored with aniseed and orange zest or orange-flower water, decorated with bones or skulls, and baked for the Day of the Dead in Mexico.

YAKI-SOBA PAN-BRIOCHE

Or hot dog buns, filled with hot noodles.

BRIOCHE TOAST

... with pâté, chutney, and cornichons.

BEIGNETS

Pieces of brioche dough deep-fried and sprinkled with sugar.

Babas & Savarins

Where dough becomes a batter: Babas are made with the same liquid-to-flour ratio as all the other bun and bread mixes on the continuum, plus plenty of egg and melted butter. The same batter is used for savarins, which are baked in a ring-shaped mold—either in individual molds or a single, large one.

For 6 individual babas, or 1 large savarin [A]

INGREDIENTS
1½ tsp instant yeast [B]
2 cups bread flour [C]
¼ tsp salt
1 tbsp sugar [D]
⅔ cup milk [E] [F]
3 eggs [G]
5 tbsp unsalted butter, melted and cooled [H]

FOR THE RUM SYRUP [I] [J]
1 cup boiling water
1½ cups sugar
1–5 tbsp rum, according to taste

1 Measure the yeast, flour, salt, and sugar into a large bowl with enough room for the final batter to double during its rise. Make a well in the center.

2 Warm the milk (not too hot or it will scramble the eggs) and pour into the flour with the beaten eggs. Mix, add the melted butter, and stir to make a homogenous batter.

3 Scrape the batter into thoroughly buttered molds. Fill them roughly halfway, and no farther.

4 Once the batter has almost reached the top of its containers it's ready to be baked. Glaze with beaten egg or yolk, if you like. The rise takes about 45 minutes in my warmish kitchen. Do keep an eye out, however. You don't want dough erupting all over your surfaces.

5 Bake in a 375°F oven: Individual babas will need 15–20 minutes; for a savarin, allow 20–25 minutes.

6 While the babas bake, make the syrup. Pour the boiling water over the sugar and stir until dissolved, then stir in the rum.

7 Remove the cooked babas from the oven and let cool a little, then unmold onto a dish suitable for their drenching in syrup.

8 Pour about half of the syrup over the babas and leave them to absorb it for about 10 minutes. Turn the babas upside-down and drizzle over the rest of the syrup. Serve as they are, or with whipped cream and fruit. ᴷ

LEEWAY

A This makes a good quantity for six 5-oz molds (special baba molds, deep muffin pans, ramekins, and dariole molds can all be used) or a 10-in savarin mold.

B If you're using yeast that needs to be activated first, mix ½ cake compressed fresh or 1½ tsp active dry yeast in the warm milk with 1 tsp of the sugar, and leave for 15 minutes to froth. Add it at step 2 and proceed as usual, but give the mix two rises, the first in the mixing bowl. Once it has doubled, stir it and pour into the baking molds for its second rise. Bake when the mix almost reaches the rim.

C Many baba recipes call for all-purpose rather than bread flour. A photo finish, as far as I'm concerned.

D A sweeter batter can be made with up to 3 tbsp sugar.

E Replace the milk with water. As with choux pastry, it will give a crisper result.

F Make a nondairy version with coconut milk and peanut oil in place of the milk and butter.

G Use 2 eggs and 1 yolk, reserving the other white for glazing the tops before baking.

H A richer batter can be made with as much as 7 tbsp butter. Note, however, that fat has a retarding effect on yeast, so the rise will be slower.

I The syrup here is thicker than the classic, which is made with 1 cup sugar to 1⅔ cups water.

J You can, of course, flavor the syrup otherwise—see pages 434-8.

K Elizabeth David only adds the syrup when serving, reheating the babas in the oven before pouring it over. I prefer them chilled and rum-logged.

BANANA & SPICE

Any attempt to flavor a rum baba must be made in the expectation that the rum will do its damnedest to drown it out. I found this out the hard way when making a spiced banana variant, whose distinct ingredients were blindsided by the bold intervention of El Dorado rum. That said, the buns I hadn't soused tasted great, toasted and spread with a tangy cultured butter from Normandy. Adapt our starting point, using 2 cups flour plus 1 tsp each of ground cinnamon and cloves. Reduce the warm milk quantity to 6 tbsp and use brown sugar. Add ¼ cup puréed very ripe banana and 1 tsp vanilla extract to the mix along with the butter. If you find the banana more appealing than the booze, try it with a plain sugar syrup and no rum.

COCONUT & BROWN SUGAR

Of all the flavorings in my baba line-up, this was the one my tasters picked out. But I must confess to a shortcoming in my data collection: There may have been a bias toward the coconut-brown-sugar babas, caused by their preparation in individual savarin molds, which made them look like exceptionally cute doughnuts, all the more so for their coconut fur. As I dressed them with rum and cream, I was reminded of a dessert from the Formica-tabled cafés of my youth, the sorts of places that smelled of vinegar, fried bacon, and cigarette smoke. The so-called "brown derby" was a doughnut with a scoop of ice cream in its hole, topped with whipped cream, chocolate sauce, and chopped nuts. Consider this an alternative way to serve your baba if you dislike booze or the texture of drenched sponge. For the coconut babas, mix ½ cup dried shredded coconut into the flour with 2 tbsp dark brown sugar. Coconut milk can be used in place of cow's milk.

CORNMEAL & BUTTERMILK

An idea inspired by a recipe for an eggy, yeasted Croatian cornbread that was tantalizingly close to our starting point. I mixed up 50/50 bread flour and fine cornmeal and used warmed buttermilk—if you want to make your own buttermilk substitute, see page 37. The yellow batter rose pretty vigorously. The buttermilk gave the finished buns a distinct tang. As for the corn, it made them a little more robust than the classic baba. Don't be tempted to use all cornmeal, however, unless you want to exfoliate your tongue.

LIME

Many chefs prefer to keep their babas plain, for fear of interfering with the rum's flavor, but will make an exception for orange or lemon zest, or a combination of the two. Or lime, which has a special affinity for rum, as you'll know if you've ever ended up dancing on the table after a glass or two of rum punch. Come to think of it, once you've zested the limes for the babas, you'll have the juice to spare, so you might as well go ahead and make the punch. The classic mnemonic is "one of sour, two of sweet, three of strong, and four of weak," the sour being lime juice; the sweet being sugar syrup; the strong, rum; and the weak, fruit juice (a mix of orange, mango, and passion fruit just tastes *right*). Decant it into glasses over ice and add a dash of Angostura bitters and a grating of nutmeg. The syrup is made with equal volumes of sugar and hot water.

RYE & TOKAJI

Marie Leszczynska, the Polish wife of Louis XV, is often credited with introducing the baba to the French. Marie-Antoine Carême recalls gargantuan babas in the royal dining room, accompanied by a large pitcher containing a mixture of sweet Malaga wine and *eau de tanaisie* (tansy, an herbaceous perennial, which has bright yellow flowers and tastes of rosemary or ginger, depending on who you ask). Leszczynska claimed the babas should be made with rye flour and flavored with Hungarian wine. Rye has its merits, but can't match white wheat flour when it comes to the sort of light, open-textured bun that's receptive to a dousing in syrup. Mind you, if the syrup were flavored with Tokaji, one might be persuaded otherwise.

SAFFRON & RAISIN

According to Louis-Eustache Ude, chef during the 1930s at Crockford's, the gaming club in St. James's in London, the classic flavoring for a baba was an aromatic mixture of saffron, currants, raisins, and Madeira. *The Oxford Companion to Sugar and Sweets* confirms the saffron and currants, noting that references to rum syrup began to appear only in the 1840s, by which time the baba had been around for centuries. Add a few pinches of ground saffron to the warming milk at step 2 and stir in a handful of raisins just after the melted butter. A similar combination of saffron and dried fruit is used to flavor the yeasted dough for the saffron loaves and buns traditional in Cornwall, England. If only a Penzance pirate had been a little clumsier with his ration of grog, Cornwall might have had another feather in its catering hairnet.

Cornbread, Polenta & Gnocchi

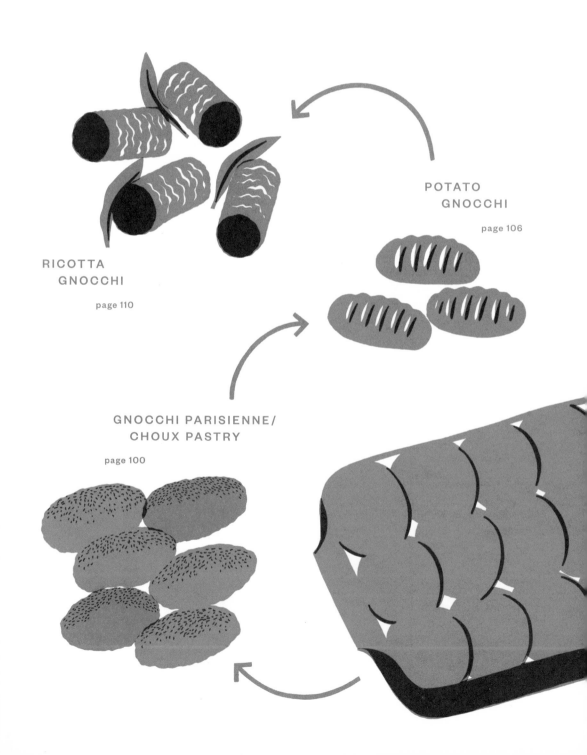

POTATO
GNOCCHI

page 106

RICOTTA
GNOCCHI

page 110

GNOCCHI PARISIENNE/
CHOUX PASTRY

page 100

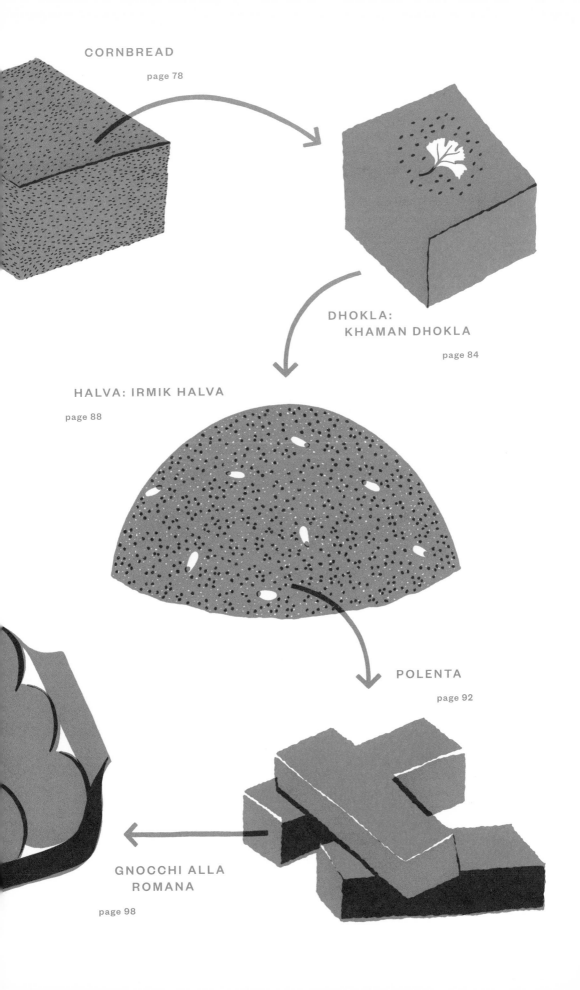

CORNBREAD

page 78

DHOKLA:
KHAMAN DHOKLA

page 84

HALVA: IRMIK HALVA

page 88

POLENTA

page 92

GNOCCHI ALLA
ROMANA

page 98

This continuum takes as its common theme the transformation of grain and liquid into hearty staples. By its end, my hope is that you will be delving into your kitchen cupboards for long-neglected grains on the brink of staleness or annexation by weevils. Making cornbread, polenta, or gnocchi can be immensely satisfying and, as you'll see, there's endless room for experimentation.

C The cornbread at the start of the continuum is closer to the bouncier
O variety eaten in the north of the U.S. than the sparer Southern sort.
R It's soda bread's first cousin once removed. Both are mixed up hastily,
N so they can make it into the oven while the leavener still has some
B oomph. Both call for similar quantities of grain and baking soda,
R with optional, modest additions of fat and sweetness. Cornbread
E requires a bit more buttermilk, but the one remove really lies in
A the addition of egg. Recipes for cornbread tend to stipulate two or
D three. Soda bread is usually eggless, meaning that it comes together
as a kneadable dough. Cornbread could only conceivably be kneaded in a world where its preparation formed the basis of the penal system. The eggs give it a batter consistency and, when baked, a moist, cakelike texture more suited to cutting into chunks or wedges than thin slices. Unadorned by savory ingredients like bacon or cheese, the corn's natural sweetness makes cornbread taste pretty cake-like, too.

Cornmeal is available in several colors and grades. The color makes little difference to the eating quality of the finished bread—but the grind size really does. Plain cornbread made with coarse meal will be sandy in texture, with a distinctively farmyardy flavor. Aficionados recommend stone-ground corn, which includes some of the hull and germ, preserving more of the fat and therefore the flavor. The higher fat content also shortens its shelf life, which means you're unlikely to find it in a mainstream supermarket.

Another alternative is Mexican masa harina, the fine flour made with nixtamal—corn that has been cooked, washed in a lime solution, and (usually) hulled—which yields a winning combination of wheaty softness and the sweetness of corn. Whichever cornmeal you're using, you'll find the best results come from baking the batter in a cast-iron pan or skillet, having heated your fat (preferably lard or bacon fat) in the pan beforehand.

D American visitors to Gujarat in northwest India might feel homesick
H at the sight of khaman dhokla, whose spongy depths and division
O into substantial cubes give it a distinct look of cornbread. The batter,
K however, is made with chickpea flour, and on closer inspection
L the crumb is more earth-toned, like a Rajasthani palace; maize is
A the Technicolor yellow of Oz's brick road. Like cornbread, dhokla
consists of flour, a binding liquid, a leavener, and small amounts of salt, fat, and sugar. It owes its springier texture to being steamed, rather than baked; its mouthfeel is moist, bordering on creamy.

Some versions of dhokla have chopped vegetables mixed into the batter, although you may feel its traditionally extravagant garnish renders this unnecessary. First, mustard seeds and cumin seeds are heated in ghee or oil, to release their flavors, then poured over the dhokla while it's still hot from the steamer. The scented oil seeps into the pores, all the more so if you've taken the trouble (as per syrup drizzled over a cake) to prick the surface beforehand. Finally, the top is sprinkled with a vibrant mix of chopped cilantro, shredded coconut, and finely sliced rings of fresh red chili. The finished dish looks like a game of quoits abandoned after an unexpected spring snowfall.

The comparison with drizzle cake is extended by the addition of a lemony element to the batter—citric acid or lemon juice, or both. In India, the citric acid normally comes in the form of a branded product called Eno, a "fruit salt" sold as a stomach settler. In the absence of Eno, you might make an ersatz version by mixing equal quantities of baking soda and citric acid. Eno lends the sarcastic edge you get with tamarind; you might find the sharpness a little unnerving to begin with. And yet, for me, the first bite led to another, and another, and before I knew it I was off to the Indian mini-mart to stock up on chickpea flour.

Instead of pharmaceutical fruit salts, traditional dhokla derives its rise and tang from the slow fermentation of ground, soaked raw pulses and/or rice in yogurt. Many classic Indian recipes depend on this technique, including idli (small, steamed white cakes), dosas (large, thin pancakes), uttapam (smaller and thicker pancakes with ingredients like tomato or coconut mixed into the batter, page 133), and vadai (a sort of deep-fried, filled doughnut). As with sourdough bread and *beghrir* (Moroccan semolina pancakes, page 134), it's fair to say that the more time-consuming method has the edge when it comes to flavor. Nonetheless, the cheat method yields perfectly delicious results, and has the advantage that you're more likely to get on and make your dhokla, as opposed to sit around intending to do it the hard way. If, however, you do have the time and inclination to make a proper fermented dhokla, using chana dal (page 86), check that your blender is capable of turning soaked chickpeas into a batter. The first time I tried, the blades of my dear old Moulinex chased the pulses round and round, fruitlessly, like Sylvester pursuing Tweety.

H It's possible to vary the dhokla by following the starting point but
A using different grains. Corn is used, but rarely. A more popular
L variant, sooji or rava dhokla, is made with semolina, although I find
V it a bit plain. Like many products of the British educational system,
A my attitude to semolina was formed by repellent, porridge-like semolina pudding, scraped untouched into the waste bin by school cooks the country over. Halva changed all that. Specifically, irmik halva, the sweet semolina pudding from Turkey that furnishes our starting point. The semolina is first toasted in butter or oil, then warmed sweetened milk is added, and the mixture is gently simmered and

stirred until the desired texture is achieved. The toasting produces a popcorn-like aroma of the sort that has propped up the movie industry for a century. It's gorgeous. It's worth noting that halva (the word is derived from the Arabic for "sweet") can be made with any one of a wide range of ingredients besides grain, including fruit, vegetables, or cheese. An especially popular type is made with tahini— although had I included it in this book, it would have sat on the sugar continuum, as a variant of fudge. Cereal-based halvas are simpler to make than the fudgy tahini variety, but don't expect them to be much less sweet if you stick to authentic levels of sugar.

The volume of liquid to grain in halva is the reverse of cornbread and dhokla—i.e. 2:1, rather than 1:2. This reflects the difference in cooking method; halva is made on the stovetop, and thus exposed to fiercer heat, even when the burners are turned down low. The grain thus absorbs the liquid more quickly and thoroughly, although the precise rate and degree of absorption can be controlled by the cook. For irmik halva, the pan can be removed from the heat while its contents are still a damp mass, somewhere between the wetness of oatmeal and the firmer consistency of mashed potato—although it's more common to continue cooking until the halva takes on the consistency of wet dough, with an elasticity that will eventually see it pull away from the sides of the pan. Once it has attained this texture, you can be sure that the mixture will set, and can pour it, as is traditional, into an elaborately shaped mold.

Prettifying halva can be a challenge. Toasted nuts are sometimes used, or you could take inspiration from dhokla's gorgeous garnish and scatter your halva with rose petals, pomegranate seeds, and chopped pistachios. Either that, or accept the fact that, at base, irmik halva looks like government-issue pudding, as frumpy and functional as a dome of masticated manila folders. Its beauty is all on the inside. Nuts or dried fruit are sometimes toasted with the grain, or the cooking liquid sweetened with something other than sugar, say a rich honey, or fruity *pekmez*, a syrup made from condensed grape, fig, or mulberry juice. In India, where halva probably arrived with the Mughals, the pudding is primped with spices like cardamom or cinnamon. Greek semolina halva is juicy with citrus- and cinnamon-flavored syrup.

That said, halva is too various in its incarnations to be written off after a single try. Made with a coarser semolina, halva takes on a crumb texture that, soaked in sweet syrup, rather reminds me of the steamed puddings I made in home economics. Likewise, this sort of halva could happily be served warm with custard sauce, although my local Turkish restaurant opts for vanilla ice cream. At the other end of the grain-grade spectrum, cornstarch mixed with milk yields the halva better known as blancmange, number three on the FBI's list of the ten most egregious offenders against international cuisine, after bubble tea and those pizzas with mini-burgers in the crust.

The savory equivalent of irmik halva is polenta. Historically, polenta was a generic term for any mushy, cooked grain. These days it is usually made with cornmeal, but before Columbus brought his boatload of fancy foreign foodstuffs to Europe, it was variously made with spelt, millet, barley, chestnut, or chickpea flours. Corn soon wiped out its competitors, although buckwheat held firm in some northern regions, where *taragna*, or "black polenta," can still be found to this day. If you've ever cooked with buckwheat, you'll know that "black" in this case isn't terribly black, or even brownish-black, to borrow from mascara terminology. If it's boot-black polenta you're after, best to dye your cornmeal with squid ink.

As a rule of thumb, for polenta the ratio of liquid to grain is 3:1 or 4:1. Some cooks opt for a far longer dilution, in the belief that a very slow simmer gives the best result. Bill Buford describes the three stages of his polenta over its three-hour cooking period as "soupy but thirsty," then "shiny and cakey and coming off the sides," and finally elastic and modestly caramelized from "being baked in its own liquid lava." You could, however, labor over a corn polenta for a week and still fail to convince some people of its merits. My husband says it has a subtlety he can't be bothered to appreciate. Goethe blamed it both for the sickly appearance of Italian peasants in the Tyrol and—sparing the reader no detail—his own constipation. In *Between the Woods and the Water*, the second of three books chronicling his journey on foot from the Hook of Holland to Constantinople in the 1930s, Patrick Leigh Fermor describes eating polenta for the first time, in Transylvania, where it was known as *mamaliga*. "I had been warned against it," he writes. For a man facing foot-blisters the size of jellyfish, diseased and unscrupulous prostitutes, and the looming prospect of war, you might think the mouthfeel of Romanian corn porridge the least of his troubles. In the event, he "perversely found it rather good." Whoever warned him off it plainly hadn't taken his nationality and class into consideration. If there's anything that binds the English upper-middle classes and the hazel-eyed shepherds of the Carpathians, it's negligibly flavorful stodge.

Cold polenta sets, meaning that it can be cut into slices. Stuff these into a soft bread roll with something piquant and uplifting, say mortadella and mostarda di cremona, in the same way you might cut the starch-overdose of a chip butty (page 34) with ketchup. Or bake the pieces and serve them with butter and cheese, in the manner of gnocchi alla Romana—which are, after all, made by the same method as both polenta and halva. For the gnocchi, semolina and milk are simmered together, then a little egg is beaten in, along with some butter and cheese. The batter is spread out in a shallow pan and left to cool and firm up so it can be cut into pieces, ready to bake and serve.

Like spaghetti carbonara, gnocchi alla Romana makes a lunch hearty enough to induce an afternoon nap, potentially right there on the gingham tablecloth. (It's a wonder Rome was built at all, let alone in a day.) By the time you wake up, a filament of drool attaching you to the placemat, it'll be time for an aperitivo. In Rome, gnocchi are traditionally eaten on Thursdays, a tradition whose origins Claudia Roden admits she was unable to unearth. Some say the heartiness of the dish sets you up for Friday's fast. I wonder if the mixture of semolina, milk, egg, and butter might have been a cheap, filling dish to make on the day before payday. Few recipes call for much else, although one of Elizabeth David's variations includes some cooked ham. Follow the starting point, adding about ⅔ cup finely diced ham and stirring it in with the egg. Adding egg to the soft semolina mixture might remind you of making choux pastry. The same faith in providence is called for, to pass through the jumbo-curdle stage to the hard-won, lustrous smoothness of the finished batter.

c Choux, as it happens, is the next starting point on the continuum,
H where it also goes by its alias, gnocchi Parisienne. If gnocchi alla
o Romana is a meal to build an empire on, gnocchi Parisienne are
U altogether lighter and more elegant, but are still served in much
X the same ways as other gnocchi: with heaps of grated Parmesan, baked or simmered in a sauce, or pan-fried with butter and sage. Alternatively, the choux can be piped into lengths or little balls and baked to make éclairs or profiteroles. Deep-fry spoonfuls of the same dough and you have beignets: Shake over some confectioners' sugar and eat while still warm, with a café au lait and a resolution to eat more healthily just as soon as you've polished off the batch.

P O T A T O Potato gnocchi, also called gnocchi Piedmontese, consist
    of warm, starchy potato mixed with flour, and in some cases egg,
G to form a dough that is then rolled into small dumplings. Potato
N gnocchi are gnocchi-come-lately—so much so that the recipe did
o not appear in Italian cookbooks until the early twentieth century,
c when it specified a whopping 2:1 flour to potato weight ratio.
c Modern recipes vary a great deal, although 5:1 potato to flour
H is fairly typical, and most recommend using as little flour as the
I dough's coherence will allow.

There is little I can add to the reams written on the subject of potato gnocchi—other than, ditch reading the blow-by-blow instructions and make them a few times. If there was ever a place where experience trumps theory, potato gnocchi occupy it. Sidle a potato or two into the oven while you're baking, scrape out the flesh, and have a go while it's still warm. The first lesson in the gnocchi-maker's handbook is to test one—a gnocco, I suppose—before you make the rest. If it holds together in the pan, and hits the right balance between softness and resistance to the teeth, proceed. If your gnocco disappears in a puff of murky flour-water, keep adjusting the mixture, adding flour in patient increments—you're looking for the elusive sweet spot between cohesion and lightness.

RICOTTA The same applies to ricotta gnocchi, in which drained
ricotta takes the place of potato. The cheese is lightly mixed with
G a little flour and egg, plus some Parmesan for flavor, then rolled into
N small dumplings, ready to cook. As the mixture is more of a wet paste
O than a dough, ricotta gnocchi are shaped singly, rather than rolling
C the mixture into a snake and then chopping it into pieces, as you
C would for potato gnocchi. As ever, it's a wise precaution to test-cook
H a couple of your gnocchi before you invest more time in shaping and
I cooking the rest.

The starting point given here has never failed me, and the mixture is
also highly amenable to the addition of other ingredients. Think of
these as gardener's gnocchi: This is a recipe that should be shared with
anyone in possession of a vegetable patch. Ricotta gnocchi sit happily
next to all sorts of lightly cooked produce, and not only the obvious
accompaniment of tomato, garlic, and basil. In summer, try serving
them with fava beans and leeks, with a little tarragon butter. In the
autumn, roasted butternut squash with pears and sage makes a warming
treat with spinach and ricotta gnocchi. Come winter, in the interests
of heartiness, you may want to up the quantity of gnocchi per serving,
and consider giving them a turn around the skillet with some shaved
Brussels sprouts, chestnuts, and cranberries. Any excess dumplings
can be served in a broth, as is typical in Italy, or in a more substantial
mushroom or pea soup.

Cornbread

This is the style of cornbread made in the northern states of the U.S., where cornmeal is mixed with wheat flour and a little sugar. Serve it alongside bacon and eggs, with pulled pork, or simply sliced in half and filled with cream cheese and chopped pickled jalapeños. Leftover cornbread is put to similar uses as yeast-risen bread: French toast, stuffing, and bread pudding. Note that the ingredients are almost the same as for griddle pancakes (page [136]), with 1 cup of cornmeal and an extra egg thrown in.

For a deep 8-in square or 9-in round pan, or a 12-cup muffin pan

INGREDIENTS
1 cup fine cornmeal [A] [B]
1 cup all-purpose flour [A] [B]
½ tsp baking soda [C]
1 tsp salt
1 tbsp sugar [D] [E]
1 cup buttermilk [F]
2 eggs
1–2 tbsp melted fat or oil [G]

1 Put the cornmeal, flour, baking soda, salt, and sugar in a bowl. Whisk them together and make a well in the center.

2 Beat the wet ingredients together, add to the dry ingredients, and mix quickly.
No need to be *too* thorough.

3 Pour the batter into a greased round or square pan (cast-iron preferably) or a 12-cup muffin pan, then bake in a 350°F oven for 25–30 minutes, or 15–20 minutes for muffins, or until a skewer inserted into the center comes out clean. [H]
Ideally the greased pan should be put in the oven to heat before the batter is added. If you're using butter, take care not to let it burn.

4 Let cool slightly, then cut into squares or slices.
Eat on the day or wrap tightly and freeze for up to 3 months.

LEEWAY

A   Coarse cornmeal can be substituted for fine—you'll need 1 cup.

B   Adjust the cornmeal-to-flour ratio—anything between 3:1 and 1:3. Some cornbreads, such as caraway (page [80]) and raisin and orange (page [82]), are made with cornmeal only; these tend to be drier and more rustic.

C   Some cooks use 1 tsp baking powder in addition to the soda. Or use 2 tsp baking powder and no soda (but see under [F] below). Soda gives a more tender bread.

D   Use any sort of sugar—white, brown, maple syrup, molasses. Or leave it out entirely, if you prefer.

E   Some recipes suggest as much as ¾ cup sugar (though I found even ⅓ cup a bit too cake-sweet for my tastes).

F   Replace the buttermilk with sour cream or plain yogurt made pourable with a little water or milk. Or make your own by mixing 1 cup of the milk and 1 tbsp lemon juice. Let stand for 5 minutes before using. Alternatively, replacing the buttermilk with pineapple juice will give a lovely brown crust and a mild pineapple flavor. There's no need to use an acidic liquid if you're using baking powder instead of soda—milk or even water will do.

G   Use any oil (not your posh stuff). Lard, bacon fat, or butter all lend an excellent flavor.

H   Some cooks bake their cornbread at a lower temperature for longer—e.g. 325°F for 40–45 minutes.

BACON

Everything's bigger in America. Except for bacon. After triple-decker burgers, sandwiches requiring the temporary dislocation of your jaw, and burritos as brawny as a Mexican wrestler's forearm, it can be a surprise to find that American bacon comes in narrow, fat-streaked strips as floppy as the ribbon in Pollyanna's bonnet. Admittedly, they are served with omelets stuffed with blue cheese, and buffalo wings, and stacks of pancakes drenched in butter and syrup, but still. As a Brit, accustomed to a more substantial bacon slice, I can only assume that Americans like streaky bacon because its fat can be rendered very quickly. Southerners in particular hold bacon fat in high regard, and cornbread is one of the many ways they put it to use. The salty, smoky savoriness of bacon fat turns the cornmeal, which has a sweetness that can make it cakey, into a more natural partner for eggs. Cook the bacon slices in a single layer over a low to medium heat until the fat renders. If you end up with more fat than you need, add all of it anyway. Crumble the bacon into your cornbread batter.

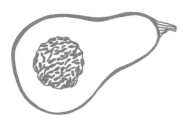

BUTTERNUT SQUASH, FETA & CHILI

In Moldova and Greece, cubes of feta-like cheese are commonly added to cornbreads. Feta and butternut squash is a classic combination, and makes a bread so bright it could be a cut-out by Henri Matisse. For the cornbread, make as per our starting point, but along with the wet ingredients stir in 1½ cups butternut squash cut into ½-in dice (no need to pre-cook), ½–¾ cup diced feta, and dried red pepper flakes to taste. You might also add cumin and oregano—lovely served with a stack of barbecued lamb chops. While the coals are whitening, stir up the cornbread batter and put it in the oven. Rinse a can or two of black beans and mix with finely chopped tomato, red onion, and cilantro leaves. Dress with a vinaigrette of lime juice and mild olive oil. Slip off your shoes, open a beer, and waggle your toes while the cornbread cooks, the flavors in your salad mingle, and drips of lamb fat vaporize on the coals. A simple, colorful, delicious dinner quick enough to make after work.

CARAWAY

This all-corn, no-wheat variation is based on Maria Kaneva-Johnson's recipe for a Serbian quick bread called *proja*. Sticklers for authenticity will want to use lard as the fat component, and eat the bread for breakfast with scrambled eggs or a sharp white cheese, or as an appetizer with clotted cream and *ajvar*, a sticky combination of charred red bell peppers and garlic originating in Serbia. Reminiscent of the cornbread muffins I once ate in Arizona, with thick, cold cream cheese and nose-tingling chili jelly: a cowboy's cream tea. Most cornbreads contain a combination of sour liquid and leavener, to lend lightness, but Kaneva-Johnson's doesn't, and has a denser texture despite its higher liquid-to-cornmeal ratio. More fat is brushed over the bread halfway through the baking time, which guards against dryness. Make as per the starting point, except use only 1 cup coarse cornmeal and no all-purpose flour, ¼ tsp salt, 1 tsp caraway seeds, 1⅔ cups milk mixed with 1 egg, and 1 tbsp oil. Pour into a well-greased 8-in round pan. After 25 minutes in the oven, when it should be just set, remove and brush over ½ tbsp melted butter mixed with ½ tbsp sunflower oil. Return to the oven to bake for up to 20 minutes, keeping your eye on it after the first 10; you're looking for a light golden brown.

CHEESE

Another kind of *proja* (see caraway, above) is made with cottage cheese stirred into the batter. In the U.S., grated hard cheeses like Cheddar or Monterey Jack—about 1 cup for our starting-point quantity—are often stirred into cornbread batter just before baking. An alternative is to put half of the plain batter in the greased pan, then sprinkle over a generous helping of cheese and not-too-wet tomato salsa; spread over the rest of the batter and bake. A distantly related dish, native to Paraguay and northeastern Argentina, is *sopa Paraguaya*, a bread that thinks it's a soup. Some say it owes its name to the notable wetness of the batter. It's traditional to eat *sopa Paraguaya* at weddings, where it's served with beer or whisky. Dice 1 large onion and simmer in ½ cup water with 1 tsp salt for 10 minutes, then set aside. Cream 5 tbsp butter, then add 4 egg yolks, one at a time, reserving the whites for later. Add 1 cup diced *queso fresco* or paneer, 1 cup roughly chopped sweet corn kernels, and the onion with its cooking water. Mix together. Slowly add 1½ cups fine cornmeal and 1 cup buttermilk, in alternating increments. Beat the egg whites to soft peaks and fold into the batter. Pour into a greased, deep, 8-in square pan and bake in the center of a 400°F oven for 30–35 minutes until golden brown.

CUSTARD

An unusual variation on cornbread that, if the moon is in the right phase, will have an integral layer of custard. It's a little sweeter than cornbread made to our starting point, and a great deal wetter, calling for a 3:2 ratio of liquid to grain. The following recipe comes from *The Farmer's Bulletin No.1236: Corn and Its Uses as Food*, issued by the U.S. Department of Agriculture in 1923. Grease a deep 8-in square pan with no less than 2 tbsp butter and place in a 350°F oven to heat. Vigorously whisk 2 eggs and ¼ cup sugar together. In another bowl, sift ⅓ cup all-purpose flour, 1 tsp baking soda, and 1 tsp salt into 1⅔ cups fine cornmeal. Add 1 cup each of milk and buttermilk to the egg-sugar mixture and stir into the dry ingredients. Pour into the hot pan and spread out evenly. Pour over 1 cup heavy cream, without stirring, then bake at 350°F for 30 minutes. Use double the amount of sugar and add 1 tsp vanilla extract to the liquid for a more conventionally custardy, cakelike confection, but the unadorned version is more interesting.

ONION

Anyone who finds the vegetable content of British fish and chips too high should familiarize themselves with hush puppies, the walnut-sized balls of cornmeal and onion batter that are served in the American South as a classic side order for fried fish or shrimp. The batter is very similar to our starting point for cornbread, except for the higher ratio of cornmeal to wheat flour, and the addition of onion. Mix ¾ cup fine cornmeal with ¼ cup all-purpose flour, ½ cup buttermilk, ½ tsp baking powder, ½ tsp salt, 1 tsp sugar, 1 finely chopped small onion, and 1 egg. Deep-fry 4 or 5 baubles of batter at a time in oil heated to 350°F, using two wetted soup spoons to scoop up the batter and push it into the oil. If, after a minute or two, the baubles don't flip over of their own accord, give them a nudge with a slotted spoon. Leave for a minute longer, then remove with a slotted spoon and drain briefly on paper towels. Keep the cooked hush puppies hot in a 200°F oven until the entire batch is done.

RAISIN & ORANGE

As one of the few comestibles available during the German/Italian occupation of Greece in the Second World War, cornbread, or *bobota*, gained a bad rep, and to this day it's considered an inferior food by the older generation. *Bobota* is, in fact, something of a catch-all term that can, depending on where in Greece you find yourself, mean a plain bread, a mush, or something more like a cake containing raisins and orange juice, glazed with honey. On the Ionian island of Zakynthos, a version is made with chopped walnuts, cinnamon, clove, and aniseed. Six thousand miles away, in the Dominican Republic, a sweet cornbread is baked with raisins, cinnamon, and evaporated milk. It's called *pan de mais*, which is what poor Blanche DuBois mutters over and over as she twists her dish towel at the end of *A Streetcar Named Desire*. This recipe differs from our starting point in calling exclusively for cornmeal—no wheat, no eggs. The result is a coarser, crumblier texture, so you might want to add the egg back in if you're planning to cut your (non-authentic) version into neat-ish pieces. Mix 1⅓ cups fine cornmeal with ½ cup sugar, 1 tsp baking powder, ½ tsp baking soda, a pinch of salt, and ⅓ cup raisins. Add 1 cup orange juice, ¼ cup water, and 2 tbsp olive oil. Stir and pour the mixture into an oiled 7-in square pan, then transfer, quickly, to a 350°F oven and bake for 25–30 minutes. If you like, you can paint the warm finished cake with a honey syrup. Let cool in the pan before cutting into pieces.

RED BELL PEPPER, SWEET CORN & CILANTRO

The first and still the most memorable cornbread I ever tasted was at Bobby Flay's Mesa Grill in New York, made with a mixture of blue and yellow cornmeal. Flay claims blue corn has more flavor, because it's grown organically in small quantities. Others say the difference in flavor is undetectable. But who cares? It's blue! Truly, madly, properly blue. (Blue, according to Buxton in *Dougal and the Blue Cat*, is beautiful and best. And you don't argue with Buxton.) Use blue cornmeal, or a mixture of blue and yellow, for these muffins, which are similar to Flay's but adapted to our starting point. Cook ½ small onion, diced, with a minced clove of garlic, in 1 tbsp oil and 2 tbsp butter until soft. Mix into the dry ingredients, with the buttermilk and egg, plus a handful of finely diced red bell pepper, 3–4 heaped tbsp fresh or frozen sweet corn kernels, and 1–2 tbsp chopped cilantro. Add pepper flakes or chopped fresh jalapeño for a mischievous whisper of heat.

RYE

As old-school American as succotash. The combination of rye and corn is known as "rye and injun" in New England (cornmeal is sometimes known as "Indian meal"—hence "injun"). In *Walden*, his hymn to self-sufficiency, Henry David Thoreau names rye and corn as his preferred combination of flours for hoe cakes, made with the same batter as our starting point for cornbread, then fried in bacon fat or vegetable oil a few tablespoons at a time, like pancakes. Thoreau recalls turning the cakes "as carefully as an Egyptian his hatching eggs. They were a real cereal fruit which I ripened, and they had to my senses a fragrance like that of other noble fruits, which I kept in as long as possible by wrapping them in cloths." Ever the experimenter, Thoreau tries other breads without leaveners, wishing "to escape the trivialness of carrying a bottle-full in my pocket, which would sometimes pop and discharge its contents to my discomfiture." Make up the batter for your own rye and injun hoe cakes by following the starting point, using a 50/50 mix of rye flour and fine cornmeal and, in place of the buttermilk, plain milk with 2 tbsp molasses added (the molasses will activate the soda). Cook over a medium heat in a hot buttered skillet, as you would pancakes, flipping them when the underside is golden brown.

Dhokla: Khaman Dhokla

A snack so pretty it could sit happily in a pâtisserie. Under its red, white, and green decoration, khaman dhokla resembles a cake, but is made with chickpea flour and tastes distinctly savory. It is steamed, like a sweet sponge pudding, resulting in a dreamily moist texture. There are other types of batter for dhokla—the traditional kind is made with a fermented mix of pulses and rice—but this sort is the simplest to make and extremely good to eat. As with cornbread, here we use a liquid-to-flour ratio of 1:2, plus a little salt, sugar, fat, and leavening agent.

For an 8-in round pan

INGREDIENTS
1½ cups chickpea flour [A]
1 tsp salt
1 tsp sugar
¾ cup water [B]
1 tbsp vegetable oil
1 tsp Eno (page [73]) [C]

TO FINISH
1–2 tsp each of mustard seeds and cumin seeds [D]
2–3 tbsp vegetable oil
Sliced fresh chili, dried shredded coconut, and cilantro leaves—optional

1 Configure your steamer. You'll need a lidded pot that will accommodate your dhokla pan, and something to elevate the pan above the water level. Add some water to the pot and bring to a boil, then reduce to a simmer.
   I do this in the bottom part of my pressure cooker, using the vegetable steaming basket, inverted, as a stand for the dhokla pan.

2 Mix the chickpea flour, salt, and sugar with the water and vegetable oil to make a smooth batter.

3 Once the water in the pot is simmering, add the Eno to the batter and stir it in thoroughly. Pour the batter into a greased 8-in round pan.

4 Lower the pan onto the stand above the water and steam, covered, for 15–25 minutes. Check it's cooked by touching the surface with your fingertip—it should feel set but springy—then remove from the steamer.

5 Heat the mustard seeds and cumin seeds in 2–3 tbsp vegetable oil until they pop.
   You will need a splatter guard over the pan to stop the seeds flying everywhere.

6 Pour the seeds and oil over the warm dhokla, then sprinkle with other garnishes, if using.

7 Cut into squares to serve. It is traditional to accompany this with a chutney made by pounding together cilantro leaves, mint leaves, green chili, fresh ginger, lemon juice, and salt.

LEEWAY

A Chickpea flour is also called besan or gram flour.

B Some cooks prefer yogurt or a mix of yogurt and water.

C A similar concoction to Eno can be made by thoroughly combining equal amounts of baking soda and citric acid. If you dislike the sharp taste of citric acid, use 2 tsp baking powder in place of the Eno.

D Make the flavored oil with other spices (whole or ground), curry leaves, red pepper flakes, or a mixture. If you're using ground spices, take care that the pan isn't too dry, and don't fry them for too long, as they're apt to burn.

BURNT ONION

Time was a gentleman might take a stroll through Soho in London and find himself propositioned by a prostitute. Or offered an origami envelope of cocaine. Or have his pocket picked by a mascara-smudged transvestite with holes in her stockings. These days you might as well be in an airport retail development for all the edge in the air. Until midnight strikes, that is, and the duty managers of the pintxos bars and East Asian BBQ concepts and informal dim-sum lounges punch in the codes on their security systems. No one knows where the carts come from; they must rise from backstreet manholes or emerge from the stage doors of dark theaters. Then the frying begins. Londoners with otherwise impeccable gastronomic credentials, men and women about town who know their natives from their Pacifics and their *yudofu* from their *agedashi* tofu, are suddenly overcome by unspeakable urges. Oh, the remorse the next morning! Had it not been for the irresistible aroma of browning onion they might never have bitten into that frankfurter, the ingredients of which bear little thinking about, crammed into a pappy bun of carcinogenic whiteness and squirted with a zigzag of unbranded ketchup. Fried onions deserve better. They get it in India, where they're used freely in vegetarian dishes, and as part of the tarka in dal (page 252). I tried some on top of a dhokla, pissaladière-style, and, even better, cooked into the batter. Dice or thinly slice 1 medium-sized onion. Fry until soft and nicely brown then stir into a dhokla batter made as per the starting point, but using only ½ cup water and leaving out the oil—the onions will yield moisture of their own, and the oil used to fry them will contribute its flavor. Instead of cumin, add a few pinches of nigella seeds to the mustard seeds and spread over the top of the cooked dhokla, along with a scattering of cilantro leaves.

CHANA DAL

Our starting point, using chickpea flour, is a lot quicker than the traditional recipe for dhokla, where the batter is made with dried split chickpeas, soaked, blended until smooth, and left to ferment overnight. Similar batters are used for idli and dosas, pancakes made with a combination of pulses and rice, but for these you'll need a blender capable of turning the soaked pulses into a smooth batter. For the plain chana (no-rice) version, rinse and then soak 1 cup chana dal for about 6 hours or overnight. Drain and grind all but ¼ cup of the soaked dal with 1 chopped green chili, 1 tbsp grated fresh ginger, and up to 1 cup water until you have a thick-ish batter. Add the reserved dal and stir in 2 tbsp plain yogurt, 1 tsp lemon juice, ½ tsp ground turmeric, and ½ tsp salt. Set aside to ferment for 6 hours or overnight. Before cooking, stir in 1 tsp Eno or ½ tsp baking soda. Steam the batter in an 8-in round pan for 15–20 minutes or until an inserted skewer comes out clean. Fry spices in oil to pour over the top, then garnish.

COCONUT

Finding that I only had 1 cup chickpea flour left, rather than schlep to the Indian supermarket, I topped up my supply of chickpea flour with ½ cup dried shredded coconut, replaced the water with coconut milk, and used 2 tsp baking powder instead of Eno. It worked a treat. The savory flavor of chickpea still dominated, but was complemented by the sweetness of coconut. Next time I added the same ground spices Mark Hix uses in his chickpea and coconut curry to the batter—clove, cinnamon, cardamom, coriander, fennel, garam masala, and turmeric— and for the garnish, I piled on more coconut and sliced green chili.

GARLIC, ROSEMARY & BLACK PEPPER

Given the Italian fondness for chickpeas, it isn't much of a leap to apply Italian principles to a dhokla—in this instance, the flavors used to make *farinata*, the chickpea flatbread from Liguria. The sharp taste of Eno would be incongruous, so use the 2 tsp baking powder suggested under Leeway instead. Toward the end of the steaming time, cook a few crushed garlic cloves in a little olive oil, then remove them and gently heat some finely chopped needles of rosemary in the garlic- infused oil. Pour this over the warm chickpea "dhokla" and give it a good grind of coarse black pepper, then cut it into squares.

RED BELL PEPPER & CHORIZO

This re-working of the dhokla idea makes for perfect picnic food. Make up the batter as per the method, but use 2 tsp baking powder rather than Eno. As you're stirring all the ingredients together, add ¼ cup finely diced, roasted red bell pepper and 4 oz cured Spanish chorizo that you've cut into tiny pieces with kitchen scissors (besides the question of whether it would cook through properly, Mexican ground chorizo would be too coarse). Pour the batter into an oiled, deep, 8-in foil dish and steam for 15 minutes. Remove, wrap in more foil, and carry in one hand, with a half-bottle of chilly fino sherry in the other. Ask a friend to bring glasses (because it *has* to be glass for sherry) and the best green olives they can find. Meet under a fig tree if remotely possible.

SEMOLINA

If you're used to the more assertively flavored chickpea flour, dhokla made with *rava*, or semolina, can lack the fine, creamy texture lent by besan, and be comparatively bland, like a khaman dhokla after a couple of cycles in the washing machine. The blandness can work in your favor, however, if you're working with subtly flavored ingredients that might be disrupted by the beaniness of chickpea.

Halva: Irmik Halva

The term "halva" means sweet, and covers a broad range of sugary treats. Irmik halva belongs to the grain branch of the halva family, and is a simple, well-loved Turkish dessert. It was once a fixture of Ottoman-era picnics, served after barbecued lamb, and today you might find it served for breakfast in Ankara tripe restaurants, or prepared in domestic kitchens for a wake. The toasted semolina gives it a wonderful flavor, reminiscent of popcorn or, if you add a pinch of salt, digestive biscuits or graham crackers.

For a 6-in dome-shaped cereal bowl, or 6 small molds [A]

INGREDIENTS
1 stick unsalted butter
1 cup coarse semolina [B]
2½ cups milk [C D E]
1 cup sugar [E F]
2–3 tbsp toasted pine nuts—optional

1   Melt half of the butter in a medium-sized saucepan over a medium heat, then add the semolina and cook it, stirring frequently, until golden.
    Take care lest its entrancing fragrance lull you into leaving it too long—you don't want it to pass from golden to dark brown.

2   Put the milk in another saucepan set over a medium heat. Add the sugar and the remaining butter, letting them dissolve and melt before slowly stirring into the semolina.

3   Cook over a low heat, stirring now and then, until the mixture starts to thicken and come away from the sides of the pan. Toasted pine nuts can be added at this point.
    If you prefer to serve the halva loose and fluffy, stop cooking when the mixture is like mashed potato and spoon onto plates.

4   Scrape into a bowl or individual molds and pat down. Leave at room temperature to set.
    You'll know it has when you press the edges and it comes away from the mold cleanly. How long this takes will depend on the size of the bowl, and how wet the semolina was when you stopped cooking it. Small individual dishes can take as little as 15 minutes, but bank on a couple of hours for the larger version.

LEEWAY

A Some halva-makers wait until the mixture has cooled a bit, then hand-form it into shapes.

B Fine semolina can be used for halva, but for irmik halva it needs to be coarse.

C Authentic irmik halva recipes often call for a 2:1 ratio of milk to semolina, but I find that quantity of liquid tends to evaporate very quickly. The more generous 2½ cups milk here gives the semolina time to cook a little.

D Similar Greek recipes call for a spiced sugar syrup in place of the milk. This will mean braving much spitting and cracking as it's stirred into the hot pan of toasted semolina. (See pages 434-8 for syrup-flavoring ideas.)

E Some recipes call for a 50/50 mix of water and milk rather than all milk; others call for canned condensed milk and omit the sugar.

F Feel free to reduce the sugar quantity—½ cup is plenty to my tooth.

CHICKPEA

Some describe *Mysore pak* as a fudge, others as a type of shortbread, but for the purposes of this book, it sits with halva. It's as rich and sweet as the eponymous palace where the dish was first prepared is extravagant. (*Pak*, incidentally, means sweet.) It departs from the other halvas in this section in that the water and sugar are cooked to the thread stage—see page [404]—before the grain is added. Cook 2 cups sugar in ½ cup water to 223–234°F, or the thread stage, then gradually—to avoid lumps—stir in 1 cup sifted chickpea flour. Toasting the chickpea flour first is optional, as is adding some ground cardamom or saffron for extra flavor. Gradually beat in 1 cup hot melted ghee. After the mixture froths it should start to pull away from the sides of the pan. When it does, pour into a 7- to 8-in dish and let set before cutting into pieces.

CORNMEAL & MOLASSES

"Indian pudding" is a sweet cornmeal mush that's especially popular in New England. It's made with milk and molasses and is served like halva. The grain—cornmeal, a.k.a. Indian meal—mixture is baked in the oven, or cooked slowly over heat until a spoon can stand up in it. Food historians believe that Indian pudding may be an American descendant of hasty pudding, as mentioned in "Yankee Doodle": *And there we saw the men and boys/As thick as hasty pudding.* Hasty pudding, made with oat or wheat meal, was popular in Britain in the seventeenth century, but had largely disappeared from cookbooks by the nineteenth. Like Yorkshire pudding (page [117]), both Indian and hasty puddings were often served before a meat course, with the intention of suppressing the appetite, in case the ensuing measly portions of meat proved disappointing. Over time Indian pudding has become sweeter and it is now more commonly served as a dessert. Start by pouring ½ cup of coarse cornmeal into 4 cups warm milk, bringing it to a boil over a medium heat, and then reducing to as low a simmer as possible. Stir for 20 minutes before adding ½ cup molasses, 4 tbsp butter, ¼ tsp salt, and ½ tsp ground ginger and/or cinnamon. Pour the mixture into a buttered 8-in round baking dish. Bake at 250°F for about 2½ hours, by which time it should resemble a perfectly baked custard—set, but still slightly wobbly in the center. Nowadays Indian pudding is usually served with ice cream, but in the eighteenth century Tobias Smollett noted that it was typically spread out on a platter, before a cavity was made in the middle and a knob of butter and generous spoonful of sugar or molasses put into it, there to be transformed into a caramel sauce by the heat of the pudding. You ate from the outside in, dipping your spoon into the central reservoir of sauce as you went. In the Veneto, in Italy, a comparable dish was made with crumbled leftover polenta, stirred up with molasses, milk, dried fruit, candied citrus peel, and toasted pine nuts—a jazzy corn granola.

DATE & VANILLA

Fly to Oman. Buy a dish-dash in a souk. Fly back and spend the next six months making halva sweetened with date syrup. You'll find the flattering cut of your new garment very handy. Date syrup tastes like maple syrup that's migrated south for the simpler life. Make the halva as per the starting point, but use 1 cup date syrup in place of the sugar, add 2 tsp vanilla extract and a pinch of salt, and leave out the pine nuts. Finish with salted candied walnuts or pecans.

POMEGRANATE & ORANGE

Silky white rice flour makes for a silky halva, I've discovered. First I cooked 1 cup rice flour in a mixture of 1 tbsp butter and 2 tbsp peanut oil until lightly browned. Next, I added 2½ cups of freshly squeezed orange juice, with pulp, and 2 tbsp of pomegranate molasses. Then I added sugar, tablespoon by tablespoon, until the mixture was sweet, but not so much that it undermined the enlivening sourness of orange and pomegranate. I left my fruity halva to set, then diced and scattered it over Greek yogurt with chopped pistachios. When my husband tasted it, he said he'd happily eat it with cheese, as it tasted the way he wished *membrillo* (quince paste) tasted—less sweet, with more pronounced fruity flavors. He was on to something. It proved terrific with mature English Cheddar, and a more than acceptable replacement for the jelly in a peanut butter sandwich.

SAFFRON, ROSE, CINNAMON & ALMOND

This *zerde* from Azerbaijan could be a relative of irmik halva. *Zerde* normally refers to a saffron-scented rice pudding served at weddings in Turkey, but this recipe contains no rice—just ground almonds and a little semolina. Anya von Bremzen describes it as silky and refreshing. In a medium saucepan, combine 1¼ cups ground almonds with 5 cups milk and ¼–⅓ cup sugar. Bring to a boil, then remove from the heat and add ¼ tsp saffron threads. In a separate pan, cook ¼ cup coarse semolina in 1 tbsp butter until brown, stirring constantly, then pour in the sweet almond-milk mixture and bring to a boil. Simmer, uncovered, stirring occasionally until it thickens—this should take 15–20 minutes. Remove from the heat and stir in 2 tsp rosewater, ¼ cup slivered almonds, and ½ tsp ground cinnamon. Pour into 8 individual molds and chill, then serve with a little more cinnamon sprinkled over.

Polenta

Polenta is made either by cooking cornmeal to the consistency of mashed potato, and serving as is; or cooking cornmeal the same way, leaving it to set, and then cutting it into pieces before it is fried or grilled. The mash-textured "wet" sort is usually mixed with lots of butter and cheese, unless it's intended as a side dish for a hearty, sticky stew, in which case its blandness comes as a relief and it needs less embellishment. Polenta fanatics avoid using metal implements or tableware, which are said to affect the flavor, preferring wooden stirrers and cutting the finished polenta with string. Saves on dishwashing.

For enough polenta to serve 3–4 as a side

INGREDIENTS
3 cups water [A] [B]
1 tsp salt
1 cup coarse cornmeal [C]
¼ tsp white pepper
Butter, olive oil, cream, cheese—optional

1   Put the water and salt in a saucepan over a medium heat. [D]

2   Once it has come to a boil, swirl the water, then pour in the cornmeal in a steady stream, whisking all the while to minimize lumps.
    Some cooks avoid lumps by first mixing the cornmeal with some of the water.

3   Keep cooking over a low heat, stirring constantly, or at least enough to prevent the mixture from sticking to the bottom of the pan, until it has the texture you're after.

4   Add the pepper and taste for seasoning, adding any butter, olive oil, cream, or cheese as desired. [E]

    FOR WET POLENTA
    Simply judge when it reaches the right texture.
    Starting with a longer dilution will help keep the polenta in a mush state—start with 6 cups liquid to 1 cup cornmeal—as will additions of butter, olive oil, cream, and cheese. Note that the polenta will naturally firm up if left.

FOR SET POLENTA

When the mixture pulls away from the sides of the pan, scrape it into a buttered or oiled dish and leave at room temperature to firm up.

Set polenta can be cut into pieces and grilled, fried, or used like gnocchi.

LEEWAY

A   As little as 2 cups water will do, and is preferable if you want the polenta to set quickly and have a dry-ish texture. Some cooks use as many as 8 cups of water. It really depends on how long you want to cook and stir your polenta. Remember that you can always add more hot water as you go.

B   Stock in place of some or all of the water will give a richer flavor. Milk will give a creamier texture.

C   Polenta was originally made with all sorts of grains and meals—spelt, farro, buckwheat, teff, chestnut. You can, of course, use fine polenta, but the result will be a little thinner and less flavorful.

D   For extra texture and flavor, first cook onion and garlic or a mirepoix (diced onion, carrot, and celery) in oil, then add the water and proceed as opposite.

E   Whole sweet corn kernels can be added to polenta for extra bite. Clearly, canned kernels will need draining first, but otherwise the sweet corn need only be stirred in toward the end of cooking.

CAULIFLOWER, CAPER & RAISIN

Plain wet polenta can be bland, but don't write it off until you've tried it as a foil or base for other ingredients. Just as mashed potato mixed with cabbage and onion makes champ, try combining wet polenta with kale and beans to make Tuscan *polenta incatenata* ("polenta in chains"), or break set polenta into pieces and serve it with the very Sicilian mixture of cauliflower, caper buds, and garlic. Think of it as a stuffing in search of a cavity. Cook ¾ cup coarse cornmeal in 1½ cups water as per the starting point, until it pulls away from the sides of the pan, then scrape it onto a plate to set. Resist the temptation to smooth it. While it cools, cut a small cauliflower into bite-sized florets, toss them in olive oil, and roast for 30 minutes at 400°F, until soft and a little charred, then set aside. Reduce the oven temperature to 350°F and toast a few tablespoons of pine nuts until golden. Break the polenta into penny-size pieces. Heat some olive oil in a skillet over a medium heat and cook 2 minced garlic cloves until just golden. Add 2 tbsp salted capers, rinsed and dried, and 2 tbsp raisins. After a few minutes add the cauliflower and polenta. Cook for a few more minutes, then add 1 tbsp anchovy paste, 1 tsp wine vinegar, and 1 tbsp water. Stir and remove from the heat. Add the toasted pine nuts and a big handful of chopped flat-leaf parsley, season and toss well, then serve.

CHEESE GRITS

I'd assumed that cheese grits are to *polenta al formaggio* as pasta parcels are to tortelloni. Not so. Grits call for hominy, a stone-ground, alkalized cornmeal that's white, rather than yellow, and more flavorful. That said, grits from the American South are made with non-hominy white corn. Not that it matters a great deal either way, when the subtle notes of corn will be shouted into submission by strident cheese. Use 2 cups each of water and milk to 1 cup coarse cornmeal. Follow the starting point up to step [3], then cover the pan and cook over a low to medium heat for 20–30 minutes, until the texture resembles very creamy mashed potato. Off the heat, stir in 4 tbsp butter and anything between 1 and 4 cups grated cheese. Whereas Cheddar, or a mixture of Cheddar and Monterey Jack, is typical for grits, polenta is open to all types of Italian cheese—Parmesan, fontina, Gorgonzola, mozzarella...*o tutte e quattro*.

CHESTNUT & RED WINE

In November it's traditional for Tuscans to sit around the fire enjoying freshly roasted chestnuts with a glass of new red wine. Andrea Pieroni notes that chestnut-meal polenta made with new red wine was once a common cough remedy in northern Tuscany. Sure sounds better than a synthetic lemon and honey lozenge. Try 2½ cups chestnut flour simmered in 2 cups each of water and red wine. Aim to develop your chest infection around the third Thursday in November, to coincide with the arrival of the Beaujolais Nouveau (even if the cure doesn't work, you'll have a glass left over to dampen your sorrows). Chestnut polenta can also be made by stirring unsweetened chestnut purée into just-cooked cornmeal polenta.

FONDUE

When you see the words "delicious" and "polenta" in close proximity, you know the phrases "plenty of cheese" or "lots of butter" cannot be far away. Ferran Adrià cuts to the chase and makes polenta *gratin*. In addition to unctuous fontina, from the mountainous Valle d'Aosta, many cheeses are used to enrich polenta. Forced to share a steak *tagliata* I had planned to eat alone, I made a fondue-inspired polenta, *polenta alla fonduta*, cooking ½ cup coarse cornmeal in 1½ cups lightly salted water and ¼ cup Picpoul de Pinet—a wine rarely spotted, I imagine, at fondue parties, but the only kind in my rack with the requisite tartness. I finished the polenta over a low heat, stirring in a handful each of grated Gruyère and Emmental until melted, then a teaspoon of kirsch, a squeeze of lemon, and a hint of white pepper. Keeping the polenta warm, I flick-flacked the steak in a hot pan, gave it a few minutes to relax, then sliced it over arugula leaves dressed with a few tears of lemon juice. I served the polenta in miniature Le Creuset pots, on the basis that pale yellow grain edged with steak blood is not a good look. This fondue polenta is a bit like *aligot*, the cheese-enriched mashed potato from the Auvergne region of France.

MILLET

Ken Albala regrets the obsolescence of millet as a European food source, given its rich, nutty flavor, and passes on the Renaissance chef Bartolomeo Scappi's suggestion to simmer it in milk or meat broth, with a piece of salted pork jowl or cervelat sausage. Once the grain is cooked, Scappi adds grated cheese, egg, cinnamon, pepper, and saffron. But millet is making a comeback. Maria Speck gives the following outline for cooking millet polenta. Soften some diced scallions with bay leaf in olive oil, add the millet, and cook for a few minutes. Add twice the millet's volume in water and bring to a boil, then turn down the heat and simmer, stirring, for 15–20 minutes. Add the same volume of plain yogurt as millet, along with plenty of chopped fresh herbs, and sprinkle with Parmesan. Simon Rogan made a millet risotto with blue cheese and pear at Roganic, his pop-up in London's Marylebone. Sandor Katz relates a method for fermented millet porridge, in which the grain is soaked in salted water in a covered jar for 24–48 hours before being drained, rinsed, and simmered in fresh water, with the optional additions of oregano, paprika, turmeric, and cumin. Olive oil and lemon juice are added, and when thickened the porridge is poured into a dish and left to set. It is served in slices, as they are or toasted.

OKRA

Flying back from Antigua, we had a longish, Friday-night layover in Barbados. Rather than hang around the airport browsing patchwork handbags and vast watches with titanium bezels and integral heat-seeking harpoon guns, we wanted a beer and some proper Bajan seafood. The lady at information suggested Oistins. In the taxi, I fell to imagining a breezy, beachside restaurant with an open kitchen and a smart-casual clientele of very thin people in expensive off-white linenwear. Nothing could have been further from the truth. Oistins is not even a restaurant. It's a village—or was—now entirely given over, by all appearances, to the preparation and consumption of seafood. It might bear comparison to boisterous, bargain-basement resort towns like Magaluf or Juan les Pins were it not for its odd atmosphere of unforced, ungarish authenticity. Friday night is "fish fry," when you're likely to eat flying fish and *coucou,* cornmeal cooked with okra, served with a portion of plantain on the side. The queues for the dozens of food stalls reflect the Caribbean attitude to urgency, so grab a cold Banks and enjoy the wait. The next challenge is to find a spare seat at one of about a thousand communal tables before your food goes cold. We chose to stand, sipping our beers and watching couples of varying ability try out their moves on the perilously sprung dance floor. It was worth the trip, especially by comparison with a lifetime of layover panini and clammy wraps. For the *coucou,* simmer chopped okra (1 cup per cup of cornmeal—coarse or fine) until just cooked. Drain, reserving the water and using it, plus however much extra you need, to cook your cornmeal, together with ½ tsp salt, 1 tsp sugar, and 1–2 tbsp butter. Stir in the okra when the cornmeal is done. Replace some of the water with coconut milk for an extra Antillean lilt.

PANELLE

The batter for *panelle*, the street-snack from Palermo in Sicily, is made by simmering chickpea flour and salt in hot water until the mixture pulls away from the sides of the pan. At this point the batter is spread out on an oiled surface or baking sheet, to a depth of about ½ in, and cooled until it takes on a dense yet flexible consistency, not unlike top-of-the-range carpet underlay. The rubbery dough is then cut into pieces and either deep-fried or grilled. They taste like egg, fries, *and* peas in one soft mouthful. Utter bliss, in other words. *Panelle* are also made in Provence, in France, and may be served for dessert, sprinkled with sugar. The Niçoise term is *panisso*, a cognate of the Italian word *panissa*, which is a generic term—as was "polenta"—for any mushy, cooked grain.

PORCINI & BLUEBERRY

Cooking polenta in stock is one way to infuse it with flavor. Soak 2 handfuls of dried porcini in 2 cups warm water, with a few pinches each of salt and sugar, and let infuse overnight. Fine-strain it the next day and your porcini stock is ready. Use this stock to cook a heaped ½ cup coarse cornmeal, adding a little extra hot water if needed. Throw in a handful of blueberries at the end, and the chopped-up rehydrated porcini if you don't have any other plans for them. Serve the polenta on the side of wild boar stew, roast guinea fowl, or venison sausages and enjoy the intermittent bursts of fresh berry.

PORK

Scrapple found its way to Pennsylvania from northern Germany. Scraps of pork are cooked with cereal in stock, then left to set in a loaf pan. It's thought to be descended from a dish made with blood and buckwheat. In the U.S., however, blood albumin was used in the sugar-refining process, which kept the price of animal blood high, so pork was used instead, combined with inexpensive cornmeal. Scrapple is most commonly served for breakfast, with eggs or syrup and maybe apples on the side. Variations include goetta, made with oats, which is popular in Cincinnati, while in the Carolinas, "liver mush" is often eaten in a sandwich with grape jelly. The method for making scrapple is straightforward. The meat scraps—or fancy modern cuts—are simmered with aromatics, yielding a broth. The cooked meat is then set aside, and the stock strained and skimmed. Enough of the latter is set aside to cook the cornmeal (using the same ratio as our starting point, 3:1). Meanwhile, any skin is removed from the meat, which is then taken off the bone, and cut or pulled into pieces. When the polenta is as thick as mashed potato, the meat is stirred in and the mixture transferred to a loaf pan. Finally, the scrapple is left to solidify for a few hours, until it's ready to be sliced and fried. And boy, does it need that pan-tan. Uncooked scrapple looks like the Dish of the Day at the Ministry of Plenty. Old recipes call for about 1 cup fine cornmeal per pound of meat, but you'll find a good deal of elasticity in the ratios.

SQUID INK

Shiny-black and squeaky as a rubber onesie: pervert's polenta. For 1 cup coarse cornmeal, add 2 sachets squid ink while the polenta is still wet enough to be easily stirred. Serve with pan-fried fish—a fillet of red mullet with crispy skin would be ideal.

Gnocchi alla Romana

In effect, gnocchi alla Romana are rounds of set polenta made with semolina and milk, and enriched with egg. No need to make a sauce. Simply arrange your gnocchi in a baking dish, dot generously with butter, and sprinkle over plenty of Parmesan. In the oven, the little dumplings will puff up and crisp, and the cheese and butter melt. Serve with tartly dressed, bitter leaves. The single most important tip with gnocchi alla Romana is to be good and hungry when you sit down to them.

For a main course for 4, or an appetizer for 6

INGREDIENTS
6 cups milk [A] [B]
½ tsp salt
1½ cups fine semolina [C] [D]
1 stick butter [E]
2½ cups freshly grated Parmesan [E]
1 egg [F]

1 Heat the milk in a saucepan with the salt until warm.
   Infuse the milk with a flavor at this point, if you fancy it.

2 Off the heat, gradually sprinkle in the semolina, while whisking, then return to a low heat, continuing to whisk.

3 Cook, stirring continuously with a wooden or silicone spoon, for 5–8 minutes, until the mixture is thick, elastic, and pulling away from the sides of the pan.

4 Still over the heat, stir in 4 tbsp of the butter and 1½ cups of the cheese, along with any other seasonings, then remove from the heat and let cool a little.

5 Beat in the egg.
   It can look a bit curdled and unpromising to start with. Persevere until everything is integrated.

6 Scrape the mixture into a moistened shallow pan or silicone mold, and use a wet offset spatula to smooth the surface. You're aiming for a depth of about ½ in. [G]

7 Leave to cool and set.
   This will take about 1 hour in the fridge, longer at room temperature.

8 Cut into rounds or squares. Overlap a little in a greased baking dish, then dot with the remaining butter and sprinkle with the rest of the cheese. Bake at 400°F for 15–20 minutes.

LEEWAY

A Use whole, lowfat, or skim milk. Add some water if you're a bit short.

B Freshly grated nutmeg is a traditional, if optional, addition to the milk at step 1.

C Some recipes call for 1½ cups semolina *flour*, milled very fine like cake flour. Or use 1½ cups coarse semolina instead if you don't mind a more knobbly texture.

D Make the gnocchi with cornmeal instead of semolina: coarse or fine, whichever you prefer—you'll need 1½ cups of either.

E Reduce the butter and/or cheese, but remember these ingredients create the flavor.

F Some recipes omit the egg, which works just fine, but the gnocchi will be a little looser and have less puff when baked. You can also use 2 yolks rather than 1 whole egg.

G For a less rustic look, spoon into silicone molds and unmold once the mixture has had a chance to set in the fridge. Quenelles are another option.

Gnocchi Parisienne / Choux Pastry

The versatile batter can be boiled for gnocchi, fried for beignets, or baked to make any number of choux pastries like éclairs, gougères, and profiteroles. To account for these variations, the method splits after step [4]. The gnocchi and beignets are pretty simple. Choux pastry is marginally more challenging; the egg must be added judiciously to achieve the right consistency. Some churro-makers use choux as their dough, as it amounts to an enriched version of the more common recipe on page [150].

For enough gnocchi to serve 4, 20–24 profiteroles or beignets, or 12 cream puffs or éclairs

INGREDIENTS
1 cup all-purpose flour [A] [B]
1 cup water [C]
Pinch of salt
4 tbsp butter
4 large or 3 extra-large eggs [D]
Freshly grated nutmeg—optional [E]

[1] Sift the flour. Put the water and salt into a saucepan set over a medium heat, and melt the butter in it. Bring to a boil, then remove from the heat. Stir and keep on stirring…

[2] … and stirring, while you tip in the sifted flour. Mix to a paste consistency, then return to a low-ish heat and cook, still stirring, for a minute or two. The mixture should start to pull away from the sides of the pan. Set aside for about 5 minutes to cool—you want to add the eggs without scrambling them.

[3] Beat in the eggs with a whisk or wooden spoon, one by one and thoroughly, adding plenty of air. Aim for a batter that's shiny and smooth, but still shapeable.
For gnocchi and beignets, there's no need to be too precise about the texture, but for choux, according to Nancy Birtwhistle, when you lift the whisk or spoon out of the mix, a "V" shape should be hanging from it—a bit thicker than dropping consistency.

[4] Some cooks let gnocchi and beignet batter rest for 30 minutes before cooking; it will keep in the fridge for 12 hours. Once mixed, choux needs to be piped and then baked or frozen.
If the batter has been in the fridge, bring it to room temperature before starting to cook.

FOR GNOCCHI PARISIENNE

Test-cook 1 tsp of your batter in boiling water, to make sure it holds together, then spoon into a pastry bag fitted with a ¾-in tip. Pipe the batter directly into a large pan of salted boiling water, using wetted scissors to cut 1¼- to 1½-in lengths. Don't cook too many gnocchi at a time. Simmer for 3–4 minutes, by which time they will be floating on the surface, then use a slotted spoon to lift them onto paper towels to drain.

The cooked gnocchi can be sautéed, or spread in a shallow baking dish and heated in the oven with butter and cheese, or mixed with a sauce.

FOR BEIGNETS

Deep-fry 1–2 tsp scoops of the batter, a few at a time, in 375°F oil for about 4 minutes (cut into a beignet of the first batch to check it's cooked through). Drain on paper towels and sprinkle with confectioners' sugar, or serve with a fruit purée.

If you're new to deep-frying, see page [17].

FOR ÉCLAIRS, PROFITEROLES, CREAM PUFFS, OR GOUGÈRES

Pipe or spoon the batter onto a slightly wetted baking sheet in fingers, balls, a ring of balls, etc. For éclairs or profiteroles, bake at 400°F for 20 minutes, then reduce the oven temperature to 350°F and bake for 10 minutes longer (or 15–20 minutes for larger cream puffs). Remove and immediately slit the bottom or side to allow the steam to escape.

LEEWAY

A For choux pastry, some cooks prefer white bread flour for its extra gluten, which helps choux stretch.

B For extra-crisp choux pastry, replace 10 percent of the flour with rice flour.

C When making choux pastry or beignets, use half water and half milk, as Michel Roux Jr. does. Milk will give a better flavor, water a crisper texture. The combination of milk and water is also said to yield the best Yorkshire pudding—choux pastry's bluff English cousin.

D A Hungarian gnocchi recipe calls for ⅔ cup each of all-purpose flour and milk, plus 5½ tbsp butter and 6 egg yolks.

E For gnocchi, stir in some freshly grated nutmeg at the end of step [3], if you like.

CHEESE

The world's best canapé. Gougères are native to Burgundy, although the cheese most often stipulated is Swiss Gruyère. As the French are not known for their embrace of foreign ingredients, this can be taken as a serious endorsement. Choux pastry is so named for the cabbage-like striations on its surface when cooked, but it has been known by various names, including *pâte royale*. Which makes a gougère, *pace* Vincent Vega, a royale with cheese. Use about ¾ cup grated cheese, stirring most of it in after all the egg has been incorporated. Pipe into small puffs and sprinkle the rest of the Gruyère over the top. You might choose to add ½ tsp dried thyme to the batter, or ½ small onion, grated—but as with cheese soufflé and straws, the unsurpassable flavor enhancer is mustard. I have made choux with mustard and no cheese whatsoever and found it had a surprisingly cheesy tang: Add 1 tsp mustard powder or 1 tbsp coarse-grain mustard to your batter. In Brazil, sour tapioca flour, made from cassava, is used for a variation on choux called *pão de queijo*. These little cheese puffs are eaten at breakfast or as a snack.

COCOA

Chocolate pastry is so often a disappointment, but it works well in choux. Ice chocolate-pastry éclairs with a pale coffee glaze and they look like the pâtisserie classic in negative—both familiar and strange. Like a good simile. Sift 1 heaped tbsp unsweetened cocoa powder with the flour—this gives a dark and distinct chocolate flavor. Add 2 tbsp sugar at step [1] if it's a cakelike effect you're after. Cocoa without sugar works in savory variations. Chad Robertson of the Tartine Bakery in San Francisco mixes cocoa with rye flour as a base for gougères (see cheese above), replacing about 15 percent of the flour weight with rye.

FENNEL

A surefire way to avoid the disappointment of unpuffed choux is to deep-fry the paste instead of baking it. The Italian chef Bartolomeo Scappi was making fritters with choux batter in the sixteenth century. Around Lent, in Spain, a similar treat is made with a slightly sweetened choux pastry flavored with ground fennel seeds: Try 1 tsp per 1 cup of flour. *Buñuelos de viento*, commonly eaten on All Saints' Day and sometimes charmingly translated as "nun's farts," are also choux-based. The pastry is made with milk, rather than water, and might be flavored with a little lemon zest and brandy, before being fried in olive oil. In the 1830s, Thomas Roscoe described the night he visited a festival in Triana by crossing the lamp-lit bridge of boats that connected the district with Seville, on the other side of the Guadalquivir, recalling the "innumerable flickering lights of the gipsies vending their buñuelos," fried in pots over charcoal fires.

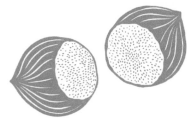

HAZELNUT

Swings and roundabouts: What you gain in flavor you lose in texture. Add ½ cup ground toasted hazelnuts along with the flour and you'll have a choux with a thicker, coarser texture than its wheat-flour equivalent. Unlike ordinary choux, however, which can seem a little plain unfilled or un-iced, this hazelnut version works well as a stand-alone puff, served with coffee, or on the side of a raspberry crème Chantilly (cream whipped with a little confectioners' sugar, vanilla, and crushed raspberries). If your guests complain that they prefer their choux filled, hand them the pastry bag and tell them to get on with it.

LARD

In Naples, the choux paste used for gnocchi is made with lard. Told you it was dangerous there. When I mixed up a batch, simply replacing the butter with the same quantity of lard, the texture and fragrance of hot water, flour, and fat reminded me of the pastry for pork pies (fortunately, the pigginess was lost in the baked choux). The main difference was the color of the finished puffs, paler than those made with butter or oil. Neapolitan bakers source their lard from the city's best salumerie and use it for their sfogliatella, the many-layered, clam-shaped, ricotta-filled pastry known by Italian-Americans, and *Sopranos* fans, as "shfooyadell." Thumb its leaves like a flip-book and you'll see the image of your waistband expanding to mobster proportions. Filled with a mere dollop of whipped cream, lard choux buns are positively healthy by comparison.

OLIVE OIL

Olive oil works perfectly well in choux batter in place of butter, and can be substituted like for like. Some say they can taste it. I can't. For me, the flavor of baked flour dominates. Sampled side by side, the flavor difference between butter, lard, and olive oil was minor, which, if cost is a consideration, makes a pretty convincing case for lard. Still, olive oil has its devotees, and cheaper oils could undoubtedly be used in its place. Dan Lepard makes his black olive gougères with olive oil choux. I made some for a dairy-averse friend by leaving out the cheese, but keeping the chopped black olives and finely chopped thyme, added to the water and oil before the flour went in.

ORANGE-FLOWER WATER & ALMOND

Marie-Antoine Carême used orange-flower water to flavor his choux batter. He made the batter into little puffs, decorating them with finely chopped almonds mixed with sugar, using egg white as a fixative.

They were then returned to the cooling oven to set. Orange-flower water is a common flavoring for crêpes—and choux batter could be seen as a crêpe mix with lots of egg. Orange-flower waters vary in strength, so start with 1 tsp per 1 cup flour, added after half of the eggs have been incorporated.

POTATO

Pommes Dauphines. Missing, presumed extinct. Why? A French fry crossed with a doughnut in the form of a crispy, golden jawbreaker. Back in the day they might be presented in a nest of *pommes allumettes,* as a double-potato side dish for simply cooked poultry. André Simon notes that *pommes Elizabeth* are *Dauphines* stuffed with creamed spinach. Combine 2 heaped cups mashed potatoes with a choux batter made to our starting point. Scoop the mixture with a melon baller and deep-fry in batches at 350°F.

PROSCIUTTO & PECORINO

Giorgio Locatelli describes a choux-type fritter available from snack bars on Sicilian beaches. Grated cheese and diced *prosciutto crudo* are added to the mixture after the eggs, along with parsley and garlic. Salami is another authentic addition, according to *The Silver Spoon*. Add ½ cup diced prosciutto and 2 handfuls of grated pecorino to your choux batter, once you've finished adding the egg.

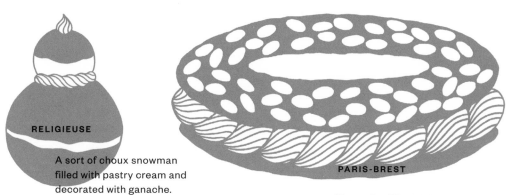

RELIGIEUSE

A sort of choux snowman filled with pastry cream and decorated with ganache.

PARIS-BREST

Choux ring filled with praline cream and garnished with sliced almonds and confectioners' sugar.

DAN LEPARD'S BAKED BRIE IN CHOUX

Butter individual ramekins, half-fill with choux, and bake, then slice off the top, fill with diced Brie, and return to the oven until the cheese melts.

MINI CHOUX PUFFS AS A SOUP GARNISH

ZEPPOLE

page 113

LE PONT-NEUF

Puff pastry shell containing choux and pastry cream.

ÉCLAIR AU SÉSAME NOIR

... at pâtisserie Sadaharu Aoki in Paris.

TULUMBA

A deep-fried, syrup-saturated choux pastry that's popular in Turkey, Albania, Macedonia, and other countries of the former Ottoman Empire.

CROQUEMBOUCHE

A tower of choux buns filled with pastry cream and bound with strands of spun sugar.

Potato Gnocchi

A simple mixture of warm riced potato, mixed to a dough with flour (and maybe egg), shaped into little dumplings and boiled. When potato gnocchi are good, they're very, very good. When they're bad, they're boring. Starchy potatoes are a *sine qua non*, but note that they should have some strength of flavor, too.

For enough gnocchi to serve 4 as a main course,
or 6 as an appetizer

INGREDIENTS
2¼ lb starchy potatoes [A]
1¼–2 cups all-purpose flour [B] [C] [D] [E]
1 tsp salt
½ tsp black pepper
Freshly grated nutmeg—optional [F]
2 egg yolks [G]

1 Steam, bake, or boil the potatoes in their skins until just cooked. Remove the skins when the potatoes are cool enough to handle, but still hot.
The warmth will help gluten development in the flour. Many cooks prefer steaming or baking, to minimize the wetness in the potato.

2 Push the potatoes through a ricer, mouli grater, or sieve.
Mash made with a hand-held masher will do, as long as it's very smooth.

3 Spread the potato out on a work surface evenly scattered with ⅔ cup flour. Sprinkle over another ⅔ cup flour, then season with salt and pepper and, if you like, freshly grated nutmeg. Add the lightly beaten egg yolks, distributing them evenly across the floured potato.

4 Using your fingers, quickly and lightly form the mixture into a dough.

5 Take a tennis-ball-sized quantity and roll it into a sausage on a lightly floured surface.
Now is a good time to cook a few to check that the dough is cohesive. If it isn't, more flour is needed. You can always pull off a piece of dough and see what it takes to make it work; sometimes nothing does, in which case I suggest you cut your losses and make bubble and squeak or ham hash. The flour in the dough will make it nice and crispy.

6   Make your gnocchi square, or indent rounds with your thumb, or make ridged logs by rolling short lengths off a fork or a gnocchi paddle. Keep the size regular so they cook at the same speed. Once each piece is made, transfer to a floured tray.
If you're not cooking your gnocchi immediately, shake a thin veil of flour over them. This will help keep them intact for a short time.

7   Cook, in batches, in a large pan of boiling salted water. They'll need about a minute or two to bob to the surface. Leave for a further 30 seconds or so, then remove with a slotted spoon.
Don't keep your gnocchi uncooked for longer than a few hours—they will start to get sticky and lose their form. But you can cook them ahead: As soon as they're done, drop them into iced water, then drain thoroughly, pat dry, and keep in the fridge for up to 2 days. Reheat in a pan or in the oven with butter or a sauce. Or freeze the uncooked gnocchi on trays, then transfer to a freezer bag. Gnocchi can be cooked from frozen, but in small batches (maybe in multiple pans), because adding too many at once will bring down the water temperature so much that the gnocchi will dissolve before they cook through. For the same reason, keep any gnocchi destined for the freezer on the small side.

LEEWAY
A   The best starchy, dry potatoes to use for gnocchi in the U.S. are russets. According to Giorgio Locatelli, Desiree is the best British option, while Piacentine or Spunto are the ideal Italian varieties.
B   White bread flour or 00 flour can be used.
C   Some cooks add baking powder to the flour for lightness; try 1 tsp for this quantity, or use self-rising flour.
D   Some recipes call for as little as 3–4 tbsp flour per 2¼ lb potato.
E   Add some grated Parmesan along with the flour—about ¼ cup for this quantity.
F   Nutmeg is particularly welcome with less flavorful potatoes, which might otherwise fail to mask the flavor of lightly cooked flour. A grating of Parmesan or a splash of grappa can also be used as flavor enhancers.
G   Egg is contentious. It helps the dough cohere, but some say it makes the finished gnocchi heavy. Some recipes omit egg entirely, at the cost of its cohesiveness; others recommend using just whites, or a whole egg. Play around. They're only gnocchi.

BEET

Hands-down, the pinkest gnocchi. Not the easiest to make, however, as beets vary considerably in their water content. If yours are too wet, you'll end up using so much flour to make a cohesive dough that the lightness essential to good gnocchi will be lost. Many chefs suggest roasting the beets first, thereby dehydrating them, rather than boiling or steaming them; others do boil their beets, then dry them in the oven. At the Tribeca Grill in Manhattan, they boil 5 large Idaho potatoes and 2 beets for 20 minutes and rice them, then spread them out on a baking sheet and let them dry in a low oven (150°F) for about 20 minutes. The mixture is then combined with 2 eggs, ½ cup finely grated Parmesan, 2 cups all-purpose flour, 1 tsp salt, and ½ tsp white pepper, kneaded, wrapped in plastic wrap, and stored in the fridge for a few hours, after which it's ready to roll and cut into gnocchi.

CHOCOLATE

Chocolate gnocchi come from Friuli in northeastern Italy. They are sugarless, and served as a *primo*, not a dessert. Follow our starting point, using 1½ cups flour and 1 cup unsweetened cocoa powder to 1 lb potatoes and 1 medium egg yolk. Typical sauces might include tomato and zucchini cooked with garlic, a venison ragù, or a mixture of tuna *bottarga* and *lampascioni*. *Lampascioni* score about an eight in the game of obscure ingredients; in looks, and taste, they resemble small alliums, but are in fact a variety of *muscari*, or grape hyacinth. Demand for them has grown to the extent that they are now cultivated in Puglia, to supplement the wild kind harvested across southern Italy. They are notably bitter, and need cooking for their natural sugars to express themselves: Most often they are simply boiled or roasted, then served with oil and vinegar, although some cook them with wine or tomatoes, or reduce them to a jamlike consistency to spread on toast.

PARSNIP

Kate Colquhoun suggests mixing parsnips with potato for gnocchi; the parsnips should be peeled, diced, and roasted at 400°F until tender, but not crisp on the outside, then mashed. For a 2½-cup mixture of mashed potato and parsnip, add ½ cup finely grated Parmesan and a grating of fresh nutmeg to half the starting-point amount of the flour, also halving the quantities of egg and seasoning.

POTATO FARLS

Irish potato farls use a similar dough to gnocchi, but they're a good deal easier to make. Peel 2¼ lb potatoes and cut into chunks, then simmer until soft. Mash or rice with 7 tbsp butter. Season, then stir in ¾ cup flour and ½ tsp baking powder. Shape the dough into two equal balls. Roll each out to the dimensions of a salad plate and cut into quarters— "farl" means fourth. Melt a lump of butter in a skillet over medium heat, and fry the farls until golden brown on both sides. Farls are not as rule-bound as gnocchi: You can make them with leftover mash. Eat with a little more butter, or alongside bacon and eggs.

PUMPKIN

M.F.K. Fisher enjoyed no gnocchi so much as the pumpkin variety— *gnocchi di zucca*—she tried in Lugano. Note that her recipe allows for the use of canned pumpkin. Mix 2 cups unsweetened puréed pumpkin with 2 lightly beaten eggs, ½–1 cup flour, ½ tsp baking powder, 1 tsp ground white pepper, nutmeg, salt, and a little crushed garlic. Once you've mixed up the dough, follow the method from step 5. Fisher suggests serving *gnocchi di zucca* with poultry, game, or pork or as a meal on their own. I toss them in butter, Parmesan, and crushed amaretti biscuits.

RICE

In Emilia Romagna, gnocchi are made with rice. Simmer 1 cup short-grain rice until tender. Drain, transfer to a bowl with 2 lightly beaten eggs and enough bread crumbs to make a dough, then season. As with most gnocchi, you can add a little butter, grated cheese, or nutmeg at this stage. Form the mixture into small balls, and cook in good stock, a few at a time, for a few minutes. Serve with butter and cheese.

SZILVÁS GOMBÓC

A Hungarian dumpling made with gnocchi dough. In Germany, they are known as *Zwetschgenknödel*. The pits are removed from plums and replaced with sugar lumps. The gnocchi dough is then fashioned around the fruit, and the dumplings simmered for about 10 minutes, drained, and tossed in a pan of buttery bread crumbs. Cut one in half and it looks a bit like a lychee.

WALNUT

Monica Galetti's gluten-free variation on potato gnocchi calls for grated walnuts. You'd better grate them carefully. No fingernails, please. (Okay, blitz them in a grinder or food processor, but not too finely.) Stir ¾ cup each of grated Parmesan and walnuts into 2½ cups mashed potato with 1 whole egg, plus 1 yolk. Make as per the starting point, but once boiled, refresh the gnocchi in iced water, drain, then shallow-fry in a mix of oil and butter. Galetti serves these with venison in a chocolate sauce. Or try them with arugula leaves lightly dressed in olive oil and lemon juice and dotted with Gorgonzola.

Ricotta Gnocchi

The lightest of all gnocchi, and the easiest to make well. Relatively quick, too, once the ricotta has been drained. As with potato gnocchi, the flour—again, used in the smallest quantity possible—helps the main ingredient cohere. Ricotta gnocchi are excellent with summer vegetables and leaves, or floated in a light broth.

For about 32 cork-shaped gnocchi, enough to serve 2 as a small main course or 4 as an appetizer

INGREDIENTS
1 cup whole-milk ricotta
⅓ cup all-purpose flour [A] [B]
½ cup finely grated Parmesan [B]
1 egg, beaten [A] [C]
Grating of nutmeg
Fine semolina or rice flour for dusting

1   Drain the ricotta for at least 30 minutes or, preferably, overnight in the fridge.

2   Spread out the ricotta on a plate, then evenly sprinkle over the flour, Parmesan, egg, and nutmeg, and quickly form into a soft, wet dough.
    As for potato gnocchi, you want to handle the dough as little as possible.

3   Flour your hands. Roll about 2 tsp of the mixture into a cork shape or a ball, drop it onto a plate of semolina or rice flour, and dust it with a fine veil of the semolina or rice flour.
    If the mixture seems too wet to roll, try dropping a dollop of mixture onto your lightly floured plate, and using a fork rather than your hands to fashion it into a shape.

4   Bring some salted water to a boil in a large saucepan and submerge your first gnocco. It should hold together and bob up to the surface after about a minute. Leave it to simmer for a minute more, before lifting it out with a strainer or slotted spoon and testing it for texture. If it passes, form the rest of the mix into your chosen shapes. If it falls apart, add a little more flour and test again.
    The idea is to get the ricotta mix to cohere with as little flour as possible. This achieved, you can freeze the uncooked gnocchi. Place on a lightly floured tray, spaced apart and in a single layer; once frozen, transfer to a freezer bag. Cook from frozen, but not too many at a time.

5 Cook your gnocchi in batches. If you're not serving them immediately, or tossing them straight into a pan of sauce, keep the cooked and drained gnocchi warm in a covered dish in the oven at 200°F.

You may find that having two pans of simmering water on the go makes this less laborious.

LEEWAY

A If you don't drain the ricotta overnight, it may need more flour. Some cooks use equal weights of ricotta and flour, and a yolk rather than a whole egg, without bothering to drain the ricotta at all. It's an economical way of making the ricotta go further.

B Jacob Kenedy uses 1 cup fresh homemade bread crumbs instead of flour, and pecorino rather than Parmesan.

C Elizabeth David's recipe calls for 2 eggs, 4 tbsp soft butter, 3 heaped tbsp of flour, and ¼ cup Parmesan to 1 cup ricotta, mixed up, then rested in the fridge overnight.

BUTTERNUT SQUASH

Mixed with ricotta, the flesh of the squash, ocher as a Roman house-front in late afternoon, takes on a pale, chalky quality recalling the pastel-colored, crumbly confectionery known as Edinburgh rock. And the gnocchi are pretty sweet themselves, even mixed with some Parmesan and salt. Simply add heaped ¾ cup dry, mashed butternut squash to the ricotta mixture at step 2. You can use roasted, mashed pumpkin the same way, so jot a note on the calendar to serve pumpkin-ricotta gnocchi around the time you're making jack-o'-lanterns.

GOAT'S OR SHEEP'S CHEESE

Italian cookbooks often stipulate sheep's ricotta for ricotta gnocchi, though you'll be lucky to find a supplier. Keep a couple of Sardinian ewes on your Juliet balcony—but be warned, they'll nibble holes in your clothespin bag. Alternatively, add some hairy-beast charisma to your blander cow's ricotta by replacing the Parmesan in our starting point with a strong, hard sheep's cheese, a well-aged pecorino, or a goat's cheese (chèvre). Replacing some of the ricotta with a full-fat, soft goat's cheese yields a less striking difference in flavor, but the texture is out of this world.

LEMON

The Zuni Cafe in San Francisco bases its ricotta gnocchi on the Elizabeth David recipe, and might flavor the batter with freshly grated nutmeg, or sage cooked in butter, or chopped lemon zest. Judy Rodgers, the late chef-proprietor, noted that ricotta gnocchi lend themselves to many partners, as long as they are "tender and delicate." Flageolet beans, for example, with extra virgin olive oil and black pepper, or zucchini matchsticks. Bank on 1–2 tbsp lemon zest to each cup of ricotta, mixing it in with the flour, cheese, etc. As Rodgers specifies chopped, as opposed to grated lemon zest, assume that means very finely chopped.

SPINACH

The Italians have a commendable habit of giving even the heaviest-handed cooks their due. There's a kind of lumpy almond-flavored macaroon called *brutti ma buoni*—"ugly but good" (page 291). Spinach and ricotta gnocchi are called *malfatti*—"badly made." (They are also known as spinach *nudi*, as they are, in essence, pasta-less spinach and ricotta pasta parcels.) *Malfatti* are more reliable than potato gnocchi, with a dreamy texture. The spinach can be swapped for other greens like chard, nettles, or herbs. Opinions vary quite widely on the proportion of greens to cheese. *The Silver Spoon*, for example, calls for 25 oz of spinach to 1 cup of ricotta, yolks rather than whole eggs, and flour only for dusting—but I use 7 oz spinach, a more common amount for 1 cup ricotta. The spinach is wilted in nothing other than the water that clings to its leaves after washing and shaking. When cool, squeeze dry. You should have 2 handfuls. Chop quite finely. (Mix with a few tablespoons of finely chopped parsley and a minced garlic clove, if you like.) Add to the ricotta with the flour, Parmesan, and egg, and form the dough into walnut-size balls. Chill on a tray in the fridge for 30 minutes. Cook the gnocchi in the usual way, but remove them from the water as soon as they have surfaced.

VANILLA

Mixing up the dough for plain gnocchi with ricotta, egg, and a little flour, I was put in mind of cheesecake, and wondered whether sweet ricotta gnocchi might be any good. They weren't. Poaching didn't agree with them. There is, however, an entirely successful deep-fried, more floury Italian variant that's just one of many Italian confections that go by the name of *zeppole*. Mix 1 cup all-purpose flour with 1 cup ricotta, 2 eggs, 2 tsp baking powder, and ¼ tsp vanilla extract. Leave for about 10 minutes while the gluten expands, then form into walnut-size balls. Deep-fry until golden, a few at a time, and serve hot with an extra shake of sugar—as is, or with added cinnamon. Or a mix of cinnamon and aniseed. Sweet gnocchi aren't unheard of, incidentally. The Bentley Restaurant and Bar in Sydney, Australia, serves orange ricotta dumplings with strawberry purée and cinnamon sugar.

Batter

CRÊPES, YORKSHIRE
PUDDING & POPOVERS

page 122

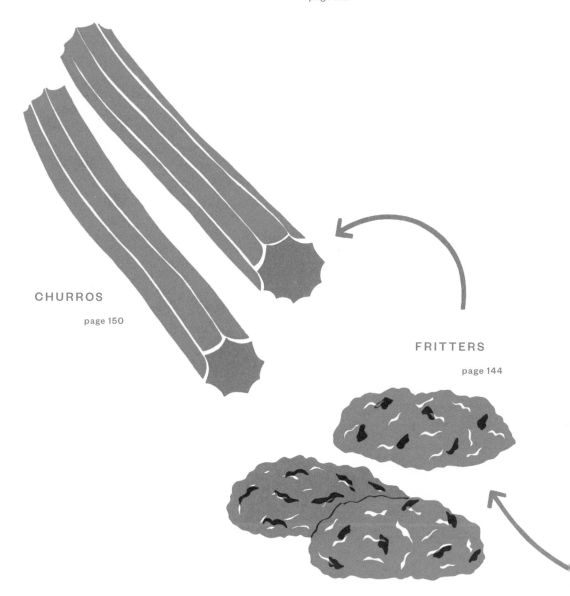

CHURROS

page 150

FRITTERS

page 144

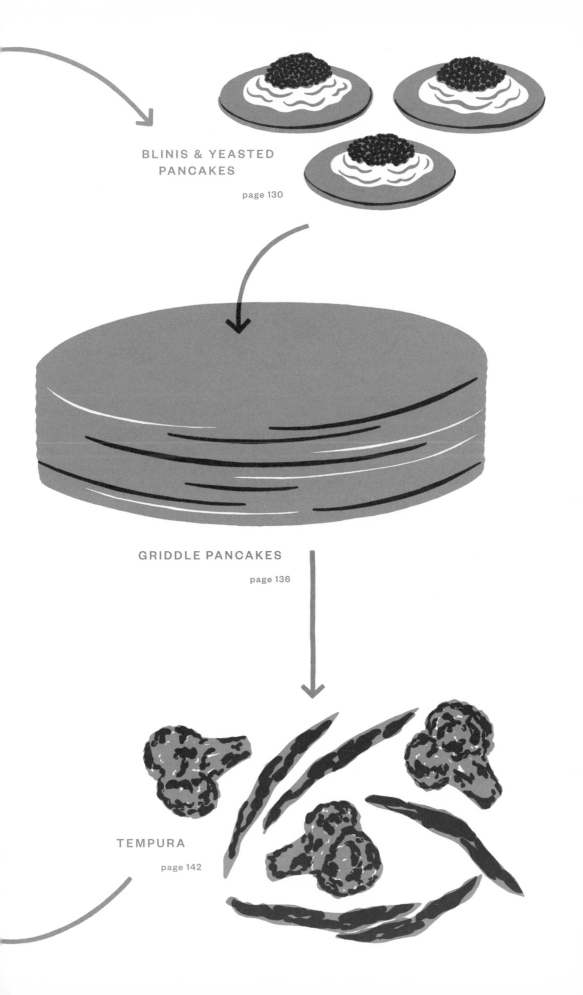

BLINIS & YEASTED
PANCAKES

page 130

GRIDDLE PANCAKES

page 136

TEMPURA

page 142

The reason why Americans eat stacks of pancakes for breakfast, and the British don't, must surely be the different ways we measure ingredients. To make batter to a metric or imperial recipe involves setting up your scales, weighing your flour, finding the measuring jug (it's in the dishwasher), and measuring out your milk—far too complex at a time of day when you're still trying to remember what your name is. In the U.S., you dig out your measuring cup and fill it with flour, adding a teaspoon each of sugar and baking powder. Mix in an egg, a cup of milk, and salt to taste. Easy as New Orleans.

The one-of-everything recipe will make enough pancakes for two or three people. If you want more, you can double, quadruple, or even duodecuple the mix with no problem. Enrich the batter with extra egg, a little sugar, or melted butter, if desired. But, as any six-year-old knows, the best way to supercharge your pancakes is to interleave the stack with butter and syrup, so that the last one is cast adrift on a maple-flavored golden pond.

C
R
Ê
P
E
S

But I am getting ahead of myself. The batter continuum starts with crêpes, the 10-denier stocking to the griddle pancake's woolly tights. Crêpe batter must be thin enough to cover the surface of the pan with a single tilt of the wrist, so it needs to be more dilute. As noted above, the ratio of liquid to flour in griddle-pancake batter is 1:1. In crêpe batter it's closer to 3:2. Its looser consistency belies the strength that allows the cooked crêpes to be so thin without falling apart. I tend to make my crêpe batter with a cup each of flour and liquid, rest it, then stir in between an extra ¼ cup and ½ cup of liquid, just before cooking, to achieve the ideal consistency. Never worry about the first crêpe in a batch, incidentally; its sole job is to soak up excess fat in the pan, and to train your hand, like your first attempt at the windmill hole in miniature golf.

I have forgotten the birthdays of close family members and my own wedding anniversary, but never Shrove Tuesday. And yet inherent to this sacred crêpe ritual, it seems, is its suppression for the other 364 days of the year: Compiling a list of ideas for the illustrations on page [129] persuaded me that every Tuesday should be Mardi Gras. I've become obsessive about the kind of *crespelle* I used to eat in cheap Italian restaurants in London's Soho—three pale crêpes stuffed with ricotta and spinach, snugly nestled in their white oval dish under a bedspread of béchamel—a dish so gentle it makes other comfort food seem like a kick in the teeth. Grate over some Parmesan, if you like, but black pepper would be as unwelcome as a profanity in church.

The Breton-style galettes served at Asterix on the King's Road were bolder in flavor: thin buckwheat crêpes, generously filled, then folded into neat brown parcels ready for delivery to your stomach. Ratatouille and Gruyère was my stuffing of choice, and is now. Galettes are made with the same proportions of flour and liquid as crêpes, but water is often substituted for the milk, lending a crisper texture. In fact, if crispness is your thing, replacing a third of the milk in the starting point for crêpes with water will yield good results.

The very same mixture, cooked in hot fat in the oven, will make Yorkshire pudding with a brown, crunchy crust. An all-milk batter makes softer, paler Yorkshire pud—more Harrogate than Barnsley.

Y O R K S H I R E The late British food broadcaster Derek Cooper
considered Yorkshire pudding "a triumphant opening batsman,"
P recalling the days when it was served with gravy in advance of
U the Sunday roast. The idea was to blunt the appetite, lest one's
D meager portion of pricey meat disappoint. It's a cunning trick. The
D lightness of the pudding in the mouth belies the share of stomach
I space it will shortly occupy. This is worth bearing in mind if, in
N the U.S., you are ever presented with a pre-meal basket of warm
G popovers.

P O P O V E R S Popovers are made with a very similar batter to crêpes and Yorkshire pudding, but tend to be eggier. It's the extra rise afforded by the egg that gave them their name: They pop over the brim of their pans, which are shaped like upturned Pilgrim Fathers' capotains. It's dangerously easy to eat too many. As Dr. Seuss advises in "My Uncle Terwilliger on the Art of Eating Popovers," best to eat the solid parts, but spit out the air.

Popover batter is often flavored with herbs, spices, cheese, or a combination, and the finished product stuffed with scrambled eggs or sandwich fillings, or served on the side of soup. Such mucking about might receive short shrift "up north" in England, but even there it's not unknown for a slice of cold Yorkshire pudding to be smothered with golden syrup or jam. And it was once common practice to pour the batter over fruit to make a dessert not unlike the French clafoutis.

Were clafoutis to have a fully-fledged place in *Lateral Cooking*, it could sit on either the batter or custard continuums. It's equally legitimate to think of clafoutis as a batter, or a baked custard stabilized with a little flour. Whichever definition you prefer, clafoutis is usually sweetened and poured over cherries.

In France, the great clafoutis debate is not over its status as batter or custard, but whether it should be considered a flan or a cake. The Académie Française reckons on the former; the residents of its native region, Limousin, the latter. Respectfully, I offer another question for their consideration. Is it nice? No matter how many recipes I try, I've always found clafoutis either rubbery or stodgy, with a deadening effect on the freshness of the fruit. Given the same ingredients, I'd opt for a delicate crêpe served with a compote; hot, crisp fritters; or, if time is not of the essence, warm blinis with homemade jam.

In its native Russia, the test of a great blini is its ability to absorb perilous quantities of butter. Hence the frequent use of both yeast and whisked egg in the batter, the aim being to achieve maximum sponginess. This is the approach I've taken in the starting point. Nonetheless, blinis are just as likely to be yeastless, relying solely on eggs for their lift. Modern blinis may also be made in the same way as griddle pancakes, using a chemical leavener like baking powder. Both alternatives are notably quicker, but at the expense of the tang of yeast. Some of the traditional flavor can be reinstated by replacing up to half of the wheat flour with buckwheat or rye flour.

As with griddle pancakes, yeasted blinis can be made with equal volumes of flour and milk. Put 1 cup flour, 1 tsp sugar, and ½ tsp instant yeast in a jug big enough to let the batter rise, and add 1 cup milk. If you mean to cook your blinis as soon as possible, first warm the milk until hand-hot, so as to activate the yeast immediately. If you're leaving it overnight in the fridge, cold milk is fine. Once the batter has risen, add the eggs and salt, and ready your pan.

Blinis have become a New Year's Day tradition in the Segnit household, partly because of the convenience of that overnight rise. I find bouncy blinis and bright smoked salmon, with the zing and tickle of lemon and dill, a more propitious start to the year than the burp of bacon, eggs, and sausages. By all means cook your blinis one by one in a dedicated blini pan, but note that the novelty of its dinky diameter will wear off quickly when there's a crowd to feed. And you'll miss out on the satisfaction of achieving the spot-on size and circularity by virtue of your pouring skills. Alan Davidson says the ideal blini should be 4 in across. I reckon that, like Marie Antoinette's breasts, they should be the same diameter as a Champagne saucer. Either way, flip your blinis with one hand while dandling the glass—filled with last night's leftovers— between two fingers of the other. Serve the blinis wearing a long satin nightdress and kohl smudged around your eyes. The mood you're after is mid-period Katharine Hepburn, putting on a good domestic show while exchanging leisurely wisecracks with your husband.

G R I D D L E   P A N C A K E S   It's not unheard of to flavor blinis: Caraway seeds or some grated vegetables, such as potato or zucchini, are the traditional options, stirred into the blini batter before cooking. Griddle pancakes are more commonly enhanced with sweet ingredients, such as sliced banana, blueberries, and chocolate chips. Pancake houses offer wild variations on the theme: pineapple upside-down pancakes, red velvet pancakes with a sour cream topping, cinnamon-roll-flavored pancakes. For me, however, plain wins every time. As with popcorn, the contrast between salty butter and simple sweetness makes a virtue of the subtly toasted taste of cooked batter. Griddle pancake enthusiasts frequently cite buttermilk and cornmeal pancakes—a twist on plain, if you like—as unimprovable when it comes to flavor.

In my worn old *Reader's Digest Complete Guide to Cookery*, there's a recipe for fried-onion-ring batter that's almost interchangeable with our starting point for griddle pancakes. I prefer a thinner, crisper batter for fritters, the sort made with water, rather than dairy, and no egg.

Shizuo Tsuji describes the ideal tempura batter as having "a lacy,
E golden effect… not a thick armour-like pancake casing." Water,
M rather than milk, is used for the last three starting points on the
P batter continuum, but as with blinis and griddle pancakes, the
U 1:1 ratio of liquid to flour remains constant. Most tempura batters
R call for 1 cup flour, 1 cup cold water, and 1 egg, or just the egg
A yolk or white.

There are also recipes that do without the egg altogether, relying on the gluten content of wetted white wheat flour to make the batter cohere. By contrast, making tempura the traditional way is more a matter of *avoiding* gluten formation. In many recipes, this is achieved by replacing some of the wheat flour with gluten-free cornstarch or white rice flour. For the same reason, the batter should be mixed up only when you're ready to use it. As beating encourages the formation of gluten, the batter-maker's quest for smoothness ends here: Tempura embraces the lump. Enjoy this moment of abandon while you can, because, like most Japanese cooking, tempura is a precise art.

At dedicated restaurants, or *tempura-ya*, the appropriate cooking oil is carefully selected for each ingredient, sometimes blended with several others to create the perfect medium, then discarded after a single use. Likewise, the batter's consistency is adjusted to suit each ingredient. An experienced tempura chef will let the batter drip from a chopstick to check the consistency is exactly right, whether it be for lotus root (the unpromising-looking vegetable that resembles a slice of loofah), shrimp head, wagyu beef, julienned carrot, quail's egg, or *shirako* (cod's sperm sac, if you're wondering)—all of which will have been painstakingly sourced. You'll find the starting point is more relaxed.

The Italian equivalent of tempura is *fritto misto*. Depending on the region, you might be served lightly battered artichoke hearts, squash blossoms, sweetbreads, calf's liver, sage leaves, anchovies, thin slices of lemon, or wedges of custard—sufficiently *misto*, in other words, to keep things interesting. Waverley Root thought the fine local olive oil made Liguria an excellent place to sample *fritto misto*, noting that *magro* and *grasso* versions existed, for fasting and non-fasting days respectively. Root lists wisteria petals, mushrooms, salsify (oyster plant), and hairy borage leaves as possible ingredients; some of the more delicate items, he writes, are used more for the flavor they impart to the batter than for their own sake. Of course, the special joy of a good restaurant *fritto misto* is having someone else stand over the deep fryer, so you can enjoy it without smelling like you've just finished your shift at a fast food joint.

F Deep-frying at home: It isn't only the lingering fragrance of dirty oil
R that puts me off. Second only, in its ability to induce cold insomniac
I sweats, to the public-information film about the boy reaching for
T a frisbee in an electricity substation ("JIMMYYYYY!") was the one
T about deep-fryer fires. Fortunately—or unfortunately, depending on
E which way you look at it—my mother was far too busy deep-frying
R fritters of apple and canned pineapple rings to watch the TV and
S discover what mortal danger she was putting us in. At school, fritters
appeared on the menu under the exotic alias "kromeskies." The name
comes from Poland via France. To please his Polish consort, Marie
Leszczynska, Louis XV had his chefs devise dishes that reminded
her of home, like the dessert that would become rum baba, and the
kromeski—a generic term, fairly interchangeable with croquette, and
similarly amenable to all sorts of fillings, seafood, meat, or vegetable.
I suspect Queen Marie would not have found my school catering very
regal. Our kromeskies were made from leftover ground meat, wrapped
in bacon and fried in batter.

I'd completely forgotten about kromeskies until they cropped up
at the swanky Ledbury in London's Notting Hill. Theirs are made of
organic pork, with celeriac baked in ash, hazelnuts, and wood sorrel.
Chef Jean-Georges Vongerichten makes crabmeat kromeski, topped
with tropical fruits and served on mustard microgreens. From a greasy
staple of the school lunch, the kromeski has returned to its aristocratic
origins: a fritter with airs. The British chef Sally Clarke calls a fritter
a fritter. Years ago, at her restaurant on Kensington Church Street,
I ate apple fritters. They came dusted with cinnamon confectioners'
sugar. The fact that I can't remember whether or not they were served
with ice cream is a testament to their deliciousness—the batter was
perfectly crisp and dry and the apple ring sliced to the ideal thickness
so that it was fluffy and soft. Between the two lay a millimeter of
exquisite goo made by the mingling of batter and fruit juice.

Although they tend toward the unsophisticated, there is still plenty
of variation in fritter batters. For the fritter batter here, however, I've
decided to keep things simple, not only to furnish a practicable starting
point, but because the batter is an excellent all-rounder. Again, it calls
for 1 cup flour and 1 cup cold water, but no egg. A touch of baking
powder will lend the required lightness—or, as with tempura, swap
the water for a carbonated drink like soda water or beer, which will
do the same job as the chemical leavener.

C Churros are the final starting point on the batter continuum. Like
H everything other than crêpes, churro batter calls for equal volumes
U of flour and liquid, but in this case the liquid is boiling water. A pinch
R of salt is added but no egg. It's as brutally direct as the Spanish sun.
R The heat of the water encourages gluten to form instantaneously,
O with a result something between a batter and a dough, thick enough
S to be pushed through the churro extruder.

In Jerez, I queued outside a churrería while the paving slabs were still wet from their early-morning hose-down. It was 9 A.M. on a Saturday and the queue already described two sides of the plaza. Time moves slowly in Andalusia, never more so than when you're shuffling toward a man piping a yard-long coil of batter into a cauldron of hot oil from a cross between a fire hose and a hypodermic needle. When cooked, the coil, ridged to increase its surface area, is removed from the oil with tongs and scissored into lengths.

I was virtually having a hypoglycemic episode by the time I reached the front of the queue. With shaking hand I exchanged my euro for a white paper bag of hot dough sticks and a fistful of sugar sachets, and retreated to a table in the center of the square. It was only by casting an eye on my neighbors that I realized my mistake—I had no hot chocolate to dip my churros into. The queue was now making inroads on a third side. So I ate a hot sugar-crusted dough stick on its own, then half of a second, which was as much as I could manage. A churro without a rich, milky accompaniment is no more edible than fries without salt and ketchup. I relocated to the non-churro café on the other side of the plaza and bought a milky coffee, the kind you find in continental Europe that tastes like the cheap fondant-filled chocolates in boxes of mixed Christmas candies, and a vanilla ice cream. Taking frequent sips of coffee I pushed my last, barely warm churro into my bauble of ice cream and demolished the lot.

Crêpes, Yorkshire Pudding & Popovers

The same mixture used to make delicate crêpes, nibbled by chic Parisians *à pied*, is used to make Yorkshire pudding, stout stalwart of the British roast dinner. The culinary *entente cordiale* breaks down, however, when it comes to the cooking technique, so if you're making Yorkshires, note how the method differs. Popovers are an American version of Yorkshire puddings, but they use more egg. Popover batter is often flavored, and the finished items might be filled in the manner of a choux puff.

For 8 (8-in) crêpes, 8–12 individual or an 8-in square Yorkshire pudding(s), or 6 popovers

INGREDIENTS
1 cup all-purpose flour ^{A B C D}
A few pinches of salt
1–2 eggs ^{D E}
1½ cups milk ^F
Butter, lard, or bland oil ^G

1 Put the flour in a bowl and whisk in the salt.
   The quick whisk takes the place of sifting the flour.

2 Make a well in the center and whisk in the egg as far as possible, then slowly pour in 1 cup of the milk, whisking and drawing the flour into the liquid to make a smooth batter. Gradually whisk in the remaining ½ cup milk, holding some back if you think it will make the batter too runny.

3 Ideally, let the batter rest for 30 minutes.
   This will give the flour a chance to absorb the liquid fully, and for the gluten to relax. If you're planning to leave the mixture for longer than a few hours, put it in the fridge, where it will keep for at least 24 hours.

   FOR CRÊPES
   Heat a little butter in a skillet and swirl it around. Pour off the excess into a small heatproof bowl and keep it to grease the pan lightly as you go. Turn the heat to medium–high, then, once the pan is good and hot, give the batter a stir and pour just enough into the pan to cover the bottom. Let the crêpe brown on its underside—this will take 30–90 seconds. Flip and cook until golden on the other side.

I think the heat, rather than the quantity of egg or fat in the batter, is what matters most when making crêpes. Keep the cooked crêpes warm in a 240°F oven. Once cooled, crêpes can be wrapped in a freezer bag (interleaved with parchment paper) and kept in the fridge for up to 3 days, or frozen for 1 month. Either way, they'll need to be brought to room temperature before being reheated.

FOR YORKSHIRE PUDDING OR POPOVERS

Pour the batter into greased, preheated pan(s). Popovers should be cooked in special popover pans, but muffins pans or custard cups will do. For individual Yorkshire puddings, bake at 425°F for 20 minutes; for one large Yorkshire pudding or popovers, reduce the heat to 375°F (after the initial 20 minutes at 425°F) and continue to bake for 10–20 minutes longer.

Popovers need longer to cook than individual Yorkshires, because the mixture is deeper in the pans.

LEEWAY

A   All-purpose flour is best for crêpes, as you want them to be thin, but I've sometimes resorted to self-rising out of necessity, and the results weren't unacceptably puffy.

B   The higher gluten content of white bread or 00 flour can give a better rise to Yorkshire pudding and popovers than all-purpose flour.

C   Gluten-free flours will work for crêpes, but not for puddings or popovers.

D   For spongier Yorkshire puddings, double the flour and use as many as 4 eggs.

E   Using 2 eggs will give crêpes an eggier flavor and a spongier texture, and will make your Yorkshire puddings puff up high. Yorkshire pudding recipes vary in the quantity of eggs they use: 1 is standard, but use as many as 4 if you prefer a deep, soft pudding to the crisper type. Popovers will need at least 2 eggs.

F   Use all milk, or thin the mixture with water at step 2 for a slightly crisper crêpe. For crispy Yorkshire puddings, use 1 cup milk and ½ cup water.

G   A few tablespoons of melted butter (or bland oil) may be added to crêpe batter, to help prevent the mixture from sticking to the pan. Butter will also enrich the batter's flavor. Lard, butter, or oil can be used to grease the pans for Yorkshire puddings and popovers.

Crêpes, Yorkshire Pudding & Popovers
→ Flavors & Variations

BUCKWHEAT

In medieval Europe, "Saracen" was a catch-all term for anything vaguely from the East. Where buckwheat actually originated is a matter for debate, but the clue persists in its Italian and French names, *grano saraceno* and *sarrasin*. Buckwheat crêpes, a specialty of Normandy, are known as *galettes de sarrasin*. The inclusion of wheat flour in modern versions of the recipe makes for a more negotiable batter and a softer crêpe: *Galettes de sarrasin* can be a little medieval when made with buckwheat *tout seul*. They often have their curved edges folded over the filling, making a square with a window in the center that begs for the bulging eye of an egg yolk. It's traditional to serve savory ingredients with (or in) *galettes de sarrasin*, sweet with wheat-flour crêpes. Taste a *sarrasin* on its own, however, and you may find its distinct cocoa-malt flavor a harmonious match for Nutella. Substitute the same quantity of buckwheat flour for the wheat flour.

CHEESE

Are the Yanks and Brits divided by a common pudding? Popovers, according to James Beard, are more than just an American version of Yorkshire pudding, but there's little to tell between the recipes. The difference is in their appearance. Popovers are always made in individual portions, and their exuberant puff is to the modest Yorkshire what the Macy's Parade is to the plowing demonstration at an English agricultural show. Popovers also differ in that they're served in a bread basket, rather than on a plate under a blanket of gravy. At BLT Steak, the U.S. restaurant chain, they serve Gruyère popovers so revered they come with a postcard detailing chef Brian Moyers' recipe. Moyers uses warmed milk in his batter, which accelerates the gluten development in the flour, ensuring maximum pop in his overs. Eaten warm from the oven, with sweet butter and good salt, they're like big, boisterous gougères—which makes sense, when you consider how similar the ingredients are for choux pastry. In Burgundy, gougères are served as hors d'oeuvres with a glass of wine, whereas a Cheddar popover would make a perfect accompaniment to a decent pint of ale. See for yourself by using 2 eggs in our starting point, and stirring up to 1 cup grated cheese into the prepared batter. Sprinkle on a little extra cheese before the popovers go into the oven. In the absence of popover pans, use deep muffin pans or custard cups.

CHESTNUT

Noting the affinity of chestnut for orange, the nature writer Richard Mabey suggests using chestnut flour for *crêpes Suzette*. Chestnut flour has a strong fragrance of cocoa, with a tang of sharp dairy, rather like Green & Black's dark milk chocolate. Replace up to half of the wheat flour in our starting point with chestnut flour. The forager John Wright singles out birch sap as a fitting accompaniment to chestnut crêpes. Birch syrup contains a mixture of glucose and fructose, and when cooked down it takes on a more caramel, less vanilla character than maple syrup, which is mostly sucrose. If you are, as you read this, on your way to the woods to start tapping the birch trees, note that it takes a hundred liters of sap to make one of syrup.

COCONUT & TURMERIC

Next time you're in Brittany, France, order a crêpe and a side salad. Dress the salad, then tip it over the crêpe. Fold, then eat as you watch the locals splutter cider into their napkins. The idea is inspired by the Vietnamese street-food crêpe, *bánh xèo*. Made with rice flour, coconut milk, and turmeric, this "sizzling cake" is thin, like a crêpe, and is eaten folded over a mixture of shredded vegetables, lots of herbs, chilies, and maybe some meat or seafood, and served with a dipping sauce like *nuoc cham*. Malaysian *roti jala* is made with a similar mixture, scribbled over the base of the pan to make a netlike crêpe served as a side to curry. For *bánh xèo*, follow the crêpe method, using 1 cup rice flour and a 50/50 mix of water and coconut milk, and adding a pinch of ground turmeric. The turmeric will turn the crêpe decidedly yellow. The batter needs its 30-minute rest. Pour it into a lightly oiled wok and swirl to make a thin crêpe about 8 in in diameter. (My first attempt turned out a bit thick, which, added to its yellowness, gave it the appearance and eating quality of a dishwashing sponge.) Arrange some washed, drained bean sprouts, chopped cilantro, and scallion in a line slightly off-center. Many recipes call for a mixture of stir-fried pork belly and shrimp to be added with the bean sprouts. Let the batter cook for a few minutes (some chefs cover the wok for a short spell), then decant onto a plate, using a spatula to fold the crêpe over the filling as you do so. Serve with lettuce leaves, plenty of fresh mint, and maybe some dill and basil too. *Nuoc cham* is the usual dipping sauce—mince 1 garlic clove with 1 tbsp sugar, then mix in 2 tbsp each of fish sauce and lime juice. Add finely chopped red chili if you like it hot.

CREAM & SHERRY

Hannah Glasse calls for sack (Falstaff's favorite fortified wine), cream, and a great deal of eggs to make a thin crêpe. The following recipe scales down Glasse's 1747 original, and keeps a similar proportion of liquid to flour as our starting point for crêpes. At step [2], beat ⅔ cup each of sherry and cream with 9 eggs, a pinch of salt, and ½ cup sugar. Season with a sneeze of cinnamon, nutmeg, and mace. Mix into your flour. Light cream is ideal here, but heavy cream thinned with milk is also fine. Glasse notes that the crêpes will not be crisp—you need water to make a crêpe crisp—but will be very good. The sack and spice combination lends a subtle fruitcakiness that it would be a shame to mask with a strong syrup or sauce. A little melted butter and sugar is all that's needed. Don't worry, by the way, if you can't find sack—that bottle of sweet cream sherry you failed to get rid of in the church raffle will do just fine.

FINES HERBES

Next time you're bedbound with the flu and your husband/butler/unexpectedly soft-hearted prison guard offers you aspirin and a bowl of cream of tomato soup, wave it away and suggest, in your most emotionally manipulative croak, that a *consommé Celestine* might just stand an outside chance of forestalling your death, not that anyone could *possibly* spare the time to make you one... Cough, consumptively, as your carer makes his way to the kitchen, there to prepare a rich, meaty broth and clarify it to pinging translucency, before adding a *crêpe aux fines herbes* sliced into delicate ribbons. Some chefs interpret "fines herbes" as nothing more than chives, but what would be really—*cough*—marvelous is a combination of chives, parsley, chervil, and tarragon. As long as it's no trouble.

GINGER

In what is said to be the first recorded recipe for Yorkshire pudding, in her *Art of Cookery* (1747), Hannah Glasse suggests using ground ginger or nutmeg in the batter. Fifty years later, John Perkins included grated ginger in the batter for his "common pancake," which he recommends frying in lard. Try adding 2 tsp ground ginger (or 4 tsp finely grated fresh ginger), along with 2 tsp sugar and ½ tsp vanilla extract, to your crêpe batter. Ginger was still a standard batter flavoring in the 1850s, going by *The Household Encyclopedia*, which also suggests making it with weak beer or "clean snow" when eggs are scarce. Beer can be used for its leavening effect on batter, and the use of snow to the same purpose is corroborated by a letter from "a young housekeeper" to *The Atlantic* in 1865: "When snow falls every day for four months, as it does in New England, eggs get exceedingly cheap in the prudent household. Then one can smile to think how she circumvents the grocer, and pray the clouds to lay a good nestful every week."

LEMON

Coming home hungry from school one day I was gripped by a very rare desire to cook. What I wanted to make was a stack of crêpes, cemented with a mixture of tuna and Branston Pickle. The recipe is omitted from this book on grounds of taste. It hit the spot at the time, though. I ate the whole thing, cut into wedges. For a while I believed I was the inventor of the crêpe cake. Not so. A torte made of layered crêpes is popular in Hungary, the layers sandwiched together with chocolate ganache (page 380) or fruit compote. In Michel Roux Jr.'s version, the crêpes are made with a mix of whole wheat and white flour, flavored with lemon zest and sandwiched with lemon curd. Lemon is the crêpe's natural chaperone, even more so than tuna and pickle. Bump up the lemoniness by using buttermilk in place of the milk in our starting point. Allow for 2 zested lemons per cup of flour.

ORANGE

Karl Uhlemann fills orange-flavored crêpes with a cooled sabayon (page 514) made with orange juice and white wine. Add 2 tsp finely grated orange zest per cup of flour. This dish, called *crêpes Bohemian,* sounds a deal less stressful to make than its infamous cousin *Suzette*—a dish that owes its unfashionability both to overexposure and the need to prepare it to order. When *crêpes Suzette* are good, they're delicate as lace handkerchiefs, and will have been flambéed in just the right proportions of butter, orange, and Cointreau or Grand Marnier. When they're bad, it's as if the handkerchief has been sneezed into and then dropped in a puddle of cheap whisky marmalade. Legend has it that *crêpes Suzette* was invented accidentally, in 1895, by Henri Charpentier, a sixteen-year-old chef at the Café de Paris in Monte Carlo. By his account, Charpentier was making a batch of crêpes in cordial when the sugary syrup caught alight. As he was cooking for—and in front of—no less a voluptuary than the Prince of Wales, he felt unable to admit his mistake, and carried on regardless. Luckily Bertie loved the results so much he asked for it to be named after his dining companion. Later, Charpentier worked with Escoffier at the Savoy in London, before making his way to New York, where he cooked at Delmonico's. After the failure of an ambitious project at the Rockefeller Center and a stint in Chicago, Charpentier moved to the West Coast, where he ran a fourteen-cover BYOB restaurant in the living room of his Redondo Beach house, serving classic French cuisine to gourmands who may have waited for up to a year for their table. Never say the pop-up is a recent invention.

PANDAN

According to Wendy Hutton, the Indonesian crêpe *bujan dalam selimut* translates as "bachelor in a blanket." Insofar as they are crêpelike and rolled around a sticky coconut stuffing, they're not unlike the coconut and turmeric crêpes on page 125, apart from the addition of pandan flavoring extract and a good deal of vivid green coloring. This may account for their relationship status—you wouldn't want to share your blanket with anyone that color. Pandan, or screwpine, tastes so much like basmati rice that it's often used to make the cheap, non-basmati kind seem more expensive. Its aromatic, toasty quality is a natural match for the coconut, although you might consider adding a sour or bitter ingredient like dried fruit, tropical fruit, or chai spices to offset the intense sweetness. Fresh pandan leaves can be used in place of extract—infuse 1 cup coconut milk by warming it with 4 leaves that have been scratched with a fork, then strain. Stuff the cooked crêpes with grated fresh or dried shredded coconut simmered for about 15 minutes with palm or brown sugar and enough water to keep it just moist, like the inside of a Mounds bar. Equal weights of coconut and sugar are typical, but I prefer half that amount of sugar, plus a few pinches of salt. You'll need about 2–3 tbsp in each crêpe, rolled up and tucked in as neatly as you can. Serve at room temperature.

VANILLA

Joël Robuchon flavors the milk for his crêpes with a vanilla bean and seeds. In the U.S., vanilla extract is sometimes used in the German crêpe also known as a Dutch baby (less of an identity crisis than it sounds, Dutch being a corruption of Deutsch). Most recipes call for equal volumes of milk and flour, although some omit milk entirely, relying on the egg to bind the flour and ultimately making for a much softer texture, recalling an omelet. Heat the oven to 425°F. Put 2 tbsp butter and 1 tbsp bland oil into an 8-in round pan and slide into the oven to heat. Mix the following, as per our starting point: 5 tbsp flour, a few pinches of salt, 1 extra large egg, 5 tbsp milk, and 1 tsp vanilla extract. No rest is required. Remove the hot pan from the oven and carefully swirl the fat around in it, then pour in the batter. Return to the oven and bake for 10–12 minutes. Serve with sugar and lemon, or crème fraîche and honey.

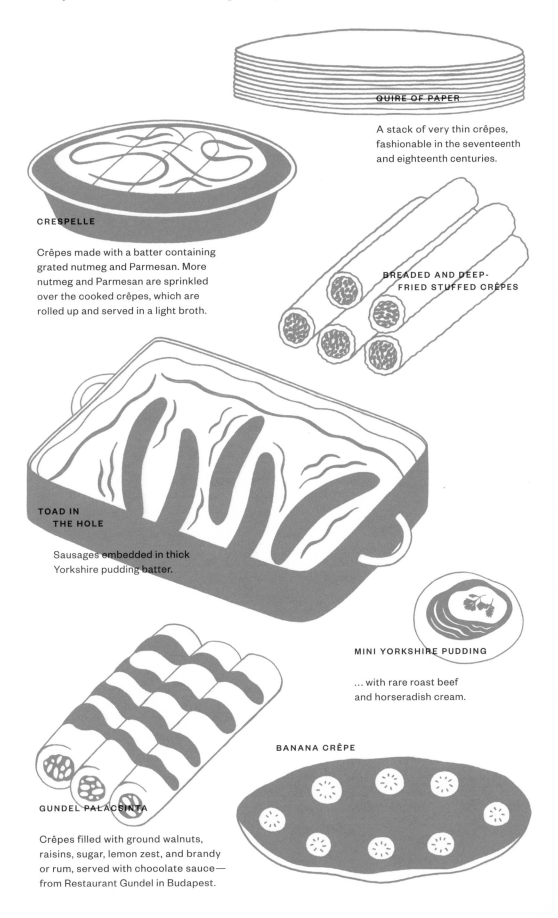

QUIRE OF PAPER

A stack of very thin crêpes, fashionable in the seventeenth and eighteenth centuries.

CRESPELLE

Crêpes made with a batter containing grated nutmeg and Parmesan. More nutmeg and Parmesan are sprinkled over the cooked crêpes, which are rolled up and served in a light broth.

BREADED AND DEEP-FRIED STUFFED CRÊPES

TOAD IN THE HOLE

Sausages embedded in thick Yorkshire pudding batter.

MINI YORKSHIRE PUDDING

… with rare roast beef and horseradish cream.

BANANA CRÊPE

GUNDEL PALACSINTA

Crêpes filled with ground walnuts, raisins, sugar, lemon zest, and brandy or rum, served with chocolate sauce—from Restaurant Gundel in Budapest.

Blinis & Yeasted Pancakes

This starting point calls for both yeast and egg, yielding the lightest, spongiest pancakes, equally happy doused in butter or under the more conventional sour cream and smoked salmon or caviar. The batter can be ready to use in an hour, but if you're making blinis for breakfast or brunch, it's easier to mix up the batter and let it rise slowly in the fridge overnight. As with bread, a slower rise means more flavor. Blinis can also be made without yeast—see [E] under Leeway.

For about 18 blinis [A]

INGREDIENTS
1 cup flour [B] [C]
1 tsp sugar
1 tsp instant yeast [D] [E]
1 cup milk
A few pinches of salt
1 egg
1–2 tbsp melted butter or bland oil—optional

1 Put the flour, sugar, and yeast in a bowl or pitcher large enough for the batter to rise.

2 Warm the milk to hand-hot and whisk into the dry ingredients.
If you're leaving the batter to rise all day or overnight, the milk does not have to be warmed.

3 Cover and set aside to rise for an hour or two.
Or place in the fridge for a longer, or overnight, rise.

4 When you're ready to cook, whisk in the salt, then the egg— and the butter or oil, if using.
For thicker, bouncier pancakes, try stirring the yolk into the batter, then beating the white to soft peaks and folding it in.

5 Heat your blini pan or skillet over a medium heat. Put a little butter in it and swirl it around, then pour any excess into a small heatproof bowl. Use this to lubricate the pan, sparingly, as needed. Add 1 tbsp batter, which should spread to a diameter of about 3 in. You'll probably be able to cook 3 or 4 at a time. Cook until small holes appear on the surface of the pancake, about 1–2 minutes, then flip and cook until colored underneath.
Keep your cooked pancakes warm in a foil-covered dish in a 240°F oven.

6 Blini batter will keep for 3 days in the fridge (although don't expect any air beaten into the egg to last that long). Cooked blinis can be kept in an airtight container for a few days, or frozen for up to a month.

LEEWAY

A The given quantity makes 18 blinis about 3 in across. If you want 12 blinis of 4-in diameter, use about 2 tbsp batter for each one.

B Use 50/50 buckwheat and wheat flour for classic buckwheat blinis. You could also use fine cornmeal or rye flour in place of the buckwheat. A little more milk may be needed to achieve the right pouring consistency.

C You can use whole wheat flour, but add about ¼ cup more milk.

D If you're using the sort of yeast that needs to be activated, add the sugar and either ½ small cake fresh or 1 tsp active dry yeast to the warmed milk. Allow 15 minutes for it to froth up, then mix into the flour and proceed from step 3.

E If you lack yeast or time, it's not unthinkable to make blinis using the same method as for griddle pancakes (page [136]), but do use some buckwheat or rye flour to restore a measure of blini-ness.

BARLEY

It was once common in Russia to make blinis with barley flour. For something so simple to make, there was a surprising amount of dissent about the *exact* method. Where should the batter for barley blini be mixed? Was it best made on the riverbank, the lakeshore, or the fringes of the forest? The aim being to capture beneficial airborne yeasts, much as the more evangelical modern breadmaker might take his sourdough mother for a walk in the hills. It was also traditional to put the first blini of the batch on the windowsill, as a gift to an impoverished passerby. This would cause nothing short of war between the squirrels and magpies that hang out in my urban garden. Elizabeth David described barley flour as an acquired taste—"earthy and rather primitive" and thought that barley meal, yeast-risen pancakes were particularly delicious. Make them to our starting point, using 50/50 white bread and barley flours. Or follow David's recipe in *English Bread and Yeast Cookery*, by adding an extra egg and diluting the batter to a more crêpe-like consistency—add ¼ cup more milk. Use this to make large, thin pancakes, and serve them in a stack, layered with cheese.

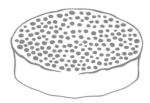

CRUMPETS & PIKELETS

A few weeks into a six-month assignment to the U.S., a colleague asked me what I was homesick for. Crumpets, I said, after a pause whose brevity surprised us both. Describe, she said. "They're like pancakes," I said, "except they're thick. And have lots of holes on the top. And if you pull them apart they have *fronds*. Not unlike a sea sponge, I suppose. If you eat them untoasted, they're almost jelly-like." "Okay," said my new colleague. "I'm pretty sure we don't have those here. Could you make one?" I demurred. Nobody actually *made* crumpets. They grew in the package, like hydrogenated corn snacks. The batter for crumpets is, in fact, very easy to make. They're just a little tricky to cook. Follow the starting point, but instead of adding an egg before you cook the batter, thoroughly stir in 1 tsp baking powder and set aside for 10 minutes. Place a greased ring, about 4 in in diameter, in a greased skillet over a low to medium heat, and pour a crumpet's worth of batter into the ring. Cook for a few minutes before removing the ring, then keep cooking as holes begin to appear and the surface gradually dries out. Check the underside to make sure it's not burning. After 10 minutes, the crumpet should be ready to flip for a quick brown on the top. The difficulty is in getting the center cooked. Best, at least to start with, to restrict them to a depth of about ½ in, and see if they cook through. If they don't, or you don't have the appropriate rings, go for pikelets instead. Pour the batter into a hot skillet until the blob is roughly the size of a griddle pancake. Likewise, cook them as you would a pancake, flipping them when the underside is cooked and the top has begun to develop holes. I've found that the texture of crumpets and pikelets is better if you allow them to cool before toasting.

LENTIL & RICE

Uttapam, a kind of pancake commonly eaten for breakfast in India, is made with a mixture of rice and lentils that has been left to soak overnight and, via fermentation, develop a mild tanginess. While an uttapam is often the same size as a blini, a thinner version of the batter might be used for the more crêpe-size dosa. Orese Fahey advises that different types of rice and lentils can be used to create variations on dosa batter, as long as you stick to a 2:1 ratio of rice to lentils. She also makes the case for the dessert dosa, wherein the pancake is wrapped around fresh fruit, applesauce, and whipped cream; the sour pancake makes a delicious contrast to the sweet filling. Sandor Katz notes how fenugreek seeds are often added to these batters, not only for flavor but also for their microbial content, which assists in the fermentation process. As well as for uttapam and dosas, the batter is used both for spongy little steamed cakes called idli, and larger cakes such as dhokla (page 86). All of which is to say, the batter is highly adaptable. Rather than syrup, Indian pancakes are served with a sweet chutney— a mixture of freshly grated coconut, cilantro leaves, and green chili is typical. To make the batter, rinse ⅔ cup white rice and ⅓ cup urad dal, then cover with cold water and let soak overnight. The next morning, drain, transfer to a powerful blender, and blitz, with a little water, to make a smooth batter. Then add ½ tsp salt and enough water to make a thick, pouring consistency—you can add more water later if you think the batter needs it. Set aside for about 8 hours at warm room temperature to allow the batter to ferment. Prepare some ingredients to sprinkle over the pancake as it cooks, if you like— say, tomato, grated coconut, onion, and cilantro leaves, chopped fresh chili, mustard and/or fenugreek seeds. Cook the pancakes on a heated, oiled (or nonstick) flat griddle pan or *tawa*, set over a medium heat, pouring about 3 tbsp batter from a ladle for each one and sprinkling over any toppings while the surface is still wet and sticky. Oil the perimeter of the pancake as its first side cooks, then flip and cook until it starts to color, peeping underneath to check. For dosas, the batter is diluted with water to light-cream consistency and cooked like a crêpe in a large, flat, lightly oiled skillet.

OAT

You could be forgiven for thinking a Staffordshire oatcake was a form of cracker. It is, in fact, a yeasted pancake made with oat meal, once popular among that English county's vast army of pottery workers— and still, now our mugs come from China, sold by the stackload from cafés in Stoke-on-Trent. They tend to be served on the side of a "full

English breakfast" (sausages, bacon, eggs, fried tomatoes and mushrooms, and sometimes baked beans)—or around one, in the manner of that dismal, clammy new staple: the wrap. They're a little more bready in flavor than other yeasted pancakes; hot, rolled with grated, melting Cheddar, they make a comforting alternative to a toasted sandwich. Simon Majumdar speculates that the Staffordshire oatcake will likely have disappeared within a generation, only to be found in some history books and "demonstrations at a Potteries folk museum." I propose we all do our bit by whipping up a batch now and then. Make as per blinis, except with 1 cup milk *and* 1 cup water, and no egg. As to the flour, use a 50/50 mix of Scottish oat meal and wheat flour. Most recipes call for fine oat meal, but medium is okay too. Choose a wide, light skillet or crêpe pan—you should be aiming for a thin pancake roughly 9 in across, more like a crêpe than a blini.

RYE

As Nordic as seasonal affective disorder. The grain is hardy and thirsty, with an appetizing sourness and an unappetizingly mousy color. The texture of rye pancakes tends to be drier and rougher than other varieties; the taste is bracingly savory, and lends itself exceptionally well to smoked fish. Follow our starting point, using 50/50 rye and white bread flours. For a consistency loose enough to pour, the batter will need 1½ cups milk for each 1 cup combined flours—possibly a little more. Eat on a crag, cursing the pointlessness of human existence.

SEMOLINA

Beghrir are Moroccan yeasted pancakes made with semolina and a mixture of milk and water. This makes for quite a thin batter—but that's as it should be, since the idea is to pour it onto the griddle or pan to a depth shallow enough that the *beghrir* can be cooked on one side only, but still cooked through. If the prospect of tossing crêpes gives you performance anxiety, *beghrir* are for you. Most griddle pancakes develop small holes on their surface as they cook; examine them closely, and you'll see that they're so smooth-edged and perfectly round that they look like the results of an immemorial process of erosion. In *beghrir* the holes appear so quickly, and in such profusion, that it's as if you were watching them develop in time-lapse. According to Moroccan legend, each *beghrir* should have a thousand holes, but only the sort of fool who had been out in the sun without his hat would bother to count them, in case his pancake gets cold. *Beghrir* must be eaten hot, with butter and honey, grabbed from a vendor and eaten in the street, one hand cupped to stop the butter-drips from staining your camel-leather *babouches*. *Beghrir*-eaters outside the Maghreb will note the compromise they strike between the crumpet and the crêpe—they combine the bouncy, honeycomb structure of the former, so receptive to melting butter, with the tender lightness of the latter. Some like to supplement the honey and butter with a little orange-flower water, or replace them with a shake of confectioners' sugar. *Amlou*, another authentic accompaniment, is harder to come by, but worth seeking out.

A mixture of almond butter, honey, and argan oil, it's a dreamily exotic alternative to peanut butter: what Scheherazade would have on toast, with her feet up watching *Ski Sunday* on television. To make *beghrir*, follow the method for blinis, but use ¾ cup semolina flour and ¼ cup all-purpose flour, and ¾ cup water mixed with ¼ cup milk. At step 4, whisk in 1 tsp baking powder and ¼ tsp salt with the egg. Remember, there's no need to flip. You can make *beghrir* whatever size you like—I make them with 4–5 tbsp batter each, i.e. roughly the size of a side plate. You can use ¾ cup fine semolina instead of the semolina flour, but the texture of the pancakes will be inferior, and the batter will need to be loosened with a few extra tablespoons of milk.

SOURDOUGH

If your sourdough "mother" (or starter) overfloweth, suffer not to throw her away. Decant her by the spoonful onto a low to medium hot griddle pan and make blinis. She is, after all, a batter of flour, yeast, and water. Add egg and/or oil in similar proportions to our starting point for a more traditional pancake texture, and a little baking powder for extra lift. The sourdough flavor will be strong, but the resulting blinis are excellent eaten warm with thin slices of mature Cheddar and chutney. Cut the starter with extra flour for a less insistent tang. In Alaska, sourdough pancakes are commonly eaten for breakfast, served with reindeer sausage or rosehip jelly. Elderberries are sometimes mixed into the dough. Alaskan miners were highly dependent on their starter cultures, which supplied them with precious bread and pancakes—and on cold nights they would take them to bed, clutching them to their chests to keep them warm and alive. These men slept with their mothers, in other words, which makes them lucky they were nicknamed "sourdoughs," and not something far nastier.

Griddle Pancakes

A.k.a. drop biscuits, or pikelets, as they're called in Australia. I tend to call them American pancakes because that's how I envisage them, served by a gum-chewing waitress in a remote diner with a fizzing neon sign. Also, because an American measuring cup makes them so quick to mix and commit to memory: 1 cup each of flour and milk, 1 egg, and 1 tsp each of sugar and baking powder. If you can count to one, you can make griddle pancakes. This batter can also be used for waffles.

For about 18 pancakes

INGREDIENTS
1 cup all-purpose flour [A] [B]
1 tsp baking powder [B] [C]
1 tsp sugar [D]
1–2 pinches of salt
1 egg [E]
1 cup milk [F]
1–2 tbsp melted butter or bland oil—optional

1   Put the flour and baking powder into a bowl, then whisk in the sugar and salt. Make a well in the center.
    It's best to cook the pancakes soon after the wet ingredients are added.

2   Beat in the egg as far as possible, then pour the milk in gradually, whisking and drawing the flour into the liquid to make a smooth batter. Add the melted butter or oil, if using.

3   Over a medium heat, wipe a heavy-based skillet or griddle pan with a little bland oil or butter, or a mixture of the two. Pour on a generous tablespoon of batter per pancake. The mix should spread, then abruptly stop. Thin it a little, if necessary. When the pancakes begin to look bubbly, flip them and cook until their other sides are golden brown.
    Keep your cooked pancakes warm in a foil-covered dish in a 240°F oven.

4   Unused batter can be kept in the fridge for a few days. Any uneaten pancakes can be frozen, then reheated in the toaster straight from the freezer.

LEEWAY

A   The pancakes can be made with a mix of flours. Cornmeal is always a winner. A very good gluten-free pancake can be made with fine cornmeal and buttermilk, using double the quantity of egg.

B   Self-rising flour can be used instead of all-purpose flour and baking powder.

C   Use ¼ tsp baking soda instead of the 1 tsp baking powder, but you'll need an activating, acidic ingredient too, such as buttermilk—or a homemade substitute, see page 79—in place of the milk.

D   Go heavier on the sugar, if you prefer, e.g. 2 tbsp instead of 1 tsp.

E   For a fluffier pancake, mix just the egg yolk into the milk at step 2, then beat the white to soft peaks and fold into the batter just before you cook it. The results are so light as to remove the need for baking powder.

F   Use only ½ cup milk, and you'll have a pretty standard recipe for what we Brits call Scotch pancakes.

BLOOD

Veriohukaiset is a Finnish pancake made with pig's blood. The blood is first whisked until light, then mixed with beer, rye and wheat flours, egg, and fried onion. The batter is seasoned, and sometimes a little dried marjoram is added. *Veriohukaiset* are often served with lingonberry jam. If you've ever eaten blood sausage with apples, or with mixed peel in *sanguinaccio*, the Italian blood-pudding dessert, you'll know how agreeably fruit flavors contrast with the iron-richness of cooked blood. Blood is very thick (thicker than water, anyway), so these pancakes call for a higher ratio of liquid to flour than typical griddle pancakes. No egg is needed, I suppose because blood supplies its own coagulants, but add one if you like. For 1 cup flour, use 1 cup strained blood and ½ cup beer instead of the milk. Sweeten with 1–2 tbsp light corn syrup. Note that fresh blood is highly perishable, and you need to take advice on storage from your supplier.

BUTTERMILK

Buttermilk sounds more luxurious than it is. The word always puts me in mind of Jersey milk, with its high butterfat content and golden tint. Buttermilk, in fact, is the thin, milky by-product of butter and cheese production. Flavorwise it's not dissimilar to yogurt. It owes its prevalence in the U.S. to Dutch settlers, who brought with them their national habit of drinking it by the glass with a meal. It owes its popularity, however, to the fluffiness it lends to pancake batter made with chemical leaveners. You can make ersatz buttermilk by adding a squeeze of lemon juice to milk and letting it stand at room temperature for a few minutes, or by mixing equal amounts of milk and plain yogurt. Use it in place of milk in our starting point and, if you have it, use ¼ tsp baking soda instead of the baking powder—you'll need to cook the batter fairly soon after it's mixed. Chef Tom Kerridge makes very enriched buttermilk pancakes to serve with gin-cured salmon, adding about 3 tbsp sugar and 4 tbsp melted butter to a batter made with 1 cup flour.

CHOCOLATE

Chef Marcus Samuelsson makes real chocolate pancakes using a fair amount of butter in the batter, cooking them in clarified butter, and sprinkling over a few grains of *fleur de sel* to bring out the flavor. By all means try it, but first ask yourself this: Doesn't the pleasure of eating a Nutella-spread crêpe, or drizzling a dark, hot chocolate sauce on a waffle, come from the contrast of intense chocolate and bland, mildly salty batter? The contrast is only increased if you enhance your chocolate sauce with Cognac and vanilla, as James Beard liked to. Mixing chocolate into your pancakes can compromise its intensity. I gave it three chances: I made one batch with a store-bought chocolate milk, one with cocoa powder, and one with good bar chocolate. Despite tasting richly chocolatey out of the bottle, the chocolate milk yielded a dun-brown pancake not immediately identifiable as chocolate-flavored, although it did have a pleasant maltiness that worked well with the addition of chocolate chips. Cocoa powder had the edge on the chocolate bar when it came to depth of flavor; the cocoa pancakes were like very thin, satisfyingly dark chocolate cakes. Furthermore, cocoa is unadulterated chocolate, which leaves you plenty of scope to add sugar, fat, and vanilla to taste. For cocoa pancakes, make a paste from ¼ cup unsweetened cocoa powder and a little of the milk, warmed, and whisk it into the batter at the end of step ², once the rest of the milk has been whisked in.

CHRISTMAS OR PLUM PUDDING

A flavor variation for Scotch pancake, from Chef Gary Rhodes. His hope that these festive pancakes might achieve Christmas-tradition status, on the basis that they're lighter than the steamed pudding, has, after about twenty years, proved forlorn. This may be down to his serving suggestion: a stack of the things, drenched in a vanilla and rum syrup, rum custard sauce, and extra-thick cream. Lighter than the steamed plum pudding? I'd say it was a close call. And, in any case, Christmas dinner has to be heavy. How else to justify the sofa and *Moonraker* for the seventh time? Also, Christmas pudding looks better set on fire. Light a stack of pancakes and it will look like an arson attack on a multistory parking lot. Come to think of it, forget Christmas. Treat these as fruitcake-flavored pancakes. I've tinkered with Rhodes's recipe to conform with our starting-point quantities: For each 1 cup flour, add ½ tsp apple pie spice, ¼ cup raisins, 2 tbsp chopped candied cherries, 1 tbsp chopped mixed candied peel, and 2 tbsp sugar.

CREAM

A crêpe is like a desert island—the best part is the coast. And this is where the waffle comes into its own. All those toasty, crispy ridges, delimiting cuboid rockpools of melted butter or ice cream: the best bits of crêpe geo-mapped on a grid. Using a blini batter will lend extra puff and an appetizing whiff of yeast, but a griddle pancake batter is a quicker and easier option when your family members are sitting, forks at the ready, impatient at the breakfast bar. The best waffle batter M.F.K. Fisher ever tried, she says, was made with equal volumes of heavy cream and flour. For 1 cup each cream and flour, use 2 eggs and 2 tbsp melted butter. No chemical leavener is needed, although you'll be in for a fair amount of beating. Separate the eggs. First beat the whites (Fisher doesn't say, but I'm guessing to soft peaks). Beat the yolks for 5 minutes, then gradually and alternately beat in the flour and cream. Beat in the butter, then fold in the egg whites. Before you reach for a sugary accompaniment, consider the great American soul-food combination of fried chicken and waffles. This was a dish served to hungry jazz bands and their danced-out audiences in the early hours of the morning, in the indeterminate space between late dinner and early breakfast, when the palate might fancy a bit of both.

MAC 'N' CHEESE

Data recently published by the U.S. Census Bureau indicate that population growth has slowed to its lowest level since the Depression. I attribute this to the number of things Americans find better than sex. For Garrison Keillor, it's sweet corn (see opposite). For restaurant owner Kenny Shopsin, it's pancakes. For me, it's the imminent worldwide ban on the phrase "better than sex." Still, check out Kenny's mac 'n' cheese pancakes. They're better than sex! They came about when a customer at Kenny's NYC diner couldn't choose between his two favorite dishes. Naturally, Kenny's response was to abolish the distinction. Now he can't make enough of them, even if they're pretty strange to behold. The ivory tubes of macaroni poke out of the pancakes, like unspeakable valve-ends in a particularly visceral cut of variety meat. Other flavors on his pancake menu include pear and pine nut, and granola and *charoset* (page 282). Once your griddle pancake is nice and bubbly, top with about 1 tbsp cooked macaroni, followed by 1 tbsp grated cheese.

POTATO

Not all blinis are made with yeast. Some rely on beaten egg white alone for the rise. In Eastern Europe, egg-leavened potato blinis might be made simply by adding grated potato to the batter. But there are other ways to make a potato pancake. In the U.S., chef Thomas Keller uses mash—specifically, mashed Yukon Gold potatoes, which have yellow flesh and a buttery flavor to match. Keller prizes them for their ability to absorb the cream he uses in the batter. For 1 lb potatoes, cooked and mashed, he adds 2 tbsp all-purpose flour, 2 whole eggs and 1 yolk, and 2–3 tbsp crème fraîche. Lindsey Bareham's recipe calls for 1 heaped cup potato flour in place of fresh mashed potato flesh, mixed with 1½ cups cold water, a pinch of salt, and no fewer than 6 eggs. Give the eggs a good beating, she says, before adding the potato flour, salt, and enough of the water to give the batter a heavy-cream consistency. Let rest for about half an hour before whisking again, and then cooking the potato pancakes on a greased griddle pan. Serve with syrup, lemon juice, sugar.

RICOTTA

Ricotta pancakes are for the sun-tousled, loose-linened, barefooted occupants of cream-interior penthouses or villas by the sea. Their pancakes are made on spotless, *very* expensive skillets and drizzled with maple syrup from a bottle whose neck remains perpetually crustless. Their children do not smear blueberry compote on their faces. These people browse through Donna Hay cookbooks without noticing how spotless and white everything looks. After an early breakfast they jog beside the ocean accompanied by a dog that neither sheds nor farts. Your life is not like theirs. But you can, at least, try the pancakes. The ricotta is usually added to the pancake batter over and above the standard ingredients—so follow the starting point, but whisk in about ½ cup ricotta with the milk. It's common to add the finely grated zest of a lemon, too.

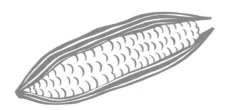

SWEET CORN

Sweet corn, writes Garrison Keillor, was the family weakness. "We were prepared to resist atheistic communism, immoral Hollywood, hard liquor, gambling and dancing, smoking, fornication, but if Satan had come around with sweet corn we at least would have listened." I, on the other hand, bought some sweet corn the other day that had the sole advantage of keeping me on the path of virtue, its flavor having taken on the bleakness of the 200,000-acre field it was grown in. When sweet corn is good, however—when its kernels are plump little pouches of savory sweetness—you can see Keillor's point. The high sugar content of both sweet corn and cornmeal makes for a batter that needs no additional sweetening. Venezuelan *cachapas* are a type of sweet corn pancake made by grinding fresh kernels with salt, egg, and butter. The variety of sweet corn used in Venezuela is so starchy—the kernels release a pearly liquid when they are pulverized—that no flour or milk is needed to create a luxuriously thick batter, stippled with nibs of whole kernels. Once cooked, the pancake is folded over a generous helping of *queso blanco*, the mild, white, Latin American cheese you might replace with some mozzarella or halloumi. The finished result is closer to an omelet than a pancake, rather like the Japanese sweet omelet known as *tamagoyaki* that sits atop egg nigiri. Peruvian *humitas* are made with a similar mixture, which is packed into dried corn husks and steamed. I once inadvertently left a batch of *cachapa* batter out overnight—either because I was tired, or because I wanted accidentally to stumble on something incredible, can't remember which—and discovered the next morning that it had fermented slightly. The resulting pancakes sacrificed a little of the *cachapas'* sweetness for a pleasing tang, reminiscent of Indian dhokla or idli. The recipe here works for the sort of sweet corn widely available in the U.K. and U.S., but without the authentic starchiness, you do have to rely on the egg and a small amount of flour to make the batter cohere. Blend 4 ears' worth of sweet corn kernels with 1 egg, ½ tsp salt, and 6 tbsp all-purpose flour. Let rest for 20 minutes. Before cooking, drip a few tablespoons of batter on the griddle pan to check for cohesiveness and add more flour (or more egg) if it doesn't hold together. Cook over a low to medium heat, and watch like an overprotective parent, as the sweet corn's natural sugars make these pancakes prone to burn; they should be about 7- to 8-in in diameter.

Tempura

Japanese tempura consists of assorted vegetables or seafood held in a fine, lacy batter. The batter is so light and crisp you might describe it as short, as in a pastry or cookie dough. Similarly, the aim of tempura batter is to minimize gluten formation, so very cold water is used and the ingredients are mixed only briefly. To the same end, this version calls for a combination of wheat and gluten-free flours. Taking gluten-suppression a step farther, some cooks mix up batches of batter as they fry, thus ensuring minimal gluten is formed in the time between preparation and cooking.

For 32 bite-size pieces, an appetizer for 4

INGREDIENTS
½ cup all-purpose flour [A]
½ cup cornstarch [A]
¼ tsp salt
1 egg yolk [B]
1 cup ice-cold water [C]
Vegetable oil for deep-frying [D]
Vegetables and/or seafood [E]

FOR THE DIPPING SAUCE
½ cup dashi
2 tbsp soy sauce
2 tbsp mirin
2 tsp sugar

1 Sift the flours with the salt, then set aside. Mix the dipping sauce ingredients together in a small saucepan and warm to dissolve the sugar, then let cool.
   This is all you can do in advance. The rest happens when you're ready to eat—although cooked tempura can be spread out on a baking sheet and kept warm in a 200°F oven with the door ajar for at least half an hour.

2 In a bowl or pitcher big enough to accommodate the flour, lightly beat the egg yolk, then mix in the iced water with a few strokes of a chopstick or fork.

3 Add the flour, all at once, and mix very roughly with another few strokes.
   If it looks lumpy, you're doing it right.

4 Heat the oil in a deep fryer or large pan to 350°F.

Never fill a pan more than a third full of oil. Test the temperature of the oil with a drop of batter. It should sink, then quickly resurface. If it sinks and stays sunk, the oil is too cold. If it floats instantaneously, and starts to color, the oil is too hot. If you are new to deep-frying, see page [17].

5 Dip *dry* tempura ingredients in the batter and carefully lower into the hot oil.

Don't try to cook too many pieces of tempura at once, as this will lower the temperature of the oil and result in sub-optimal crispness. Give the oil a chance to reheat between batches. Root vegetables will take about 4 minutes to cook, soft vegetables and seafood 2–3 minutes.

LEEWAY

[A] Use 1 cup all-purpose flour and no cornstarch. You can also replace the cornstarch with ½ cup rice flour.

[B] Some recipes call for a whole egg, others just the white. You can also do without egg completely; in which case, use 1 cup all-purpose flour (rather than a mix of all-purpose and cornstarch or rice flour), as the gluten in the wheat flour helps the batter cohere.

[C] Use chilled fizzy water in place of still—the carbonation will give the batter extra lightness. Achieve a similar effect with still water by mixing a few pinches of baking soda into the flour at step [1].

[D] In tempura houses, chefs use a blend of sesame, canola, and soybean oils for frying, lending a distinct fragrance to the food; sesame seeds can also be added to the batter.

[E] I aim for cork-size pieces of bell pepper, eggplant, sweet potato, carrot, cauliflower, broccoli, shiitake caps, lotus root, and white fish, or whole sugar snap peas and shrimp.

Fritters

A word to cover a multitude of sins. Our starting-point fritter batter is the sort that encases pieces of meat, fish, fruit, and vegetables—or even chocolate bars—but the term could cover the previous starting point, tempura, and the following, churros. Many recipes for batter include an egg, or just an egg white beaten to soft peaks and folded in just before the frying starts, in which case the quantity of water should be reduced by a couple of tablespoons. According to Leiths Cookery School, peanut, sunflower, and vegetable are the best oils for deep-frying.

For 4 fish fillets, or 4 apples, or 2 eggplants cut into rings

INGREDIENTS
1 cup all-purpose flour ᴬ
½ tsp salt
½ tsp baking powder ᴬ ᴮ
1 cup water ᶜ
Vegetable oil for deep-frying

1 Put the flour, salt, and baking powder into a bowl, then whisk together. Make a well in the center.

2 Just before you're ready to heat the oil, gradually pour the water into the well, and whisk, drawing the flour into the liquid to make a batter.
You're aiming for a consistency that coats the back of the spoon—you may not need all the water. If you prefer to make the batter in advance, omit the baking powder and stir it in when you're ready to fry.

3 Heat the oil in a deep fryer or large pan to 350°F.
Never fill a pan more than a third full of oil. To test the temperature of the oil, drop in a little batter: it should sink for a few seconds, then float to the surface. If the oil is not hot enough, the batter will stay sunk; too hot and the batter will float immediately and start to color. If you are new to deep-frying, see page ^{17}.

4 Make sure whatever you're battering is as dry as possible, then coat it in a little flour. Dip into the batter, allow any excess to drip off, then carefully put into the hot oil. Turn once, halfway through the cooking time: An apple ring or eggplant slice should take 3–5 minutes, a fish fillet 6–8 minutes. Remove with a slotted spoon and drain on paper towels.

LEEWAY

A Self-rising flour can be used, in which case the baking powder can be reduced to ¼ tsp or done without altogether.

B If you don't have baking powder, add ¼ tsp baking soda instead. Alternatively, use fizzy water or another fizzy liquid like beer in place of the water.

C Some cooks prefer to use milk. Note that it will make the batter less crisp.

BEER

Specifying the beer in a batter has become the prevailing means in British pubs to distinguish fish and chips from, well, fish and chips. Anyone who claims they can tell their Stella from their Peroni once it's been mixed with flour and fried in boiling oil needs to ask the barman how much lager they've actually drunk. For fruit fritters, Fiona Beckett suggests "bog-standard lager." Nathan Myhrvold and W. Wayt Gibbs, writing in *Scientific American*, say that the chief advantage of beer over other liquids is that some of its carbon dioxide is preserved during the making of the batter. This means that when your fritter or piece of fish is immersed in hot oil, the bubbles froth, expanding the batter and giving it a light texture. Beer also contains foaming agents, to create a head, which give its bubbles extra staying power. Follow our starting point, substituting beer for the water.

BUCKWHEAT & GRAPPA

There's a batter-based snack from the Italian Alps known as *sciatt*, a Valtellinese dialect word for toad. The name is a frank admission: They're ugly as hell, nuggets of deep-fried thick batter with cubes of cheese in the middle. Use a ratio of 3:1 all-purpose to buckwheat flour and start with ¾ cup fizzy water with a dash of grappa in it, then thin further if necessary. Serve on a lily pad of green leaves.

CHICKPEA

Vegan cheese is without doubt the most repulsive thing I have ever put in my mouth—and I say that having been taken to the hospital, aged three, after taking a bite out of a frog I had caught in the cup of my Thermos. Vegan cheese tastes like wet dogs smell. For complex reasons, I was at a vegan food festival when I first encountered it, and then urgently needed something to mask the taste. Thankfully, on the outskirts of the festival, I found a quiet stand selling Indian food, made with real, identifiable ingredients. I bought a paper bag of warm *batata vada*—palm-sized, frittered balls of mashed potato mixed with green chili, herbs, and spices that not only banished the taste of dog from my palate, but actually seemed to cleanse it, perhaps because of the reputed mouth-freshening qualities of fenugreek. Like pakoras and onion bhajis, *batata vada* balls are cooked in a spiced chickpea batter, which lends them a deliciously savory sulfurousness. Make as per the starting point, but using 1 cup chickpea flour, and go gently with the water—you may need as little as ½ cup. At step [1], add to the flour ½ tsp ground fenugreek and ¼ tsp salt, plus ½ tsp each of ground coriander and cumin if you fancy something more elaborately spicy. For the interior, heat 2 tbsp bland oil and fry 1 tbsp finely chopped fresh ginger with 1–2 finely chopped green chilies, 2 tsp mustard seeds, 1 tsp cumin seeds, and, if you have it, ¼ tsp asafetida. Mix into 2½ cups salted mashed potato with 1 tbsp chopped cilantro and ¼ tsp ground turmeric. Form the mixture into balls, dip into the batter, and deep-fry.

COLA

Defiantly unhealthy. It was a cola batter that helped Abel Gonzales Jr. win one of his many fried-food awards at the Texas State Fair. His dish consisted of fried strands of cola batter, topped with a cola syrup, whipped cream, cinnamon sugar, and a cherry for good luck. For the batter, replace the water and baking powder with cola. Make it for Morgan Spurlock next time he drops in for dinner.

CORNMEAL

Cornmeal lends a satisfying sweet-savoriness to breads and batters—and corndogs. I was living in Minneapolis when the movie *Se7en* came out. It left me so traumatized that my companion took me straight to the bar for a stiff drink and a stabilizing snack. Corndogs are frankfurters dipped in a thick, sugared cornmeal batter, deep-fried, and impaled on a popsicle stick: hand-held depravity. I've seen the movie since and wasn't so disturbed second time around, but I still have nightmares about the corndogs. More appetizing to try shrimp fried in cornmeal batter, or catfish, or green chilies stuffed with cheese. This is a thick, soft batter, so milk is used instead of the water in our starting point. Some might even add an egg, which would make it the same as the starting point for griddle pancakes. Mix ½ cup cornmeal with ½ cup all-purpose flour, 1 tsp baking powder, 1 tsp sugar, 1 cup milk, and ½ tsp salt. If you're curious about corndogs, dab some frankfurters dry, impale them on sticks, then dip them in the batter (poured into a tall receptacle, so you can immerse the long sausages). Deep-fry a few at a time, with sticks pointing up, in oil heated to 350°F for 3–4 minutes.

CURRY

Tom Norrington-Davies recommends adding a "smidgeon" of curry powder to the batter for fish and chips. If you live in London, as I do, the curry-chip combination is an odd one, but in the north of England curry sauce and chips is as unremarkable as a cup of tea with your evening meal. In Wales, it's almost as common to put curry sauce on your chips as it is salt and vinegar. I used a bit more than a smidgeon, and it was excellent: 1–2 tsp supermarket curry powder added to the flour will do nicely.

EGGNOG

Medieval batters were made with wine or ale, cream, and far greater quantities of egg than is customary today. They were a little like a stabilized custard, similar to the cream and sherry crêpe batter on page [125]. Many were made with ale barm, the froth that collects on the surface of beer as it ferments. The practice was common until the eighteenth century, when barm was replaced with egg whites to give a greater lightness of texture. Still, if you happen to live near a brewery, flutter your eyelashes at the yeasty chap at reception. If he gives you some barm in return, try it in batter, and use the rest to make some barm bread, or barm cakes, the Lancashire buns traditionally stuffed with fries or blood sausage. The word "barm," incidentally, gives us "barmy," as in "frothy of temperament"—an etymological tidbit you can feed the guy at the brewery as his eyes glaze over. For an eggnog batter, whisk 1 tbsp sherry and 1 egg into ⅔ cup water before adding it to the flour, then grate in some nutmeg at the end of step [2].

SAFFRON

Elizabeth David notes that yeasted pancake mixture can be diluted to make a good fritter batter, passing on, while she's at it, a fifteenth-century recipe for an apple-fritter batter made with beer yeast, wheat flour, saffron, and salt. Jane Grigson cites a saffron batter for apple fritters that includes black pepper, lamenting the fact that modern batter recipes omit such spices, which have a "gingerlike" if less assertive quality. Oyster and salt-cod fritters are often made with saffron batter. Janet Mendel makes the batter for salt-cod fritters using the water the fish was simmered in, mixing it with saffron, parsley, garlic, and an egg yolk, then stirring in flour and baking powder. She stirs through the cooked, flaked salt cod, then beats the egg white until stiff and folds that in. The finished fritters are served with molasses, and are rather reminiscent of Vietnamese caramelized fish dishes. A similar batter, Mendel explains, is used for the Spanish equivalent of tempura, *rebozados*. The great Renaissance gastronome Bartolomeo Platina (1421–1481) gives a recipe for sage leaves fried in a sweetened saffron and cinnamon batter. Using a pestle and mortar, grind a couple of pinches of saffron strands to a powder and add to the flour at step [1]. This will give a pronounced saffron flavor, and a batter the color of a maple leaf in autumn.

SHELLFISH

Traditionally the batter for shellfish fritters was made with milk, or a combination of milk and the liquor from inside oyster or clam shells, with the optional supplements of anchovy essence or sauce, cream, and/or cayenne. Recently chefs have found ways to make more of the briny flavor of oyster juice. Heston Blumenthal mixes it with passion-fruit juice to make an aspic, then sets a raw oyster in it. Nathan Outlaw discovered, by chance, that the juice was particularly good for curing raw mackerel, which gave him the idea of mixing it with cucumber juice. A recipe for oyster fritters in *The White House Cookbook* (1887) calls for 1 cup each of oyster liquor and milk, some salt, 4 eggs, and enough flour to "make a batter like griddle cakes." The oysters are then dipped in the batter and fried in a mixture of butter and lard.

Fritters → Other Directions

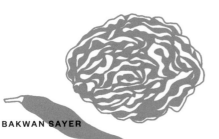

BAKWAN SAYER

Indonesian fritters made with strips of cabbage, carrot, and scallion, served with green chilies.

FRUTTO MISTO

Mixed fruit fritters—apple, banana, pineapple, orange, mango, and not-quite-ripe apricots or plums—served with a sauce.

FALAFEL IN PITA

BREAD PAKORA

Popular Indian snack of plain bread or sandwiches cooked in besan batter.

SWEET CORN, PEA & BLACK BEAN FRITTERS

… made with a thick, binding batter—use ¼–½ the amount of liquid in the starting point.

CALAMARI STUFFED IN A BUN

… with lots of herbs and tartar sauce (page 530).

ELDERFLOWER

Also consider apple blossom, acacia blossom, and locust flowers.

Churros

Think of them as bottom-of-the-range doughnuts, or simply batter fritters, but plain old churros have held their own where lighter, prettier, or trendier treats have been forgotten. Impressive, given how high-maintenance they are. They must be eaten fresh from the fryer. And you'll need a pastry bag, or plastic extruding machine, to pipe the batter through the star-shaped tip that gives churros their characteristic ridged surface—which has a sugar-catching ability unmatched by the cylinder or ball. Serve your churros with a dipping cup of rich hot cocoa, a milky coffee, or, inauthentically, a milky chai.

For 12 sticks about 5 in long

INGREDIENTS
1 cup all-purpose flour [A]
¼ tsp salt
1 cup boiling water [B] [C]
Sunflower or vegetable oil for deep-frying
Confectioners' or granulated sugar for sprinkling [D]

1 Put the flour into a bowl, then stir in the salt. Make a well in the center.

2 Add the boiling water to the flour and mix with a wooden spoon until smooth. The dough will be pretty stiff. Let it rest for about 10 minutes.

3 Heat the oil in a deep fryer or large pan to 375°F.
   Never fill a pan more than a third full of oil. To test the temperature of the oil, drop in a teaspoonful of batter: It should turn golden in about 30 seconds. If you are new to deep-frying, see page [17].

4 Pipe the mixture directly into the hot oil through a star-shaped nozzle, using scissors to snip off a length every 5 in or so. Cook, in small batches, for 2–4 minutes, before lifting out and draining on paper towels.

5 Serve hot, sprinkled with confectioners' or granulated sugar.

LEEWAY

A For a lighter texture, use self-rising flour, or add 1 tsp baking powder to the all-purpose flour. For sweeter churros, add a few tablespoons of sugar to the flour.

B For softer churros, try a combination of milk and water.

C Some cooks add a little vanilla extract to the water.

D Some mix the sugar with ground cinnamon—a ratio of 4:1 is good.

Roux

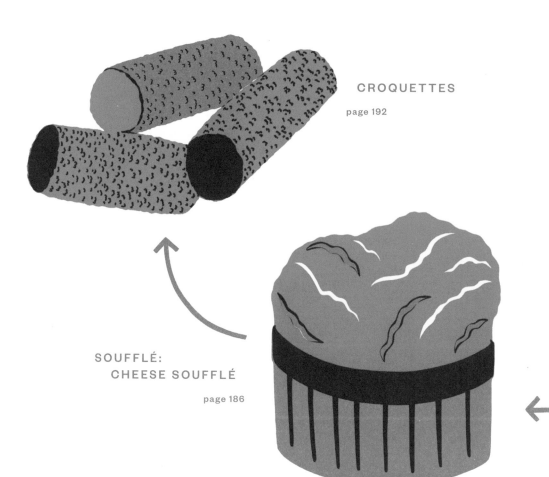

GUMBO

page 162

CROQUETTES

page 192

SOUFFLÉ:
CHEESE SOUFFLÉ

page 186

ESPAGNOLE

page 168

VELOUTÉ

page 174

BÉCHAMEL &
WHITE SAUCE

page 180

The legendary Marie-Antoine Carême once said that roux—the simple, cooked mixture of flour and fat—was as indispensable to chefs as ink is to writers. These days, excepting a handful of romantic contrarians, chef-defenders of the roux are about as common as writers who choose the pen over the PowerBook.

It was in 1973 that Henri Gault and Christian Millau, of the eponymous French restaurant guide, published their manifesto for a radical *nouvelle cuisine*. Their intention was to liberate chefs from the suffocating rules of *la grande cuisine*—the tradition of elaborate French cooking established and codified by Auguste Escoffier, and Carême before him. They laid out ten rules for a freer, more imaginative way of cooking, encouraging the *nouvelle cuisinier* to serve rarer meat and fish, shorten his menus, experiment with unusual flavor combinations, keep an eye on the healthiness of his dishes, use fresher ingredients, and generally take a more open-minded approach to his craft. It was the sort of paradox in which francophone culture exults: a set of rules for being less rule-bound. Nonetheless, the gist was clear: freedom from a systematized approach to cooking, with the strict adherence to recipes that it entailed.

Of all the aristocratic pillars of the *ancien régime*, pompous old roux was the first to be dragged to the guillotine. All those heavy, rich espagnoles and béchamels: how mediocre, thought Gault and Millau—how pretentious, how *inane* they were. Off with their heads, along with Madeira, red wine, flour, cheese, veal stock, and meat glaze—although cream, butter, pure *jus*, and truffles were (somewhat arbitrarily) spared the chop.

In large part, the precepts of *la grande cuisine* grew out of the emergence, in the late nineteenth century, of the large luxury hotels where so many of the finest restaurants were located. Here, in his vast kitchen, the chef was kept at a remove from buying ingredients, and was expected to put whatever produce was acquired for him at the service of classic, documented recipes. A century on, many early practitioners of *nouvelle cuisine* were chef-proprietors of their own modest establishments, often outside Paris. They would shop daily in local markets, consciously fondling, weighing, *feeling* the ingredients. The old guard sniffed at a practice they saw as scarcely more sophisticated than the efforts of housewives, but the writing was on the kitchen whiteboard. Today, even if the single-pea-on-a-plate excesses of *nouvelle cuisine* seem as outdated as the blowsy over-elaboration it displaced, many of the principles laid out in Gault and Millau's manifesto, like the adherence to local, seasonal produce, are as orthodox to contemporary cooking as Nike-swooshes of balsamic reduction and visible kitchen staff.

Poor old roux has never recovered. Consult your *Larousse* and you can begin to see why. Classic sauce cookery is founded on five basic recipes—the "mother" sauces, three of which were roux-based:

espagnole, velouté, and béchamel (the other two were hollandaise and sauce tomate, in case you were wondering). Each "mother" went on to have as many offspring as a devout nineteenth-century fishwife practicing the rhythm method. In older editions of *Larousse* these variations were laid out in a perversely user-unfriendly way. If you've never seen a copy, imagine trying to navigate your way through a medieval French hill town, without a map, along streets named after members of an interbred local aristocracy while simultaneously trying to commit to memory the groceries in a prewar Fortnum & Mason catalogue: lobster roe, truffle shavings, smoked oysters, blanched brain, chopped capers, gilded aspic. Young chefs were expected not only to learn all the variations, but which dishes they were meant to accompany. It's easy to see why many kitchens started to cut corners, while a creative new wave sought a fresher, less fussy alternative.

Four years after the publication of the *nouvelle* manifesto, Julia Child wrote an essay for *New York* magazine covering her recent travels in France and her frank assessment of *nouvelle cuisine*. Child sides neither with the traditionalists nor the *enfants terribles*, suggesting instead that good cooking might do well to borrow from both camps, and is itself more important than strict adherence to either orthodoxy. For her, the banishment of roux was an act of needless vandalism, especially in light of the *nouvelle* sauces "like liquefied bouillon cubes" that she encountered—one memorably bad example completely drowning her *magret de canard*. She held out for the revival of the traditional demi-glace, not least because its thickening with flour stopped it from becoming oppressively dark brown in flavor.

More than forty years after Child's plea, the roux is still waiting for its comeback. Especially in cheffy circles, it remains the preparation *non grata*, notable by its omission from all but a few contemporary chefs' cookbooks. Simon Hopkinson is a fan. Why spurn a delicious, well-made béchamel, he asks, for a "modish over-reduced, flour-free" sauce. Clifford A. Wright is likewise baffled by the snobbish attitude of modern restaurants to roux-based sauces and soups, recommending that home cooks redress the balance as we "seek good food, not fashion." After all, a roux, according to Michael Ruhlman, is "potentially the most elegant and refined way of thickening a sauce."

I refer so liberally to the roux camp for a simple reason: You're nuts if you don't add it to your repertoire. It's so easy to master, yet so transformative of the humblest dish. Even if you don't find yourself making a velouté or a béchamel very often, to become a proficient roux-maker is to possess the secret of good gravy, which is basically a roux made from the wonderfully sticky semi-burnt bits stuck to your roasting pan. Once you've taken out a chicken, for instance, and put it aside to rest, remove all but 2–3 tbsp of the fat, stir in the same amount of flour, and cook for a few minutes before gradually adding about 2½ cups stock, water, and/or wine. Whisk, or stir vigorously, taking care to see off any lumps, as you try to scrape up as much as possible of the sticky bits and incorporate them into the gravy. Once that's done, let it simmer while the meat continues to rest. The only problem with this method of gravy preparation is the danger of not having enough. Good gravy is always hugely appreciated—I have certainly never heard it described as mediocre, pretentious, or inane, but that might be the benefit of it being called gravy, as opposed to Sauce Duc Marquisat de la Mothe-Houdancourt.

The demise of roux might also be attributed to the internationalization of home cooking. Now that the most unambitious domestic cook's repertoire often extends to self-saucing dishes like tagines and curries, tomato-based pastas, and soy-based Asian dishes, roux-based sauces can struggle to find a place. But an espagnole, made with beef stock and a few aromatics, or a velouté, its paler equivalent made with veal, chicken, or fish stock, can bring together a plate of plainly cooked meat (or fish) and vegetables as little else can—say over sausages and mash, or as a sauce for the sort of lean ingredient that doesn't yield much juice. There are few better ways of elevating your cooking than learning to make your own sauces from homemade stock.

Growing up in the 1970s, I ate a lot of roux-based meals. The school cooks of Hampshire County Council did not hold with *fumet* or *jus*. They served chicken supreme, or cod or eggs Mornay—grand cuisine for little people—which we ate with a knife and fork off china plates, as opposed to the indented prison-style plastic trays by which today's schoolchildren are taught to associate eating food with punishment. Admittedly the vegetables of my youth could have done with being a shade more *nouvelle*, but the sauce was so nice it almost made up for them. There were curries, too, made with a roux flavored with curry powder—essentially a mildly spicy variant on gravy. I consumed that gloopy school curry under duress, and years later was speechless with wonder at my first proper curry-house korma, sweet and dreamily aromatic with cashews, cilantro, and saffron. But how I love the smell of old-fashioned school curry now. When I caught a whiff of it the other day, on the concourse of Waterloo Station, I wheeled on one heel, half-expecting to see Mrs. Pearce, the school cook, wielding a dripping ladle. The smell, to my obscure disappointment, was coming from the Japanese food concession.

The Japanese call school curry "navy curry," having picked up the partiality from British sailors and adapted it to local tastes, in a culinary take on the Telephone game. It's a long way from rogan josh. Tadashi Ono and Harris Salat give a recipe for pork shoulder curry that calls for cheese, honey, ketchup, and coffee, and is served with salad, a boiled egg, and a glass of milk. Many Japanese eat curry at least once a week, and while it's often served with rice, south-Asian style, *karē* flavor has spread like knotweed to national favorites like potato croquettes and ramen. Several brands of instant curry roux are available in bar form, like slabs of chunky chocolate. The "Vermont" version contains apple, honey, Gouda, and Cheddar: a British bastardization of Indian food reimagined by the Japanese with an American-Dutch flavor profile. Serve it with blini and toast the authenticity police with a glass of ouzo. What the hell.

G Given its roots in French culture, it's less surprising that Louisianan
U cuisine should have adopted the roux, albeit riffing on it as they
M might on a jazz standard to produce something peculiarly their own.
B Dark roux is to a classic French roux as *True Detective* is to *Inspector*
O *Maigret*—swampy, occult, and deliciously degenerate. It plays a
crucial role in Cajun and Creole dishes, flavoring and thickening gumbos and sauce piquante, which is a bit like gumbo plus tomatoes. Dark roux usually exchanges butter for oil, or a hard fat like lard or margarine, because it needs to cook without burning for at least an hour, if not two, until it's somewhere between the color of an old penny and midnight on the bayou. It is, for this reason, sometimes known as "chocolate roux." In flavor terms, while you could argue that it shares some of chocolate's deep, empyreumatic qualities, it's more reminiscent of well-fried chicken, and imparts a lugubrious, heavy-lidded drawl of silty savoriness to soups and stews.

A couple of blocks from the northern terminus of the Canal Street trolley in New Orleans, there's a famous restaurant called Liuzza's by the Track, whose clapboard exterior and creaky sign turned me starry-(and stripey-) eyed with Americophilia the first time I visited. Billy Gruber, the proprietor, tells the story of one of his customers, who took a sip of the house gumbo and declared that "Billy must have stepped in it." In time, Gruber realized that this was high praise. Make your own dark roux, and by the time it's ready your hair will smell as if you've been up all night worshipping some unspeakable deity in the form of a crayfish. For the sake of convenience, and your hair, you might consider making a large quantity and keeping batches in the fridge or freezer. While others on the continuum don't take anything like as long to pull together, any roux can be made ahead and stored in the fridge or freezer, ready to deploy whenever you have a soup or stew that needs thickening.

The price paid for darkening the roux for so long is that it loses some of its thickening power. There's no consensus about quite how much it loses, so it's probably better to assume that a dark roux made with 1 cup oil and 1 cup flour will thicken about 2 quarts liquid to a gumbo-like consistency, i.e. closer to a hearty soup than a stew. If that's not thick enough for your purposes, make up a small amount of golden roux (page 174) and add it to the mix. Two other thickening options for gumbo involve the addition of filé or okra. Note that the frogspawn-like mucilaginousness of filé is harder to control than that of okra. Heat your stew too fast once the filé is added and it'll only be good for hanging wallpaper. That aside, filé has the most wonderful, exotic flavor. The powdered leaf of the sassafras tree, a member of the laurel family, it shares a eucalyptus note with its relation, the bay leaf, and has a similar leaden-green color when dried. Its distinct sour-fruitiness comes as a refreshing contrast to the richness of dark roux and the sweetness of the "holy trinity" of onion, green bell pepper, and celery that forms the basis of so much Louisianan cooking. Filé may also remind you of tea with lemon or of tamarind. Don't worry, however, if neither filé nor okra are to your taste; the roux will suffice.

With this in mind, let us turn our attention to the roux continuum. We start with the dark roux used for gumbo, which is cooked long and slow and, as a consequence, loses some of its thickening power. We then move through brown, then golden, to the pale roux used for béchamel, and further still to the thickest versions of pale roux, for soufflés and croquettes. There are almost as many recommended roux-to-liquid ratios as there are cookbooks that contain them. The following are rules of thumb for the quantity of roux needed, in the preparations along the continuum, to thicken 4 cups of liquid. (In the starting points, I give precise quantities, which is more a matter of preference than diktat.)

- ½ cup each of oil (or lard) and flour to stock for gumbo roux
- 4–6 tbsp each of fat and flour to stock for espagnole or velouté
- 7–8 tbsp each of butter and flour to milk for béchamel
- ½–¾ cup each of butter and flour to milk for a soufflé base
- ¾ cup butter and 1 cup flour to milk or stock for croquettes

E In color, brown roux is essentially indistinguishable from the lighter
S shades of dark roux, but as it's generally made in smaller quantities
P than its Cajun cousin, it doesn't involve quite so much standing
A around and stirring. Its classic application is in espagnole sauce.
G Espagnole is made with a brown roux mixed with a mirepoix of
N finely diced onion, carrot, and celery, some bacon, and a good dark
O stock, usually beef. Tomatoes and other aromatic ingredients might
L be added to bump up the flavor. Then it's simmered, skimmed,
E and strained to a thick, shiny consistency ready to use or flavor
further, say with bitter orange to serve with duck, or with Madeira and mushrooms for steak.

According to Anne Willan, espagnoles were "once the glory of the French kitchen," where these days chefs prefer to make their sauces by thickening beef or brown veal stock with slurries of cornstarch or potato starch, or by reducing a good bone stock. All very well if you have gallons of beef stock sloshing about, or easy access to a prehistoric cave full of bones. Failing this, I recommend making a fairly basic beef stew, using a mix of beef stew meat and something on the bone, like oxtail or short ribs. Add chunks of carrot, onion, and celery, a squeeze of tomato paste, some red wine, a bouquet garni, and a bit more liquid than you might normally use, then slow-cook it—see page [238] for more guidance. With the beef, vegetables, and just a little of the liquid, make delicious pot pies topped with rough puff pastry (page 574). Strain, cool, and de-fat the balance of the liquid and you'll have an excellent beef "stock" that can form the basis of an espagnole.

Traditional French cooking tends to match its roux to the ingredients used to turn them into sauces—dark roux with dark stock, light with light, white with milk—but there's no good reason not to mix things up a little. In the American South, a dark roux is made by cooking flour in pan drippings from fried chicken, steak, or bacon. Milk is then added and the mixture stirred to create "country" or "pan" gravy. Add Cheddar to make a sauce for macaroni and cheese embellished with the toasty flavor of dark roux—a kind of mac 'n' rarebit.

V E L O U T É That's not to pooh-pooh the classic approach. A golden roux with a light stock is the basis for a velouté sauce—think of it as espagnole's blonde sister—or a main course like *blanquette de veau*, which regularly tops the polls for France's favorite dish. Veal is cooked in a mixture of golden roux, light stock, cream, small white onions, and button mushrooms. Elizabeth David considered the dish insipid, but only in comparison to stews that combined veal and tomatoes, which she reckoned have a special affinity for each other. It's worth noting that David was writing at a time when *blanquettes* were more common than tomato-based dishes, whereas today the situation is very much the reverse, and the restraint of a *blanquette* can be a pleasurably plain departure from such strong flavors. My husband makes a *blanquette de dinde* a few days after Christmas, with leftover turkey and stock made from the carcass. After a week of roast potatoes, buttered Brussels sprouts with chestnuts, clods of cold stuffing, smoked salmon pâté, ham sandwiches, mince pies, Pedro Ximénez sherry, and chocolate geranium creams, its calm creaminess is like switching off the TV.

B É C H A M E L Next stop on the roux continuum is béchamel, the thick, flavored white sauce under which ingredients unwind when they're in the mood for a box set. Conceived in the seventeenth century, by the eighteenth béchamel was all the rage among the French upper classes. Today it is most at home in comfort food like mac 'n' cheese, fish pie, or chicken pot pie. It puts the *aah* in lasagne and moussaka. Enriched with cheese, to make Mornay sauce, it's poured over cauliflower or mixed with chopped parsley to accompany ham. While Nigella Lawson says that béarnaise is her favorite sauce, she admits that béchamel is the most essential.

S O U F F L É A soufflé is a thick white sauce that's had a big intake of breath. If I'm planning one, I generally make a starting-point quantity of thick white sauce as a base, reserving enough for the soufflé and keeping the rest in the fridge to dilute with wine or stock for whatever sauce I fancy later in the week. For the soufflé, I'll flavor the roux base with a vegetable purée, or some cheese, then add the egg yolks before beating the whites and folding them in. The indispensable quality of the soufflé-maker, says James Beard, is nonchalance. Soufflés are like horses: Never let them sense that you're nervous. By all accounts, Beard himself was the Robert Mitchum of soufflé-making nonchalance. All the sacred rules, he believed, such as chilling the uncooked soufflé in the fridge, and not opening the oven door during cooking, could safely be flouted—as long as a) you kept your cool, in case any anxious vibes be communicated to the soufflé, and b) you beat your egg whites to soft peaks, the kind that *start* to fold over when you take out the beaters, but never quite get there.

A successful soufflé is also, I suspect, a fair bit to do with knowing your oven and cookware. To achieve a perfectly cooked center is a matter of trial and error, so it's wise to try to isolate one variable—whether that be the dish used, the temperature of the oven, or the temperature of the uncooked mixture when it went into the oven—and keep the other conditions constant until you hit the jackpot. It's impossible to tell by eye if the center of a soufflé is cooked through or still wet; it's perfectly safe to open the oven door and, with suitably Beardean nonchalance, dip in a strand of dried spaghetti to see if it comes out clean. Or, if you're making individual ramekin-sized soufflés, make a few extra, taking them out at intervals and noting which cooking time works best. A few standardized trials will be of more use to you than any guidelines in a recipe book, plus you'll get an idea of how long the soufflé stays *soufflé*. The roux-based variety will stand tall longer than any made with pastry cream, ganache, or a simple purée, but not so long that you can afford to dally once it's out of the oven. There are few gastronomic sights more melancholy than a soufflé collapsing like a risqué joke in a roomful of puritans.

C
R
O
Q
U
E
T
T
E
S
Croquettes get a bad press in the U.K., where they're associated with school lunch, but in Spain they come studded with *jamón* or fibrous with *bacalao*, and are heaven with a dipping pot of allioli and a cold *caña* of draft beer. Take a bite of *croqueta* and the bread-crumbed crust gives way to thick, creamy roux. In Belgium, *garnaalkroketten* are a national delicacy, made with tiny brown shrimp suspended in a hot, soupy center, like a hand-held chowder. In the Netherlands, dedicated outlets like Van Dobben sell *kroketten* and their smaller, rounder cousins *bitterballen* in classic flavors like chicken, beef, and veal, and, more exotically, satay and goulash. *Bitterballen*, incidentally, are so called not because they're bitter themselves but because they were traditionally served with a shot of *jenever*, a gin-like form of aromatic bitters.

I once had a lunchtime meeting in Amsterdam after staying up too late the night before, drinking too much and too variously, and spending a sleepless, dehydrated night on the houseboat we had rented. Lunch was being served in the office. We sat in plumply upholstered, and, crucially, reclinable executive chairs around a conference table, at the center of which was a cardboard box full of hot *kroketten* so golden and crispy-looking you could almost hear them nestling against each other. The idea was to pick up a roll—the very sweet, very white sort the Dutch really dig—smear it with yellow mustard, cram in a croquette, and sink your teeth into it. Soft, crunch, soft. Bliss.

A hangover loves carbs, all the more so if they yield a rich, beefy roux when you bite into them. The life-saving qualities of no-frills fast food. That said, it's no longer beyond possibility for croquettes to crop up on swankier menus, albeit with fancier fillings. The Catalan chef Sergi Arola makes his croquettes with Gorgonzola, while the Scot Martin Wishart uses smoked haddock; Ernesto Iaccarino, chef at Don Alfonso 1890, near Naples in Italy, shapes his croquettes into cubes, in a manner reminiscent of sliced *crema fritta*, or *panelle*, the irresistible Sicilian chickpea-flour fritters. Iaccarino makes a pair of olive oil roux—one using wheat flour, the other with tapioca flour—and combines them with horseradish-infused milk. Once set, the mixture is cut into cubes and coated with turmeric-spiked bread crumbs, then fried and served with jasmine-scented yogurt. One example serves to show all the different methods you can use to flavor a croquette.

And so chefs creep back roux-ward, not via the venerable sauces of *la grande cuisine*, but with a new spirit of thrift, of spinning out leftovers in a delicious and accessible way, with plenty of scope for creative interpretation. That is, the kind of *nouvelle cuisine ancienne* that might take hold if someone came up with a ten-point manifesto for it.

Gumbo

The earliest published recipes for gumbo didn't include a roux; now most do. The finished dish is usually served as a main-course stew, with long-grain rice and a garnish of chopped parsley and thin green slices of scallion. Other than that, what goes into the gumbo and its seasoning varies wildly. Keith Floyd makes the inevitable jazz analogy: Know the tune, and you can improvise the rest, "with plenty of heart and soul."

For a stew for 6, or soup for 8 [A]

INGREDIENTS
1 cup vegetable oil [B] [C]
1 cup all-purpose flour [C]
Fat or oil for frying
2¼ lb chicken pieces [D]
1 lb spicy smoked sausage, sliced [D]
1 large onion, diced
1 green bell pepper, diced
2–3 celery stalks, diced
3–4 garlic cloves, minced
3 bay leaves [E]
¼ tsp cayenne [E]
1½ tsp salt
2 quarts warm chicken stock [F]
5–6 tbsp chopped parsley
4–8 scallions, green parts only, finely sliced
Long-grain rice, for serving

1 First make your roux. Heat the oil in a cast-iron skillet or heavy-based saucepan over a medium heat. Slowly stir in the flour. Cook for 30–45 minutes over a low heat, stirring intermittently, until the roux is dark brown.
   Making a dark roux in the oven is an easier option: Stir the flour into the hot fat in an ovenproof pan on the stovetop, then transfer to a 350°F oven and cook for 1½–2 hours, stirring every 15 minutes.

2 When you're ready to make the gumbo, heat some fat or oil in a skillet and brown the meat one type at a time, then transfer to a stockpot (or large saucepan). Add the onion, green bell pepper, celery, and garlic to the skillet and cook until softened, then transfer them to the stockpot, too.

3 Put the stockpot on a medium heat and add the roux, bay leaves, cayenne, and salt, then stir in the warm stock. [G]

4 Bring to a boil, then simmer slowly, uncovered, for as long as your ingredients need to cook through—in the case of chicken pieces and sausage, about 1 hour.

You may need to top up the cooking liquid if it falls below the level of the ingredients.

5 Skim off any fat, then stir in the parsley and scallion. ᴳ ᴴ

6 Ladle the gumbo into deep soup plates, preferably with a mound of cooked rice in the center.

A crusty baguette, a judicious sprinkling of Tabasco, and a cold beer would be welcome, too.

LEEWAY

A Extend your gumbo by using more stock, roux, and rice.

B Use lard or rendered bacon fat instead of oil.

C It's worth making a double batch of roux—the excess will keep for months in the fridge and up to a year in the freezer.

D Many ingredients make it into gumbo—fish, shellfish, game, or poultry—although red meat is less common. In the case of seafood, the roux, aromatics, and stock (preferably homemade) are simmered for an hour or so, for the flavors to develop and combine, before the fish or shellfish is added for the brief period it needs to cook through. See Flavors & Variations for examples.

E Typical additional seasonings include dried or fresh thyme, dried oregano, Tabasco, Worcestershire sauce, paprika, and white pepper.

F Replace 1 cup of the stock with a 14-oz can of crushed tomatoes or 1 cup white wine to enhance it further.

G Thicken your gumbo with okra—more common with seafood than with meat. Cut the fingers into ½-in slices and either stir them in at step [3], if you like them soft and stewed; or, for a bit of bite, fry them in vegetable oil for a few minutes and then stir in at step [5].

H Filé powder is an alternative thickener that's mostly used with meat. Be warned: It will become horribly stringy if the gumbo is brought back to a high heat after it's been added. For this reason, some people prefer to stir ½ tsp or so into their own bowl at the table. Alternatively, add 1 tbsp filé powder per 4 cups stock, off the heat, at step [5].

BLOOD SAUSAGE, SPICY SAUSAGE & SMOKED HAM

Looking for cheap, flavorful ingredients for my gumbo, I returned from my butcher's in London with pretty much the same things I might have bought in Baton Rouge—a ham hock, a pound of spicy sausage, and an 8-oz pyramidal block of blood sausage. Blood sausage *can* be found in Louisiana, but the federal hygiene people get a little nervy about it, so, for an easy life, the local restaurants tend to give it a miss. It's always worth tracking some down if you can, as it lends the same brooding depth to gumbo as it does to the Asturian bean stew *fabada* (page [246]). Follow our starting point, using the ham hock in place of the chicken pieces. As with any broth or stew, let the cooking time be guided by your ingredients, i.e., how long it takes to cook them through while retaining a good texture. In this case, at step [4] the ham hock will need a slow simmering for 2–3 hours. Both spicy and blood sausages can be sliced and added an hour before the cooking time is up. Remove the ham hock, cut the meat into bite-sized pieces, and return them to the pan to reheat before serving your gumbo with rice and garnish.

CRAYFISH

"Cajun" is a corruption of Acadian, Acadia being a historical French colony roughly corresponding to present-day Nova Scotia, New Brunswick, and Prince Edward Island. After the British invaded in the eighteenth century, many of the inhabitants were deported, a good proportion ending up in francophone Louisiana. The story goes that so close was the Acadians' relationship with the Canadian lobster that it followed them south, losing so much body weight during its two-thousand-mile swim that it was transformed into crayfish. Aesop need lose no sleep, but a small crustacean that teems in sluggish creeks and is otherwise known as the mudbug needs all the mythologizing it can get. Much of the crayfish consumed in Louisiana is raised locally, in vast natural wetlands, farmed in rotation with rice. Louisiana *is* a bowl of gumbo, the bayou a rich brown as if made with a dark roux. One way to make a crayfish gumbo is to follow the starting point, leaving out the chicken pieces and adding 2¼ lb cleaned, whole, shell-on crayfish about 45 minutes into step [4]. If the crayfish are in their shells, as they should be, you can use water rather than stock. Most recipes for crayfish gumbo call for tomatoes and Creole seasoning. If you don't have a tub of the branded stuff (e.g. Tony Chachere, Paul Prudhomme, or Emeril Lagasse) in your pantry, make some by thoroughly mixing

3 tbsp paprika, 2 tbsp garlic powder, 1 tbsp onion powder, 1 tbsp dried thyme, 1 tbsp dried oregano, 2 tsp black pepper, 2 tsp salt, and 1 tsp cayenne. Use 1–2 tbsp in a gumbo made according to our starting point.

GAME

Fat rendered from duck, goose, or chicken can all be used to make an excellent roux for a game gumbo. At Prejean's Cajun restaurant in Lafayette, they use lard in the pheasant and quail gumbo that sells in vast quantities every year at the New Orleans Jazz Festival. For something similar, adapting our starting point, use 2 boned pheasant, 2 boned quail, 1 lb *andouille* (a coarse, smoked pork sausage that you might approximate with Polish kabanos), and 8 oz finer-ground smoked fresh sausage (hard to get in the U.K., so I use a spiced sausage). With the bay leaf, add 2 tbsp paprika, ¼ tsp white pepper, and ¼ tsp black pepper. Once the meat is cooked through, add a few dashes of Tabasco with the parsley and scallions as well as, if you can find it, 1–2 tsp of the liquid flavoring/browning product called Kitchen Bouquet. Simmer for 5 minutes longer before serving with rice.

SEAFOOD

Some say gumbo has its roots in another soup/stew from the Francophonie—bouillabaisse. The *Times Picayune* columnist Lolis Eric Ellie disagrees. He claims the dish has African heritage. If gumbo *could* trace its origins to a European dish, you might say it was closest to paella, which is made with the distinctly gumboesque combination of rice (albeit short-, not long-grain), bell peppers, onion, spices, and, usually, sausage and shellfish. What gumbo and bouillabaisse do share, however, is the addition, sometimes, of a wisp of emulsified sauce in the broth. In gumbo's case, this will be mayonnaise, from the potato salad some cooks add to the bowl in place of rice. (Grits and potatoes were once common alternatives to rice in gumbo, and the tradition persists in the domestic kitchens of the South, if less so in its restaurants.) In bouillabaisse, the sauce will be *rouille*, and the fish used is generally of the finned kind, whereas in gumbo shellfish predominates, especially in the touristy versions involving shrimp, oysters, and a shellfish stock. Put down your camera and piña colada and make a shellfish gumbo by following our starting point, omitting the chicken and using fish or shellfish stock. Simmer at step 4 for 45 minutes before adding 1½–2¼ lb shrimp, shucked oysters, crabmeat, or crayfish in any combination you choose. Simmer for 10 minutes and serve with rice.

SMOKED HADDOCK, MUSSEL & OKRA

More Lossiemouth in Scotland than Louisiana, admittedly, but a combination of mussels and smoked haddock is appropriately intense and unpretentious. You don't even have to use a stock: Water will suffice with such pungent ingredients. Follow the starting point, without using chicken or sausage, as far as step 4. When the broth has simmered for 30 minutes, cut 8 oz okra into ½-in slices. For those who haven't tried it, okra is like a cross between a zucchini and a shooting star. Throw the okra into a skillet with some vegetable oil, and you'll note the tiny white strands that ping and snap like elastic. Pretty entertaining, as vegetables go. Add the okra to the broth, along with 8 oz of smoked haddock fillet, skinned and cut into chunks, and 2¼ lb mussels in their shells, scrubbed. Simmer gently for 5–7 minutes, then serve with rice, parsley, and scallions. Like a rice-y chowder, but rowdier.

SQUIRREL & OYSTER

This surf-and-turf gumbo variation comes from *Housekeeping in Old Virginia* (1879) by Marion Cabell Tyree, and is seasoned with cloves, allspice, black and red pepper, parsley, and thyme. It's thickened with filé. Newcomers to squirrel might heed the journalist Vincent Graff: It's as fiddly to eat as quail, he advises, "without the reward at the end of it." André Simon is more enthusiastic. Gray squirrel, he notes, is "the fatter and the best to eat, resembling very closely the warren rabbit in texture of flesh and flavor." Others have compared the taste to wild boar, or a cross between duck and lamb, especially if the squirrel had lived on nuts and berries. Like many animals, the flavor of squirrel meat is influenced by its diet, which is why squirrels that live in pine forests, and whose flesh thus tastes of turpentine, are best left in peace. Whereas the squirrels that live in the park across the street from my house, who subsist on KFC and discarded burrito ends, are truly delectable. A typical squirrel weighs about a pound, bones included, so you'll need to allow half a squirrel, plus 4–6 oysters, per person.

SWEET POTATO, LEEK, LIMA BEAN & FILÉ

The dark roux used in gumbo is made with oil rather than butter, and so can be used as the basis of a vegan stew. The authenticity of a gumbo without crayfish eyes or alligator wattle might be called into question, yet the toasty richness of dark roux is so characteristic that it can make a soup made with nothing more than vegetables taste like the real deal. Cooking flour for an extended period, as in a dark roux, creates flavor molecules similar to those produced when bones are roasted for stock. If you cook a lot of meat-free dishes, dark roux is a very handy preparation to have at your disposal—it will keep for a few months in the fridge and even longer in the freezer. For my vegan gumbo, I use sweet potato, because I love it, and lima beans because their cooking water can be used as the stock. Leeks pull off the allium trick of adding depth of flavor and a textural contrast to the other two vegetables. Some people may find them a bit slimy, though sliminess is not a demerit in gumbo—both of the typical thickening agents, okra and filé, contribute sliminess to a degree. Soak 1½ cups dried lima beans for at least 5 hours or overnight, then cook until soft (about 30–40 minutes); drain and reserve the cooking water. Follow the starting point, but brown 4 leeks, cut into chunks, instead of the meat, then add the onion, green bell pepper, and celery to the skillet. When the vegetables are soft, transfer to the stockpot with the cooked beans and their cooking water, topping up with tap water to make 6 cups. Add 4 cups sweet potato cut into chunks and a little fresh thyme, along with the bay leaves and cayenne. A gentle simmer for 35–40 minutes should be plenty. Add the parsley and scallions, remove the pan from the heat, give it a few minutes, then stir in 1 tbsp filé powder.

Z'HERBES

Z'herbes is a soupier sort of gumbo made with bundles of greens, traditionally served by Catholics on Maundy Thursday. These days the version made by Leah Chase at the New Orleans restaurant Dooky Chase attracts diners of every denomination. *Z'herbes* is often referred to as the vegetarian gumbo, but other than at Lent, when it is served meat-free, it usually fits the description only in the French sense—i.e. it contains meat. Ham bones, sausage, and bone broth are common inclusions; some even make use of beef or veal. Sara Roahen describes *z'herbes* as "mulchy, bitter, strangely sweet, zinging with cayenne pepper, meatier than an NFL locker room, and inordinately refreshing." The best time of year to make *z'herbes* is not Easter, but the second week in January, when the greens you optimistically bought for your New Year juicing drive have begun to wilt in the fridge. Any greens will do, but a wide selection is preferable—collards, spinach, mustard, turnip, cabbage, carrot tops, chard, parsley, watercress, dandelion, arugula, lettuce, tarragon, thyme. Some *z'herbiers* use twelve, in honor of the apostles, but most (including Leah Chase) stipulate any odd number, other than unlucky thirteen. Legend has it that for every different green you add, you make a friend; this is too much trouble nowadays, when you can make several thousand by posting a photo of a kitten in a tank top. Whether you blend the gumbo is up to you, but if you choose not to, expect tangles of greens to hang down your chin like Spanish moss from a tree. Mine reminded me of Portuguese *caldo verde*, a broth made with greens and sausage and thickened with floury potato as opposed to a roux. For a *z'herbes* in line with our starting point, leave out the chicken and use double the quantity of sausage, then add ham stock and 1 tsp Tabasco with the bay leaves, cayenne, and 2¾–3½ lb cleaned, chopped greens. Simmer for an hour, then remove from the heat and stir in 1 tbsp filé powder.

Espagnole

Espagnole is made with a brown roux, a few aromatics, and some good brown stock. Properly prepared, espagnole is glossy and rich enough to be used sparingly, most often in bringing together a plate of simply cooked meat and vegetables. It also makes a superior gravy for sausages and mash, in which case you needn't be sparing in the least.

For 2–4 cups, depending on the level of reduction and whether wine is used

INGREDIENTS
5 + 1 tbsp vegetable oil (corn, sunflower, peanut)
3 tbsp finely diced lean bacon (or ham) [A]
1 small onion or 1 large shallot, finely diced
1 carrot, finely diced
1 celery stalk, finely diced
5 tbsp all-purpose flour [B]
4 cups good-quality brown veal or beef stock
1 bouquet garni of fresh herbs
2–3 tbsp tomato paste [C]
Scant 1 cup wine—optional [D]
Salt

1   Heat 1 tbsp of the oil in a small skillet and cook the bacon over a medium heat until its fat runs. Add the onion, carrot, and celery and cook until they start to turn golden, then set aside. Warm the stock while you're doing this.

2   Heat the remaining 5 tbsp oil in a heavy-based saucepan. Stir or whisk in the flour. Cook over a low to medium heat, stirring constantly, for about 5 minutes, or until the mixture turns a pecan shade of brown.

3   Off the heat, gradually add the warm stock to the roux, whisking vigorously to see off any lumps. [E]

4   Return the pan to the stovetop on a medium–high heat. Add the cooked bacon and vegetables, plus the bouquet garni, tomato paste, and wine, if using. Bring to a boil, stirring regularly, then turn down to a simmer.

5 Continue simmering, slowly, to reduce the sauce by about a quarter to a half, skimming as necessary and stirring regularly. The end result should be glossy and concentrated. Check the seasoning, then strain the sauce.
Reducing by half might take 35–40 minutes for this quantity. F

6 If you're not serving the sauce immediately, keep it warm in a heatproof jug sitting in a pan of barely simmering water. Or let it cool, then keep in the fridge for a few days or freeze for up to a year.
Espagnole reheats very well, and welcomes the addition of other ingredients.

LEEWAY

A Many recipes also call for a few tablespoons of chopped mushrooms to be cooked with the bacon and vegetables.

B Some cooks use pre-browned flour, spreading it out on a baking sheet and cooking it at 350°F, turning it over every few minutes until much of it is a light brown color.

C A deseeded, skinned tomato can be added instead of tomato paste. Take care not to overdo the tomato, which can give the sauce a store-bought tang.

D White wine was once quite commonly added to beef sauces. Madeira famously makes a delicious sauce.

E It's often said that cold liquid should be added to hot roux and vice versa, but I find lumps far easier to avoid by adding warm liquid to the hot roux.

F The long simmer is important. For a more refined sauce, keep about 1 cup of the stock back while you warm the rest at step 1. Then add half of the cold stock to the simmering sauce 10 minutes into step 5; this will coax any scum and fat to the surface, making it easier to skim off. Repeat with the rest of the cold stock about 10 minutes later.

BITTER ORANGE

Bigarade sauce is reason enough to prepare an espagnole. It's what makes duck "*à l'orange,*" although Jane Grigson recommends it (made with venison or beef stock) for venison, and for salt pork glazed with mustard, orange juice, brown sugar, and marmalade. Seeing as bigarade sits next to Big Mac in my rigorously indexed cook's journal, I let my mind waddle to the notion of a duck burger, served in a robust bun with an orange sauce and half a chalk stream of watercress. A Bigarade Mac. A duck burger is not an original idea. Comptoir Gascon in London serves a burger made with a mix of raw and confit duck, topped with a slice of foie gras and a little chutney. Michel Roux Jr. grinds a mixture of fat and skin with the duck meat, to guard against excessive leanness, then stuffs Vacherin cheese into the middle, just to be sure. I served my duck burger, a simple patty of ground, seasoned meat, to my husband with a bit of a fanfare, knowing that the bitter orange sauce was excellent—luscious, piquant, and fruity. Two bites in, he leaned over, placed a hand on my shoulder, and whispered: "Don't make this again." To him it tasted like a duckpond smells, and I had to agree. There are many planets for the gastronaut to explore, but not all of them are friendly. Next time I'll stick with simply fried duck breasts. For the sauce, julienne (very finely) the zest of 3 Seville oranges, or 2 sweet oranges plus 1 lemon, then juice the fruit. Boil the zest in the juice until the liquid has reduced by half, then add 2 cups espagnole sauce and simmer for 5 minutes, skimming if necessary. Remove from the heat, check the seasoning, and stir in 1 tbsp butter and an optional dash of Cointreau or Grand Marnier.

CHESTNUT & GAME

"An extremely rich roux can be made using chestnut flour," according to John Wright, in his *River Cottage Hedgerow Handbook*. He suggests a game pie, made with as many woodland creatures as you can bag with your blunderbuss. I'd mix one part chestnut flour to three of wheat, for a hint of that rich flavor. Chestnut flour is gluten-free and will work fine in a roux: It can be straight-swapped for wheat flour. That said, I'd still be inclined to cut the chestnut flour with something less strident—wheat flour, as mentioned, or a gluten-free mix if you're a gluten-avoider.

DEMI-GLACE

One of those culinary terms whose meaning I forget no sooner than I've looked it up. Commit the sauce to memory by focusing on the demi and ignoring the glace. The clue is in the name: It's made of half espagnole and half beef, veal, or brown chicken stock. Bring them to a boil together, then reduce by half. Once cooled, it's ready to freeze in small portions, especially useful if you're a restaurateur with cooked-to-order dishes like Steak Diane on the menu. Steak Diane is a flambéed dish from New York that was fashionable in the 1970s. It was decades later that I first tried it, but then I'm as square as a *nouvelle cuisine* plate. It was a Friday night in early summer, and my sister and I were the only customers at a cliffside pub near Land's End. The proprietor, who also turned out to be the waiter, sommelier, chef, cloakroom assistant, and barman, perhaps because the original occupants of these roles had all thrown themselves off the cliff, took our orders and then disregarded them entirely. You're having the Steak Diane, he said, and disappeared into the kitchen to fetch meat, some matches, and the first of many bottles of red wine. While he fried the flattened steaks on the guéridon next to our table, he explained how he'd moved there to escape the pressures of life in London, where he'd worked "in the theater." He set the steaks aside to rest, softened some finely chopped shallot and garlic in butter, then added Cognac, which he lit with a match. Once the flame had subsided, he added a small wineglass of demi-glace and a teaspoon each of Dijon mustard and Worcestershire sauce, reminiscing, as he did so, about his initial unpopularity among the villagers. Not only did they stay away from the pub, but they swerved him in the street and refused to make eye contact in the post office. The steaks were returned to the pan. Gradually he came to be accepted, to the extent that he had recently been invited to join the Women's Institute. Then disaster had struck. He won first prize in the raffle at the summer fair. The moment he held the Yardley talc and bath-cube set in his hands, he felt the August air crackle with frost, and his bookings dried up. My sister and I adored him. He told us tall tales of London in the 1960s as he made us *crêpes Suzette*, one after another until the crêpe batter was all used up. It was quite clear that his specialties were tableside dishes because the kitchen was too lonely. We returned the next summer, looking forward to more tales of alcoholic fist-fights in the West End of London, but he'd gone. The pub had the same layout, the same furniture, and the same horse brasses, but the food was frozen stuff from a national catering supplier. Every table was packed.

DIABLE

A devil to define. French bourgeois recipes for sauce diable amount to espagnole tickled up with cayenne, mustard, or both. The chef Daniel Boulud, meanwhile, maintains that anything named diable in French cooking is coated in mustard, bread-crumbed, and broiled. He gives a recipe for chicken served with a "diable" sauce made from 2 tbsp Dijon mustard, 1 tbsp each of tomato ketchup and A.1. steak sauce, 1 tsp Worcestershire sauce, and a few drops of Tabasco. Rather like the aggressive brother of Marie Rose, the pale-pink sauce in a classic English shrimp cocktail. I mixed some Bouludian sauce diable, substituting HP sauce for A.1., and dolloped it on the side of bubble and squeak with fried egg. Rachel Khoo serves the classic French version of the sauce with similarly unassuming sausages and mash. Follow the starting point for espagnole, adding ¼ tsp cayenne at the end.

FRUIT & NUT

Sauce romaine is unusual among variations on espagnole, being sweet and sour, with additions of fruit and nut, and thus more redolent of medieval cooking than French bourgeois cuisine. Assuming you've already made your espagnole, start by making a *gastrique*—a caramel with vinegar added, i.e. not unlike the knock-off balsamic that smooth-talking market trader in Modena, Italy, sold to you for 45 euros. To a simple dish of steak and wilted spinach, sauce romaine adds the kind of exclamation marks that punctuate punch-ups in *Batman* (the TV show, not the po-faced movies). Caramelize 2 tbsp sugar, add ½ cup red or white wine vinegar, and cook until it starts to caramelize again. Pour in 1 cup espagnole and bring to a boil. Then simmer with half a handful of raisins. Check the seasoning, stir in 1–2 tbsp toasted pine nuts, and serve immediately.

MUSTARD, VINEGAR & ONION (ROBERT)

At Dinner, Heston Blumenthal's restaurant in the Mandarin Oriental Hotel in Knightsbridge, I ate pork with sauce Robert, a preparation allegedly described by Rabelais as "so salubrious and so essential." Which version of sauce Robert he was referring to is hard to pin down. The recipe has (probably) been around for more than six hundred years. In essence it consists of onions cooked in butter with meat stock (or espagnole), mustard, and vinegar. Blumenthal's version is unusual in that he adds reduced pork stock, heated to 175°F, to butter-softened shallots, garlic, and bacon, lets them infuse for 20 minutes, then adds thyme and sage and lets them infuse for 5 minutes longer. According to Blumenthal, this keeps the sauce fresh-flavored. In place of vinegar, lemon juice is whisked into the strained sauce with coarse-grain mustard until everything emulsifies. For the old-school version, cook 2 finely chopped onions in 2 tbsp butter until soft, then add 4 tsp white wine and 2 tsp wine vinegar and reduce to almost nothing. Add 2 cups espagnole or demi-glace and heat through, then strain. Whisk a little of the warm sauce into 1 tbsp Dijon mustard, then stir this mixture back into the remaining sauce.

TOMATO, MUSHROOM & WHITE WINE (CHASSEUR)

Sauce chasseur might seem oddly named, given that its defining ingredient puts one more in mind of a retiree pottering about in his greenhouse than a sinewy survivalist fording a stream with his rifle cocked. Still, you have to hand it to this sauce for outliving the decline of French bourgeois cooking. Arguably it has done so by reinventing itself as an all-in-one dish. Chicken is the usual meat but rabbit was once popular, and the companionability of the other ingredients is such that pretty much any meat will do. In the late nineteenth century, during the Paris siege, when the zoo could no longer afford to feed the animals, Chef Choron of Voisins made his chasseur with elephant trunk. Soften 2 tbsp finely chopped shallots or onion in 2 tbsp butter, then add 1½ cups sliced mushrooms and let them turn golden and release their juices. Pour in half a glass of white wine with 1–2 tbsp of brandy and cook off the alcohol for a few minutes before adding 1 cup espagnole and ½ cup tomato paste. Bring to a boil, then simmer for a few minutes, adding chopped parsley and a little more butter. Or, you can replace the espagnole with chicken stock and make chicken chasseur, following the starting point for stew on page 238. The sauce won't match the intensity of a classic espagnole made with beef stock, but the one-pot method using skin-on, bone-in poultry will yield excellent results, and is far quicker, giving you time to flick through your *guide culinaire* in search of other sauces to turn into casseroles.

Velouté

Espagnole's fair sister, made in the same way but with a paler roux and lighter stock—chicken, fish, or white veal. Think of velouté as a more formal way of making gravy for roast chicken. It is crucial to use a pronounced-tasting stock for velouté, so do taste it before you proceed.

For about 4 cups, 6–8 servings

INGREDIENTS
4 cups good-quality chicken, fish, or veal stock [A]
Scant 1 cup dry white wine
5 tbsp butter
5 tbsp all-purpose flour
A squeeze of lemon juice—optional [B]
Salt

1 Warm the stock with the wine.

2 In another, heavy-based saucepan, melt the butter over a low to medium heat, then whisk in the flour. Cook for a few minutes, stirring constantly, until the mixture turns pale beige. [A]

3 Off the heat, gradually add the warmed stock, whisking vigorously to see off any lumps. [C]

4 Simmer the sauce for 30–45 minutes, stirring occasionally and skimming when the need arises.
   This will be long enough for any starchiness yielded by the flour to subside.

5 Strain the sauce, add a few drops of lemon juice if you like, and season to taste. [D] [E]

6 If you're not serving your velouté sauce immediately, keep it warm in a heatproof pitcher sitting in a pan of barely simmering water. Or let it cool, then keep it in the fridge for a few days or freeze for up to a year.
   Velouté reheats very well, and welcomes the addition of other ingredients.

LEEWAY

A   As with espagnole, some recipes for velouté recommend flavoring the sauce further with a mirepoix. Finely dice 1 small onion, 1 carrot, and 1 celery stalk, then cook them in the butter until soft, but not brown, before adding the flour. Other cooks simply add 1–2 tbsp finely chopped mushrooms after the stock at step [3].

B   The lemon juice is optional, but a few drops will brighten the sauce.

C   A more assiduous way to make this is to add about three-quarters of the stock, warmed, at step [3], then add the rest, cold, in a few increments, to the simmering pot. This helps bring impurities to the surface, where they can be carefully skimmed off.

D   For a richer, softer flavor, add heavy cream or crème fraîche (anything between 2 and 6 tbsp) at the end and return the pan to the heat to warm through gently.

E   Or whisk in a little flavored butter, such as the anchovy and seaweed options given under seafood on page [178].

BERCY

A wine sauce named after a neighborhood in the 12th arrondissement of Paris. Pleasurable, at least after a few glasses, to imagine vines clinging to the shiny metal facets of the Opéra Bastille, or giraffes puckering their lips to pluck a bunch of grapes hanging off that artificial crag at the Zoo de Vincennes. Bercy, sad to say, owes its wine association not to its terroir, but to the warehouses that lined its section of the Seine. In its eighteenth-century heyday, the neighborhood was so awash with wine that local restaurants dispensed with their wine lists; their customers would no more have considered paying for a glass of Pomerol than we would a glass of tap water. Now, in common with once-industrial areas the world over, the warehouses have been converted into swanky shops and bars. Soften 4 tbsp finely chopped shallots or onion in 4 tbsp butter, moisten with white wine, and reduce until it's all but disappeared, then add 2 cups velouté made with fish stock. Bring it to a boil, then simmer for 5–10 minutes. Finish with 1–2 tbsp butter and some chopped parsley. Serve with fried, poached, or broiled fish of any sort. A variation on Bercy to serve with meat replaces the fish velouté with demi-glace, and the butter with bone marrow.

CURRY

If you've ever made the curry base given in Kris Dhillon's excellent *The Curry Secret: Indian Restaurant Cookery at Home*, a pungent gloop of blended onion, garlic, and ginger, you'll have wondered how anything so sulfurous-smelling could have remained a secret long enough for Dhillon to write about it. Once cooked and spiced, however, the super-alliaceous base undergoes a tasty transformation. Nonetheless, the sensitive of nose may prefer to make a roux-based curry sauce: a *blanquette*, basically, with curry flavors added. This approach is popular both with the Japanese, and with the British school cooks of my childhood, who stirred shreds of leftover chicken into it. Pub curry is conceived along much the same lines, and is roughly the color of a very old ginger cat with a distinct flavor of fenugreek. Escoffier's velouté-based curry sauce was predictably ritzier. He created Poularde Edward VII for the British king's coronation: chicken stuffed with truffles and foie gras, on a bed of more truffles, served with a curry sauce in lip service to the jewel in Bertie's crown. For school lunch/ pub curry, simply add 2 tsp bought curry powder to the flour when making your roux.

LEMON

In *Unmentionable Cuisine*, Calvin W. Schwabe gives a Russian recipe for brains in lemon sauce. (A little like my brains feel after a night on the Stolichnaya.) The sauce here is, in fact, a velouté made with veal stock and flavored with plenty of grated lemon zest and "a little" lemon juice and sugar. Once it's simmered for a while, add parboiled brains and some chopped dill. Bring to a boil and serve. Allemande sauce (page 179) is the more common choice for brains—an enriched velouté finished, like Schwabe's sauce, with a brisk spritz of lemon juice.

MUSHROOM & CHERVIL

Velouté means "velvety": a plush coating for the throat. In its incarnation as a soup, historically the texture of velouté would have been down to a roux and a finishing liaison of egg yolks and cream. But since the advent of the blender, thick, soft soups are available at the touch of a button, and a velouté might be made with nothing more than stock and vegetables. The following recipe of Marco Pierre White's calls for a roux and a blender; it's flavored with a combination of mushrooms and chervil. Sweat 1 small onion and 1 small leek, both finely chopped, in 3½ tbsp butter, then stir in 3 tbsp flour to make a light roux. Add 2¼ lb sliced mushrooms, then 3 cups chicken stock. Bring to a boil, stirring regularly. Add 2 cups each of milk and cream and bring back to a boil, then season and simmer for about 8 minutes. Purée, sieve, and check seasoning. Froth to cappuccino-top consistency with a hand blender, then finish with chervil leaves. The common ground shared by soups and roux-based sauces was also spotted by Campbell's, whose condensed "cream of" soups are widely used to make mac 'n' cheese, and sauces for pot pie fillings or for the green-bean casserole that graces twenty million American tables every Thanksgiving.

PEANUT BUTTER

An Ambrose Heath recipe. Lightly brown 2 tbsp butter and add 2 tbsp peanut butter. When well mixed, stir in 2 tbsp flour and cook until brown. Add 1⅔ cups chicken stock and, over a medium heat, stir the sauce while it thickens. Season to taste. "Interesting" with ham or roast chicken, says Heath.

SAFFRON, PASTIS & TOMATO

A sort of bouillabaisse sauce. This is excellent with shellfish, and with the shellfish-flavored red mullet, but I'm most likely to make this vibrant, aniseedy sauce for a tranche of bright white cod, fresh from the North Sea in winter. As your 4 cups of fish stock are warming, add a good pinch of saffron to it, along with 1 tbsp pastis. Once the stock has been mixed into the roux, add 3–4 skinned, deseeded, chopped tomatoes. Be sure to give your sauce the recommended minimum 30-minute simmer, so the tomato mellows. In summer, a little torn basil would be a welcome finishing touch.

SEAFOOD

The crayfish shells, oyster juice, and lobster corals used to make the classic seafood veloutés in *Larousse* are all very well if you fancy an extended marine-themed treasure hunt before you've even gotten your apron on, but shellfish butter, anchovy butter, and seaweed butter offer delicious and pragmatic substitutes. To make shellfish butter is quite an involved process, so we'll leave it aside here. For anchovy butter, blend half a dozen anchovies with 1 stick unsalted butter, 1 minced garlic clove, a pinch of cayenne, and a few drops of lemon juice. And a simple seaweed butter can be made by grinding 2 sheets of toasted nori to a powder and mixing it into 1 stick unsalted butter. Expect this to be a dark sea-green. Potted shrimp could be considered as another form of seafood butter, and can be bought from fish merchants and fancier supermarkets. For a seafood sauce to go with fried, poached, or broiled fish, soften 2 tbsp finely chopped shallot or onion in 2 tbsp butter. Add a glass of dry white wine or vermouth and reduce by half, then add 1 cup velouté and reduce by half again. Finish by whisking in any of the butters above, checking for flavor and salinity as you go.

TARRAGON

As with so many sauces, tarragon can turn a velouté into something very beautiful. You can make a quick version of tarragon velouté in the pan you've used to sear a chicken breast or a portion of seafood. Set the protein aside somewhere warm, then add no more than 1–2 tsp fat to the still-warm pan. Whisk in 1–2 tsp flour, then, after a minute or two, add 1 cup stock and simmer for 5 minutes. Finish with a teaspoon of chopped tarragon—and a little heavy cream or crème fraîche, if you like. Modern versions of this classic tend to dispense with the flour and stock in favor of loads of cream, reduced to an unctuous thickness, but both my arteries and my palate prefer it the old-fashioned way. If fresh tarragon is hard to come by, note that freeze-dried is good.

VEAL

Anthony Bourdain is quite clear on the matter. *Blanquette de veau* should be pale. The rice should be white. The plate too. The temptation to add vegetables should be resisted at all costs. It's a *blanquette*, for Pete's sake. See if you dare serve this without reaching for a handful of chopped parsley—it's as hard as eating a sugary doughnut without licking your lips. I wonder what Bourdain would make of Philippe Delacourcelle's version. Delacourcelle adds star anise to the veal during cooking, and a little ground cardamom to the butter used for the roux.

Still as pale as oatmeal, but far more exotically flavored than a classic *blanquette*. Bourdain simmers cubed veal neck or shoulder in water with a mirepoix and bouquet garni until tender. To a blonde roux, he adds the liquid the veal was cooked in, followed by the veal plus some boiled pearl onions, white mushrooms, white pepper, and salt. Bourdain finishes his *blanquette* with some egg yolk and a little lemon juice, as in an allemande—see below.

YOLK & BUTTER OR CREAM (ALLEMANDE)

Sauce allemande was one of Carême's original mother sauces, but was demoted by absorption into velouté. It is, after all, simply a velouté enriched with egg yolks and butter or cream. Many maintain that the stock used should be veal, but Escoffier was open to any white stock, and Philippe Legendre at Taillevent in Paris opts for snail stock in his celebrated allemande. The name, incidentally, verges on racist: The allemande is teutonically pale, where espagnole is a swarthier brown. Some chefs still use the alternative name of sauce Parisienne, a result of wartime anti-German sentiment, much as the British royal family ditched Saxe-Coburg-Gotha for Windsor. For a velouté made with 2 cups stock, use 2 yolks mixed with 6 tbsp melted, unsalted butter or ½ cup heavy cream. Temper the egg mixture (i.e. whisk in a little warm sauce), then add to the remaining velouté and gently warm through, finishing with a squeeze of lemon juice. Sauce allemande is often served with simply cooked fish or chicken, or as an alternative to béchamel as the unifying medium in a savory pie.

Béchamel & White Sauce

Béchamel is made with an even paler roux than velouté and is diluted with infused milk rather than stock. It's a fast, simple, versatile sauce that's made with ingredients you're likely to have to hand. Minus the aromatics it's called white sauce, which is sometimes a better choice for the savory flavor variations (and always for the sweet).

For about 4 cups, 6–8 servings [A]

INGREDIENTS
4 cups milk [B]
½ onion, with a bay leaf nailed to it with a clove or two—a.k.a. a *clouté*
7 tbsp butter or other fat [C]
7 tbsp all-purpose flour [C]
Salt and white pepper
Nutmeg—optional [D]

1   First flavor the milk by scalding it with the onion *clouté*.
    Remove from the heat and let infuse before straining.
    Scalding means bringing just to a boil. The infusing will take at least
    10 minutes. The onion, bay, and clove are what distinguish béchamel from
    white sauce. They can provide a fragrant backdrop for other flavors,
    but if they're likely to clash with them, or risk being overpowered,
    leave them out.

2   In another, heavy-based saucepan, melt the butter over
    a medium heat, then whisk in the flour. Cook over a low to
    medium heat, stirring constantly, without allowing the roux
    to darken beyond a pale sand color. [E]

3   Off the heat, gradually add the warm milk, whisking vigorously
    to see off any lumps. Turn up the heat to medium–high and
    bring to a boil, stirring constantly.

4   Lower the heat and simmer gently for anything between
    8 and 40 minutes, stirring frequently. Season with salt, pepper,
    and nutmeg. [F]
    Often 15 minutes is called for, but the longer simmer is recommended
    for a finer flavor and texture. Do stay close to it, stirring occasionally
    so the sauce doesn't stick to the pan and burn.

5 Strain into a heatproof pitcher and cover with plastic wrap or lightly buttered parchment paper. Set the pitcher in a pan of barely simmering water to keep warm, if serving imminently. Or let cool and store in the fridge for up to 5 days, or freeze for up to 3 months.

The sauce reheats well, although it will have thickened further and you may need to add a little extra milk to loosen it. Reheat it gently and whisk as you do.

LEEWAY

A The finished quantity will be smaller if you opt for a longer simmer at step 4.

B Use any sort of milk, or a mixture of milk and cream if you're after something richer. Michel Roux makes a coconut-milk béchamel flavored with soy sauce and minced garlic. These quantities are for a thick but pourable sauce.

C If you want a thinner sauce, simply add more milk at step 4.

D Nutmeg is optional, but recommended; do try to use freshly grated.

E A finely chopped shallot, softened in the butter before the flour is added, can give many savory sauces a stronger-flavored backbone.

F The sauce can be enriched by whisking in some heavy cream or crème fraîche. For this quantity, use about ½ cup and add it to the sauce at the end of its simmer, giving it another 5 minutes over a gentle heat.

ANCHOVY

I used to frequent a brasserie in Chelsea, in London, primarily because I had a crush on the barman. This was nothing unusual: Everyone had a crush on all the staff, who were beautiful to a (wo)man. My barman was distinguished by his imperfections: He had a slightly brutish nose and an insufficiently defined chin, which, in the manner of these things, oddly intensified his beauty by reducing it. Since the brasserie had table service, I never got to speak to him, but I would sit in his eyeline, drinking black coffee or citron pressé in an effort to seem blasé and Parisian and unconcerned about anything so bourgeois, banal, and figure-compromising as food. Casting him smoky glances over my copy of *The Second Sex*, I would suppress the agonizing hunger pangs brought on when a waiter passed by with a *croque monsieur* or steak sandwich and *frites*. One morning I showed up and he wasn't there. I sulked into my *café filtre* until I realized his absence meant I could actually eat something. The brasserie made their *croques monsieurs* the proper way—slim, with not too much ham or Gruyère, modestly topped with béchamel speckled brown under the broiler, and served with a little facial tickler of frisée. I had just taken my last, slightly too large bite of *croque*, chasing it with what remained of the frisée, when my barman walked in. He looked over and didn't avert his gaze. "Excuse me," he said. Unable, as I was, to open my mouth, I thought the most blasé and Parisian thing would be to raise an eyebrow. "You have salad on your chin." I learned to make my *croques monsieurs* at home after that. I think they work best with anchovy béchamel, and fish breath is of no concern when you're slumped dateless on your sofa in your pajamas. Jane Grigson recommends pounding 8 anchovy fillets in 4 tbsp butter, then adding this to the starting-point béchamel before straining.

BACON & CORNMEAL

My husband's comeback of choice when I criticize him for not washing the pan after a Saturday-morning fry-up: *I was saving it for white gravy.* The gravy in question, a specialty of the American South, is a white sauce made with bacon, sausage, or pork drippings, served with fried chicken, sliced ham, or steak, and mopped up with biscuits—the savory scone-a-like type, not British biscuits/cookies (see page [23]). Some cooks use wheat flour for the roux, but cornmeal is also common, in which case the result is called "sawmill gravy," on account of its rougher texture. Retain 2 tbsp bacon/sausage fat in your skillet, then stir in 2 tbsp flour to make the roux, followed by 1⅔ cups warm milk and plenty of seasoning. Keep simmering until you have a thick sauce consistency, making sure to loosen as much as possible of the sticky residue left in the pan by the meat. Some will come off as you stir in the flour, and the harder bits should dissolve in the warming milk with a bit of encouragement from your spoon.

BRANDY

Brandy butter, the dense, wincingly sweet, and strongly flavored hard sauce traditionally served with British Christmas pudding and mince pies, is essentially sozzled cake frosting. Delia Smith's boozy sauce is a very different proposition: Denis Thatcher to brandy butter's Maggie. Which is to say it's pleasantly, bumblingly bland—but rather wonderful served with a strident classic like plum pudding. (The comforting blanket of béchamel in a lasagne or moussaka works on much the same principle.) For something similar, make a white sauce according to the starting point, omitting the *clouté* and the salt and pepper. Once it has simmered for 15 minutes at step 4, add ⅔ cup sugar and stir for a couple of minutes. Turn the heat down to its lowest setting and add ¾ cup brandy and 1¼ cups heavy cream. Gently warm through, then taste for brandy levels. Remove from the heat and cover the surface with plastic wrap or buttered parchment paper. The quantity of brandy is about double what Smith uses, but I've had guests who like it even punchier. You can swap the brandy for the same amount of Calvados, rum, whisky, or sweet–medium golden fortified wine.

EGGPLANT & CHEESE

In Turkey, a dish called *hunkar begendi* ("sultan's delight") consists of lamb braised with tomatoes, served on a creamy, smoky eggplant béchamel enriched with *kasseri*—a sheep's or goat's cheese—and seasoned with freshly grated nutmeg. Jeremy Round won the 1982 *Guardian*/Mouton Cadet cooking competition with his version; he thought that Cheddar worked better than the *kasseri*. Char 3 lb eggplants on a griddle pan or in a 400°F oven until collapsed and soft, then scoop out the flesh and soak in lightly salted water for 30 minutes. Before you dump the results in the trash and head for the takeout, note that Round warns that it will look like "grubby rags." Squeeze out any excess moisture, then mash, or blitz in a food processor. Make a roux with 4 tbsp each of butter and flour, then add 2 cups warm milk. Cook for 3 minutes before adding the eggplant purée along with ⅔ cup grated Cheddar. Stir off the heat, mixing in the cheese as it melts, and season. Serve with lamb braised in onion, tomato, garlic, and herbs.

MORNAY (CHEESE)

The roux-based sauce that would not die. There might be more *au courant* ways to make a similar sauce, but who wants fashion-forward cauliflower cheese? Or directional eggs Mornay? Insistent seekers after novelty would do better to make their cheese sauce in the time-honored manner, and use it in ways less familiar to British palates.

The French classic, *endives au jambon*, is made with whole heads of Belgian endive, simmered (10 minutes should be enough) and then rolled in ham that's been spread with mustard so the apex of each one sticks out like a pig's foot in pink flares. Next they're lined up in a baking dish, covered in Mornay sauce, scattered with some extra grated cheese, and baked at 350°F until bubbling—about 20 minutes. Or consider Anna Del Conte's eggplant chips fried in garlic and parsley, mixed with ziti pasta tossed in a bay-scented Mornay: mac 'n' cheese meets Ottolenghi. For a classic Mornay, stir ¾–1 cup grated cheese into a just-finished 2 cups béchamel, off the heat, until melted—too much heat and your sauce is liable to split. Traditionally a Mornay calls for 50/50 Gruyère and Parmesan; even the stronger varieties of Cheddar don't impart flavor quite so efficiently. Taste for seasoning after adding the cheese, because its saltiness will vary. Add a teaspoon or two of mustard if you like, and/or a few tablespoons of butter and an egg yolk or two for richness (but not the last if you intend to *gratinée* your Mornay). Other common additions include cayenne, shallots, nutmeg, a dash of Worcestershire sauce, Tabasco, or kirsch. Cumin and caraway are worth considering, too.

ONION (SOUBISE)

Onions were once boiled with honey and the strained liquid used as a cough syrup. I reckon I'd prefer a zigzag of Robitussin on my hot dog. Onion water is put to more appetizing use in the thick béchamel known as soubise. This sauce is one of the many casualties of the roux's general unfashionability, and while it still makes an occasional appearance with its classic partner, lamb, back in the day it was served with rabbit, duck, chicken, and even fish. Vegetarians should note that the balance soubise strikes between sweet and sulfurous makes it an equally fitting match for robust mushroom dishes, hard-cooked eggs, or mixed roast vegetables, and it makes a good filling for an omelet. Simmer 2 large chopped onions in 2 cups salted water, then strain when soft, retaining the water as well as the onion. Mix the onion-cooking water with 2 cups milk and use to make a béchamel as per our starting point. Return the cooked onion (puréed, if you prefer) to the finished sauce, together with a little freshly grated nutmeg. Check for seasoning, then heat gently to warm the onion. For a more elaborate version, finish with Calvados and crème fraîche.

PARSLEY

As in a couple of slices of pink country-style ham, draped in white sauce speckled green, with some carrot rounds and yellow boiled potatoes on the side. Thankfully, this dish is still served at St. John restaurant, whose chef, Fergus Henderson, advises adding the milk when your roux smells of "biscuit" to prevent it from overcooking. He makes a thick sauce—½ cup of butter and ¾ cup flour and to 2½ cups milk—then suggests thinning it to your liking with the ham's cooking water. He specifies a big bunch of curly parsley, chopped. Served with white fish, the same sauce will benefit from an additional half a handful of chopped chives or dill.

SHERRY & CREAM

We were in New York. "Let's go to the 21 Club," I said. "Nah," said my friend. "It's so touristy." I pointed out that I was a tourist. My friend wanted to take me to some new place in Brooklyn. Bolivian dim sum served by unicyclists with plaid shirts and waxed moustaches. "I can get that in London," I said. To me, the 21 Club was foreign: old-fashioned America at its most eccentric. Wrought-iron gates guarded by life-size ornamental jockeys. Inside it was like a toy shop that went out in a hurricane and got blown into a speakeasy. And it was in *All About Eve*. My friend relented and joined me for lunch. I had the famous chicken hash. Back home, I found the recipe in my father-in-law's copy of Molly O'Neill's *New York Cookbook*. The method for the white sauce is unusual in that it involves a long cook in the oven, as opposed to on the stovetop. It's made with 2 tbsp each of butter and flour and 2 cups milk, then simmered for a couple of minutes. Add ¼ tsp white pepper and a dash each of Tabasco and Worcestershire sauces. Cover and cook in a 300°F oven for 1½ hours. When the time is up, strain the sauce, then return it to the pan with 2 cups diced poached chicken breast, ¼ cup sherry, and ½ cup light cream. Warm, gently, for 5 minutes. Temper 2 egg yolks (i.e. whisk in a little warm sauce), then add to the remaining sauce and cook on a low heat until the sauce thickens. Serve on wild rice and spinach, or with waffles or toast. Sprinkle with grated Gruyère and run under a hot broiler until golden and bubbling, if you like.

VANILLA

Custard powder is a mixture of cornstarch, vanilla flavoring, and yellow coloring. It makes for a slightly less silky custard sauce than the type thickened only by egg yolks. Egg-avoiders might find that a vanilla-flavored white sauce has the edge over a custard made with powder, not only because cooked flour lends a less blowsy texture than cornstarch, but because you can let the roux darken more than is usual for a white sauce, introducing a hint of shortbread flavor. Infuse 2 cups milk with 1 split vanilla bean, then stir in 4 tbsp sugar (or more to taste) when the heat is reduced to a simmer at step 4.

Soufflé: Cheese Soufflé

The basis of savory soufflés is a thick, flavored white sauce, enriched with egg yolks before the whites are folded in. In the oven, the mixture creeps up the side of the dish, and eventually beyond it. The theory is that simple. The rest is practice.

For an 8-in soufflé, or 6 (5-oz) individual soufflés [A]

INGREDIENTS

For the dish(es): 1 tbsp butter, melted, and 4 tbsp finely grated
    Parmesan or fine bread crumbs [B]
2 cups milk
5 tbsp butter
5 tbsp all-purpose flour
4 egg yolks [C]
1½ cups grated cheese, plus a little extra to sprinkle over the top [D]
Salt and white pepper
5 egg whites, at room temperature [C] [E]
Pinch of cream of tartar or ½ tsp lemon juice

1   Thoroughly brush the dish(es) with melted butter. Sprinkle in the Parmesan or bread crumbs, then tilt in all directions until entirely covered. Tip out any remaining cheese or crumbs.
There's no need to tie a paper collar around your dish(es),
unless you plan to add a good deal more egg white than here.

2   Warm the milk in a saucepan.
You can infuse the milk, as you would for béchamel (page [180]),
for an extra flavor dimension.

3   In another, heavy-based saucepan, melt the butter over a medium heat, then whisk in the flour. Cook, stirring constantly, over a low to medium heat for 2 minutes, without allowing the roux to darken beyond a pale sand color.

4   Off the heat, gradually add the warm milk, whisking or stirring vigorously to see off any lumps. Turn up the heat to medium–high and bring to a boil, stirring all the time.

5   Reduce the heat and simmer for 5 minutes. Remove from the heat, and let cool a little before stirring in the egg yolks.
Once the yolks have been added, the soufflé base can be cooled, covered, and refrigerated for up to 2 days. When you're ready to use the base, you'll need to reheat it gently, so it's hot enough to melt the cheese.

6 Add the grated cheese, letting it melt for a few minutes before mixing it in. Season, noting that the air in the soufflé will tamp the flavor somewhat. Transfer to a large mixing bowl.

7 In a clean glass or metal bowl, beat the egg whites until frothy, then add the cream of tartar and keep beating to soft peaks. Peaks are defined as soft when you lift out the beaters and the peaks begin to droop, but stop short of folding over completely.

8 Fold a third of the egg whites into your soufflé base, then carefully fold in the rest, aiming to retain as much of the air you've beaten into them as possible. Adding a small amount first loosens the mixture, making it easier to incorporate the rest.

9 Pour into your buttered, dusted soufflé dish(es) and smooth the surface, then run a knife around the edge to discourage it from clinging. Sprinkle the extra grated cheese over the top.

10 Place on a preheated baking sheet, on a low shelf, in a 350°F oven, and bake for 20–35 minutes for a large soufflé, depending on whether you like your soufflé wet and wobbly, or cakey. Individual soufflés will need about 15 minutes.

11 Serve immediately. Nothing deflates the mood like a subsiding soufflé.

LEEWAY

A Use a 15 x 10-in jelly roll or sheet pan to make a soufflé roulade. Bake it for 15–25 minutes, until firm yet springy.

B For sweet soufflés, use sugar or fine cake crumbs. Sweet soufflés—e.g. chocolate or coffee—can be made with white sauce as a base, although pastry cream (page 498) or ganache (page 380) are more conventional.

C Chilled eggs can be brought to room temperature by leaving them (unbroken, naturally) in warm tap water for a few minutes.

D Gruyère is the classic soufflé cheese, but Comté and aged Gouda, or a mix of any one of these with Parmesan, are worthy substitutes. Even strong varieties of Cheddar are likely to be disappointing.

E The extra egg white will give your soufflés a boost. Most soufflé recipes call for one more white than yolk.

CAULIFLOWER, CHEESE & CUMIN

Craig Claiborne writes that all main-course soufflés are essentially made the same way, and so can be varied "at will" once the basic principle is learned. Soufflé recipes are as rare in modern cookbooks as tips on how to spread an avocado on toast are rife, and what instances there are tend to be classics. So there's plenty of scope for some experimentation. I find the Middle Eastern combination of cauliflower and cumin strangely satisfying in soufflé form, at once airy and dense, like walking through an edible cloud in a souk. Steam half a large cauliflower's worth of florets until soft, then blitz to a rough purée. Make up the starting-point soufflé base, using half the quantities of butter, flour, and milk and adding 2 tsp ground cumin at the outset of step [5], then stirring in only 2 egg yolks at the end of this step. After the 1½ cups of cheese has melted at step [6], stir in about 1 cup of the cauliflower purée and proceed from step [7], using only 3 egg whites. The replacement of some of the white sauce with purée means that the soufflé will need a longer cooking time: about 30–45 minutes for a large soufflé, or 20–22 minutes for individual ones.

CHOCOLATE

There are many different starting points for a sweet soufflé. In the case of chocolate, you might fold your beaten egg whites into a ganache, a chocolate pastry cream, a mixture of melted chocolate and egg yolks (in which case you will essentially be baking a chocolate mousse), or even a puréed, chocolate-flavored rice pudding. Hubert Keller makes a white-sauce-based chocolate soufflé flavored with vanilla and rum. Naturally you'll want to try all five approaches to see which you like best. Without wishing to be tendentious, I should add that the flour in a roux makes for a very light, cakelike soufflé—quite wonderful. Follow our starting point, adding ¾ cup grated dark, 70%-cocoa chocolate, ¼ cup sugar, 1 tbsp rum, and 1 tsp vanilla extract at step [6], in place of the cheese, stirring after a few minutes to make sure the sugar dissolves completely and the chocolate is evenly distributed.

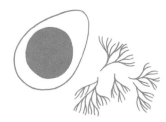

EGG & DILL

Egg soufflé—an edible tautology? While researching roux variations, I came across a recipe for egg croquettes in *The Constance Spry Cookery Book*. In comparison to the salty, punchily flavored ingredients of your standard croquette, boiled egg seemed rather demure. But the idea stuck around, and I found myself curious about how egg-flecked soufflé might work. Early one morning, I cooked the first few and sat down, napkin tucked into pajamas, facing a brimming ramekin and some buttered toast "soldiers" of Special Forces sturdiness. I loved the little pieces of boiled egg, held in frothy suspension and gently seasoned with dill. I switched off the *Today* program and sat watching the birds hopping around the garden while I twiddled my toes in my fluffy slippers. This must be mindfulness, I thought, as I reached for my second helping. The next batch came out of the oven just as my husband had roused himself, his face crumpled like the first draft of this page. I silently passed him his soufflé and waited for the praise. "Some of the egg has gone lumpy," he grouched. Remember that the soufflé base can be made, and the ramekins prepared, in advance, then you just need to spend a few minutes beating the egg whites and folding them into the mixture while the oven heats. Follow the starting point, stirring in 3–4 fairly well chopped hard-cooked eggs, 1 tbsp chopped fresh dill, and ½ tsp white pepper at step 6, instead of the cheese.

GINGER

Ginger soufflé was a favorite of James Beard. In a letter to Helen Evans Brown, he praised her version "with gobs of preserved ginger in it." I had a go, resisting the temptation to add ground ginger, gingerbread spices, or cardamom. The sweetened white sauce stayed elegantly plain. Brown's soufflé calls for more egg than our starting point, but the method is the same. Make a roux with 3 tbsp each of butter and flour and cook it for a minute or so, then stir in ¾ cup warm milk, continuing to stir until the mixture is thick and smooth. Lightly beat 5 egg yolks with a little of the warm white sauce, then add it to the rest. Stir in ½ cup sugar and ½ cup finely chopped preserved ginger. Beat 6 egg whites to soft peaks, then fold a third into the sauce to loosen it, followed by the rest. Pour into a buttered and sugar-dusted 1½-quart soufflé dish. Bake at 375°F for 25–30 minutes until risen and lightly browned. Serve with sweetened whipped cream.

GRAND MARNIER

Hugh Fearnley-Whittingstall recalls taking a date to Lapérouse, the legendary restaurant overlooking the Île St Louis in Paris, and spotting a bargain bottle of Château Petrus on the *carte des vins*. It was only when the free glass of Champagne arrived that he wondered if the management had extra reason to be glad of his custom. The bottle cost

£650, not £65: He'd got the exchange rate wrong. Thankfully, the food was sublime, the soufflé Lapérouse world-beating... "crusty on the outside, light and moussey under the crust, and completely gooey and saucy in the middle." Butter the ramekins and dust with sugar. Make as per our starting point, at step 6 stirring in 2 tbsp marmalade, 2 tbsp Grand Marnier, and ¼ tsp vanilla extract instead of the cheese.

RICE PUDDING

An alternative to roux, ganache, or pastry cream as a base for a sweet soufflé is blended rice pudding. Philip Howard uses it at his restaurant The Square in London, and in the *Sweet* volume of his two-volume cookbook gives a recipe for individual Peach Melba soufflés (he blends rice pudding and peach purée before whisking in the egg whites). The dishes are lined with dried almond-cake crumbs, and the soufflés served with a sharp raspberry sauce and a vanilla and almond ice cream. Howard believes that no sweet soufflé is complete without a scoop of ice cream dropped into it: "The sensation of eating a hot, full-bodied soufflé with a cold melting ice cream is one of the greatest dessert pleasures." For a domestic, vanilla-flavored version, make a rice pudding with ½ cup short-grain rice, 2 cups whole milk (or a mix of milk and cream), ¼ cup sugar, 1 split vanilla bean, and a pinch of salt. Purée enough of it to fill 1¼ cups—enjoy any leftover pud as a cook's treat—and fold in 5 egg whites beaten to soft peaks with 6 tbsp sugar. Bake in 4 ramekins on a preheated baking sheet for no more than 8–9 minutes at 350°F, carefully rotating the sheet halfway through the cooking time. If you prefer your soufflé with the rice grains left intact, seek out Hungarian *rizskoch*.

SPINACH & RICOTTA

When our parents came to visit us in London in the mid-1980s, my sister and I, considering ourselves girls about town, took them to Langan's Brasserie in Mayfair, which was a place celebrities went and therefore somewhere my mother might have read about in the papers. "Don't expect to see anyone famous," I said, with a teenage scowl. "London really isn't like that." We were shown to a table between Rod Stewart and half the England soccer team. My parents sniggered behind their menus. Gary Lineker folded an asparagus spear into his mouth while I studiedly didn't watch. This was not only to broadcast my metropolitan indifference but also because I was genuinely more interested in my appetizer, a Langan's classic: spinach and ricotta soufflé with an anchovy sauce. There was, and is, no Langan's cookbook—imagine that now, when you can sell fish sticks out of a knackered old Citroën H van and score a TV-book deal—but here is my own interpretation, adapting the starting point. Leave out the 1½ cups grated cheese. Wilt a pound of washed spinach in a large wok for 2–3 minutes with nothing but the droplets of water clinging to its leaves; squeeze, finely chop, and set aside. Prepare 6 ramekins as per step 1, then make up a white sauce following steps 2 to 4, using 1⅔ cups milk and 4 tbsp each of butter and flour. Let the sauce simmer over a low heat for 5 minutes, then remove from the heat and cool a little before stirring in just 3 egg yolks. Transfer the mixture to a large bowl and thoroughly stir in the spinach, along with ½ cup ricotta and ¼ cup finely grated Parmesan. Season with salt, pepper, and about a quarter of a nutmeg, freshly grated. Beat 4 egg whites to soft peaks, then fold a quarter of them into the spinach mixture with a metal spoon, followed by the rest. Divide among the prepared ramekins, sprinkling over some more grated Parmesan, if you like. Bake the soufflés on a preheated baking sheet at 350°F for 20–25 minutes until they are risen and light brown. While you're waiting for the soufflés to rise, make the anchovy sauce: Warm scant 1 cup crème fraîche in a small pan, or in the microwave, with 1½ tsp anchovy paste, a dash of Worcestershire sauce, and a few drops of Tabasco. Make a small incision in each just-cooked soufflé, pour over a little of the anchovy sauce, and serve the rest alongside.

Croquettes: Chicken Croquettes

Roux-based croquettes are further testament to the adaptability of white sauce—it's a mixture that takes particularly kindly to being deep-fried. Whereas a pourable white sauce calls for 3½–4 tbsp each of butter and flour per 2 cups milk, and a soufflé base 4–6 tbsp, this variation demands 6 tbsp fat and 8 of flour, making it close in texture to a cooked polenta.

For 15 cylindrical croquettes about 2½ in long

INGREDIENTS
2 cups milk [A]
6 tbsp butter
½ cup all-purpose flour [B]
⅓–⅔ cup finely diced, cooked chicken [C]
Salt and white pepper
1 egg, beaten
1½ cups dry bread crumbs
Vegetable oil for deep-frying

1   Warm the milk in a saucepan.
    You can infuse the milk, as you would for béchamel (page [180]), for an extra flavor dimension.

2   In another, heavy-based saucepan, melt the butter over a medium heat, sprinkle over the flour, and whisk or stir in vigorously. Cook, stirring constantly, for 2 minutes, without allowing the roux to darken beyond a pale sand color. [D]

3   Off the heat, gradually add the warm milk, whisking or stirring vigorously to see off any lumps. Turn up the heat to medium–high and bring to a boil, stirring all the time.

4   Simmer for 5 minutes. Remove from the heat and let cool a little, then stir in the chicken and check for seasoning. [E]

5   Spread the croquette mixture out on a sheet pan, to a depth of about ¾ in. Let cool, then chill for at least 2 hours.

6   Have three shallow bowls ready: one of flour, another of beaten egg, and a third of fine bread crumbs. Remove the chilled mixture from the fridge not long before you're due to cook the croquettes and fashion into the classic cylinders or ball shapes.

7 Flour each croquette all over, then dip in the beaten egg and then the bread crumbs, aiming for a comprehensive coating.

8 Deep-fry in oil heated to 350°F, a few at a time, for a couple of minutes each side or until crisp and golden. Keep the cooked croquettes warm in a 225°F oven. F
If you are new to deep-frying, see page 17.

LEEWAY

A As with most béchamel-like sauces, a combination of milk and stock can be used.

B It's typical to use marginally more flour than fat.

C When it comes to coating and frying the croquettes, it helps to keep any added pieces quite small, so the finished croquettes are smooth and less inclined to leak.

D Make the roux around some onion, or other chopped vegetables (finely diced red bell pepper makes an excellent flavoring), that you plan to keep in the finished croquettes. Make sure you dice the vegetables finely enough, and give them time to soften sufficiently in the butter before adding the flour.

E Constance Spry recommends starting with a more dilute white sauce and reducing it, on the basis that a longer, gentler reduction will result in a more concentrated flavor. (See serrano ham, page 196, for a recipe that works along similar lines.)

F Croquettes can be baked instead of being deep-fried, but they will be given to oozing.

ASPARAGUS

I like to use the woody ends of asparagus to infuse the milk for croquette-making, before straining them out and using the milk to cook the middle parts of the asparagus stalks, subsequently draining and puréeing those. The resulting asparagus-infused milk is then used to make a thick croquette base, to which the puréed asparagus is added (in place of the chicken). The croquettes are fashioned into rough rounds about the size of new potatoes, then breaded and deep-fried. Serve with the tender, al dente asparagus tips—no need for any sauce, if the insides of your croquettes are as creamy as they should be. Use about 18 asparagus spears for the starting-point quantity.

BEEF

On a business trip to Tokyo my colleague suggested I try beef karaoke. What could this be? A strip of tofu doing a tuneless imitation of prime rib? A medley of protein-crazed Shania Twain covers? *Korroke*, my colleague repeated. A corruption of "croquette." These are like the sort of mini cottage pies you might be served if there were any such thing as a British fast-food chain. Delicious, and salvation to the bleary-eyed salaryman, stumbling to his bullet train after a night on the *shochu*. Nonetheless, the mashed-potato base of Japanese croquettes lacks the inimitable creaminess furnished by a thick white sauce. In the Netherlands, *bitterballen* are spherical *kroketten* typically served with evening drinks. Beef *bitterballen* are often based on beef stock, rather than milk, and are a revelation when made with espagnole (page 168). Follow the starting point for croquettes, using 6 tbsp butter to ½ cup flour, and 2 cups of a good-quality beef stock. If you're not using a naturally gelatinous, homemade beef stock, stir 2 soaked and squeezed-out leaves of gelatin into the cooked croquette mixture once it has cooled a little, at step 4, before you stir in the chopped, cooked beef (instead of the chicken).

MUSHROOM & CIDER

Asturias is a fertile, mountainous region of northwestern Spain, a place of sea mists and damp valleys, well suited to mushrooms and alcoholic cider production. According to local myth, mischievous *duendes de seta*, or mushroom sprites, steal into cider mills at night and drink themselves silly. It's why the *paraguas de pequeñito* ("little fellow's umbrella"), the species of mushroom under which the *duendes* are said to sit, has such a large, drooping cap: to help hungover goblins keep the sun out of their eyes. None of this is true, but you may wish it were after tasting one of these croquettes: The combination of piquant cider and musty mushroom is almost mythically delicious. Gently cook 1½ cups trimmed and diced mushrooms in some butter until soft, then follow our starting point, replacing the chicken with the mushrooms, and ½ cup of the milk with a none-too-dry hard cider.

OLIVE

Classic croquette ingredients are salty. So why shouldn't the olive have a croquette to call its own? By my reckoning black, or a mixture of black and green, works best. Nice to make the roux in our starting point with 6 tbsp olive oil instead of the butter. Chop ¾ cup pitted olives, and consider infusing the milk with 1 lightly crushed garlic clove, warming it gently and leaving for a few minutes before tasting for strength; discard the clove once the desired depth of flavor is achieved. Garlic milkshake is an acquired taste, but remind yourself that you're doing this for the sake of the croquettes.

ORANGE & CINNAMON

Sweet croquettes: no reason why not. I made a batch with milk infused with orange zest and cinnamon. For 2 cups milk, use the grated zest of 2 navel oranges, a 4-in cinnamon stick, and ¼ tsp ground cinnamon. Use all ground cinnamon (adding an extra ¼ tsp) if you're in a hurry, but the stick will give a nicer flavor. You'll need to strain out the aromatics at the end of step 1. You could also add sugar to the white sauce, although better in my view to serve the croquettes hot and sugar-sprinkled. Proceed from step 5 of the method, cutting the mixture into triangles and adding a few pinches of crushed fennel seeds to the bread crumbs. Eat them straight from the deep fryer and imagine you're at a Saint's Day *feria*.

SAFFRON, PEA & RED BELL PEPPER

A painting "is an experience," not a representation of it, thought Mark Rothko. He was rarely so reductive as to interpret his work, but of *Green and Tangerine on Red* (1956), he related the red to "the normal, happier side of living," and the green rectangle above it to "the black clouds or worries that always hang over us." This croquette is called *Green and Red on Saffron* and symbolizes the pleasures of paella without the worry of washing a large cast-iron pan with rice stuck to the bottom. While the 2 cups milk is warming, infuse it with two pinches of powdered saffron. Cook the peas and finely diced red bell pepper—a handful of each will be about right—in 1 tbsp olive oil for a few minutes, then add them at step 4, in place of the chicken.

SALT COD

On a hot day in July I had an unseasonally comfort-seeking yen for fish pie. On the way to the fresh-fish market I ran through the task ahead of me. Whisking the roux, stirring the béchamel, tweezering bones from the fish, peeling, boiling, and mashing potatoes. By the time I reached the fish market the yen had vanished. Maybe just a quick one at the tapas bar next door. A *copita* of stern fino was set before me. I ordered a plate of salt-cod *croquetas*; they arrived still spitting from the deep fryer. I took my first bite, then ordered a second plate, and a third to be on the safe side. Then another glass of fino, just to be on the comprehensively insured side of safe. *Croquetas de bacalao* or *jamón* are standard fare in tapas bars, but Roux at the Landau in London serves something a notch or three swankier, coated in a handsome black crumb made with squid ink, and served with a fennel purée. You'll need to soak salt cod for 24 hours, with several changes of water, then pick it over, removing any bones, before shredding it: 5 oz (prior to soaking) is a good amount for a base made with our starting-point quantities. Soften 1 finely chopped small onion in 2 tbsp olive oil. Add the shredded salt cod and cook for a few minutes, then set aside. Make up a batch of croquette base, adding the salt-cod mix at step 4, in place of the chicken.

SERRANO HAM

Nacho Manzano is famous for his serrano-ham croquettes. He puts their reputation partly down to the long cooking time of his white sauce: 30–45 minutes, rather than the 5 minutes stipulated in our starting point. Manzano also starts with only 3½ tbsp butter and 6½ tbsp flour per 2 cups milk, cooking 3–4 tbsp diced serrano in the butter before adding the flour. Season once the croquette base has cooked for a while, so that you can judge how much salt the ham has already contributed. Chill the mixture for 24 hours, then pick up the method from step 6, using sunflower oil as the deep-frying medium.

SHRIMP

The Belgian specialty of *garnaalkroketten* contain the *crangon crangon* or *crevette grise* shrimp, which is tiny and tasty. In Ostend, some of the catch is still harvested the old way, by *crevettiers* on horseback. The *crevettier* sits on his hardy cob, up to its girth in the sea, wearing yellow oilskins and scooping up shrimp in his net, dreaming of landing a movie contract or at least a cigarette advertising campaign in Southeast Asia. (Or maybe just of buying a boat.) *Garnaalkroketten* are consumed by the plateful with plenty of good Belgian beer. There is, perhaps, a kind of correlation at work here: Countries that love a good beer seem also to love a good croquette. Some recipes call for a 50/50 mix of milk and shellfish bisque, resulting in a harmoniously persimmon-colored medium for the shrimp, which turn brown when cooked. These same shrimp are known as brown shrimp in the U.K. (no relation to the brown shrimp found in the Gulf of Mexico); the San Francisco "bay shrimp" is similar. Many cooks enrich the croquette base with egg yolk, and sometimes grated cheese.

SWEETBREAD

You might think it extravagant to use the king of all variety meat in a croquette, but sweetbreads needn't be expensive, especially if you are prepared to use lamb's. One thing that makes sweetbreads more popular in professional kitchens than in domestic kitchens is their time-consuming, fiddly preparation. Ideally, they should be soaked and blanched before the deft removal of their gristly, sinewy, and fatty bits, leaving the membrane intact. If you do cut the membrane, and your cutting board is strewn with debris too untidy to serve to anyone but the dog, you can always make croquettes. André Simon gives a recipe including fresh peeled mushrooms, ham, and "if possible, a truffle cut into small dice"—all added, along with cut, blanched sweetbreads, to 1 cup very thick white sauce enriched with 2–3 egg yolks.

Stock, Soup & Stew

STOCK: BROWN
CHICKEN STOCK

page 208

RISOTTO:
RISOTTO BIANCO

page 266

UNSTIRRED RICE:
KEDGEREE

page 258

DAL: TARKA
CHANA DAL

page 252

BEAN STEW:
FABADA

page 246

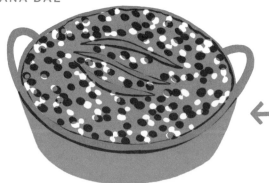

BROTH: POT AU FEU

page 218

PURÉED SOUP:
VEGETABLE SOUP

page 226

CHOWDER

page 232

STEW: LAMB &
VEGETABLE STEW

page 238

S
T
O
C
K
Turning water into stock may not quite warrant miracle status, but it almost does, and it's considerably easier to achieve for the unanointed. Like breadmaking, stockmaking is a habit worth acquiring and requires very little hands-on time from the cook. A good chicken stock can be ready in the time it takes to watch a movie. Many cookbooks claim that bouillon cubes will do in most circumstances. Don't believe a word of it. It is merely what the consensus thinks you want to hear: You're busy (so buy stuff that will save you time).

Powdered or cubed bouillon can give your cooking the same thin, repetitive backbeat that the Linn 9000 sequencer gave to Stock, Aitken, and Waterman records. If you're making a dish where stock is a prominent feature, like French onion soup, it's hard to avoid the effort proper stock demands. Treat your guests to white truffles, exotic flavor combinations, or a rare citrus fruit with an unpronounceable name, but good stock trumps the lot and sticks as much in the mind as it does on the lips. In the early stages of planning this book I drew up a list of the best things I have ever eaten, and it was remarkable how many of the dishes depended on stock for their deliciousness.

Stockmakers are like survivalists or the self-employed. They hoard bones and peelings with the ardor of a post-apocalyptic shack-dweller happening on a scrap of corrugated iron, or a freelancer with a shopping bag full of stationery receipts. The mildly committed might intervene at the sight of a chicken carcass about to be tipped into the trash; a true fanatic will watch like a spaniel while you carve the roast. I veer between the two extremes. I was at a friend's house the other day and was about to ask, quite casually, if I could have the pile of chicken bones left over from lunch, when another guest claimed them for her pet parrots. I folded my ziplock bag back into my handbag with good grace. But my Christmas-card list is now two addresses shorter.

The lessons you learn making stock and broth apply to most of the dishes on this continuum. Little technical skill is required to make a soup or stew. This sort of cooking depends more on your feel for ingredients, cooking times and temperatures, taste and flavor. The challenge is to broker the best deal between solids and liquids. Optimal texture and flavor is the dividend. The opportunity to adjust and improve flavor during the cooking period is particularly satisfying. Baking rarely affords such luxury—once your buns are in the oven, your bets have been placed.

I use chicken stock as the exemplar for our starting point. Pampered parrots notwithstanding, chicken stock is doubtless so familiar due to the ready availability of carcasses. Once you really get hooked on homemade stock, however, you may find your frozen hoard of Sunday-roast debris insufficient. With any luck your local butcher, if you have one, will supply raw bones and scraps for free or next to nothing, especially if you buy the occasional pound of chuck or T-bone from him. Chicken carcasses and ham bones constitute the unofficial loyalty scheme of the independent butcher. (Same thing goes for fish heads and bones from the fish merchant.) There are, however, other options if your shopping is restricted to the supermarket, or you're short of time.

The first option is to use a combination of bones and meat. Chicken thighs lend excellent flavor and viscosity, thanks to their relative proportions of skin, bone, and flesh, and can furnish a quart of very good stock in about 40 minutes. In a 2-quart saucepan, brown 2¼ lb chicken thighs quickly in a little bland oil, stirring from time to time. Browning contributes depth of flavor to all stocks, soups, and stews, and will make what is often referred to as a "brown stock." (A "white stock" is made with bones and meat in the raw.) For a sweeter, more caramelized stock, make a mirepoix of diced onion, carrot, and celery once the chicken is underway and add that, too. Pour in 6 cups *boiling* water (which will speed things up, and won't affect the flavor, although it will make the liquid a bit cloudy). Reduce the heat and simmer very softly for at least 30 minutes before straining. One advantage of this quick method is that the meat will not have been boiled into inedibility, so you're only an onion and some Arborio away from a very good chicken risotto. Note that the flavor of this stock is mild, as it should be for a risotto. It will also make a superior vegetable soup, lending both flavor and body, but for chicken noodle soup you'll probably want to reduce the stock to concentrate its flavor. By how much depends a bit on how tasty the original chicken was, and so frequent tasting is essential. Remember to add a few grains of salt to each tasting to bring out the flavor.

To cooks with less than 40 minutes to spare, I would recommend layering flavor into double-diluted store-bought stock. This can be done in 10–15 minutes. Extra water is added for the simple reason that at its recommended dilution, most convenience stock has a whiff of canned meat, if not cat food, which is disguisable in a busy soup or stew, but brutally exposed in a dish that features stock more prominently. The idea is to give your additive-laden stock a top note of actual food, like cladding your cinder-block bungalow in handsome split-oak clapboards. I once simmered a sliced leek, a handful of frozen peas, some asparagus trimmings, and a pinch of fennel seeds in some store-bought vegetable stock for just 10 minutes. Strained, it made one of my best-ever asparagus risottos. Likewise, for French onion soup, simmer a small quantity of ground beef, some fresh thyme, and a dash of dry sherry in the stock for 10 minutes, then strain. Organized cooks might freeze small quantities of ground meat to add a truer flavor to dilute stock (a rare reason to buy strangely creepy ground poultry). Note, however, that without bones your stock will lack the viscosity that separates truly epic stock from the plain good stuff—although you can cheat here too, with the cautious application of gelatin, as long as you're not planning to boil the liquid afterward.

The differences between stock, broth, and soup are as murky as a consommé shouldn't be. Alan Davidson maintains that "broth occupies an intermediate position between stock and soup," and this is the position I have taken in the continuum. In the case of broth, the solid ingredients are generally consumed with the liquid, whereas they are discarded for stock. The simplicity of this distinction is clouded by cooking waters, which can be categorized neither as broths nor stocks. This is not to say they aren't worthy of consideration. Cabbage water, for instance, is a mainstay of good gravy, and potato water can lend the crust of homemade bread a deeply satisfying crunch. If you've used water to boil something, pause before pouring it down the sink. Fuchsia Dunlop notes that in China, the waters used to cook both fermented black beans and sprouted soybeans are used as stock. It's traditional in the Périgord to prepare a soup called *bougras* from cabbage and the water used to cook blood sausage. Cooking waters may not merit valuable freezer space, but they are too rich and easy a source of flavor to discard without thought.

When I think of broth, I envisage a translucent, unthickened, and intensely flavored liquid served in one of three weights: at its lightest, the thin, clear soup known as consommé; more substantially, and with tidbits floating in it, in the case of Thai *tom yum* or Italian *pasta in brodo*; and at its heartiest with assorted chunks of meat or fish, as in French *pot au feu* and bouillabaisse. I use *pot au feu* as the starting point for broth—which, in its simplicity of preparation, differs negligibly from stock. Apart from deciding whether or not to brown the meat and vegetables, and choosing your aromatics, all you need do is work out the optimum simmering time for each of your ingredients, and add them to the pot in the right order.

With most meat broths, the key is not so much how quickly you can cook them, as identifying the sweet spot whereby a pleasingly soft texture is achieved without cooking them for so long that the flavor leaches out. (There is generally some leeway, especially when you're cooking meat on the bone, or tough cuts from the hard-working parts of the animal like legs and shoulder.) Removing the fat from the broth is probably the biggest hassle with dishes such as these, and even that is a cinch if you cook it a day in advance, chilling the broth overnight so that the fat solidifies on top. I like Elizabeth David's suggestion to time the cooking so that the meats are ready to serve for lunch or dinner with a little broth, and cornichons and mustard alongside. The remainder of the broth can then be stored in the fridge for the following day, when it will invariably taste better, and is more easily de-fatted.

PURÉED SOUP The next starting point on the continuum is puréed soup. Again, the method is straightforward. Start as if making a broth, but once the solids are cooked through, purée them with the liquid. As with broth, the key technical consideration is how long it will take your ingredients to cook. In most cases, they should be cooked for long enough to make them purée-able, but no longer, so as not to take the edge off their freshness. Note that some types of soup are to be found under other starting points—for example, lentil soup under dal (page 254), nut soups under tarator (page 306), and avgolemono, the Greek chicken stock and lemon soup, under crème anglaise (page 487). However, "puréed soup" covers many classics, like cream of tomato, vichyssoise, watercress, mushroom, and curried root vegetable.

The liquid nature of soup is what makes it so adaptable: You can almost always add or subtract (by reduction), making it the ideal training ground for the culinary ad-libber. It's where I started, although in the early days I was so lashed to the recipe book I probably would have looked up how to butter the bread I was serving on the side. The odds and ends in your salad crisper and vegetable rack are a good (which is to say low-stakes) source of improvisatory material. Other than remembering that a single portion of soup amounts to 1–1¼ cups, there are two guidelines worth following. Firstly, err on the side of too little liquid. It's usually quicker and easier to dilute an intense soup than it is to embolden, or thicken, a watery one. Simply submerge your ingredients in your chosen cooking liquid, or follow this rule of thumb: 1 onion and 1½ lb of vegetables will need 5 cups of liquid. Secondly, it's worth having some notion of the result you're aiming for. A bubbling pot of soup on the stovetop is a tempting call to incessant fiddling. Even if you're making something that calls for a range of ingredients, like minestrone, tinkerers might want to rein themselves in. An unadorned purée of one or two ingredients can be the essence of good eating—the tomato and carrot soup on page 230 being a case in point.

C The definition of chowder is not just murky; it's as slippery as the
H eel you might find lurking in its depths. In contemporary cooking,
O chowder is generally considered a soup, in line with its position
W on the continuum between soup and stew, but historically it was
D hearty enough for salty types with Queequegian appetites to eat
E it as the main meal of the day. The word itself is thought to be
R derived from the French *chaudière*, or cauldron. The story goes that fishermen would gather around the communal cookhouse *chaudière*, each contributing some fish in exchange for a share of the meal. The custom took hold, and spread along the Atlantic seaboard all the way down to New England.

The earliest documented chowders were very simple and made with the catch of the day. Salt pork would be laid on the bottom of the *chaudière*, followed by layers of potato, onion, butter, and fish fillets. A mixture of stock made from the fish heads and bones, milk, and seasoning would be poured over, before the dish was cooked for half an hour. Hardtack was added when the chowder was nearly done, dissolving into and thickening the broth. You might point out that cooking fish fillets for 30 minutes isn't going to do their texture any favors, and you would be right. The compensation is in the flavor.

Modern recipes stipulate a shorter cooking time—often just a few minutes—so a highly flavorful fish stock is essential to achieving a similar depth of character. A terrific seafood stock can be ready in as little as 20 minutes, so while the total cooking time will still hover around the half-hour mark, the fish in your chowder will be sable-soft.

The starting-point quantities for chowder can easily be committed to memory: They're along similar lines to the puréed soup, using a pound of potato and one of fish instead of the vegetables, and splitting the 5 cups of liquid between stock and milk. Bacon is optional. Some cooks would mash some of the potato to thicken the broth, but this can be achieved in other ways—by beginning with a roux (as in our starting point) or by finishing with heavy cream. Chowder simply must not be watery: Fishermen see quite enough water all day.

Hardtack, or ship's biscuits, may no longer be everyone's thickening agent of choice, but the small crackers commonly supplied with bought soups in the U.S. are a welcome alternative. When I was first handed a package, in a Minneapolis diner, I gave the waitress the kind of indulgent smile you might give a toddler presenting you with a single, disconnected section of toy train track. But it didn't take long to discover that pushing a salty, soup-softened cracker into a paste in the roof of your mouth is an addictively pleasant experience.

S The progression from soup to chowder describes a gentle ascent
T toward heartiness, continuing on to stew. I find that even seasoned
E improvisational soupmakers balk at being inventive with a stew.
W Often the risk of spoiling expensive meat or fish is a justifiable cause for caution. As, of course, is the possibility of ending up with a main course that nobody wants to eat. In most cases, however, you can throw open your pantry doors and be bold, especially if you keep the following questions in mind.

1 What are the main features of the dish I'm making—meat, fish, poultry, vegetables?
2 What liquid am I cooking them in—water, stock, wine, juice, tomatoes, milk, a mixture? And how much of it? A small amount for a braise, or plenty for a stew?
3 What aromatics am I using—a mirepoix, a "holy trinity" (onion, celery, green bell pepper), bouquet garni, spices, herbs, cocoa?
4 Am I going to thicken it? If so, how—with a roux, mashed vegetables, beurre manié, cornstarch, cream, ground nuts?
5 How long will it need to cook?
6 How am I going to cook it? In the oven, on the stovetop, or in a slow cooker?

If you need any convincing re: unconventional flavor combinations, allow me to direct your attention to the duck with chocolate and Marsala on page 242, or Vietnamese duck and orange on page 245.

Alternatively, if you've never tried poultry cooked with pomegranate and walnuts (*fesenjan*), take a look at pages 310–14. Along with other Persian, Indian, and Moorish nut-based stews, such as korma and *carne en salsa de almendras*, *fesenjan* can be found on the nuts continuum (which would, in theory, intersect with this continuum, as the methods have much in common).

B
E
A
N
Bean stew and dal are the next two starting points. Most recipes call for the pulses to be soaked before cooking. For the simplest bean stews, all the ingredients are then put in a pan and cooked together, as in the example recipe, the classic Asturian dish known as *fabada*.

S
T
E
W
In some variations, like Boston baked beans, the pulses are soaked and cooked until tender *before* they're combined with the meat and aromatics. This approach may derive from a precaution: making sure the beans are soft before mixing them with more expensive ingredients, or keeping them separate from salted meats, as some cooks believe salt prevents pulses from ever softening. Opinions on this, and whether beans should be given a long soak before cooking, differ considerably. I soak whenever possible. When it isn't, a quicker method is to boil the beans for about 10 minutes, let them soak in the hot cooking water for an hour, rinse, and then cook as if you'd soaked them overnight.

In some recipes, canned (i.e. precooked) beans are a perfectly workable option. You might narrowly get away with using canned *fabes* (or big lima beans) in a *fabada*, because it contains a decidedly flavorful mixture of smoked and unsmoked pork, chorizo, and morcilla, but the superiority of dry beans in this context lies in their slow plumping-up in the cooking liquid, the deliciousness of which is partly down to the flavor of the beans themselves. Some *fabada* recipes call for a little saffron, but I prefer it without. The dish needs no other embellishment than the seasoning in the sausages; it's a happy marriage of meat and beans that no other ingredient should put asunder. I have read modern recipes that claim you can do without the morcilla. Ignore these with extreme prejudice. They are written by the sorts of people who thought The Doors could go on without Jim Morrison. Leave the morcilla on the side of your plate, if you must, but it has to go into the pot, where it lends the broth a darkness as solemn as "Riders on the Storm."

Researching bean stews left me clear about one thing: The world needs more bean stew recipes. Or at least a few that don't combine pork and beans. Ken Albala points out that bean dishes were historically excluded from cookbooks because they were considered coarse; if you had to eat them, you probably knew how to prepare them. Meanwhile, bar the odd cassoulet, I couldn't recall ever seeing a bean stew on a restaurant menu. Or any bean-seafood combinations. I had, as my research revealed, forgotten about Iberian variations on *fabes con almejas*, dry white beans (of varying types) with clams. In *Larousse* I found a recipe for flageolets cooked with salt cod in place of the more traditional salted meats. Jane Grigson's *Fish Cookery* contains only one dry bean recipe, although it is a corker. In *haricots à l'anchoïade*, the little white beans are cooked and mixed, still warm, with anchovy mayonnaise. A spoonful of these, in place of the usual sugary tomato sort, will bring out the best in your breakfast sausages and bacon.

As for meat- or fish-free bean recipes, the newfangled veggie-centric cookbooks I looked at had little to say. This may be for want of appropriate salty ingredients to infuse the beans with flavor, as ham or seafood can. There's miso, of course, or seaweed, or olives, but in my experience few have yielded very satisfactory results. Of those I tried, the most effective was a combination of soy sauce with burnt eggplant and paprika; the recipe this inspired (page 248) passes the crucial bean stew test—it needs nothing other than a bowl, a fork, and a basket of crusty bread. Similarly, the Greek dish of lima beans with honey, tomato, and dill (page 251) is one of my favorites in the book, and can be made saltier with a scattering of feta cubes. Incidentally, while I was looking for vegetarian bean recipes, I kept coming across *ful medames*, eaten in Egypt by every social class at every mealtime. It's too simple to be called a stew, made as it is with nothing but dried beans that are boiled and fully or partially mashed. Lemon wedges, crushed garlic, parsley, cumin, olive oil, fresh flatbread, and (often) hard-cooked eggs are then handed around to complement your hill of beans.

D A similar principle applies to dal, monotonous without the pickles,
A chutneys, raita, rotis, and fresh herbs commonly served with it. Poke
L me in the eye with a cinnamon stick but I never saw the point of dal until I made it myself. I'd eaten dal in every shade and consistency; dals as thick as the swamps of the Ganges-Brahmaputra Delta and as thin as Ceylon tea, dals sneering with tamarind and so laden with medicinal turmeric and dusty cumin that they tasted like a failing hospital. It wasn't until I settled on a tarka chana dal recipe, a hybrid of several I tried during a month in which I cooked nothing but Indian food, and made it over and over again, that I realized it had become a comfort food I craved like a dish from my childhood—a rare compliment from my gastric subconscious.

Naming principles in Indian food tend to be as plain as its flavors are complex: "Tarka chana dal" is dal made with chana and embellished by a tarka. Chana is a small, split, skinned chickpea, simmered to softness. Tarka adds pizazz: It's essentially a fry-up of aromatics, a pan of sizzling ghee infused with, say, cinnamon sticks, cloves, bay, mustard seeds, curry leaves, cardamom pods, sliced onion, and chopped tomato. This is stirred into the dal at the end of its simmer, transforming it from contemplative recluse to the life of the party. The aroma is enough to reawaken anyone's appetite. Tarkas should be used more widely, and not just for dal. Yotam Ottolenghi applies something similar to a sweet corn chowder, dry-frying ground cumin and coriander seeds before adding butter, smoked paprika, white pepper, and salt.

UNSTIRRED From lentils to rice: Broadly the same principle applies to the starting point for unstirred rice as it does to that for dal—the grain is hydrated with flavored water or stock to create a comforting one-bowl dish. The technique is highly adaptable; it can be used to make kedgeree, jambalaya, or an inauthentic but delicious sort of vegetable biryani. All three can be made with water rather than stock, as their ingredients are so strongly flavored: kedgeree with its pungent smoked fish and curry spices; jambalaya with its slow-cooked "holy trinity" of onion, celery, and green bell pepper, plus skin-on, bone-in chicken, shellfish, and spicy sausage; vegetable biryani with onions, garlic, vegetables, and an aromatic curry paste. It's rather as if you were making a delicious broth and cooking rice at the same time. Use the absorption method, and a reliable liquid-to-rice ratio, and you'll end up with a complete meal in half an hour.

The usual means of cooking risotto is a high-maintenance variation on the absorption method. Instead of trapping the rice in an enclosed space and forcing it to take up all the stock or water that's poured into it, risotto rice is gradually fed liquid in small amounts, allowing the grains to hydrate slowly while the starch is simultaneously coaxed out of them by stirring, thus rendering the remaining liquid somewhat creamy. For 2 cups short- or medium-grain rice, our starting point for unstirred rice calls for 3⅓ cups stock. In risotto's case, assume this is the minimum you'll use—it can sometimes take up to 50 percent more to cook the rice perfectly. Risotto has attracted its share of prescriptivists, who will tell you that no risotto is ready until a spoon will stand up in it, or that its surface should describe a gentle wave like Le Corbusier's Ronchamp chapel. Take it from me: The only reliable test is to put some in your mouth. A grain between the teeth will tell you if it's done, or better still, very nearly done, at which point it can be removed from the heat.

The risotto police may also insist on water as the liquid, on the basis that it allows you to appreciate the flavors of the other ingredients—including, of course, the rice. The idea is appealing. I would also like to be the sort of person who can appreciate the stitchwork on a piece of clothing. But I'm not. Even with strongly flavored feature ingredients, risotto made with water is too subtle for me. The weaker "white" stocks often stipulated by Italian food writers seem much more like it. The rice benefits from the leg-up in flavor, and there's a boost in body, too. Unreduced, the quick chicken-thigh stock outlined earlier is an option, although I prefer my risotto more boldly flavored. My ideal is Mark Hix's heavenly butternut squash risotto (page 268): Made with the squash peelings, and enhanced by typical aromatics, the stock only takes an hour to prepare. You won't get to watch a movie while it bubbles away, but you could get started on a box set.

Stock: Brown Chicken Stock

Homemade stocks are the elixirs that underpin really good soups, stews, and sauces. I use chicken as the example for our starting point simply because it's easy to procure the raw materials. This is a classic method using standard ingredients, but some faster alternatives that yield very satisfying results are given on page [201]. No one new to stock need get too hung up on the technicalities. You really can just put all that remains of a roast chicken, broken up, in a big pot, cover it with water, and simmer on a low, low heat for a couple of hours to create the basis of a fabulous risotto or noodle dish.

For about 3 cups flavorsome stock—how flavorsome will depend on the cooking time and level of reduction

INGREDIENTS
2¼ lb chicken carcasses/bones/pieces [A] [B]
1 onion, quartered (but not peeled) [C]
1 celery stalk, cut into a few pieces [C]
1 carrot, cut into a few pieces [C]
Tomato paste, wine, or vermouth—optional
4–6 cups water, or enough to cover [D]
Salt
A few parsley stalks [C]
1 bay leaf [C]
1 tsp black peppercorns [C]
2 egg whites, to clarify—optional

1   Brown the scraps/pieces in a large saucepan or stockpot over a medium to high heat using a little bland oil. (For larger quantities than those given above, you'll need to work in batches, in which case you might prefer to do the browning in a 400°F oven. This will, however, carry a risk of burning, and anything remotely singed will need to be excluded from the pot.) The vegetables can also be browned, but if you'd rather avoid the resulting sweetness, add them raw at step 4.

2   Add the tomato paste, wine, or vermouth, if using, and let cook for 1 minute. Pour the water into the pot and place over a medium to high heat.
    Tomato paste, or a few tablespoons wine or vermouth, will enrich the stock. Starting with cold water helps keep the stock clear, as fewer insoluble proteins are drawn out of the bones. If clarity is less important than speed, use boiling water; it won't make any difference to the flavor.

3 Just as the liquid approaches boiling point, turn down to a slow simmer. Skim away any scum as it rises to the surface. If it's a clear stock you're after, a slow simmer means a barely perceptible shimmer. If clarity isn't a consideration, it can go a little bubblier.

4 Season with a little salt, if desired, and add the parsley, bay, and peppercorns when the scum desists. Add the vegetables too, if you didn't at the browning stage. Received opinion recommends not salting until the very end of the cooking process. I'm in the minority who add a little salt early on (¼ tsp for these quantities), knowing that I won't reduce the finished stock so much that the extra salt will make it unpalatable. Some cooks prefer to add the herbs and vegetables considerably later—say an hour before the simmering time is up—as they begin to lose their fresh flavor if cooked for too long. Nonetheless, as in a stew, there's nothing wrong with slowly cooking them for a few hours.

5 Cook, uncovered, for 2–3 hours, skimming as necessary. Alternatively, slide the pot, partially covered, into a 200°F oven and leave it there for 3–4 hours. The low temperature will yield a fine-tasting, uncloudy stock.

6 Strain the stock ᴱ (through cheesecloth, if you have it), then pour back into the pan and simmer to reduce as required. Taste and add salt, depending on the stock's ultimate use. Once cool, your stock can be refrigerated for 1 week or frozen for 6 months. Short of burning the pan dry, it's impossible to over-reduce: You can always re-dilute. You can under-reduce, however. If you're using the stock immediately, remove as much fat as you can by skimming or blotting the surface with paper towels. If time permits, cool and then chill the broth, so the fat solidifies on top and can be easily lifted off.

7 If you want to clarify your stock, you have two choices. After you've strained and chilled it and removed the fat from the top, whisk the egg whites, then add them to the cool stock in a pan. Slowly bring it to a gentle simmer and cook for 30–40 minutes, by which time the egg white will have formed a raft that can be lifted off, along with all of the impurities it collected as it rose to the surface. The downside of this technique is that it can also remove some of the stock's flavor, so it's common to whisk the egg with some extra raw ingredients, say a little ground meat. The other method, as recommended by Heston Blumenthal, is to freeze the cooled stock in an ice-cube tray, then transfer the cubes to a cheesecloth-lined sieve set over a bowl. Cover and leave in the fridge while the stock drips itself clear—this can take a day or two. It's the gelatin in the stock that makes the Blumenthal method work, so it can't be used for vegetable stock (unless gelatin has been added).

A Pale or "white" chicken stock is made with raw bones. Some cooks think you get a cleaner flavor if you rinse the bones in cold water first. Continue from step 2.

B Frozen and fresh bones/carcasses can be mixed if you give them all a good few hours of simmering. The same goes for frozen meat, as long as it has reached its required safe internal temperature before you finish. Clearly, large pieces of meat or anything on the bone will take longer.

C Chicken stock can be flavored with a wide range of aromatics, or, conversely, left as it is if you'd rather keep it neutral (and thus adaptable). Options include turnip, parsnip, sweet potato, watercress, lettuce, red or yellow bell peppers, zucchini, kale, bok choy, bean sprouts, green beans, mushrooms or mushroom peelings, sweet corn cobs (stripped of kernels), celeriac, Swiss chard, tomato, cucumber, bouquet-garni herbs, juniper berries, cilantro leaf/stalk, coriander seeds, ginger, lemongrass, garlic (a whole bulb sliced in half horizontally), celery leaves, star anise, fennel seeds, and allspice. Avoid asparagus, beet, broccoli, cauliflower, curly endive, globe artichoke, green bell peppers, radicchio, spinach, and Brussels sprouts. They're variously too bitter, sulfurous, or earthy. Note that squash and potato peelings cause cloudiness.

D Most meat stock recipes call for 2¼ lb bones/meat to 4–6 cups water, or a little more than enough to cover the solids. It may need a bit more every now and then to keep everything submerged. Naturally, the smaller the quantity of water, the quicker the stock will intensify—even more so when the solids are packed tightly into the pan.

E Once you've strained out the bones and aromatics from your first stock, you can use them again, as Ferran Adrià recommends, to make a second stock, which can be used in place of water the next time you make stock. This way, you can tell people who brag about making their own stock that you make *your* own stock with your own stock.

BEEF

For a brown beef stock, follow the starting point, using beef bones instead of chicken, but simmer the stock with the pan partly covered, and for 4–5 hours, before straining and reducing as necessary. I must confess that I have never been pleased with any of the beef stocks I have made using just bones. Avoid disappointment by making broth instead (page 218); the flavor of bones *and* meat is always a success.

DASHI

Dashi is a Japanese seaweed-based stock. It can be made with just two ingredients: kombu seaweed and water. Buying the ingredients has historically been the most challenging thing about dashi, but they are now easily available online. To make kombu dashi, immerse ½ oz dried kombu in 2 quarts water and place over a medium heat. Turn down to a simmer just before the water reaches boiling point; keeping the heat low is crucial to achieving a delicate flavor. Cook for 20 minutes, strain, and cool. To make *katsuo* dashi, the fishy version, gently submerge 2 oz *katsuobushi* (dried tuna shavings) in the finished kombu dashi. Place over a low heat and when the water seems on the point of trembling, take off the heat and leave for 5 minutes, then strain. Use right away, or cool and keep in the fridge for up to 2 days; opinions differ on the advisability of freezing dashi. If you'd rather avoid the expense and hassle of seaweed and tuna shavings, instant dashi powder is available. Tim Anderson prefers it to from-scratch dashi, at least for home cooking, and says it has the added benefit of being great sprinkled on fries. Aside from its use in miso soup, noodle dishes, and *chawanmushi* (page 471), dashi has many non-Japanese applications: Consider it for soups, chowders, stews, and bean and rice dishes on this continuum.

FISH

Even if you have no immediate call for the head and bones your fish merchant has removed from the portion of white fish you have just bought, ask for them anyway. Ask nicely and he may even trim the gills (which impart a nasty flavor to stock) and chop the bones into small pieces if you doubt the heft of your own knife collection. Back home, you can bag and freeze them for another day, but why wait? This stock is made very quickly, and, restricting ourselves to this continuum alone, can be used for watercress or nettle soup, chowders, fish stews, risotto and paella-type dishes, Thai soups, and curries. For some other uses, see gumbo (page 162) and *romesco de peix* (page 315), as well as velouté (page 174) and beurre blanc (page 534) sauces. I've specified white fish, as oily fish are not usually recommended for stock. That said, salmon stock is good for salmon chowder or soup, so if you have the bones and debris, give it a try to see whether you like it. It's made the same way as white fish stock. For either, follow the starting point, but tend to the lower end of the solids-to-water ratio—2¼ lb to 4 cups is ideal. Try to include at least one fish head: It lends body. And for extra flavor intensity, slowly sweat the fish bones in butter before adding the water. Grate or finely dice the vegetables, as they'll need to yield their flavor during the relatively short simmering time of 20–30 minutes—any longer and the fish bones can start to yield strange flavors. It's not typical to reduce fish stock, but some recipes suggest removing the fish solids after 20 minutes, then adding the vegetables—i.e. flavoring the stock and reducing it at the same time. Some cooks omit the carrot in favor of fennel, either in the form of diced bulb or a pinch of seeds. Escoffier's fish stock is notably less sweet, calling only for onion, parsley, lemon juice, and white wine to be added to the fish and water. Zakary Pellacio, formerly chef at The Fatty Crab in New York, makes a very aromatic fish stock with lemon zest, white peppercorns, coriander seeds, star anise, onion, fennel bulb, garlic, and white wine. However austere or elaborate your version, once you've strained it, let it cool, then refrigerate and use within 4 days, or freeze for up to 3 months.

GAME BIRD

In Balzac's *Eugénie Grandet*, Felix, penny-pinching father of the eponymous heroine, instructs the servant to make stock with wild ravens, pronouncing them "the game that makes the best broth on earth." Crane stock also has its fans. Hunters in the U.S. refer to sandhill crane as "the rib-eye of the sky." But ravens are brainy, and cranes have a life span of a thousand years. Lucky, then, that squabs yield a stock that's "almost beefy in intensity," according to Hugh Fearnley-Whittingstall. Elizabeth David suggests adding a squab to a broth of lean beef and chicken, to boost the richness—a good use for a "rather dull little bird." There's usually no reason not to mix poultry in stocks, although waterfowl can have an unwelcome fishiness that will only become more pronounced in stock form. As for what vegetables you might include, parsnips are a particularly delicious addition to game stock.

LAMB

I suspect the reason otherwise-sensible Brits habitually throw away the debris from cooked leg of lamb, lamb breast, and chops is because lamb stock means Scotch Broth, which in turn means pearl barley, which could serve as a gristle substitute for vegans who like their food to recall what they're missing. Lamb should be stamped with the word "harira," as a reminder of the soup traditionally served to break the fast during Ramadan in Morocco. Harira might contain rice or small pasta, chickpeas, tomatoes, spices, and cilantro. Additions can include saffron, the North African spice mix ras-el-hanout, a fried egg, or a little sourdough starter, stirred in toward the end of the simmering, to give the soup a distinctive tang you might otherwise achieve with a squeeze of lemon juice. Rice or couscous pilafs present a similar opportunity for the experimental cook, and lamb stock makes a fitting background for the combination of eggplant, onion, and dried apricots (page 260) or a luxurious lamb biryani. Watch out for an excess of fat in the stock, which will make it greasy and too farmyardy in flavor. Follow the starting point, but simmer the stock for 3–6 hours before straining and reducing. It's common to add tomatoes and/or thyme to lamb stock, along with the vegetables and bay.

MUSHROOM

An intense mushroom stock can be made by cooking nothing other than chopped button mushrooms over a low heat until they release their liquid—just remember to stop before it all evaporates. For a more typical, longer stock, cook a mirepoix of 1 onion, 1 carrot, and 1 celery stalk, all chopped, in 2 tbsp butter for 3 minutes, then add 2¼ lb sliced button mushrooms. Once the mushrooms have begun to give up their moisture, add 2 quarts water and a bouquet garni. Simmer for about 20 minutes, let stand for 10, then strain. For a more complex and layered version, add 2 oz dried mushrooms, soaked in hot water for 15 minutes, once the stock is simmering. Leeks make a good addition to the mirepoix, or add a little wine in place of some of the water.

PEA POD

Double your green points by making a stock out of your empty pea pods before composting them. Pea pod stock, an essential component of *risi e bisi*, is quintessentially Venetian: dazzling on the surface, murky and fathomless beneath. Some recipes call for the addition of fennel, but try it without first, to appreciate the freshness and savory depth of pure pea. As for the newfangled addition of pancetta: *Va' al diavolo*. Let the pea have its moment in the sun. Pea pod stock is also excellent for vegetarian pasta dishes. Marx Rumpolt, head cook to the Elector of Mainz and author of *Ein new Kochbuch* (1581), suggests the use of pea stock in a sauce made with egg yolk, vinegar, butter, and chopped fresh herbs—a kind of proto-béarnaise—to serve with poached eggs. For *risi e bisi*, shell 2¼ lb peas, set them aside, then wash the pods and pat them dry. In a saucepan, soften the pods in butter for a few minutes, then add 4 cups water and simmer for a further 30 minutes. Strain and set the liquid aside. Soften an onion in butter without browning it. Add the freshly shelled peas and cook for 1 minute before pouring in the stock and bringing to a simmer. After 10 minutes, add 1¼ cups of risotto rice and cook gently, stirring regularly, until al dente. Add parsley to freshen and Parmesan to enrich, but only in modest amounts if you want the flavor of rice and pea to be detectable (you do). If you have a spare 15 minutes, it can be worth blending and straining the pod stock for a *risi e bisi* that's murky but a whole lot deeper.

PORK

Hugh Fearnley-Whittingstall's recipe for pork stock resembles our starting point, except that he recommends roasting the pork bones at 400°F for 10–15 minutes—a shorter time than chicken or beef bones—then simmering the stock for 3–5 hours. The result will be a fitting substitute for chicken stock in most recipes, but will come into its own in gumbo, bean stews, pea or lentil soups, paella-style rice dishes, pork with clams, and the Polish braised cabbage dish *kapusta*. Pork stock is also great for cooking greens, for binding the masa mix in Mexican tamales, or as a medium for ramen noodles. If you're after an aspic to fill the cavity of pork pies, or just a sticky stock, add a pig's foot to up the gelatin content. Pork stock is as intrinsic to Chinese cuisine as veal stock is to classic French, and it's often mixed with chicken or shellfish for a fuller flavor. A good pork and chicken stock can be made with pork ribs and chicken carcasses or pieces. When the scum has desisted, add a little sliced fresh ginger with a dash of Shaoxing wine, plus the chopped white parts of 1 or 2 scallions.

SHELLFISH

Their shells are so delicious that crustaceans can't resist eating their own: Lobsters have specially adapted grinders in their stomachs to deal with the most chitinous bits. Unless you have something similar, I'd recommend making a stock with their shells instead. It's quick and easy, and will make your seafood dishes taste like you've dropped anchor at a secret little place on the Amalfi coast. Serve it as a sauce on simply cooked fish, or for risotto, paella, chowder, bisque, or gumbo. Use the starting-point quantities of 2¼ lb shells to 4–6 cups stock. If you're short of shells, supplement them with de-gilled fish heads and bones. Simmering the shells in water with a few aromatics will yield a light flavor, but for something deeper, first brown the shells in oil or butter with a fennel-enhanced mirepoix, then add a squeeze of tomato paste and a dash of brandy before pouring in the water. Most recipes stipulate a maximum cooking time of 30 minutes, but the Louisiana-raised chef John Besh takes 2 hours over his. For a bisque-y effect, blend the simmered stock, shells and all, before straining out the gritty bits with a fine or cheesecloth-lined sieve. (Leave out any very hard pieces of crab or lobster if you don't want to ruin the blade of your blender or food processor.)

SHIITAKE & KOMBU

A combination of mushrooms and seaweed makes an excellent stock for soup or noodles. Rinse the mushrooms but not the seaweed. In a pan, soak 1 oz (about 6) dried shiitake mushrooms and a 6-in piece of kombu in 6 cups water. After about 15 minutes, place the pan over a medium heat and bring to a simmer. When the stock has been simmering for 3 minutes, remove the kombu and let the stock simmer for a further 12 minutes. Include the shiitakes in your dish, or set them aside for something else. The cooled stock should be refrigerated and used within 3 days.

TURKEY

Of course you can't go for a long walk the day after Thanksgiving. *Somebody* has to keep an eye on the stock. Rather than a curry to use up the leftover bird, use it for a *blanquette de dinde* (page 159), agreeably plain after the seasonal excess, or a gumbo (page 162) as murky as the plot of a TV soap opera. Simply swap turkey for chicken in our starting point for stock; as the turkey is roasted already, there's no need to brown it, so start at step 2.

VEAL

Caldo sin jamón ni gallina, no vale una sardina, say the Spanish— "Stock without ham or chicken isn't worth a sardine." This may be intended as a poke in the eye to the French, so fond of veal stock, pale and rich and neutrally meaty. Michael Ruhlman is rhapsodic: Veal stock, in his view, is up there with the Goldberg Variations and Plato's cave allegory. Make it Ruhlman's way by chopping 2 lb veal bones into 3-in pieces and roasting them, in a pan large enough to spread them out a bit, at 450°F for 45 minutes, turning occasionally. Remove, then turn the oven down to 180°F, and transfer the bones and sticky pan scrapings to a 2-quart ovenproof pot. Pour in 5½ cups water, return to the oven, and cook, uncovered, for 8–10 hours. Whatever length of simmering you decide on, set a timer to add 1 diced onion, 1 diced carrot, and 1 bay leaf for the final hour. Strain through a cheesecloth-lined sieve and you should have about 4 cups of veal stock. You're now seven-eighths of the way to very, very good French onion soup. Just be careful to avoid "stock shock," the trauma caused by the unthinking act of pouring your precious liquid down the sink while retaining what should be the discards.

VEGETABLE

Of all the stocks that come in cubes, vegetable stock must be the least like its fresh counterpart. It's not really clear to me why you'd choose it over plain salted water. A quick, all-purpose vegetable stock can be made with finely diced or grated carrot, onion, and celery, plus some bay leaves, peppercorns, and parsley. Work on the basis of 2 onions, 2 carrots, 2 celery stalks, 12 peppercorns, and a small bunch of parsley to 4 cups of cold water. Bring to a boil and simmer very slowly for 10 minutes, let it rest for 5, then strain. This will yield a light, fresh flavor. For a rich, brown vegetable stock, do as above, but cook the vegetables in oil (or oil and butter) until golden before adding the water, and increase the simmering time to 1 hour. Vegetable stock can be a little sweet, so for a balancing savoriness consider adding soy sauce, Parmesan rind, lentils, shiitake mushrooms, rinsed and drained fermented black beans, or a dab of Marmite. Vegetarians looking for an alternative to the classic mirepoix trio of onion, carrot, and celery might consult pea pod stock (page [213]), lentil broth (page [222]), or butternut squash risotto (page [268]); see also c under Leeway (page [210]) for a list of ingredients to use or avoid in stocks.

Stock → Other Directions

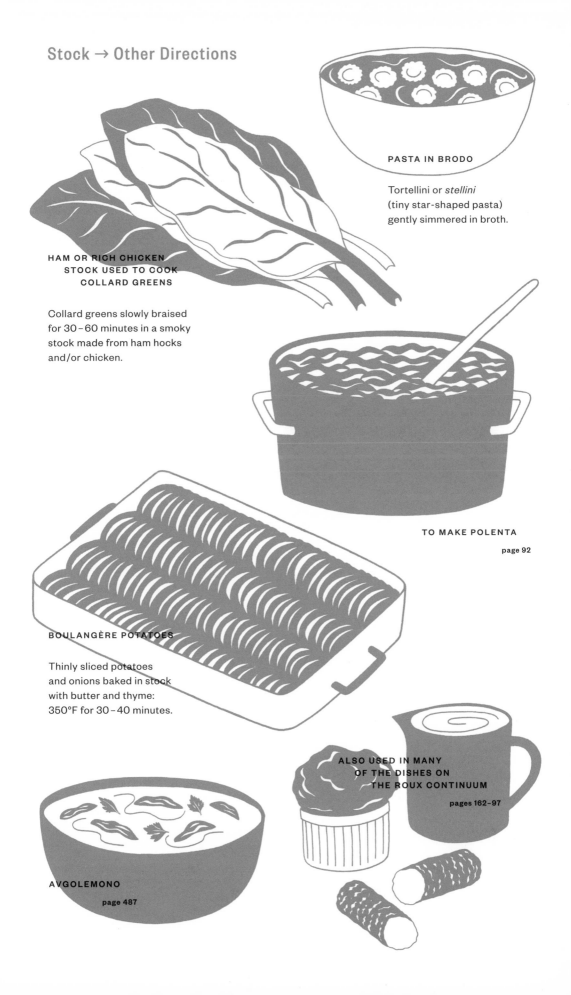

PASTA IN BRODO

Tortellini or *stellini* (tiny star-shaped pasta) gently simmered in broth.

HAM OR RICH CHICKEN STOCK USED TO COOK COLLARD GREENS

Collard greens slowly braised for 30–60 minutes in a smoky stock made from ham hocks and/or chicken.

TO MAKE POLENTA

page 92

BOULANGÈRE POTATOES

Thinly sliced potatoes and onions baked in stock with butter and thyme: 350°F for 30–40 minutes.

ALSO USED IN MANY OF THE DISHES ON THE ROUX CONTINUUM

pages 162–97

AVGOLEMONO

page 487

Broth: Pot au Feu

Broth is a stock with benefits—the ingredients that create it are eaten rather than discarded. *Pot au feu* is a good basic example. It's a "poem of the French soul," according to Daniel Boulud, and one that takes a good while to compose. Marlene Dietrich liked to make it in the lulls between scenes. It doesn't, however, require a lot of attention, so there'll be plenty of time to run your lines and pluck your eyebrows. As with stock, you may or may not brown the ingredients before adding cold water, bringing it slowly to a simmer, and turning the heat right down for a slow, slow cook. Unlike stock, you need to know when to retrieve the meat from the pot so it doesn't overcook—your best bet is simply to extract a sample and taste it.

For a broth and main course for 10–12

INGREDIENTS

3 lb boneless beef (shank, chuck, flank, brisket), in large pieces A
4 lb bone-in beef (shank, short rib, oxtail), in large pieces A
4 medium carrots, peeled and cut into large chunks B
4 celery stalks, cut in half B
4 medium onions, peeled (but left whole), 2 studded with a clove B
4 leeks, trimmed, rinsed, and cut into large chunks B
1 bouquet garni of bay leaf, parsley, and thyme
8 black peppercorns
½ tsp salt
1 lb marrow bones, cut into 2-in pieces, tied up in cheesecloth
    if possible—optional A

1   Place the meat in a pan or stockpot large enough to hold all your ingredients, pour in enough cold water to cover by a couple of inches, then set over a medium heat.
    If you're including types of meat that require notably different cooking times, start by adding those that need to cook the longest and then calculate when to add the others.

2   Just as your broth approaches boiling point, turn it down to a very slow simmer. If scum has begun to collect on the surface, skim until it desists (or it's just a thin, white froth), then add the vegetables, bouquet garni, peppercorns, and salt. Partially cover the pan, using a baking sheet if you don't have a lid big enough, and let the broth simmer for 2½–3 hours. C
    You may need to use a heat diffuser to slow the cooking sufficiently.
    If you prefer your vegetables less cooked, add them a bit later.

3 Add more boiling water or stock when necessary to keep the ingredients immersed.
But don't add so much that you risk diluting the delicious broth.

4 If using, add the marrow-bone pieces 2 hours into the cooking.

5 About half an hour after adding the bone pieces, check the meats to see if they are cooked. If they could do with a little longer, return them to the pan. If they're ready, remove and keep them warm if serving imminently, or cool and refrigerate if serving later. Discard the bouquet garni, strain the broth, and adjust the seasoning.
If you're serving the broth immediately, remove as much fat as you can by skimming or blotting the surface with paper towels. If time permits, cool and then chill the broth, so the fat solidifies on top and can be easily lifted off. If you decide you want a thicker broth, simmer to reduce it, mash some of the strained-out vegetables, and return them, or use a beurre manié (page 242) or a cornstarch slurry.

6 Traditionally, the broth is served as an appetizer, and the meat as a main course with cornichons and mustard.

LEEWAY
A The number and types of beef cuts vary a great deal, but a mixture of lean beef stew meat, bone-in stewing cuts, and bones is common. Other additions include garlic sausage, a small stewing chicken, ham hock, slab bacon, or tongue. A Provençal cook might add lamb, tomatoes, juniper, and white wine.
B The types and quantities of vegetables are highly negotiable. Celeriac, turnip, potato, whole peeled shallots, and quartered cabbage all have their advocates. The cabbage might be cooked separately, in some ladled-off broth, to prevent it from contributing too much sulfurous funk to the stockpot. Note that potato may make the broth cloudy.
C If you'd rather use the oven, put the broth in a 250°F oven at the end of step 2, and cook, partially covered, setting the timer for 2 hours as a reminder to add the marrow bones. You may need to check that the ingredients remain immersed, and add more boiling water if they're not.

CHICKEN

In my twenties I made friends with an elderly man who was selling his house and going to live on a tiny boat. As part of his clear-out he gave me a lidded pot in the shape of a chicken. I thought it was for keeping eggs in, but he assured me it was a "chicken brick," and as it was slightly larger than a medium-size chicken, and therefore able to accommodate one, that's how I used it. In those days I went out most evenings, except on Sunday, when I would scatter the nest-shaped base of the brick with diced onion, carrot, celery, and bacon, sit a chicken on it, pour over some bought stock and white wine, put the hen-shaped lid on, and then slide it into a 350°F oven with an accompanying brood of baking potatoes. Ninety minutes later I had a delicious, comforting dinner that had called for very little effort and would need minimal clearing-up. Quite an advantage over the nine-pan roast. The following night, I'd strain the stock, then reduce it at a determined boil until it was deliciously concentrated. Shredded leftover chicken, some of the vegetable bits, and a nest or two of egg tagliatelle could then be added to the pan, and the finished pasta, glistening with broth, served with toasted pine nuts and chopped parsley. An entire winter of Sundays I made this meal; I still can't watch *University Challenge* on the TV without pining for the smack of sticky chicken stock. If I'd known about Hainanese chicken rice, I might have added it to my lazy Sunday-to-Monday repertoire. It's an interesting variation on broth, with the chicken cooked very lightly, creating a notably soft, almost jelly-like texture. There are several traditional ways to cook Hainanese chicken, some of which call for the bird to be placed in and out of hot and cold water as if at a plunge spa. This is one of the simpler versions. In a large saucepan, cover a 2¾–3¼ lb whole chicken, breast down, with cold water, add a little sliced fresh ginger and scallion, and bring it up to a simmer. Let it bubble gently for 15 minutes, then remove from the heat, cover the pan tightly, and leave for 30 minutes before removing it from the stock, which is used to cook the rice. Chop the cooked chicken into chunks and brush with toasted sesame oil. Serve with dipping sauces, like a sweetened soy sauce diluted with water, or a paste of fresh ginger and garlic, fried golden and salted.

FISH

There's a fish restaurant in a cove in Ibiza, Spain, that you can't reach by car or phone. The result is a peculiar mix of customers rich enough to arrive by yacht, or dogged enough to hike over the bluff from the neighboring beach. All, however, wear the self-satisfied smirk that comes of having schlepped there once before and been turned away, every last table having been taken by an identical mix of bronzed socialites and sweaty ramblers who had been required to reserve in person. The first time I went, finding—sure enough—every last table taken, I made a reservation for the following week and walked back to the beach for a sulk. I was just fishing in my tote bag for the remains of a bag of potato chips when my husband emerged from the sea holding aloft a car key attached to a rental-company fob. He had been snorkeling about twenty feet out, he explained, when he spotted an octopus that had made its home in a cookie tin on the ocean floor. Crikey, I thought. Clearly such vast quantities of drugs had been excreted by visitors to Ibiza that the sea itself was now hallucinogenic. He had hovered above the octopus for a while before noticing that it was repeatedly unfurling one tentacle in a particular direction. Just out of its reach something glinted on the seabed. The car key. It looked un-rusty, as if it had been dropped recently. My husband made a tour of the beach, asking the sunbathers if they had dropped anything. "Mmff," said a man sitting by a rock with his wife and three kids, and took them without so much as a thank you, or an expression of surprise that a complete stranger had just emerged from the sea with his keys, let alone the fact that they had been located by a benevolent cephalopod. We returned to the cove a week later for lunch and sat at a trestle table overlooking the water, snug up against our fellow diners. Nearby, vast stockpots bubbled away on a wood-burning stove. The menu was simple to the point of peremptoriness. You could have the single dish on offer or buzz off. It was *bullet de peix*, a traditional Ibizan stew of the morning's catch, with potatoes and saffron. I suppose it can go either way with single-dish restaurants: Practice either makes perfect or profoundly bored. In this case, we suspected the latter. The catch of the day was bony and earthy-tasting, the yellow broth thin and sour as the patron's welcome. Save yourself the bother and make a *bullet* properly at home. Soften garlic with some peeled chopped tomato in olive oil for 15 minutes, then add some firm potatoes cut into chunks. Pour in a glug of white wine and enough fish stock to cover. Add salt and saffron, then simmer until the potatoes are cooked through. As with most seafood broths and stews, the fish goes in last, simmered for the few minutes it takes to cook. Add some shellfish too, if you like. Your first course consists of the fish and potato with a little of the stock and a dollop of allioli. For the second, a simple dish of rice and cuttlefish or squid is cooked in the remainder of the stock. Later the same afternoon, burping saffron-scented bubbles through his snorkel, my husband went back to visit his octopus friend and complained about the lackluster lunch he'd waited a week to eat. The octopus unfurled its tentacle. This time it was pointing north. We duly drove in that direction until we reached Aguas Blancas, a beautiful beach with an Argentinian-run *chiringuito*, where we sat chewing superb steak and chimichurri baguettes and drinking cold *cañas* of Mahou, staring out over the bright waters at the mysterious ski-jump island of Tagomago.

HAM AND PORK BELLY / BACON

Time was men walked the streets of Spain hiring out ham bones by the minute for housewives to use in their bean pot. In England, it's rare to make ham stock *per se*, since the water used to boil a ham can so easily be added to a soup, or bacon be added to a mirepoix. The chef Richard

Corrigan, however, does make his own non-by-product ham stock, rating it up there with the "cheffiest *jus de veau*," and recalling that his mother would add it to leftover colcannon. It's so usual for pea soup to contain ham stock that it's surprising to learn that it was once routinely made with other stocks, including pork, mutton, beef, and poultry, according to Robert Kemp Philp, author of *The Family Save-all* (1861); he also notes that a ham-shank bone, the root of a tongue, or some pieces of red herring would suffice. (The red herring is a red herring: Philp means strong kipper.) To cook a country-style ham, place it in a deep pan and cover with cold water. Bring to a boil, then reduce to a simmer, allowing 20 minutes per pound plus an extra 20 minutes, or until the temperature in the center of the ham reaches 165°F. David Chang, founder of Momofuku, advises that the *katsuobushi* (dried tuna shavings) usually used to make Japanese dashi (page 211) can be replaced with pork belly. Put a 6 x 3-in piece of dried kombu in 4 cups cold water and bring it to a simmer, then immediately remove the pan from the heat and let the seaweed steep for 10 minutes. Take the kombu from the pan and set aside. Add 4 oz pork belly to the warm water, bring it back to a simmer, then turn down very low and give it 30 minutes while you ponder how to use the cooked seaweed. Strain, cool, and chill the broth, then remove the fat. The broth will keep in the fridge, covered, for a few days; use it to make a meaty miso soup, or to cook your own buckwheat noodles (page 30).

LENTIL

There aren't many occasions in life that call for lentil broth, but it's wise to be prepared. Arabella Boxer's recipe for mushroom soup requires 6 tbsp of brown or green lentils to be cooked in 2½ cups lightly salted water, yielding about 1¼ cups liquid; the lentils are set aside for a different dish (which is what merits its inclusion in the broth section). In a similar vein, Elizabeth David urges us not to throw away the cooking water from cannellini beans. Note that the lima beans with honey, tomato, and dill (page 251) taste markedly better made with the water the dry beans have been cooked in. Bean broths are so good, in fact, that you can comfort yourself, when confronted with a batch of beans that refuse to soften, with the thought that you'll have *something* worth eating (or cooking with) at the end of it. What makes them so interesting is their savory depth, in contrast to vegetable stock made with onion, carrot, and celery, which has a tendency to be sweet. Use pulse broth in soups, noodle dishes, pilafs, or something paella-esque.

OCTOPUS

Greek fishermen bash their octopuses against rocks to tenderize them. Frank Walter Lane notes that, to the same end, islanders in Honolulu treat their catch to a long washing-machine cycle. Any octopuses reading this are advised to move to Japan, where they'll at least get a massage before they're cooked. *O' bror e purpo* is a Neapolitan octopus broth served from street stalls with lots of black pepper and a twist of lemon. It's meant to be excellent if you have a cold. Gennaro Contaldo rinses a whole 2¾-lb octopus, then brings 6 cups water to a boil with 1 tsp salt, 4 bay leaves, and 15 black peppercorns. He then takes the octopus by its head and dips it into the hot water. This will curl the tentacles—it would certainly curl mine—before the whole thing is submerged. Put a lid on the pot and simmer over a low to medium heat for about 1¼ hours or until it's tender. Serve the broth, and cut up the octopus to use in a salad or pasta or rice dish, once your cold subsides and sense of taste returns.

RABBIT

The game meat in *Larousse*'s consommé is taken off the bone and turned into the hodgepodge known as a salpicon, which can be used, among other things, for croquettes (page 192), rissoles, stuffing, small pies, or canapés. That makes it a broth by this book's definition. Whether a consommé counts as a broth or a stock would surely have been beside the point to the self-proclaimed "very fussy consommé maniac" Egon Ronay. Keep the stockpot going too long and the consommé will be too dark, he mutters; go heavy on the vegetables and the consommé will be too acidic. If the cook has been miserly with their meat, using cheap cuts, and not beef shank—or, heaven help us, just bones—the results will be "bland and empty." Ronay singles out the British chef Brian Turner as his kind of consommé-maker, praising Turner's rabbit consommé for its balance—light with a touch of meat essence—and cleanness. To try Turner's version, add 3 rabbit carcasses to 3½ quarts cold water and bring to a boil, then skim. Add 1 leek, 4 celery stalks, 1 onion, 2 carrots, all chopped, plus a 14-oz can of tomatoes, 1 bay leaf, a few juniper berries, a sprig of thyme, and some parsley stalks. Simmer for 2–2½ hours, then strain and let cool. Finely chop another 3 rabbit carcasses with a cleaver. Blend 1 lb large, open mushrooms with 1 carrot, 1 onion, 1 leek, 1 garlic clove, 2 tsp juniper berries, 1 tsp tomato paste, and 2 egg whites. Thoroughly stir this mixture into the cold rabbit stock. Bring to a boil, add a stalk each of thyme and rosemary, and keep stirring frequently until a crust forms. Reduce to a simmer and cook for 1½ hours. Line a sieve with cheesecloth and carefully tip the crust onto the cheesecloth, straining the consommé through it. Season, and garnish as desired.

RED BRAISE

Hypernatremia is a word I learned after trying a recipe for a Chinese pork stew, then frantically googling my symptoms to see if I was about to die from a heart attack (it refers to a level of sodium in the blood above 145 mmol/L). The combination of tachycardia, extreme thirst, and sudden exhaustion brought on by the ingestion of industrial quantities of soy sauce was unpleasant, of course, but the dish was so compelling in other respects that I made it a few more times before investigating the possibility of a similar-tasting dish minus ingredients that make you feel as if you've just completed the *Marathon des Sables*. Here is a hybrid of a pot au feu and a red braise. Brown a 2-in piece of fresh ginger, sliced, and 4 crushed garlic cloves in a little bland oil. Add a split pig's foot and 2¼ lb pork shoulder, cut into large chunks. Brown them a little before adding 6 tbsp Shaoxing wine or dry sherry, 3 tbsp dark soy sauce, 2 tbsp light soy sauce, 2 pieces of cassia bark, 2 star anise, 3 strips of orange peel, 1 tbsp molasses, 2 tbsp brown sugar, and 1 cup water. Bring to a boil, then cover tightly and transfer to a 325°F oven to cook for half an hour. Add 12 fat, spicy sausages (not chorizo) and return to the oven to cook for 1 hour longer. To serve, cut the shoulder, sausages, and pig's foot into smaller pieces. Remove any surplus broth and thicken what's left in the pan by adding a little cornstarch mixed with water, then simmering for a few minutes. Serve with rice and stir-fried greens. Use any leftover stock as a poaching medium or a base for noodle soups.

SAUSAGE

In my marketing days it was once my duty and honor to visit a washing-machine factory in Italy. Try as I might to be businesslike, a regal air came over me as I was shown around the floor, hands clasped behind my back, Duke of Edinburgh-style, nodding with heavy-lidded half-attention at a robot arm inserting the impeller in a centrifugal pump. We moved on to drum assembly. A young guy with a shock of un-mussable black hair and a criminal charisma straight out of Pasolini's *Ragazzi di Vita* was bending sheets of hole-punched metal into cylinders. "Wow," I breathed, "they're made by hand." My host, fussy in trim moustache and starched white lab coat, beamed, under the impression that someone, finally, was showing an interest in his manufacturing process, and not the little Adonis grimacing against the metal's resistance. I was rewarded for my curiosity with a seven-course lunch at a trattoria just outside the town of Fabriano, where I ate a *primo* of *strozzapreti* that I still yearn for every time I crank the dial to Delicates. *Strozzapreti* are thin, rolled strips of pasta, around 4 in in length, served in this instance with sausage and vegetables in a broth so golden it looked as if an egg yolk had been stirred into it. The *secondo* was wild boar with chunky, cubed roast potatoes cooked with rosemary; then a ewe's-milk cheese, farmyardy as a nuzzle from a gregarious sheep, followed by a plate of figs that when cut in half were blood-red flecked with old ivory, like a well-aged steak. We drank a voluble Rosso Conero and finished the meal with a shot of the local grappa and a strong, dark coffee. Not strong enough, alas, to keep me awake back in the meeting room during a lengthy explanation of the latest advance in washing-machine technology, something called fuzzy logic. I felt my blinks begin to lengthen. Logic rapidly lost ground to fuzziness. And then I woke with a start to see my host, so happy back on the factory floor to have found an eager student, unable to disguise his disappointment. I flew back to London only marginally less ignorant about washing machines, but an instant expert on *strozzapreti in brodo*. It's not impossible to find *strozzapreti* outside of Le Marche, but other good-quality dried pasta will do as a substitute, so long as it's not too thick. Tagliatelle is a good bet. This *pasta in brodo* will serve 2. First soften 1 onion, 1 carrot, and 1 celery stalk, all finely chopped, in a little olive oil, then add 2 skinned, roughly crumbled, top-quality, fat, fresh pork sausages and brown them. Add 1¼ cups hot water and 1 tsp salt. Simmer very gently for 15 minutes, before adding the pasta and cooking until it is al dente. Serve in large bowls with a little of everything. Ravioli stuffed with butternut squash are also good cooked and served in *salsiccie brodo*—sausage broth—especially with a flotilla of shaved Parmesan.

VEGETABLE

I first came across the idea of a meat-free *bollito misto* in a book about vegetarian slow-cooking by Robin Robertson. She softens shallots, garlic, and celery in olive oil, then transfers them to the slow cooker with potatoes, carrots, tomatoes, stock, bay leaves, and seasoning, and cooks the whole lot for 5–8 hours, adding some seitan (wheat gluten) and vegetarian sausage just before the end. To me, seitan has an unpleasantly doughy flavor and I'd rather leave it out. I made my *bollito* on the stovetop with turnip, sugar snap peas, Yukon Gold potatoes, pattypan squash, ricotta gnocchi (page 110), bundles of thin green beans bound with string, and scrubbed radishes with their leaves. The radish idea I borrowed from Deborah Madison, who serves her vegetarian *bollito misto* with olive oil and fresh herbs (but also suggests flavored butter as an alternative), as well as the traditional accompaniment for the meat version, salsa verde (page 543). It is tempting to offer all three. Boiled vegetables can be a little samey, particularly if they've been boiled in the same water, so it's nice to have the contrasting condiments—one herb-fresh, one rich, and one salty—to shake things up a bit.

Puréed Soup: Vegetable Soup

As easy as making a broth and then blending the mixture, but it's hard to make something truly outstanding. Preparing a puréed vegetable soup is one of the true tests of a cook's tastebuds. As with stocks, broths, and stews, use the ingredient quantities here as a rough guide—an extra carrot or onion isn't going to hurt. If you're a bit short of a pound, potato makes a reliable back-up to most vegetables, but soup is also a good place to experiment with more unusual combinations, like the pea and pear on page [229].

For 4 servings [A]

INGREDIENTS
1 onion, diced [B]
2 tbsp butter or oil
1½ lb vegetables, rinsed, peeled, and chopped if necessary [C] [D]
5 cups water or stock [E]
Herbs or spices—optional [F]
Salt
Vinegar or lemon juice—optional [G]

[1] Gently soften the onion in the butter or oil for 8–10 minutes.
The longer you cook, the sweeter the taste. Use oil, butter, or a mixture of butter and oil. If using just butter, watch that it doesn't start to burn. Some cooks prefer oil for soups that will be served chilled.

[2] Add the prepared vegetables. Let them cook in the hot fat for 1–2 minutes if you want to enrich and sweeten the soup a little further.

[3] Add the water or stock, bring to a boil, and then reduce to a simmer. Salt modestly.
Use hot or cold water or stock. Bank on simmering for as long as the vegetables need to soften.

[4] Cool a little, remove any hard or unwanted aromatics, then blend or semi-blend as preferred. Thin with stock or water, if required. Taste and adjust the seasoning.
Reheat gently before serving. If adding cream or cheese, reheat the soup very gently.

LEEWAY

A A typical serving of soup is 1–1¼ cups.

B Alternatively, start with a mirepoix (diced onion, carrot, and celery), augmented with chopped bacon or chorizo, if you like—or, for leafy vegetable soups, a mixture of potato and onion. You might also add some chopped garlic when the onion is nearly softened. Omit the onion if you don't want the richness and sweetness it brings.

C Roots, mushrooms, eggplant, squashes, cooked beans, tomato, and brassicas all work to the 1 onion and 1½ lb vegetables to 5 cups liquid rule.

D If using leeks, or leafy greens like radish tops or watercress, mix them with potato—see page [230].

E Stock made from cubes or powders is the standard liquid in so many soup recipes, but water will often give a better flavor, especially if you're softening the vegetables in butter, or finishing the soup with a bit of crème fraîche or cream. A mix of water and milk is good, too. Replace some of the liquid with a few tablespoons of wine, fruit juice, or coconut cream.

F Add hard aromatics—thyme, rosemary, star anise, cumin seeds, cinnamon, cloves, parsley stalks—once the onion has about 1 minute left to go at step [1], remembering to remove them before blending. Add soft herbs like tarragon, basil, mint, and cilantro just before the blending at step [4], or use as a garnish.

G Vegetable soups can be very sweet, so always consider adding a sour ingredient to balance the taste. Taste a little of the soup on a spoon with a few drops of vinegar or lemon juice first—1 teaspoon may be enough for the panful. Also consider yogurt, buttermilk, or crème fraîche.

Puréed Soup → Flavors & Variations

ASPARAGUS

Soup royalty, to be served in Spode. Made according to our starting point, asparagus soup would be a little thin. You might take this as a sign of its refinement—but it *is* possible to be too thin (not to mention too rich). Some recipes call for a little flour as thickener, others for potato, as in the radish-top variation on page 230. Tastes good, but it's a bit blowsy in texture—and asparagus soup must be silky and elegant. My advice is to buy more asparagus and up the ratio of stalk to stock, allowing at least 1 lb 10 oz asparagus to 5 cups liquid. However classy your asparagus, fiber will almost certainly be a problem. There are several ways to approach this. You can peel the fibrous stalk-ends, or make a simple stock out of them, and cook the rest of the spears in it. Or, like me, you can strain them out of the blended soup at the end. Make as per the starting point, using just onion or shallot at step 1. A notable variation, given by Diana Kennedy, is asparagus and orange soup, which calls for scallions rather than onions, and substitutes some of the stock with orange juice, adding the zest too, in an orangey echo of sauce maltaise (page 522).

CANNELLINI BEAN & SAGE

Our starting point works perfectly well with dry beans—once cooked, 1½ cups will be about right for 4 servings. (As a rule of thumb, dry beans double in weight once cooked.) But you will need to add more boiling water as you go, to allow for evaporation during the beans' lengthy cooking time. No need to worry if you haven't soaked your beans overnight. You can simply rinse and cook them, in the expectation that they'll need a longer simmering time than if soaked. As to exactly how long, it's hard to say: Cannellini beans can take anything from 45 minutes to 3 hours, partly depending on their age and size. You might think of pressure cooking as a sure bet, if speed is a priority, but be warned that many cooks think it compromises the flavor and texture of beans. The issue of salt opens up another debate. Most reliable sources agree that salting the beans early during their simmering is a good idea, even if it adds a little to the cooking time. Other cooks claim that adding salt during the soaking gives the best flavor. You'd be forgiven for throwing up your hands and opting for canned beans. But know that in this everyone is pretty much agreed— they don't taste as good as dry. I think the difference is tolerable. Drained of their liquid, 3 (15-oz) cans will yield about 3¾ cups beans, which will be enough for a hearty soup made up with 5 cups stock. Whatever the provenance of the beans may be, for the soup base it is preferable to use a mirepoix, rather than onion alone, and to add 3 chopped sage leaves or ½ tsp dried sage at step 3. I sometimes forgo puréeing the mixture and serve it with *pa amb oli*, the Balearic answer to bruschetta: a slice of rustic white bread, rubbed with garlic and tomato, drizzled with olive oil, and sprinkled with salt.

LEEK & OAT MEAL

Vichy O'ssoise? It's said that the leek was introduced to Ireland by Saint Patrick, an escaped slave from Rome, where the allium was a popular vegetable. (Before its arrival, the following type of soup was made with nettles or chives.) The oat content is small, but it does lend an irresistibly creamy texture to the soup, something for which vichyssoise has to rely on actual cream. Significant, perhaps, that the word "porridge" is a sixteenth-century corruption of "pottage": The association of oats and thick soups is long-standing. Cook 4 cups of sliced leeks and 1½ cups diced potato in a little butter and oil until soft. Pour in 5 cups hot chicken stock, add ½ tsp salt and ⅓ cup pinhead or coarse Scottish oat meal, and simmer for 25 minutes. Taste, and imagine how good the mixture would be with roast partridge—a hybrid of polenta and stuffing. Blend, adding as much as 2 cups more water, for a thick soup consistency. Adjust seasoning and reheat, if necessary.

PEA

Not the sliceable sludge of Dickensian penury, made with dry pulses (see pease pudding on page 257), but the green garden-pea soup of Austenesque pertness. Most recipes call for a diced potato to be added to the softening onion, to give body; 3⅓ cups frozen peas and 1⅔ cups diced potato will be enough for 5 cups water. If you'd prefer to skip the potato, 5 cups peas will give a good flavor and texture. Use fresh peas by all means, if you can get your hands on the truly fresh—you'll need 2¼ lb if you're buying them in pods. A handful or two of shredded romaine lettuce leaves will lend depth to the flavor of pea by matching and extending its sweet earthiness. Add for the last minute of cooking. Lindsey Bareham likes to add canned pears to a pea soup that's very quick to make, since there are no onions to soften. The flavor is quite unusual—identifiably pear-y. Cook 3 cups frozen peas in salted water for a few minutes, then drain. Remove the fruit from 2 (14-oz) cans of pears in juice (not syrup), and add cold water to the juice to make 3¾ cups. Use the liquid to blend the peas with the pears. Reheat and season with salt, white pepper, and 2 tbsp chopped fresh mint or mint jelly.

PUMPKIN WITH THAI SPICE

October is the hungriest month, the stores and stalls glazed in appetizing oranges and browns: maple, pecan, gingerbread, caramel, cinnamon, pumpkin. Ah, pumpkins. What to do with all that flesh once you've hollowed them out to make jack-o'-lanterns? Pumpkin pie is not for me. Tastes like a vegetarian lobster bisque set with wallpaper paste.

Ravioli will take care of a few thimblefuls. So it's pumpkin soup, at least until Guy Fawkes Night, when I can throw the remaining flesh on the bonfire. Of all the variations—pumpkin and mushroom, pumpkin and apple, pumpkin and sweet corn—pumpkin and Thai flavors is my favorite. Pumpkin and coconut blend into something so soft and seamless you'd be slipping into your onesie were it not for the hot and highly complex curry paste the combination demands (plus the impolite fish sauce). Pumpkin may sound inauthentic in a Thai context, but it is used in soups there, cut into cubes for a broth, rather than puréed as it is in this recipe. Follow the starting point, softening 1 chopped onion or 2 chopped shallots at step [1]. Add 2 tbsp Thai green curry paste (Mae Ploy is good) and cook for a minute or two. Stir in 6 cups chopped pumpkin flesh, then 2½ cups each of stock and coconut milk, 2 tbsp fish sauce, and 1 tbsp brown sugar. A fresh or frozen lime leaf will add a fresh, sweet top note. When the pumpkin is cooked, let it cool a bit, fish out and discard the lime leaf, blend, adjust the seasoning, and garnish with chopped coriander, sliced chili, and a sprinkle of sesame seeds.

RADISH LEAF / WATERCRESS / LEEK / LETTUCE / NETTLE

Instead of a mirepoix, a soup made of greens is usually started with a combination of onion and potato, which contribute a mild, comforting bass note underneath the strident, iron-rich chlorophyll. For a classic watercress soup, follow the starting point but simmer—ideally in a mixture of water and milk—the diced potato (about 2 cups) and onion until soft, then add the cress (12–14 oz) for the few minutes it takes the stalks to soften. The same principle can be applied to leek, lettuce, and nettle—the latter measured, according to one sadomasochistic recipe I came across, by the handful. Jenny Baker makes radish leaf soup using both stalks and leaves with the potato-onion base, simmered for 15 minutes, and seasoned with salt, pepper, and a little nutmeg to taste.

TOMATO & CARROT

I am a veteran of too many carrot soup recipes. Most are okay, some almost good, but none worth writing home about. Same goes for tomato. Leafing through a book of Arabella Boxer's *Vogue* columns, I came across a recipe for both: carrot and tomato soup. It hadn't even crossed my mind. Carroty *meh* + tomatoey zing = amazing. Boxer's original recipe was for a cold soup, with lots of buttermilk added at the blending stage, but I was just as taken with it hot from the blender, sans buttermilk. Note the absence of additional aromatics. Not so much as a bay leaf. It's one of those heaven-sent combinations that would be diminished by embellishment. Chop peeled carrots into 2 heaped cups of coins and sweat them in 2 tbsp butter for a few minutes. Add 2 cups skinned, chopped fresh tomatoes and cook for another few minutes. Pour in 4 cups chicken stock (double-diluted if you're using a cube) and season with sea salt, ½ tsp sugar, and some pepper. Simmer gently, lid on, for 35 minutes, then blend. If you plan on serving it cold, use only 3¼ cups stock, blending the finished, cooled soup with a scant cup of buttermilk, and chill before serving.

TURNIP WITH BROWN BREAD & BROWNED BUTTER

Whatever its rustic reputation, I think of turnip as the white-collar rutabaga. It has a silkier texture and a more refined vegetal flavor; the cruciferous bite without the sulfurous stink. Even so, Michael Smith, whose recipe follows, advises against telling your guests what this soup is made from until they've tasted it. Brown 4 tbsp butter in a pan, then add 5 cups diced turnips and ⅓ cup chopped onion. Sweat, lid on, over a low heat until the turnip is tender (about 25 minutes). Cut 2 slices of dry brown bread into cubes, and fry them in 1 tbsp olive oil until crisp and brown. Add the bread to the turnips with 4 cups cold chicken or veal stock, bring to a simmer, and cook gently for 20 minutes longer. Blend, seasoning with salt, pepper, and freshly grated nutmeg. Serve with a garnish of watercress or chopped cooked chestnuts.

Chowder

A hearty, creamy soup that would once invariably have featured seafood. These days it's more open to interpretation. Nonetheless, this starting point calls for ingredients in keeping with its earlier incarnations. Oyster crackers are the traditional garnish for chowder. Make enough for 4 servings by rubbing 4 tbsp unsalted butter into 2 cups all-purpose flour, then stirring in 1 tsp salt, 1 tsp sugar, and 2 tsp baking powder. Add most of ⅔ cup water and mix to a dough, adding the rest only if necessary. Let rest at room temperature for 30 minutes, then roll out to a ¼-in thickness, and either press out rounds about the size of a quarter, or cut into small squares. Bake on a greased baking sheet at 325°F for 20 minutes, rotating the sheet halfway through.

For 4 servings [A]

INGREDIENTS
1 fish head and bones for stock, or 2½ cups warm fish stock
2 tbsp butter [B]
4 oz sliced bacon, cut into lardons [C]
1 large onion, diced [D]
2–3 tsp all-purpose flour [E]
1 lb (about 3 cups) potatoes, peeled and cut into ¾-in dice [F] [G]
1 bay leaf [H]
Salt
2½ cups milk
1 lb haddock fillet, skinned and cut into bite-sized pieces [I]
¼ tsp white pepper
2–4 tbsp cream—optional

1   If you're making fresh stock, simmer the de-gilled fish head and bones in 3 cups salted water for 20–30 minutes to make a stock. Strain through a cheesecloth-lined sieve and set aside. Making your own fish stock is quick and simple, and really pays dividends in chowder—see page [211] for more details.

2   Melt the butter in a saucepan and cook the bacon until it's turning crisp at the edges. Remove with a slotted spoon.

3   Use the bacon fat and butter left in the pan to soften the onion. Golden is okay, but don't let the onion brown.

4 Off the heat, sprinkle the flour into the onion and stir it in. Cook for 1 minute.

5 Pour in the warm stock gradually, stirring to dilute the oniony roux, and deglazing the pan as you do.

6 Add the bacon, potato, and bay leaf, then season modestly with salt. Bring to a boil and reduce to a simmer.
The bacon will salt the soup, as will the fish.

7 Cook for 10–15 minutes until the potato is soft.

8 Add the milk, bring back to a simmer, then stir in the fish, cover the pan, turn the heat down to low, and let the fish cook for 4–5 minutes. Remove from the heat, add more salt to taste, and gently stir in the pepper—and the cream, if using.

9 Serve the chowder with oyster crackers, or with saltines, crusty bread, or sweet corn fritters.

LEEWAY

A As with most soups, this is a fairly elastic recipe. To serve 6, for instance, you could add another potato and 1 cup more liquid.

B Use 2 tbsp oil instead of the butter, although the flavor of the latter is hard to beat.

C Bacon is optional, but if you're not using it, I urge you to make a good, strong fish stock. Or consider experimenting with seaweed.

D As an alternative to onion, use scallions, leeks, or a mix of leeks and onion. Garlic is particularly good with shellfish chowders.

E Not all chowders rely on flour as a thickener. In some, a portion of the potato is mashed and stirred back in, or butter/cream is added. I've seen as much as ½ cup heavy cream added to the quantity here, but 2–4 tbsp stirred in when the fish is cooked gives pretty rich results.

F Any potato will do, but a variety that holds its shape is preferable.

G Replace or mix the potato with sweet potato, pumpkin, or other root vegetables.

H Thyme is the other classic aromatic for chowder. Alternatives include celery salt, cayenne, and mace.

I Mix the fish—white fish, shellfish, salmon, and smoked fish can all intermingle promiscuously.

BAKED POTATO

A chowder where potato, ever the support act, takes top billing. Highly recommended if you're in the mood for something buttery. Skip step [1] of the method, and instead rub 2 large baking potatoes (about 8 oz each) with oil, sprinkle with sea salt, and bake in the oven at 400°F. They should be good and soft in 1 hour 20 minutes. Cut the cooked spuds in half and scoop out most of their flesh. Return the potato skins to the oven for 10 minutes on each side. Then follow the method from steps [2] to [7], adding the potato flesh at step [6], still including the diced raw potato, which is important for texture and will give the flavor an extra dimension, especially if you use a different potato variety. For the liquid, a mild vegetable or chicken stock is best. Garnish with extra bacon, fried to a crisp, plus some chives, sour cream, and chopped scallions, dressing the crispy potato skins with the same. Serve a laden skin on the side of the soup for a rich feast. Or eat the skins while they're warm (they don't reheat well) and have the soup the next day.

CLAM

Among many other things, *Moby-Dick* is a powerful appetite stimulant. In Chapter 15, "Chowder," a ravenous Ishmael and Queequeg, fearing that the landlady at the Try Pots in Nantucket is about to fob them off with a single clam between them, are relieved to be served two smoking-hot bowls of clam chowder. "It was made of small juicy clams, scarcely bigger than hazel nuts, mixed with pounded ship biscuit, and salted pork cut up into little flakes; the whole enriched with butter, and plentifully seasoned with pepper and salt." Mrs. Hussey, the proprietor's wife, "a freckled woman with yellow hair and a yellow gown," looks not unlike a chowder herself. By Ishmael's account, the Try Pots is the "fishiest of all fishy places," where even the milk tastes of fish, a phenomenon that puzzles Ishmael until he takes a stroll along the beach and sees the Husseys' "brindled cow feeding on fish remnants." Adapt our starting point, using 4 lb clams in their shells in place of the 1 lb fish. In a large saucepan that has a lid, reduce 1 cup dry white wine by half, then add 2 cups hot water. Turn the heat down to medium and add the cleaned clams. Apply the lid and let cook for 4–5 minutes, shaking the pan halfway through the cooking time. When the time is up, check if most of the clams are open. If not, replace the lid and check every minute until they are. Then remove the clams from their shells. Do this over the cooking pan so as to catch as much of their liquor as possible. Discard any clams that failed to open. Now follow the method from step [2], using the clam-cooking liquid (strained through a cheesecloth-lined sieve) in place of fish stock, and adding the clams where you would have added the fish—they will only need a minute or two to reheat. Tom Kerridge makes a chowder with cockles, potato, and sweet corn kernels, drizzling the finished dish with sweetened vinegar in a nod to an English seaside classic.

MUSSEL & GARLIC

Like a *moules marinière*, but with the fries pre-dunked, and *so* much sauce you're gonna need a bigger bread basket. Sliced baguette is the obvious choice, but I'd recommend the potato bread on page [51] for its miraculous absorbency. Mussel and garlic chowder deviates from our starting point in a similar way to the clam version, opposite. The shellfish cooking liquid furnishes the stock, but here it's flavored with garlic and wine, so the result is a far richer soup. Over a medium heat, in a lidded pan with room for all the mussels, melt 1–2 tbsp butter and cook 2–3 minced garlic cloves until just turning golden. Turn the heat up to high and add 1 cup dry white wine. Bring to a boil and simmer for 1 minute. Add 4 lb scrubbed and debearded mussels. Cover and leave for 2 minutes, then stir and re-cover. If the mussels haven't opened already, check them every minute to see if most of them have opened— this can take up to 8 minutes if they have particularly thick shells. As soon as they're open, remove the lid and liberate the mussels from their shells, discarding any that remain closed. Reserve the liquid and add enough water to make 2½ cups: This will be your stock. Follow the method from steps [3] to [7]—you'll find the intense flavors of mussel and garlic obviate the need for bacon. Add the cooked mussels at step [8] and briefly heat through. If the mussels are a bit big for your tastes, cut each one into 2 or 3 pieces.

RED WINE

The first documented recipe for chowder appeared in an anonymous poem published by *The Boston Evening Post* in 1751:

> First lay some Onions to keep the Pork from burning
> Because in Chouder there can be not turning;
> Then lay some Pork in slices very thin,
> Thus you in Chouder always must begin.
> Next lay some Fish cut crossways very nice
> Then season well with Pepper, Salt, and Spice;
> Parsley, Sweet-Marjoram, Savory, and Thyme,
> Then Biscuit next which must be soak'd some Time.
> Thus your Foundation laid, you will be able
> To raise a Chouder, high as Tower of Babel;
> For by repeating o'er the Same again,
> You may make a Chouder for a thousand men.
> Last a Bottle of Claret, with Water eno; to smother 'em,
> You'll have a Mess which some call *Omnium gather 'em*.

Recipe writers might question the poet's failure to specify stovetop or oven; poets, the advisability of rhyming "Thyme" with "Time." And red wine with fish? Historically, to be fair, the pairing was less unusual. Best to avoid a tannic Bordeaux in favor of a young Beaujolais. Even so, it's an idea to mellow the wine first by cooking it.

SMOKED HADDOCK & POTATO

Cullen skink is the famous Scots soup made with smoked haddock and potatoes. It's not unlike our starting point for chowder, but simpler. No need for stock or bacon. Simply put the diced potatoes and chopped onion in a saucepan, add 2½ cups water, and simmer until both are soft (about 10–15 minutes). Similarly, put the smoked haddock ("finnan haddie") in another pan and pour in 2½ cups milk, add a bay leaf, and simmer until cooked (no more than 10 minutes). Remove the fish and retain the milk, which will now be as fishy as milk from the Husseys' brindled cow (see clam, page [234]). Flake the fish, removing any bones as you go. Remove roughly half of the cooked potatoes and onions from their cooking water, mash, then return them to their pan, along with the flaked fish and milk. Warm through and serve sprinkled with parsley or chives and with a side of oatcakes (page [33]) or bannocks, squashed biscuitlike breads made with oat or barley meal and cooked on a griddle pan. Parsnip was traditionally popular with smoked fish; using it in place of half the potato yields a tasty variation.

SWEET CORN, SWEET POTATO & CRÈME FRAÎCHE

Sweet corn chowder is best kept simple—the earthiness of the corn isn't improved by the classic chowder herbs, bay or thyme. Crème fraîche offsets the sweetness of the vegetables. If possible, use a French crème fraîche from Isigny: Its flavor, somewhere between Greek yogurt and a Camembert on the cusp of maturing, is well worth the small price premium. Make as per the starting point, making sweet corn stock instead of fish stock at step [1]: Strip the kernels from 4 ears of sweet corn and set aside; immerse the shorn cobs in 4 cups water with ½ tsp salt and simmer for about 20 minutes. Reserve 2½ cups of the stock and compost the cobs. Pick up the method from step [3], using just butter or oil to soften the onion. Use sweet potato instead of potato, and add it and the sweet corn kernels with the milk and salt at step [6]. Bring to a simmer and cook for 10 minutes. Add 4 tbsp crème fraîche and heat through gently. Theodore Roosevelt liked to eat his fish chowder with popcorn instead of oyster crackers. If you decide to follow his lead, add a few pieces at a time, to let them absorb a little soup without entirely losing their crunch. Salted corn nuts also make an excellent garnish.

TOMATO (MANHATTAN CLAM CHOWDER)

Caused a right hoo-ha in 1934, when it first appeared in print:
J. George Frederick called the invention of tomato and clam chowder
the most controversial in American culinary history, "exceeding easily
the strawberry shortcake controversy." Maine assemblyman Cleveland
Sleeper introduced a bill to make it illegal to add tomato to clam
chowder. Eleanor Early, writing in 1940, called it a "terrible pink
mixture," claiming that clams and tomatoes had no more compatibility
than horseradish and ice cream. How times change. The tomato-clam
drink Clamato (launched in 1966) is a staple of American convenience
stores, and if horseradish ice cream isn't already available in your local
gelateria, it's only a matter of time. To see what all the fuss was about,
follow the starting point, but make a shellfish stock (page 214) rather
than a fish stock at step 1. Then follow the method from step 2, adding,
along with the onion, 1 carrot, 1 green bell pepper, and 1 celery stalk,
all finely chopped, and 3–4 crushed garlic cloves. When the vegetables
are soft, stir in 2 tbsp tomato paste and cook for a minute before adding
1 potato, the shellfish stock, a bay leaf, a few sprigs of thyme, and a little
salt and pepper. Simmer until the diced potatoes are just cooked through.
When they are, add a 14-oz can of crushed tomatoes and a few pinches
of pepper flakes. Give it 15 minutes longer, then add 2¼ lb scrubbed
clams, cover, and simmer until they're all opened. You're supposed to
wait until the next day to eat the chowder, preferably leaving it outside.
I left mine on a stoop in Brooklyn and by the following morning someone
had started a microbrewery in it.

Stew: Lamb & Vegetable Stew

A one-pot dish of meat or fish and vegetables. The example here is a straightforward lamb and vegetable stew, but the Flavors & Variations include a curry and a tagine, as well as classic French casseroles. For our starting point, the stew is cooked in the oven, but the stovetop can be used instead. If you are cooking a stew on the stovetop, use a diffuser to tamp the heat, if possible—it will make an appreciable difference to the texture of any meat or fish.

For 4 servings, made in a lidded, 3-quart ovenproof pot [A]

INGREDIENTS
4 tbsp butter, or 2–3 tbsp oil [B]
2 lb boneless shoulder or leg of lamb, diced [C] [D] [E]
2 onions, roughly chopped [F]
2 carrots, roughly chopped [F]
2 celery stalks, roughly chopped [F]
8 oz slab bacon, cut into lardons or strips [F]
3–4 garlic cloves, minced [F]
1 tbsp all-purpose flour [G]
3 cups hot stock [H]
1 bouquet garni [I]

[1] Heat the butter or oil in your ovenproof pot and brown the meat, in batches if necessary. Remove with a slotted spoon.

[2] Add more fat if needed and, when it is hot, soften the onion, carrot, and celery with the bacon over a medium heat for about 10 minutes. Add the garlic and cook until it's just turning golden.

[3] Off the heat, sprinkle in the flour and stir it in. Return to the heat and cook for 1 minute.
If the bacon and meat have rendered a lot of fat, you may want to remove all but about 1 tbsp of it before adding the flour.

[4] Pour in the hot stock gradually, stirring to deglaze the pot as you do. Return the meat to the pot and add the bouquet garni.

[5] Bring to a boil, then reduce to a simmer and transfer to a 325°F oven. Cook for 1½–2 hours.
Larger lamb cuts and bone-in pieces like shank will need longer.

6   Serve—or, better still, cool and leave in the fridge for a day or two, to allow the flavors to develop and the fat to rise to the top for easy removal.

LEEWAY

A   If the lid is a bit loose, interpose a piece of foil or parchment paper between it and the pot. This will prevent steam from escaping, and thus the stew from drying out and ultimately burning, especially if you're tending toward the lesser amount of liquid. If your pot isn't suitable for stovetop cooking, start the stew in a heavy-based pan, preheat the pot in the oven, and then transfer the stew to it at step [5]. While a bigger pot will do, the ideal is to have the ingredients packed tightly and covered with the minimal amount of liquid, in order to furnish the most intense results.

B   Use oil if the flavor principle or cuisine is more suited to it, say for a tagine or Chinese braise.

C   If you're buying meat on the bone, ask for 50 percent extra weight—i.e. 3 lb.

D   Shoulder is a good choice for a lamb stew, but neck is another option, as are breast and shank (adjust cooking times according to the cut).

E   Err on the side of larger pieces, which are harder to overcook and look more appetizing in the finished dish.

F   The above is a classic set of flavorings, but you may omit or substitute freely. Onion, red bell pepper, and tomato makes a good base for most meats.

G   As an alternative to thickening with wheat flour, stir in a mixture of cornstarch and cold water just before the end of cooking (see Vietnamese duck and orange, page [245]). Or, if the ingredients allow, you might mash or purée a small portion of the vegetables and stir that back into the finished stew. Also note the beurre manié on page [242].

H   Use more or less liquid but adjust the flour accordingly: 1 tsp per 1 cup stock will yield a moderately thick sauce. It's conventional to add enough liquid to cover the ingredients by about an inch. If you're using less (that is, making a braise) ensure that your pot has a tight-fitting lid, so the contents will cook properly. The stock can be partially or entirely replaced with the same volume of wine or chopped tomatoes.

I   A fresh bouquet garni can make a huge difference to the finished flavor. A solitary bay leaf or a few sprigs of thyme are good, too; 1 tsp dried mixed herbs will suffice. If you're adding any spices, add whole ones at step [2], and ground at step [3] once the flour has been absorbed, checking the pot isn't too dry in case they burn.

BEEF IN BEER

The world's second-best application for beer is called *carbonnade* in the francophone south of Belgium, *stoofvlees* in the Flemish north. The stew is the same, even if the *stoofvlees* is considerably more likely to come with fries. Delia Smith warns against tasting the stew before it has been cooking for at least 2½ hours, as it will need that time for the bitterness lent by the beer to mellow; Garrett Oliver, owner of the Brooklyn Brewery, suggests that 1½ hours should be long enough. He also notes that "used correctly, beer has much to add to cuisine across a wide range of cooking applications," an observation about as enthusiastic as the gym entry in my husband's school report. ("A good effort in swimming and basketball. A pleasant boy.") How tepid you feel about your *stoofvlees* will partly depend on the type and amount of beer you use. I use Mackeson's milk stout, black as hot tar, mixed with beef stock, but any dark beer will do. Escoffier called for a lambic—see page 516—although I'd save that for drinking. Follow the starting point, using the same weight of stewing beef, and forgetting the carrot and celery, but using at least twice as much onion, sliced rather than chunked. For the liquid, use 50/50 beef stock and beer, plus 1 heaped tbsp sugar, 1 tbsp Dijon mustard, and 4 tsp cider vinegar or wine vinegar. A bouquet garni is pretty much nonnegotiable. Anne Willan also adds ½ tsp freshly grated nutmeg. It's not uncommon to pave the top with toasted slices of bread spread with mustard; food writer Mimi Sheraton records a *carbonnade* served with a sort of gingerbread topping. If you're not serving it with fries, go for plenty of plain potatoes, boiled or mashed, or ribbons of egg pasta. I can't speak for every dark ale, but on occasion I've replaced the beef with a dozen fat pork sausages (left whole and briefly browned), cooked it for no more than 45 minutes, and found the small remnant of bitterness welcome.

CHANFANA

A stew from the Beira region of Portugal. Traditionally made with goat, modern versions are just as likely to contain lamb or mutton. Some say the dish dates to the Peninsular war, when Napoleon's Grande Armée polished off all the best livestock, leaving the Portuguese with a bunch of old goats. Necessity can be the mother of a decent stew, however, and marinated slowly in red wine the meat becomes nicely tenderized— up to a point. According to Celia Pedroso and Lucy Pepper, the dish still requires "good teeth." The aromatics are pretty inventive, too. The mixture is unlike any I've come across—mint, bay, parsley, and paprika, alongside onion and garlic. The dish also merits mention for requiring neither softening nor browning. The ingredients are loaded into a lidded (preferably earthenware) ovenproof pot, layered if you like, immersed in red wine, left to mingle for an age, then given a long, slow cook in the oven. Marinate 4½ lb diced goat or mutton for 8 hours (in the fridge) in 3 cups red wine, 1 bulb's worth of chopped garlic,

6 tbsp chopped parsley, ¼ cup chopped mint, 1 tsp paprika, 1 tbsp salt, 1 tsp piri piri seasoning or pepper flakes, and a few dots of lard. When ready to cook, stir and add a bit more wine if the meat has absorbed a lot. Cover, transfer to a 325°F oven, and cook for 3 hours. Serve with boiled potatoes and a multi-colored fan of interdental brushes.

CHICKEN & WINE

On the basis that he's married to someone who writes about food, people assume my husband eats like a king. So when they ask about the best meal I've ever cooked for him, they're often disappointed at the answer. On our last night at a vacation cottage on Dartmoor, it so happened that I had most of the ingredients for a *coq au vin* to hand. What I didn't have (brandy, shallots, bread) was supplied by the delightfully well-stocked village shop. I cut up a chicken, and proceeded as per our starting point, flambéing the bird in a miniature of Courvoisier. Opposite the cottage was the absurdly attractive Drewe Arms, so I slid the Pyrex dish into a 1970s oven set to 300°F, and we strolled across the road for a sharpener. The pub was just as a Devon country pub should be: thatched, with a choice of small rooms, furnished with tongue-and-groove benches and a floor of enormous flagstones. There was no bar; you bought your pint from a hatch opening onto the taproom, full of kegs wrapped in blankets as if recovering from their traumatic journey from the brewery. A chalkboard listed simple hearty classics—lamb chops, pie and mash. We caved, and ordered. Halfway through dinner, I tiptoed over the road to remove the poor, scorned chicken from the oven. I think I might even have apologized as I left it to cool on the counter and returned to my bread pudding. The following morning, standing in the driving rain, looking at the junction of three paths heading out of the parking lot, arguing as to which one led to which tor, we cut our losses and got back in the car. Time for an early lunch. What I produced from the foil wrapper wasn't much to look at: *coq au vin* sandwiches. The purple sauce had seeped into the bread, leaving it soggy and vaguely toxic-looking. The chicken, however, was juicy, mildly truffly in flavor, and the wet bread nutty and fruity. At that moment a soggy sandwich, eaten amid the mild background note of dirty engine oil, staring out at a bog while infuriated rain lashed the windscreen, became and has remained the single most delicious thing my husband has apparently ever consumed. Regarding the *vin*,

Waverley Root reckons that reds from Chinon or Bourgueil combine best with meat in cooking, while *coq au vin* "is never better than when made with Touraine wine." He also observes that the Franche-Comté version is made with Château-Chalon, a rich, sweet wine he likens to "a mountain Sauternes." Rose Gray and Ruth Rogers's *River Cafe Two Easy* gives eleven recipes for "birds with wine," including slow-roast chicken in vermouth, roast partridge in *vin santo*, pheasant in Chardonnay, and roast grouse with Chianti Classico. To make a classic *coq au vin*, adapt the starting point by using a 2½ lb cut-up chicken in place of the lamb, and red wine for the liquid. Celery is optional. The traditional finish is to cook little onions and bacon lardons in butter for 10 minutes, add button mushrooms for 5 more, then—assuming the onions are now soft enough to eat—stir the lot into the stew just before serving. To thicken it, make beurre manié (kneaded butter) by mixing equal proportions of unsalted butter and all-purpose flour to a paste. Stir a teaspoon of the mix at a time into the finished stew, allowing a minute of cooking after each addition, until the sauce is as thick as you want it. The same flavoring principles and garnish apply to beef bourguignon: Simply follow the starting point, using beef in place of lamb and red wine for the liquid.

DUCK WITH CHOCOLATE & MARSALA

The ingredients I'd choose for my desert-island dish would be duck, garlic, fennel, chili, a bar of Green & Black's Raisin & Hazelnut chocolate, and a bottle of Marco de Bartoli Marsala. I could then choose between getting drunk, eating the chocolate, and throwing the rest in the sea, or making something like this opulent Sicilian dish from Jacob Kenedy's *Bocca: Cookbook*. Follow the starting point, using a cut-up duck. Brown the seasoned duck pieces for 5–10 minutes on each side, then remove the triple-bypass-worth of fat that will have collected in the pan. Pour in 1 tbsp olive oil, then soften 1 onion and 2 garlic cloves (all finely chopped), followed by a 1¼-in cinnamon stick, ½ tsp pepper flakes, and a pinch of salt. Cook over a low heat for 10–15 minutes. Add 1 tsp crushed fennel seeds, ½ cup raisins, and ⅓ cup pine nuts and cook for 2 minutes longer. Return the duck to the pan. Pour in 1 cup dry Marsala or oloroso sherry with ⅓ cup red or white wine vinegar. Cover tightly and simmer very gently until the duck is tender and the sauce is thick—about 1 hour. Skim off as much of the fat as possible from the top of the sauce, then stir in ⅓ cup chopped dark chocolate, taste, and season. Sprinkle with parsley and (maybe) a little more chili. Serve with couscous—a nod to the dish's supposed Arab heritage—or, as Kenedy recommends, spinach sautéed with a little garlic and chili.

OSSO BUCO

Bone Hole. Sounds like the kind of gay bar you might have found in Manhattan's Meatpacking District before the dreary fashionistas took over. Osso buco is, of course, a veal stew from Lombardy, made plush by the marrow seeping from the bone, to the extent that you may wish to take off your shoes and simply stand in it. What marrow remains you scoop out from the cavity, leaving the "buco" in the "osso." So I was delighted when a friend told me he was serving it for dinner. I arrived with a purposefully sharpened appetite, to find that although he had already chopped the garlic and parsley for the gremolata, the lemon-zesty garnish traditionally sprinkled over the finished dish, the veal lay on the kitchen counter, brutally, unapologetically raw. My offers to help were politely refused. "No, no. You *relax*." I was handed a glass of Gavi di Gavi. I inhaled its citric and herbal aromas, which only served to remind me of the gremolata and the stew that it wouldn't be garnishing for several hours. An hour and a half into the osso buco's simmer a mutiny was brewing. Another guest *made himself an omelet*. Without offering to share it. Appallingly rude, in other circumstances, but tonight it was every man for himself. At 10.45, those guests who hadn't passed out drunk on the sofa were presented with steaming plates of veal stew on soft, creamy saffron risotto. It was actually worth the wait. It restored the power of speech. How often does a meal do that? Follow the starting point, using six 1¼-in slices of veal shank, and browning them in olive oil rather than butter. Chop the mirepoix more finely than you would for a beef stew. Once you've softened it, and lightly colored the garlic, add ½ cup dry white wine and cook for a few minutes. Pour in 2 (14-oz) cans crushed tomatoes, 1 cup water, the finely chopped needles from a sprig of rosemary, and the leaves from 4 sprigs of thyme. Season with salt and pepper. Bring to a boil, then cover, transfer to a 300°F oven, and cook for 3 hours. Serve with saffron risotto, polenta, or mashed potatoes. Without the veal, the recipe comes very close to cacciatore; in fact, some recipes are pretty much interchangeable, other than replacing the veal with rabbit or chicken, and holding the gremolata. Other versions of cacciatore might include bell peppers or mushrooms. You'll find the French equivalent, chasseur, on page [173].

SAAG GOSHT

Hard to imagine grumbly, socialist spinach could be so lavish, but in the Indian dish saag gosht, yogurt arbitrates between a wealth of it and the lamb juices, creating a velvety sauce. (Feel free to use other kinds of meat, but adjust the cooking time if necessary.) Start either by quickly cooking 2¼ lb fresh spinach in just the rinsing water clinging to its leaves, then squeezing thoroughly and chopping it, or by thawing 8 oz frozen chopped spinach and squeezing it well. Follow our starting point, browning the lamb in oil. Exclude the carrot, celery, and bacon in favor of 2 tbsp finely chopped fresh ginger, added with the garlic. No need to add flour at step [3], as the spinach does the thickening. Instead, stir in 1 tbsp ground coriander, 1 tsp mustard powder, 1 tsp ground cumin, 1 tsp ground turmeric, ½ tsp ground black pepper, ¼ tsp freshly grated nutmeg, and chili powder or pepper flakes to taste, then cook for 1 minute. Return the lamb, with the spinach, to the pan and stir in 1¼ cups plain yogurt and 1 tsp salt. Cover and cook in a 325°F oven for 2 hours, adding a little hot water if it begins to dry out toward the end. Serve with rice or flatbreads (page [28]) and chutney.

SEAFOOD

The main challenge for the maker of seafood stew lies in achieving a good depth of flavor in the broth. Few types of seafood can withstand more than 10 minutes of cooking, so unlike a stew made with meat or dry beans, a tasty broth will need to be made separately, before the star ingredient is added—scaled and gutted whole fish, fillets, crustaceans, bivalves, or a mixture—and letting it poach for the short time it needs. A fish stock made with heads, bones, and/or shells can often taste so exquisite as to need no further embellishment—or can be flavored with curry or tagine aromatics. Alternatively, use it to dilute a nut paste, as in *romesco de peix* (page **315**). In the absence of stock ingredients, try a tomato base instead, and flavor it with some of the following: onion, leeks, garlic, celery, fennel, bell pepper, thyme, bay leaf, tarragon, saffron, bacon, chorizo, sausage, chili, white wine, or pastis. Or, more unusually, make a red braise (page **223**) and use the spicy, pork-infused liquid as a broth. A handy shortcut to deliciousness is to add a handful or two of mussels or clams, which will open as they cook and impart their juices to the cooking liquid; also consider adding a little fish sauce, anchovy sauce or paste, or seaweed as a booster.

TAGINE

The trouble with eating out in Marrakech is the volume of sensory information competing for your poor tourist-brain's attention. At a restaurant in the medina, I picked at my plate of couscous, lamb, and apricots in a vast room tiled in blue and white, and half off its rocker with ornate mirrors, rugs, cushions, and little fountains spurting fans of golden light. A few feet away, a man playing some kind of lute spun the tassel on his fez in time with the music. Even the walk to the restaurant was remarkable: We were picked up at our riad by a small boy, who led us, in his bright-red djellaba, through a moonlit maze of back streets; like a parched reversal of *Don't Look Now*, our diminutive guide stayed several paces ahead but never quite out of sight. Oddly, the tagine that lingers most in my mind for its flavor, I ate in a Corsican seaside café—reached not thanks to a hooded child, but a hired Fiat Punto. That afternoon we had walked the final stretch of the island's long-distance mountain trail, the GR20, and we arrived at the café after a cooling, twilit swim that had only left us hungrier. The sinewy look of the chicken leg, sticking out of the stew as if appealing for help, suggested it had seen a bit of exercise itself, but that only made it more appropriate in a slow-cooked dish like a tagine. Afterward we skipped the baklava and mint tea and hit the ice cream parlor across the square, where our waitress gamely supplied miniature beach-shovels of every flavor they served, until my teeth ached as badly as my legs. For a chicken tagine, follow the starting point, using a 2½ lb cut-up bird (or a mix of legs and thighs) in place of the lamb, and olive oil rather than butter. With the flour, add 1 tsp each of ground cumin and turmeric, plus ½ tsp ground cinnamon. Return the browned chicken to the pot with a drained 15-oz can of chickpeas and some pitted green olives if you like. For the liquid, go for a 50/50 mix of white wine and chicken stock—or, if you want to avoid the alcohol, all chicken stock. For a red-meat tagine, follow the instructions for chicken, but use 2 lb diced, boneless lamb or beef stew meat, and a mix of red wine and beef stock. Add 8–12 prunes or dried apricots with the chickpeas. Serve either tagine with couscous, sprinkled with parsley, cilantro, and/or toasted pine nuts.

VIETNAMESE DUCK & ORANGE

Rick Stein has said that of all the recipes in his *Far Eastern Odyssey* TV series, the duck braised in spiced orange juice is the one everyone should try. He's right. The distinct sulfurousness of cooked orange juice is one of its high points. The sauce can be used with other meats (chicken legs, beef short ribs) but duck is nonpareil. The mix of aromatics bears comparison with the sort used in Chinese master stock, although the lemongrass pushes it in a Southeast Asian direction. It's much like our starting point for stew, method-wise, except it's cooked entirely on the stovetop. Cut up and brown a 5½-lb duck. Set aside and remove all but 2 tbsp fat from the pan. Use this to fry 5 tbsp each of minced garlic and fresh ginger together until golden. Pour in 4 cups orange juice, ¼ cup fish sauce, 1 tbsp sugar, 5 whole star anise, 4 whole red bird's eye chilies, and 2 finely chopped stalks of lemongrass. Season with black pepper. Return the duck pieces to the pan and simmer very slowly for 1½ hours, partially covered. Slice the white parts of 8 scallions lengthwise, add to the pan, and cook for a further 30 minutes. Remove the duck and keep it warm while you skim the excess fat from the liquid, then simmer vigorously to concentrate the flavors. Finally, to thicken the stew, mix ½ tsp cornstarch with 1 tsp cold water, add to the pot, and simmer for a final minute. For an easier time at the table, you might remove the bone and gristle from the duck—it should slip away easily—before warming it through in the sauce. Garnish with the sliced green remainder of the scallions, shredded cilantro, sliced red chili, and sesame seeds. Try not to eat it all, as the dish benefits from being fed back into itself: Make a duck stock from the carcass, then add it to the leftovers for a second serving the following night, so intense in flavor it may well push your eyeballs out on helical springs.

Bean Stew: Fabada

A stew from the mountainous Spanish region of Asturias, *fabada* is made with large white beans and a mixture of pork cuts and sausages. It's hefty, as so many pork and bean dishes are, and the inclusion of morcilla, a blood sausage, makes it rich and sumptuous. It's traditional to serve it with crusty bread and hard cider. Marvel, as you undo the top button of your jeans, that in Asturias it's not unusual to serve *fabada* as an appetizer. The method for *fabada* requires little more than putting ingredients into a pot, but for many of the other bean stews in the Flavors & Variations section, you'll need to brown the onions and meat, or precook the beans.

For 6–8 servings [A]

INGREDIENTS
1 lb dry jumbo or large lima beans [B]
1 large onion, diced [C]
2–3 garlic cloves, minced [C]
2 lb mixture of cured pork belly, morcilla, and Spanish chorizo sausages, all left whole [D]
4 oz slab bacon, cut into lardons or strips
Salt

1   Soak the beans in plenty of water for at least 8 hours, or overnight.

2   Drain and rinse the beans. Transfer them to a pan large enough to hold all of the ingredients and cover them with cold water. Bring to a boil and cook for 10 minutes, then turn down to a simmer, and skim off the scum until it desists.

3   Add the onion and garlic and return to a simmer.

4   Prick the morcilla and chorizo and add to the pan, along with the pork belly and bacon lardons.

5   Pour in enough boiling water to cover. Return to a simmer and cook, partially covered, on the lowest heat for 2 hours, or longer if the beans need it. Regularly shuffle the pan (try not to stir, for fear of breaking up the ingredients) and check the water level; you don't want the pan to boil dry and burn. Once the beans are fairly tender, sprinkle over some salt. [E]
Some cooks prefer to salt the beans earlier; others believe that doing so breaks their skin.

6 Adjust the seasoning and chop the meat into bite-sized pieces. Serve with crusty bread.

LEEWAY

A The proportion of bean to meat is up to you. You could easily double the amount of beans without increasing the meat. *Fabada* freezes pretty well for several months.

B If your beans are old and you're worried they might not soften, cook them until just tender first, then add the other ingredients and simmer for 1½ hours.

C While the occasional recipe calls for paprika or saffron, *fabada* usually relies on the spiced sausages and smoky bacon for its seasoning. Some recipes even go as far as leaving out the onion and garlic.

D For a variation on *fabada*, with meat and root vegetables, add the latter 1 hour into the cooking to preserve their texture and flavor. If you're using tomato, or any other especially acidic ingredients, it's best to add them after the beans have softened.

E If you prefer to cook your *fabada* in the oven, cover the pot tightly and cook at 325°F for about 2 hours after bringing it to a simmer at step 5.

BOSTON BAKED BEANS

Make *fabada* look like fast food. Despite their small size, navy beans can take a good deal of cooking. Bostonians leave nothing to chance. They soak them overnight, simmer them on the stovetop for an hour or so, transfer them to a clay or ceramic bean pot with some pork and a few aromatic ingredients, and cook them in the oven for 4–5 hours, or even overnight. Time-consuming, but pretty hands-off. The beans are traditionally eaten with Boston brown bread, which is made with a special blend of whole wheat and rye flours and cornmeal, and milk mixed with molasses. Boston brown bread is steamed for 2 hours, then left in the pan for another hour before being unmolded. Why there isn't a saying like "She has the patience of a Boston cook" is beyond me. The first published recipe for Boston baked beans calls for nothing but pork and beans, but like a tall story the recipe has been embellished over the years. The following is on the fussy side, but feel free to simplify. Soak 1 lb dry navy beans for about 8 hours, then rinse them and transfer them to a pan of fresh water. Bring to a boil and simmer for 1–2 hours, or until tender. Meanwhile, chop a large onion and cut 8 oz slab bacon into lardons or strips. Drain the cooked beans, reserving the stock, and transfer about a quarter of the beans to a lidded 2½-quart bean pot or earthenware casserole. Scatter a quarter of the onion and bacon over before ladling in another layer of beans. Keep going until you've used all the ingredients. Mix 2 cups of the bean-cooking water with 2 tbsp molasses (or dark brown sugar), 1 tbsp tomato paste, 1 tbsp mustard powder, and 1 tsp salt. Pour the mixture over the beans until they're submerged to a depth of 1–2 in, adding more stock if necessary. Cook, covered, in a 300°F oven for at least 3 hours. Check the liquid from time to time, adding more of the hot bean-cooking water, or plain hot water, if it drops below the surface of the beans.

BURNT EGGPLANT, SOY & PAPRIKA BORLOTTI

I told my mother I had made a burnt-eggplant stew. "Never mind," she said. "You can always have cheese on toast." "No, Mum, you don't understand," I said, just as I would have done thirty years earlier, when she looked askance at the latest LP by Einstürzende Neubauten. "Burnt is *fashionable*." Silence at the other end of the line. "How," she asked, "do you tell if it's fashionable or just burnt?" "Context," I said, but I knew I'd lost her. Eggplant gives a meaty quality to stock, all the more so if you've roasted it good and hard. It lends as much substance to this meat-free dish as a special advisor to a blustering politician. The broth is made with a little soy sauce and mirin—enough to put the beans in a deep, dark, salty mood, but not so much that they'll taste noticeably Asian. Dry borlotti beans (an Italian variety of cranberry beans) are worth seeking out for this dish. Never judge a bean by its cover—although the Rosalia-marble skin of dry borlotti is hard not to admire, even if it turns a mottled mid-brown when cooked. Once soaked, the beans can be cooked in as little as 25 minutes, by which time they will have both tripled the deliciousness of the broth and plumped up to the extent that the dish easily qualifies as a main course for 4. Chop 2 eggplants into 1¼-in chunks and roast in a little peanut oil, together with 12 halved cherry tomatoes, for 30 minutes at 400°F. While you're waiting, dice 1 onion and soften it in oil, adding 3 minced garlic cloves and a pinch of fennel seeds for the last few minutes. Squeeze in 1 generous tbsp tomato paste, stir to mix it in, and cook for 1 minute. Add 1⅓ cups soaked and drained borlotti (or cranberry) beans, 4 cups boiling water, 1 tbsp soy sauce, 2 tbsp mirin, and 1 tsp smoked paprika. Simmer slowly for 30–40 minutes or until the beans are good and soft, adding extra boiling water if necessary. Drain any excess water from the beans and mix in the eggplant and tomatoes, then season and add a squeeze of lemon juice. (Instead of cooking the dry borlotti or cranberry beans in 4 cups water, you can use 2 (15-oz) cans of pinto or cannellini beans, drained, adding just a splash of water to the stew.)

CHUCKWAGON BEANS

I once took part in a cattle roundup in Arizona. Hitching my horse for the night, I was disappointed to find that one of the ranch hands had driven up to the camp and dropped off some flowery-padded deckchairs as bedding, the dirt being too real a surface for our tender city slickers' bones. I slipped off my boots and cracked open a beer, while some fellow fairweather cowboys made up a pitcher of G&T with the Tanqueray they had asked the ranch hand to bring in his truck with the deckchairs. The camp cook heated the beans and fried the steaks on an open fire. We ate in the dark, under a night sky feverish with stars. We polished off the Tanqueray and retired to our old cushions drunk. I woke three hours later with a terrible thirst. The wrangler had fallen asleep with his arm around my bottle of water. My sweet, sweet bottle of water. He was snoring and had his finger on the trigger of his gun. So there I lay for hours, my throat a desert, propitiating the rain gods, as I listened to the restless horses lapping water from their tin buckets. In Ken Albala's recipe, 2 cups dry large lima beans are soaked overnight, then cooked until almost tender (about 30 minutes), before being layered with 2 lb tenderized, floured round steak cut into 4 pieces. Mix 1 tbsp brown sugar, ½ tsp mustard powder, 1 cup tomato juice, and 1 tbsp bacon fat, and pour this over the beef and beans. Chop an onion and sprinkle it on top. Cook at a minimal simmer until the meat is tender (at least 2 hours), adding water as necessary.

FEIJOADA

Feijoada, the national dish of Brazil, owes its good looks to the shiny little black beans it's made with. It's tough to make a fully authentic version unless you have a proper Brazilian butcher nearby, but I urge you to improvise nonetheless, as in my view it's not the smoked beef tongue or *carne seca* (dried beef), nice as they are, that make this dish such a joy. It's the carnival of side dishes that goes with it: sour sliced orange; bitter greens finely shredded and fried with garlic; spicy malagueta peppers; sweet, mild rice; and my favorite, *farofa* (toasted cassava flour), which is delectably sweet-salty-savory, like pulverized graham crackers. In Rio, it's the done thing to go to the beach after *feijoada*, but I've only ever eaten it in London, where the oily shores of the Thames offer little incentive for sun-worship. If you know a Brazilian butcher, ask for his *feijoada* recipe. Otherwise, try this approximation. Use 1 lb dry black beans and 2¼ lb mixed beef and pork. The aim with the meats is to achieve some variation in flavor and texture; my last *feijoada* contained pork ribs, spicy sausages, and a piece of corned brisket. Follow our starting point, but soften the onion and garlic in lard or vegetable oil before adding to the soaked and drained beans with 2 bay leaves. Cook for as long as the meat needs to soften—mine took 2½ hours. If you think the stew needs thickening, remove some of the beans and blend them, then return to the pot and simmer for a little longer. Remove any bones from the meat and discard, then chop the meat into bite-sized pieces and reunite it with the beans. Don't skimp on the side dishes—they really are the point. Coerce your guests into preparing one each over a pitcher of ice-cold caipirinhas.

FLAGEOLETS WITH SALT COD

Flageolet (pronounced *fla*-zhee-o-lay) beans are just about small enough to insert in the holes of the woodwind instrument with which they share their name. Some are the color of Camembert cheese, but most are a shabby-chic pastel green, as if Tic-Tacs were running a Farrow & Ball promotion. Flageolets contain less starch than most other beans, so cook down to a smooth, rather genteel texture. *Larousse* proclaims them "perhaps the finest of all pulses," and a classic accompaniment to blade of pork or leg of lamb. It also gives a recipe for salt cod with flageolets: an interesting stand-in for salted pork, which pescatarians might apply to other bean stews. Note that the beans are given a long soak and, along with the cod, a very short cook, so this dish represents a deviation from the starting point. Soak 2⅔ cups dry flageolets in plenty of water for 24 hours. Do the same to 2¼ lb salt cod cut into 4 pieces, changing the water a few times over the 24 hours. The following day, simmer the beans in fresh water for 30 minutes with 1 roughly chopped carrot, 1 halved onion studded with 2 cloves, 3 crushed garlic cloves, and 1 bouquet garni. Drain (keeping the stock for soup) and discard all but the beans. Drain the soaked cod, pat dry, and sprinkle over some black pepper before browning both sides in peanut oil. Put the beans in an ovenproof dish and place the fish on top. Scatter on 3 minced garlic cloves. Pour over 1 cup crème fraîche, then cook in a 400°F oven for about 20 minutes. Serve with chopped chervil. Rick Stein uses flageolet beans along roughly the same, albeit more elaborate, lines in his bouillabaisse-cassoulet hybrid.

HONEY, TOMATO & DILL BEANS

Gigantes—fasolia gigantes, or giant Greek beans—would serve as a handy travel pillow for a shrew. The following is a slight adaption of a recipe by the Greek cooking expert Diane Kochilas. Jumbo lima beans (sometimes called butter beans) make a fine substitute, not least because this recipe makes them live up to their alternative name. Somehow, the sweet-and-sour combination of tomato, vinegar, and honey, with the unusual addition of fresh dill, draws out the beans' butteriness. The results are more-ishly rich. I first cooked this dish as a side to an excellent leg of lamb I needn't have bothered with. It was the bean-pot my guests went at like locusts. Like good butter, this needs no other accompaniment than a basket of crisp French bread. Soak 1 lb dry jumbo lima beans for 8 hours. Drain the beans before boiling them in fresh water for 10 minutes, then simmering for 20, or until they are just cooked. In a separate, ovenproof pot, fry 2 chopped onions in 2 tbsp olive oil until they are lightly golden. Drain the beans, reserving their cooking water, and add them to the onions with another 3 tbsp olive oil, 2 (14-oz) cans of crushed tomatoes, 2 cups of the bean-cooking water, and 2 tbsp honey. Stir, then cover tightly with a lid or foil. Cook in a 375°F oven for 1 hour, adding more of the bean water if needed. Assuming the sauce looks good and thick, stir in a chopped bunch of dill, 4 tbsp red wine vinegar, 2 tbsp tomato paste, and salt and pepper to taste, then return to the oven for 30 minutes longer. Kochilas serves these with crumbled feta on the top.

WHITE BEANS, CLAMS & CIDER

Beans are a staple of the cash-poor, time-rich cook. But not in this dish: If there's a faster recipe that achieves such intensity of flavor, I'd like to know about it. Scrub 2¼ lb clams. In a large saucepan, soften 2 minced large garlic cloves in 2 tbsp olive oil until just turning golden, then add 1 cup hard cider. Bring to a boil and simmer for 1 minute. Add the clams, apply the lid, and cook for 4–5 minutes. They're ready when most of them have opened—check them every minute after 2 minutes. Meanwhile, warm a drained 15-oz jar or can of white beans (if you prefer a clam-heavy dish) or double that amount (if you prefer a bean dish with clams). Try to use beans in a jar from a Spanish grocer; they're far tastier. Cannellini or lima beans are both fine. These go especially well with littleneck clams as, being a similar size, they become lodged in the shells, and, infused with garlicky liquor, are transformed into creamy little vegetarian bivalves themselves. The first quantity will feed 4, the latter 6. Mix the warm beans with the clams, sprinkle with parsley, and serve with good crusty bread.

Dal: Tarka Chana Dal

Dal doubles as the name of the dish and its main ingredient, lentils. Tarka is the fragrant mixture of oil and spices (and sometimes tomatoes and onions) that is stirred into the lentils when they're just about cooked. Not all dals include tarka, but maybe they should. The recipe that follows calls for split chana dal, an Indian variety of chickpea that's smaller and darker-skinned than our familar chickpea (or garbanzo bean). They are easily mistaken for yellow split peas, which can be substituted, and don't need soaking, but the chana dal taste marginally better. Consider this a scaled-down version of the previous starting point for bean stew—you're essentially applying the absorption method to produce softly cooked lentils with a small amount of liquid, which can be mopped up with homemade chapatis (page [29]). Serve with yogurt, chutney, and poppadoms, too. If you prefer your dal more soup-like you'll need to make it wetter: See [B] under Leeway.

For 4 as a main dish, or 8 as a side

INGREDIENTS
1⅓ cups dry chana dal [A]
3 cups water [B] [C]
½ large onion, diced
1 tbsp finely chopped fresh ginger
½ tsp ground turmeric
Salt

FOR THE TARKA [D]
2 tbsp bland oil or ghee
½ large onion, sliced
1 cinnamon stick
4 cloves
4 cardamom pods
2 tomatoes, roughly diced
1 tsp garam masala
½ tsp ground cumin
½ tsp ground coriander

1   Rinse and pick over the chana dal. Soak for 30 minutes, then drain.

2   Transfer the chana dal to a pan with the water. Bring it to a boil, then reduce to a simmer.

³ Skim off any scum and, once it desists, add the onion, ginger, and turmeric.

⁴ Simmer, uncovered, for 50 minutes, stirring occasionally, and judiciously adding boiling water if the dal is drying out. Add salt after about 20 minutes. ᴱ

⁵ When the chana dal is almost cooked, make the tarka. Heat the oil or ghee in a skillet and fry the sliced onion and whole spices. When the onions are soft and tinged with brown, add the tomato, followed by the ground spices, and cook for a further minute.

⁶ Stir the tarka into the dal and warm through if necessary. Garnish, if you like. ᶠ

LEEWAY

ᴬ Urad dal, toor dal, Mysore dal, and moong dal can all be used in place of chana dal. These can cook in as little as 20 minutes. Just be careful with split urad dal, which has a tendency toward *over*-softening. Use a mix of lentils for a complexly flavored and textured composite dal.

ᴮ This ratio of lentils to liquid yields a mashed-potato consistency. For a soupy consistency, increase the water to 5 cups.

ᶜ Replace some of the liquid with coconut milk, stock, or tamarind water.

ᴰ The tarka here is basic. It can be embellished with any number of the following: curry leaves, asafetida, tomato paste, whole or sliced garlic, cumin seeds, and mustard seeds. (See pages ²⁵⁴, ²⁵⁶ and ²⁵⁷ for more tarka ideas.)

ᴱ Ingredients that can be added 10 minutes before the dal is ready: chopped fresh spinach, frozen peas, or other cooked pulses such as canned chickpeas or kidney beans. As a rule, acidic ingredients are held back until the lentils are soft.

ᶠ Garnish with (toasted) shredded coconut, fine strands of fried fresh ginger, fried whole garlic cloves, cilantro, basil, or mint, crushed toasted coriander seeds, garam masala, Bombay mix, or roasted salted cashews.

COCONUT, RAISIN & CASHEW DAL

The Bengali specialty of *cholar dal narkel diye* is the sort of dal you could sell at a fairground. It has a sportive sprinkle of sugar added at the end of cooking, and is served with a sweet, multi-textured, lucky-dip garnish, and a luchi, a thin, round bread that looks like a clutch bag and is ideal for scooping up mouthfuls of sweet, soft stodge. Follow the starting point, using chana dal and adding 1 bay leaf, 2 cloves, and 2 cardamom pods at step ³. While the dal is cooking, make the following tarka. Chop a palm-sized piece of fresh coconut into ½-in dice and fry in oil or ghee until brown, adding 1 tbsp each of golden raisins and cashews when the coconut is golden. Set the fruit and nuts aside and use the same oil or ghee to fry 1 bay leaf, 1 cinnamon stick, 2 cloves, 2 cardamom pods, and ½ tsp pepper flakes. Drain any excess water from the dal if necessary, but retain it in case the dish needs moistening later. Stir the fruit and nuts and the spice mixture into the dal, along with 1–3 tsp sugar.

LENTIL, APRICOT & CUMIN SOUP

Not a dal, but this fabulous soup (from Armenia, according to David Ansel) is vibrant enough to be sold on the streets of Mumbai. The secondary ingredients pull the lentil base in opposite directions—cumin is gloomy, bitter, and earthy, while apricot is bright, sweet, and floral. It's like listening to The Smiths on a glorious summer afternoon. Dice 1 large onion and 2 carrots. Soften them in olive oil in a covered pan over a low heat for 10 minutes. Add 2 tsp ground cumin, replace the lid, and give it all another 10 minutes. Add 1¼ cups rinsed split red lentils and 4 cups water, bring to a boil, and simmer for about 20 minutes until the lentils are soft. Remove from the heat and stir in 1 cup sliced dried apricots, 1 tsp salt, and a scant cup more hot water. Blend in batches, then gently reheat and serve.

LENTILLES AU CURRY

I wanted to find out how dal principles might be applied to Puy lentils. In contrast to the masoor or urad lentils used in India, tiny, slate-green Puy lentils resist disintegration, retaining an elegant French integrity. Rather than mix the cooked lentils with a tarka of roughly chopped onions and whole spices, as you would for Indian dal, it seemed more appropriate to mix them with a delicate curry oil before serving them under some plain fried seafood with a little cumin-roasted cauliflower on the side. The curry oil is adapted from a Raymond Blanc recipe, although my version calls for more curry powder: I found it needed an extra kick of heat to register. Carefully toast 1 tbsp Madras curry powder in a dry skillet over a low to medium heat for 5 minutes. Add 6 tbsp warmed extra virgin olive oil, along with 1 lemongrass stalk, bruised and finely chopped, 2 lime leaves, thinly sliced, the grated zest and juice of ½ lime, and a pinch of salt. Take off the heat and let infuse for at least an hour, then strain through a cheesecloth-lined sieve before use. To serve 2, cook 1 cup rinsed Puy lentils with 1 large diced shallot in 3 cups simmering water until the lentils are softened—this will take about 25 minutes. While the lentils are still warm, mix in the curry oil and a squeeze of lemon juice.

MAKHANI DAL

While the coconut, raisin, and cashew dal opposite is enriched with sugar, fruit, and nuts, *makhani* dal is slow-cooked, then enhanced with butter and cream. *Makhani* means "buttery," and the dish lives up to its name. It's the dal equivalent of Joël Robuchon's famously opulent *purée de pomme de terre*, except you don't even have to pretend to want anything else to go with it. A pulse dish heavily enriched with dairy products is unusual in any cuisine, and you may be taken aback by your first mouthful. Lentils are often described as meaty, but here they taste positively beefy. Add some peas and you'll have a vegetarian keema. It's not uncommon to mix in some kidney beans or chana dal, but I prefer to make *makhani* dal with just urad dal—the sort with the skin still on, so they stay intact during the slow cook while their insides turn creamy. The method departs from our starting point in being a little more involved—once you've cooked the dal, made the tarka, and mixed them together, the dish goes into the oven for a long time before the butter and cream are stirred in. Soak 1¼ cups whole black urad dal for 12 hours. In fresh water, bring the dal to a boil and cook hard for 10 minutes, then reduce to a simmer and cook for 60 minutes longer. When the scum desists, add 2 chopped green chilies, 1 black cardamom pod, and ½ tsp ground turmeric. After the hour of simmering, when the dal is soft, melt 2 tbsp butter or ghee in a small skillet and gently cook 2 tsp sweet paprika, 1 tsp ground coriander, 1 tsp ground cumin, and ½ tsp chili powder. After 1 minute, add 1 cup boiled and puréed onion, 1 tsp tomato paste, 8 crushed garlic cloves, and 1 tbsp chopped fresh ginger. Cook gently for 2 minutes, then add to the lentils, along with 2 skinned, deseeded, and diced tomatoes, ⅓ tsp freshly grated nutmeg, 3 tbsp garam masala, and enough water to make the dal pourable. Transfer to a 325°F oven and cook, uncovered, for 3 hours, checking the water level several times and replenishing with hot water if necessary. About 30 minutes before the cooking time is up, remove the pot from the oven and stir in 1 stick butter, ⅔ cup heavy cream, and 2 tsp salt. An option at this stage is to drain and rinse half a 15-oz can of chickpeas or kidney beans and add them too. Serve with homemade flatbreads (page 28).

MISIR WOT

This Ethiopian dish is made with red lentils, onions, garlic, and berbere—an admirably complex mixture traditional in Ethiopian and Eritrean cuisine, which comprises chili, other hot aromatics like black pepper, ginger, and clove, plus ajwain, allspice, cardamom, cinnamon, coriander seed, cumin, fenugreek, and nutmeg. In most cases *misir wot* is made like a standard lentil soup, although some recipes take an approach more along the lines of our starting point: cooking the lentils first, then frying the onion, garlic, and berbere together like a tarka and stirring them into the lentils. The version that most piqued my interest, however, was more akin to a risotto, in that the cooking liquid was added in increments (even if, in this instance, there's no need to keep stirring). Once the water has been absorbed, the lentils are allowed to catch—i.e. stick to the bottom of the pan and start to caramelize—before the next few tablespoons of water are added. It's a culinary game of chicken: How far are you prepared to let the lentils darken before you give them a scrape? The process is repeated until the lentils are cooked. To finish, it's traditional to add a spiced, clarified butter called *niter kibbeh*. Dice 1 large onion and soften it in oil or ghee in a medium-sized saucepan. Add 4 crushed garlic cloves and 2 tbsp tomato paste and cook for a few minutes, then add the berbere with 1⅓ cups lentils and ½ cup hot water to start. Salt when the lentils are almost soft. If you're new to berbere, I would recommend starting with 2 or 3 tsp—you can add more toward the end of cooking if desired.

PANCHMEL DAL

A Rajasthani dal made with five different pulses ("panch" means five): moong dal, chana dal, skinless black urad dal, toor dal, and either moth beans (matki) or split red lentils (masoor dal). Soaking in a glass bowl, the pulses look very pretty, like the colored gravel in a tropical fish tank. The recipe has a Jain heritage, and so contains no onion or garlic. What sets it apart is the side dish of *baati*, a bread made with 1 cup coarse whole wheat flour and ½ tsp salt, mixed (rather like pie pastry) to a bread-crumb texture with 4 tbsp ghee, then brought together into a dough with water and salt. The dough is then fashioned into small patties and cooked over a charcoal fire or baked at 350°F until golden—10–15 minutes on each side. The finished *baatis* are soaked in melted ghee, then broken into pieces and dunked in the dal. The other accompanying dish is a *churma*—crumbs of *baati*, fried in ghee and then sweetened with jaggery, a kind of unrefined dark sugar. Coconut, almond, and cardamom are all optional additions for the *baati* and *churma*. Soak ¼ cup of each dal in water for 2 hours, then drain and cook as per the starting point (but leave out the onion). For the tarka, fry a pinch of asafetida in oil or ghee with 4 or 5 cloves and ½ tsp cumin seeds for 1 minute, then add 1 tsp each of ground cumin and coriander and ½ tsp chili powder. Cook for 1 minute longer, then add 3 chopped tomatoes. Mix the tarka into the dal and serve with a sprinkle of garam masala, plus the *baatis* and *churma*.

PARIPPU

An everyday Sri Lankan dal made with red lentils and coconut cream. Follow the starting point, using red split lentils—which only need rinsing, not soaking. At step ³, when the scum has desisted, add 6 tbsp coconut cream, 1 chopped green chili, ½ tsp ground coriander, and ½ tsp ground cumin with the diced onion and ground turmeric, but leave out the ginger. Simmer for 20–30 minutes until the lentils are soft, or longer if you like them on the mushy side. Make a simple tarka with 1 tsp cumin seeds and 1 tsp brown mustard seeds cooked in the oil until they start to pop (use a splatter guard to stop them flying everywhere), then add ½ large onion, sliced, plus a few curry leaves if you have them. Stir it into the dal and heat for a few minutes. Serve with rice and sliced chilies, or the coconut flatbread on page [32].

PEASE PUDDING

I was describing traditional English pease pudding to an Indian friend. "It's like dal," I said, "but without any of the aromatics." Let's just say he remained unconvinced. It didn't help when I added that it was traditional to boil it in a piece of old cloth. He had forcibly repatriated himself by the time I told him that the dish was often finished with butter and/or cream, and a sprinkling of white pepper or mint. His loss: I love it. Jane Grigson recalls that pease pudding, made with yellow split peas, was sold at the butcher's in her youth: You bought it by the slice. For a sliceable pudding, use the ratios in our starting point. At step [3], add the diced onion (obviously no turmeric or ginger) and, if liked, a little butter to the peas in their cooking water. Salt after 20 minutes. After 50 minutes, blend the mixture with more butter plus white pepper, and, if liked, a little cream. Scrape into a loaf pan to set if you do intend to slice it. Serve in a floury bun with fried fish or a slice of ham, or as a side for the butcher's plumpest sausages.

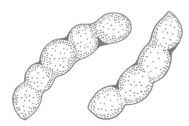

TAMARIND DAL

A dal with edge. Tamarind and lime give soft, comforting lentils a racy makeover. It's what I want to eat if I come down with a cold in July. You'll need some tamarind water, so put 1 tsp tamarind pulp to soak in 2 tbsp boiling water, leave for 30 minutes, then strain and discard what's left of the pulp. Try making this one with toor dal, which is the most popular lentil in India and, compared to other varieties, has a slighter blander flavor, and a mildly gelatinous texture when cooked. You can buy it in a shiny, "oily" form, with a longer shelf-life; just remember to give it an extra-attentive rinse before use. Follow the starting point, using an extra 1 cup cooking water from the outset, as the consistency should be quite runny. The cooking time will be about 45 minutes. To make the tarka, fry 2 minced garlic cloves and 1 chopped green chili in oil. After a few minutes, add 3 chopped tomatoes and 1 tsp each of ground coriander and ground cumin. Stir into the toor dal with the tamarind water and the juice of 1 lime. Serve with lime wedges, cilantro leaves, and thick, creamy plain yogurt.

Unstirred Rice: Kedgeree

Not the usual way to make kedgeree, but it works well and is a deal less fiddly—a benefit if you fancy making it for breakfast or brunch. Once the lid is on, you can quickly prep the eggs and garnish, knowing that in half an hour you'll have perfectly cooked rice and fish. The method is easily adapted to the oven— you'll find examples in the Flavors & Variations section, or see [G] under Leeway.

For a main course or substantial breakfast for 6

INGREDIENTS
1 medium onion, diced
2 tbsp butter or bland oil
1 tbsp garam masala [A]
Chili powder, to taste
½ tsp ground turmeric
2¾ cups hot fish stock or water
1½ tsp salt (less if the stock is very salty)
⅓ cup frozen peas
2 cups white basmati rice, rinsed and drained [B] [C] [D]
10 oz smoked haddock fillet, cut into bite-sized pieces, any
    stray bones removed [E] [F]
6 eggs
A little butter or cream, to finish
Chopped parsley or cilantro and fresh chilies, for garnish

1   In a large saucepan with a tight-fitting lid, soften the onion in the butter or oil over a medium heat.

2   Stir in the garam masala, chili, and turmeric and cook for 1 minute.

3   Pour in the hot stock or water, add the salt, and stir.

4   Add the peas and bring to a boil, then add the rice and fish, stir, reduce to a low to medium heat, and cover. You should be able to hear the contents of the pan gently simmering. Set the timer for 10 minutes. Once the time is up, leave the pan covered, but remove from the heat and let rest for 20 minutes. [G]

5   While the rice is cooking, hard-cook the eggs for 6–8 minutes, depending on how soft or set you like the yolks. Let cool a little, then peel and cut each egg into 4 or 6 wedges.

6   When the 20-minute rest is over, remove the pan lid and check to see if the rice is cooked. If it isn't quite, replace the lid and leave it for a few more minutes. Sprinkle over a few tablespoons of boiling water before you cover if it's looking a little dry.

7   With a fork, fluff the rice grains with the butter or cream and serve garnished with the eggs, parsley or cilantro, and chilies. Avoid too much stirring, as it can turn the rice mushy.

LEEWAY

A   In place of garam masala, use your favorite bought curry powder, or custom blend. You may want to add some whole spices, too: cinnamon sticks, cloves, split cardamom pods.

B   Long-grain rice (*not* easy-cook) can be cooked to this method and time. As can short-grain rice, if you use 3⅓ cups of stock or water, although note that short-grain is not appropriate for kedgeree.

C   Brown basmati and long-grain rice will need 30 minutes simmering and 5 minutes resting time, using the same ratio of rice to liquid; although note that some long-grain rice can take longer. Cooking times for brown rice tend to vary more—it's fine to take the lid off and check.

D   Use the same method to cook plain rice. Pour the hot stock or water into the pan and allow 1–3 tsp oil or butter to melt into it, then add the rinsed and drained rice, along with ½ tsp salt. You can also use the oven method at G.

E   The same technique can be applied to any raw meat, fish, or vegetables that will cook in the allotted time. If in doubt, precook or partially precook it by browning, roasting, frying, broiling, or poaching. If you opt for the latter, the poaching water could be used as stock to cook the rice.

F   You can be pretty flexible with the quantities—say up to twice this amount of fish.

G   If you prefer to cook the rice in the oven, use an ovenproof pot or baking dish that will go on the stovetop. Once all the ingredients are in the pot at step 4, cover it tightly and put it on the center shelf of a 325°F oven. White basmati and long-grain rice will need about 25 minutes, as will white short-grain, although in the latter case you'll need to increase the liquid to 3⅓ cups for 2 cups rice. Brown basmati and long-grain will need more like 30–35 minutes, but note that brands do vary. It's fine to take the lid off and check, but remove the lid only briefly before returning the pot or dish to the oven if needed.

ARROZ CON POLLO

A few summers ago my husband and I chanced upon an isolated *chiringuito* on the Playa de Zahara near Cadiz in Spain. As we paid for a couple of beers we spotted, behind the beach shack, a gas burner the size of a bicycle wheel. Precariously balanced on it was a paella pan full of *arroz con pollo*. No vegetables. No herbs or spices. Just rice with bits of chicken in it. A paper plateful cost a euro and was one of the best meals I've ever eaten, largely because it was made with the sort of dark, sticky chicken stock that somehow tastes profound. Eating outdoors actually diminishes intensity of flavor, for the simple reason that the wind on which irresistible cooking smells are borne also whisks them away from your olfactory bulb, and I had to marvel at how good my lunch must have been to taste so incredible *al aire libre*. Make the quick chicken stock with chicken thighs as described on page [201], adding ½ tsp salt. Simmer for 45 minutes, then strain, skim, and reduce to 3⅓ cups. Follow our starting point, using the cooked, boned chicken, cut into pieces, in place of the fish, and cooking some garlic with the onion. Omit the eggs, peas, and kedgeree flavorings. Use short-grain paella rice rather than basmati. Garnish with a sprinkle of cayenne and some chopped parsley.

EGGPLANT, CHICKPEA, APRICOT & PINE NUT

Classic pilaf flavors, for when you lack the time for the fuss of pilaf. The idea with pilaf is to keep the grains separate, so you absolutely must give the rice a good rinse first to rid it of starch. Leave out the fish, peas, spices, and garnish used for kedgeree. For 2 servings, dice 1 large or 2 medium eggplants, toss them in oil, then cook with the onion at step [1], allowing everything to soften and brown before adding 2–3 crushed garlic cloves. Sprinkle in ½ tsp ground cinnamon, ¼ tsp ground turmeric, and 2 tsp ground coriander. Allow 30 seconds before adding 1 tbsp tomato paste and cooking for 30 seconds longer. Stir in 1¼ cups cooked chickpeas (canned are fine, and organic have a notably better flavor and texture) and 12 dried apricots cut into strips. If you've cooked your own chickpeas, use 1½ cups of the cooking water as stock; if not, plain water will do. Add ¾ tsp salt and bring back to a boil. Stir in 1 cup rinsed and drained brown basmati rice, then cook as per step [4], giving it 30 minutes, followed by a 5-minute rest. Pile onto plates and zigzag over some Sriracha or other chili sauce. Garnish with plenty of toasted pine nuts. If the carnivore in you is feeling left out, first fry 8 oz ground lamb (not too lean) for a few minutes, then set it aside before continuing with the onion and eggplant. Add the ground lamb back in with the rice. The combination of meat, pulses, nuts, fruit, and spices crops up in various forms across the Middle East. In addition, Alan Davidson makes reference to Caribbean pilafs, very loosely based on their Middle Eastern counterparts in their combination of pork, peanut, olives, brown sugar, and Worcestershire sauce.

FAVA BEAN, ONION & DILL

The kind of side dish to steal the show. Takes its cue from *baghali polo*, the Persian rice dish sometimes served with charcoal-grilled meat or fish. The flavor comes from plenty of sliced onion, fried hot-dog brown, and enough butter to flatter the basmati rice. Dill adds a balancing freshness and can be augmented with mint and/or parsley. You can make this on the stovetop, but as I most often serve this at barbecues, I prefer the oven method. This makes enough to serve 6 as a side. Assuming you're barbecuing smaller items like kebabs and merguez sausages, as opposed to an entire lamb, if you add the rice to the water just as the charcoal is glowing red and turning white, everything should be roughly synchronized. This means the onions (3 medium) will need their long, slow frying ahead of time, in an ovenproof pot or dish. When the charcoal's ready, add 2¾ cups boiling water, 1½ tsp salt, and 1 tbsp butter to the onions in the pan and bring back to a boil. Stir in 2 cups white basmati rice and put into a 325°F oven for 25 minutes. When the time is up, gently stir in a couple of handfuls of cooked, shelled, and skinned fava beans (or more, if you don't mind skinning them), 2–3 tbsp butter, and lots of chopped herbs. A pile of the rice and a skewer of lamb will be all your guests need, bar a spicy red and the rain to hold off. Once or twice I have saved myself the trouble of skinning the fava beans by using shiny green edamame instead, but it's a questionable economy; the flavor isn't as good.

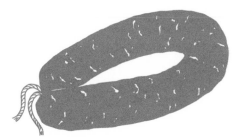

JAMBALAYA

Mother's on Poydras Street in New Orleans serves the most memorable jambalaya I've ever eaten, the soft rice smoky and piquant with sausage and cayenne, fragrant with herbs, and deeply savory with chicken stock and celery. Cut 12 oz chicken (boned breast or thigh is fine) into small pieces. Set a large pan over a medium-high heat and brown 8 oz sliced spicy, smoky sausage with the chicken in a little vegetable oil. Add 1 medium onion, 1 green bell pepper, and 2 celery stalks, all diced, and 2 minced garlic cloves. Stir, then add 1 heaped tsp dried oregano, 1 bay leaf, ¼ tsp cayenne, 1½ tsp salt, and a good grinding of black pepper, followed by the 2¾ cups chicken stock (or use boiling water and ½ tsp more salt). Stir, bring to a boil, and add 2 cups long-grain rice. Bring back to a boil, then reduce the heat to low to medium, cover, and cook for 10 minutes. Remove from the heat and leave for about 20 minutes longer with the pan still covered. Fluff, then serve with sliced scallions and a splash of Tabasco.

KHEER

I had long been curious about the Hindu festival of Diwali, and so planned a trip to Leicester, where the biggest celebrations in Britain are held. I asked a friend to come with me. "It's the festival of light," I explained, failing, largely due to my near-total ignorance, to make it sound vaguely enticing. I tried a different tack. "It's really the festival of candy," I said, but I'd lost her by then. I arrived alone on Belgrave Road, "the Golden Mile," famous for its Indian restaurants and sari-sellers. It was a cold, gray November day and I had four hours before the festivities were due to begin. I had been given a recommendation for a Gujarati restaurant, and took a table with the intention of making my meal there last as long as possible. I ordered the special thali. The appetizer consisted of a seemingly endless supply of *farsan*, a pick-and-mix selection of vegetables dipped in chickpea-flour batter, like a vegan *fritto misto*. Next the thali arrived. The removal of its poppadom lid revealed two curries—one of smoky mashed eggplant, the other of mixed vegetables—plus plain rice, a thin, earthy dal, a fruity chutney with a tamarind edge, a chilly raita, and a salad with whole spice seeds and cilantro leaves mixed into it. The chapatis arrived regally, on a plate of their own. I ate everything slowly, savoring every dish. The waiter cleared my plate and returned with a bowl. Kheer, he announced, a special for Diwali. This was bad news for me. Kheer is rice pudding. I wouldn't eat rice pudding if it were the last food on earth. I examined the bowl. Admittedly it looked different from the glutinous horror of my school days. It was thinner, and the rice grains were defined and separate, as they might be in a savory dish. I could see pistachios and toasted almonds. It smelled not of baby posset but of cinnamon, cardamom, and caramelized milk. And instead of a blob of jam it was garnished with gold leaf. Still. It was *rice pudding*. Blech! Then I looked out the window, at the street busy with Diwali-goers carrying boxes of fireworks and candies. They looked cold and fed up. So I took a tiny hamster-ish nibble on the tip of my spoon. Little by little, as the cinnamon and caramel sweet-talked my palate, I came to realize it was exquisite. Three hours after I'd sat down, the waiter brought me the check like he meant it. Our familiar rice puddings are usually made with short-grain rice—say 6 tbsp rice with 4 cups milk and 2–3 tbsp sugar—and are baked, uncovered, in a 300°F oven for 2 hours. Kheer is made on the stovetop, with long-grain rice simmered slowly (a diffuser will be handy) so the milk thickens and caramelizes. From our starting point, it's possible to make something very like kheer—without the risk of the milk boiling over, or the patience to wait for the rice to cook through (it takes longer to cook in milk or coconut milk than it does in water). In a large saucepan with a lid, melt 2 tbsp butter in 2¾ cups boiling water with a pinch of salt. Stir in 2 cups rinsed and drained white basmati rice, cover with a lid, and reduce to a gentle simmer. After 10 minutes, remove the pan from the heat and leave, covered, for 20 minutes longer. Meanwhile, put 2 (4-in) pieces of cinnamon stick, 6 cracked cardamom pods, and 6 cloves in scant 1 cup milk and microwave on high for 60 seconds (you might also add a pinch of saffron). Let the spices infuse. When the 30 minutes are up, check the rice is cooked. Strain the spice-infused milk, mix with half a 14-oz can of sweetened condensed milk (adding a touch of rosewater, if you like), and stir gently into the rice. To loosen the kheer, add as much of the remaining condensed milk as you like. This should be enough for 6–8. Serve hot or cold, in bowls, decorated with pistachios, rose petals, and a little silver or gold leaf.

KITCHURI

Kitchuri is a mixture of lentils and rice, a fragrant heap of dots and dashes that, decoded, might reveal how a staple for sixteenth-century Hindustani peasants became kedgeree, the mildly curried breakfast dish enjoyed by Bertie Wooster. I make it following our starting point, first cooking 2 onions, sliced rather than diced, in butter and oil until they are lightly browned. Then I add the spices—usually a mixture of ground cumin, coriander, and garam masala—and finally 1 cup of rinsed split red lentils and 1 cup rinsed basmati rice. Pour in 3⅓ cups boiling water and add ½ tsp salt, then simmer, covered, on the lowest heat for 10 minutes. Remove from the heat, still covered, and let stand for 20 minutes. Adjust the seasoning before serving with flatbreads (page 28), poppadoms, chutney, pickles, and (inauthentically) a fried egg.

PAELLA

The small, busy cove had no natural shade, so to avoid the lunchtime sun we had no choice but to retire to the restaurant. When our paella arrived, I served us both a modest spoonful from the surface. "You know what?" I said to my husband. "I feel a bit faint. You wouldn't fetch my fan from the car, would you?" Left alone at the table, I dislodged a large section of *socarrat* and ferried it directly to my mouth. *Socarrat* is the layer of crispy rice that, with a modicum of luck and skill, forms on the bottom of the paella. My husband returned. "You've got to see this," he said. "A basket of the most *adorable* puppies. Just there, behind the bins." Puppies! I hurried off to see them. When I returned, the paella had been ransacked and the rest of the *socarrat* had gone. To this day I don't know what had happened to those puppies. Another mystery is what constitutes an authentic paella. Some say that to qualify as the real deal a paella must be cooked in the Spanish countryside, over an open fire, at the weekend, by a man. We had returned home from vacation. It was a Tuesday in London. And I was a woman. At a gas stove. Unqualified, that is, in every particular. An approximation of paella can be made by adapting the starting point for unstirred rice— either the stovetop or oven version—to paella-ish ingredients, as the method works as well with the short- and medium-grain rice required by paella as it does with long-grain. But then there's the *socarrat*, whose utter deliciousness comes at a price: an authentic, thin-bottomed, wide, shallow, lidless, non-nonstick paella pan. No lid, in turn, means you need to get the ratio of stock to rice exactly right—it's far higher than in our starting point—and judge the heat carefully, so it's absorbed at the right speed to cook the rice through before the dish dries out. Adapting the recipe to your stove and cooking vessel is a matter of trial and error. To make sure my paellas cook evenly I generally use two gas burners and rotate the pan by 45 degrees every 2–3 minutes. To practice my *socarrat* skills I use the following inexpensive, low-maintenance set of ingredients in a 12-in paella pan (makes enough for 3 generous servings). Slowly soften 1 large diced onion in 3 tbsp olive oil. Add 4 crushed garlic cloves and cook until golden. Push the onion and garlic to the edge of the pan and brown 3 spicy, fat pork sausages, sliced, and 2 chicken thighs, cut into bite-sized pieces. Meanwhile, stir 2 tbsp dry white wine, 2 tsp smoked sweet paprika, 1 tsp thyme leaves (fresh or dried), a few pinches of cayenne, and ⅛ tsp powdered saffron into 3 cups hot chicken stock. Once the sausages and chicken pieces are browned, stir in a handful of halved green beans and the same of frozen peas, then pour in the stock mixture. Bring to a simmer. Pour 1¼ cups paella rice evenly into the stock, spreading it out with a spoon. The trick now is to keep as much of the stock as possible at a low simmer—the rice at the edges of the paella will be particularly prone to undercooking, so if your pan is bigger than 10 in, you'll probably need to move it around. The rice will need 20–30 minutes to cook through. When it has—or almost has, and the liquid is dropping beneath the ingredient line—it's time to pay attention to the *socarrat* (assuming that your relationship can take the strain of sharing it). Move the pan to the largest burner on the stovetop and whack up the heat. After a few minutes, check the hardness of the rice at the bottom with a prod of a fork, or pull back a little of the rice and take a peek at the color—it's best to look in the center. If it's not crispy or golden enough yet, keep a watchful eye on it—you don't want your *socarrat* burnt, or cooked for so long that the rest of the rice goes mushy. Serve using a slotted or flexible metal spatula, or whatever implement will dislodge as much of the *socarrat* as possible.

ROASTED VEGETABLE SPICED RICE

Inspired by the exotically spiced biryani dishes eaten at lavish banquets, and thought to have been introduced to India by the Mughals. Well, that, and my husband's inability to use the last of anything. Our fridge is full of tiny Tupperware boxes containing a tablespoon of tuna salad, two soggy spears of roasted asparagus, a pinch of grated Parmesan. In the crisper, you'll find a single carrot, a lone zucchini, a quarter-cauliflower, and a sixth of a red onion, its layers separating like parched petals. My husband defends all this as sound environmental practice, but in truth his need to retain very small portions of food is akin to his reluctance to leave parties: He just can't bear the finality. For 2 generous helpings, chop a few double handfuls of vegetables into bite-sized pieces, put them in a large roasting pan with a tablespoon or two of peanut oil, and roast at 400°F for about 25 minutes. Transfer the vegetables to a large saucepan and pour in 1½ cups boiling water, then add 3 tbsp good-quality biryani paste and 1 tsp salt. You might also add some frozen peas, green beans, and/or a few cardamom pods. Bring to a boil. Stir in 1 cup rinsed and drained white basmati rice and reduce to a simmer, then cook as per the starting point. Serve with chopped cilantro, toasted sliced almonds, plain yogurt or raita, and a stack of poppadoms.

Risotto: Risotto Bianco

For all its plainness, risotto bianco would make an excellent side dish to a stew or a simply cooked piece of fish. Its neutrality also means it can be easily and productively flavored. Whereas in the starting point for unstirred rice, precise quantities can be given for the liquid, with risotto the cook must respond to the ingredients at hand, continuing to feed the grains with warm stock until they're on the point of being cooked all the way through. It's the starch released by the grains as they cook, and are stirred, that thickens the stock and lends the dish its signature creaminess. Carnaroli rice is more given to this than other varieties. Add butter and cream at the end of cooking for an extra-luxurious consistency, although some chefs prefer to use olive oil when the risotto features seafood or green vegetables.

For a main course for 4, or a side dish for 6 [A]

INGREDIENTS
3½–5 cups stock or water [B] [C]
1 medium onion, or 2 shallots, finely chopped [D]
1 tbsp each of butter and olive oil
2 cups risotto rice [E]
1 small glass of white wine [F]
¼ cup finely grated Parmesan
Salt

1   Make your stock (page [208]), or reheat if already made. Keep it warm over a very gentle heat. If you're using water rather than stock, bring it to a boil, then let it cool a little.

2   Over a low to medium heat, soften the onion or shallots in the butter and oil.
    This will take 8–10 minutes. Don't let the onion or shallots color. You might also add other aromatics here.

3   Add the rice and stir to coat it with the butter and oil. Cook for 1–2 minutes.
    Until you hear it "crack," as many recipes have it. My hearing is not *that* good.

4   Add the wine and let it evaporate almost entirely.
    Skip the wine if you'd rather. But it's a small amount. No one ever got tipsy on risotto.

5 Start adding the warm stock, ladle by ladle, stirring often enough that the rice doesn't stick. If it is sticking, turn down the heat. Start tasting the rice after about 12 minutes. ᴳ

It can help to set a timer. Some like their risotto chalky—with a little white spot in the center of the grain—others comprehensively cooked through. The precise temperature of the stock, the size of the pan, and the variety of rice will all have an effect on the speed of the cooking. Stir gently, to avoid mashing the rice grains.

6 When the rice is perfectly cooked, add the Parmesan, salt to taste, and serve.

Some cooks add a final ladle of stock before removing the risotto from the heat, to insure against dryness; others add butter, olive oil, or a splash of dry white vermouth.

LEEWAY

ᴬ Giorgio Locatelli advises against making more than 10 servings in one go, at least in a domestic kitchen.

ᴮ In Marcella Hazan's opinion, risotto stock should be on the lighter side, as opposed to a richer, more French-style stock. You may prefer the flavor of a brown stock.

ᶜ Both Judy Rodgers and Jacob Kenedy advocate water over stock. Rodgers says it gives the "clean rice" flavor its due. They will, of course, be using top-notch rice, butter, cheese, etc. A white risotto is as unforgiving as a white swimsuit; short cuts and penny-pinching will be mercilessly revealed. Some cooks even stipulate bottled mineral water.

ᴰ Jamie Oliver adds a little finely chopped celery with the onion in his risotto bianco. Fennel is often added to seafood risotto. Garlic can be added to the onion or shallots toward the end of their softening time.

ᴱ It's said that Carnaroli makes a creamier risotto; Arborio stays firmer. Both are good.

ᶠ Dry white vermouth can be used in place of wine at step 4, but expect it to leave a definite aromatic trace in the finished risotto. Where suitable, red wine is also a possibility.

ᴳ I've gone with the classic method. Judy Rodgers, however, suggests adding half the stock up front and letting it cook out before starting with the incremental additions and regular stirring. She also recommends a saucepan rather than a low, wide pan—a good tip if you're making a risotto for 1 or 2, when the volume of ingredients is small, and the stock can evaporate too quickly.

BLUEBERRY

To prepare *The Silver Spoon*'s blueberry risotto, adapt our starting point by making a vegetable stock (page [216]) at step [1], then adding a few handfuls of blueberries once the white wine has evaporated at step [4]. Keep a few berries back for the garnish. Blueberries are sometimes added to mushroom risotto in northern Italian restaurants. *The Silver Spoon* also gives a recipe for strawberry risotto, in which the crushed berries are added once the rice has cooked for roughly 10 minutes. In contrast to the blueberry risotto, there's no call for Parmesan, but both are finished with cream.

BUTTERNUT SQUASH & FENNEL

The Ivy's butternut squash risotto is unusual, in that it tastes as good made at home, following the recipe in the restaurant's legendary cookbook, as it does at the restaurant itself. And that's not to disparage the chefs: The recipe is just a bona-fide classic. This is in part down to the fennel seeds, but it's the stock made from squash peel that lends the dish its deep, dark bass note, just as bones do to meat stock, and pea pods to *risi e bisi* (page [213]). The recipe is more or less in keeping with our starting point, but I give Mark Hix's quantities anyway, since there is no sense in meddling with perfection. Make the stock with the peel of 1 butternut squash, 3⅔ cups chopped carrots, 3 sliced leeks, 6 peeled garlic cloves, a small bunch of fresh thyme, some parsley stalks (leaves stripped off and set aside for the risotto), 1 tsp fennel seeds, 20 black peppercorns, a pinch of saffron, 7 tbsp white wine, ½ cup tomato paste, and 3 quarts water. Cook the vegetables and garlic in a little vegetable oil for 5 minutes, without allowing them to color, before adding the aromatics and water. Simmer for 1 hour, so the flavor of the stock can deepen. Strain the stock, reserving 6 cups for the risotto, and chilling or freezing the rest for another time. Cook 4 cups diced, peeled butternut squash in half of the reserved stock until just tender, then remove with a slotted spoon and set aside. Add the rest of the stock to the pan and warm. Heat 4 tsp vegetable oil in a heavy-based pan and soften 8 finely chopped shallots over a low heat for a few minutes. Add 1⅔ cups Carnaroli or Arborio rice and stir for 1–2 minutes, then start adding the stock. When the rice is almost cooked, add the squash. Stir in the chopped parsley leaves, 7 tbsp unsalted butter, and 1 cup grated Parmesan. Check the seasoning and serve.

CHICKEN LIVER

The sort of risotto where the feature ingredient is cooked separately and folded in when the rice is almost cooked. I say risotto, but this version includes some of chef Peter Gordon's unconventional ideas, and they might not play well with your Italian grandmother. Follow our starting point, but use a brown chicken stock. Cook the onion or shallots with a star anise. Use red, not white wine. Stir in 1 tsp soy sauce when you've used about half of the stock. Fry 10–14 oz chicken livers (any sinew and greenish-tinged parts removed, then chopped or left whole, as you prefer) until just cooked through, and stir into the almost-finished risotto. This will only take a few minutes. Deglaze the liver pan with 1–2 tbsp stock and add that too. Treat yourself to a glass of Barbaresco. If soy is too far out for your tastes, follow the chef Valter Maccioni, of Antico Masetto in Tuscany, and add either an anchovy or anchovy paste to your chicken liver risotto. Then again, he recommends basmati over Arborio or Carnaroli, so nothing is sacred. *Mio Dio!*

CITRUS

Judy Rodgers notes that her citrus risotto pleases cooks and diners alike. Soften ½ cup finely diced yellow onion in 2 tbsp unsalted butter, then stir in 2 cups Carnaroli or Arborio rice. Start to gradually add between 4 and 5 cups chicken stock (there's no wine in this risotto). Add 16 chopped, skinned segments of pink or red grapefruit and 8 of ripe lime, plus any juice that collected when you chopped them. When the rice is done, remove from the heat and vigorously stir in ¼ cup mascarpone, so the citrus is "reduced to pretty flecks in the creamy rice." Rodgers suggests serving this as a bed for shrimp sautéed in their shells. Seared scallops are the obvious alternative.

JERUSALEM ARTICHOKE

I came across a recipe for Jerusalem artichoke risotto that recommends serving it for a Valentine's Day dinner. Either the author has their globes and Jerusalems mixed up, or they were being mischievous. The tubers play such havoc with most people's digestion that they should be sold in joke shops. Others are unaffected. Lucky them: The flavor is wonderful. Peel 6 Jerusalem artichokes and cut them into ⅛-in slices. Heat your chicken, veal, or vegetable stock and simmer the artichoke slices in it until tender. Remove them with a slotted spoon and set aside. Follow the starting point, adding the cooked artichoke slices to the risotto after the first ladle of stock has evaporated. Garlic is particularly pally with the flavor of Jerusalem artichoke.

MUTTON

Elizabeth David cites a *Risotto in capro Roman*, a Venetian recipe, and one of the few Italian rice dishes to make use of mutton. When the onion has softened, add 5–7 oz diced raw mutton to the same pan and brown. Add ½ cup skinned and diced tomato, followed by a glass of white wine, enough meat broth to cover, and seasoning. Apply the lid and simmer gently until the meat is almost cooked (check a piece after 10 minutes to see how it's coming along). Add 1¼ cups risotto rice and return to a simmer, now uncovered, until it has absorbed all the stock in the pan. Continue adding up to 4½ cups stock gradually, only stirring in Parmesan and butter when almost all of the stock has been absorbed. David suggests swapping a wooden spoon for a wooden fork toward the end of cooking, to avoid crushing the rice grains. Note that this calls for just under two thirds of the starting-point quantity of rice.

PRAWN (SHRIMP)

If you're lucky enough to find a source of great-tasting shrimp, go back immediately, buy more, and make a risotto. You'll need 10 oz shell-on, raw medium shrimp, but opt for 1 lb if you're feeling particularly flush. Bring 3½ cups salted water to a boil, reduce the heat to medium-low, and cook the shrimp for 2 minutes. Remove them with a slotted spoon and turn off the heat. When they're cool enough, peel the shrimp, retaining the debris, including the heads if you have them. Remove and discard any dark veins. Heat some butter in a saucepan and fry the shrimp debris for a few minutes. Add the shrimp-cooking water and bring to a simmer. After about 20 minutes, strain this stock, then return it to the pan over a low heat to keep warm while you make the risotto as per the starting point, adding some minced garlic at step 2. The cooked shrimp can be added when the rice seems a few minutes away from being cooked. If you run out of stock, hot water will do. Some cooks fry raw shrimp in butter and add them just before the risotto is finished, but poaching them in the stock you're about to use ensures their flavor is dispersed throughout the dish—which is, after all, the point of risotto.

RADICCHIO & GORGONZOLA

Radicchio, the red-blooded member of the chicory family, is highly prized in the Veneto region of northern Italy. The Verona variety is compact and round: the most throwable radicchio, and the easiest to come by. Treviso, especially tardivo Treviso, which has a pronounced bittersweet taste, is particularly revered, and appears in market stalls in midwinter. It has thick, white, rippling limbs, as if it's been harvested from an underwater garden in the lagoon. Hot pork fat, and a local cheese called Montasio, were traditional Venetian pairings for radicchio, but in recent years it has formed a winning partnership with an ingredient from the other side of northern Italy. Now radicchio and Gorgonzola are combined in just about every Italian dish you can imagine: panini, bruschetta, sauces for pasta, and risotto. They're a good-looking pair—the ivory cheese with its fine blue tracery, and the pink-and-white strips of leaf, make as pretty a picture as Florentine marbled paper. But it's their collaboration on the palate that really distinguishes them. The slightly metallic, grassy flavor of the raw radicchio harmonizes with similar notes in the cheese, and the bitter leaves sluice the mouth of Gorgonzola's richness and pungency. Gorgonzola may have a reputation for smelliness, but you'll probably have to go to Italy to find one that's properly pungent. Most of the stuff available outside Italy is sold young and sweet—i.e. pale, easily spreadable, and, if you try it with your eyes closed, tasting like freshly churned butter with a mild electric current running through it. Cook 1 sliced head of radicchio with the onion or shallots, then add the rice and proceed as per our starting point, stirring in about ⅔ cup cubed Gorgonzola at the end. Finish with Parmesan.

SAFFRON (RISOTTO MILANESE)

The classic partner to osso buco (page 242), so ask the butcher for some marrow bones when you're buying the veal. For a risotto Milanese made as per our starting point, add approximately 2 tbsp of the extracted marrow to the butter you're using to soften the onion or shallots, and do include some minced garlic. Use veal or light beef stock, if possible. Add the saffron—a healthy pinch of strands, ground to a powder using a pestle and mortar—with the rice. I like to make too much saffron risotto, then flatten the leftovers into an omelet shape, coat it in bread crumbs, and fry in butter until golden. If this sounds a bit frugal-housewife, know that *risotto al salto*, as it's called, was once a favorite at the glamorous Ristorante Savini in Milan, the kind of place you might take a dissolute Hungarian duke after he'd fallen asleep halfway through *Nabucco* at La Scala.

Nuts

MARZIPAN

page 280

NUT STEW:
FESENJAN

page 310

NUT SAUCE:
TARATOR

page 304

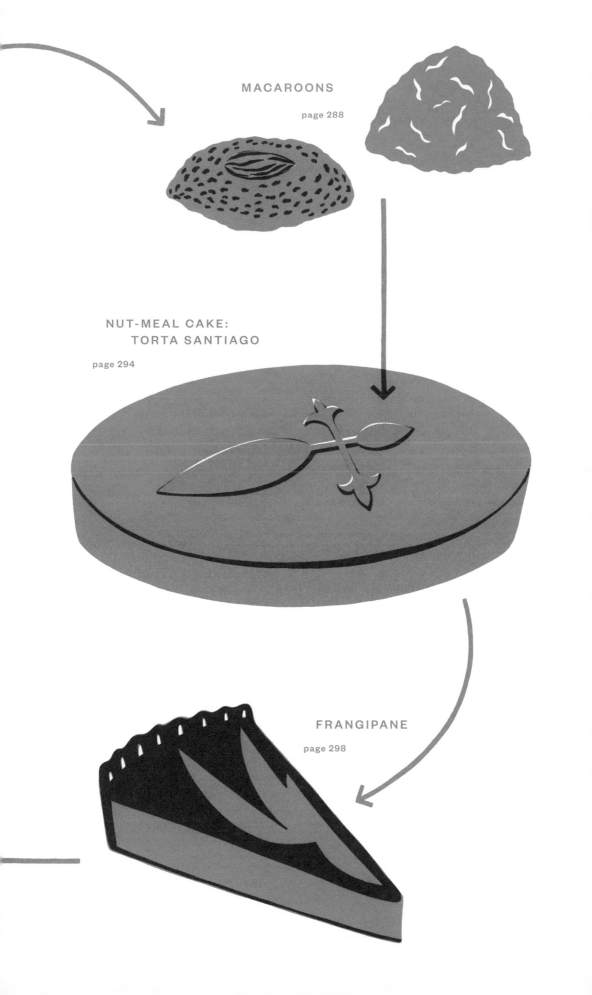

MACAROONS

page 288

NUT-MEAL CAKE:
TORTA SANTIAGO

page 294

FRANGIPANE

page 298

M A R Z I P A N Marzipan is the unluckiest guest at a wedding, stuck between dry fruitcake and uptight royal icing. It can only be thanks to the famous British sense of humor that we would mark so joyous an occasion with such a godawful cake. No wonder more and more couples get married abroad.

Having a soft spot for marzipan, I'm often tempted to peel it away from its dreary neighbors, before the DJ drops "We Are Family" and the caterers scrape two hundred slices of barely touched cake into the trash. In Britain, other than in wedding and Christmas cakes, marzipan is a rare sight outside of convenience stores that keep an eccentric line in confectionery. Search among the Polish wafers and Ethiopian marshmallows and you might discover a lozenge of marzipan seemingly wrapped in the original publicity material for *Die Fledermaus*. These treasure hunts become redundant once you realize how easy it is to make basic marzipan, using equal weights of sugar and ground almonds and just enough raw egg white to bind to a dough. Give it a brief knead. Then eat.

That's the basic version. For the finer, extra-pliable, and more labor-intensive marzipan, you'll need to blanch, skin, and grind the almonds yourself, then make a hard-ball sugar syrup—see page [405]. Next, make a praline by mixing the nut meal with most of the syrup, then bake, break, and re-grind it, adding more syrup as needed to make a dough. Harder work, but the advantage here is the absence of raw egg, with its shorter shelf-life and risk of food poisoning. (Simpler no-egg and cooked-egg versions of marzipan are outlined on page [281].)

Marzipan is, of course, edible Play-Doh, as will be plain from the windows of Italian pasticcerie, which are thronged with fat friars, bucktoothed lions, and reproachful frogs that we can only assume are edible. Less plastically minded cooks might coat marzipan cubes in chocolate, coarse-grate it onto puff pastry for *palmiers*, or roll it in stollen. In Spain, marzipan is flavored with aniseed liqueur, or lemon and cinnamon, then fashioned into cigar shapes, wrapped in thin pastry, and fried to make *casadielles*. It's not obligatory for marzipan to taste like marzipan. The signature bitter-almond flavor that's disliked by so many comes not from the nuts but from an added extract. The nuts used for the paste are the sweet, lightly flavored variety, and most of their faint bitter-almond flavor can be masked if you prefer. I say most, as a mild aftertaste persists unless the nuts are ground very finely. That said, not all marzipan is made of almonds—see the peanut, pistachio, and walnut options on pages [283, 284,] and [285] respectively.

Marzipan can also be baked or broiled. Glaze it first and it will turn an appetizing gradated brown, like a loaf, as noted by the pâtissiers who fashion it into miniature boules, braids, and baguettes. To my eye, the particular shades of brown and ivory it will take on lend themselves perfectly to faux porcini mushrooms, although you'll need to balance them on their stalks in the oven to get a brown cap and pale stem effect. In Toledo, in Spain, which prides itself on its marzipan, the same technique is used for bite-sized bones, snails, and fish, or coiled and elaborately decorated snakes; you'll also find little baked marzipan cups filled with sweet pastes of crystallized potato, egg yolk, or chestnut.

MACAROONS There's scarcely a foil wrapper between marzipan and the next starting point on the nuts continuum, macaroons. A late-sixteenth-century source collapses the distinction altogether. What it calls macaroons are, in fact, small baked pieces of marzipan. Although these days the two preparations are distinct, macaroons are still very close to marzipan, whether in the form of those puffy coconut domes zigzagged with melted chocolate; the flatter, cracked-almond disks decorated with a solitary nut; or the tastefully varicolored, sandwiched variety that in certain quarters have become as essential a lifestyle accessory as a pinched expression or a dog the size of a gerbil. All are baked mixtures of ground nuts, sugar, and egg white. Another variation on this mixture is the meringue called dacquoise (page 426), which can be found on the sugar continuum. Unlike macaroons, dacquoise also contains a little cornstarch, and it's cooked for longer and at a lower temperature.

NUT-MEAL CAKE Rather than just the white, some cooks add whole eggs to macaroons made from coconut, to counter its tendency to dryness. This gives a spongier, more cakelike texture akin to the next starting point on the continuum, that splendid nut-meal cake from Galicia in Spain called *torta Santiago*. Arguably, this is the best known of a variety of cakes that pitch the same weights of ground almonds and sugar against whole egg. The *torta* is flavored with citrus zest and often with a touch of cinnamon too. As with macaroons, you simply beat the egg with sugar, fold in the dry ingredients, and bake. It's the custom for pilgrims who have completed their walk to Santiago de Compostela to celebrate with a slice of the *torta*, which is graced by the cross of St. James reversed out of confectioners' sugar on the top; every pastelería, café, and restaurant in town sells it.

I once undertook an unintended pilgrimage to Santiago. On the drive out of London to the airport my then husband-to-be, who suffers from a condition known as freeway priapism, which compels him, poor man, to pass other vehicles for no other reason than that they're not going as fast as he would like them to, allowed himself one last Honda and rocketed past the turnoff to the airport. We found ourselves in what I now know to be Britain's third-longest gap between exits. "It's fine," he said, ignoring the stationary London-bound traffic on the other side of the freeway. We watched our flight depart from the comfort of our car seats. Five hours and a hefty surcharge later, we were on a flight to a remote airstrip three hundred miles from our destination. We had anticipated lunch in Santiago. Instead we arrived to find the city resounding with the clatter of closing metal shutters. The one place that was still open smelled of sweat and served the kind of tapas that make you grateful for small portions. Only the *torta Santiago* was edible, presumably because it had been made somewhere else. At the table next to ours a septuagenarian couple from Nîmes told us they had walked a total of 778 miles, "seventeen and a half of them today." I nobly resisted the temptation to compare their ordeal to mine. The next day my boyfriend got down on one knee and produced the engagement ring that had been seeping anxiety into his luggage. Completing the Camino de Santiago has traditionally been considered a penance. If it had cured him of his freeway priapism, and shown us both that we could put up with entirely avoidable six-hour car journeys without murdering one another, that was good enough for me. Reader... well, you know.

If you've ever made Claudia Roden's famous orange and almond cake, you'll note that Santiago cake is quite similar. The main difference comes down to her addition of whole, cooked, pulped oranges—everything bar the seeds. Making the cake is something of a pilgrimage in itself, starting with the two-hour slog of boiling the oranges (although you can always hitch a ride to the shrine, and cook your—pierced—oranges in the microwave for a few minutes). Roden's recipe shows how liberally additions can be made to the basic Santiago-style batter. Nut-meal cakes have a moist texture that puts them at ease on a dessert plate with a dollop of crème fraîche. The one drawback, Roden's lovely burnt-sienna creation excepted, is that they tend to unsightliness. You can see why the bakers of Santiago reached for their sugar shakers.

F Take your Santiago-cake batter, add the same weight of butter as
R each of the other ingredients (sugar, ground almonds, egg) and
A you'll have the starting point for frangipane. The addition of butter
N necessitates a change in method, however: Instead of beating the
G sugar with the eggs, it's creamed with the butter. Frangipane is
I what provides the filling of Bakewell tarts, and in French tarts sets
P fruit like fanned pears or halved apricots in place. It also makes
A a good cake batter. The ingredients are, after all, the same as
N for butter cake (page [336]), except ground nuts are used in place
E of all-purpose flour.

"Franchipane" first cropped up in cookbooks in the seventeenth century, but referred at the time to a tart filled with pastry cream and often enhanced with nuts or crushed macaroons. The name can be traced back to the Frangipani, powerful aristocrats in medieval Rome. In the early seventeenth century, one of their descendants living in Grasse invented a means of liquidizing perfumes in alcohol, and lent the family name to the resulting scent, a heady mixture of orris (derived from iris roots), spice, civet, and musk that was often used to perfume gloves. The similarity, on the nose, to the aroma of *Plumeria alba* flowers was so striking that the plant itself came to be known as "frangipani." According to the Perfume Society, this was the first and only instance of a plant taking its name from a fragrance, rather than the other way around. The Perfume Society describes the smell of frangipani flowers as creamy, peachy, and soft, which might account for the seventeenth-century pastry cream adopting the name, particularly given the flavor notes shared by fruits such as peach and the almonds or macaroons included in the pastry cream. It is unclear precisely why the term frangipane began to be applied to the thicker, cakelike preparation it denotes today, although the semantic shift is recent, dating to the latter half of the twentieth century.

Other than in tarts and cakes, frangipane has all sorts of uses. You might pipe it into the cavities of cored apples for baking, or peach halves for broiling; dot it among the fruit in a strudel before you roll it up; fold it into croissants; or mix in just enough all-purpose flour to turn it into a dough, and roll it out for cookies. It's one of those preparations that's worth making in greater quantities than immediate circumstances might demand—all the more so, in fact, as it is the best-tasting raw batter you will ever lick off a spoon. There's no need to feel that this is in any way transgressive, at least not if you think of it as a sweet version of the nut dips and sauces that furnish the next starting point on the continuum.

There are many flavor variations on the basic combination of raw ground nuts, supplemented with bread crumbs, garlic, and herbs, and then emulsified with a mixture of oil and vinegar or lemon juice. Romesco, for example, is a savory Catalan sauce made of almonds and/or hazelnuts, roasted red bell peppers, tomatoes, and sherry vinegar. Since I first encountered it at Moro in London, I've found it hard to stop making it. A good romesco achieves a perfect poise between sweetness, sharpness, and a deep, nut-buttery savoriness that elevates roast meat, fish, or vegetables to truly awe-inspiring heights of deliciousness. It's my favorite in a category where it's hard to pick a favorite, but I've chosen tarator as the starting point because it's eaten as a sauce, a dip, and a soup, which usefully demonstrates, for the experimental cook, how broadly applicable the basic principle can be.

The term "tarator" originated in Turkey, where it was used to describe a blend of pounded walnuts and vinegar. It's easy to imagine how an oily paste thinned with vinegar might serve as a creamy dressing with a sharper side. The Levantine-Arab version of tarator is made with ground sesame seeds (in the form of tahini), lemon juice in place of the vinegar, and a little crushed garlic. Depending on its intended use—it is, for example, the region's most popular sauce for fish dishes—it may or may not be thinned to a more pourable consistency with water. More elaborate recipes might call for bread crumbs and/or olive oil, and may dispense with blended smoothness in favor of a chunkier texture. In Bulgaria, pounded walnuts are mixed with sour yogurt, grated or diced cucumber, and dill, and eaten chilled as a soup. From the simple starting point of pounded nuts or seeds, offset by something acidic, the possibilities branch and multiply.

Contemporary chefs have been finding ingenious ways to elaborate on the basic principle. Doug Ducap makes a hazelnut and cashew tarator with dried thyme, serving it with lamb "corn dogs" cooked in falafel batter. Andrew McConnell, of Cumulus Inc. in Melbourne, puts sliced garlic in lemon and red wine vinegar to "cook," then adds roughly chopped, toasted pine nuts, parsley, sumac, and olive oil. He serves this over chargrilled sardines, laid on sourdough toast spread with onion cooked with oil, red wine vinegar, and raisins, and garnished with dill. Greg Malouf sprinkles a mixture of toasted, skinned, and finely chopped walnuts, chopped onion, cilantro, red chili, sumac, lemon juice, and extra virgin olive oil over gently cooked fillet of salmon coated with a blend of yogurt, tahini, lemon juice, and garlic. His tarator is served at room temperature and is probably the neatest you'll ever see, certainly compared to the sauce served with skewers of deep-fried mussels on the banks of the Bosphorus.

Cosmopolitan tarator has many like-minded cousins. Some are less well known, like French *lou sassoun*, a mixture of nuts, mint, fennel, anchovies, olive oil, and lemon juice; or *pipián*, a Mexican sauce made with pounded sunflower seeds and epazote, an herb otherwise known as Mexican tea. Others, like mole and pesto, are world-famous. Picada, the Catalan sauce commonly considered a sister to romesco, mixes garlic, nuts, toasted bread, and olive oil, pounded in a mortar with herbs and/or spices. It's either served as a sauce or added to a stew or rice dish just before serving. Paula Wolfert goes so far as to call picada "the future of cooking." Given the piquant and roasted flavors it contributes to cooked dishes, on top of its enriching and thickening properties, it's easy to understand her enthusiasm, whether you follow the traditional route or try an adaptation of your own devising.

N If you're a fan of picada, you might also consider Persian *fesenjan*,
U our final starting point on the nuts continuum. *Fesenjan* presides
T over a grand family of luxurious nut-thickened stews, including
Indian korma, Georgian *satsivi*, and African *mafe*. *Fesenjan* can
S feature all sorts of meat, fish, or vegetables, but duck or pheasant
T are typical. The sauce is made with pomegranate (either juice,
E or a mix of stock and pomegranate molasses) and thickened
W with ground toasted walnuts. It might be only moderately spiced,
say with cinnamon and saffron, but the wondrous sweet-sourness contributed by the pomegranate makes a tagine, by comparison, taste about as exotic as Irish stew.

As with most of the recipes on the nuts continuum, *fesenjan* is pretty simple to make. Follow the classic stew method: Brown the meat and set it aside while you soften some onions. Return the meat to the pan, add any aromatics and other flavorings, and stir in the liquid and ground nuts. Bring to a boil, then turn the heat right down to a gentle simmer and cook the *fesenjan*, tightly covered, until the meat is tender and the sauce has thickened.

Mafe, or peanut stew, which is indigenous to Mali but popular across West Africa, also follows our starting point, but here the liquid is supplied by tomatoes, and the nuts come in the form of peanut butter (*mafe* translates as "peanut-butter sauce"). Turkish Circassian chicken is similar, but in this case the meat is poached with onions, carrots, and spices, before being removed and boned while the stock reduces. The chicken is added back to the concentrated stock with enough ground walnuts to make a thick sauce. Like *satsivi*, it's served at room temperature. And like most stews, it benefits from being left overnight after cooking—tomorr-inated, as I like to say. On a very hot day I tried some leftover Circassian chicken, cool from the fridge, and it was as soothing as a *vitello tonnato*.

The dishes in the nut stew family are a cinch to adapt. Take the starting point and apply it to any nut, nut butter, or purée you fancy; feel free to vary the liquid beyond the classic stock, wine, or fruit juice. *Aji de gallina*, for example, is a Peruvian dish of chicken cooked in evaporated milk with hot, fruity *aji amarillo* chilies and cumin, and thickened with walnuts or peanuts. As with many of these nut dishes, cheaper bread crumbs or crushed crackers may be substituted for some of the nuts. Such is their cost that there are few traditional recipes that rely on pistachios, at least in the quantities required by *fesenjan* and its cognates, but if money is no object, a pistachio sauce is particularly good with a fine-flavored oily fish like red mullet.

Marzipan

A simple mixture of ground almonds and sugar, marzipan can be eaten as confectionery, or fashioned into edible decorations as plain as the balls traditionally used to top British Simnel cakes at Easter, or as elaborate as a basket of miniature fruits. In the U.S., almonds and sugar mixed to these proportions might be referred to as almond paste, whereas "marzipan" will contain a higher proportion of sugar; the grind of the nut will also be finer, not unlike supermarket marzipan in the U.K.

For about 14 oz or 36 (¾-in) cubes [A]

INGREDIENTS
2 cups ground almonds [B] [C] [D]
1 cup sifted confectioners' sugar [D] [E]
½ cup superfine sugar [D] [E]
Pinch of salt—optional
A few drops of almond extract or other flavoring—optional [F]
1 egg white, lightly beaten [G] [H]

1 Thoroughly mix the ground almonds with the confectioners' sugar, superfine sugar, and, if using, salt.

2 Make a well in the center, add flavoring if using, and gradually incorporate just enough egg white to bring the dry ingredients together into a kneadable dough.

3 Knead for a few minutes, then refrigerate to firm up a bit.
   If you're planning on using it for *petits fours* or dipped chocolates, it helps to fashion the marzipan into a ¾-in-thick square or rectangle while it's still soft.

4 When ready to use the marzipan, bring it to room temperature.
   If you're rolling out your marzipan, e.g. to cover a cake, do so on a sprinkling of confectioners' sugar to prevent it from sticking.

5 Well wrapped, the marzipan will keep for 1 month in the fridge or 6 months in a freezer.
   Reduce the amount of sugar and the marzipan won't keep as long.

LEEWAY

A For a flavor-testing quantity, use 5 tbsp ground almonds, 3 tbsp confectioners' sugar, and 1 tbsp superfine sugar.

B Other nuts can be used—see Flavors & Variations.

C If your almonds aren't already ground, blanch them in boiling water for 3 minutes, then slip their skins off. Grinding your own almonds will leave them damper than those bought already ground, and they will need less binding agent.

D If you want a less sweet marzipan, use twice the quantity of nuts.

E For a softer texture, forget the superfine and just use 2 cups of confectioners' sugar.

F Some cooks replace the almond extract with vanilla extract, and many recipes call for ½–1 tsp brandy or sherry. There are all sorts of flavoring options, but if you add more moisture, you might want to up the ground almond content to make the dough less tacky. This will be more of an issue if you plan to roll out or model the marzipan, less so if you're coating it for chocolates.

G There are no-egg versions of marzipan that use other liquids for binding. Claudia Roden's recipe for Toledo marzipan uses a few drops of almond extract in water. Some recipes call for glucose or corn syrup.

H If you'd prefer to use cooked egg, there are versions in which whole eggs and sugar are beaten over heat to the ribbon stage—see page [514]. Any flavorings are added off the heat and the mixture is beaten constantly until cool. The almonds are then folded in and the dough mixed and kneaded.

ANISE

Used in the marzipan-like filling for *casadielles* ("homebodies") from Asturias in northern Spain. *Casadielles* are rough rectangles of pastry, similar to strudel (page 556), but bound with anís instead of egg, filled with the nut mixture, and pinched at each end before being deep-fried and dusted with confectioners' sugar. Think of them as baklava's slovenly cousin, baggy where their Middle Eastern relatives are neat and tight. Recipes vary. The proportion of nuts to sugar is, in some versions, higher than in our starting point. Anise-flavored liqueurs from Spain may be less well known than French pastis and Italian sambuca, but Anís del Toro is immortalized in Hemingway's short story "Hills Like White Elephants." A man and a girl are drinking beer in the sun outside a station bar. The girl notices the bull logo on a beaded curtain and asks to try some. "It tastes like licorice," she says, after her first sip. "Everything tastes of licorice. Especially all the things you've waited so long for, like absinthe." If the idea of everything tasting of licorice fills you more with dread than longing, take note (and heart) that some *casadielles* are flavored with sherry or wine.

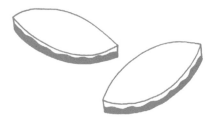

CALISSONS D'AIX

Calissons d'Aix are lozenge-shaped sweets from Aix-en-Provence, made from a mixture of ground almonds, honey, and candied melon, brought together with Grand Marnier and orange-flower water, and then finished with glacé icing as white and shiny as the hull of a motor yacht in the marina at Antibes. In the mouth they're a little like a British wedding cake, minus the cake bit. One theory goes that they were created to celebrate the nuptials of *Le bon roi* René of Anjou to Jeanne de Laval in 1452. If celebrate is the right word. History records that the princess was less than keen to marry a man twice her age. Forced marriage notwithstanding, *calissons* are well worth making yourself. Candied melon is fairly easy to find in France, although you'll get far better results by candying your own. A decent substitute can be made by soaking mixed candied peel in orange brandy.

CHAROSET

As your Jewish friends will tell you, *charoset* is the one part of the Passover Seder meal worth eating down to the scrapings (not that there's a great deal of competition—a bone, some horseradish, lettuce, salt water, and some matzo cracker). *Charoset* is a sweet paste of fruit, nuts, spices, and red wine, intended to resemble the clay, or *cheres*, enslaved Israelites were forced to use as building material in ancient Egypt. There are many varieties, but the earliest documented recipe is rather like a marzipan that predates sugar, containing dates, walnuts, sesame, and red wine vinegar. The Ashkenazi version more widely encountered today calls for apple, cinnamon, walnuts, and red wine.

HONEY

You might try swapping egg white for runny honey as the binder for marzipan. I wondered whether almond-flower honey might be just the thing, recalling a drive around Majorca in February, when the fields were a blizzard of almond blossom. I made some enquiries. Almond-flower honey is by all accounts vile—"bitter and not suitable for human palates," says *The Backyard Beekeeper's Honey Handbook*. Apiarists who, for the pollination season, take their bees to California, where four-fifths of the world's crop of almonds is grown, must thoroughly scrub their hives afterward, to rid them of all traces of the thick, foul-tasting honey. Orange-flower it is, then.

LEMON

Local law requires marzipan from Toledo, in Spain, to be made with 50 percent sweet almonds and 45 percent sugar, with the remainder taken up by essential ingredients like the preservative citric acid. To make a virtue of this necessity, I made a lemon marzipan, adding lemon zest, a little juice, and a cymbal-ping of citric acid, turning the flavor of lemon zest into tart lemon. It was fantastic covered in dark chocolate; uncovered, it was rather like eating little cubes of concentrated lemon drizzle cake. For each cup of ground almonds, use the finely grated zest of 1 lemon, 1 tsp lemon juice, a pinch of citric acid, and just enough egg white or sugar syrup to bind. I also came across a recipe for a lemon marzipan that calls for soaking a dozen dried lemon peels in water for 2 days, changing the water every 4 hours. The peel is then rinsed and simmered in water for about an hour, by which time it should have become soft enough to purée. Measure the purée and put it in a pan with the same volume of ground almonds and twice its volume of superfine sugar. Cook on low, stirring, until the mixture pulls away from the sides of the pan. When cool, knead it with confectioners' sugar—again about the same volume as the purée. Roll the mix into small balls and leave for a day before eating.

PEANUT

Although peanuts are technically not nuts, but legumes, and aren't as interchangeable as almonds or walnuts, they can be used to make a marzipan-like confection. In Mexico, peanuts are ground up with sugar and vanilla and sold, under the de la Rosa brand, as *dulce de cacahuate estilo marzipan*. The packaging looks like a make-up compact from the 1950s. If you've ever eaten a Reese's Peanut Butter Cup, the marrow of a Starbar, or peanut butter on a teaspoon you've first dipped, wet, into the sugar bowl, you'll have an idea of what it tastes like.

PISTACHIO

Aside from the smooth, lipped shell seemingly designed by Arne Jacobsen, the great visual pleasure of the pistachio is its incongruous green, so appetizing when the nut is sliced or chopped. Ground, on the other hand, it takes on the appearance of wood lichen, which is handy for adding that extra touch of authenticity to a Yule log. The pistachio is "mildly exotic," writes Waverley Root, but not so remarkable, in his opinion, as to justify the prices growers charge for it. The marzipan I made with supermarket pistachios mounted no challenge to Root's judgment. Made with *Sicilian* pistachios, it would have caused him to reconsider.

POIRE

For one reason or another I was alone in Paris. From my hotel, which was handily close to the local recycling center, I might just have been able to make out the Eiffel Tower on the horizon had it not been for the vast extractor fan outside my window. It was so depressing I wanted to lie on the bed and watch *Asia Business Report* while chewing inattentively on a club sandwich served with a trio of cocktail onions and six stale potato chips. Nonetheless, I roused myself, taking to the streets with only a cheap telescopic umbrella between my gray suede shoes and the glowering sky. I walked until I found myself in a *quartier* that I vaguely recognized, where I came across a restaurant so bustling and cozy and stereotypically Parisian it might have featured in a late-period Woody Allen movie. The waiter showed me to a bijou table with a view of the street. I ordered *steak-frites* and a carafe of ordinary red Bordeaux. When I was in my twenties I ate alone in restaurants all the time. Here, in a city where solo dining carries less social stigma, I was reminded of the feeling of independence it gives—perhaps because, by lending purpose and the structure of a meal to time spent alone, it frees you from the obligation of missing human company. All too soon my plate of *nougat glacé* was reduced to streaks of white like Monet's *Snow at Giverny*. The waiter suggested a digestif. I said yes, and not only because I was reluctant to leave the snug interior, with its spill of golden light on dark wood, the locomotive hiss of the coffee machine, and the break-up/post-affair recriminations playing out in dumb show at the bar. It was also because I was *expected* not to hurry. I ordered a *poire*, the highly potent eau-de-vie that tastes like a white jelly bean caught in a beam of winter sunlight through a clear cathedral window. It arrived in what looked like a test tube, laid on a bed of crushed ice, with a brandy balloon standing stoutly in wait. Its very logic demanded I take my time. The rain lifted and the usual Parisian zoetrope of lovers, old ladies, and tiny clockwork dogs returned to the boulevard. On my walk back to the hotel, I stopped in at a supermarket and, hoping to prolong the feeling, bought a bottle of *poire William* so I could enjoy a second glass before bed. No sooner had I walked into the lobby than the dream evaporated, and the bottle remained unopened, until, months later in London, I wanted to make marzipan with a traditional addition of kirsch, but found I didn't have any.

Out came the *poire*. I fitted the marzipan into a small pan, poured over the same depth of *poire*-infused dark chocolate ganache (page 380), and left it to set, then sliced it into small rectangles with every intention of dipping them in tempered chocolate. I never quite got around to it. The combination of creamy dark ganache, almond, and pear was superb, recalling a *belle Hélène*, albeit after Hélène had hit the bottle. Maybe she had been in Paris *toute seule*.

RUM TRUFFLE

"The Catalan preoccupation with shit," writes the art critic Robert Hughes, "would make Sigmund Freud proud." On January 6 every year, the Feast of the Kings, all good children are given pretty sweetmeats lovingly fashioned from marzipan, while naughty children receive *caca i carbo*, "shit and coal" (except no one can be bothered to make the coal). Some pâtissiers strive for maximum authenticity by finishing their cocoa-dusted lumps with sugar-sculpted flies. If you're not by now thoroughly disgusted, try this rum truffle variation of marzipan, which masks the bitter-almond flavor that puts so many people off: Use 4 tsp sifted unsweetened cocoa powder and 1 tsp rum to each cup of ground almonds.

STICKY GINGER PUDDING

Marzipan's fashionable, contemporary counterpart is variously called a "power ball," "raw truffle," or "energy bite," and is made with ground nuts and the kind of sweetener considered nutritionally superior to white sugar, like puréed dates or maple syrup. You can play fairly fast and loose with the idea, adding spices, flavor extracts, and nut butters as you fancy, as long as you end up with a firm, rollable paste. For a sticky ginger pudding flavor version, add the following to the bowl of a food processor: 1 cup ground hazelnuts, 1 cup ground almonds, ½ cup chopped medjool dates, 2 tsp vanilla extract, 2 tsp molasses, 1½ tsp ground ginger, and a few pinches of salt. Pulse until the mixture is fairly smooth, and beginning to form into a dough. Shape into 12 balls, or, as I prefer, 6 small bars ("fun size," in chocolate-bar parlance).

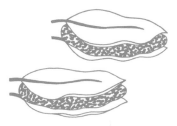

WALNUT

According to *The Anonymous Andalusian Cookbook*, compiled in the early thirteenth century, *jawzinaq* is a form of marzipan made with ground walnuts and sugar syrup. The Swiss chocolatier Läderach makes a walnut marzipan covered in white chocolate, then dipped in dark chocolate, and topped with a walnut, while the Australian company Zotter makes a 50%-cocoa chocolate bar filled with a walnut and rum marzipan. I made something similar, using our starting point recipe for marzipan, and found it hard initially to tell it apart from almond marzipan—until the walnut crept up on me. Much of the walnut's distinctive flavor is contained in the skin, which is very difficult to remove entirely. Many chefs' recipes call for skinned walnuts, which is all very well if you have an eager apprentice ready and willing to do it for you. Don't bother, is my advice. The tannic bitterness lent by the skin is as essential to the character of walnut as pointy ears are to Nosferatu. *Nociata* is an Italian confection that's somewhere between a marzipan and a praline, made with equal volumes of honey and finely chopped (rather than ground) walnuts. The honey and walnuts are heated until the honey turns red, then the mixture is turned onto a marble block, rolled out to about ⅓ in, and cut into pieces. Once it has cooled a little, the pieces are sandwiched between fresh bay leaves, which lend their own flavor; you peel the leaves back to eat the sweet.

Marzipan → Other Directions

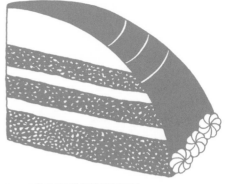

CLAUDIA RODEN'S MAJORCAN GUINEA FOWL

Stuffed with marzipan, prunes, blanched almonds, dried apricots, and sugar.

SWEDISH PRINCESSTORTE

Layers of sponge cake, jam, pastry cream, and whipped cream, covered with green marzipan.

MARZIPAN LATTICE ON A FRUIT TART

MOROCCAN M'HENCHA

Marzipan wrapped in phyllo pastry, rolled into a coil, and baked, then sprinkled with confectioners' sugar.

MARZIPAN-STUFFED DATES

MARZIPANSCHWEIN

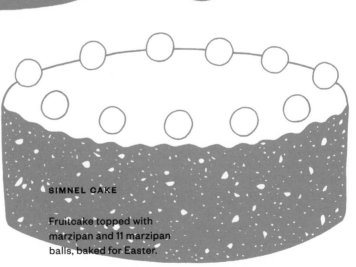

SIMNEL CAKE

Fruitcake topped with marzipan and 11 marzipan balls, baked for Easter.

Macaroons

Like marzipan, macaroons are made with equal weights of sugar and ground almonds mixed with egg white, but a lot more egg white is used. For our starting point, the egg whites are beaten with the sugar, as for meringue, lending the finished confection its characteristic domed shape. A faster, flatter version can be made with the same ingredients by hand-beating the egg whites until foamy before folding into the nuts and sugar.

For 18 macaroons of about 3-in diameter

INGREDIENTS
2 egg whites
Pinch of salt
1 cup superfine or granulated sugar [A] [B] [C]
2 cups ground almonds [A] [D]
Rice paper—optional, but recommended

1 Beat the egg whites with the salt until frothy. [E]

2 As you beat, add the sugar gradually. The mixture should become stiff and shiny.

3 Fold in the nuts to make a mixture that can be piped, or fashioned with a pair of spoons, into 1½-in rounds. [F] [G]

4 Leaving a little room for the macaroons to spread, place on a baking sheet lined with rice paper or a silicone mat. In the absence of these, grease the sheet well.
   Rice paper is preferable.

5 Bake at 350°F for around 20 minutes until turning golden on top, then cool on a rack.

6 When cool, roughly tear around the rice paper (if using) to set your macaroons free.
   Store in an airtight container.

LEEWAY

A The ratio of sugar to ground nuts varies from recipe to recipe: Try 4 cups of ground nuts to 1 cup of sugar. Or you could go for a more meringuelike 1 cup of ground nuts to 2 cups of sugar.

B Using 1 cup confectioners' sugar and ½ cup granulated sugar will soften the texture of the finished macaroons.

C Using all or part brown sugar will boost the flavor of both sugar and nuts.

D Other nuts can be used: See Flavors & Variations.

E As noted, the beating involved in this method gives the macaroons their distinctive domed shape. If you're not bothered about the rise, give the egg whites a quick whisk by hand, then stir into the sugar and ground nuts.

F Some recipes call for 1 tsp to 1 tbsp cornstarch or rice flour, which will absorb excess moisture.

G For almond macaroons, gently nestle a whole almond on top of each one before baking.

ALMOND & RASPBERRY

Michel Roux makes a raspberry powder for macaroons, drying fresh raspberries in a low oven and then grinding them. I'm more likely to grab freeze-dried raspberries in the baking section of the supermarket, and crush them well. Either way, the raspberry retains its distinctive character, making for as vivid and spiky a contrast with the sandy macaroon as the pinkness of prickly pears in the dun-colored Sonoran Desert. Add a little almond extract to the mixture, and the resulting marzipan and jam-like flavors will yield what you might call Bakewell macaroons. Follow our starting point, adding ½ cup crushed dried raspberries with the nuts at step ³.

AMARETTI

When I first worked in Soho, in London, many of the local restaurants were still Italian, and at lunchtime my colleagues and I would gorge on breadsticks and cheap bowls of pasta. Too full for dessert, we got our sweet fix in the form of flaming sambuca shots and Lazzaroni amaretti cookies, whose paper wrappers we'd set alight, as is the custom, and watch float to the ceiling like burning wishes. Mine was always that I didn't have to go back to work that afternoon. Steadily the old Italian joints were replaced with Thai restaurants and sushi bars, which I'd assumed was just the march of fashion, but on reflection might have been linked to the insurance implications of encouraging tabletop arson. Years later I was disappointed to find that diners in Italy were far too cool to set fire to anything other than a chain of Dunhill cigarettes; now, of course, they can't even do that. There are two types of amaretti, *morbidi* and *secchi* (soft and dry). Lazzaroni's amaretti are the dry type, making them hard to duplicate in a domestic kitchen. Why bother, you may ask, especially as the bought version comes in such attractive packaging? The answer is simple: to understand what wonders can be achieved by a few basic tweaks to our starting point for macaroons. The following might not be quite to Lazzaroni standards of neatness, but they're very good to eat. In old-fashioned recipes some of the bitter-almond character would have been lent by apricot kernels, but current advice is to avoid them entirely, as they contain trace amounts of cyanide. No matter: A good-quality almond extract will provide flavor in spades. Beat 2 egg whites with ½ tsp egg white powder until foamy, add ¼ tsp cream of tartar, and keep on beating until soft peaks form. Add ½ cup sugar, 2 tbsp at a time, beating for a minute to stiff peaks after each addition. In another bowl, thoroughly combine 2¼ cups ground almonds, 2 cups confectioners' sugar, and ¼ tsp baking soda. Sift the mixture, and fold into the egg white mixture with 2 tsp almond extract. Transfer to a pastry bag, and pipe into 2-in domes on a silicone mat or well-greased baking sheet. At this point you might sprinkle with some sugar pearls, if you have them. Let set at room temperature for about 30 minutes, then bake at 275°F for 25 minutes. Turn the oven up to 350°F and bake for 10 minutes longer. Transfer to a rack to cool.

COCONUT

For coconut macaroons, whisk a whole egg with a little salt before thoroughly mixing in 1 cup dried shredded coconut and ½ cup sugar. The inclusion of the yolk makes for a spongier macaroon, and the additional moisture offsets some of the coconut's dryness. Shape and bake as per the starting point. Decorate with a zigzag of chocolate once cooled. If you prefer old-fashioned pyramid macaroons, shape the mixture into small mounds, topping with a candied cherry if desired. If they simply must be pink, stir a little red food coloring in with the nuts and sugar. They'll need longer in the oven—more like 25 minutes.

HAZELNUT & CHOCOLATE

In Italy, *brutti ma buoni* ("ugly but good") cookies are as popular as their spelling and preparation are various. Most recipes I've come across call for the egg and sugar to be heated in one way or another. Either a meringue is made and gently warmed before the nuts are added; or the egg, sugar, and nuts are processed together, then heated in a pan; or, as a third alternative, the sugar and egg white are stirred for 5 minutes in a double boiler before being beaten to peaks. But you'll also find *brutti ma buoni* made with a cold mixture, as per our starting point. You'll need to make sure the egg whites are beaten to firm peaks, so the cookies are robust enough to hold their messy shape as they're baked. Use a mixture of ground and coarsely chopped nuts for an authentic knobbly finish. That's the *brutti* part covered. For the *buoni*, add a little cocoa powder and vanilla extract to flatter the naturally beautiful flavor of hazelnut. The only unforgivable tweak is to make the cookies attractive to look at: Where's the fun in *belli e buoni*?

MACADAMIA & BROWN SUGAR

In their shell, macadamias, the premium-priced nuts originally grown in Australia, look like the kind of large wooden beads that Hampstead ladies wear to the theater. Eating a shelled one is like taking a bite out of a porcelain teacup—brittle and extremely fine. Concentrate and the flavor might remind you of Brazil nut. Both taste a little like coconut once you've chewed the sugary juice away. A less attentive munch may yield little more than a kinship with bland cooking oil, which is unsurprising given how oily macadamias are; so oily, in fact, that's it's a fool's game trying to make nut meal out of them. As with other fatty nuts, chilling before you grind them will have a temporary effect, but they will still melt into nut butter. Best to accept that its texture is the macadamia's best feature and use it in coarse chunks in an almond macaroon. Go with ⅔ cup roughly chopped macadamias, folded in at step 3. Using brown sugar in place of white gives the macaroons extra flavor and teases out a hint of butteriness in the macadamia. To loosen the batter, I add a few teaspoons of maple syrup too.

OATMEAL & RAISIN

The first time I saw the launch ad for "breakfast cookies"—a sort of edible oval précis of cereal and milk—I was bemused. When were cookies ever *not* for breakfast? In my youth, before concerns over calorific intake brought an abrupt end to those halcyon days of eating anything, anytime, in unlimited quantities, I often scoffed Garibaldis and Fig Newtons with my sugary coffee before setting off for school or work. Intrigued, nonetheless, by the potential for timeslot-specific refreshments, I wrote to Smirnoff with my suggestion for breakfast vodka. I took the lack of response as a sure sign they were about to launch their own version without crediting me. Breakfast cookies slipped my mind until I tried making macaroons with oats instead of nuts. I had the chewiness of whole oats in mind, but the fineness of the oatmeal I used made for slabs of petrified porridge the likes of which a Highland shepherd might keep in his sporran for desperate times. To achieve proper cookie status they needed a coarser texture and more sweetness, so taking inspiration from the wonderful Anzac cookie, the second batch combined 1¼ cups rolled oats, 6 tbsp granulated sugar, 2 tbsp dark brown sugar, 1 tbsp corn syrup, 2 tbsp raisins, and ¼ tsp baking soda with the whisked egg whites. Opt for the hand-whisk method at E under Leeway for a super-quick breakfast version: They'll take 5 minutes to mix up and can be baking while you jump in the shower/trim your nostril-hairs for that 10 A.M. presentation.

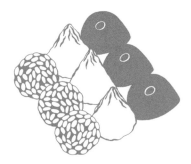

POTATO

Panellets are nut-based cookies from Catalonia that are eaten with a glass of sweet wine on and around All Saints' Day. A common variation calls for the inclusion of mashed potato—either ordinary spud or sweet potato. Try adding ¾ cup cooked, mashed sweet potato to the starting point. Include enough egg yolk—rather than white—to bind, and some finely grated lemon zest for flavor. Once chilled, fashion the dough into balls. Roll them in egg white and then in chopped, untoasted pine nuts or hazelnuts (about the same amount as the almonds in the starting point) before baking for about 15 minutes at 400°F.

WALNUT, CHEESE & CAYENNE

My low-carb, gluten-free friend was coming to dinner and I didn't want her to miss out on the nice cheese I'd bought. I made savory macaroons for her, taking my cue from the crackers on page [353], in which the sugar is replaced by the same weight of Red Leicester cheese. I mixed 1 cup ground almonds with 6 tbsp chopped walnuts, 1 cup finely grated Parmesan, ¼ tsp cayenne pepper, and just enough of a whole beaten egg to make a dough. I rolled it into small balls, flattened them with the heel of my hand, and baked them at 350°F for 12–15 minutes. "I think I'm allergic to nuts," said my friend. I smiled and handed her the glorious Bartlett pear I'd bought specially for the leftovers lunch I was planning for the following day, plus the magnificent cheeseboard. "And dairy," she added, looking at the Camembert like it was an improvised explosive device. She took the pear, though. When I cleared her plate I found she'd cut the pear into quarters, but not taken a single bite. Fussiness I can handle, but the waste singed my soul. I lost a friend, but gained some excellent walnut and cheese crackers.

Nut-Meal Cake: Torta Santiago

This Spanish nut-meal cake is normally made in wide, shallow, round pans, and so often looks like a tart filling removed from its pastry shell (and some versions are baked in a pastry shell). Using an 8-in pan will make a more conventional-looking cake—one that will tend toward the upper end of the given baking time. Like marzipan and macaroons, *torta Santiago* is made with equal weights of ground almonds and sugar, but here the entire egg is used, not just the white.

For a 9- to 10-in cake [A]

INGREDIENTS
4 large or 3 extra large eggs [B] [C]
1 cup superfine or granulated sugar [D]
2 cups ground almonds [E]
1 tsp baking powder [F]
Finely grated zest of 2 oranges or lemons [G]
2 tsp ground cinnamon [G]
Confectioners' sugar, to decorate [H]

1 Beat the eggs with the sugar until the mixture becomes pale and voluminous.
   You can do this with an electric beater, but a vigorous assault with a whisk will do.

2 Mix together the ground nuts, baking powder, citrus zest, and cinnamon (or other flavorings), then fold them into the egg and sugar mixture.

3 Scrape the batter into a well-buttered pan. Bake at 350°F for 20–30 minutes. When a skewer inserted into the center comes out clean, the cake is ready.
   You might also dust the pan with flour or ground nuts, as the mixture is sticky. These cakes need watching, as they form a sugary crust that's prone to burn. Start to check at around 17 minutes. If yours is getting too brown, cover it with a loose tent of foil.

4 When the cake is cool, cut a St. James's cross template out of paper, lay it on the cake, and sift confectioners' sugar over it. Carefully remove the template.

LEEWAY

A Use ¼ cup sugar and ½ cup ground almonds, ⅛ tsp baking powder, and 1 egg to fill 2 darioles or ramekins; reduce the baking time to 18–25 minutes.

B As with butter cake, roughly the same weight of eggs is used as each of the other ingredients (nuts and sugar). An extra yolk or two can be added for a richer, moister cake.

C Some recipes recommend beating the yolks of the eggs and the sugar together before adding the almonds and aromatics, then folding in the whites of the eggs beaten to soft peaks.

D The ratio of sugar to nuts is adaptable. Rick Stein's recipe calls for 3 cups ground almonds to ½ cup sugar.

E Other ground nuts can be used—see Flavors & Variations.

F Baking powder is not essential, but it makes the cake notably lighter.

G Ferran Adrià suggests port as an alternative flavoring.

H Forget the confectioners'-sugar cross and decorate with sliced almonds, scattered over the cake before baking.

HAZELNUT

Anyone who prefers hazelnuts to almonds will be glad to know that there are many hazelnut variations on the classic Galician *torta Santiago*. The Slovenian version is often topped with a caramel butter frosting, the Austrian a mocha. The food writer Carol Field adds candied orange peel to hers and finishes it with a chocolate glaze. My favorite is the plain cake noted by Elizabeth Karmel, which is served with a gooseberry sauce made with sour cream. Edward Behr's *The Art of Eating Cookbook* includes an Italian equivalent, *torta di nocciole*, to which a little cocoa powder is typically added—a fairly common enhancement in hazelnut cakes and cookies. The cocoa lends depth, as will a little instant coffee (1 tbsp dissolved in 1 tsp boiling water will do the trick). In Behr's opinion, however, the cocoa is a distraction, and the cake is best served with a zabaglione made with Barolo or Moscato, or nothing but a glass of Moscato d'Asti.

HONEY & CRÈME FRAÎCHE

Andrée Maze, better known as La Mazille, author of the classic *La Bonne Cuisine de Périgord*, was a collector of recipes in the Elizabeth David mold. She gives a recipe for a hazelnut cake that's similar to *torta Santiago*, but with honey replacing the sugar. I had a pot of good heather honey that I wanted to try in a cake, but I plumped for almonds over hazelnuts because they provide a more neutral-flavored background. I also added a little crème fraîche to the batter, to offset some of the sweetness. The finished cake had a subtle but exquisite flavor, and the sour edge from the cream made it so interesting that I nixed my plan to serve it with a compote of greengages and had only a glass of ice-cold creamy milk on the side. Follow the starting point, but replace *half* the sugar (½ cup) with ⅓ cup of honey (gently heated if it has hardened in the jar). Fold in the crème fraîche with the nuts: Aim for 1 tbsp for every ½ cup ground nuts.

LIME & CASSIA

Santiago cakes are traditionally flavored with citrus zest and cinnamon. This variation calls for the combination of cassia and lime zest: so assertively spicy as to threaten the cake's dedication to a saint. Cassia is Charlton Heston to cinnamon's Montgomery Clift—stronger and less complex. Where cinnamon comes in delicate cigarillo-like scrolls, cassia is like a partly unfurled Gran Corona, thick and stippled and often broken into rough shards. Grind some and sprinkle a pinch onto a just-cut slice of lime. The fragrance may well remind you of cola. Accordingly, I recommend brown sugar in this cake variation, for its caramelized quality. For an 8-in cake, I used 2 eggs, ½ cup packed light brown sugar, 2 tbsp dark brown sugar, 1¼ cups ground almonds, the finely grated zest of 3 limes (as well as, or instead of, orange or lemon zest), 2 tsp freshly ground cassia, and ¼ tsp freshly grated nutmeg.

ORANGE-CHOCOLATE

Claudia Roden's famous almond and orange cake could be considered a variation on *torta Santiago*: 2 cooked, whole, puréed oranges are added to 2½ cups of ground almonds, 1¼ cups sugar, and 6 eggs, along with 1 tsp baking powder. It's all mixed up in a food processor. The only drawback of the recipe is that it's tempting to wheel it out too often. To prevent déjà-vu, try a choc-orange variation—or rather orange-choc, as the fruit dominates at these proportions. You can increase the cocoa content or add some grated dark chocolate if you want to level things out. For a deep 7-in pan, use 1¼ cups ground almonds, ⅔ cup sugar, ¼ cup unsweetened cocoa powder, 3 eggs, 1 cooked and puréed whole navel orange, and a pinch of salt. Last time I made this, the orange was on the juicy side, and I wanted to add a dash of Cointreau, so I mixed in a few tablespoons of flour to absorb some of the excess moisture. As with most cakes of this type, crème fraîche on the side is a must, as is a cup of coffee. Readers of *The Flavor Thesaurus* may recall that I'm a fan of the orange-coffee combination; I recommend replacing the cocoa powder in the cake batter with 4 tsp instant coffee granules dissolved in 1 tsp boiling water.

PECAN

According to Ken Albala, the original 1925 recipe for pecan pie was the work of a corn syrup manufacturer. The nut, sugar, and egg ratios are fairly similar to our starting point—1½ heaped cups pecan halves to 1 cup sugar and 3 eggs—but a great deal of syrup (1 cup) is added, as well as a few tablespoons of melted butter, a teaspoon of vanilla, and a pinch of salt. All of which means the cooked filling differs from the butter-cake texture of *torta Santiago*. It's more of a glistening, transparent, super-sweet jellified custard embedded with nuts. Bake in an 8-in pastry shell, on the lowest shelf, at 350°F for 50–60 minutes.

WALNUT

The advantage of Santiago-style nut cakes is that they can be in the oven within a matter of minutes. The disadvantage is that they are so delicious, they deter your dinner guests from leaving. Pellegrino Artusi reports that his guests found his *torta di noci*, made with ground walnut meal, "exquisite." All I can say is the cake I made with ground walnuts and a grating of blood orange zest, served with coffee and a glass of Armagnac, kept our friends dabbing at their plates for stray crumbs long after the ostentatious yawning had started. With hindsight, it might have been wiser to kill the evening dead with a white chocolate trifle and a shot of Mulligan's Irish Cream Hint of Mint.

Frangipane

Frangipane adds an equal volume of butter as sugar to the nut-meal cake ingredients. While it makes a fantastic cake, frangipane is more often associated with tarts. It furnishes Bakewells with their classic filling, or fanned apples and pears with their soft context in the tarts that fill the windows of French bakeries.

For an 8-in cake, or 3 cups tart filling [A] [B]

INGREDIENTS
¾ cup unsalted butter, just soft enough to beat [C]
¾ cup sugar [C]
3 large eggs [D]
1½ cups ground almonds [E] [F]
1 tsp almond extract—optional [G]
Pinch of salt

1 Cream the soft butter and sugar together until light and fluffy. [H]

2 Beat in the eggs, one at a time.

3 Thoroughly stir in the nuts. [H]
Add any liquid flavorings here.

4 Scrape the mixture into a buttered and lined deep 8-in cake pan or a baked tart shell (page [566]). Bake at 350°F for 25–35 minutes, starting to test from 25.
Use the skewer test—when the frangipane is done, a skewer inserted into the center should come out clean.

LEEWAY

A   For a quantity to fill 2 ramekins, about 1 cup, use ¼ cup each of butter and sugar and ½ cup ground nuts, plus 1 egg; bake for 15–20 minutes. To make a deep 10-in cake, use 1 cup each of butter and sugar, and 2 cups ground nuts, plus 4 eggs, and bake for 30–40 minutes.

B   This quantity will also be enough for a 9-in Bakewell tart—do use the almond extract. Scrape the frangipane mixture into a baked tart shell that has been cooled and spread with a layer of jam. Sprinkle with sliced almonds and bake as per step [4].

C   As with a butter cake (page [336]), you can use half the quantities in the starting point and still get good results—just remember to reduce the pan size too.

D   Or 2 extra large eggs will suffice. Use more eggs if you want a fluffier, puffier frangipane for a cake (the puff might be less desirable in a tart).

E   Nuts other than almonds can be used—see the Flavors & Variations section.

F   Add 1 tbsp flour per 1 cup nut meal for a more robust texture. Wheat or rice flours, or fine cornmeal, will all do the job. Worth considering if you're adding wet ingredients to the mix.

G   Flavor your frangipane with 1 tsp vanilla extract, rosewater, or rum.

H   Some cooks mix the egg yolks into the creamed butter and sugar, then fold in the beaten egg whites after the nuts. This will lighten a cake, but may be too puffy for a tart.

CASHEW

A brief (if enjoyable) survey of French pâtisseries revealed that cashews are about as welcome as Dr. Atkins. Maybe it's the way they look. They lack the vivid color of pistachio, the elegant shape of the almond, or the cerebral intricacy of the walnut. Untoasted, unsalted cashews are fetal in appearance, mundane in flavor. The best that Frederic Rosengarten has to say about the "bland" cashew is that it's sometimes used to extend almond. I tried cashew on its own in a frangipane, and could see his point. It tasted like the filling of a treacle tart might if you'd run out of treacle and resorted to plain sugar syrup instead. Malcolm Livingston II, pastry chef at WD~50 and Noma, brooks no blandness by smoking his cashews and using them for a nougatine.

FRIANDS

Leftover egg whites needn't always mean meringues. Friands, the little French-style cakes so popular Down Under, are so much more fun to eat. Think of them as a riff on frangipane. My volume formula is easy to remember—1:2:3:4, plus an egg white for (approximately) every ⅓ cup of the sugar. So: ½ cup all-purpose flour, 1 cup butter, 1½ cups almond flour, 2 cups confectioners' sugar, and 6 egg whites. As with frangipane, you can play around with the proportions. In a bowl, mix together ½ cup all-purpose flour, 1½ cups ground almonds, 2 cups sifted confectioners' sugar, and a pinch of salt, then make a well in the center. Whisk 6 egg whites—a hand-whisk will do—until frothy, then pour into the well and mix a little before stirring in 1 cup melted and cooled unsalted butter. You may also want to add the finely grated zest of a lemon or the seeds of a vanilla bean and 1 cup raspberries or blueberries. Pour into 10 small silicone molds or well-buttered pans and bake at 350°F for 15–20 minutes until golden.

OLIVE OIL & CHOCOLATE

Nigella Lawson's recipe for this frangipane-like cake calls for olive oil rather than butter. Compared to our starting point, it contains a little more sugar, which will offset the harshness of the cocoa. Mix 6 tbsp unsweetened cocoa powder with ½ cup boiling water. When combined it resembles a glossy ganache. Don't be taken in. It may initially taste chocolatey, but quickly develops a powerful bitterness, like aspirin. While the cocoa is cooling, and your gag reflex subsides, whisk 3 eggs with ⅔ cup nonvirgin olive oil and 1 cup sugar. Once the sugar has dissolved, whisk in the cocoa mixture and 2 tsp vanilla extract. Taste again and you should just about be able to detect the olive oil. Mix in 1½ cups ground almonds, ½ tsp baking soda, and a pinch of salt. Put into a lightly oiled 9-in pan lined with parchment paper and bake at 325°F for 45 minutes. The results have a moist, fudgy texture that suits chocolate cake very well.

ORANGE-FLOWER WATER

Old recipes for frangipane, or "franchipane," did not always contain nuts. It was originally a pastry cream (page [498]), which can be found on our custard continuum. A recipe in *The Professed Cook* (1769) calls for 3 eggs, 1 pint of cream, 2 or 3 spoonfuls of flour, and a "proper" quantity of sugar. Once the custard was cooked, some crushed almond cookies, lemon peel, butter, a couple of egg yolks, orange flowers, and orange-flower water were stirred in. In *English Food*, Jane Grigson gives a similar recipe for a baked custard, except it calls for ground almonds rather than crushed cookies and sherry rather than orange-flower water. According to *The Oxford Companion to Sugar and Sweets*, the derivation of frangipane is frangipani, a flower (otherwise known as plumeria) used by French glovemakers to perfume their wares.

PINE NUT

I bought a packet of ground pine nuts to try them in a frangipane in place of almonds. As expected, the flavor was mildly resinous, but the grind of the meal came as a surprise. It was as fine as wheat flour, which meant the batter (made to frangipane quantities) was too dense when cooked. A little baking powder improved matters. Some cooks use a little leavener in their frangipanes for a fluffier texture. As to the pine-nut meal, let's just say I won't be restocking once the packet is finished. It's expensive, for one thing, and the resulting tart paled in comparison to Italian *torta di pinoli*, an almond frangipane cake covered with whole pine nuts: Mix in scant ½ cup pine nuts at the end of step [3], then scatter another ½ cup or so pine nuts on top before baking.

PISTACHIO

Used in early frangipane recipes, but prohibitively expensive for all but the swankiest pâtisseries and restaurants. At The Square in Mayfair they make a pistachio frangipane with chopped ripe figs folded into it. The mixture is then piped into *kataifi* pastry, and served with vanilla and almond panna cotta, thyme ice cream, and fig pulp. Pistachio and grapefruit are well matched, perhaps because (as Waverley Root observes) the flavor of pistachio is more suggestive of a spice than a nut, and grapefruit is famously fond of spice, especially cinnamon. I once baked a pistachio frangipane over segments of pink grapefruit. The results were like an extreme fruit crisp. If they eat desserts in deep space, this is what they'll taste like.

RUM

Raymond Blanc includes 1 tbsp rum or Cognac in the filling for his *galette des rois* ("king cake"), effectively a frangipane calling for ⅓ cup butter, ¾ cup confectioners' sugar, and ¾ cup ground almonds plus 1 egg, and 1 extra yolk). This will fill 14 oz puff pastry, rolled into two circles, the lower and upper being 8-in and 9-in diameter respectively. Spread the frangipane over the lower circle, leaving a ¾-in margin all around the edge and painting it with yet another yolk. (Blanc suggests grating chocolate over the frangipane, or covering it with slices of fried quince.) Lay the upper layer of pastry over the lower, chanting a low-pitched invocation, and seal around the edges. Chill for an hour, in both senses of the word. Brush the top with more yolk and score a pattern in it, traditionally a fan of spokes that curve as they near the edge, but you might prefer a grid of diamond shapes, a sprig of laurel leaves, or a cameo of Elvis with the collar of his jumpsuit turned up. Bake at 350°F for 45 minutes. *Galettes des rois* are traditionally eaten on January 6, at Epiphany, the *rois* being the Magi visiting the infant Christ. Whoever finds the bean or charm customarily baked into the cake gets to wear a crown for the day (or to spend it on the phone trying to get a dentist's appointment). Dorie Greenspan notes that French pâtisseries now sell *galettes des rois* from Christmas to the end of January, and that the almond cream might be flavored with rose or clementine. Pithiviers, which is not dissimilar, is made year-round, and often contains a layer of jam on top of the frangipane.

SPICY CHOCOLATE

Rather than frangipane, my spicy choc cakes are made along friand lines (page 300). If you've ever pressed your face to the window of a pâtisserie and wanted *all* of the cakes, this flavor is for you. It's inspired by an outstanding iced cookie recipe by Yotam Ottolenghi and Sami Tamimi who, in turn, were inspired by Israeli *duvshanyot* or German pfeffernüsse. It tastes like a bite out of every cake in the shop: ginger cake, fruitcake, chocolate cake, citrus cake, spice cake, and, thanks to the glacé icing, lemon drizzle cake. Cover 3 tbsp dried currants in rum or brandy and let soak for a few hours, or a few days. In a large bowl, mix together 1 cup ground almonds, ⅓ cup flour, 1⅓ cups sifted confectioners' sugar, 2 tsp unsweetened cocoa powder, ½ tsp each of ground cinnamon, ground allspice, ground ginger, and freshly grated nutmeg, ¼ tsp salt, the finely grated zest of 1 lemon and 1 orange, and ½ tsp vanilla extract. In a separate bowl, whisk 4 large egg whites to a foam, then fold them into the ground almond mixture until well combined. Stir in ⅔ cup melted butter, ½ cup coarsely grated dark, 70%-cocoa chocolate, and the drained currants until just about combined. Pour into 10–12 small cake pans or molds (bars/midi-muffins) and bake at 350°F for 15–20 minutes. When they've cooled a little, glaze with an icing made from ¾ cup confectioners' sugar and 2 tbsp lemon juice, and finish with little jewels of mixed candied peel.

Frangipane → Other Directions

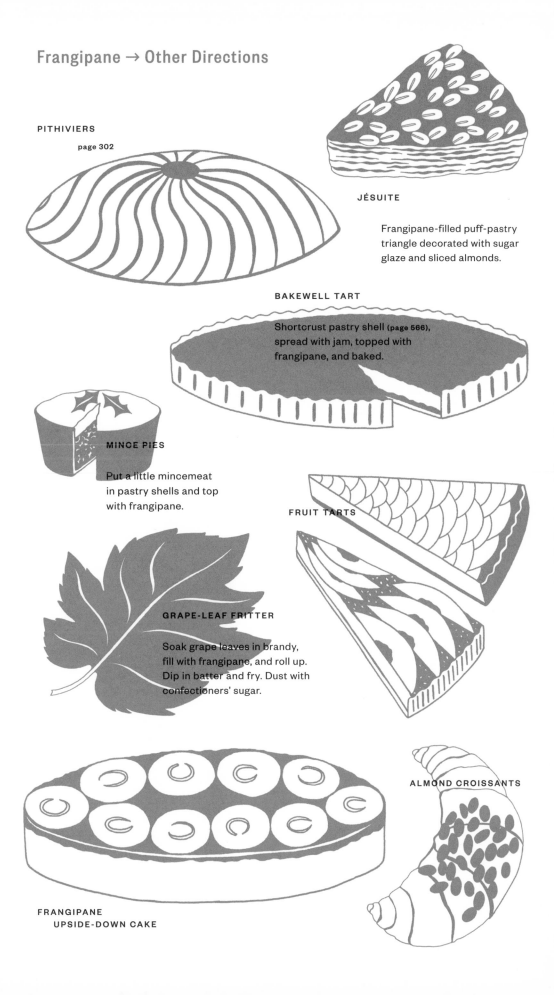

PITHIVIERS

page 302

JÉSUITE

Frangipane-filled puff-pastry triangle decorated with sugar glaze and sliced almonds.

BAKEWELL TART

Shortcrust pastry shell **(page 566)**, spread with jam, topped with frangipane, and baked.

MINCE PIES

Put a little mincemeat in pastry shells and top with frangipane.

FRUIT TARTS

GRAPE-LEAF FRITTER

Soak grape leaves in brandy, fill with frangipane, and roll up. Dip in batter and fry. Dust with confectioners' sugar.

FRANGIPANE UPSIDE-DOWN CAKE

ALMOND CROISSANTS

Nut Sauce: Tarator

The term "tarator" applies to any number of preparations, but for our purposes refers to a pounded walnut and garlic sauce, sometimes mixed with yogurt to make a cold soup—see page [306]. The proportions of the starting-point ingredients are pretty adaptable, and tarator can be made with equal *weights* of the principal ingredients (in this case bread, milk, nuts, and oil).

For scant 1 cup sauce

INGREDIENTS
2 slices of white bread, preferably a bit dry [A]
½ cup milk or water
1 cup chopped walnuts [B]
1 garlic clove, roughly chopped [C]
½ tsp salt
½ cup olive oil [B]
1 small bunch of dill, chopped [D]
1–4 tbsp lemon juice or red wine vinegar [E]
Chopped walnuts, chopped dill, and/or walnut oil, for garnish

1 Put the bread, shorn of its crusts, to soak in the milk or water until soft, then squeeze dry.

2 Place the nuts in a blender or small food processor and pulverize. Add the squeezed-out bread, together with the garlic and salt, then blitz to a coarse or smooth paste according to taste. [F]

3 With the motor running, slowly drizzle in the olive oil.

4 Stir in the chopped dill, then add lemon juice or vinegar, tasting as you go.

5 Check the seasoning, then chill. Allow time for the flavors to meld, if possible.

6 Garnish with chopped walnuts, dill, or a drizzle of walnut oil, or all three.

LEEWAY

A The bread can be replaced by more ground nuts, if you prefer.

B Use skinned almonds, hazelnuts, or pine nuts, preferably blanched or toasted first to intensify their flavor. Walnuts can be hard to grind—it may be easier to use a pestle and mortar. Claudia Roden makes her pine nut tarator sauce for fish with fish stock instead of oil. Leanne Kitchen uses blanched almonds in her recipe, and adds a small amount of ground cinnamon.

C Some cooks use as many as 5 garlic cloves.

D Sally Butcher uses cilantro and summer savory in place of dill in her walnut tarator sauce to serve with fried vegetables. Herbs can be omitted—it'll still be tarator.

E Some recipes call for a lot more acidity—4 tbsp lemon juice or vinegar is a pretty authentic quantity, but I find it too sour, and tend to use just 2 tbsp.

F The time-honored (and time-consuming) means of preparation is with a pestle and mortar. Pound the garlic with the salt first, then add the walnuts in stages, pounding until you have a paste. Then repeat with the bread. Either transfer to a blender or food processor and pick up from step 3, or gradually whisk in the olive oil by hand, as you would for a vinaigrette, then continue from step 4.

CUCUMBER & YOGURT SOUP

Also known as tarator, this Bulgarian soup takes the starting-point sauce as its base. At step 4, add just 1 tbsp lemon juice or vinegar, then transfer the mixture to a bowl and whisk in 2 cups plain yogurt. Add 1 peeled, deseeded, and diced English cucumber and stir well. Taste and season, adding more lemon juice or vinegar if you like, plus as much cold water as necessary to thin to your desired texture. Some cooks use sour cream, or a mix of sour cream and yogurt, to give a richer texture, then refrigerate. Others prefer the cucumber with its skin on, or grated, or mixed with some diced fennel. Serve chilled.

EGGPLANT, WALNUT & RED BELL PEPPER

Gas stations should sell eggplants next to the barbecue charcoal. Left to char and soften as the embers cool, barbecued eggplant will develop the smokiness and silken texture to take the *meh* out of your *melitzanosalata*—(roughly) the Greek equivalent of *baba ghanoush*. There are many versions, and while roasted eggplant flesh is common to all of them, nuts aren't—although my favorite combines eggplant with walnuts, roasted garlic and red bell pepper, red wine vinegar, olive oil, parsley, and seasoning. Not dissimilar, that is, to romesco (page 315), which is probably why I like it. In a food processor, reduce 2 roasted garlic cloves and 1 cup chopped walnuts to a paste, adding 2 tbsp olive oil in increments. Gradually add the scraped-out flesh of 2 barbecued eggplants and 1 roasted, skinned red bell pepper, 6 more tbsp olive oil, 2 tbsp lemon juice, and 1 tbsp red wine vinegar, plus salt and pepper. If you don't have a food processor, make the paste using a pestle and mortar and beat in the other ingredients. Garnish with plenty of chopped parsley and eat with flatbreads (page 28) fresh from the grill.

GARLIC & ALMOND SOUP

Ajo blanco translates as "white garlic," and while there are dozens of allegedly authentic variations on this almond-based soup, the garlic is nonnegotiable. As is sunshine. *Ajo blanco* is a swim you can drink. Try to make this at the cooler time of morning, so you don't get hot and bothered, and the soup has enough time to chill. Make an almond, garlic, and bread paste (no dill) as per our starting point for nut sauce, but with three times the amount of bread, nuts, and garlic. Transfer to a blender with ½ cup olive oil and ½ tsp salt and blitz. With the motor running, slowly add 3 cups cold water until the soup has a creamy consistency. Finish with up to 3 tbsp sherry vinegar and additional salt to taste. Refrigerate for a couple of hours. Relax in the garden with a glass of very cold Tio Pepe and some green olives while you consider your garnish options. Diced ripe melon, quince jelly, apple, pear, Muscat grapes, or, as recommended by Frank Camorra, a grape granita? In more remote parts of Andalusia, *ajo blanco* is served with roast potato, but I'd opt for a little nebula of olive-oil droplets.

LOU SAUSSOUN

Jenny Baker describes a nut-based sauce from the Var (*lou saussoun* is a regional term for "poor man"). To make about ½ cup, pound 3 sprigs' worth of mint leaves with ½ tsp fennel seeds using a pestle and mortar. Add ½ cup ground almonds and 6 anchovy fillets, and beat in 1–2 tbsp olive oil and enough water to make a paste. Taste, and add salt and/or a squeeze of lemon, if required. Serve in a little pot with an extra sprig of mint and eat, thinly spread on crackers. Reminded of Vietnamese cuisine by the combination of mint and pungent fish, I served it on white-rice crackers. *Cerneux*, from Touraine, is a similarly obscure nut-based spread described by Waverley Root. It's made with green walnuts steeped in the juice of green grapes, and garnished with chopped chervil. Quite tart, records Root, but it sharpens the appetite.

PEAR & WALNUT

Intxaursalsa, from the Basque Country, is a "walnut cream" made from the ground nuts, cooked in milk with sugar and cinnamon, and served in small portions at room temperature with whipped cream or vanilla ice cream. Thomas Keller's exquisite walnut soup is more complicated. He makes a purée of pear that's been cooked in a stock of sugar and Sauvignon Blanc. Next, he simmers roasted, skinned walnuts in cream infused with vanilla, and strains it. The pear purée and nut cream are then combined, and the soup is served cold with a little walnut oil. You might feel bad about discarding the nuts; no doubt their grainy texture wouldn't impress the Michelin inspectors, but at the domestic table, they may be welcome. You could make a hybrid of the French Laundry and Basque versions—a *kellerintxaursalsa*. I find the mixture of fruit, nut, vanilla, and cream delectable, like a whole serving of the god-given concoction at the bottom of a sundae glass. The bonus of cooking the Keller version was discovering how good pears are when poached in Sauvignon Blanc. I'll never go back to red.

PESTO

Being served pesto at a special meal is like being given socks for Christmas. When a friend took me for lunch at Assaggi, a pricey Italian restaurant in Notting Hill, and insisted everyone have the pesto, my heart sank. She was paying. How could I object? The pasta, a fresh tagliolini, arrived tightly ravelled like a miniature Egyptian mummy. The pesto was made with seven herbs, the exact constituency of which was a secret. Suffice to say it was perfectly balanced, like a stroll in an herb garden in summer, and made the dominance of basil in ordinary pesto seem crude and overbearing. In place of pine nuts, it contained walnuts, which lent a pleasing bitterness. I've since tried to recreate it at home, mixing basil, parsley, chervil, mint, thyme, rosemary, and sage, with good results that nonetheless fall mysteriously short of the mark. Pesto Trapanese is a Sicilian variant from the western port of Trapani, where local cooks, catering to homesick Genoese sailors, supposedly created an approximation of Ligurian pesto using their indigenous small-leaved basil, almonds instead of pine nuts or walnuts, and fleshy ripe tomatoes. Cheese was generally omitted, although pecorino features in some versions, as do other Sicilian specialties like anchovies, pepper flakes, and even mint. Delicious, but you can't help but think the main effect of pesto Trapanese would be to remind the Ligurian sea dogs that they were five hundred miles from home. For a classic basil pesto, pound ½ cup toasted pine nuts with 1 garlic clove, 1 cup basil leaves, and a few pinches of sea salt to make a paste-like consistency. Transfer to a dish and stir in up to 4 tbsp extra virgin olive oil as well as ½ cup finely grated Parmesan. Check for seasoning, adding a little lemon juice if you like. Alternatively, blitz the ingredients in a blender. For pesto Trapanese, use ½ cup blanched almonds, 2 garlic cloves, ½ cup basil or mint leaves, 1 lb skinned raw tomatoes, and ¼–½ cup extra virgin olive oil, plus salt and pepper. Eat with linguine, from a shallow bowl, dreaming of pine nuts and Paganini.

PICADA

A sauce so transformative it deserves its own Disney movie. Use picada to thicken stews, to flavor bean or lentil dishes, to stir into steamed clams (for *almejas de palamós*), to serve alongside roasted meat, fish, or vegetables, or simply spread on slices of French bread. Toast or fry 1 slice of crustless white bread, then pound it with 1–2 garlic cloves, a handful each of skinned toasted almonds and hazelnuts, ¼ tsp sea salt, and the leaves of a few sprigs of flat-leaf parsley. Some versions call for a pinch of saffron, others for a hint of chocolate. You can dilute it further with a little oil, water, or stock. Single-nut versions are just as common as the almond-and-hazel combination.

WALNUT & CREAM

Walnuts can be as bitter as a washed-up salesman in a motel bar and grill. This is particularly apparent when they're ground, but their harsh edge can be softened with some thick white cream. On the Italian Riviera, *salsa di noci* is served at room temperature with hot pasta. It's made with pounded walnuts, garlic, parsley, olive oil, and heavy cream. Escoffier gives a recipe for a rather similar-sounding sauce, made with coarsely chopped walnuts, sour cream, freshly grated horseradish, dill, sherry vinegar, salt, and pepper. On a slightly grander note, Elizabeth David recounts a description by Sir Harry Luke, briefly British Chief Commissioner in Transcaucasia, of a salmon trout unique to Lake Sevan in Armenia, served with its own amber-hued caviar and a sauce of fresh walnuts mixed with buffalo cream and a touch of horseradish.

Nut Sauce → Other Directions

THINNED FURTHER WITH
OIL TO MAKE A DRESSING

**AS A STUFFING FOR
APRICOTS OR FIGS**

... with pine nuts and mostarda
di Cremona soaked in Campari,
wrapped in bacon, and broiled
until crisp.

**AS A GARNISH FOR SOUP,
OR TO ENRICH A STEW**

**ON THIN TOASTS,
LIKE TAPENADE**

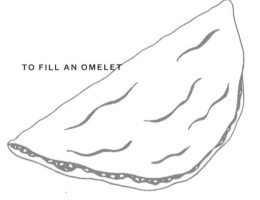

TO FILL AN OMELET

TO MAKE PALMIERS

Spread a sheet of puff pastry with
pesto and sprinkle with grated
Parmesan. Roll one long side to
the middle, then the other to join it.
Cut into ½-in slices and bake at
400°F for 10–15 minutes.

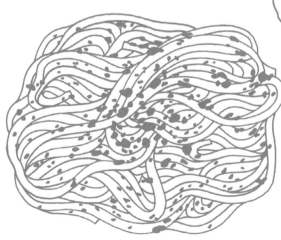

**STIRRED THROUGH
PASTA, LIKE PESTO**

**MIXED WITH A LITTLE
SHREDDED MEAT
TO MAKE EMPANADAS**

Nut Stew: Fesenjan

Imagine a korma on opium. *Fesenjan* is a Persian stew that has all the tastes covered—sweet, salty, and savory—but it's the exotic, sour and bitter notes of pomegranate and walnut that make it so memorable. It's a sumptuous treat. The Persian rice dish *chelow* is the authentic accompaniment: It's flavored with butter and saffron, and is fairly elaborate to prepare. So I've opted for plain white rice.

For 4 servings

INGREDIENTS
2 cups chopped, lightly toasted walnuts ^A
3 to 3¼-lb chicken or duck, cut into pieces ^B
Olive oil or ghee for frying
1 large onion, finely diced
½ tsp ground cinnamon ^{C D}
Pinch of powdered saffron ^{C D}
2 cups pomegranate juice ^{A E}
1–2 tbsp pomegranate molasses ^F
1–2 tbsp sugar or honey
1 tsp salt
Chopped parsley and/or pomegranate seeds, for garnish
White basmati rice, for serving

1 Grind the walnuts. Better still, pound using a pestle and mortar. Walnuts tend to get claggy when blitzed in a machine. If you have time, try refrigerating them first, but if they still don't pulverize in your grinder/blender/processor, you might find it faster to use a pestle and mortar, or a strong plastic bag and a rolling pin.

2 In a pan large enough to hold all of the ingredients, brown the poultry pieces in oil or ghee, in batches if necessary. Remove with a slotted spoon and set aside.

3 In the same pan, soften the onion. You may need to supplement the fat, or, if you're using duck, remove some.

4 Stir in the cinnamon, saffron, and any other ground spices and cook for 1–2 minutes.

5 Return the poultry pieces to the pot. Add the walnuts, pomegranate juice, molasses, sugar, and salt. Stir thoroughly and bring to a boil, then reduce to a simmer.

6 Simmer slowly for as long as the meat needs to cook through and the sauce to thicken.

Chicken or duck pieces will take about 1 hour. If you have the time, the poultry is likely to become more tender if cooked in a 325°F oven, under a tight-fitting lid or foil, for 1½ hours.

7 Taste and adjust the seasoning, if necessary.

8 Garnish with chopped parsley. Pomegranate seeds look good, too. Serve with rice.

LEEWAY

A The ratio of ground walnuts to pomegranate juice varies from recipe to recipe, anything from 1:1 to 1:4. This would be between 1:1 and 1:2 for volume. Whatever proportions you use, the finished dish should have a thick and creamy sauce.

B Lamb, quail, and pheasant are also traditional, but eggplant slices, meatballs, and fish can be given the *fesenjan* treatment. If you're using an ingredient that does not need a long simmer—say fish or quail—cook the sauce for 30 minutes before you add it, allowing the flavors to develop and meld.

C Spices vary a good deal from recipe to recipe. Some call for turmeric rather than saffron. Others add black pepper or fenugreek.

D Some cooks add 1–2 tbsp tomato paste with the spices at step 4.

E The pomegranate juice can be freshly squeezed or store-bought, and partially supplemented with chicken stock if you don't want your *fesenjan* too fruity.

F In the absence of pomegranate molasses, use a mixture of honey and lemon juice.

AJI DE GALLINA

A Peruvian dish of chicken in a creamy sauce, made with walnuts, garlic, chili, and bread, and often cheese and evaporated milk. *Aji* means "chili pepper," and *gallina* translates as "hen," but in Lima, you're just as likely to be served a plate of creamy guinea pig. If the kids are back from school and there's no getting near the hutch without being spotted, you can substitute shrimp, hard-cooked eggs, sweet corn, or squash. The type of chili specifically denoted by *aji* is *aji Amarillo*, a bright yellow pepper that scores a 7/10 rating for heat. If you can't find this either in fresh or paste form, Martin Morales, owner of the London-based Peruvian restaurant Ceviche, suggests that the heat and flavor can be roughly reproduced with an orange Scotch bonnet chili, an orange or red bell pepper, and a squeeze of orange juice. If this sounds too fiery—Scotch bonnet is at least twice as hot as the *aji Amarillo*—you can make a similar dish with a milder chili, orange in color if possible. According to Maria Baez Kijac, indigenous Peruvians used walnuts and peanuts as thickeners until the Spanish shipped up with their almonds and pine nuts. Poach a cut-up chicken with carrots, onion, and garlic in water until cooked through. Remove; strain and reduce the stock to 1 cup. Soften an onion, 4 garlic cloves, and deseeded chilies/bell peppers in some oil until light golden. Add the stock, 1 tbsp ground cumin, and ¼ cup ground nuts (walnuts or peanuts) and simmer for a few minutes. Blend 4–5 handfuls of bread crumbs or of cracker crumbs with a 12-oz can of evaporated milk and add to the sauce. Shred the chicken meat from the bone and add to the sauce, along with 1 cup grated Parmesan, to reheat. (If Parmesan sounds like an odd ingredient for a traditional Peruvian dish, note that there was a large influx of Italian immigrants to Peru in the mid-nineteenth century.) Some garnish their *aji de gallina* with a sprinkle of turmeric, hard-cooked eggs, and olives, and serve it with rice and new potatoes. The price of authenticity, in this case, is a finished dish straight out of a 1950s all-color cookbook.

CARNE EN SALSA DE ALMENDRAS

Cancel that cooking-school vacation in the Tuscan hills. Reserve an apartment within walking distance of La Boqueria in Barcelona. You'll need somewhere with a decent kitchen, a magnetic strip of knives that don't shy at onions, and some outside space, even if it's only a foot-wide strip of crumbly balconet. You'll need somewhere to sit, or lean, with a cold Estrella and a tapa of *sobrassada* spread on toast, while your *carne en salsa de almendras* mutters on the stove. The *carne* is typically chunks of pork shoulder, although Claudia Roden's faster version calls for meatballs made with veal and/or pork. Which you choose will depend on how much Spanish you summoned, faced with the blood-stained *carnicero* at the market, leaning impatiently on his cleaver. The technique for *carne en salsa* is similar to *fesenjan*. For 2¼ lb pork, you'll want about 1 cup each of stock and dry white wine. The meat is cut into roughly 1¼-in dice, browned in olive oil, and set aside, then the onions are softened. Chicken stock, white wine, and aromatics (½ tsp smoked paprika, a sprig of thyme, a bay leaf, a pinch of saffron) are added before the meat is returned to the pot, brought to a boil, and tightly covered, then gently simmered for 1½ hours. The almonds, bread, and garlic are stirred in at the end, in the form of a pounded sauce called picada (page 308). The dish is served as either a tapa or a main course. In the latter case, Rick Stein suggests boiled potatoes or steamed rice and green vegetables as accompaniments.

CIRCASSIAN CHICKEN

Until the mid-nineteenth century, Circassia was a small independent nation on the northeastern shore of the Black Sea. After the Russians annexed the country, many ethnic Circassians were expelled and formed a diaspora across the Ottoman Empire. Circassian chicken may be so called because of its paleness, recalling the skin tone of the legendary Circassian women (as an ideal of femininity, the "Circassian beauty" can trace her origins to the late Middle Ages). The recipe is fairly simple, so it's worth seeking out the best-quality ingredients. As with *fesenjan*, the chicken is cooked first, but poached as opposed to browned or stewed. Use enough water to cover the chicken by an inch or so. Because the poaching liquid is essentially your stock, treat it as such, and cook the meat with typical stock ingredients—carrot, onion, celery, bay, parsley, garlic, and peppercorns, and maybe some cardamom pods and cloves too. Clifford A. Wright's version includes coriander seeds, leek, and allspice berries. Remove the cooked chicken meat from the bones and skin, and set aside. Reduce the stock to about 2 cups. Grind 1½ cups chopped, lightly toasted walnuts with 2 slices of stock-dampened bread. Soften 2 garlic cloves with a chopped onion and a pinch each of paprika and cayenne, then mix with the ground walnuts. Gradually add enough stock to achieve a thick but pourable sauce (some cooks add a little cream here too). Mix the chicken with the sauce, holding back a bit of sauce to pour over the top. Gently warm 2–3 tsp paprika and a few pinches of cayenne in 2 tbsp walnut oil, then drizzle it over the dish so it gathers in red puddles like dying post-Soviet lakes. Scatter with chopped parsley. Circassian chicken is best served at room temperature, and is therefore a shoo-in for picnics. (Evelyn Rose suggests using it to fill pastry shells—a nice idea, as it is a little like a *vol-au-vent* sauce.) Take the rusty-red oil along in a bottle, plus some good bread and a salad of diced cucumber, tomato, and radishes in a lemony dressing. Then fruit and Turkish Delight for dessert.

KORMA

I had my first London curry-house experience aged eighteen, a gauche girl recently arrived from rural Hampshire. Wary of chili heat, I was coerced by my more worldly sister into trying a korma. I was won over by my first mouthful, and not a little surprised that Indian food could be as soft and comforting as Christmas turkey in clove-warm, creamy bread sauce. As Pat Chapman points out, in India, korma refers more to a technique than a single dish; the term is said to be Middle Eastern in origin, and means "braise." Chapman goes on to give a recipe for Kashmiri *mirchwangan* korma, which calls for red wine, bottled beets, and plenty of red chili. You're unlikely to encounter that in your local Taj Mahal. Nonetheless, don't knock the thick, rich, ivory-colored sauce we Brits commonly understand as korma—the kind with layers of spices, and almonds, cashews, or coconut, or a mixture of all three— until you've made it yourself. To serve 2, cut 10 oz skinless, boneless chicken breast into bite-sized chunks and marinate them in 1 cup plain yogurt while you get on with the chopping and pounding. Soften 1 finely chopped onion in oil. For the paste, blend or pound 2 shallots or 1 small onion, 1 tbsp dried shredded coconut, ¼ cup blanched almonds, 2 green chilies with the seeds and seams removed, 3 garlic cloves, a thumb of fresh ginger, minced, 1 tsp ground cumin, 2 tsp ground coriander, a pinch each of ground cloves, cardamom, and cinnamon, and 1 tsp salt. Add to the softened onion in its pan and cook over a low heat for 1 minute. Add the chicken with its yogurt marinade. Bring this to a simmer, slowly, then cook over a low heat, covered, for 45 minutes, stirring occasionally. Add a little hot water if it looks like it's drying out. Toward the end of cooking, stir in 5 tbsp ground almonds or cashews. While I've specified pre-ground spices, the dish will be immeasurably improved if you toast and grind your own spice mix.

MAFE

Mafe (pronounced "ma-fay") needs a global ambassador. It could do for Senegalese food what green curry did for Thai. It is also very hospitable to whatever you have in your pantry, but one nonnegotiable ingredient is peanut. In Senegal, you might visit the market to buy a large, clear plastic bag full of fresh peanut butter. And I mean large. It can be used as a pillow when you stop for a much-needed breather on the way home. Huge quantities of peanut are not mandatory in *mafe*, but you will need enough to offset the acidity of the tomato. The stew can be made with lamb, beef, or chicken, or a selection of chunky-cut vegetables—carrots, say, with potato, yuca (cassava), turnips, okra, and cabbage wedges. Season 2¼ lb meat, brown it, and set aside. Finely chop 1 onion and 1 green bell pepper and soften in peanut oil, adding minced fresh chili to taste. Return the meat to the pan. Whisk ½ cup smooth peanut butter into 2 cups hot stock and pour it into the pan with a 14-oz can of crushed tomatoes. Add a bay leaf and a few sprigs of thyme. Season and cook at the lowest simmer, stirring occasionally, until the meat is cooked through and tender. Season with salt and black pepper. Serve with white rice.

ROMESCO DE PEIX

Romesco de peix is a main-course variation on romesco sauce—and, like picada (page 308), it is Catalan in origin. It might, in fact, be considered an elaboration of picada. Nuts, bread, oil, and garlic form its backbone, but roasted tomatoes and ñora peppers are added too. The *peix* is usually monkfish, but you can use any fish that holds together sufficiently, or shellfish if you like. Make a romesco by de-stemming and deseeding 2 dried ñora peppers (ancho or pasilla chilies are acceptable substitutes) and soaking them in hot water for at least 30 minutes. Roast 3 or 4 fleshy tomatoes and half a garlic bulb in some olive oil at 400°F until charred and soft. After dispensing with their skins, scrape into a blender with 1 torn-up slice of toasted white bread, 1 cup ground toasted nuts (almonds, hazelnuts, or a mixture), 1 tsp salt, and the soaked ñora. Blitz to a thick paste with up to ½ cup olive oil. Add red wine vinegar to taste (1–3 tsp is typical) and set aside at room temperature. Transfer the romesco to a pan big enough to hold the fish too. Add a small glass of dry white wine and 1¼ cups fish stock. Bring to a boil, then turn the heat down and simmer slowly for about 10 minutes. Taste and adjust the seasoning, if necessary. Add the fish (or shellfish) to the sauce and cook for 4–5 minutes longer, or as long as it takes to cook through. Some prefer to season and flour the fish fillets and fry them for a minute on each side before adding them to the sauce to finish cooking—this helps the fish hold together. Garnish with chopped parsley and serve with bread.

Cake & Cookies

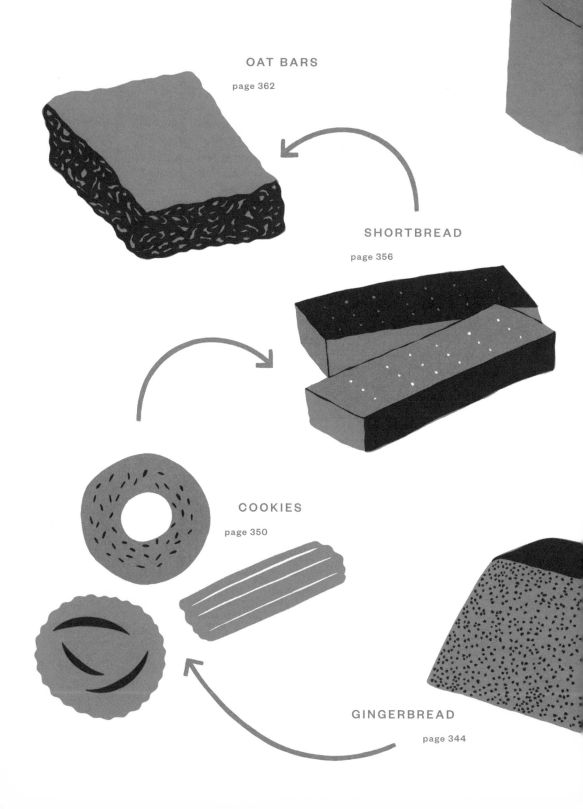

OAT BARS

page 362

SHORTBREAD

page 356

COOKIES

page 350

GINGERBREAD

page 344

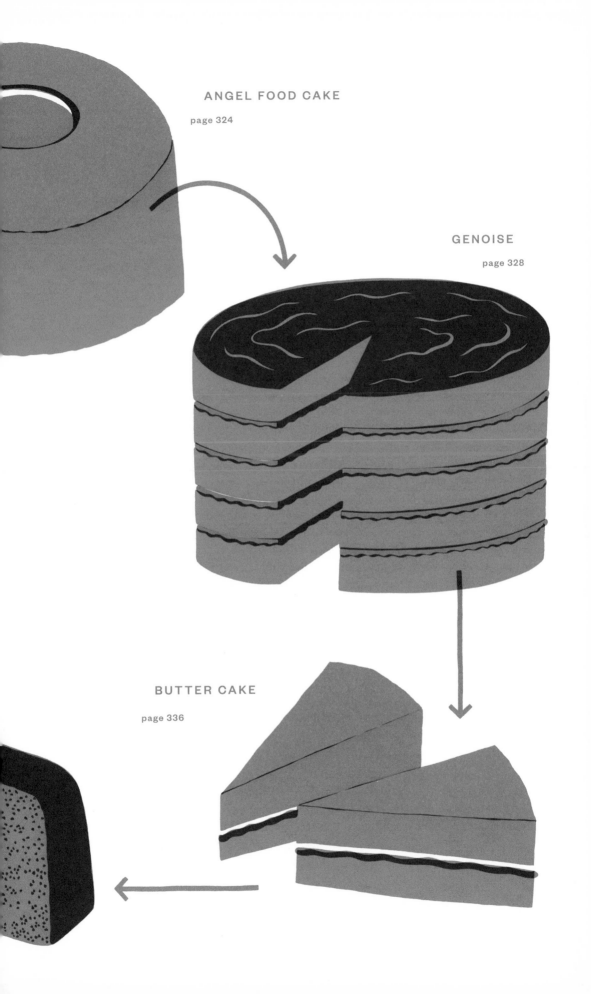

ANGEL FOOD CAKE

page 324

GENOISE

page 328

BUTTER CAKE

page 336

The aroma of a Victoria sandwich cake being baked derives from just four ingredients—flour, sugar, butter, and egg. If you concentrate, you can tell them apart: the toasty flour, the smell of warm butter, the cotton-candy smog of caramelizing sugar, the sweet sulfurous notes of gently cooked egg. It's as heady and innocent as a freshly bathed baby. I say four, but arguably there's a fifth ingredient. Or perhaps a fourth-and-a-bit—the near-odorless leavening agent. Before baking powder and baking soda, or their coarser predecessors like pearlash, were easily available, the baker relied on eggs, yeast, or, less commonly, beer, to put the spring in their sponge. Thus yeasted cakes like buns and babas sit on the bread continuum, since the methods used to make them have more in common with bread. This chapter deals with egg and/or powder-risen cakes and their flatter cookie brethren. You might argue that egg is the defining point of difference in the cakes and cookies described herein. The quantity (if any) used, and how; from the cakes at one end of the continuum, aerated with beaten egg whites, through the solitary yolk-as-dough-binder, to eggless shortbread and oat bars at the other extreme.

A   We'll start with the most egg-risen of all: angel food cake. It is, in
N   essence, a flour-fortified meringue. Both share a dry, somewhat
G   tiresome sweetness, but where meringue is as brittle as a New
E   York socialite, angel food cake is its softer, more mallowesque,
L   Midwestern cousin. Study the recipes and you'll see why. Angel
    food cake has a higher ratio of egg to sugar than meringue. But
F   its origins are identical. Lots of egg whites are beaten with a little
O   cream of tartar and maybe some flavoring, before half of the sugar
O   is added, gradually, to form a billowing, shiny white mass, like a
D   dowdy egg's extravagant daydream. The rest of the sugar, along
    with a modest amount of flour, are then folded in. Typically, angel
C   food cake is baked in a pan shaped like a giant O. When the cake is
A   unmolded, its stippled, golden exterior makes it look like a lichen-
K   covered fertility stone of great antiquity. Inside it's as white as chalk.
E   Serve it at a garden party and you risk being overrun by pagans.

Its greatest devotees are health-conscious cake addicts who revere it for its absence of fat, the first and signal irony of which is that it is usually accompanied by large quantities of whipped cream—which, in turn, posits a gâteau variation on the Gaia hypothesis. Extract the most fattening bits from a cake, and the system will provide them by other means. The second irony is that the enormity of the standard angel food cake cancels out any of the benefits of using zero fat. I bought the specified tube pan, then never used it, either from a fear that we'd never be able to eat a cake that size, or the fear that we would. That, or I just never got around to it. Rather than splash out on another piece of equipment, consider demoting the angel to cherub and making your cake in a loaf pan. The recipe also works very well in dariole molds, which is handy to know if you're rationing your treats, or trying out adventurous flavor variations.

Like angel food cake, Genoise relies entirely on beaten eggs for its lift. Both are categorized as foam cakes. Where angel food cake is made with only the whites, Genoise calls for whole eggs. Further, where many recipes for Genoise call for equal weights of flour and sugar—about an ounce of each per egg—angel food cake calls for double the flour weight in sugar. A stand mixer will make Genoise far less trouble, but armed with only a portable electric mixer, you'll soon discover why it has traditionally been more popular with pâtissiers than domestic cooks. It's fiddly and time-consuming: You will need to melt (and consider clarifying) the butter, beat the eggs and sugar in a double boiler, thoroughly fold in the flour without reducing the volume of beaten froth too much, and, finally, carefully fold in the butter, which beaten egg whites like about as much as slugs do salt. All this effort for what to amateur eyes is a rather dry, dull cake. The benefits of Genoise to the pro are the ease of shaping that comes of its tight crumb, and its dryness, which means it can be topped with mousses and crèmes without turning soggy. It can also take a dousing of syrup—an open invitation to create fanciful layers of flavor. Only when a Genoise has been filled can its qualities be properly appreciated.

The Portuguese make a Genoise-type cake called *pão de castela*. In the seventeenth century, merchants took the *pão* to Japan, where it became known as *kasutera*, and caught on with the locals partly because it contained no dairy products. It is now a regional specialty of the Nagasaki prefecture, where the Portuguese merchants came ashore. At the Fukusaya bakery, famed for its *kasutera*, the batter is hand-whisked by rows of chefs, dressed in what look like radiation-adapted beekeeping suits, rhythmically whirling balloon whisks the width of tennis rackets around tilted copper bowls of egg. The batter is then decanted into long, rectangular pans and baked until it attains its characteristic crème-caramel livery—a rich yolk-yellow on the inside, dark brown on the out. This is thanks to the malt syrup or honey added over and above the sugar content of a typical Genoise. The plank-like lengths of cake are cut into smaller portions and wrapped in the sort of sumptuous packaging you associate with Fifth Avenue boutiques or fine Champagne houses. Like Champagne, Fukusaya *kasutera* is aged before it's sold. Everyone knows that soups and stews can benefit from a day or two's rest in the fridge—a process known as tomorr-inating in the Segnit household. The same principle applies to cakes and cookies. Recipes for parkin (page [345]) generally recommend a week of keeping before you cut it. According to James Beard, shortbread needs a week to attain optimal shortbreadiness. And you'll find the flavors in butter cake are much more pronounced once the cake has been out of the oven for a day or two. It's surely only a matter of time before artisan bakers are equipped with temperature-controlled *caves de pâtisserie*, or that we start to lay down gâteaux for special occasions.

Anyone put off by the prospect of setting up a double boiler might be interested in the version of Genoise that doesn't call for the eggs to be heated first. A good deal of beating is, nonetheless, still required. The main difference between the heated and non-heated versions is that the former is more robust. You'll notice this when you fold in the flour. The uncooked version is more given to losing its puff, and, when you take it out of the oven, to deflating a little. Naturally, this is unimportant when the height of your cake isn't an issue. A Swiss roll is made via the unheated method. So are French madeleines, the little shell-shaped cakes that I rarely find as good to eat as they are to look at. Nonetheless, madeleines could scarcely have inspired seven volumes of remembrance without there being something to be said for them—although it should be noted that Proust's narrator dips his madeleine in linden flower tea, thus circumventing the problem of dryness. Without the tea, *À La Recherche du Temps Perdu* might have been a novella.

B   Next, the butter cake. Or pound cake. Or, in France, the *quatre*

U   *quarts*, the four quarters, so called because of its equal weights

T   of sugar, butter, flour, and egg. No need for a clever mnemonic to

T   commit that to memory. What I particularly love about this starting

E   point is that you can replace the flour with ground nuts, for a fluffy

R   frangipane/almond cake (page 298), or, with a minor tweak to the
method, melted chocolate for a sumptuous chocolate cake (page 396).

C   Where angel food cake and Genoise are made by the foam method,

A   butter cake relies on the creaming method, in which the sugar is

K   beaten with the butter rather than the egg. This requires the butter

E   to be soft, which tends to put the damper on a spontaneous urge
to bake cake. Anyone who's tried to cream cold butter will recognize the four stages of declining impetus: 1) develop tendinitis/impatience with declogging the mixer beaters; 2) eat too many sugar-crusted butter nuggets out of the bowl; 3) set the remainder aside to reach a workable temperature; 4) get caught up in the afternoon showing of *Seven Brides for Seven Brothers*. By the time Howard Keel breaks into "Spring, Spring, Spring," you'll have a bowl of over-softened butter and no cakemaking inclination whatsoever. Faced with rock-hard butter, Dan Lepard's tip is to apply heat (in a pan or microwave) until a third of the butter is melted, transfer it to the mixing bowl, and leave it for 5 minutes before proceeding.

Butter cake can be made with no leavener other than eggs and the air that you've creamed into the fat by pushing the sugar through it. As a rule, however, most recipes call for a little baking powder, for extra lightness and an awful lot less beating. Another advantage of the butter cake is its tolerance for all sorts of flavoring ingredients. Liqueurs and spirits, zest, oil-based extracts, seeds, nuts, and fruit can all be added to the dry ingredients—in contrast to foam cakes, where, as in meringue, the egg whites can easily be deflated by careless additions, leaving you with a frothy white soup on your hands.

It might seem remarkable how conservative cake flavoring has remained compared to, say, the fanciful flavors Baskin-Robbins was adding to ice cream as far back as the 1950s. But the custard base of ice cream is even more tolerant of additions than butter cake. The recent annexation of Manhattan, and whole boroughs of London, by the cupcake industry has yielded its fair share of innovative butter cake recipes, but by and large the classics like chocolate and vanilla prevail. The new popularity of red velvet cake is telling: the same old chocolate and vanilla butter cake, just in a different color.

GINGERBREAD Ginger, of course, is another perennial favorite, at least in Europe and Australia. The classic dark, spicy gingerbread cake, or loaf, furnishes the next starting point on the continuum. Gingerbread requires equal weights of sugar and flour, just like the butter cake, but instead of an equal weight of butter, only half is used—the other half is replaced with syrup. The egg is greatly reduced, to just one per cake, but there's more milk used than in the butter cake. Only one egg means that a small quantity of baking soda is added to give some lift; the soda is activated by the acidity in the golden syrup or light molasses. Sticky gingerbread cakes are made by the melting method, which means the butter, sugar, and syrup are warmed in a pan until all is melted, then mixed into the dry ingredients, followed by the egg and the milk. As you might imagine, the batter is notably wet. The result, once baked, is a juicy, dense cake.

Other flavored sticky cakes rely on similarly acidic ingredients— cocoa powder, say, or honey or citrus juice—to activate the baking soda. Baking powder can be substituted if you're making your sticky loaf with nonacidic ingredients. This cake is perfectly amenable to experimentation, but be prepared for it to take one or two more attempts to perfect than a butter cake or a Genoise.

This is mainly because a sticky loaf cake is a one-recipe lesson in why cakes sink. The high sugar content makes it especially prone to subsidence. Furthermore, the lengthy spell in the oven may tempt you to check how it's doing before the batter has properly set. The quantity of leavener needs to be just right so the loaf doesn't expand too quickly, then deflate later on. On top of this, the loaf shape requires a certain amount of experimentation with heat and cooking times, so you end up with a cake that is neither burnt on the sides nor raw in the middle. Take heart from the fact that you'll often see mild indentations in professionally made loaf cakes.

COOKIES Omitting the milk and half of the granulated sugar will turn sticky gingerbread loaf into gingerbread cookies: Roll the warm just-mixed dough between your palms to make walnut-sized balls, then bake to make domed, tender cookies. Omit the egg, too, and cookies made in the same way will be flat, cracked, and, once cooled, hard on the teeth like an old-fashioned gingersnap—the dunking cookie nonpareil. Egg or no egg, once the dough is chilled, rolled out to a depth of about ⅛ in, cut into gingerbread people or dainty fluted rounds, and baked, the difference between the types of cookies will be negligible.

It's a commonplace that liberties are out of bounds to the baker, baking being more of a science than an art, etc., etc. There are authorities on the matter who would have you weigh water and measure your sugar on microchemist's scales. Fair enough, if your goal is to reproduce something you've seen in a swanky bakery's cookbook, but compare ten recipes for chocolate chip cookies, say, or a layer cake, and the breadth of variation will be salutary. Never more so than for cookies. Dan Lepard has it right about cookies: They're "the ultimate in foolproof baking. There's so little that can go wrong... there is a paradise of tweaks and simple changes that can be made to most recipes, enough to keep an inventive cook busy for a decade."

Use the sugar, butter, and flour proportions as a starting point from which you should, within reason, be unafraid to deviate. The same applies to the next point along the continuum, shortbread: the polestar of cookie recipes, the first I learned, and promisingly easy to commit to memory—a simple 1:2:5 ratio of three ingredients. To help remember which ingredient corresponds to which number, my handy mnemonic is Short Bread Formula: Sugar, Butter, Flour.

s   Shortbread is made with just the three ingredients and a small, but
H   essential, pinch of salt. The creaming method is ideal. Once you've
o   made a paste of the butter and sugar, mix in the flour and salt, and
R   the dough is ready to bake. The only liquid is the water in the butter,
T   ensuring that very little gluten is developed and, assuming you
B   haven't gone mad stirring in the flour (and thus developing the
R   gluten), the texture of the baked shortbread will be crumbly and
E   short. If you only have rock-hard butter on hand, you can rub the
A   cubed butter into the flour, then stir in the sugar and salt and bring
D   the dough together with some egg yolk. It will still be short—just
not as much as if made by the creaming method. In place of the egg yolk, some rub-in recipes recommend pressing the crumb mixture into a prepared pan, but this can be at the expense of the shortbread's cohesiveness after baking, and it can be tricky to cut into shapes—especially the traditional Scottish petticoat tails.

The main flavor of shortbread is butter. Historically, however, it was enhanced with many of the aromatics that have similarly fallen out of fashion in cakes. Shetlanders favored caraway seeds (and they used a griddle pan to cook the shortbread). On the mainland, a Christmas variation called Pitchaithly shortbread contained a mixture of toasted almonds and caraway and was decorated with whole almonds or citrus peel. Mrs. Beeton uses the same aromatics in a very low-sugar, 1:4:13 shortbread. The Nevis Bakery, run by Archie Paterson, in the foothills of Ben Nevis, has offered demerara, double-chocolate and ginger, chai, Earl Grey, and lavender flavor variants, all of which are worth putting the teakettle on for. I was once given pink peppercorn shortbread. It looked very pretty, rosy as a Scotsman's knees, but pink peppercorns taste like hairspray and have a similar effect on the back of my throat.

Other common variations on the standard shortbread recipe include swapping a little of the wheat flour for a different cereal. Cornmeal or coconut flour will have a noticeable effect on the flavor, as well as the texture; cornstarch and rice flour the texture only. I had high hopes for manioc flour, made from cassava. So toothsome, like a little pile of crushed digestive biscuits or graham crackers, sprinkled over or served on the side of Brazilian dishes, but its distinctive character was not apparent in a shortbread. Save it for *feijoada* (page 250).

o And so we arrive at oat bars (or flapjacks, as they're called in the
A U.K.). Here the egg, an option in cookies and shortbread, is omitted,
T and the flour replaced by oats, which are naturally gluten-free. In
   the absence of egg or gluten, the finished cookie is kept together by
B the caramel mixture of hot butter and sugar. Like gingerbread, oat
A bars are made by the melting method, so they will be ready for the
R oven in just 10 minutes. Nonetheless, you have to wait until they
S have cooled sufficiently for the caramel to set, which can take a
good while. (If possible, it's an idea to make them the day before you serve them.) The great advantage of the oat bar—and what merits its inclusion here—is that the recipe is so open to variation. You can add nuts, seeds, chocolate, and fruit—both fresh and dried. They can be made with coconut oil if you are vegan, or molasses if you like punchy flavors. Do what you like with oat bars as long as you don't try to make them too healthy; skimping on the fat and sugar will leave you with something closer to muesli. Not that there's anything wrong with muesli. It's just a pain to slice.

Angel Food Cake

The size of a typical angel food cake is all the more impressive considering that it is entirely down to beaten egg whites. No other leaveners are used. Its dryness and open texture give angel food cake something of the look of a millstone, belying the lightness that accounts for its divine name.

For a 10-in angel food cake/tube pan [A] [B]

INGREDIENTS
1 cup cake flour [C]
Pinch of salt
1½ cups sugar [D]
10 extra large or 12 large egg whites, at room temperature
1 tsp cream of tartar [E]
1 tsp vanilla extract [F]

1   Sift the flour with the salt and half the sugar. Sift again and set aside.

2   Beat the egg whites until foamy. Add the cream of tartar and beat to soft peaks.
    If your eggs have been in the fridge, sit them in warm water for 5 minutes before cracking and separating them.

3   Gradually beat the remaining sugar into the egg whites to reach stiff peaks. Beat in the vanilla.
    Don't let the mixture get too stiff (i.e. when it begins to look dry), or you'll struggle to incorporate the flour.

4   Gradually fold in the sifted flour and sugar mixture.
    One method is to sift a quarter of the mixture over the surface of the meringue, then fold it in, aiming to retain as much of the beaten-in air as possible. Repeat until all the flour mixture is incorporated, delving deep to catch any flour languishing at the bottom of the bowl.

5   Pour into an *ungreased* pan (not the nonstick sort). Firmly bang the pan against a work surface, then "cut" the mixture through with a knife in several places.
    Both the banging and cutting are to knock out any large air bubbles introduced by the transfer from mixing bowl to pan.

6 Bake immediately on the lower-middle shelf of a 325°F oven.
It should take about 45 minutes.

But check 10 minutes before the time is up. When it's ready, the cake should spring back when you press it in the center with your finger.

7 Let the cake cool in the pan, open-side down. Ideally, place the hole in the center of the pan over a bottle, so that the cake sits suspended on the neck of the bottle.

Some tube pans have legs or an extra-long tube in the center, so you can upend them and allow air in underneath.

8 After about an hour's cooling, run a knife around the edge of the cake before unmolding it. Use a serrated knife to slice it. Be gentle.

9 The cake will keep for 2–3 days. It doesn't freeze well.

LEEWAY

A A fifth of this quantity will fill 3 dariole molds—count on 30–35 minutes baking time. Or, for a 9 x 5 x 3-in (8-cup) loaf pan, use 5 egg whites, ¾ cup sugar, ⅔ cup cake flour, ½ tsp cream of tartar, and ½ tsp vanilla extract, and allow for 40 minutes baking time. At step 7 the pan can simply be inverted on a cooling rack.

B Angel food cake is never baked in a standard round cake pan. It needs an ungreased (not nonstick) pan with narrow sides to cling to.

C It's permissible to use the same quantity of all-purpose flour. To make a gluten-free version, you'll need to use a special gluten-free flour mix. Ground almonds, cornstarch, etc. will not work.

D You can use either granulated or superfine sugar.

E In place of the cream of tartar, you can use the same quantity of lemon juice or white wine vinegar.

F Avoid oil- or fat-based flavorings, which will deflate the egg peaks irreparably. You can get away with beating in up to 1–2 tbsp flavoring, once the egg white has stiffened at the end of step 3. Try lemon juice with zest for a lemon cake or, for a coffee version, 2 tbsp instant coffee granules dissolved in 2 tsp hot water and then cooled.

Angel Food Cake → Flavors & Variations

ALMOND & ROSE

Pity the pre-First World War American prairie farmer. A 1912 edition of *Prairie Farmer Magazine* urges its readers to "try mixing almond and rose together as a flavor for angel food cake. It is delicious." As if harsh winters, summer droughts, European wheat quotas, railroad companies overcharging for transportation, and cows requiring manual assistance in labor weren't enough, here's this magazine expecting you to slip an apron over your dungarees and whisk up a delicate cake infused with the flavors of the Maghreb. At least the mechanical eggbeater had been invented by then. In place of 1 tsp vanilla, beat ¼ tsp almond extract and 2 tsp rosewater into the egg whites at the end of step [3].

BUTTERSCOTCH

If the world were a fairer place, butterscotch angel food cake would usurp the standard recipe: It's less of a flavor variation than a wholesale improvement. Not long after angel food cake became the most popular cake in North America, cookbook writers started to put spins on the recipe. Butterscotch is one of the most widely documented, and is as simple as the straight substitution of light brown sugar for white. As a rule, using brown sugar in cakes will give moister, stickier results than white, which can't go amiss when your cake is fat-free.

CLEMENTINE

As with meringues, the basis of angel food cake is foamed egg white, which can make the cake difficult to flavor—the addition of oil or fat will tend to deflate the bubbles. Citrus peel is handy in this instance, as its minimal oil content will not be enough to flatten your froth. Lemon is probably the most common flavoring, but I wanted to use clementine, mourning as I do each claw of beautifully perfumed peel dropped into the trash unzested. The peel of four clementines, Microplaned into zesty flecks, flavored an angel food loaf cake—see A under Leeway. Returned to the fruit bowl, my grated clementines, matte and ridge-marked, looked as cold and forlorn as newly shorn sheep. So I puréed them and put them in a *torta Santiago* (page [294]). By teatime I had two clementine-flavored cakes to offer my friends. The nut-meal cake was luscious with a tart edge. The angel food cake had a restrained elegance and wore the clementine like a fragrance it had stepped through. Carmen versus the Spanish Ambassador's wife.

HARD BOILINGS

Such is the rock 'n' roll reputation of sugar, these days, that contemporary Lemmys might drop the Marlboro reds and Jack Daniels from their riders in favor of plain dangerous quantities of angel food cake, made with crushed hard candies. Or "hard boilings," as the Scots call them, with that inimitable Scottish ability to make a sweet your grandmother might produce from her handbag sound like an initiation ceremony at a youth detention facility. Acid drops (a.k.a. lemon drops) are surely the hardest of all hard candy. Laura Mason notes how confectionery manufacture was made easier after the discovery that acid, in the form of cream of tartar (potassium bitartrate), prevented sugar from crystallizing at high temperatures, so that the transparent, gemlike hard candies we know today could reliably be produced in large quantities. Subsequently, she writes, they went "quite quickly from being a technical novelty to something banal." Other forms of acid, like vinegar or lemon juice, were substitutable—as they are in many toffee recipes—but cream of tartar had the advantage of being cheap, reliable, easy to store, and flavorless. Acid drops are no more than sugar, water, cream of tartar, and a drop of lemon essence. In Scotland, they're dyed livid green and called "soor plooms," although they're only marginally more sour than the plums you'll find at the supermarket there. To make the rock 'n' roll cake, cover the hard candies with a dish towel (or a bandanna) and bash them into fine sugar crystals with a rolling pin (or the heel of your guitar). You'll want 5–6 tbsp for a cake made with 10–12 egg whites, folded in at the same time as the last addition of flour mixture at step 4.

STRACCIATELLA

Stracciatella has only the second-best name in the gelateria. *Primo premio* goes to *fior di latte*, "flower of milk," a term suggestive of such tender ephemerality that ice would be the only possible hope of preserving it. It's a mixture of fresh cream, milk, and sugar—no eggs, vanilla, or other ingredients—so unless the gelateria is within a hoof-clatter of the milking parlor, best to stick to coffee and hazelnut. Name aside, nothing beats *stracciatella* for looks, the flakes of dark chocolate jutting from the off-white cream like quartzite formations in snow. The trouble comes with the eating of it, as the ice cream chills the inside of your mouth to the point that the chocolate can't melt. It accounts for the weird, pasty-cardboardy sensation of all ice cream involving solid chocolate. In a cake, however, the chocolate can yield on your tongue as it should, and its bitterness is thrown into relief against the very sweet cake. Using a sharp knife, cut 2 oz dark, 70%-cocoa chocolate into thin shards. Fold them into a cake batter made with 10–12 egg whites, at the same time as the last of the flour mixture at step 4.

Genoise

Like angel food cake, Genoise relies entirely on egg and air for its leavening. It differs in containing yolks, more flour, and a little butter, thus sitting somewhere between angel food cake and butter cake. Genoise is light, a tad dry, and, consequently, prized by pâtissiers: It welcomes adornment. Flavored syrups, mousses, buttercreams, fruit, and whipped cream can be piled on without fear of sogginess. This starting point requires equal weights of flour and sugar (approximately an ounce of each per egg), which is standard in Europe. In the U.S., equal volumes are typical, so you'll find American versions have less flour per cake.

For 2 shallow or 1 deep 8-in round cake(s) [A] [B]

INGREDIENTS
4 tbsp unsalted butter [C]
1 cup all-purpose flour [D]
Pinch of salt
4 extra large eggs, at room temperature
⅔ cup sugar
1 tsp vanilla extract

1   Melt the butter and let cool. Butter and lightly flour the cake pan(s), then line the bottom with parchment paper.

2   Sift the flour with the salt and set aside. Keep the sifter to hand.

3   Beat the eggs and sugar in a double boiler (or a heatproof bowl set over—but not touching—a pan of barely simmering water), until the mixture feels warm to a dipped finger, or reaches about 110°F. [E]
    Starting with room-temperature eggs, this should take about 5 minutes.

4   Remove from the heat and keep beating until the mixture holds its shape for 5 seconds after falling from the beaters.
    Using a portable mixer, this will take about 10 minutes, or a bit less if you put the eggs and sugar in a stand mixer once heated.

5   Sift about a third of the flour over the eggs and sugar. Fold it in thoroughly with a metal spoon, but try to minimize the amount of air that gets knocked out of the mix. Continue to sift and fold until all the flour is fully incorporated into the batter.
    Delve down to the bottom of the bowl a few times, because the flour will collect there.

6   Place a ladleful of the batter in another bowl and fold the butter into it, aiming to leave any butter solids behind in their pan. Fold in the vanilla, then briefly fold the butter mixture into the rest of the batter.

Some cooks skip this tempering stage, instead drizzling the cooled butter around the edge of the main bowl of batter and folding it in. If your butter is hot, however, you'll need to temper it as above.

7   Pour carefully into the prepared pan(s). Level the top(s) with a light hand.

Don't push the air out by being too heavy-handed with the spoon or spatula.

8   Bake immediately at 350°F for 20–30 minutes.

Start checking after 20 minutes—when ready, the edges of the cake should have shrunk away from the sides of the pan, and the center should spring back when you press it gently with your finger.

9   The cake can be cooled and kept wrapped at room temperature for a week.

If iced with buttercream or sugar glaze, the cake can be kept in an airtight tin for 4–5 days, but try to wrap the sponge part if possible. If filled or topped with cream or cream cheese, it will need to go in the fridge. This is less than ideal for a sponge, so eat it within 3 days.

LEEWAY

A   For a 6-in springform pan, use 2 eggs, ½ cup flour, ⅓ cup sugar, and 2 tbsp melted butter. Bake for 20–25 minutes, checking after 15. For a 9-in springform pan, use 5 eggs, 1¼ cups flour, ¾ cup sugar, and 4–5 tbsp melted butter. Bake for 25–35 minutes, checking after 25.

B   If making a layer cake, 1 deep cake cut into 3 (or 4, for the more skilled) usually looks better than 2-pan layers.

C   Some recipes call for 3 tbsp bland oil, at room temperature, in place of the butter. Alternatively, the cake can be made entirely without fat.

D   Some recipes recommend a 50/50 mix of all-purpose flour and a gluten-free flour like potato or cornstarch— amounting to an ersatz cake flour. Or use ⅔ cup cake flour.

E   There are several low-rise variations on Genoise that follow the same (or similar) ingredients and method, but without heating the eggs and sugar. These include madeleines (page [332]), savoiardi (page [333]), and Swiss roll (page [334]).

BROWN BUTTER BAY

Wasn't there a Shirley Temple song about Brown Butter Bay? There should have been. It's a good flavor for cake, and makes a Genoise highly suited to its classic accompaniment of berries and cream. If you're already melting butter, browning is only a step further. Start with about 10 percent more butter than you need for the cake, to allow for wastage. In a pan—preferably a light-colored one that lets you keep an eye on the browning—over a medium heat, melt the butter with a few torn bay leaves, then let it foam and turn amber. Remove from the heat before it goes dark. Strain, and use before it re-solidifies. To accentuate the bay flavor, consider making a syrup (page 432) infused with bay leaves and pouring it over the finished cake. Fresh or dried leaves can be used, but fresh will yield their flavor faster.

CHOCOLATE

Chocolate Genoise is the sponge at the heart of a classic Black Forest gâteau, even if its flavor lacks the dark depths of the *Schwarzwald* itself. The strength of the cocoa should not be too assertive, or it will blunt the impact of the gâteau's dousing in kirsch. The Queen's favorite birthday cake is a chocolate Genoise simply layered with a rich chocolate ganache. According to the royal chef Darren McGrady, Her Majesty's favorite *tea* cake is "chocolate biscuit cake" or tiffin cake. I wonder whether she longs for this cake, made with broken-up cookies, on her birthday too, but feels obliged to choose a more regal plinth on which to mount the royal candles? I once made a chocolate Genoise for my friend James's birthday. James favors food with low nutritive value—salty, oily potato chips, fried chicken from no states other than Kentucky, chocolate with a cocoa content no higher than 20 percent. Recently back from New York, and having noted how well a Crunchie bar might serve as a scale model of a skyscraper, I set about making a chocolate Manhattan. First I baked a few sheets of chocolate Genoise—it's an excellent cake for cutting into shapes—and then left them and a sharp knife to my husband, who was appointed chief architect and builder. When I returned, there were two blocks of New York. Just like I'd imagined it. Towering buildings and everything. The streets paved with ganache. Yellow fondant taxis. My husband was on the point of excavating a subway tunnel in the Genoise and modeling a little graffiti-tagged gray fondant A-train to emerge from it. The cake was a delight to behold, but not so easy to cut into pieces. We settled down with a round of Black Russians and picked buildings off the cityscape at random, like Godzilla. Depending on how dark and chocolatey you want your Genoise, replace ¼ cup of all-purpose flour with the same volume of unsweetened cocoa powder, making sure you sift the flour and cocoa together several times so they're well mingled. Some recipes that stipulate a lot of cocoa also call for a little extra sugar to help balance the bitterness.

COFFEE

Coffee will ensure an authentically log-colored Genoise in your *bûche de noël*: Use 2 tbsp instant coffee dissolved in 2 tsp hot water, and let cool before adding with the butter at step 6. Plus, it tastes great with the vanilla whipped cream and marrons glacés you'd be a Scrooge not to roll up into it. All that remains to be done is the thick chocolate frosting, distressed to resemble bark, a growth of pistachio-crumb lichen, and a meringue mushroom or two, if you can make them small enough. Try to take it as a compliment if someone dumps it on the fire.

GREEN TEA

In Japan, green tea is a popular flavoring, in particular for cakes made in the Genoise style, wherein the delicacy of matcha won't be spoiled by chemical leaveners or masked by butter. Not unlike true pistachio, the color can tend to the queasy, but looks rather handsome set off by dark chocolate. Use 2 tsp matcha green tea, sifted in with the flour. The Paris-based Japanese pâtissier Sadaharu Aoki combines green tea and chocolate in his take on opéra cake, the neat, quadrilateral stack of layered sponge and crème pâtissière that will make your heart sing if you like beautifully bound books.

JOCONDE

Joconde is a close relative of the Genoise. Its name is said to be a measure of high regard: The joconde is to sponge cakes as the *Mona Lisa* is to portraits of enigmatic young noblewomen. It departs from Genoise in calling for ground almonds in place of most of the flour and, as in savoiardi (page 333), for the egg yolks and whites to be beaten separately. It's baked in a jelly-roll/sheet pan and used to make opéra cakes (see green tea, above) or, if you fancy yourself a bit of a Leonardo, to make joconde imprime, where a design is baked into the sponge using a cookie paste in a contrasting color. Not only is this good fun, but if you're using your imprime to line a pan before filling it with mousse or bavarois, there'll be plenty of trimmings to nibble on. First, for your dark-chocolate design, make a paste by mixing together ½ cup confectioners' sugar, ¼ cup butter, ¼ cup egg whites, and 6 tbsp flour, plus 2 tbsp unsweetened cocoa powder. Pipe your design on a silicone mat laid on a baking sheet. If your design is text-based, remember it will have to be mirror-writing. Freeze for an hour, then make the joconde. For two 12 x 8-in sheet pans, beat 3 egg whites until frothy, add ¼ tsp cream of tartar, then keep beating, gradually adding 3 tbsp sugar, until the mixture stands up in soft peaks. Set aside, and immediately beat together 3 yolks, 1 cup ground almonds, and 1 cup confectioners' sugar until pale and soft. Sift 3 tbsp flour evenly over the yolk and almond mix, then gently fold in a third of the egg whites, followed by the rest. Fold 1–2 tbsp cooled melted butter thoroughly into the mixture. When your design has been in the freezer for about 50 minutes, set the oven to 350°F. Pour the joconde over the frozen design, gently level it with an offset spatula, and bake for 7–10 minutes until the cake is a pale golden brown. While you're waiting for the cake to cool a little, liberally dust another silicone mat or sheet of parchment paper with confectioners' sugar. Flip the cooled cake onto it and peel off the silicone or parchment from the top. In the case of smaller cakes, some chefs claim that a joconde made with more flour than nut meal makes the cake more flexible, and therefore less likely to break if you're using it to line little ring molds.

LEMON

Lemon cake is so good with a sharp lemon frosting that bolder combinations seldom get a look-in, especially if they involve darker flavors. Not so at Aureole, Charlie Palmer's restaurant in New York, where they make a dessert of lemon Genoise in coffee gelatin with an espresso ice cream. The pairing of lemon and coffee is not unusual in the U.S., where an espresso may well be served with a twist of lemon peel on the saucer. Everyone agrees you won't find it in Italy—which makes it, of course, the sort of utterly unimportant controversy that has gourmet forums swarming with authenticity police, the culinary equivalents of Comic Book Guy in *The Simpsons*. "I've been to Italy *three times* and *never once* seen this." All that aside, if something works well with coffee, chances are it works with chocolate too. In *The Particular Sadness of Lemon Cake*, the sadness in question belongs to nine-year-old Rose, who finds she can taste her mother's emotions in chocolate-frosted lemon cake. Curious to see whether I too had the gift, I made a very lemony Genoise and iced it with a dark chocolate ganache. Somewhere amid the mildly floral citrus and dark tang of chocolate I swear I could sense something. I wasn't sure, so had another slice, and sat dusting the crumbs from my cardigan and eyeing a third slice when I distinctly heard someone say, "Why don't you stop stuffing your face and get on with writing your book?" It sounded a lot like my husband. Fold the finely grated zest of 2–3 lemons into the butter and batter mixture instead of the vanilla extract at step [6].

ORANGE-FLOWER WATER

Madeleines de Commercy are the pretty little shell-shaped cakes that look like guest soaps, and, all too often, are about as nice to eat. The only one I've ever had that wasn't unpleasantly dry was undercooked. Still, the madeleine remains popular because of its enchanting form. The celebrity endorsement from Proust can't hurt, either. Madeleines are like glasses with plain lenses. Their sole function is to make you look clever. The following variation would sit between a Genoise and a butter cake, based as it is on the *unheated* Genoise method, but made with butter cake proportions. Beat 2 large eggs with ½ cup sugar until pale and fluffy. Sift over ¾ cup all-purpose flour with a pinch of salt and fold in, then stir in scant ½ cup cooled melted butter and 1 tsp orange-flower water. Variations include replacing 1 tbsp of the sugar with honey, using self-rising flour, adding baking powder to all-purpose flour, replacing ¼ cup of the flour with the same of ground almonds, or adding finely grated lemon zest instead of orange-flower water. Many recipes stipulate letting the batter rest for a few hours, so as to allow the gluten in the flour to develop, so the cake grows a little bump on its non-grooved side. The most useful tip is to test, and test again, until you find the batter quantity per madeleine, and cooking time, to suit your oven and your baking sheet. If your madeleine pan has 12 indentations, use 3 or 6 to start with, noting (or photographing) how much you've filled the indentations. Transfer to a 350°F oven and start checking from about 10 minutes, tinkering with the fill and cooking time until you hit the sweet spot. Unless you have a Proustian memory, write the final result down somewhere. You're aiming to give the cakes a good browning without overcooking the middle. Any cakes that turn out too dry may be dunked in linden flower tea.

QUINCE

One of the great benefits of Genoise is its hospitability to unusual flavors via the medium of syrup. And syrup is one of the few means of capturing the otherworldly flavor of quince. Like apple and pear, quince is a member of the *Rosaceae* family, and would look more like a cross between the two were it not for its fine coating of fuzz, as if it were grown in the bag of a vacuum cleaner and not on a tree. They are too hard and sour to eat raw, shortcomings that only make their aromatic qualities more striking. Cooked, they taste like a sunny autumn afternoon in the twelfth century. Rinse off the fluff but don't peel. Core and chop a pound of fruit (i.e. about 2 large quinces). Place in a pan with 1½ cups water and 1 cup sugar and bring to a simmer. Cook until soft and use in a pie or crisp, or serve as they are, with a dollop of thick yogurt and a scattering of toasted nuts. Strain the remaining liquid, thicken it with more sugar if necessary, and drizzle over a Genoise. You'll need about 4 tbsp syrup for each layer of an 8-in round cake. Quince syrup can also be mixed with prosecco or with sugar, water, lemon juice, and ice to make a sort of quince *pressé*: We'll call it a Wife of Bath.

SAVOIARDI/SAVOY BISCUITS

A swoon in cookie form. Pale, fragile, and sugared, these are also known as ladyfingers or boudoir cookies. Think twice about giving them to the handyman with his coffee. The ingredients are the same as a butter-free Genoise—¼ cup flour and 2½ tbsp sugar per egg—but the method is different. No double boiler is called for, and the yolks and whites of the egg are beaten separately. The egg yolks are beaten with half the sugar, and a little vanilla extract, to the point where the mixture holds its shape for 5 seconds after it falls from the beaters. This should take 5–10 minutes with a portable mixer, less with a stand mixer. Sift over the flour with a pinch of salt, but don't fold in. In another bowl, beat the egg whites, adding a few pinches of cream of tartar when they begin to foam. Continue beating to soft peaks, then gradually add the rest of the sugar, tablespoon by tablespoon, and beat to stiff peaks. Fold the meringue into the yolk and flour mixture in a few batches until just combined. Taking care not to knock out too much air, spoon the mixture into a pastry bag fitted with a ⅝-in plain tip and pipe 3½- to 4-in lengths onto a lightly greased or parchment-lined baking sheet (or use a ladyfinger pan). Sprinkle with sugar and bake at 350°F for 8 minutes. If you're making your savoiardi to stand sentry around a Charlotte Russe, try to make sure they're the same length. If you're making them for a tiramisù, you can get away with greater irregularity. Or forget the cookies and bake the batter in a jelly-roll or sheet pan, slicing the results into fingers. You won't get the pretty cross-sectional ellipses when your tiramisù is sliced, but then looks were never its strong point anyway.

SWISS ROLL

Like madeleines and savoiardi, a Swiss roll (a.k.a. jelly roll) is made to the Genoise method, bar the double boiler—simply beat the room-temperature eggs and sugar to ribbon stage, then follow our starting point from step ⁵. Use 3 eggs for ½ cup sugar, ¾ cup flour, and 1 tbsp melted butter mixed with 1 tsp vanilla extract. Bake in a greased and lined jelly-roll/sheet pan, about 12 x 8 in, for 12–15 minutes until golden and springy. Shake some sugar over a piece of parchment paper just bigger than the pan. Unmold the sponge onto it. Working while the sponge is still warm, trim off the rough edges with a serrated knife. Score, from top to bottom, a line about ¾ in in from one of the short sides—this will make it easier to roll the center in on itself. Spread jam evenly over the sponge (you'll need at least ½ cup). Use the parchment to help you roll it up as tightly and neatly as possible. A thin layer of buttercream under the jam will be particularly welcome.

Genoise → Other Directions

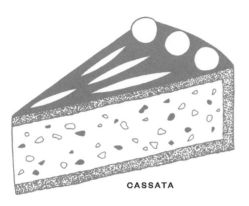

CASSATA

A Genoise sponge case filled with sweetened ricotta and candied fruits.

TRIFLE

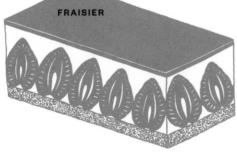

PUNSCHKRAPFEN

Cubes of rum and apricot cake sandwiched between layers of Genoise and covered with pink fondant icing.

BAKED ALASKA

A Genoise base topped with ice cream, then entirely encased in Italian meringue (page 428) and baked.

FRAISIER

CHARLOTTE ROYALE

Slices of Swiss roll are used to line a mold. This is then filled with bavarois, before being unmolded and glazed.

MONT BLANC

Slice of Swiss roll topped with rum and chestnut cream, then piped with more chestnut cream.

Butter Cake

As pound cake once was, this butter cake, called *quatre quarts* in France, is made with equal weights of sugar, butter, flour, and eggs. A little leavener and vanilla is included here too. It's okay to deviate—some cooks like to use a bit more sugar and less flour for a moister cake. Excessive dryness can also be avoided by replacing some of the flour with the same volume of ground almonds: ¼ or ½ cup will make a notable difference—over 1 cup and you'll be in frangipane (page [298]) territory.

For 2 shallow or 1 deep 8-in round cake(s) or a 9 x 5 x 3-in loaf [A] [B]

INGREDIENTS
Scant 1 cup unsalted butter, softened [C] [D]
1 cup sugar
Pinch of salt
4 large or 3 extra large eggs [E]
1 tsp vanilla extract—optional
1⅔ cups all-purpose flour [F]
1 tsp baking powder
2 tbsp milk [G]

1   Prepare the pan(s) by greasing lightly and lining the bottom with parchment paper. Use a wooden spoon to cream the soft (not melting) butter and sugar with a pinch of salt until the mixture is pale and fluffy.

2   Lightly beat the eggs with the vanilla extract, if using. Gradually beat the egg mixture into the butter and sugar, then sift in the flour and the baking powder and stir as little as is needed to combine thoroughly. Finally, stir in the milk.

3   Spoon or scrape the batter into the prepared pan(s).

4   Bake at 350°F for 20–25 minutes for 2 shallow cakes (to make a 2-layer cake), 45–55 minutes for a deep cake, or 60–70 minutes for a loaf cake. They are cooked when the top of the cake springs back to the touch, or when a skewer inserted into the center comes out clean.

LEEWAY

A This quantity of batter will also make 20–24 fairy cakes (as opposed to cupcake size) in fluted paper cups. Bake for 14–18 minutes.

B 4 tbsp butter, ¼ cup sugar, 6½ tbsp flour, 1 large egg, and ½ tbsp milk will make just over ⅔ cup batter.

C If your butter is soft enough, you can use the all-in-one method, wherein all the ingredients are beaten together in a bowl, for 1–2 minutes with an electric mixer, or 3 minutes by hand. Compared to the traditional method, this can make for a slightly denser cake, so you may prefer to use self-rising flour in addition to the baking powder.

D For a lower-fat cake, you can reduce the butter weight by two thirds and add the full butter weight of apple purée or applesauce. For example, instead of a scant cup (7 oz), use 5 tbsp (2½ oz) butter, and add ¾ cup (7 oz) apple purée. The cake may need longer to bake.

E Replace 1 of the eggs with 2 yolks for a moister crumb (but don't replace all of them).

F You can replace the all-purpose flour with the same amount of cake flour, or use a mix of the two.

G The milk is not essential: It just loosens the mixture a bit.

Butter Cake → Flavors & Variations

BUCKWHEAT & ALMOND

Buckwheat was once used by peasants in the Italian Tyrol to make a layered butter cake known as *la torta di grano saraceno*. Like pound cake, it calls for equal weights of flour, sugar, butter, and eggs, and, in addition, ground almonds. For an 8-in cake, use ¾ cup each of butter and sugar, 1½ cups of ground almonds, 1¼ cups of buckwheat flour, 3 large eggs beaten with 3 tbsp milk, and 1 tsp baking powder. Omit the vanilla in order to preserve the flavors of the buckwheat and almond. Jam is the usual filling. Top the baked, cooled cake with a shake of confectioners' sugar. Overall the cake has a slightly cornlike quality, with a subtle sweetness you wouldn't want to overwhelm with an excess of extracts (or jam, for that matter); whipped cream would be a better filling. Texturewise, too, the cake recalls corn: Its high flour content makes it dry and a little sandy, like cornbread.

CARROT

What happened to carrot cake? It used to be awful. Hmm, you'd think, perched on a repurposed pew in the cathedral café. Why did I order *this*? The incongruity of cake made from root vegetables was just that: an incongruity, entirely as tiresome as it sounded. Then something happened. Left-leaning cakemakers started grating the carrots more finely, or hit upon exactly the right spice mix. Or maybe the frosting just got deeper. Some recipes depart only minimally from our starting point, substituting brown for white sugar, adding spices and the same volume of grated carrot as flour. It's not uncommon for the butter to be replaced by oil; tasted side-by-side, most people preferred the oil-based cake, which has the extra benefit of not relying on the creaming method. For an 8-in square pan, put 1⅔ cups all-purpose flour, 1 cup packed light brown sugar, 2 tsp cinnamon, 2 tsp apple-pie spice, 2 tsp baking powder, and ¼ tsp baking soda in a mixing bowl. Whisk 3 extra large eggs with 1 cup oil (peanut, sunflower, or canola) for 2 minutes—by hand is fine. Add 1 tsp vanilla extract toward the end. Pour the egg mixture into the dry mix and stir until nearly combined before stirring in scant 2 cups finely grated carrot. Pour into an oiled, lined pan and bake at 325°F for 45–50 minutes, or until a skewer inserted into the center comes out clean. Grated orange zest, raisins soaked in orange juice, and/or chopped walnuts can be added with the carrots. For the frosting, mix ⅔ cup confectioners' sugar into 1 cup soft cream cheese. The cake will keep, wrapped and in the fridge, for 3 days.

CHOCOLATE

Sachertorte may be more famous, but my mother's chocolate cake is miles better. Had she only refrained from jotting the recipe down for every neighbor, distant relation, and door-to-door cleaning-products salesperson, she might have trademarked it, and I'd be dictating this sentence from a vicuña-covered davenport while muscular flunkies washed my feet with Champagne. When I left home for London I took solace in the chocolate fudge cake they used to serve at Kettner's, in Soho, although I've since learned it was made with a packaged mix. It's possible to make chocolate butter cake by replacing some of the flour in our starting point with cocoa powder, but what elevated the Kettner's/package-mix cake was the use of oil instead of butter, which counters the drying effect of cocoa in a way that butter doesn't. To make your own chocolate cake mix, sift together 1⅓ cups self-rising flour, ⅓ cup unsweetened cocoa powder, ½ tsp salt, ½ tsp baking soda, and 1 cup sugar. When the need for cake strikes, tip the dry mix into a bowl and excavate a well. In a jug, beat together 3 extra large eggs, 1 cup vegetable oil, and 2 tsp vanilla extract. Tip the wet ingredients into the well, mix everything together, and divide the batter between 2 greased and lined 8-in round cake pans. Bake at 350°F for 20–25 minutes, when a skewer should come out clean. Remove from the oven and let cool. For the fudge frosting, melt ⅓ cup butter with 3 tbsp cocoa powder and 3 tbsp milk, stirring all into a smooth paste. Then stir in 2 cups sifted confectioners' sugar; don't skip the sifting. Mix to a homogenous brown, allowing the frosting a few minutes to thicken before spreading just under half of it on the bottom layer and the rest on the top. If you prefer to use butter in your chocolate cake, note that a professional cakemaker might freeze a butter cake once it's cooled— it will be moister when thawed.

ELDERFLOWER

The fragrance and flavor of elderflower is a musky commingling of blackcurrant leaf, floral lemon oil, and an English hedgerow after a shower in June. Ideal, then, as a flavoring for dainty fairy cakes, to serve after cucumber sandwiches and a chamomile tisane—the very essence of a decorous garden tea, even if the only grass you own is the clump of municipal park stuck to the sole of your trainers. Like its vanilla equivalent, elderflower sugar can be a lovely thing to have on hand: Layer about 1 tbsp fresh blooms per ½ cup sugar and leave to "elderflowerise" for up to 6 months. For a stronger hit, Jane Scotter and Harry Astley add the blossoms from 4 large elderflower heads directly into a cake batter. Out of season, you'll have to resort to elderflower cordial. For ½ cup sugar, 7 tbsp butter, and ¾ cup flour, add 3 tbsp cordial beaten into the 2 eggs in place of the milk and vanilla. Note that the sugariness of the syrup will give the cakes a light crust, and you'll find the flavor as mild as a vicar's small talk— so an elderflower glacé icing is a must if you hope to create a stir amid the croquet hoops. About 1½ tbsp cordial mixed with 1 cup sifted confectioners' sugar will be enough to top 12 fairy cakes.

FRUITCAKE

This is a far simpler adaptation than you might expect. (Or than I expected.) A good fruitcake can be as straightforward a matter as stirring the fruit into a standard butter cake batter, after the eggs and flour have been mixed in. How much dried or glacé/candied fruit and mixed candied citrus fruit peel is up to you, but a good rule of thumb is to use the same volume as the flour (1⅔ cups) if the results are to qualify as bona-fide fruitcake, as opposed to a cake with some fruit in it. For something denser, more akin to a Christmas fruitcake, triple that amount. A few handfuls of almonds or walnuts can be thrown in to keep your teeth interested. Consider flavoring the crumb with a small amount of sweet spice (freshly grated nutmeg, apple-pie or pumpkin-pie spice, ground cinnamon), an ooze of molasses, some finely grated citrus zest, a dram of dark spirit, or any combination thereof. Some recipes call for vanilla extract, but vanilla is so ubiquitous, why not seize the opportunity to omit it? Brown is the usual sugar of choice; white will taste odd, unless you supplement it with molasses, or, indeed, dark brown sugar. As for the flour, you might experiment by substituting rye flour for about half of the wheat flour, or a gluten-free flour like buckwheat, semolina, nut meal, or cornmeal for a third or so of the wheat flour. For an 8-in cake, use 1 cup packed brown sugar, scant 1 cup butter, 1⅔ cups flour, 4 large eggs, about 4⅓ cups dried vine fruits (raisins, currants, etc.) soaked in 3 tbsp dark spirit (or sherry, or tea), ⅓ cup each of chopped glacé/candied fruit and mixed candied citrus peel, 1 tsp spice, 1 tbsp citrus zest, 2 tsp light molasses, and ½ tsp salt. Bake at 300°F for 2½ hours. For a 6-in round cake, halve these quantities and bake for just 2 hours. For a 10-in cake, double the quantities and bake for 3–3½ hours. Whichever size you make, you'll need to line the inside and outside of the cake pan with parchment paper to protect the cake during its long spell in the oven. As it bakes, keep an eye on the top as well, tenting it with foil if it's getting too dark. The baked cake will benefit from being very well wrapped and kept for a while, sprinkled with a tablespoon of rum or brandy every week or so. The same mixture can also be used to make Christmassy fairy cakes. Spoon into small fluted paper cups in a muffin pan and bake at 325°F for about 25 minutes. One of the earliest fruitcakes I remember making was for the annual baking competition at my elementary school. My mother, still wary after my performances in ballet competitions with my back to the judging panel, took things in hand and made much of the fruitcake herself. It lost to a buttercream hedgehog. The whole murky business taught me two valuable lessons: that cheating doesn't pay, and that (going by my mother's indignation) it definitely wasn't the taking part that counted.

LANGUES DE CHAT / TUILES

Mix 2 tbsp butter, 2 tbsp sugar, and 3 rounded tbsp flour per egg white for *langues de chat*, or tuiles—pliable cookies that can be fashioned into curls, cups, and spirals. The shaping and baking require a little more skill than for their sugary cousins, brandy snaps (page 347), but with a bit of practice, or cheating with a stencil, you'll soon get the hang of it. Follow the method to the end of step 2, omitting the egg yolks, baking powder, and milk. Vanilla is optional, but if you are using it, limit it to ¼ tsp extract per egg white. Transfer the batter to a pastry bag fitted with a ¾-in tip. Lightly grease two baking sheets, or line them with silicone mats or parchment paper, and pipe 3-in lengths of the batter onto them, leaving an inch or so in between to allow for spreading. Tap the trays on your worktop to dispel any air bubbles, then bake at 350°F for 5–7 minutes. Once they're out of the oven, give your *langues* a minute before taking a metal spatula to them, to check if they're ready to shape. For variation, add ground spices to the flour, or sprinkle sesame seeds or sliced almonds over the top before baking.

NAKED

Put down the vanilla bottle. Your Victoria sandwich should be as naked as a calendar girl—except for the filling of raspberry jam, and the light sprinkling of sugar—allowing the Women's Institute judges to check that it's golden and evenly baked. Expect to be marked down for any tell-tale criss-crosses left by the cooling rack.

PEANUT BUTTER

Cooking with peanut butter can be a little touch and go. The flavor works well in this batter but, unlike most cakes, it's at its best soon after you make it. As the days pass, the beaniness of the legumes gets ever more apparent. Add ¾ cup of peanut butter, creaming it in with the butter and sugar. Omit the vanilla but keep the baking powder. Loosen the mix with some extra milk: about 4 tbsp. You might also add a few pinches of salt (or use salted butter), and a 50/50 combination of white and brown sugar is good.

POLENTA & PINEAPPLE

Cornmeal is evidently an aphrodisiac either side of the Adriatic. In Bosnia, "sweetheart cake" is made with cornmeal, sometimes studded with pieces of walnut or chocolate and, once baked, soaked in lemon, wine, or an anise-flavored syrup. In Italy, a variety of polenta cake flavored with Maraschino, grappa, or rum is known as *amor* polenta. Some polenta cakes simply adapt our starting point for butter cake, using half flour and half (coarse or fine) polenta. Cornmeal cakes can, of course, be made with no other flour than cornmeal—see page 82. I made a polenta cake for my friend Bruna, from Brazil, where corn-based cakes like *bolo de fubá* are very popular. Rather than soaking it in booze or citrus, I made it with pineapple—another Brazilian weakness. She might have eaten it all if my husband hadn't tucked in too. Normally agnostic about cornmeal cakes, he claimed this one was different, on the basis that it reminded him of two-day-old, leftover pineapple upside-down cake (a good thing, apparently). Follow the butter-cake method, replacing ⅔ cup of the flour with fine cornmeal. Use light brown sugar in place of white, if you have it. I used scant 1 cup butter, 1 cup all-purpose flour, ⅔ cup fine cornmeal, and 1 cup sugar (although you can reduce this as the pineapple and cornmeal are both pretty sweet). Drain 2 (15-oz) cans of pineapple pieces (about 2 cups drained weight), or the equivalent amount of fresh, and dab dry with paper towels. Once all the flour is mixed into the batter, stir in the pineapple. Continue as per our starting point, although note that the cake may need a little longer in the oven to pass the skewer test.

YOGURT

I made the *gâteau au yaourt* French kids are taught to make at school, using the yogurt pot as a measuring cup. Crikey, I thought. This is why French women don't get fat. It was cheap-tasting and clammy. I double-checked the recipe online, only to find that I was not alone in finding it unpleasant. So let's leave the cake to little Hippolyte and Mathilde. If yogurt cake appeals on health grounds, make the Lebanese version on page 472. It's much nicer: more of a cheesecake than a sponge, but tangy and delicious, and low in sugar, flour, and fat.

Butter Cake → Other Directions

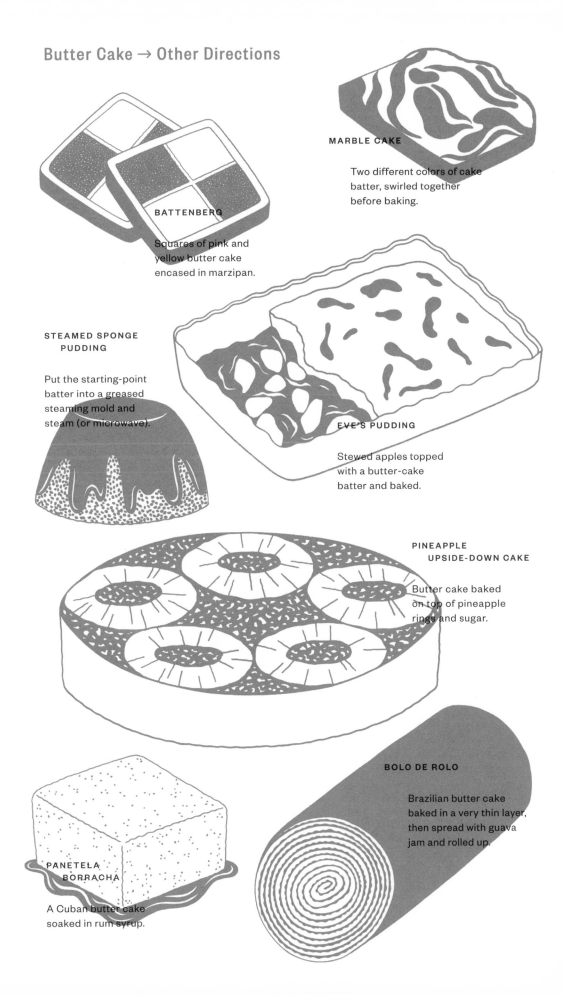

MARBLE CAKE

Two different colors of cake batter, swirled together before baking.

BATTENBERG

Squares of pink and yellow butter cake encased in marzipan.

STEAMED SPONGE PUDDING

Put the starting-point batter into a greased steaming mold and steam (or microwave).

EVE'S PUDDING

Stewed apples topped with a butter-cake batter and baked.

PINEAPPLE UPSIDE-DOWN CAKE

Butter cake baked on top of pineapple rings and sugar.

BOLO DE ROLO

Brazilian butter cake baked in a very thin layer, then spread with guava jam and rolled up.

PANETELA BORRACHA

A Cuban butter cake soaked in rum syrup.

Gingerbread

Gingerbread marks the transition on the continuum from cake to cookies. With minor tweaks to the ingredients and method you can take this in either direction. The batter is very wet, thanks to the quantity of melted butter, sugar, syrup, and milk, resulting in a moist, dense cake. Egg, so important for the leavening of the previous three cakes, plays only a minor role in the rest of the cake continuum. For gingerbread cookies (page 348), the milk and half of the sugar are omitted, yielding a drier, rollable dough.

For a 9 x 5 x 3-in (8-cup) loaf pan A

INGREDIENTS
½ cup unsalted butter
1 cup packed brown sugar B C D
¼ cup golden syrup or light molasses, or a mix B D E
1⅔ cups all-purpose flour
½ tsp baking soda F
1 heaped tbsp ground ginger G
2 tsp apple-pie spice H
Pinch of salt
½ cup milk
1 egg, beaten

1 Melt the butter with the sugar and syrup in a small saucepan over a low heat until smooth.

2 Meanwhile, sift the flour, baking soda, spices, and salt into bowl. Make a well in the center.

3 Pour the butter mixture and the milk into the dry ingredients and thoroughly combine without over-beating. Mix in the egg.

4 Pour into the greased or lined loaf pan.
A parchment loaf-pan liner will help protect the cake from burning.

5 Bake immediately at 350°F for 35–45 minutes or until a skewer inserted into the center comes out clean.
Start checking from 35 minutes. You may need to cover the top loosely with foil to stop it from burning before the cake is fully cooked.

6 If possible, wrap the cake tightly in parchment or wax paper and keep it for a few days. The flavor will improve, and the texture will become moister and stickier.

LEEWAY

A Make an 8-in square parkin by using ½ cup packed brown sugar and ½ cup syrup (50/50 golden syrup and molasses). Add ⅔ cup medium Scottish oat meal and an extra ½ tsp baking soda to the dry ingredients, then proceed as opposite, baking the cake at 325°F for 30–35 minutes. Wrap and leave for a few days before eating.

B For an extra-sticky loaf cake, use double the syrup and half the sugar quantities (i.e. ½ cup each syrup and sugar).

C Use light or dark brown sugar. The latter has a stronger flavor, which you can tamp down by mixing it with white sugar. Using only white sugar is fine, but you'll need molasses rather than golden syrup to get a proper gingerbread flavor, and the squidgy texture of the baked loaf will take longer to develop.

D Sticky cakes like this are prone to sinking, due to their high proportion of sugar; I find some are better baked at 300–325°F for slightly longer.

E I make my gingerbread with a 50/50 mix of molasses and golden syrup, as I love the licorice tang of the former, but 100 percent golden syrup mixed with dark brown sugar will still yield a dark cake. You might also use the syrup from a jar of candied ginger or honey.

F For a loaf cake, some cooks add 1 tsp baking powder along with the baking soda.

G *The Joy of Cooking* calls for ½ cup very finely chopped fresh ginger in place of ground ginger. Fans of ginger might like a combination of fresh, ground, and candied.

H In many gingerbread recipes, the ginger is augmented by other spices: cinnamon, nutmeg, cardamom, clove, and allspice are all common. Finely grated citrus zests might be mixed in too.

ALMOND & GINGER

Dijon France, is famous for its gingerbread as well as its mustard. The half-timbered premises of Mulot et Petitjean, rather appetizing themselves in their red-and-cream paintwork, are the perfect place to sample *pain d'épices*. Besides the plain variety, they sell a version containing nuggets of candied fruit, and another studded with big pieces of pale almond, creating, against the reddish-brown background of the crumb, a visual effect not unlike Spanish *salchichón*. Recently Mulot and Petitjean have been working with the late Bernard Loiseau's company to create a range of more exotically flavored *pains d'épices*— bergamot, five-spice, and Morello cherry. The last is said to be good with game and cheeses, and excellent toasted. For almond gingerbread, add 1 cup chunkily chopped blanched almonds to our starting point recipe, mixed in with the egg at step [3].

CHOCOLATE & GINGER

When McVitie's launched the chocolate variant of their famous ginger cake in the U.K., ginger nuts like me assumed they'd used chocolate *and* ginger. They hadn't (the invertebrates). Here's the opportunity they missed: a chocolate gingerbread loaf. Use only 1⅓ cups flour and sift it with ⅓ cup unsweetened cocoa powder, the baking soda, spices, and salt. Add the butter, sugar, and golden syrup, as per our starting point, and the milk and egg, then stir in ⅓ cup each of chopped candied ginger and dark chocolate chips. Bake for 45 minutes. This is the rare sort of sticky loaf that is not improved by a slick of butter.

COCONUT MASALA

Marks & Spencer used to sell sweet curried popcorn. I must have been the only person who liked it. I went in search of some only a few weeks after its first appearance on the shelf and it had gone for good. I visit it, head bowed and hands respectfully behind my back, in my food-and-drink garden of remembrance, interred alongside Maynard's Salad Gums, Royal Scot cookies, Milk Tray's Lime Barrel, the Lion Bar (as was), a veal cobbler my mum used to make until she lost the recipe, and the whitebait served at The King's Head in Wickham, where I worked for a bit. Some favorites have risen from the dead. I managed to resurrect Rowntree's much-mourned Cabana bar for an entry in *The Flavor Thesaurus*. And I was amazed to find a Chinese takeout in Clerkenwell that makes spring rolls the way I remember them from my teenage years: big, ugly, and filled to their folded ends with earthy bean sprouts. M&S's curried popcorn contained a mix of spices, coconut, and nigella seeds that invites reinterpretation along the gingerbread cookie lines described on page [348]. Use 1 cup flour, ⅔ cup dried shredded coconut, ¼ cup golden syrup, ½ cup packed brown sugar, 1 tsp garam masala, 1 tsp ground coriander, and a pinch of nigella seeds. You might consider replacing the butter with the same amount of ghee.

COFFEE & CARDAMOM

Coffee and cardamom struck me as an ideal combination for a sticky gingerbread-style loaf. I was so right I was almost wrong. The roasted notes in the coffee recalled the molasses in gingerbread, and cardamom is a member of the ginger family. My loaf, in other words, tasted like gingerbread, but less so. It turns out that the strident fieriness of ginger is key to gingerbread's success: If you plan a shot across its bows, be bold with the aromatics. For an unambiguous coffee and cardamom flavor—or *garwa*, as they call it in the Middle East—add the crushed seeds of 4 cardamom pods to the dry mix in our starting point, and stir 5 tsp instant coffee into 2 tbsp of the milk, heated to help the coffee dissolve. Use golden syrup on its own or mixed with 1 tbsp molasses.

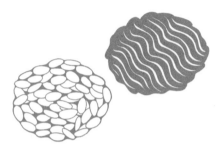

FLORENTINES & BRANDY SNAPS

Forget spinach. In Europe, the term "Florentine" generally refers to a lacy, chewy variety of cookie: a toffee with benefits. They are pretty enough to pin to your sweater. Like edible Andrew Logan brooches. Roughly speaking, the Florentine mixture is a simplified version of its gingerbread-cookie counterpart, but once the Florentines are baked they are so flat they look like the marks a previous batch of cookies left on your baking sheet. To make about 20 Florentines, melt 2 tbsp golden syrup, ¼ cup sugar, and ¼ cup unsalted butter together, then stir into ¼ cup all-purpose flour with 2 cups of sliced or chopped fruit and nuts. Choose from diced candied fruit, candied ginger, or candied angelica; slivered or sliced almonds; chopped hazelnuts or pistachios. For brandy snaps, use the same mixture as for Florentines but omit the fruit and nuts and mix in 1 tsp ground ginger with the flour. Once the ingredients are all combined, transfer teaspoonfuls onto a nonstick baking sheet, leaving each an inch or so of elbow room. The brandy-snap batter can be left in mounds, but the Florentine batter should be gently spread out with the back of a teaspoon. Bake at 350°F for 8–10 minutes. Once they're dark golden, remove from the oven. Let Florentines harden for about 1 minute (judge their readiness by poking at the edges with a metal spatula), then lift them off and transfer to a cooling rack to await their coating (or two) of melted chocolate on the smooth side. As for brandy snaps, wrap them while they're still warm and pliable around the handle of a wooden spoon, or anything similarly circular in cross-section. Don't dawdle, because they harden pretty quickly (although they can be re-softened if necessary by a short stint back in the oven).

GINGERBREAD COOKIES

Elizabeth I had gingerbread people made to the likeness of her guests. It's a good idea: Anyone who shuns your baking can have their head snapped off, voodoo-style, when they leave. Reduce the brown sugar to ½ cup and omit the milk. At the end of step 1, let the butter mix cool for 10 minutes before stirring it into the dry ingredients. Fashion the warm dough into rounds, rolling walnut-sized quantities into balls between your palms, and baking immediately, spaced out on a lightly greased or parchment-lined baking sheet. Alternatively, let the dough cool, then refrigerate for at least 30 minutes, before rolling it out to make gingerbread men or neat shapes. In either case, bake at 350°F for 10–15 minutes. If you like a harder ginger cookie, like an old-fashioned gingersnap, omit the egg too. Makes 20–22 (3-in) cookies.

GOLDEN SYRUP

I was so thin as a kid that my mother used to leave the lid off the golden syrup can and surreptitiously fail to police it. I ate it on oatmeal made with one part oats to two parts sugar, or on stacks of Mother's Pride white buttered toast. My limbs remained twiggy while my teeth fell out one by one. Golden syrup is familiar in most Anglophone Commonwealth countries, but is mysteriously unknown in Europe. Americans have corn syrup, which to me tastes like elevator music to golden syrup's classic British pop (maple syrup is Miles Davis, wasted in a cake batter). With no ground ginger but a bit of help from a couple of teaspoons of vanilla extract, golden syrup makes for a milder, cooler sticky loaf. Retain the baking soda, as these super-sweet syrups are surprisingly acidic (both golden syrup and molasses have a pH between 5 and 6).

HONEY

Honey cake, or *lekach*, is traditionally served for Rosh Hashanah, the Jewish New Year, in the hope of sweetening the year to come. Jewish friends tell me the cake is so widely disliked it can easily hang around the house for a year before it's thrown away to make way for the next one. Honey cake is often horribly dry (it's known as "the choker" in some circles). No risk of choking here: The quantity of sugar in this adaptation of the starting point lends the cake a pleasing moistness, further enhanced by the use of oil instead of butter. Sift and then thoroughly mix together 1⅔ cups flour, ½ tsp baking soda, 2 tsp ground cinnamon, 2 tsp apple-pie spice, ½ tsp freshly grated nutmeg, and a few pinches of salt. In a separate bowl, mix together ½ cup each of vegetable oil and cold coffee, ¼ cup honey, ½ cup each granulated and light brown sugar, and 1 egg. Make a well in the center of the dry ingredients and pour in the wet mixture. Mix well, then pour the batter into a lined 9 x 5 x 3-in (8-cup) loaf pan and bake at 325°F for 45–55 minutes. Check on it after about 30 minutes—you may need to cover the top with a loose tent of foil to stop it darkening too much. Let cool for 15 minutes before unmolding. The flavor of the cake will depend, to some extent, on what type of honey you've used. Buckwheat honey ("malty, spicy, assertive, and memorable," according to Marie Simmons) is the choice of Ruth Reichl, who suggests eating the cake in toasted slices spread with cream cheese.

MALT LOAF

Store-bought malt loaf is dense enough to lag the walls of a black hole. This variation is a little lighter, and less likely to bond irreversibly to the roof of your mouth. But the brewery-floor pungency of barley malt, plus the sweetness of dried fruit, make it indisputably malt-loafy, and with a half-decent overarm it could still take out a window. Follow our starting point, leaving out the spices, substituting barley malt syrup for the golden syrup, and omitting the butter and milk in favor of ⅔ cup golden raisins and ½ cup cold tea. Put the raisins in the pan at the outset, to heat with the malt syrup and sugar. Bake the loaf at a slightly lower temperature—325°F—for 35–45 minutes. Keep wrapped for at least a day or two if you can, then reward your patience with a slice spread with plenty of butter.

TOMATO SOUP

Sylvia Plath made tomato soup cake the day she wrote "Death & Co." It was once known as a "depression cake," not, as it happens, with reference to Plath's mental condition, but because it was one of those cakes popular during the 1930s for its low quantities of expensive ingredients like eggs, butter, and milk, in favor of cheap sugar. On a cheerier note, the cake is a lovely reddish-ginger, like fox fur, and wonderfully springy in texture. M.F.K. Fisher calls it Mystery Cake, on the basis that it's best not to tell people what's in it before they give it a try. To my mind its flavor is less like tomato soup than the can it comes in, but to my husband's it has the sweet and slightly estranged spiciness of carrot cake. Early recipes stipulate the creaming method and sometimes call for lard rather than butter, but this later version substitutes oil for hard fat, obliging, in effect, a non-melting method. Mix 1¼ cups flour and ¾ cup granulated sugar with ½ tsp each of baking powder and baking soda, 1 tsp ground cinnamon, and ½ tsp each of ground allspice and cloves. Make a well in the center, then add a premixed combination of 1 egg, 2 tbsp vegetable oil, and half a can of Campbell's condensed cream of tomato soup. Whisk for a couple of minutes, then pour into an 8½ x 4½ x 2½-in (6-cup) loaf pan. Bake for 40 minutes at 275°F. Consider frosting the loaf with cream cheese sweetened with confectioners' sugar: cheese and tomato cake.

Cookies

This starting point is close to the recipe for gingerbread cookies without the spices and the syrup. The egg can be left out, but it does help to make a cohesive dough. By weight, it's a very easy ratio to remember—1:1:2 butter, sugar, and flour. *Larousse* demands the same proportions of ingredients bar the baking powder to make *pâte sablée*, a French sweet pastry. And like sweet pastry, this dough will need chilling if it's to be rolled out and cut into shapes. However, if you want fat, round cookies, walnut-sized balls of dough can be rolled between your palms and then baked immediately. Bear in mind that this recipe is only a starting point. Experiment. You might find that you prefer to use 1 cup of sugar, which is more in keeping with American cookie recipes.

For 20–24 cookies

INGREDIENTS
½ cup unsalted butter
½ cup sugar ᴬ ᴮ
1 tsp vanilla extract
1 egg or 2 egg yolks ᶜ
1⅔ cups flour ᴰ ᴱ
½ tsp baking powder ᶠ
Pinch of salt
Chopped nuts, raisins—optional ᴳ

¹ Cream the butter with the sugar in a large bowl.
   Start by softening the butter with a fork if it's still a little hard.
   Then add the sugar and cream them together until pale and fluffy.
   It's crucial that the butter is not warm or melting when you start—
   this would make the finished cookies greasy and flat.

² Beat the vanilla extract with the egg and stir into the butter
   and sugar mixture.

³ Sift in the flour, baking powder, and salt and stir as little
   as is needed to combine thoroughly. If using chocolate chips,
   nuts, or raisins, stir them through now.
   Too much stirring will develop excess gluten. In some cookie recipes,
   when a shorter texture is called for, the egg is added after the flour,
   to keep gluten formation to a minimum.

4   If you're rolling out the dough, pat it flat, cover in plastic wrap, and leave in the fridge to firm up for about 30 minutes. When you're ready to bake, roll out the dough to a thickness of ¼ in and cut out your shapes. Or fashion the just-made dough into a log, then wrap and refrigerate until it's firm enough to cut into ¼-in slices. The instant-gratification route is to hand-roll the mixture into walnut-sized balls and place them on a baking sheet (only greased if it isn't nonstick), spacing them an inch apart, before using the tines of a fork to flatten them a bit.

5   Bake at 350°F for about 15 minutes, by which time the cookies should be browning at the edges and underneath. Rotate the sheet halfway through if your oven seems to have hot spots. Make sure the oven is truly at heat, or the butter in the dough can start to melt before it starts to cook. If you think your cookies are done, but aren't sure, take them out. You can always put them back in for another minute or two if they turn out not to be.

6   Remove the cookies from the baking sheet to a cooling rack. Once cool, quickly stash in an airtight tin before you eat them all.
    Let the cookies firm up for a few minutes before removing them from the baking sheet.

LEEWAY

A   The finer the sugar, the more the biscuits will spread in the oven.

B   You can replace 2 tbsp sugar with 1 tbsp syrup—all of the sugar if you like—but note that syrups contain water, and will make the finished cookies less crisp.

C   Egg is optional, but make sure the butter and sugar are well creamed in order that the flour can be incorporated. You may want to add the flour in increments.

D   Self-rising flour can be used, but drop the baking powder.

E   For chocolate cookies, replace up to 3 tbsp of the flour with the same quantity of unsweetened cocoa powder.

F   The baking powder is optional, but it creates airier cookies. Don't replace it with baking soda, as there's not enough acidity in the other ingredients to activate it, and your cookies will have a metallic flavor.

G   Add as many chocolate chips, chopped nuts, or raisins as you like at the end of step 3.

CHOCOLATE CHIP

Cookie is the obligatory term for these, even for Brits. Offer someone a chocolate chip *biscuit* and you'll sound like a dowager duchess. Make these according to our starting point, stirring in, at the end of step ³, roughly the same amount of chopped chocolate as sugar. Or maybe a bit more, to compensate for the stingily chipped commercial sort. Use half white and half muscovado sugar, if possible. Bake for no more than 8 minutes if you like your cookies soft; otherwise, follow the cooking time in the starting point. Let your cookies firm up on the baking sheet for a few minutes before transferring them to a cooling rack. Heaven with a dog-eared copy of *Black Beauty* and a glass of cold milk.

FIG, ALMOND & FENNEL BISCOTTI

Biscotti—the poster cookie for the low-fat lifestyle. Made without butter or oil, these parched and petrified sweetmeats are desperate for a drink. Hence their place on the coffee-chain counter. They wouldn't stand a chance in a bakery, next to an éclair or a strawberry tartlet. In any case, to hell with coffee. Biscotti are at their best dipped into wine, as anyone who has softened *cantuccini* in a glass of *vin santo* will know. They are very easy to make, and demonstrate what happens when you subtract all the butter from the starting point for cookies. Beat ½ cup sugar with 1 egg until the mixture is thick and pale, add a few pinches of fennel seeds, then stir in 1⅔ cups flour, ½ tsp baking powder, and a pinch or two of salt. Bring together to form a dough, then knead in 1¼–1½ cups in total of roughly chopped, toasted nuts (almonds are classic). Split the dough in half, then roll each half into a log. Place the logs on a parchment-lined or nonstick baking sheet— not too close together as they will expand a bit as they cook—and bake at 250°F for 1 hour. Remove from the oven and immediately cut into ½-in slices using a serrated knife (you may need to slip an oven mitt on your other hand to steady the logs). Return the slices to the baking sheet and bake for 30–40 minutes longer, turning them over about halfway through. When they're ready, they should be golden. Cool your biscotti on a rack, then store in an airtight tin or jar for up to a month. For a version to serve on a cheeseboard, use pistachios, hazelnuts, walnuts, or almonds, all cut into pea-size pieces; cut the rolls into very thin slices after their first bake, and re-bake for as long as is needed to turn them golden.

GINGER

Grasmere gingerbread, sold from a tiny shop in England's Lake District, looks more like shortbread than classic syrup (or honey) gingerbread used to make gingerbread men (page [348]). It's more crumbly than chewy or snappish. I rather prefer the packaging to the contents. Mind you, there wouldn't be queues backing up to Stone Arthur if everyone felt the same way. The exact formulation of the gingerbread created in 1854 by Sarah Nelson remains a secret of Kentucky Fried proportions, but Jane Grigson gives a recipe that she claims is better. It's more in line, ingredient-ratio-wise, with our starting point for cookies, although it's made into a dough using a just-the-butter melting method. Mix ½ cup packed light brown sugar, 2 cups flour or 1¾ cups Scottish fine oat meal, 1 tsp ground ginger, and ¼ tsp baking powder in a bowl, then bring it all together with ⅔ cup melted, tepid, lightly salted butter. Press into a thin layer in an 8-in square pan, and bake for 30–35 minutes at 350°F until the top is golden brown. Mark into pieces immediately, then let cool before storing in an airtight tin.

LIME & CLOVE

A favorite pairing of chef Peter Gordon, who uses them with pine nuts in a shortbread, and in a cream to serve alongside banana and ginger cheesecake. Of all the citrus and spice combinations, this is up there with the most boisterous; you may want to fix the cookie tin with a padlock. Best to follow Gordon in crushing whole cloves rather than using ready-ground. Freshly ground, the fruitiness of clove is that much more apparent. And lime zest is spicy. As with many of the best combinations, it's hard to tell where one aromatic ends and the other begins. Follow the starting point, but drop the vanilla. For ½ cup of brown sugar, ½ cup butter, and 1⅔ cups flour, use the finely grated zest of 3 limes and ½ tsp freshly ground cloves. A grinding of black pepper gives an interesting edge. Lime and clove also coincide in a sweet Barbadian syrup, or liqueur, called Falernum. It can be bought off the shelf, or homemade with rum, lime zest, cloves, and ginger. There are many variations, but lime and clove is the *sine qua non*.

RED LEICESTER & OTHER CHEESES

Naturally, when we stay with our Italian-American cousins in New York, we're treated to great food and wine. They point us toward the best groceries and markets, and recommend with gestural intensity the most interesting new restaurants on the scene. And when they're not looking, I sneak into the nearest drugstore and buy peanut butter and cheese crackers. They do justice to neither ingredient, but I'm crazy about them. Just as well they're not available in the U.K. They come in a lurid shade of orange, and are probably colored with annato, a natural extract from the seeds of the achiote tree, used at low levels to make butter look like it's come from pasture-fed cows, and to make Red Leicester cheese red. I used the latter to make cheese crackers, planning to sandwich them with a 50/50 mix of smooth peanut butter and cream cheese. But you can't leave cheese crackers on the cooling rack and expect many of them to survive. By the time I came to make my PB&C crackers, there was one cracker's worth left—that is, two halves—enough, nonetheless, to establish their wholesomeness compared to the drugstore crackers' trashy friability. But much more usefully, I learned that the ½ cup sugar in our starting point for cookies can be replaced with 1 cup grated cheese, using the 2 egg yolks to bring the dough together. Cream the butter, then mix in the flour, baking powder, cheese, and 1 tsp mustard powder in place of the vanilla. Cracker doughs like this will probably need to be chilled if they get too soft. Stephen Bull makes a cheese cracker with 1½ cups crumbled blue cheese, 1 cup butter, and 1⅔ cups flour, adding 1 tsp salt plus a whole egg. The resulting mixture is very soft, so Bull freezes it, so as to be able to roll it out to less than ⅛-in thickness and press out the crackers. Bake them at 375°F for 12 minutes. If you prefer your cheese with, rather than in, your crackers, see pages 28, 31, and 33 for several cracker recipes. Or try the biscotti variation given under fig, almond, and fennel (page 352) or whole wheat digestives (opposite).

TURKISH DELIGHT

Turkish Delight makes an exotic addition to cookies. You'll need 6–8 cubes of Turkish Delight for a dough made to our starting point: Use a sharp knife to cut the cubes into ¼-in dice, tossing them in the drifts of confectioners' sugar that collects in the box, to stop them becoming exasperatingly sticky. (They also make a good substitute for mixed candied peel in yeasted buns and fruitcakes.) The rose flavor is sphinxlike in its subtlety, so keep the cookie dough fairly neutral in flavor—perhaps just a touch of vanilla or cinnamon. Chopped pistachios are a classic pairing.

WALNUT

We were staying in a vacation rental on a Cornish creek, and planned to have supper at the local pub. It was a warm October evening. We had a drink on the little beach at the foot of the cottage garden, then walked along the coast path by flashlight, only to find the pub kitchen unexpectedly closed. Back at the cottage, the cupboards were all but bare. We were both over the limit for driving, and so isolated that ordering a pizza would have struck our immediate neighbors as an improbable idea from the future. We had no choice but make do with what we had. Some butter and milk. A third of a bottle of whisky. An assortment of half-eaten cheese, a brown paper bag of walnuts in their shells. And my husband's muesli, brought in his suitcase from London. No bread, or wine. I pounded some of the nuts, creamed the butter, and mixed them with the muesli to a ratio of roughly 1:1:2. Then I added a tot of hot milk, fashioned the dough into a rough, flat circle, and cooked it on the stovetop. We wrapped the warm oatcake in a napkin, then packed up the rest of the walnuts and the cheeses— most of a Cornish Quartz Cheddar, a heel of Comté, and an unopened package of Roquefort. Recalling an excellent cheese and whisky pairing I tried at the insistence of the bloke who used to work in Milroy's, the whisky shop in Soho in London, I grabbed the bottle of Laphroaig. We returned to the beach in our woolliest sweaters and sat on a thick rug, leaning back on the tortured trunk of a long-dead tree. By the light of a full moon, we ate our picnic while the black water fizzed in and out of the shingle.

WHOLE WHEAT DIGESTIVES

A.k.a. the *reader's* cookie. (The chocolate sort is to be avoided. We won't stand for smears on the pages.) Three digestives, a glass of cold milk, and a good book is, for me at least, as sure a path to serotonin release as a trip to Disneyland for a seven-year-old. Digestives can be made with half the sugar in our starting point—hence their other name, "semi-sweet." It's not the easiest dough to work with, and will almost certainly need to be chilled in the fridge. As you'd imagine, whole wheat flour predominates, with added bran for the lovely rough texture. Use granulated sugar and make sure there is either salt in the butter, or add a little more than you would for a cookie. Salt is as essential to the character of a digestive as it is to a fisherman's beard. Graham crackers are the digestive's American cousin, but often contain a little cinnamon and molasses, or honey, in addition to the sugar. For the British digestive, make up a dough in the same way as you would for our starting point: Use ¼ cup granulated sugar, ⅓ cup butter, 2 tbsp lard, 1 cup whole wheat flour, ½ cup all-purpose flour, ¼ cup wheat bran, ½ tsp baking powder, ¼ tsp vanilla extract, and ¼ tsp salt. No egg. Chill the dough for at least 30 minutes at step 4, then roll out to a thickness of ⅛ in and cut out 3-in circles, docking them with a dough docker, or stabbing them at regular intervals with a knitting needle or similar. Bake as per the starting point.

Shortbread

The ratio for shortbread is 1:2:5. Useful as long as you remember which number applies to which ingredient. I rely on a mnemonic, Short Bread Formula. Sugar, Butter, Flour. Don't forget the pinch of salt. Note that in comparison to the previous starting point for cookies, the large quantity of butter makes any egg redundant, although some cooks use it. Shortbread is very low in sugar compared to all the other cakes and cookies. Classic and memorable as it may be, the shortbread formula is not set in stone. James Martin uses three times this amount of butter.

For a 7- to 8-in round, or about 20 fingers [A]

INGREDIENTS
¼ cup sugar [B]
½ cup unsalted butter, softened slightly [C]
1¼ cups all-purpose flour [D]
Pinch of salt
1 egg yolk—optional [E]

1 Cream the sugar and butter until combined.
    The butter should be cool and soft when you start, not melting, because this will affect the texture of the finished shortbread.

2 Add the flour and salt, stirring with a spoon to form a dough.
    If the dough is too dry, an egg yolk will bring it together, although for the shortest texture, it might be better to hold some of the flour back initially.

3 Either press the dough into a greased 7- to 8-in round pan, then score and prick it as attractively as possible, or roll out the dough to a thickness of ¼ in and cut into shapes. Or use your hands to roll it into walnut-sized balls, placing them on a greased baking sheet and pressing their tops with the tines of a fork.
    Let rest in the fridge for 30 minutes if you have time.

4 Bake at 325°F for about 45 minutes for a round, 10–20 minutes for individual cookies, depending on how thick they are.
    Some bake their shortbread for 15–20 minutes at 350°F, in common with most standard cookie recipes, but a longer bake will give a toastier flavor, and the surface a distinctly un-Scottish tan.

5 Store in an airtight container.
    Shortbread should keep for a week, even two.

LEEWAY

A For 6 hand-rolled cookies—both a good quantity and a quick means of testing flavor variations—use 1 rounded tbsp sugar, 2½ tbsp butter, and 6 tbsp flour. To make enough for an 8- to 9-in square pan, use ⅓ cup sugar, ⅔ cup butter, and 1⅔ cups flour.

B You could think of Viennese whirls as a variation of shortbread, made with confectioners' sugar and a high proportion of butter to flour. This makes a soft paste that can be piped into swirly rosettes and fingers.

C Some cooks deploy the rubbing-in method for shortbread. It's an option if your butter is hard, but you will almost certainly need to add some egg yolk to bring the dough together.

D Replace 5–7 tbsp of the flour with rice flour, cornstarch, semolina, or potato starch. These gluten-free flours will lend an even shorter texture. You can substitute cake flour for all-purpose.

E Heston Blumenthal adds a little baking powder to his shortbread, and also includes egg yolk, which contains the liquid necessary to activate the powder.

BLACK PEPPER

Salt is a must in shortbread, but rest easy if you have matching grinders and used the wrong one. Leiths gives a recipe for black pepper shortbread, stipulating 1 tsp peppercorns crushed in a mortar for a dough made with similar quantities as given in the starting point.

CHICKPEA

Pakora, socca, or dhokla might prompt you to file chickpea flour under "savory," but cookies made with besan argue otherwise. What they have in common with their savory counterparts is their deep, golden color, which is suggestive, if not indicative, of a richer butteriness than a regular cookie made with white wheat flour. The real gain is textural: They're so light and melting that the addition of fruit or nuts would only detract from them. Spices are another matter. Cardamom and nutmeg, as used in the Indian cookie *nan khatai*, are particularly popular during Diwali. Afghan *nan-e nodhokchi* are flavored with rose and cardamom. The besan flavor is quite strong and, if you haven't tried it in sweet cookies before, you might start by mixing it into wheat flour, as suggested for cornstarch or semolina at [D] under Leeway.

CHOCOLATE

In the U.K., it takes a minimum of 3% fat-free dry cocoa solids to qualify as a chocolate cookie (in case you were thinking of applying). Cookies that fall short of the minimum can only be called chocolate-flavored. I have yet to calculate whether Granny Boyd's cookies, from Nigella Lawson's *How to be a Domestic Goddess*, make the grade, but I don't care: This is my favorite chocolate cookie dough by a country mile. The ratio is more or less in line with our starting point for shortbread; there's just a little less flour than you might expect, as the cocoa takes the place of some of it. Use the time you haven't wasted calculating the dry-cocoa-solids content raiding the supermarket for some really good vanilla ice cream, the indispensable accompaniment. Lawson calls for ½ cup superfine sugar, 1 cup unsalted butter, 2¼ cups self-rising flour, and ⅓ cup unsweetened cocoa powder. Make as per the starting point and bake for 5 minutes at 325°F, then reduce the heat to 300°F for 15 minutes longer.

CULTURED BUTTER

Only a swivel-eyed serial killer would eat butter by the spoonful. Clotted cream is about as fatty as social norms allow. To comply with its PDO (Protected Designation of Origin), Cornish clotted cream must contain a minimum of 55 percent butterfat. (Most British butters contain 86 percent, American at least 80 percent.) I came across a recipe for clotted cream shortbread in which half the butter in the 1:2:5 formula was replaced with clotted cream. They were lovely, but questionably named, as the water content in the cream compromised the shortness.

Butter is better. For a deeper dairy flavor, follow Michael Ruhlman's recommendation and try cultured butter. Most butter sold is of the sweet cream variety, but some smaller dairies are starting to sell the sourer, more complex cultured butter online. Or you can seek out a French or domestic European-style butter. Or make your own with heavy cream, buttermilk, and a stand mixer. The process involves washing the butter solids from the butterfat, a sensory experience that merits immediate inclusion on your bucket list: twenty fats to wash before you die.

CUSTARD

In *English Food*, Jane Grigson calls custard powder "one of our minor national tragedies." I'd like to have heard her thoughts on the recipe for custard powder found, fittingly enough, between curry powder and cyanide of potassium in *The Pharmaceutist's and Druggist's Practical Receipt Book* published in 1865. A concoction of sago flour, turmeric, bitter almond powder, and oil of cassia—like cinnamon, but harsher—is stirred into sweetened milk. Alfred Bird's powder of cornstarch, yellow coloring, and vanilla is ambrosial by comparison. (Bird invented his eggless custard powder for his wife, who suffered from an egg allergy. As love tokens go, it makes a change from flowers or frilly underpants.) Custard shortbread is made by substituting custard powder for 6 tbsp of the flour in our starting point. For a more richly custardy effect, add vanilla extract and a touch of egg-yellow food coloring or annatto.

DATE

Date slices: up your street if you like the crumbly top of a fruit crisp more than the fruit. Date is the classic, but any dried fruit, or even a very thick compote, can be used. Make sure it's thick, though—a watery fruit mixture will seep into the bottom layer of streusel and make your slice too soggy to handle. The oat streusel is made in the same basic fashion as shortbread—sugar, butter, and a mixture of flour and oats. Rub or process 14 tbsp unsalted butter into 1¼ cups flour, then stir in scant 2 cups rolled oats, ½ cup sugar, and a few pinches of salt. Simmer 14 oz pitted dates with 1 cup water until the excess water evaporates, then chop them roughly. Press half the streusel mix into a 9-in square baking dish, spreading it out evenly, followed by the dates, then the other half of the streusel. Bake at 325°F for 40 minutes. Mark into slices while still warm from the oven, then cut and transfer to a wire rack when cool enough to handle.

HONEY & GHEE

Honey is never better than when it's paired with butter, preferably salted. It was after making the *beghrir* pancakes on page [134], dripping with honeyed butter, that I picked up a tube of honey shortbread in Fortnum & Mason. On a return visit, I found that they no longer sold them, and ended up making my own approximation. It's possible to swap honey for sugar in shortbread, but note that they have very different water contents—white sugar contains as little as 0.1 percent, where honey contains anything between 12 and 23 percent (good-quality honey will typically contain less than 20 percent). The more water in your sweetener, the more the gluten in the flour will develop, compromising the shortness of your shortbread. Using ghee in place of butter is one way to compensate for excess water in your sweetener, since it's all fat. It's like clarified butter, except that it's been cooked as well, and so has a richer flavor. Some ghee has butter flavoring added, but it's not hard to find the pure sort.

LAVENDER

A modern classic. Tiny round lavender shortbreads are served on the Eurostar route that runs direct from London to Avignon in France. The idea, I suppose, is that as you hurtle past the sun-warmed stone hamlets and acres of purplish blur, the cookie provides a foretaste of your vacation. There's no shortbread on the return journey, presumably because the flavors of King's Cross station via abandoned car plants aren't fit for human consumption. Use 1 tsp lavender buds per 1¼ cups flour, plus a few drops each of orange-flower water and vanilla.

MINCEMEAT

It's December 20 or thereabouts. You roll up the sleeves of your Christmas sweater and prepare to make little mince pies. You regret it almost immediately. Sweet pastry is hard enough to roll out on the best of days, but the heating is at full blast, so the pastry sticks and stretches and melts. Your plan to delight the children by topping each pie with a pastry reindeer founders when most of the reindeer have unsettlingly long legs. You remove the first batch from the oven only to find molten mincemeat has bubbled over the sides and turned into a bituminous deposit. You look at the next batch of pastry and think about dumping it. Don't. Our starting points for sweet pastry and shortbread dough have a lot in common. Put the dough and remaining mincemeat in a bowl and give it all a good mix. Pluck out walnut-sized amounts to roll into balls using your hands, flatten the tops with the tines of a fork, then bake as per the shortbread starting point. When cool, dust with confectioners' sugar. Serve with the bald assertion that *Pastetenfüllungbälle* are a Swabian precursor of mince pies.

OLIVE OIL & OUZO

If the ouzo you brought back from Corfu isn't the same without the sunshine and bouzouki music, save your guests from unwanted late-night digestifs by using it as a flavoring. *Kourabiedes* ("clouds") is a Greek member of the international shortbread family. It's usually made with olive oil. Adapt it to our starting point by using olive oil instead of butter and increasing the flour quantity. You could also replace up to a quarter of the flour with ground almonds, if you like. For ¼ cup sugar, ½ cup olive oil, and 2 cups flour, add 2 tbsp ouzo with the oil. Mix all the ingredients together, roll into walnut-sized balls, and place on a greased baking sheet, making a depression with your thumb in the top of each one. Bake at 325°F for 30 minutes. While still warm, dust the cookies with confectioners' sugar. Some cooks sprinkle a little more ouzo over the baked cookies, but I prefer the milder version, where the flavor of the olive oil makes itself known. Variations include a Christmas *kourabiedes* flavored with brandy, and decorated with a whole clove, to signify the spices presented to Jesus by the Magi.

PECAN

A typical North American addition to shortbread. For "pecan sandies," the nuts are toasted, chopped, and added to a dough made with brown sugar, which lends a slight caramel flavor. Vanilla is usually used too, and some cookiemakers add a dash of bourbon. As with so many American cakes and cookies, pecan sandies are sweeter than their British equivalents. Use 6 tbsp brown sugar, 2 tbsp white sugar, ⅔ cup butter, 2 cups flour, ⅔ cup chopped pecans, 1 tsp vanilla extract, and ½ tsp salt. Roll into about 12 balls, then roll in white sugar and bake at 325°F for 20 minutes. Chad Robertson, owner of the San Francisco bakery Tartine, makes his sandies with maple sugar, ground pecans, and KAMUT flour, a trademarked wholegrain wheat flour, which he claims yields the sandiest texture of all "alternative" flours. (Bob's Red Mill, the Oregon-based natural-food company, maintains that KAMUT has a buttery flavor, so it really does sound perfect.) Robertson adds baking powder and, rather than roll the uncooked cookies in sugar, once they're out of the oven, he brushes them with maple syrup.

SHERBET LEMON

A fantastic and truly lemony shortbread that tastes rather like a good *tarte au citron*. The secret ingredient, citric acid, is borrowed from the recipe for Indian dhokla (page 84). Don't stint on the zest—the complex aromatics that give lemon its distinct flavor, aside from the acidity, are essential to keep the citric zing in balance. For a batch made with ¼ cup sugar, ½ cup butter, and 1¼ cups flour, add the finely grated zest of 2–3 lemons and ⅛ tsp citric acid to the mix.

Oat Bars

Called flapjacks in the U.K., these oat bars are, like gingerbread, usually made by the melting method. This means they can be in the oven very quickly. Beware, however, of trying to eat them too soon. They contain no egg or gluten to hold them together. The toffee-like combination of butter and sugar needs time to cool and set strong enough to withstand cutting. If they're not quite ready, your bars will crumble, along with any notion of portion control. Little nuggets of oat bar are very difficult to resist.

For an 8-in square, or a 9-in round [A] [B]

INGREDIENTS
½ cup packed light brown sugar [C] [D]
¼ cup golden syrup or light corn syrup [D] [E] [F]
1 cup unsalted butter [G]
4 cups quick-cooking rolled oats [H]
Pinch or two of salt
½ tsp baking soda—optional [I]

1 Melt the sugar, syrup, and butter in a small saucepan over a medium heat until smooth. Set aside to cool.

2 Pour the oats into a bowl. Stir in the salt and the baking soda, if using. Make a well in the center.

3 Pour the melted butter mixture into the dry ingredients and thoroughly combine.

4 Tip the mix into an 8-in square or 9-in round silicone mold or well-greased pan and press it in evenly and firmly.
   If you are using a silicone mold, set it on a baking sheet before you scrape the mixture into it.

5 Bake in the center of the oven at 300°F for 25–30 minutes or until golden and firm.
   If you prefer a crisper bar, bake at 375°F for 30 minutes.

6 When the bar has been out of the oven for 15 minutes, score into individual pieces. Leave the oat bars (still in the mold or pan) somewhere cool to set, preferably overnight. If you need the bars sooner, once cold, they can go into the fridge for a few hours to fix the set faster.

Don't let the bar get so cold in the fridge that it shatters when you try to cut it. If this happens, let the bar come up to room temperature and test now and then until it becomes pliable.

7 Cut the pieces. Oat bars will keep in an airtight tin for 1 week.

LEEWAY

A As a rough guide, for a 6-in square pan, use half the quantities given. For a 12 x 8-in baking pan, increase the quantities by 50 percent.

B Some say bar cookies are best made in a pan, but I prefer silicone, which makes them easier to unmold, and it is much easier to wash.

C Dark brown sugar can be used instead of light, but remember how strongly flavored it is. White sugar is fine too: It can just be a bit bland in an oat bar.

D Syrup has a higher water content than sugar, and brown sugar has a higher water content than white. If you want your bars to keep a firmer texture for longer, use 4 tsp molasses and 14 tbsp white sugar, instead of the syrup and brown sugar.

E If you're short of syrup, use 2 tbsp sugar for every tbsp you lack.

F Use other syrups, or a mix, but some—including honey and corn—contain a higher percentage of fructose, which will start to brown at a lower heat, so keep an eye on them while baking.

G Salted butter can be used for oat bars, but using unsalted and adjusting with pinches of salt gives you more control.

H Old-fashioned rolled oats don't hold together very well. Stick with quick-cooking rolled oats (not the instant sort).

I The baking soda is optional, but not if you like your oat bars browned and crispy.

BAKLAVA

Baklavas are the flipside of oat bars. Fatih Gullu, sixth-generation baklavamaker at the renowned Karakoy Gulluoglu in Istanbul, insists on the thinnest, crispiest pastry, and that the syrup must be exactly the right density, bearing in mind that it changes according to climatic conditions. A coin dropped onto a baklava from a height of two feet should shatter each layer from top to bottom, although skeptics would be ill advised to try this at their local bakery. Outside Turkey, baklava is flavored according to regional preference. Michael Krondl notes that Syrians opt for orange-flower water or rosewater, and Iranians add cardamom too. Greeks include honey in the syrup and cinnamon with the nuts. Oat bars suit similar flavoring principles. You might, however, want to adjust the size. Baklavas are small for a good reason. I make my exotic oat bars in mini tart pans, using honey, orange-flower water, and coarsely chopped pistachios.

BANANA

Flavoring the sugar, syrup, and butter mixture with banana yields an oat bar that's the dimple-cheeked offspring of banoffee pie. It's only a minor variation on the starting point, but the results will send your eyebrows to your hairline. Ideally you want a well-browned banana, but yellower specimens can be titivated with a little vanilla extract and a pinch or two of pumpkin-pie spice. Mash (or finely chop) 2–3 very ripe bananas and stir into the hot melted butter mixture before adding it to the oats at step 3.

PASSION FRUIT

Passion-fruit pulp is so concentrated in flavor it's almost like an essence in itself. Which means it can be used in butter cakes and cookies without compromising their texture. Raw passion-fruit seeds are about as easy on the teeth as fragments of lead shot in feathered game. However, when cooked, they become crunchy and are less out of place in a bar cookie than a cake. Use the pulp of 3–4 passion fruit. The water content of the fruit will ensure that the oat bar is more chewy than crunchy. This variation was inspired by an Ecuadorian drink called *colada de avena*, or colada quaker, which is made with soaked oats, a raw sugar called panela, and fruit—it's a little reminiscent of old-fashioned lemon barley water.

PEANUT, CHOCOLATE & RAISIN

I can resist Mars Bars unless there's one in my backpack after (or during, or just before) a strenuous climb up a mountain. Don't get me started on what they've done to the other mass-market chocolate bars of my youth (other than Picnic bars, which are still totally delicious). Avoid mountaintop disappointment by making your own: The following bars are so quick and easy to make, and so much more delicious than anything—bar the Picnic—you'll find in the local grocery store, that I regularly rustled them up when my babies were tiny (with the not entirely dishonest self-justification that oats are beneficial for breast-feeding). To make a 7-in round, follow the starting point, using 3 tbsp brown sugar, 2 tbsp syrup, 5 tbsp butter, and 1½ cups oats, plus 2 heaped tbsp each salted peanuts, chocolate chips, and raisins. Add the peanuts with the oats, then let the mixture cool slightly before stirring in the chocolate chips. Sprinkle the raisins into the prepared pan and cover them with the oat mix, to avoid any nasty scorched fruit on the top. Pick up from step 5 of the method.

TREACLE & ORANGE

I mourn the dessert cart in restaurants. Jingling with crystal bowls of fruit salad, hefty cheesecakes, lurid trifles, and resplendently plattered gâteaux, short of a slice or two. Like miniature mobile libraries—for *desserts*. My grandmother would always opt for the oranges in caramel, a dish I recalled when making an orange and treacle oat bar, which tasted like the sort of old-fashioned, dark Oxford marmalade Frank Cooper makes. Far too grown-up and bitter for Paddington's under-hat sandwich. I make these oat bars thin, and serve them with glacé ginger ice cream. If you're doing the same, reduce the cooking time to 10–12 minutes. Mix 2 tbsp treacle or molasses, ¼ cup granulated sugar, ½ cup butter, scant 2 cups quick-cooking rolled oats, and a pinch of salt. Stir in the finely grated zest of 2 large oranges and the juice of 1. Bake in an 8-in round pan for the usual thickness, or divide between 2 pans for the thinner sort.

Chocolate

CHOCOLATE
SAUCE

page 374

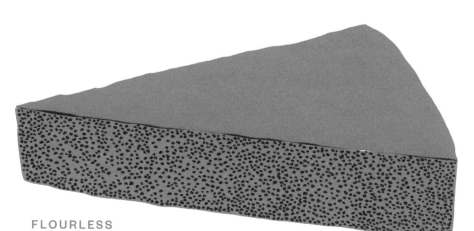

FLOURLESS
CHOCOLATE CAKE

page 396

CHOCOLATE TRUFFLES,
TART & FROSTING

page 380

CHOCOLATE MOUSSE

page 386

CHOCOLATE
TIFFIN CAKE

page 392

In all but one of the starting points on the chocolate continuum, the method is essentially identical. Melt chocolate with another ingredient. Add eggs and/or flavoring. Let it set (or encourage it to). The exception to this is chocolate sauce, whose tendency to set you want, of course, to inhibit. Chocolate is temperamental. When things go wrong, the blame usually rests with excessive heat or moisture. Which is ironic, given the conditions necessary for the cacao tree to flourish: excessive heat and moisture. Such, however, are the consequences of refinement (and chocolate is very, very refined). You lose touch with your roots.

When melting chocolate, it pays to have a little sangfroid. You will want to inspect your bowl and stirrer for moisture as obsessively as a sheriff polishes his favorite six-shooter. Water is your enemy. Wooden spoons can harbor dampness in their crevices. Steam can escape from the double boiler you thought was watertight. Beads of condensation quiver on the extractor fan, waiting to drop into the bowl. The planet is seven-tenths water: The odds are stacked against you. I have seen it written that "even a few drops of water" will cause your molten chocolate to seize—that is, turn into a grainy sludge, like the mud pies you wished were chocolate as a kid—but the "even" inverts the concern. It is the small quantities you need to watch out for. Were you, for example, to tip a good deal of water into your bowl, the chocolate might well be sufficiently saturated to avoid seizing, and therefore usable for something, if not quite what you originally had in mind. A small amount of water, on the other hand, will stick to the dry parts of the chocolate, resulting in runaway clogging and the sort of panic that takes over when Tetris outpaces your ability to play it. Whisking in fat can sometimes save seized chocolate. Sometimes it can't. No wonder Willy Wonka lost his mind.

Most of the dishes on the continuum *can* be made by first melting chocolate, then mixing it with other ingredients that have been warmed separately—the microwave is probably your safest bet. The methods in the following pages, however, rely on the simpler principle of either gently heating the chocolate *with* other ingredients—butter, for instance, as for the flourless chocolate cake on page 396—or melting the chocolate by mixing it with a hot liquid, such as cream, for a ganache.

S The first kind of ganache on the chocolate continuum is made to
A a long dilution: 1 cup chopped chocolate to 1¼ cups light cream.
U (Note that the measurements for this ganache, and the thicker
C kind that follows next on the continuum, are easier to memorize
E in weights than in volume. The sauce calls for twice the chocolate's
weight in cream; the tart/truffle ganache calls for equal weights of
chocolate and heavy cream.) This dilution will yield a rich sauce the
color of a hazelnut shell that will remain pourable for 2–3 hours at
room temperature. Left for longer, or in the fridge, the cocoa butter
in the chocolate will begin to solidify, and the sauce will need gentle
heating to be pourable again. Extra liquid flavorings help keep your

ganache saucy for longer—a splash of brandy, say, or coffee, or sugar syrup. Don't be tempted to increase the proportion of cream, though. Even with 70% cocoa content, the chocolate flavor will be too weak.

Rita Rudner once said she never understood when people asked if she had any spare change. "How can you tell? You haven't finished living your life yet." I'm the same with chocolate sauce. Leftovers are just the "more" you haven't used yet. Spread it on a croissant. Dilute it with milk for a shake. Blend it with frozen banana slices to make an *almost* healthy ice cream. Stir in a dram of Cointreau, decant into a dainty pot, and eat with a couple of thin ginger cookies. Or take a spoonful each morning in lieu of a vitamin tablet: It'll put you in a better mood, and surely can't be worse for you than a pellet of orange-flavored chalk.

T A denser form of ganache—the next stop on the continuum—is made
R with twice as much dark, 70%-cocoa chocolate as the sauce, i.e.
U 2 cups chopped chocolate to 1¼ cups heavy or whipping cream.
F Whip the mixture once it has cooled to room temperature and,
F thanks to the cream, it will become lighter and fluffier. Some serve
L it as a sort of chocolate mousse (page 370), and it's very good for
E frosting a cake. It's also sometimes flavored and sweetened slightly,
S then set in a pan and served as a truffle cake. Usually, however, it's
   left unwhipped and rolled into truffles, or set in a prebaked pastry
& shell for a chocolate tart. Add a little softened, unsalted butter for
   a silkier texture, and some sugar if you find the bitterness lent
T by a high-cocoa chocolate too much. The real interest lies, however,
A in the flavoring options available to the ganachemaker, either by
R infusing the cream with aromatics or adding an extract, spirit, or
T liqueur to the ganache while it's still runny. The trick is not to add
so much that the ganache will no longer set. 1 cup chopped 70%-cocoa chocolate can generally take on as much as 1 cup heavy cream and still set to a rollable, sliceable texture, even if it needs a night in the fridge (having first cooled to room temperature) to get there.

Milk chocolate and white chocolate need more careful management than dark, since their sugar content makes them tackier when melted. They will not, as a rule, stand the same dilution as dark chocolate and still set, and they are more heat-sensitive. I say "as a rule," because it's impossible to be definitive when there are so many brands available, and so much variation between them.

If you want to give your truffles a crisp chocolate shell, you'll need to master the art of tempering chocolate, which makes it shiny and smooth and gives a pleasing snap on the teeth. The process involves heating, then cooling, and stirring the chocolate to a rather rigid set of rules, ensuring the cocoa crystals set in the right way. Of the several ways to do this, I find the following the easiest, although it does require a thermometer (and at least 7 oz chocolate). If your chocolate is not in chocolate-chip form, cut it into small, even-sized pieces. Put about two-thirds of it in a heatproof bowl set over, but not touching, just-about-simmering water and let it melt (alternatively, melt it in short bursts in the microwave). Remove the bowl. Add the remaining third of the chocolate and stir until the temperature falls to 88–90°F in the case of dark chocolate, 84–86°F for milk, or 80–82°F for white. As soon as the temperature of the chocolate has fallen to within these ranges, it's ready to use. Dip the truffles into the tempered chocolate. Try to work quickly, because it won't stay in temper forever.

Harold McGee has remarked that cookery writers need to be precise about the sort of chocolate to use in a recipe. Proportions of cocoa butter, cocoa particles, and sugar can vary widely, and since the cocoa particles absorb liquid, and sugar becomes syrup in a liquid, a recipe developed for sugary chocolate can go horribly wrong when a premium bittersweet, 70% cocoa is substituted. That said, I find that standard supermarket bars of dark chocolate (around 45% cocoa) work for all the starting points on this continuum, as long as you don't mind the sweetness. You might add some coffee or brandy to improve the flavor.

Milk and white chocolate turn up in a fair few of the Flavors & Variations, but they only work as a straight swap for dark in chocolate sauce and mousse. In sum, the milk solids, high sugar content, and (in some cases) partial substitution of vegetable fat for pricey cocoa butter make milk and white chocolate substantively different from dark. Even diehard fans of the most candy-like chocolate will concede the superiority of dark for cooking, once its bitterness has been tamed by butter or cream plus sugar.

Here we intersect with the custard continuum. *Petits pots au chocolat* are made in a similar way to ganache, except instead of melting the chocolate in heavy cream, a warm, pourable custard is used. The results will be silkier than ganache, rather like a ladle of the brown computer-generated chocolate you see in TV commercials. In my experience, making *petits pots* this way works considerably better than baking them crème-brûlée-style in the oven, as the chocolate doesn't get the opportunity to overcook. Flavor variations can be achieved by infusing the custard with hard aromatics—see pages 487–8—or adding liquid flavorings once the chocolate has been stirred into the custard.

M You might be forgiven for thinking that *petits pots* are to chocolate
O mousses as solid chocolate bars are to Aeros: the same thing with
U the air let out. But in *petits pots* the egg is cooked, where in a classic
S mousse it is not, which is a problem if you're catering for someone
S who can't or won't eat raw egg. Some chefs dodge the issue by
E whipping a ganache and calling it chocolate mousse, and while
the results are lovely, they lack bubbles, which are as much the point
of mousse as they are of Champagne. Where mousse has a singular
advantage over *petits pots* is in its ease of preparation. The typical
method is to fold stiffly beaten egg whites into cooled, but still liquid,

melted chocolate. The process will take 10 minutes at most. My ideal chocolate mousse is made with coffee and a splash of rum: the perfect combination of complex flavor, light texture, and palate-stimulating kick. Served, of course, in a small vessel with no gouges or dimples or otherwise inaccessible interior-design features. There is no frustration like the fraction of a teaspoon of mousse dislodgeable only by the bristles of a dishwashing brush.

The best chocolate mousse I have ever eaten came not in a tiny ramekin but a huge white tureen. It was served at a cozy candlelit restaurant in London that I'm pretty sure no longer exists. The waiter would hand you a white plate and administer a dollop of wondrous reddish-brown mousse with a comically enormous silver spoon. He would then return with another tureen of whipped cream and spoon a generous amount on top. The last time I went there was on an early date. We ordered the mousse for two, which was the same as the mousse for one, except served on a larger white plate to share. The date was going passably well. We talked about Martin Amis. He preferred *London Fields* to *The Information*; I took the opposite line. It seemed a lively and mutually enlightening disagreement. The plate began to look more white than brown. We began discussing our experiences of Istanbul, or maybe it was Cardiff. I can't remember. Soon the plate was white but for the smears I hadn't yet tidied up with my index finger. "Isn't that a great mousse?" I said, dabbing my lips with my napkin. "I'll take your word for it," he said, as I clocked the spoon gleaming untouched at his elbow. The next time I saw him was nine years later and he was married with three kids.

T   The method for making chocolate tiffin cake is very similar to the
I   method for chocolate mousse, except that you beat whole eggs with
F   sugar, rather than just egg whites. Once this is folded into melted
F   chocolate and butter, you stir in some broken cookies. It's as simple
I   as that. No need to bake. Simply scrape the mixture into a pan or
N   silicone mold and let it set. Most modern recipes tend to omit the
     eggs, but if you're happy to eat the odd raw egg, I would
C   recommend keeping them in: They lend volume to the chocolate mix
A   and a more sliceable texture to the finished cake. Many egg-free
K   versions amount, essentially, to a butter ganache, which is given
E   to melting and can feel rather slippery in the hand. Nonetheless,
egg-free options are given in the Flavors & Variations section.

Chocolate tiffin cake entered my family's culinary consciousness after my mother saw Delia Smith make it on a Saturday-morning TV show. Smith called it "Belgian biscuit [i.e. cookie] cake," which I always considered a misnomer. At least in the context of chocolate, Belgium represented ambassadorial levels of refinement, a country-sized little finger raised above the oily mediocrity of British cocoa solids. This did not square with our chocolate tiffin cake, which was undoubtedly delicious. But about as refined as a belch on the forecourt of a gas station. Nowadays it seems to be more commonly known as plain old chocolate biscuit cake, chocolate fridge cake, or tiffin cake, all of which capture its lumbering unpretentiousness rather better.

Actually, it's likely that the so-called "Belgian" cake originated in Germany; the recipe is said to have been invented a century ago by Bahlsen, Germany's biggest cookie manufacturer, to encourage use of their famous Leibniz-Keks. Leibniz are a crisp, plain variation on the classic French Petit-Beurre, although not as plain as the Rich Tea cookies used in British chocolate tiffin cake, which have no *beurre* in them at all. In Germany, they call the cake *Kalter Hund*—"cold dog"— which sounds less like a cake than a particularly grueling state of narcotic withdrawal. The reality is, in fact, rather closer to the refined ideal to which British "Belgian" cake singularly fails to measure up. Like the American icebox cake, *Kalter Hund* is typically made in a loaf pan with whole cookies, layered with Teutonic precision, giving each slice the orderly appearance of something seen in the window of an upmarket pâtisserie, as opposed to a rubble of chocolate and cookie bits thrown together by your mum. If the chocolate tiffin cake did originate in Germany, it's no wonder that it's the Queen's favorite tea cake, according to the royal chef Darren McGrady. Prince William requested it for his wedding, alongside the traditional tiered and iced fruitcake. The Palace's version is topped with a generous amount of dark chocolate, and finished with white. Not quite as rustic as my mother's version, but still artless enough to have Carême weeping into his toque. At least until he tasted it.

McGrady remarks on how frequently he is asked for the recipe for his chocolate tiffin cake; likewise, testing it for this book, I was struck by how irresistible people find this sort of cake. I went through a phase of making it Italian-style—the Portuguese and Croatians make a similar version too—in the form of a salami, dusted with confectioners' sugar and served in slices after dinner with coffee. The speed with which the slices disappeared called into question the point of spending hours perfecting a quince millefeuille or fashioning a realistic potting shed out of marzipan and grated chocolate.

Which is not to say there aren't ways of sprucing up your tiffin cake. In the eastern Italian region of Le Marche, they make a version with dried figs, almonds, and walnuts laced with brandy, spices, and aniseed liqueur, then eat it with pecorino cheese. Delia Smith herself has updated the idea for adult palates, making one chocolate tiffin cake that uses amaretti cookies dipped in brandy and cider, layered with a ganache in a domed mold, and another that uses a mixture of dried sour cherries, pistachios, oatmeal cookies, and rum. I once made a white chocolate, raspberry, and pistachio version that looked very much like mortadella. All these elaborations, it has to be said, make me nostalgic for the untidy exuberance of the chocolate tiffin cake of my youth. If the Windsors can't resist it, why should we?

The continuum ends with its only cooked dish. The intensity and luscious texture of flourless chocolate cake is achieved by melting chocolate with butter, beating together sugar and eggs, then folding them into the cool chocolate mixture and baking. Aside from the spell in the oven, the method departs only minimally from chocolate tiffin cake. Note that in the absence of flour, it's akin to cooking a custard, with the liquid chocolate and butter standing in for sweetened milk or cream. This means that the cake will need to be baked at a low temperature, preferably in a water bath, until it is set but for a slight wobble in the center. Precisely when flourless chocolate cake is done is hard to determine by timer alone. It's more a question of knowing when to start repeatedly checking it. The skewer test works very well, but in contrast to a butter cake, you want the skewer to come out a little wet, with a modicum of crumb attached. A dry skewer means your cake is overcooked.

"Fallen chocolate cake" and "fallen chocolate soufflé cake" are very similar to flourless chocolate cake. The same ingredients and quantities can be used for all three, but in the "fallen" cakes the egg whites are beaten separately from the yolks and sugar, then folded into the mixture of chocolate, butter, and egg yolks. This ensures the essential amphitheater-like depression in the center of the finished cake. Take note: Murphy's law dictates that, on the rare occasion you actually want them to, soufflés deflate painfully slowly.

There are many versions of flourless chocolate cake; some call for a lot more sugar, or the addition of fruit, or some ground almonds folded into the mixture for more substance. The great advantage of our starting point is its simplicity. Just use a cup each of butter, sugar, and eggs and 1½ cups of chopped chocolate—or, if you use scales, equal weights of the four ingredients.

Chocolate Sauce

A quick-to-make chocolate sauce to pour on ice cream or sundaes, crêpes, etc. It's made with twice the *weight* of cream as chocolate. For a fuller, smoother sauce, try adding a tablespoon or more of soft, unsalted butter at the end of step [3].

For 1 ¾ cups

INGREDIENTS
1 cup chopped dark, 70%-cocoa chocolate [A] [B]
1¼ cups light cream [C] [D]
1–2 tbsp sugar or sugar syrup—optional

[1] Place the chocolate in a heatproof bowl large enough to hold the cream too.

[2] Bring the cream to a boil in a saucepan, heating it just until small bubbles appear at the edges (i.e., scald it). Remove from the heat. If you're using hard aromatics to flavor the cream, add them and let infuse until their flavor in the cream has reached the required intensity, then strain and re-scald.
     Any flavorings will need to be bold to register against the chocolate flavor.

[3] Pour the hot cream over the chocolate and leave for a minute or two to let the chocolate melt. Stir until thoroughly combined and glossy. Stir in any liquid flavorings now.
     If you prefer, you can add the chocolate to the cream. Some think this reduces the chance of the chocolate seizing.

[4] Taste for flavor and sweetness; correct if necessary.
     A few tablespoons of sugar or sugar syrup should melt easily in the still-warm mixture. If you know you prefer your chocolate sauce much sweeter than this, best to add the sugar or syrup to the warming cream at step [2].

[5] Pour the sauce into a jug and lay a piece of parchment paper or plastic wrap on the surface, to prevent a skin from forming.
     The sauce can be kept in the fridge for a week, but it may need warming to liquefy it again.

LEEWAY

A   Milk chocolate and white chocolate both require extra care when heating. Do use high-quality bars.

B   If you're out of solid chocolate, a chocolate sauce can be made with ¼ cup each of butter, unsweetened cocoa powder, sugar, syrup (corn or golden), and water, plus 1 tsp vanilla extract. Simply put them all in a pan, place over a low to medium heat, and stir constantly until you have a dark, homogenous liquid.

C   You can use half and half, or all sorts of cream. Heavy or whipping will be very rich and will eventually set solid; they can be re-liquefied by gentle heating. Alternatively, prevent your cream from setting by diluting it with milk. Custard sauce is another option. I have an old cookbook that suggests plain old milk is fine for "family occasions."

D   Jamie Oliver makes a chocolate sauce in the same way, but uses the syrup drained from 2 (15-oz) cans of pears (in place of dairy) on 1¼ cups chopped dark, 70%-cocoa chocolate.

CHERRY, LICORICE & CORIANDER SEED

The kind of tasting notes you can find in chocolate enthusiasts' online forums are a good source of inspiration for flavorings. A blend of red cherry, licorice, and cedar in a dark chocolate inspired a sauce that proved very popular with my tasting panel. To approximate cedar flavor, I used coriander seeds, which have a sawmill hint of freshly cut timber about them. Lightly toast 1 tbsp coriander seeds—and I mean lightly, just enough to tease out the flavor. Don't brown them. Add them to 1¼ cups light cream, along with 1 tsp aniseed, and scald. Let infuse for an hour. Scald the cream again, then pick up at step 3, straining the cream onto the chocolate. Once the chocolate and cream are a unified brown, stir in 2 tbsp cherry brandy. Like cakes, casseroles, and radical new hairstyle decisions, flavored sauce often seems better the day after it's made.

CHOCOLATE MINT & VODKA

According to a letter he wrote to his friend Helen Evans Brown in 1954, James Beard thought a chocolate mint was "sensational" with a properly dry martini. Having put the pairing to the test, with an After Eight and a gin martini (I presume Beard meant gin, given the time of writing) *and* a vodka martini (in case he didn't), I can only conclude that Beard was being wry. The mint smothers the botanicals and the icy booze makes the chocolate seize in the mouth. Mutually assured destruction. Adapt the means of delivery, however, and the combination *is* sensational. By opening the nasal passages, the menthol can make you more receptive to the flavor, and its cold blast only emphasizes the alcoholic heat of the spirits. It's way more fun than the 1990s party game of snorting vodka off a spoon. I ended up melting 9 After Eights in 1¼ cups scalded cream, giving the chocolates a few minutes to soften before stirring them into a homogenous sauce, adding 1 tbsp vodka, and stirring some more. The vodka seemed to open up the peppermint, as if I had fitted my tastebuds with 3D glasses. Try this with any sort of chocolate mint, but I find the sauce made with After Eights retains the musky note detectable in their vacated paper sleeves, as stimulating as the pheromones on a lover's unwashed T-shirt.

DARK CHOCOLATE & AMBERGRIS

Jean Anthelme Brillat-Savarin, author of *The Physiology of Taste* (1825), prescribed a pint of ambergris-flavored hot chocolate for the over-worked, the over-indulged, and anyone feeling a little dull around the edges. Someone should tell the Head of Flavor Variations at Berocca. Ambergris is formed in the intestines of sperm whales, as a natural defense against digestive problems caused by the beaks of the squid they ingest. It's passed as fecal matter, some of which washes up on the seashore. You're about as likely to find some, walking Fido on the beach, as you are a message in a bottle from a shipwrecked slave-trader, but that needn't dissuade you from keeping your eyes open. The problem is in identifying it. Ambergris only develops its more perfumed qualities as it ages—animalic, with notes of musk, tobacco, and leather, as I imagine the interior of the Duchess of Cornwall's Range Rover might smell. In the seventeenth century, the adventurer Sir Philibert Vernatti claimed the best ambergris was found on Mauritius, where "the hogs can smell it at a great distance, who run like mad to it, and devour it commonly before the people come to it." The comparison with truffles is hard to resist, all the more so as a typical lump of ambergris has the calcified-stone appearance of a white truffle. Both ambergris and truffle are widely synthesized, to diminishing returns. If you *do* get lucky on a beach somewhere, a perfumier will pay you handsomely. The 6½-lb lump found by Ken Wilman on the beach of the English seaside town of Morecambe in 2013 was thought to be worth around £100,000, until an international team of experts decided it wasn't ambergris but a smelly rock. In 2006, a couple who came across the real deal on a beach in South Australia earned U.S. $295,000 for their find. Brillat-Savarin suggests 60–72 grains per pound of chocolate for his cocoa. A grain is the weight of a grain of barley, internationally agreed at 64.8 mg. So 15 grains make a gram. On the basis of the Wilman estimation, this cocoa recipe will set you back between £133 and £160 in ambergris. If you have any left over, recall that in *Moby-Dick* Ishmael notes that "some wine merchants drop a few grains into claret, to flavor it."

DARK CHOCOLATE & PX

I needed a boozy chocolate sauce for an impromptu midweek dinner, so made two, one with Pedro Ximénez sherry, and another with a good-quality Jamaican rum, and offered them both with a sundae made from chocolate brownie, vanilla ice cream, and toasted hazelnuts. Indecisive, maybe, but no one objected to conducting a side-by-side chocolate-sauce tasting, and were too busy licking their spoons to notice that I'd served them a shortcut dessert. I had assumed the rum would prevail, with its familiar sweetness and higher ABV, but the PX was by far the favorite. This sweet, dark sherry shares many characteristic flavors with chocolate, and makes a luscious, fruity ganache with hints of molasses, caramel, raisin, and fig. Use 1–2 tbsp PX for our starting point chocolate and cream quantities.

DARK CHOCOLATE, ROSEMARY & LEMON

Delicious on a slice of almond cake (page ²⁹⁸), or poured over *melanzane al cioccolato*, a surprisingly delicious pairing of eggplant and chocolate that's popular in Sorrento. In one variation, steamed eggplants are stuffed with a ricotta mixture, then draped in a chocolate sauce and served warm; in another, fried strips of eggplant are cooled, dipped in a mixture of syrup and bread crumbs, then layered with chocolate sauce, candied citrus, and toasted pine nuts before being served at room temperature. You might say that given enough chocolate, ricotta, dried fruit, and roasted nuts you'd be content with boiled Birkenstock, but the eggplant must be given its due. Fried, it takes on a silky texture, and its mellow flavor, enhanced by the subtle saltiness that comes from degorging (salting) it, makes a satisfying contrast to bittersweet chocolate. In my easy version, the eggplant slices are dipped in flour and egg, then fried, which gives them a pancake-like quality, and the result is a cross between a crêpe spread with Nutella and a Neapolitan chocolate tiffin cake. To serve 4, cut 12 rounds, each about ½ in thick, from as many eggplants as needed. Sprinkle lightly with salt and let degorge for 1 hour. Meanwhile, scald 1¼ cups cream with 3 rosemary stalks and the pared zest of 1 lemon and let infuse for 2 hours. Remove the aromatics, re-scald the cream, and pour it over 1 cup chopped dark, 70%-cocoa chocolate. Leave for a few minutes, then stir until dark and glossy, and stir in ½ tsp lemon oil. Set aside to cool a little. Rinse the eggplant slices, squeeze gently, and pat dry. Dredge both sides with flour, dip in beaten egg, and fry in batches in a few inches of vegetable oil until golden. Drain on paper towels. To assemble, divide the slices into 4 sets of 3, then sandwich each set together using the chocolate sauce. Smooth some sauce around the sides, so you can't see the eggplant. Scatter with a mixture of candied peel, toasted pine nuts, and rum-soaked raisins.

MILK CHOCOLATE, COCONUT & NUTMEG

As close to a taste of paradise as you can get with everyday ingredients. Nutmeg will add refreshing top notes of citrus, floral, and pine. Make sure it's freshly grated: Pre-ground is more nut-*meh* than -meg. Follow the starting point, but use 1 cup chopped good-quality milk chocolate and 1¼ cups coconut milk—light is fine. Grate in a quarter of a whole nutmeg once the milk and chocolate are completely mixed.

WHITE CHOCOLATE

White chocolate sauce over frozen berries was a classic dessert at Le Caprice and The Ivy in London during Mark Hix's reign in the kitchens. There were foodie types who shuddered at its artlessness, but the customers loved it. Hix uses equal amounts of white chocolate and heavy cream. I make it to our starting point, which is less rich, but it still tastes like clotted custard. Lindt white chocolate is a good choice: 1 cup chopped with 1¼ cups light cream will serve 4; plan on about ¾ cup berries per serving. If you're using a bag of frozen berries, throw away the strawberries, which, once thawed, are like cold tea bags. White chocolate sauce is also good for banana crêpes, and you may find it kinder to the pears in a *belle Hélène* than dark chocolate. Add a little *poire* eau-de-vie to the latter for an intense esteriness.

Chocolate Sauce → Other Directions

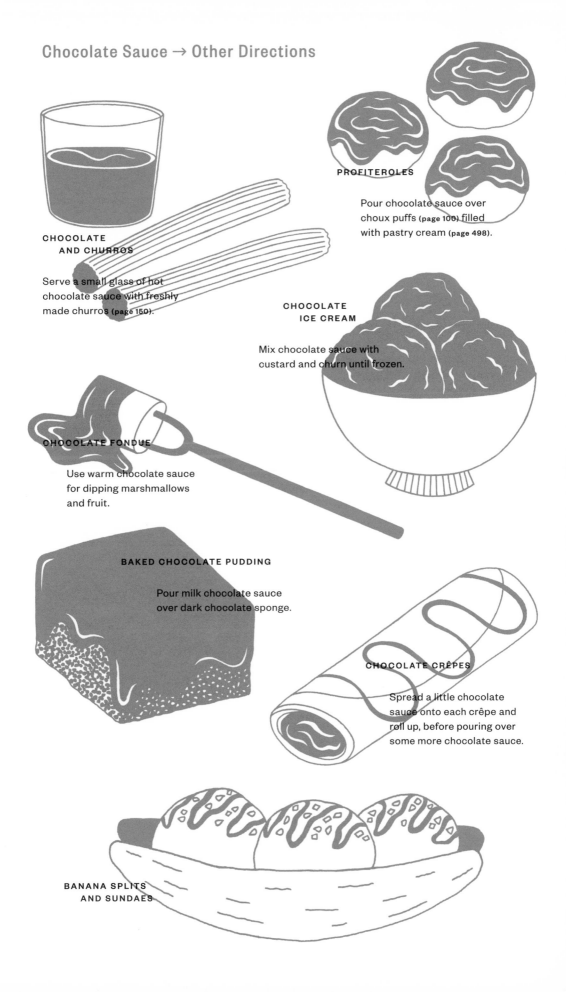

CHOCOLATE AND CHURROS

Serve a small glass of hot chocolate sauce with freshly made churros (page 150).

PROFITEROLES

Pour chocolate sauce over choux puffs (page 100) filled with pastry cream (page 498).

CHOCOLATE ICE CREAM

Mix chocolate sauce with custard and churn until frozen.

CHOCOLATE FONDUE

Use warm chocolate sauce for dipping marshmallows and fruit.

BAKED CHOCOLATE PUDDING

Pour milk chocolate sauce over dark chocolate sponge.

CHOCOLATE CRÊPES

Spread a little chocolate sauce onto each crêpe and roll up, before pouring over some more chocolate sauce.

BANANA SPLITS AND SUNDAES

Chocolate Truffles, Tart & Frosting

A simple and highly adaptable classic ganache that retains the rich flavor and melting quality of the chocolate. The snap of the bar is replaced with a creamy set to sink your teeth into, especially if you also add a little butter—2–4 tbsp soft, unsalted butter per 1 cup chopped chocolate—once the chocolate and cream are combined. Cooled, the ganache can serve as an egg-free mousse or for frosting a cake: Simply whip until light and fluffy. If you own kitchen scales, this starting point will be easier to memorize: Use equal weights of chocolate and cream.

For 30–36 truffles, or enough ganache to fill a shallow 9-in tart shell, or top and fill an 8-in cake

INGREDIENTS
2 cups chopped dark, 70%-cocoa chocolate [A]
1¼ cups heavy cream [B]
1 tsp vanilla extract—optional [C]
2–4 tbsp sugar or sugar syrup—optional [D]
Sifted unsweetened cocoa powder or confectioners' sugar—optional

1   Place the chocolate in a heatproof bowl large enough to hold the cream too.

2   Bring the cream to a boil in a saucepan, heating it just until small bubbles appear at the edges (i.e., scald it). Remove from the heat. If you're using hard aromatics to flavor the cream, add them and let infuse until their flavor in the cream has reached the required intensity, then strain and re-scald.
    Use bold flavorings to register against the chocolate flavor.

3   Pour the hot cream over the chocolate and leave for a minute or two to let the chocolate melt, then stir until thoroughly combined and glossy.
    If you prefer, you can add the chocolate to the cream.

4   Stir in any liquid flavoring.

5   Taste for flavor and sweetness; correct if necessary.
    If you're adding sugar, do so while the chocolate is still warm enough to melt it. You could use a few tablespoons of syrup instead, but don't add so much that you jeopardize the set. If you find 70% chocolate very bitter, dissolve some sugar in the cream at step [1].

FOR TRUFFLES

Transfer to a dish and let cool. For the best texture, let set at room temperature rather than in the fridge. When it has, scoop out the mixture with a melon baller or teaspoon, fashion into rough rounds, then roll in sifted cocoa powder or confectioners' sugar, or dip into tempered chocolate—see pages [369-70].

The setting takes 2–3 hours if the mixture is poured into a dish to a depth of about 1¼ in. Your truffles will keep at room temperature for 3 days.

FOR A TART

Pour your ganache into a *fully* baked pastry shell (page [566]) and let set at room temperature. When it has, decorate it with sifted cocoa powder, grated chocolate, chocolate curls, or chopped toasted hazelnuts.

The ganache will keep at room temperature for 3 days.

LEEWAY

A For 2 cups chopped good-quality milk chocolate, use ¾ cup of heavy cream; makes about 25 truffles. For 2 cups chopped good-quality white chocolate, use ⅓ cup heavy cream, and gently heat it with the white chocolate in a double boiler; makes about 20 truffles.

B Light whipping cream will also work. Or replace all or some of the cream with crème fraîche, which will lend a refreshing sour edge. Condensed milk is fine in chocolate tarts, although it is super-sweet, and you may want to use dark 85%-cocoa chocolate to compensate.

C Clearly, the more wet ingredients you use for flavoring (fruit purée, eau-de-vie, rum, etc.), the more the setting potential will be compromised.

D More sugar can be added if you prefer your ganache to be sweeter.

BANANA & MILK CHOCOLATE
Of all the nonalcoholic flavorings for milk chocolate truffles, this is the best. The esters in banana recall those found in rum, or brandy, lending the chocolate an extra dimension. In place of the cream in our starting point, use sieved banana purée, or cheat and use a pouch of baby food, like Ella's. A pouch contains about 3 tbsp, so use one, plus ½ tsp vanilla extract, and a pinch of ground cloves for every ⅓ cup chopped milk chocolate. Vanilla and clove notes are both detectable in very ripe bananas, and therefore boost what would otherwise be a rather subtle banana flavor. I once made this ganache with white chocolate, supposedly for truffles, but the mix didn't set hard enough. So I took a loaf of golden syrup cake (page 348), spread the tan slices with the ganache, and served it, shamelessly, as my own ingenious invention. I'm going to hell, but on a tide of sweet banana-flavored goo.

BLONDE
It was in 1879 that Sir William Crookes identified the fourth state of matter, plasma, or "radiant matter" as he called it. In contrast, it wasn't until 2012 that the confectionery industry owned up to a fourth state of chocolate. "Blonde" chocolate was discovered in 2004 when Frédéric Bau, executive chef at L'École du Grand Chocolat Valrhona, left some white chocolate in a double boiler for ten hours, during which time it caramelized. Valrhona spent the next eight years figuring out how to produce their accidental discovery on an industrial scale. They call their blonde chocolate "Dulcey," presumably in reference to *dulce de leche*, the caramelized milk with which it shares many flavor characteristics. Dulcey, in flavor terms, reminds me of millionaire's shortbread when the cookie, chocolate, and caramel have been munched to a pulp. If you doubt that something can be sickly *and* have finesse, give it a try. I used it to make mini tarts with a sweet pastry base, topped with a glossy dark ganache. Valrhona recommends pairing Dulcey with mildly acidic fruits, like apricot and mango, or with hazelnut, coffee, or caramel.

BLUE CHEESE
You may be surprised at how recessive blue cheese is, subsumed into creamy dark chocolate in a ganache. Disappointed, even, that the experience isn't stranger, although the presence of chocolate *and* cheese gives you double the excuse to dust off the port. The following makes about 10 truffles, a good sample quantity. Melt 2 oz blue cheese (Gorgonzola or Stilton) in ⅔ cup heavy cream, gently, and stirring all the while. Pour onto 1 cup chopped dark, 70%-cocoa chocolate, as at step 3. The set and rolled truffles are best kept wrapped in the fridge.

DARK CHOCOLATE & WATER
In a ganache, the advantage water has over cream is its neutrality—the flavor of the chocolate can express itself fully. The chocolatier Damian

Allsop uses mineral water, but has recently created a seawater variant. Chantal Coady, founder of Rococo Chocolates, recommends boiling water and dark chocolate, in line with our starting point. (Coady stipulates a 50/50 mix of 61%- and 70%-cocoa chocolate, but feel free to use all 70%.) To make enough for 6 espresso cups or shot glasses (it's intense, so a little goes a long way), pour a scant 1 cup hot water over 1¼ cups chopped chocolate, leave for 5 minutes, then thoroughly mix with an immersion blender. Coady notes that the ganache will seem thin, but will set at room temperature. The water gives this ganache a short shelf-life—bacteria grow more readily in water than in cream—so keep it in the fridge once it's set, for no more than 3 days.

IRISH COFFEE

Long before Heston, Hervé, and Ferran, Giles at our local pub blew our tiny minds with his signature Irish Coffee, deploying some unfathomable culinary sleight-of-hand to get the heavy cream to sit atop the whiskey-laced coffee, and *stay there as you drank it*. And all this without resorting to aerosol cream, which lacks the velvety texture of hand-whipped. In Giles's honor, I make this *ganache fouettée au White Lion* when I need a quick-to-make dessert that simultaneously takes care of both coffee and *digestif*. To serve 6, make a ganache with 1 cup chopped dark, 70%-cocoa chocolate and ⅔ cup heavy cream heated with 2 tbsp sugar. At step ⁴, stir in 2 tbsp Irish whiskey and 2 tsp instant coffee dissolved in 1 tsp boiling water. Let the mixture cool to room temperature (30–60 minutes), then whip until it becomes lighter and fluffier (and more matte than shiny), which will take a few minutes with a portable electric mixer. Note that, left unwhipped, the ganache will tend to harden, so whip it as soon as possible after its cooling period. Divide among 6 small glasses. Top with as much cold whipped cream as the glass will allow. Serve on a white saucer with a teaspoon. Just as you whipped it soon after cooling, eat the ganache as freshly whipped as possible, while it still has a soft-serve dreaminess. Whipped ganache is nothing if not a lesson in how chocolate likes to set.

MILK CHOCOLATE & PASSION FRUIT

A ganache that tastes like chocolate jam. Stick it in a jar with a gingham-print lid and tell your friends it comes from a rare plant, *Passiflora cacao*, whose pods contain soft beans that yield a silky brown pulp with a fruity chocolate flavor. Or tell them the truth, which is that you pushed the insides of 8 passion fruit through a sieve to separate the juice from the seeds, then brought the juice, plus 1 tbsp honey and a pinch of salt, just about to a boil, before gradually stirring in

2 cups chopped milk chocolate. The cooked juice will be thick and shiny, and 2 cups may seem like a fair bit of chocolate to incorporate. You might want to chop it finer, to help it melt quickly. As you stir, you'll understand where the jam notion came from. Check for sweetness, because some passion fruit are near-hydrochlorically sour. Pour into a prebaked tart shell and let set. As the volume of fruit juice and honey only amounts to roughly ⅔ cup, the ganache should set relatively quickly.

PEANUT BUTTER

Hillbilly praline. Make as per our starting point, but using 1 cup chopped chocolate and ¼ cup cream, then stir in ¾ cup of smooth peanut butter once the ganache is well combined. Milk or dark chocolate work equally well, but don't use white. (You have to draw the line *somewhere*.) More ambitious cooks might like the sound of Damian Allsop's award-winning chocolate flavored with roasted peanuts, fresh ginger, and soy sauce. The use of soy sounds no more peculiar than sea salt did, ten or so years ago.

TARRAGON & MUSTARD

An idea from the chocolatier William Curley, who makes a ganache of tarragon and mustard with dark chocolate. By his own admission, it's a daring mix—the woodland notes of tarragon, underwritten by mustard's warmth, are more usually found in sauces for chicken and fish. Yet other resinous herbs, such as thyme and rosemary, are uncontroversial flavorings for chocolate. You could consider swapping the tarragon for fennel, which has a similar anise flavor, but the tarragon is brighter. I prefer the warmth mustard brings to chocolate over any chili confection I've tasted. Curley makes the case for infusing the cream for flavored ganaches, rather than adding off-the-shelf potions and oils, as the flavor will be purer. In summary, add the leaves of 1 oz tarragon to 1¾ cups whipping cream, scald it, let it cool, and then leave to infuse for 2 hours. Strain the mixture, pressing it to extract as much flavor as possible. Return the infused cream to the pan, add 3 tbsp invert sugar (e.g. liquid glucose or light corn syrup), scald again, and then remove from the heat. Spoon out a few teaspoons and mix to a paste with ¾ tsp mustard powder, stirring this back into the still-warm cream and pouring the mixture over 1 lb chopped dark chocolate (Curley uses 66%-cocoa chocolate, but you may have to settle for 70%). Stir to combine, then add 6 tbsp unsalted, room-temperature butter and stir again until well mixed. This will make a hefty amount, so you may want to halve the quantities.

WHITE CHOCOLATE NOG

To give white chocolate the nog treatment is to give it its Cinderella moment. Combined, the chocolate and nutmeg taste like a spicy lemon curd, making each other seem fresher and lighter. For 2 cups chopped white chocolate, use ¼ cup heavy cream, 1 tbsp rum, and about a sixth of a whole nutmeg, freshly grated, and follow the starting-point method. If you're making truffles, roll them in finely ground vanilla sugar, and top with a further tiny pinch of fresh nutmeg.

RASPBERRIES

Filled with white
chocolate ganache.

SPLIT CHOCOLATES

Made with ganache and
caramel (page 412), or ganache
and marzipan (page 280).

AS A FILLING

Use ganache to sandwich
together meringues (page 424)
or cookies (page 350).

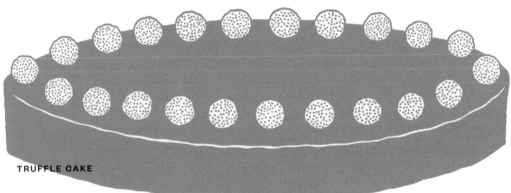

TRUFFLE CAKE

Make a chocolate truffle cake
(page 369) and decorate with
chocolate truffles.

MENDIANTS

Disks of ganache studded
with nuts and dried fruit
(also made just with chocolate).

TUNIS CAKE

Pound cake covered with
ganache and decorated
with marzipan fruit.

FOR MACAROONS

Use ganache to dip or decorate
macaroons (page 288).

Chocolate Mousse

Our previous starting point called for equal amounts of heavy cream and chocolate. Here the cream is replaced with eggs—roughly the same weight as the chocolate. Some people make their mousse with just two ingredients—egg whites, whisked and folded into melted chocolate. I prefer to mix some cold black coffee and a tot of rum into the chocolate. Not only does this embellish the flavor of the chocolate, it also lightens up the mousse. Baked chocolate puddings can be made with this mixture: Pour into buttered ramekins and cook at 400°F for 10–12 minutes. Serve them with cream. Add some extra egg white and you could call them soufflés.

For 6 individual mousses or 1 large mousse (makes 2½ cups)

INGREDIENTS

1⅓ cups chopped dark, 70%-cocoa chocolate [A]
¼–½ cup water or cold coffee [B]
4 large or 3 extra large eggs, separated [C] [D]
3 tbsp sugar—optional [E]

1   Place the chocolate in a heatproof bowl. Add the water or coffee and set the bowl over—but not touching—barely simmering water in a pan. When the chocolate has melted, remove and stir until you have a lovely, homogenous, shiny-brown mixture.
    Cold coffee will enhance the chocolate flavor.

2   In a clean bowl, beat the egg whites to soft peaks. If adding sugar, beat it in here, a tablespoon at a time.

3   Stir the egg yolks into the cooled chocolate mix.
    By the time you've beaten your egg whites, the chocolate should have cooled enough not to cook the yolks. Using the yolks is optional, but they add richness as well as a little extra volume.

4   With a large metal spoon, fold a third of the egg whites into the chocolate mixture. Then fold in the rest. Pour into individual dishes or a large serving bowl.
    The first third is folded in to loosen the mixture, making it easier to incorporate the rest without losing too much of the beaten-in air.

5   Refrigerate for at least 2 hours (longer if you're making 1 large mousse).
    The mousse will keep in the fridge for 2 days.

LEEWAY

A Good-quality milk chocolate can be used in place of dark. (For a honey and goat's cream variation, see page [388]; for white chocolate options, see pages [390] and [391].)

B Replace the water or coffee with a flavored syrup, or some of it with a spirit or liqueur. Some use cream, which will give a less acidic taste than water, but note that this will also take the edge off the chocolate flavor.

C It's okay to use fewer eggs (using more will likely dilute the chocolate flavor too much, and bring an unwelcome egginess). For example, Gordon Ramsay uses only 1 egg white for a chocolate mousse made with ⅔ cup chopped dark chocolate, 1¼ cups heavy cream, ¼ cup sugar, and 2 tbsp Amaretto. Whipped chocolate ganache is an option if you want to make something like a mousse without egg—see Irish coffee on page [383].

D Ferran Adrià pours warm cream onto chopped chocolate—à la ganache—then stirs in the unbeaten egg white, transfers the mixture to a siphon, and charges the mix into a glass. Useful if you make a lot of chocolate mousse, or you want an excuse to buy a siphon.

E The 3 tbsp sugar suggested will make a moderately sweet mousse. Anyone with a particularly sweet tooth might want to double that. If you're using chocolate with a low cocoa content, you might not need any extra sugar.

ARMAGNAC OR COGNAC

Victoria Moore considers Cognac and Armagnac "the town mouse and the country mouse of the brandy world." While Cognac has "sophistication and finesse" and is described as "smooth and sweetly woody," Armagnac is "not just more rustic, it is throaty. You can feel its guts, the hot fire, almost hear the stories that would be told over a glass of it." The difference boils down, in large part, to distillation. Cognac is double-distilled, Armagnac single, each distillation smoothing out the spirit, but removing flavor. (Irish whiskey is triple-distilled, which makes it, as a rule, lighter but less complex than single malts, which are almost always double-distilled.) Moore's distinction applies equally well to the way each spirit combines with chocolate. Cognac lends its presence to refined bonbons and classic truffles, while Armagnac turns up in homely puddings, and rarely gets to spend any time alone with chocolate without wrinkly old prune bumbling in, like Charlotte Bartlett clinging to Lucy Honeychurch in *A Room with a View*. I made a couple of mousses, one with Cognac, one with Armagnac, and preferred the latter: I'm more of a country mouse than I like to admit. In either case, dipping a spoon in the mixture of just-melted chocolate and brandy, I thought of churros (page 150) and the little glass of dipping chocolate they come with. For a mousse, add 2 tbsp Armagnac or Cognac per 1⅓ cups chopped dark chocolate. Follow the starting point, but don't add the spirit to the chocolate as it melts—instead, stir it into the *cooled* chocolate at step 3, before you add the egg yolk. Don't resist a spoonful in its luscious liquid state.

HEATHER HONEY & GOAT'S CREAM

The Mayans and Aztecs sweetened their cocoa drinks with honey. When mixing honey with chocolate, using a stronger-flavored variety like chestnut or heather will pay dividends. Heather Hills Farm in Perthshire in Scotland, makes a raw heather "Champagne of honeys," characterized by its "assertive, full-bodied, warm smoky palate of toffee, with underlying notes of plum and coffee." I made a honeyed milk chocolate mousse with goat's cream, which gave a rustic edge to the finished mousse. (But be warned: The next day it tasted like I'd infused the cream with a billy goat's beard.) To serve 4, use 1 cup chopped good-quality milk chocolate (at least 32% cocoa solids), ½ cup heavy goat's cream, and 1 tbsp heather honey. Melt all these ingredients together, then continue from step 2 of the starting point.

JASMINE

Despite being one of the most expensive flowers to turn into perfume, jasmine is the principal aroma in Chanel No. 5, Joy, and Arpège, and is present, according to *The Perfume Handbook*, in 83 percent of quality fragrances for women. In seventeenth-century Florence, Cosimo III de' Medici, epicurean and wholly disastrous Grand Duke of Tuscany, commissioned his head physician, Francesco Redi, to create a jasmine-scented chocolate. Redi, who was happy to share his recipes for chocolate infused with citron, with lemon peel, and even ambergris, guarded the jasmine version religiously. Even when the recipe did enter the public domain, it was found to be almost insurmountably tricky, requiring a vast number of jasmine buds to be layered with chocolate nibs. Picked very early in the morning, the buds would open while intermingled with the chocolate. The process was then repeated ten or twelve times to achieve the desired intensity of flavor. A similar process is used to flavor green tea leaves for the finest-quality jasmine tea, which is what is used, in turn, to flavor the chocolate in modern jasmine ganache. Redi was on to something: It can be hard to attain a sufficiently strong floral note. A short—if expensive—cut is to use a food-grade jasmine absolute (a form of essential oil).

PARFAIT AMOUR

Parfait Amour is a liqueur to make Baileys look butch. It is lavender-purple, with a somewhat flexible list of aromatic ingredients. *The Techno-Chemical Receipt Book* of 1919 stipulates oils of cinnamon, cardamom, rosemary, anise, lemon, orange, clove, chamomile, and lavender. No mention of violet, which, along with orange, is the identifying ingredient in most commercial versions available these days. As with Blue Curaçao, its purpose is to lend color, although its resemblance to methylated spirits might prove off-putting to all but the most ironically minded mixologists. Color is beside the point when it comes to flavoring dark chocolate, which the combination of violet and citrus does rather beautifully. Use 2 tbsp Parfait Amour in our starting point and taste, adding more if necessary.

STRAWBERRY OR GOOSEBERRY

You can incorporate the moussey bubbles furnished by egg white into bases other than chocolate, but a little more work is needed to recreate the firm structure that chocolate provides as it sets. The following technique recalls a bavarois (page 488), except that whipped cream is used in place of custard. I've used strawberry as an example here.

Purée 10 oz (about 2 cups) strawberries and set aside. Beat 2 egg whites to stiff peaks, adding 2–3 tbsp superfine sugar (depending on the sweetness of the berries), a tablespoon at a time, toward the end of beating. Set aside. Whip ⅔ cup heavy cream to soft peaks. Put 2 leaves of gelatin to soak in cold water for 5 minutes. Heat about a third of the strawberry purée until it's hot but not boiling. Squeeze out the gelatin leaves and thoroughly stir them into the hot purée, then stir this mixture into the cold purée. Fold a third of the egg white into the whipped cream, followed by the other two thirds. Gently fold the strawberry mix into the cream mix. Divide among 4 dessert glasses or ramekins and chill in the fridge. The quantities here are negotiable. The few times I've made this, the strawberries were sweet enough to require only a small amount of sugar; if, on the other hand, I were using gooseberries, I'd cook them with a little sugar first. The 2 leaves of gelatin give a soft set, but you could add more cream or use thick Greek yogurt instead. Using 1 egg white, instead of 2, would give less moussey results. Use none and you'd have what would be called a fool. Whichever approach you take, do make sure the strawberry purée is strongly flavored, so as to survive its dilution by cream and egg.

VANILLA
Adding the best-quality vanilla to ordinary dark chocolate is like refitting a chain-store jacket with vintage buttons. An easy upgrade. Make a syrup with ½ cup water, 5 tbsp sugar, and ½ split Madagascan vanilla bean, then use in place of the water or coffee. This removes the need for adding any sugar to the egg whites. Using an infused syrup is a simple way to flavor your mousse. For more ideas, see pages 434-8.

WHITE CHOCOLATE
If you're over the age of six, you'll probably want to offset the sweetness of white chocolate with something bitter or sour. Fruit is one option, with raspberries being the most obvious pairing. Or make some bitter, dark chocolate cases for the white chocolate mousse by melting ¼ cup chopped dark, 70%-cocoa chocolate, covering the bottom of 4 dariole molds with plastic wrap, and painting them with 2 layers of the melted chocolate. Let set, then carefully remove the plastic wrap from the chocolate cases. Fill with white chocolate mousse, made as per our starting point, but using 1⅓ cups chopped Lindt Excellence White and ¼ cup light cream. These mousses may take longer to set than dark chocolate versions, and will need to be kept refrigerated.

WHITE CHOCOLATE & DOUBLE MALT

I was invited to a tasting of some very expensive limited-edition whiskeys. I tried a 40-year-old Cally ($1,180 per bottle, for "a medley of sultanas, soft, overripe bananas, and honey on a cinnamon Danish," according to the tasting guide) and a 32-year-old Port Ellen ($3,770, for "a profound smokiness… an outstandingly dark expression"). Feeling a little chatty after a few sips, I passed on my recent discovery of how good a glass of single malt is with a few squares of high-cocoa milk chocolate. The distiller looked over one shoulder, leaned in close, and, in the anxious tones of a novice insider trader, said "frozen white Maltesers." Although I still take my dram with room-temperature, cocoa-rich, honeycomb-free chocolate, I put my distiller friend's suggestion to work in a mousse, adding some Horlicks and a little Glenfiddich to white chocolate. Slowly melt 1¼ cups chopped good-quality white chocolate with 2 tbsp heavy cream. Mix 5 tbsp Horlicks (or Ovaltine: different in flavor but nice) powder with a further 2 tbsp (cold) heavy cream, then whisk it into the melted chocolate and stir in 1 tbsp single malt. Pick up from step 2 of the starting point. White chocolate, malt, and aniseed is a good combination for the teetotaller, provided you give the malt its due by holding back on the aniseed: 1 tsp ground is ideal.

Chocolate Tiffin Cake

The methods for chocolate tiffin cake and chocolate mousse are similar. However, for the cake, butter is melted with the chocolate, rather than coffee; and whole egg, rather than just the whites, is beaten with sugar before everything is folded together. The effect of this cake should be to fill you with childish glee, even more so if you add candied cherries. If you've put away childish things, there are more grown-up versions of the cake made with brandy or rum and fashioned into neat shapes. There are egg-free variations too.

For a 7-in square or 8-in round cake pan A

INGREDIENTS
1⅓ cups chopped dark, 70%-cocoa chocolate B
1¾ sticks butter C
2 eggs D
½ cup sugar E
3 cups broken-up graham crackers or plain cookies F G
Confectioners' sugar for dusting

1 Place the chocolate in a heatproof bowl with the butter. Set the bowl over—but not touching—barely simmering water in a pan. When the chocolate and butter have melted, remove and stir until you have a lovely shiny gloop. Set aside to cool a little.
  Alternatively, carefully (i.e. in short bursts, to avoid burning) melt the chocolate and butter separately in the microwave, then mix together.

2 In a clean bowl, beat the eggs and sugar together until thick and pale.
  This is easier with an electric mixer. If you don't have one, do your best with a hand whisk.

3 With a large metal spoon, fold the egg and chocolate mixtures together to make a homogenous mid-brown mixture.
  This can take a while. Aim for exaggerated looping movements, trying to keep as much of the beaten-in air as possible.

4 Stir in the broken-up graham crackers or cookies.

5 Scrape the mixture into a pan lined with plastic wrap or parchment paper (for ease of freeing the cake once it has set). Or use a silicone mold that doesn't need lining. Or put spoonfuls in fluted paper cups. Or fashion into a salami shape and tightly wrap in plastic wrap, then cut into slices when set (make sure the graham crackers are in pea-size pieces if this is your plan).

6 Let cool a little, then ideally leave at room temperature to set. It can go into the fridge to set, but the texture won't be as smooth. If you're pressed for time, let the cake cool to room temperature before transferring it to the fridge.
If the weather—or your kitchen—is particularly warm, the cake will eventually need a blast in the cold.

7 Dust with confectioners' sugar. Cut into narrow bars or wedges. They will keep for 3–4 days in the fridge. Egg-free versions will last a few more days.

LEEWAY

A The pan size can be varied—but the deeper the cake, the longer it will take to set. For a smaller cake, use half the quantities in a 9 x 5 x 3-in (8-cup) loaf pan.

B Regular, sweeter chocolate like Cadbury Bournville will do; just omit the sugar, or use only 2–3 tbsp.

C Using 1¾ sticks butter is fairly standard, and will create an unctuous texture in the finished cake. Nonetheless, the cake will set if you use less butter, or even none, as long as you don't change the quantity or type of chocolate. Unsalted or slightly salted butter are fine, as is salted, if you're partial to the tang it contributes.

D The eggs can be left out, but note that they expand the mixture without diluting the richness (you're making a whole-egg mousse, if you like). For an egg-free cake, see the mulled chocolate variation on page 394. The cake with eggs is less given to melting than the kind without. And it slices better.

E The need for additional sugar will depend on the sweetness of the chocolate you're using—the amount suggested here is based on dark, 70%-cocoa chocolate.

F Rich Tea and digestives are the most commonly used cookies in the U.K. In the U.S., some use animal crackers.

G Add nuts, dried fruit, glacé or candied fruit, and the like with the cookies—as much as ⅔–1 cup. Other options include marshmallows, Maltesers, smashed honeycomb candy, cubes of marzipan, marrons glacés, boozy marinated cherries, candied ginger, mixed candied peel, breakfast cereal, or pretzels. You might also add 1 tbsp brandy or rum to the chocolate mixture at the end of step 1. This is a nonjudgmental cake.

Chocolate Tiffin Cake → Flavors & Variations

MULLED CHOCOLATE

Yotam Ottolenghi's reworking of chocolate tiffin cake calls for a flavored chocolate mixed in with the plain, and dispenses with the eggs. Jeremy Lee's is more akin to our starting point, but contains no sugar other than that which is present in the chocolate. For want of "decent" candied cherries, Lee uses chopped (preferably Agen) prunes instead. I love candied cherries in cakes. They were as innocent a fixture of my childhood as Paddington Bear and glittery barrettes. Still, I could see how prunes might match candied cherries for juiciness. My chocolate tiffin cake combines Lee's ideas with Ottolenghi's egg-free base. The result has a jingle of Christmas about it, without straying too far from the original. Chop 1 heaped cup pitted prunes into 4 pieces each and soak in port for at least 30 minutes. Melt ⅔ cup chopped Green & Black's Maya Gold chocolate with 1¼ cups chopped dark, 70%-cocoa chocolate, ⅓ cup golden syrup, and 1 stick unsalted butter. (In the absence of Maya Gold, spice up some dark chocolate with orange zest, nutmeg, and cinnamon.) Pick up the starting point from step 4, adding the drained prunes, ⅔ cup walnuts, and 8 oz graham crackers broken into small pieces. Coarsely chop 2 tbsp pistachios and sprinkle over the top before the chocolate sets. Once cooled, firm up in the fridge.

PINE NUT, PEEL, CURRANT & AMARETTI

Honey, I shrunk the chocolate tiffin cake. Cut into 1¼-in squares—this is to scale with the plates in my children's toy tea set—it also makes for neat little *petits fours* everyone is guaranteed to love, even if they can't quite pinpoint what they remind them of. The additional ingredients are chopped up small, so the set mixture is easily cut into pieces. In a departure from our starting point, this simply calls for chocolate and butter: There's no added sugar or egg, so the results are dense and deeply chocolatey. If you're making doll's-house portions for kids, you might want to sweeten it. For the after-dinner version, soak the currants in booze first. I use currants in this recipe, as opposed to raisins, only because they're smaller; if you want to show off, you could source some Vostizza currants, from Aigio in western Greece, singled out by *Larousse* as especially delicious, and awarded protected designation of origin status in 1993. First melt ⅔ cup chopped dark, 70%-cocoa chocolate with 1 stick unsalted butter. Stir to combine, then add the grated zests of 1 lemon and 1 orange. Stir in 3 tbsp toasted pine nuts, 1 tbsp each of finely diced candied ginger and mixed candied peel, and 4 amaretti cookies cut into pea-size pieces. Transfer to a 6-in square pan lined with plastic wrap or parchment paper and let set at room temperature before refrigerating and cutting.

RICE KRISPIES

A variation on chocolate tiffin cake that calls for cocoa powder, rather than bar chocolate. This was the first recipe I knew by heart.

The crispy crackolates called for 2 tbsp each butter, sugar, golden syrup, and unsweetened cocoa, and 1 cup Rice Krispies or cornflakes. You melted the first four ingredients in a pan, stirring the mixture together to make a fabulously fragrant chocolate syrup, then let it cool a bit before stirring in the cereal and joyfully dolloping spoonfuls into fluted paper cups. It strikes me now that you're making a form of chocolate by mixing cocoa powder, butter, and sugar, although of course good-quality dark chocolate is made with the pricier cocoa butter, and both conched and tempered to yield the correct texture and sheen; most has vanilla added to it, too, so you might want to add a few drops of vanilla extract to the crispy crackolate mix.

SPECULOOS ROCHER

The "Belgian" tiffin cake described on page [371] might be more indisputably Belgian were it made with speculoos, the more-ish little caramelized cookies I wish more British cafés would dish out with their espressos. The following, like an icebox cake, is smart enough to serve for dessert, as long as you use a good-quality milk chocolate, such as Lindt or Green & Black's. Melt ⅔ cup chopped milk chocolate with 1 tbsp unsalted butter and stir in ½ cup roasted and skinned ground hazelnuts, then set aside. In another bowl, melt ⅔ cup each chopped dark, 70%-cocoa chocolate and milk chocolate with 1¼ sticks unsalted butter; stir to combine and let cool. Beat 2 eggs with 2 tbsp sugar until thick and pale. Fold the egg mixture into the slightly cooled chocolate and butter mix. Form 4 chocolate truffles from the hazelnut mix and spread the rest over 4 speculoos cookies (Lotus Biscoff is the best known imported European brand), then place another cookie on top of each, to make sandwiches. Line an 8½ x 4½ x 2½-in (6-cup) loaf pan with plastic wrap and pour in a thin layer of the chocolate-butter-egg mixture. Pave it with plain speculoos. Cover with another layer of the chocolate-butter-egg mixture and lay the speculoos sandwiches on top. Cut the hazelnut chocolate truffles in half and slot four halves along each side, between the cookies and the edge of the pan. Cover with yet more chocolate-butter-egg mixture. Add a final layer of plain speculoos and use the remainder of the chocolate-butter-egg mixture to top it all off. Let the cake sit at room temperature for a few hours before putting it into the fridge to firm up, preferably overnight.

Flourless Chocolate Cake

The batter for this cake is wetter than that for chocolate tiffin cake and it is baked, but it's otherwise similarly made—by melting chocolate and butter together, then beating egg with sugar and folding it into the chocolate mixture. A few tweaks to the starting point and you'll have a brownie or fondant (hopefully with a runny center). If you are happy to work in weights, this cake is made with 7 oz of each ingredient.

For an 8-in round springform cake pan A B

INGREDIENTS

1½ cups chopped dark, 70%-cocoa chocolate B C
1 cup unsalted butter
Flavoring—optional D
4 large, 3 extra large, or 1 cup eggs
1 cup sugar E

1 Place the chocolate in a heatproof bowl with the butter. Set the bowl over—but not touching—barely simmering water in a pan. When the chocolate and butter have melted, remove and stir until you have a lovely shiny gloop. Add any liquid flavorings (such as vanilla or rum), if using. Set aside to cool a little.
   Alternatively, carefully (i.e. in short bursts, to avoid burning) melt the chocolate and butter separately in the microwave, then mix together.

2 In a clean, separate bowl, beat the eggs and sugar together until thick and pale. F

3 Using a large metal spoon, fold the chocolate and egg mixtures together to make a homogenous brown batter.
   This can take a while. Aim for exaggerated looping movements, keeping as much of the beaten-in air as possible.

4 Grease your springform pan generously and line its bottom with parchment paper. Transfer the batter to the pan and bake in the center of a 325°F oven.
   Most recipes recommend using a water bath. The resulting texture can be marginally better, but it's optional. If you do want to use one, wrap the base and sides of the cake pan with a large sheet of foil to make it watertight, then place it in a larger pan and pour in enough hot water to come halfway up the sides of the cake pan.

5 After about 25 minutes, check for doneness by inserting a skewer into the center of the cake.
If the skewer comes out wet, as it may well do, the cake isn't ready. When the skewer comes out slightly damp and with a few crumbs on it, the cake is probably perfect. If it comes out dry, you've overcooked the cake, but it will still be good to eat.

6 When it's done, remove from the oven and gently run a knife around the edge of the cake. A few minutes later, release the clip and carefully remove the springform ring. Let the cake cool, then transfer to the fridge to chill for at least a few hours before serving.
An overnight chill is ideal.

LEEWAY

A The cooking times given here are guidelines, as the size of pan used is open to negotiation (an inch or so either way). You'll need to check the cake while it's cooking to catch it at its ideal point.

B Some recipes (including Delia Smith's for Fallen Chocolate Soufflé) call for twice as much chocolate. Adjust the pan size accordingly.

C Don't be tempted to swap the dark chocolate for milk or white chocolate. For thoughts on using milk chocolate, see page 400.

D Add vanilla extract or other liquid flavorings to taste: up to 3 tbsp liquid is fine.

E About 1 cup sugar works well with dark, 70%-cocoa chocolate, but this amount can be reduced if you think it's too much. A less cocoa-rich chocolate may also require less sweetening. Use either granulated sugar or superfine, which just dissolves more quickly.

F Some recipes recommend beating only the egg yolks with the sugar. The whites are beaten to soft peaks separately, then folded into the mixture at the end of step 3.

AMARETTO

Add Amaretto to a flourless chocolate cake and you may find yourself transported to the Black Forest. The almond flavor is indistinguishable from the cherry flavors used in confectionery and soft drinks. If you're ever in Switzerland, don't leave without buying a supply of Sprüngli chocolate almonds to decorate your finished cake. How good can a chocolate-covered almond be, you might legitimately ask. Suffice to say I once spent an hour pricing flights to Zurich to replace the box a friend had brought back from vacation. (Sprüngli have shops in Swiss airports, so my plan was to stock up and get straight back on the next plane home.) Then I found out you can have them delivered by airmail. Make the cake while waiting for your parcel to arrive. Use 3 tbsp Amaretto for a cake made to our starting point, added at the end of step [1].

BROWNIES

Our starting point for flourless chocolate cake contains equal weights of chocolate, butter, and sugar, but you'll find recipes for the same sort of cake that call for 10–20 percent more sugar. Others might contain a little flour and cocoa. Incorporate all these variations into one and you'll have a fairly typical brownie recipe. Nuts and chocolate pieces are optional extras. The only major difference between the flourless chocolate cake and the brownie is the shape. A brownie must contain four right angles. Try any other sort of quadrilateral—or, heaven help us, a circle—and it won't taste the same. For an 8-in square pan (greased and lined), follow the starting point, using 1¼ cups sugar. At the end of step [3], fold in 6 tbsp sifted flour and ⅔ cup unsweetened cocoa powder, then ⅔ cup nuts and/or chocolate chips or chunks. Bake at 325°F, starting to check for doneness after 20 minutes, using the skewer test: If you want fudgy brownies and your skewer comes out with a bit of batter on it, you're laughing. As with flourless chocolate cake, if your brownie is on the wet side, a spell in the fridge will firm it up. Baked longer, it will be drier and more cakelike. Ice cream may be necessary.

FONDANT

Fondant: a flourless chocolate cake with flour in it. Simply add flour to our starting point and leave out half of the egg white. For example, to make 6 fondants, follow steps [1] to [3] of the starting point, melting together 1½ cups chopped dark chocolate and 1 cup unsalted butter.

Beat 1 cup sugar with 2 whole eggs, 2 yolks, and 1 tsp vanilla extract, then mix into the cooled chocolate. Fold in ¾ cup sifted flour. Divide the batter among 6 buttered and floured dariole molds, filling each one to about ½ in from the top, then bake at 400°F for about 11 minutes. Once cooked, immediately slide a knife around the edge of each fondant, upend the mold onto a plate, and, clamping mold and plate firmly together, give it one definitive shake to persuade the fondant to part from the metal. The fondants can be made up to a day in advance and chilled, but need to be brought to room temperature before cooking. Note that the cooking time assumes the oven has reached heat, and that the fondants are at room temperature; 11 minutes always works for me, but if you're making these for the first time, you may want to verify the cooking time by baking one before you commit to the rest.

GINGER

Death by Chocolate is a dessert you expect to find on a laminated menu, along with dirty-minded cocktails. Hardly suitable for a Michelin-starred restaurant like London's River Cafe. They call their indulgent flourless cake Chocolate Nemesis. As Sam Leith points out, Nemesis was the Greek goddess of retribution, ready to knock anyone guilty of hubris for a loop: It was she who lured Narcissus to his watery death. The difference, I suppose, is that "Death by Chocolate" merely presupposes your death, whereas "Chocolate Nemesis" strongly implies that you *deserve* to die. The self-loathing of the upmarket-restaurant-goer? Either way, in *River Cafe Green*, Ruth Rogers and the late Rose Gray give a recipe for a flourless chocolate ginger cake that omits the syrup required by the original Nemesis recipe. Chocolate Ellipsis? To adapt our starting point along similar lines, once the chocolate and butter are melted at step 1, stir in 3½ tbsp peeled and minced fresh ginger, along with any juice left on the board, 2 tbsp fine cornmeal, and 1 tbsp sifted unsweetened cocoa powder. Use ¾ cup sugar at step 2.

HAZELNUT

On a spring visit to Burgundy, we sat in the only bar in a drive-through village. It was tiny and wood-paneled, like the inside of a barrel. The other customers certainly looked as though they'd been marinating in brandy since 1936. We ordered two Paris goblets of chilled Aligoté, Chablis's rough-spoken young cousin, which can, as it happens, come as a refreshing change from too much good Chardonnay. Draining our glasses, we flipped a euro as to which of the village's two restaurants we'd patronize for lunch. Tails saw us sitting under lurid hanging baskets on a strip of sidewalk opposite the church. The hors d'oeuvres arrived: two warm salads of hazelnuts, green beans, and tiny potatoes in a sweet, piquant, grainy dressing so well-judged the chef could conceivably claim mustard as his second language. A roasted, corn-fed chicken leg came with matching golden mash. Three wedges of local cheese emptied our bottle of Gamay. Dessert was a slice of chocolate hazelnut cake. As she set down the plates, our matronly waitress gave a knowing smile and uttered the third-most-understood word in the world, after okay and iPhone. "Nutella." We drank coffee and more hazelnut in the form of a shot glass of homemade *noisette* liqueur, then lolled on a bench in the square like a couple of retired old men, sharing a Gitane for old times' sake and agreeing to buy the next Renault 4 that parked alongside, at whatever price the driver named. For a cake made to our starting point, fold in 1 cup roasted and skinned ground hazelnuts at the end of step [3].

LIME

Add orange zest to chocolate and it is instantly identifiable—unlike the zest of other citrus fruit, even when you add enough to blunt your Microplane. Natural oils, easily found online, are often a better bet. They are considerably more intense than common store-bought extracts, to be used by the drop rather than the teaspoon. Lime oil is particularly winning, especially with dark chocolate. Add to the melted chocolate and butter drop by drop, tasting as you go, and bearing in mind that the egg mixture will dilute the flavor to some degree. Serve the cake with a dollop of crème fraîche mixed with fresh lime zest, to restore some of the sourness and fruity top notes.

MILK CHOCOLATE

I made several flourless chocolate cakes to our starting point, using good-quality milk chocolate in place of dark, but they all had an unpleasant, rubbery texture. A bit of research revealed that flourless milk-chocolate cakes made by pastry chefs tend to include ground almonds to give a cakier texture. I tried a couple. To me, they tasted like chocolate cake made by someone who had run out of chocolate. At Tru in Chicago, they serve a flourless milk-chocolate cake with grilled-potato-skin ice cream and bacon-toffee sauce. According to its website, Tru offers an "extensive caviar program," which caught my attention, as only a few days earlier I'd walked past a bar called "Wine Workshop." I am now studying for my Bacon Sandwich Baccalaureate at a white-truffle retreat in Oregon. For flourless milk-chocolate cake, reduce the sugar and fat in the starting point—because, compared to its dark counterpart, milk chocolate contains more of both. Melt scant 1 cup chopped milk chocolate (minimum 32% cocoa solids) with 1 stick unsalted butter. Beat 2 whole eggs and 2 yolks with ⅓ cup packed light brown sugar and a pinch of salt. Fold the egg mixture into the cooled chocolate, then fold in 1¼ cups of ground almonds. Pour into an 8-in springform pan (greased and bottom-lined with parchment paper) and bake at 350°F. Start to check for doneness after 25 minutes.

MUSCOVADO

Muscovado sugar takes its name from the Spanish *mascabado*, meaning "unrefined." It's a raw sugar, rough as a bandit's chin, and hard to find in some countries. In the U.S., cooks are advised to approximate the flavor and texture of muscovado by mixing 1 tbsp unsulfured molasses with scant 1 cup packed brown sugar. According to the London-based chocolatier Paul A. Young, an inveterate muscovado fan, using it in place of refined white sugar is a simple way to add flavor to a chocolate dish. Try it in a flourless chocolate cake, made to our starting point, and note the intensity of flavor the following day: hints of black licorice minus the aniseed. Add the finely grated zest of a large orange, too, especially if you like dark, Oxford-style marmalades.

RASPBERRY & CASSIS

This variation started out as cranberry and port, a flavor combination used by Charbonnel & Walker in a favorite chocolate truffle of mine. I gave dried cranberries a luxurious soak in port and added them to the batter of a flourless chocolate cake. It wasn't particularly good. It needed fresh fruit to work, I felt, and since it wasn't the season for fresh cranberries, I turned to raspberries. By this stage I had run out of port, so I used a little crème de cassis instead. It wasn't clear if the results amounted to a chocolate cake with berries, or a berry-flavored cake with chocolate, but it didn't matter. Exclamation marks were dancing on my palate. Make as per the starting point, but using ¾ cup chopped chocolate, ½ cup unsalted butter, ½ cup sugar, and 2 large eggs. Add 2 tsp crème de cassis to the chocolate and butter at the end of step 1, then fold in a heaped ½ cup halved fresh raspberries at the end of step 3, and bake in a 7-in pan.

Sugar

CARAMEL

page 412

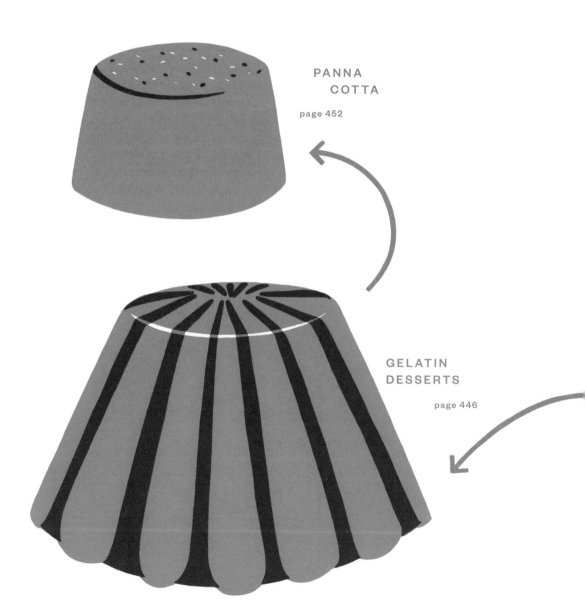

PANNA
COTTA

page 452

GELATIN
DESSERTS

page 446

FUDGE

page 418

MERINGUE

page 424

SYRUP
& CORDIAL

page 432

SORBET
& GRANITA

page 440

Received opinion has it that confectionery recipes must be followed to the letter. Start fiddling—fiddling being *Lateral Cooking*'s founding principle—and you risk catastrophe. This argument would be more persuasive were it not for the likelihood of catastrophe even when you do stick to the path. Making sweets is like riding a horse: The most experienced rider sometimes ends up in the ditch. Not even a triple-tested recipe from the most reliable source can comprehensively insure you against mishap. Months of trial and error in my own kitchen have left me in awe of the perfection on display at the confectionery counter. I therefore present the first two starting points on the continuum with a couple of pieces of advice.

C
A
R
A
M
E
L

First, accept that things may not work out as planned, and set aside some backup ingredients in case you feel like scrubbing your pan and starting over. Second, learn the old-fashioned way of testing the stages of cooked sugar. Even if you have a specialized sugar or digital thermometer, the time-honored test is indispensable when you're experimenting with ingredients and/or proportions. Pour ⅔ cup sugar and 2 tbsp hot water into a heavy-based pan. Ideally the pan should be pale on the inside, rather than black, so you can see the color of the syrup as it changes. Fill a light-colored cereal bowl with cold water and leave it within arm's reach of the stove, along with a teaspoon and a pastry brush in a mug of water. Half-fill a larger pan with cold water and keep it somewhere similarly close at hand, and stable—it will shortly be receiving your super-heated syrup pan, so you don't want it rocking or tipping over. Confectionery does tend to require this level of planning.

With everything in place, put the syrup pan over a low to medium heat and allow the sugar to dissolve in the water, giving it the odd stir. For confectionery and syrups, I prefer to use a silicone spoon, partly because they're far easier than wooden spoons to check for debris: tiny bits of food or detritus that sucrose crystals can mistake for fellow sucrose crystals and latch onto, causing unwelcome crystallization. Something as minuscule as a speck of dust can have this effect. Likewise, from time to time you may have to brush down the sides of the pan with a wet pastry brush, to prevent sucrose crystals from forming and attracting others.

Once the sugar has completely dissolved, turn the heat to medium and continue cooking the syrup without stirring. After about 2 minutes, remove ½ tsp and plunge it into your bowl of cold water. Leave it for a second or so, and if the syrup hasn't dissolved from the spoon entirely, pinch some between your thumb and finger. The first cooked-sugar stage is the "thread" stage (223–234°F), when the syrup forms a slack line. The thread strengthens as the water continues to evaporate from the sugar solution—take care not to touch it once it's beyond this point. By the time it has reached 239–241°F ("soft-ball" stage), it will form a squashable ball, not unlike the tacky stuff used to stick perfume samples to the pages of magazines. Arrest the heating here, and the mixture can be manipulated into an icing-like substance, used to make fudge or the white fondant in cream-filled candies. At 248°F—the "hard-ball" stage—the mixture will become firmer, yielding a toffee that's chewable the moment you put it in your mouth. Next comes the "soft-crack" stage, 270–290°F. This is the kind of challenging toffee generally considered to be a menace to your molars. As the temperature of the sugar mixture rises, the longer the resulting toffee will need to be in the mouth before becoming chewable. When the mixture becomes a strong thread that stiffens in the water and breaks without flexing, you've reached the "hard-crack" stage, 300–310°F, which means your sweet will be suckable. By this point, the water will have all but gone from the solution, and the sugar can get on with changing color, from lemon juice to straw, brick-red, and eventually brown.

Next comes black: the pan-shopping stage. To stop things from going too far, just as the mixture starts turning from brick to brown, remove the pan from the heat and plunge it into the larger pan of cold water. Alternatively, pour it into 6 molds, ready for crème caramel (page 474). Or, after removing the pan from the heat, carefully—it will splatter— stir in ½ cup warm cream (light or heavy). This will make a fabulous caramel sauce—enough, say, for 4 sundaes. As it cools, the sauce will firm up: After an hour you'll be able to spread it over the bottom layer of a 7- to 8-in sandwich cake. Or, instead of adding the cream, stir in ⅓ cup warm water and use it for Vietnamese fish and pork dishes (page 414) or for pouring over a vanilla panna cotta (page 411). Diluted this way it will keep in the fridge for months. Once it's cooled, taste a spoonful, noting the transformation from simple sweetness to toasty, perfumed complexity. Sugar may get a bad press, but watching its color and texture change with each step up in heat, it's hard not to marvel at the transformations its crystals harbor.

Replace the water with butter, cream, or milk, and the sugar mixture will pass through the same stages, but not necessarily at the same temperatures. Dairy solids will also create a more complex caramel flavor than cooked sugar alone. It was long believed that toffee would never take off in Japan, on account of its alien dairy smell. But in 1914, a philanthropist named Taichiro Morinaga, who had been trained in confectionery-making in the U.S., launched his milk caramels and put paid to that prejudice. Today toffees are a popular gift on Hokkaido, where honeysuckle, curry, and kelp flavors are available, not to mention Yubari King melon and "Genghis Khan." Yubari King is a variety of orange-fleshed melon that looks like a cross between a cantaloupe and a small helicopter and is said to bring luck, which is just as well considering how much they cost—about the same as a small helicopter. "Genghis Khan" is a grilled-mutton flavor based on a locally popular dish. Mutton toffees will strike you as marginally less strange if you've ever eaten Vietnamese pork or fish claypot dishes, cooked in a caramel made with fish sauce.

Cooked sugar lends a roasted flavor and a silky succulence to just about anything, which means that you need only be limited by your imagination when it comes to flavoring caramels. Well, that and your willingness to make repeated batches, to get your brilliant idea just right. In the case of toffee, aromatics are often added with the sugar and dairy at the outset. Once you've started cooking the mixture, and the caramelization is under way, it will be too hot to taste; by the time the mixture cools, it will be too late to make any alterations. Fudge is a little easier to play with, because extracts and nuts are generally added at the end, after the mixture has cooled a little. Try splitting an unflavored batch and experimenting with a few variations on theme— or simply make a few entirely different flavors.

F   Like penicillin and Play-Doh, fudge is one of those accidental
U   discoveries, made when a batch of toffee went awry. As I've noted,
D   it's easy to get toffee wrong, although to end up with fudge you
G   have to get it wrong in the right way. Fudge was originally the
E   name given to an American confection of sugar, dairy, and chocolate.
There was a late-nineteenth-century craze for it in women's colleges like Vassar, Wellesley, and Smith, where the students cooked it in chafing dishes. In *College Girls*, Lynn Peril suggests that the difficulty of making confectionery with limited equipment was half the point. Making rarebit was easy: no kudos. Fudgemaking, on the other hand, "required luck as well as kitchen finesse." Girls formed fudge cliques and swapped tips and tricks. There were times, testing fudge recipes, when I wondered if it might be easier to apply to Vassar and insinuate myself into a clique. I'm still waiting to hear—but in the meantime, all that trial and error helped elucidate the basic, three-stage process.

Which proceeds like this: 1) dissolve the sugar in milk or cream over heat; 2) cook the resulting dairy syrup to the soft-ball stage; and 3) let it cool a bit, then beat, fast, to create much smaller crystals than the sugar you started out with. It's easy to err. Jump to the cooking stage before the sugar is properly dissolved and you'll end up with crunchy fudge, which is good for nothing but the trash. Take note: *properly* dissolved. It's also quite possible to burn the mixture while heating it to the soft-ball stage. Beat too soon, too late, or too much and the crystals will be the wrong size. Undershoot the temperature and the fudge won't set. Overshoot by a few degrees and your mixture will become caramel. Just as fudge can be caramel gone wrong, caramel can be mutant fudge, because they can both be made with the same ingredients in the same proportions.

I stress *can* be made with the same ingredients, as for our purposes the ingredients are a little different. The toffee starting point calls for equal weights of sugar, syrup, butter, and cream. The fudge calls for (more or less) equal weights of sugar and cream with a little butter and syrup added. You can make caramel and fudge with just granulated sugar, but the syrup performs the useful task of suppressing crystallization, both during cooking and once the toffees are made. In the case of fudge, only a small amount of syrup is used, so as not to prevent the crucial formation of tiny crystals during the final stirring stage; crystallization is what makes fudge fudge.

M E R I N G U E If you've ever made Italian meringue, you'll know that, as with fudge, you start by cooking the sugar to soft-ball stage. The syrup is then beaten into the stiff egg whites to make a robust froth, used to top pies and desserts, or to add sweetness and structure to mousses and icings, or folded through a sorbet base. For French meringue, the most commonly made variety in domestic kitchens, plain sugar (often superfine sugar) is used rather than syrup. The cognoscenti will tell you that they whisk their French meringue by hand. Cheffy bravado, you might think, but whisking it the hard way does make it easier to tell when your foam is *à point*, whereas, with an electric mixer, you can easily beat past the sweet spot without noticing. That said, Yotam Ottolenghi and Sami Tamimi, no slouches in the meringues department, recommend using a stand mixer for the billowing sort that grace their windows.

Beaten by hand or machine, meringue, like its confectionery cousins, may be simple, but it is by no means foolproof. Meringue foam balks at too much interference, and, as anyone who has read a meringue recipe knows, the feeblest rumor of fat or grease on your bowl or beater will prevent peaks from forming. It's worth committing the three different stages of peak to memory: a soft peak will flop over into itself; firm peaks will tend downward like the necks of sorrowful anteaters; and a stiff peak will stand erect as a freshly gelled mohawk.

Once the meringue mixture is stiff, you can get away with folding in ground nuts, ground spices, or a little alcohol-based extract, but note that adding oil-based flavorings can send your egg whites back to an irreparably liquid state. Coloring requires caution for the same reason. The Meringue Girls, a bakery based in Broadway Market in East London, resorts to topical application to make their pretty, candy-striped confections, applying lines of color gel to the inside of their pastry bags before the meringue is added.

An alternative, slightly less common means of flavoring or coloring meringue is to add egg-white powder to a fruit purée or juice, then beat it with sugar. Try the strawberry-based version on page 430 and prepare to emit unguarded, ecstatic noises. This kind of meringue can be used for piping onto pies and desserts. It can also be made into nests, although they'll be on the chewy side—the water content mitigates against crispness. Another flavoring option is to replace the sugar with honey, heated to soft-ball stage, then added to beaten egg whites as per the Italian method. You might, of course, consider flavoring your own sugar syrups for Italian meringue, which brings us to the next starting point on the continuum.

Syrup is a cakewalk after caramel, fudge, and meringue. Mix equal amounts of sugar and boiling water, stir, and that's it. Simple syrup, otherwise known as "stock syrup," is surprisingly useful, partly because the flavoring options are limitless. For a syrup made with 1 cup of each ingredient, add 5 tbsp rum once the sugar has dissolved, and you'll have the best part of a classic rum baba (page 66); the coarse, open texture of a baba invites a proper drenching without succumbing to sogginess. In "Consider the Lobster," his classic account of the Maine Lobster Festival, David Foster Wallace points out that few people would go weak at the knees for lobster were it not swimming in melted butter. Similarly, the baba is a primarily a vehicle for alcoholic sugar syrup. Other spirits were used originally, but it was rum that made the dessert a hit. My guess is that rum, made with cane juice and often enhanced with cooked sugar, makes a syrup that tastes rather like caramel, and is thus both reassuringly familiar and pleasingly transgressive. Rum makes a good base for all sorts of syrupy flavor combinations. I like the unusual pairing of rum and turmeric suggested in *Spirit House: Thai Cooking* by Annette Fear and Helen Brierty. Make a simple syrup with ½ cup each of crushed light and dark palm sugar, 1 tsp salt, 1 tbsp peeled and minced fresh turmeric, 7 tbsp water, 9 tbsp coconut milk, and 2 tbsp rum. Pour over coconut and palm sugar crêpes: You'll find a pandan-infused version of these on page 127.

Honey is nature's simple syrup, and before sugar was readily available it was used to elevate relatively plain items like breads and pancakes to the status of a treat. Where honey was unavailable, or unaffordable, date syrup was used as a sweetener, or the juice of other fruit boiled down to syrupy sweetness and consistency: Figs, pomegranates, carob pods, and mulberries were, and still are, made into molasses in Turkey, Syria, and Lebanon; and in Italy, grapes were used to make *mosto cotto* ("cooked must") or *sapa*. Sugar, when it did become widely available, was prized for its clarity and neutrality of flavor: Hard to imagine what a revelation this would have been. Conjure the flavor of a toddy and you'll recall what a different character lemon takes on when sweetened with honey rather than sugar; even the mildest honey has a complexity and bitterness to it. Sugar-sweetened, the pure, floral flavor of lemon is exposed—try the lemon syrup on page 435 and see for yourself.

Sugar syrup can be used for preserving fruit, to make Italian meringue, to flavor cakes and sweets, to glaze baked goods, or to create a unifying base for fruit salad. Simple syrup also lends sweetness and body to cocktails. There has, in recent years, been something of a revival in custom-made, flavored syrups for both alcoholic and nonalcoholic drinks, the latter an echo of the late-nineteenth-century craze for "nerve tonics" and other carbonated drinks. Some, like Coca-Cola, were so successful that the manufacturers began selling their syrup for franchisees to dilute with fizzy water. Many of these drinks were based on old remedies; others claimed new benefits. Dr. Pepper, for example, served not only as a cure for exhaustion, but also for aging, smoking, and alcoholism, so long as you drank it three times a day. A ginger ale called Clicquot Club was claimed to have "brain-cleaning" properties. Those gullible Edwardians, I thought, as I sipped on a can of Red Bull, and waited for my wings to sprout.

S O R B E T Flavored syrups can also be used to make gelatin desserts, granitas, and sorbets. Sorbet shares its etymology with the Persian *shabat*, meaning "syrup." The science of ices is complex, but sorbets can be easy to improvise—as easy, for example, as mixing 2 cups of sweet fruit purée with 1 cup of simple syrup, plus an optional teaspoon of lemon juice for vibrancy. The mix is then frozen. For the smoothest texture, use an ice-cream machine. In the absence of a machine, pour the mix into a rectangular Tupperware or other freezerproof container to a depth of about 1½ in, put it in the freezer, and return every half-hour or so to break up the crystals with a fork.

More fastidious sorbetmakers might try to calculate the proportion of sugar in the mix in order to achieve the textural ideal. Sugar will lower the mixture's freezing point; too much will leave you with an unscoopable mush. Quite possibly a delicious unscoopable mush, but it's a confident host that serves Slush Puppies to any guests over the age of twelve. The ideal sugar content will be roughly 20–30 percent of the total weight of the mixture. This is easy to calculate in the case of non-sweet liquids, but a little harder with fruit, where you have to account for its own sugar content. A Brix refractometer, which measures the sugar content in any given liquid, and costs no more than half a dozen cartons of fancy-brand sorbet, will solve the problem. The lo-fi means to the same end is to use a clean, unbroken, raw egg. Float it in your sorbet mix, and if a little circle of egg protrudes from the surface, the mixture should be good to freeze. (If the egg sinks, add more sugar syrup; if too much of the egg protrudes from the surface, add more purée/water/cold coffee/whatever flavor base you're using.) I have made excellent lemon sorbet using this method, but question its reliability with thicker liquids like fibrous fruit purées. Nonetheless, success seems to have wide parameters. In the summer, when there's an abundance of cheap, ripe fruits, I often just measure out a purée and mix it with half its volume in sugar syrup. I don't recall ever making a sorbet I was unhappy with.

Note that adding a dash of booze can lower the mixture's freezing point and help make the sorbet smoother. The neutral flavor and color of vodka make it a popular choice, but you might consider treating the alcoholic ingredient as an extra layer of flavor, as in Campari with grapefruit, hard cider with apple, or Riesling with peach. As with sugar, an excess of alcohol will prevent the mixture from freezing properly. Astute readers will have worked out that alcohol can be used in place of some of the sugar, if you're looking to cut down on the latter. It might just take a bit of trial and error to find the right balance.

Fortunately, if you're not happy with the texture of your sorbet or granita, you can always let it melt, make adjustments, and refreeze.

G For those keen to limit their sugar consumption, granita is the
R better bet. Its crunchier texture is a result of its lower sugar content.
A A very decent granita can be made with notably unsweet liquids
N like grapefruit juice or strong coffee, and as little as 10 percent
I of the liquid weight in sugar. Its bitter edge makes coffee granita
T especially refreshing. In Sicily, where the heat can be oppressive
A even early on a summer morning, coffee granita is often served
for breakfast, decanted into a pretty glass with a brioche on the side, or piled into the bun to make an icy sandwich.

G Gelatin desserts are like sorbet, but easier. Once you've created
E a sweet base with juice or purée you're most of the way there. All
L that remains is to determine the right amount of gelatin to set it to
A a perfect wobble. Other than taking care to read the instructions on
T the package—different brands and grades will have their own setting
I strengths—there isn't a lot that can go wrong. To discover the
N simplicity of making a molded dessert with leaf gelatin is to wonder
how fruit gelatin mixes became so popular. I suppose good-quality leaf gelatin wasn't always as widely available as it is today. My mother only ever bought the powdered type, which she once used to make Turkish Delight. The smell that lingered in the kitchen was less Eastern promise than porcine threat, like an enraged pig in a rose garden. To this day, whenever I hydrate gelatin granules I suppress a shudder.

In truth, my sister and I had a vested interest in our mother *not* mastering the use of gelatin. For what seemed like years we saved tokens from packages of Chivers fruit gelatin mix to earn a tank of goldfish. At long last we sent off the tokens and received our fish a few weeks later by Royal Mail. In a matter of days our favorite, Georgie Best, had died. We scooped him from the surface and gave him a decent burial in the garden. Over the coming weeks the other four gave up the ghost, one by one, until we lost interest and Mum was left to flush the last one down the loo. The experience was not, however, for nothing. My sister and I learned an important lesson: What we really wanted was a dog. And no more packaged fruit gelatin for a long, long time.

In retrospect the promotion seemed like a pretty odd idea. What was the connection between gelatin and goldfish? A tenuous reference, maybe, to the days when the dried swim-bladders of sturgeon and cod were used to make isinglass, a type of gelatin popular in the nineteenth century? Marie-Antoine Carême specified isinglass for his red Champagne and orange gelatin layered with almond blancmange, served in scooped-out whole oranges cut into segments to showcase the stripes. Eventually isinglass was replaced by cheaper alternatives, including leaf gelatin, which Bompas & Parr, contemporary masters of gelatin desserts, consider the finest setting agent available. Gelatin is comprised of long, thin strands of protein which, when hydrated and heated, become a tangled mass that sets as it cools, holding in suspension any liquid it is added to; heat it and it will dissolve again. As gelatin is derived from animal parts, some cooks prefer vegetarian alternatives like agar agar and carrageen, both derived from seaweed. However, I think they yield an inferior wobble, and a gelatin dessert without a good wobble is like a clown without a honk in his horn.

The jolliness of a gelatin mold is valued in even the finest dining rooms, although curiously often as gelatin in its savory form. The Dublin-based French chef Patrick Guilbaud riffs on oyster stout by serving a Carlingford oyster in a stout aspic with a pearl made of oyster cream. Joël Robuchon serves a crab pâté under a layer of fennel aspic, topped with caviar and presented in a caviar can. Heston Blumenthal's exquisite "meat fruit" is a hyperreal mock-up of a tangerine, its peel fashioned from orange gelatin, stippled for verisimilitude, concealing an interior of smooth chicken liver parfait. A deliciously deadpan joke.

P If you prefer your gelatin less droll, make a panna cotta. Somehow
A its opacity renders the wobble more dignified. It also benefits from
N an outstanding effort-reward ratio: A delicious panna cotta can be
N made in 5 minutes, then left to set. There are more time-consuming
A approaches—rather than just heating the cream, some recipes
     require it to be cooked, as the name panna cotta suggests. The River
C Cafe's version involves boiling heavy cream, then mixing it with
O whole milk and whipped heavy cream. Nearly all recipes call for
T some milk, to tamp down the cream's richness. Given how quick they
T are to make, it's worth fiddling with your panna cotta proportions
A until you have the recipe just as you like it. Start with 50/50 milk and
cream, before upping one or the other to taste. Adjust the sweetness likewise, then work on the quantities of gelatin. Stick to one brand, and expect that you may find yourself cutting leaves into quarters. What constitutes the right amount will depend on whether you plan to unmold the dessert, in which case it will need the strength to support its own weight, not slump like a defeated sumo wrestler. If, on the other hand, you plan to serve it in individual glasses, less gelatin could be used. In either case, the set should put up a barely detectable resistance to the spoon, yielding the moment it enters the mouth.

As for flavorings, if your cream is especially good, you may prefer to add none at all. For the starting point I have used grappa, which is a traditional flavoring, and is simply added to the mixture once the gelatin has been added to the cream. Panna cotta is pretty open to experimentation. Take inspiration from cocktails and desserts, or classic custards or ice creams. Vanilla in bean form can be hard to beat, even if, when the panna cotta is unmolded, the speckled top created by the seeds looks a little like newsprint—not very pretty. My solution is to pour over the cooled, glossy brown sauce made by diluting a caramel, as outlined on page 405; the result is like a crème caramel, but creamier.

Caramel

This starting point applies both to soft, chewable caramel and the hard sort that has to be sucked or, if your teeth are up to it, crunched. If you use kitchen scales, caramel ingredients are easily memorized: equal weights of sugar, syrup (golden or corn), milk or cream, and butter. Stir in any nuts or small pieces of dried fruit at the end of step [4], once the pan is submerged in cold water. *Be really careful with the hot mixture—don't let it come into contact with your skin and, however good it smells, do not be tempted to taste it until it has cooled.*

For an 8-in square pan or silicone mold, to make 25 toffees [A]

INGREDIENTS
1 cup sugar [B]
1 cup golden syrup or light corn syrup [C] [D]
1 cup unsalted butter [E]
1 cup cream [E] [F]
1–2 tsp vanilla extract—optional [G]
Pinch of salt or ½ tsp sea salt for salted caramel—optional [G]

[1] Use a silicone mold as is, or line a pan with parchment paper and lightly oil it. Place a cereal bowl of cold water and a few teaspoons beside the stove if you plan to test the sugar-cooking stage in the traditional way, as outlined on pages [404-5]. Pour about an inch of cold water into a large pan and leave it somewhere safe and easily accessible.
You'll be plunging your hot caramel pan into this large pan to stop the cooking, so make sure it fits. Choose a caramel pan big enough for the ingredients to bubble up—bank on the caramel tripling its starting size.

[2] Put the sugar, syrup, butter, and cream into your chosen pan, preferably one with a heavy base, and place over a medium heat. Stir frequently, with a silicone or wooden spoon, to melt the sugar and butter completely.
The thinner the base of your pan, the more assiduous you'll need to be with the stirring. If the mixture separates, stir it vigorously. If this doesn't bring it together, add a few tablespoons of hot water, carefully— it will splatter—and stir again.

[3] Bring the mix to a boil. Stir constantly if you like, but strictly it's only necessary to stir every now and then, to prevent scorching, or before you take the temperature of your caramel.

The caramel can now be cooked to the texture of your choice: Cook to 248–264°F (hard-ball stage) for a soft caramel; cook to 270–290°F for a firm, but eventually chewable caramel that might stick to your teeth a bit; cook to 300–310°F (hard-crack stage) for a rock-hard sucking caramel—see page [405] for further elaboration.

4   Remove from the heat as soon as the caramel reaches the desired temperature and plunge the caramel pan into the larger pan of cold water you prepared earlier.
Small quantities of flavorings can be added here. However, if you're working toward the bottom end of the temperature range, be aware that too much cold liquid may send your caramel backward to a softer stage. To prevent this, consider pre-warming your flavorings.

5   Pour into the prepared mold or pan and let set. For pieces of a regular size, score the surface when the mixture has cooled enough to hold a line, but not cooled so much that you can't score it at all.
Start trying after 10 minutes. Hard toffee can be hammered into pieces if you don't mind irregular sizes. Caramel weeps in the open air, which is why it's common to wrap it tightly (e.g. in wax paper) or enrobe it in chocolate. Even so, most toffee will begin to soften and crystallize after a few days.

LEEWAY

A   An 8-in square pan gives an ideal depth of caramel for cutting into cubes or rectangles. Use half the quantities for a 6-in square pan—a good size for flavor-testing.
B   Brown sugar in place of white will give the caramel a more pronounced flavor.
C   Use a higher proportion of sugar to syrup—say 1½ cups sugar to ⅓ cup syrup—or even all sugar. Note, however, that a little syrup helps prevent crystallization during cooking, and once the toffee is made.
D   Replace the syrup with liquid glucose.
E   Use half the amounts of butter and cream. Or use only butter or only cream. The temperature ranges given in the method can still be used as a guide. It's worth noting that the overall fat content of the mixture will have an effect on the consistency of the finished caramel: The higher the fat content, the softer the caramel will set.
F   Use the same amount of condensed milk in place of the cream. It'll be quicker, as it's already had the water cooked out of it—the reason many manufacturers use it. On the other hand, it will need more stirring, as condensed milk is very sugary and more prone to burning.
G   A great deal of flavor comes from the caramelization of the ingredients, so you don't need any extra flavoring at all. Nonetheless, you can stir in 1–2 tsp vanilla extract, the seeds of a vanilla bean, or a little salt at the end of step 4.

CHOCOLATE

Chocolate toffee. What's not to like? First of all, people saying "what's not to like?" Second, I reckon the ingredients are better left separate. It's a fine judgment, and you may well disagree. Follow the starting point, adding ⅓–⅔ cup chopped chocolate at step 2. The results are pretty wonderful, but to my palate a toffee enrobed in chocolate, whether from Artisan du Chocolat, or in the more demotic form of a Rolo, has the edge. The point where your teeth have broken the crisp chocolate shell and are sinking into the soft, sweet-salty interior, which tastes almost warm by comparison, is surely one of the pinnacles of confectionery consumption, if not human experience. On a practical note, the chocolate coating also preserves the caramel and stops it from weeping—so chocolate-covered toffees will, in theory, outlast their chocolate-flavored counterparts.

FISH SAUCE, GINGER & GARLIC

In Vietnam, the taste for salted caramel is more than a passing trend; it's the cornerstone of a popular sauce served with pork or fish. *Thit kho to* or *ca kho to* is usually cooked in a clay pot, although a lidded saucepan will do, as long as your ingredients fit snugly into it. The salt comes in the form of fish sauce, and the resulting tastes are no less balanced for their extremity. There are many regional variations, and you might try a different one every night and not tire of it for weeks. Some call for a mix of fish sauce and soy sauce, others specify fish sauce and rice vinegar. Catfish is the usual choice, the cooking time 30–40 minutes. I apply the same flavor principle to a dish that's considerably quicker to prepare. Make a simple mixture of caramel plus warm water, as outlined on pages 404-5, remembering that any excess will keep in the fridge for months. Slice the white parts of 3 scallions. Slice the green parts and set them aside for a garnish. Put a little bland oil into a saucepan that will hold 2 salmon fillets snugly and place over a medium heat. Cook the scallion whites, 1 minced garlic clove, and 1 tbsp minced fresh ginger until their fragrance tickles your nose. Add the seasoned fish, skin-side down, and fry for 2 minutes. Turn the fish, add 2 tbsp caramel, 1 tbsp fish sauce, and 2 tsp rice vinegar. Apply the lid. The fish will be ready in about 5 minutes. Serve on white rice, garnished with slivers of scallion greens and lots of freshly ground black pepper.

LEMON

Acidic ingredients like lemon juice, vinegar, or cream of tartar were once added to toffee to prevent the recrystallization of the sugar as it cooked. These days, sugar syrups like golden syrup, liquid glucose, or corn syrup are more commonly added for that purpose. Lemons were also used to flavor the toffee, either in essence form (6 drops to 2½ cups sugar) or as grated zest. The Victorian writer Eliza Acton adds the grated zest of 1 lemon to her simple toffee mixture of 2 cups packed brown sugar and 6½ tbsp butter (noting that more butter is normally used). Rather than using a grater, I employed the Victorian zesting method, rubbing the skin of 2 unwaxed lemons with 12 sugar cubes. The roughness of the sugar teases the oil from the tiny pores in the peel, and you're not left with any flecks of zest to spoil the smoothness of the toffee. Follow our starting point, adding ¾ cup sugar to the lemon-infused sugar cubes. The resulting lemon flavor is wonderfully floral, far brighter and more complex than from bottled lemon essence, which degrades quickly. Chunkily chopped, blanched almonds were once mixed into a popular, butter-free lemon toffee called hardbake. A chewier, Starburst-style of lemon sweet can be made with sugar, syrup, and a little butter, cooked to a lower heat—around 244°F. Confectionery flavoring, color, and a spike of citric acid will lend it the requisite Easter-chick yellow and juicy tartness.

MINT JULEP

One Sunday I pounded a handful of mint leaves into a paste, then stirred it into a tablespoon of warmed bourbon. Once my batch of toffee had reached its destination heat, I added the mint-whiskey concoction and stirred. The next day I was sitting in a railroad-station café with a sensible, middle-aged colleague. Our train was delayed. I remembered I had some homemade toffees in my handbag. "Fancy one?" I said. "They're mint julep flavor." "Mint what?" she mumbled, toffee in mouth. "Julep. It's a cocktail made with bourbon and sugar syrup and fresh mint. They drink them in the American South." There was still no sign of the train. We were on our third round of toffees and I was still going on about the cocktail. I had moved on to its association with the Kentucky Derby, where mint julep is the traditional drink, when a revival in my colleague's formerly drifting interest made me wonder if she was experiencing some form of sugar rush. It turned out she was into horses—that is, betting on them. The delay on the departures display grew like a reluctantly confessed betrayal. My colleague swiped the last toffee and made for the slot machine in the corner. She stuck a pound in it. I watched as she jabbed at the lights. In short order a few coins rattled into the tray, followed by a few more, then a deluge. We had just finished counting the winnings when I looked up and realized we had missed our train. Scooping the coins into a plastic bag, my colleague led me out of the station and into a minicab that smelled of incompletely deodorized smoke. "Take us to the best cocktail bar in town," she said. We were in Portsmouth, but still.

PEANUT BRITTLE

A good place to start for the confectionery novice. (Butter toffees and creamy fudge, by contrast, need extra care, as their dairy content makes them prone to burning during their long cook at a high temperature.) Roast 1¼ cups blanched peanuts until they are golden and set aside. In a saucepan over a medium heat, bring 1 cup sugar, ⅓ cup golden syrup or light corn syrup, and ¼ cup water to a boil, then apply the lid. Leave for 4–5 minutes. (Putting on the lid removes the need to brush down the sides of the pan during the early sugar-dissolving stage.) Uncover and cook to the soft-ball stage (239–241°F). Add the peanuts. Continue to cook, stirring to prevent the mixture from sticking and burning, and brushing down the sides of the pan with a wet brush if necessary, until the caramel starts to turn brick-red, or reaches 320°F. Immediately remove from the heat and sprinkle over ¼ tsp fine salt. Stir thoroughly. If you like, add a few tablespoons unsalted butter with the salt; as with shortbread and shortcrust pastry, this will shorten the texture. Pour into an 8- to 9-in square silicone mold or oiled pan and let cool.

PRALINE

Praline is legion. There are pralines that are single nuts coated in rough sugar, like the rose kind mentioned on page 64. There's praline that is essentially fudge, such as the pecan version on page 422. Finally, there's a praline that's a variation on the peanut brittle above, made using toasted almonds or hazelnuts. Make a caramel with just ⅔ cup sugar and 2 tbsp water, as per the instructions on page 404. When it has turned dark gold, add 1–1½ cups toasted and skinned nuts. Stir to ensure the nuts are well coated, then scrape the mixture out onto a silicone mat or a lightly oiled baking sheet and flatten to a depth of one nut. When the mixture has cooled and set hard, grind it to a fine powder; note that if you grind for too long, the natural oils in the nut will turn the mixture into praline paste. Keep any excess powder in the freezer, wrapped, where you won't be tempted to put a licked finger in it, like it's some kind of Dip-n-Lik candy. Praline powder can be used in ice cream, to decorate cakes, or mixed into buttercream. Praline paste is added to crème pâtissière to make *crème pralinée*, which is used to stuff the choux puffs for Paris-Brest, or to flavor ice cream. With the addition of egg white, *crème pralinée* can be made into praline soufflés.

SALTED CARAMEL SAUCE

Make the simple caramel sauce outlined on pages 404-5, using ⅔ cup sugar, 2 tbsp water, and ½ cup cream. The flavor of the brick-red caramel goes a long way, and you can get away with adding at least another ½ cup cream without risking excessive thinness of taste or texture. A cheat's variation is to melt together 3 tbsp each dark brown sugar, butter, and corn syrup, then gradually stir in ⅔ cup heavy cream. No need to give it a long cook: The brown sugar will furnish the flavor. Whichever sauce you make, once the mixture is cool enough, stir in sea salt to taste, pinch by pinch. The non-cheat version has a complex caramel flavor with a pleasing bitter streak. The cheat version is sweeter, but spicier. You might add a splash of Calvados or bourbon to either. While *light* brown sugar will do in place of dark, the results will lack the depth of flavor to qualify as caramel sauce. Add some vanilla and a few pinches of salt and call it butterscotch. Most caramel sauces will thicken as they cool, and so might need warming up to become pourable again.

TREACLE

At Christmastime in North Wales it was traditional to gather for a *noson gyflaith*, an evening of games, stories, and toffeemaking. The toffee in question would be made with butter, sugar, treacle (which is very like molasses), and spices—what the English would call treacle toffee. The equivalent Scottish terms are as ornery as the toffee itself: "clack," "claggum," "treacle gundy," or "teasing candy." Another Scots version includes baking soda, creating a dark variation on honeycomb candy. For treacle toffee, use 1 cup packed brown sugar, ½ cup each of treacle (or molasses) and golden or corn syrup, 1 cup water, 1 cup butter, and ¼ tsp cream of tartar. Follow the starting-point method, heating the caramel to 300–310°F.

Fudge

Fudge is an exercise in sugar-crystal management. Success tastes like a caramelized butter engorged with confectioners' sugar. It has anything between a mildly elastic and a crumbly texture. As with caramel, the starting point for fudge calls for more or less equal amounts of sugar and dairy. For vanilla flavor, add the contents of a bean at the outset of step [3], or 2 tsp extract at step [5]. Raisins, chopped nuts, etc. can be added at step [5], once you've beaten the mix for a few minutes. *Be really careful with the hot mixture— don't let it come into contact with your skin and, however good it smells, do not be tempted to taste it until it has cooled.*

For a 7-in square silicone mold or pan [A]

INGREDIENTS
2 cups sugar [B]
1½ cups heavy cream [C] [D] [E]
4 tbsp butter
1 tbsp golden syrup or light corn syrup [F] [G]
Pinch of salt

1 Use a silicone mold as is, or prepare a pan by lining it with parchment paper and lightly oiling it. Place a cereal bowl of cold water and a few teaspoons beside the stove if you plan to test the sugar-cooking stage in the traditional way, as outlined on pages [404-5].

2 Find a robust pan deep enough to hold the ingredients as they bubble up.
   Remember that cream rises when it boils. For these amounts, a heavy-based 3-quart saucepan is good. (As a rule, the mix will triple in height.)

3 Put all the ingredients into the pan. Set over a moderate heat, stirring all the while, until the sugar has dissolved and the butter has melted.
   Be especially sure that the sugar has all dissolved before moving on. Brush down the sides of the pan with a wet pastry brush if you see crystals forming. Left to their own devices, these tiny clusters will attract others and ruin your fudge mix.

4 Still over a moderate heat, bring the mixture to a boil, stirring regularly to prevent the bottom from scorching, and keep cooking until it reaches the soft-ball stage (239–241°F). Remove the pan from the heat.

5   Leave for about 15 minutes, then beat until the mixture thickens
    and turns matte, but is still pourable. Use a wooden spoon if
    you're doing this by hand.

    The cooling minimizes the opportunity for large seed crystals to develop.
    Some recipes suggest you start beating at a certain temperature. As
    these can range from 98–212°F, however, I find it easier to go by time.
    Likewise, opinions vary widely as to how long to beat for—some recipes
    suggest a long time, but I generally beat just until the mix starts to
    thicken and lose its shine. By hand, this should take about 5–7 minutes
    for this quantity. It's hard work, but gratifying with it. With an electric
    mixer it'll be a matter of a few minutes.

6   Pour into the silicone mold or prepared pan and leave to set
    at room temperature. ᴴ

7   Cut into pieces and store in an airtight container, preferably
    wrapped in parchment paper. The fudge will keep for at
    least 3 weeks.

LEEWAY

A   Make a batch of fudge any smaller than this and it will
    be liable to burn. Even if it doesn't, there will be too little
    to beat at step 5.

B   Brown sugar often improves the flavor, especially as fudge
    is removed from the heat before much caramel flavor
    has had a chance to develop.

C   Use the same quantity of light cream or whole milk;
    the less fat, the icier the texture.

D   Reduce the cream to as little as scant 1 cup.

E   Some recipes stipulate condensed milk. A recipe by
    condensed-milk manufacturer Carnation calls for a 14-oz
    can of condensed milk, ⅔ cup milk, 2 cups demerara
    sugar, and ½ cup butter, made to the method here, other
    than specifying 244°F as the target temperature, and
    suggesting you beat the mixture immediately after
    removing it from the heat.

F   Golden syrup (or light corn syrup) suppresses unwelcome
    crystallization, but in this small quantity not so much as
    to hinder the crystallization required at step 5.

G   Golden syrup can be omitted. But see F above.

H   If your fudge won't set, it'll be because it wasn't brought to
    a high enough temperature at step 4. Break it into bits and
    put in a pan with a little water, then slowly dissolve over
    a moderate heat and try again. If the finished fudge has
    a crystalline texture, it's beyond repair.

BEAN

In Japan, a sweetened red-bean paste, *anko*, is made with azuki beans and sugar. Earthy in flavor, it turns up in all types of sweetmeats, classic items like pancakes and stuffed rice balls, and, less traditionally, in ice cream. Its closest relative in the West might be the mixture of peanut and sugar called *dulce de cacahuate* (page ²⁸³). Barfi, the fudge-like Indian sweet, comes in many forms, one of the most popular being made with chickpea flour, butter, and sugar. Perhaps unfair of Ken Albala, then, to give fudge the "runner's-up award for the most deranged use of beans." Sugar, corn syrup, milk, salt, cocoa powder, and bean purée are brought to soft-ball stage, and butter added, before the mixture is left to cool. Peanut butter and vanilla are then stirred in, and the whole poured into a pan to set. Albala's no. 1 most deranged use of beans is a fruitcake enhanced with mashed pinto beans. Fans of beet and chocolate cake: This is your next crazy.

BUFFALO OR YAK MILK

If the spirit of the animal is in its milk, buffalo are far gentler than their extravagant horns and stampeding habit suggest. *Mozzarella di bufala*, that mellow daydream-bubble among cheeses, is made from it, as is proper Indian paneer. Both owe their bright whiteness to the absence of carotenoids that give milk from grass-fed cows its yellow tinge. (Buffalo, sheep, and goats convert the carotene into vitamin A.) Buffalo milk has twice the fat content of cow's milk, which makes it rich and flavorsome. Aside from mozzarella, Laverstoke Park in Hampshire, England, uses its own buffalo milk to make award-winning Gouda- and Brie-style cheeses. They have been known to make fudge from it, too. In Nepal, Sherpas slowly cook down yak milk to make a toffee called *korani*. To my shame, Sherpa sweetmeats represent a lacuna in my cookbook collection, so I can't pass on any details, but from what I understand it's not dissimilar to *dulce de leche*. A boon on your granola bar when you're halfway up Everest.

CHOCOLATE

The word "fudge," as applied to confectionery, dates from late nineteenth-century America, but there it refers to a chocolate candy, as opposed to the caramelized-dairy confectionery the term denotes in the U.K. By the early twentieth century, the chocolate variety was all the rage at women's colleges like Vassar, where fudge parties were held in the dorms, and girls would cook it in a chafing dish. A recipe by a Vassar student of the time calls for 2 glasses of sugar, ¼ cake (about 2 oz) chocolate, 1 glass of milk, and a little butter. Another contemporary recipe stipulates 1 cup dark brown sugar, ½ cup milk, 2 tbsp butter, 2 cups New Orleans molasses, 4 squares of chocolate, grated, and 1 tsp vanilla. The mixture is then cooked to a hard-ball stage, which would make more of a soft toffee than a fudge. But it's best not to split hairs with a woman presiding over a pot of boiling sugar. I find making confectionery tricky enough with my modern pan, silicone mold, and digital thermometer, so I tip my toque to anyone prepared to make fudge in a chafing dish. At the turn of the twentieth century, these portable braziers were popular enough to inspire a slew of cookbooks, including Fannie Merritt Farmer's indispensable *Chafing Dish Possibilities*. "Anything constructed upon a chafing dish," announced the *Los Angeles Herald* in 1909, "brings with it an element of sociability and cheerfulness that is hard to attain in any other way. Long life to it and its pretty schoolgirl champions." A Brazilian chocolate-fudge sweet called the *brigadeiro* is simple enough to cook over a spirit lamp. Whisk ¼ cup unsweetened cocoa powder with a 14-oz can of condensed milk, eliminating any lumps, then add 1 tbsp butter and cook over a medium heat for about 10 minutes, by which time the mixture should pull away from the sides of the pan. Pour into a silicone mold, or onto oiled foil, and let cool and set. Once it has, fashion it into small balls as you would ganache for truffles, then roll them in chocolate sprinkles. If, however, you simply want to flavor your fudge with chocolate, beat in ½ cup warm, melted chocolate at step [5].

COCONUT & ORANGE

Cajeta is a type of fudge popular in Mexico and Central America. It's most often found in spreadable form, like *dulce de leche*, but it's also given a harder set for individual candies. The Costa Rican astronaut Franklin Chang-Rodriguez packed *cajeta* for his space missions, and a celebratory *cajeta espacial*—space fudge—was named in his honor. The flavors were coconut and orange—not because these are widely grown in Costa Rica (although they are), but because NASA's takeoff and reentry suit-helmet combos are colored white and orange. In the absence of a photograph of space fudge, it's anybody's guess whether the candy itself was white and orange. To make the plain brown coconut fudge popular in the Caribbean, follow the method given at [E] under Leeway, but use light brown sugar in place of demerara and coconut milk in place of the ⅔ cup milk. Britain's coconut ice candy is made in a very similar way to fudge—put sugar, milk, and butter in a pan and bring them to the soft-ball stage, before mixing in dried shredded coconut, then beating and transferring to a pan to set.

COFFEE & WALNUT

If you find yourself in Italy, with no time to spare for an espresso, save yourself about twelve seconds by knocking back a "Pocket Coffee," a bite-sized dark chocolate shaped like a treasure chest and filled with a bittersweet ristretto. Frank C. Mars was thinking along the same lines when he invented the Mars Bar—the confection we in the U.K. refer to as a Milky Way. After drinking a chocolate-malt shake in a diner, he got to wishing he could have something similar to hand whenever he wanted a nutritious snack. Forswearing the billions I would have made trademarking it, I dedicate the following coffee and walnut fudge to all human beings. Pocket Coffee Cake! Unlike the real thing it won't leave

smears of frosting on your car keys. Dissolve 2 tsp instant coffee in
1 tsp boiling water and stir into the sugar and dairy mix at step 5 (before
you start beating), then add a handful of chopped walnuts a few minutes
into the beating. If you prefer a stronger coffee flavor, use 50/50 white
and light brown sugar, and dissolve 1 tbsp instant coffee in the 1 tsp
water. The notes of caramel in the brown sugar match and enhance
similar flavor compounds created in coffee when the beans are roasted.

GINGER

Although "fudge" is a nineteenth-century American coinage, there are
methods of cooking sugar and dairy together that predate it by some
way, Scottish "tablet" being a case in point. Despite the similarity of
the recipes, tablet has a notably different texture from fudge—harder,
grainier, more brazenly sugary. A Glaswegian assault on your tooth
enamel. In the first Scottish cookbook, published in 1736, flavor
variations for tablet include ginger, orange, rose, horehound, aniseed,
and cinnamon. Horehound is related to mint, and from the 1600s was
a popular flavor for throat lozenges, which are still available today. The
herb is notably bitter; the wild-plants expert Kay Young writes that few
people like the flavor, and those that do consume it only rarely. Hardly
a ringing endorsement. Try Catherine Brown's ginger variation from
Classic Scots Cookery instead. She says tablet is harder than fudge—
it has a bite to it. Her standard tablet recipe calls for 4 cups sugar,
¾ cup each milk and butter, and a 14-oz can of condensed milk. The
night before you make your tablet, line a 9-in square pan with foil and
then with plastic wrap, and put it in the freezer. The next day, melt the
butter in the milk before adding the sugar and melting that too. Add
the condensed milk and cook to the soft-ball stage (239–241°F) before
removing it from the heat and beating it immediately, but "not too
much." Mix in ¼ cup chopped preserved ginger before pouring the
tablet into the lined pan. Leave it to set for 30 minutes before covering
with plastic wrap and placing the pan in the freezer for 1½ hours.
Remove it from the pan, leave for 10 minutes, then score and break
into small cubes. For her orange variation, Brown suggests using
orange juice in place of milk, and adding the finely grated zest of
1 orange to the mix before pouring it into the pan.

PECAN

The evening started, as had the previous three, at The Spotted Cat
on Frenchmen Street in New Orleans. We had a couple of margaritas,
listened to the band, chucked some money in the hat. Then we walked
east over Elysian Fields, wandering past the candy-colored houses and
trees festooned in glass beads until we came across a white structure

half-hidden in palm trees. We had a few drinks in what might have been a courtyard, or a part of the building that had lost its roof: I don't recall. The walls were thick with ivy, and somewhere inside was a dark room like a passenger car on a train, crowded with drinkers. Then on to another bar, more music, fried catfish, before ending the evening back in the French Quarter at Lafitte's candlelit Blacksmith Shop. "How do you feel?" asked my husband the next morning. "Like a puddle of fudge," I replied. So he went out and came back with one. A praline, NOLA-style, is a flat dollop of crystallized sugar studded with pecans, quite different from the French kind. The method is the same as for our starting point for fudge, but the freshly beaten mixture is poured onto marble in little pools to set. Use 1¾ cups packed light brown sugar, ⅔ cup butter, and ⅔ cup cream and follow the starting point, resting the mix for just 10 minutes at step [5], then beating in 1¾ cups toasted chopped pecans, ½ tsp sea salt, and 1 tsp each of bourbon and vanilla extract. Drop small puddles onto a silicone mat or sheet of parchment paper and leave at room temperature to dry. Aunt Sally's, which has sold fresh handmade pralines in the French Quarter since 1935, offers standard, triple-chocolate, café au lait, and Bananas Foster versions.

Meringue

A simple beaten mixture of sugar and egg white. The type outlined in the method below is French meringue. Italian meringue can be made with the same ingredient proportions as French, but water is added to the sugar, and the mixture is heated to form a syrup (soft-ball stage). This is beaten into the egg whites at soft-peak stage. For Swiss meringue, the mixture of sugar and egg white is warmed in a double boiler; it's used mainly for buttercream frostings. Details for both Italian and Swiss meringue are given in the Flavors & Variations section. Meringue can pose a challenge to the experimental cook—care must be taken with additional ingredients, which can deflate the foam.

For 6–8 individual meringues, or an 8-in round ^A

INGREDIENTS
4 egg whites, at room temperature ^B
½ tsp cream of tartar or lemon juice ^C
1 cup sugar ^{D E F}

1 In a clean glass or metal bowl, beat the egg whites until foamy. Add the cream of tartar or lemon juice and beat to soft peaks.
   If your eggs are not at room temperature, place them in warm water for 5 minutes before cracking them and separating the yolk from the white.

2 While beating, add 1 tbsp sugar and continue to beat until it has dissolved.
   If you're unsure how long this takes, rub a little of the mixture between your fingers. If it still feels grainy, continue beating. (I usually give each tablespoon of superfine sugar a count of ten. Naturally, granulated sugar will need a bit longer.)

3 Add the rest of the sugar, tablespoon by tablespoon, while continuing to beat, until all is incorporated and dissolved, and the meringue is shiny and stiff.
   For a meringue pie topping, see ^G under Leeway; for a marshmallowy pavlova, see ^H.

4 Transfer the meringue to a pastry bag and pipe into shapes (concentric circles or kisses), or dollop spoonfuls onto a silicone mat or parchment-lined baking sheet. Leave an inch or so between individual meringues. For a large meringue, dollop spoonfuls into a rough round, and use the back of a spoon to fashion a nest shape.

5   For individual meringues, bake at 200°F for 1¼ hours, 1½ hours for large. When cooked the meringue should lift off the silicone or parchment easily. Turn off the oven but leave the meringue in there for a few hours or overnight, until the oven is cold.

6   If you're serving the meringue with cream, assemble the dessert close to serving time, to forestall sogginess. Unfilled meringues will keep in an airtight container for 2–3 weeks.

LEEWAY

A   This quantity is also good for a roulade, made in a jelly roll pan about 12 × 9 in. The pan will need to be lined with enough parchment paper to hang over the edges slightly. Bake at 325°F for about 20 minutes, until the meringue feels firm. Carefully unmold it onto another piece of parchment and let cool before filling; use the parchment to help roll it up.

B   The whites of extra large or large eggs will be fine.

C   The acidic ingredient helps to stabilize the mixture, and is preferable but not essential. Cider vinegar or white wine vinegar could be used, too. A copper bowl has the same effect, rendering the acidic ingredient redundant.

D   You can use anything between 3½ and 5 tbsp sugar per egg white. The more sugar you use, the firmer the structure of the meringue and the crisper it will be.

E   Some recipes recommend folding in the last half of the sugar all at once with a large metal spoon, instead of gradually beating it in. Heston Blumenthal beats in half the sugar, using superfine sugar, then folds in the remainder in confectioners' sugar, which makes dissolving a non-issue.

F   For a light brown, toffee-flavored meringue, replace half of the white sugar with the same quantity of dark brown sugar. Meringues made with brown sugar will soften more quickly than those made with white.

G   For topping a pie or dessert, sift ½ tsp cornstarch per egg white into the stiff meringue at the end of step 3, and briefly beat again to incorporate. If using on a pie, start piping at the crust edge, making sure the meringue touches it, then dollop a large blob in the middle and swirl it around until the top is covered.

H   To give a chewy, marshmallow texture to the meringue for a pavlova, fold in 1 tsp white wine vinegar (or lemon juice), 2 tsp sifted cornstarch, and 1 tsp vanilla extract at the end of step 3. Bake at 250°F for 1 hour.

ALMOND

What's the difference between a dacquoise and a macaroon? Nine points, if you're a Scrabble player. More dishwashing, if you're a cook. Dacquoise is a variation on meringue that involves ground nuts. In one of its most common incarnations, disks of dacquoise are sandwiched with flavored buttercream or whipped cream, like a gâteau where the cake is replaced by meringue. Almond and hazelnut, either used separately or in combination, are the classic nuts, but these days anything goes. Dorie Greenspan uses a mix of almond and coconut, and between the layers spreads white chocolate ganache and roasted pineapple. To make a classic dacquoise, adapt our starting point by using ½ cup ground nuts, ¼ cup sugar, and 1 tsp cornstarch per egg white (4 egg whites' worth will make two 8-in disks). Having beaten in half of the sugar, tablespoon by tablespoon, beat the mixture to stiff peaks, then gently fold in the other half of the sugar mixed with the ground nuts and cornstarch. Pipe the mixture into thin disks (draw circles on the parchment paper if you want to make the layers the same size), then bake at 200°F for 1 hour. The *Meringue Cookbook* gives a recipe for a savory pecan meringue to serve on sweet potatoes at Thanksgiving. If you've balked at marshmallow used for the same purpose, note that this recipe doesn't include sugar. Beat 6 egg whites, gradually adding ¼ tsp salt, until stiff. Then fold in 1 cup chopped pecans or walnuts. Spread the meringue over warm mashed sweet potatoes and bake at 375°F for 10–15 minutes until the peaks are brown.

CARAWAY

A classic flavor for meringue, says *The Oxford Companion to Food*. The German (or Latvian, or Dutch, depending on who you believe) liqueur called kümmel is typically flavored with caraway and aniseed. Kingsley Amis recommends you get a bottle in for Christmas, as a relief to the stomach after all that plum pudding. The first sip should be as clean, chilly, and exhilarating as a lungful of air on a mountaintop. The flavor is more complex, savory-sweet, reminiscent of almost-burnt bread crust with a hint of menthol and aniseed. Fold in 2 tsp kümmel (or the same amount of ground caraway seeds) at the end of step [3].

CHOCOLATE

Belongs to another era. Like step aerobics, and g-string leotards over tights. Not my cup of tea. But if it's yours, use 2–3 tsp unsweetened cocoa powder per egg white, mixing the sifted cocoa into the sugar to be added in increments at steps [2] and [3].

COCONUT

I came into the kitchen to see the digital clock on the oven blinking, as if coming around from a disorientating dream. This could mean only one thing: We'd had a power outage overnight. I opened the freezer to find four drawerfuls of freezer bags softly slumped like Claes Oldenburg sculptures. A *feijoada* for six, pea soup for four, two dozen sausages, homemade burgers, sweet potato fries, frozen red currants, two blocks of puff pastry, and a handful of kaffir lime leaves rimed with ice as if at sun-up on a frosty morning. There was no choice but to get cooking. Necessity is the mother of confection: There was also a large quantity of raspberries, five egg whites, and two cartons of heavy cream. I'd always wanted to make a vacherin glacé—and now not only did I have the necessary ingredients, but also the freezer space, since the perishables were lined up on the kitchen table and the cartons of melted ice cream had been thrown out. First, I made a French meringue with coconut, beating 6 egg whites and 1½ cups sugar to stiff peaks, then stirring in ¼ cup dried shredded coconut. Most of the meringue I piped into two 8-in rounds, then shook over more coconut. The remainder I piped into decorative twigs, sprinkling them with crumbs of freeze-dried raspberry. While the rounds of meringue baked, I made a sorbet with the raspberries. At this point I could get dressed and pop out for a couple of fresh cartons of vanilla ice cream. After letting it soften a little, I added a deep layer of the ice cream to one of the meringues, topped it with the raspberry sorbet, and positioned the second meringue disk on top. All that remained was to invite some nonjudgmental friends over to polish off everything else. Our main course, it has to be said, was eclectic: Brazilian bean stew with pea soup and hamburgers. But the vacherin redeemed matters, piped with Chantilly cream and decorated with raspberries and meringue twigs, so festive-looking you half-expected Jayne Mansfield to jump out of it.

COFFEE

The roasted nature of coffee and cocoa means they have many flavor notes in common, but make your sweet meringue roulade with coffee, and roll it around a creamy, bitter chocolate ganache, and you'll tease out the differences in the most satisfying way. Mix 1 tbsp instant coffee into 1½ tsp boiling water and let it cool, then fold in at the end of step [3]. Bake in a parchment-lined 12 x 8-in jelly roll or sheet pan at 350°F for 20 minutes. For the ganache, follow the starting point on page [380], using 1 cup chopped dark 70%-cocoa chocolate and ⅔ cup heavy cream. Spread over the meringue and carefully roll up your roulade before it sets too hard. Keep back a few spoonfuls of each mixture and fold the meringue into the ganache for an instant mocha mousse— simple enough to qualify as a cook's treat. Coffee meringue is also excellent served with fresh cream and either raspberries or cherries.

HONEY

Honey can make an exquisitely flavored meringue. Cooking honey really accentuates its flavor, so even a mild variety like clover will yield a definite character. Honey also turns baked goods brown, so avoid it if that's not the look you're after. For use in meringues, you'll need to cook honey to the soft-ball stage (239–241°F), as you would for an Italian meringue (see below). Once cooked, the mixture will be soft, not crisp, so is best used as a topping for pies and desserts rather than meringue nests. Use 5 tbsp honey per egg white, adding it in a steady stream once the whites have been beaten to stiffness with cream of tartar. Keep beating until the meringue has cooled and become thick and glossy. Use as is to frost a cake, or, for a toasted topping on a tart or dessert, bake at 350°F for 10 minutes, assuming that whatever is underneath can take the heat.

ITALIAN MERINGUE

Italian meringue is made with sugar syrup cooked to either the soft- or hard-ball stage. It's mainly used to top pies or cakes, folded through mixtures to make extra-light mousses and buttercreams, or added to ice creams and sorbets to lend them an extra airiness, and a softer texture (once frozen) thanks to its sugar content. Italian is also the type of meringue used in baked Alaska. Apply the same proportion of sugar to egg white as for French meringue (3½–5 tbsp sugar per egg white); in this case, I use 5 tbsp per egg white. Cook scant 1 cup sugar and 5 tbsp water to the soft-ball stage (239–241°F). Beat 3 egg whites until stiff (adding ¼ tsp cream of tartar once frothy), then continue beating as you trickle in the hot syrup. Avoid pouring the sticky liquid onto the beaters or the sides of the bowl and keep beating until the mixture is cool. This will furnish enough to top an 8- to 9-in round tart or an 8-in baked Alaska. Some cooks flavor the syrup for Italian meringue: Try fennel, cardamom, coffee, coconut, or any type of tea.

MARSHMALLOW

Can be made in two basic ways. The first is a hybrid of an Italian meringue (above) and a gelatin. It has a more robust structure than the type made without egg white. Sprinkle an 8-in square silicone mold or nonstick pan with a 50/50 mix of sugar and cornstarch, or with toasted coconut. Soak 6 leaves of gelatin in cold water for 5 minutes. Then dissolve them in 5 tbsp hot (not boiling) water with 2 tsp vanilla extract. Beat 3 extra large egg whites to soft peaks, then make a syrup by cooking 1 cup + 2 tbsp sugar and 5 tbsp water to the soft-ball stage (239–241°F). Trickle the hot syrup into the egg whites while beating. Slowly pour the gelatin mix into the meringue, still beating, and keep on beating until the mixture has cooled. Scrape the mixture into the prepared mold or pan. Smooth it over, then cover with whatever you sprinkled underneath. Alternatively, for an eggless version, also 8-in square, use an electric mixer to beat 1 cup sugar with 5 tbsp water in a large bowl for 3 minutes. Soak 5 leaves of gelatin, then squeeze out the water and dissolve them in 5 tbsp hot (not boiling) water. Mix into the sugar and beat for 10 minutes longer, by which time you should have a sticky, frothy white mixture. Add 1 tsp vanilla extract and give the mixture another quick beat to incorporate. Line your mold or pan and finish the marshmallow in the same way as for the egg-white variation. Naturally, marshmallow can be flavored with something other than vanilla.

MUSTARD

The sort of off-the-wall suggestion that can make vintage branded-recipe pamphlets so entertaining. "Crown o' Gold Meat Loaf," included in an ad for French's mustard, was probably devised because French's also make cream of tartar. Imagine the benighted home economist, sweating under the directive to combine the two ingredients. To make the meatloaf, mix 1½ cups fresh bread crumbs with 1½ lb ground beef, 4 egg yolks, 5 tbsp tomato ketchup, 3 tbsp finely diced green bell pepper, 2 tbsp finely diced onion, 2 tbsp French's mustard, 1½ tbsp horseradish sauce, and 1½ tsp salt. Lightly pack into a 9-in springform pan and bake at 325°F for 30 minutes. Meanwhile, beat 4 egg whites until foamy, add ¼ tsp cream of tartar, then keep beating until very stiff. Gently fold in ¼ cup mustard. Remove the meatloaf from the oven and swirl the mustard mixture on top, then return it to the oven for 20–25 minutes, by which time the top should be golden and crisp. Incidentally, the recipe also included a "Friendly Warning"—not, I was disappointed to find, that your husband may leave you for Betty in the secretarial pool if you insist on serving him such bizarre concoctions, but that French's mustard is made with a very particular blend of spices, vinegar, and mustard seeds. Use another mustard and you risk not achieving the "best results."

ROSEWATER & PISTACHIO

A perfect, delicately flavored end to a Middle Eastern feast. And extremely pretty with it. For a meringue made with 4 egg whites and 1 cup sugar, fold in 1 tsp rosewater at the end of step [3]. Scatter over some finely chopped pistachios (2–3 tbsp) and some crystallized rose petals before baking the meringues. The results are as billowy and winsome as embroidered bed linen, if rather nicer in the mouth.

STRAWBERRY
Brent Savage, chef at the Bentley in Sydney, makes a lemon-flavored meringue by adding egg-white powder to lemon juice and sugar and beating. A similar process can be used to make a strawberry meringue—but take note, the water content in the fruit mitigates against crispness. For a crisp strawberry-flavor meringue, use freeze-dried strawberry powder (about 1 tbsp for every egg white, mixed with the sugar and added at step [3]). Using a purée base makes for more of a soft meringue, suitable for filling cakes or topping pies and desserts. It's best made using a stand mixer, but a powerful portable electric mixer will do. Pour ½ cup strawberry purée into the bowl of a stand mixer, sprinkle over 2 tbsp egg-white powder, and beat on low until dissolved. Continue to beat as you add 1 cup sugar, a tablespoon at a time, then beat on high to reach firm peaks. Fill the bottom of 6 sundae glasses with raspberries, ideally tossed in mango purée, follow with a scoop of vanilla ice cream, then pipe some of the pink meringue on top and blast it with a blowtorch. Miraculously, the meringue replicates the flavor of the freshest, sweetest strawberries imaginable, like the northern Norwegian type described by Alexander Masters as "dense with the sort of sweetness you normally only read about in children's books, force-fed by twenty-four hours of sun."

Meringue → Other Directions

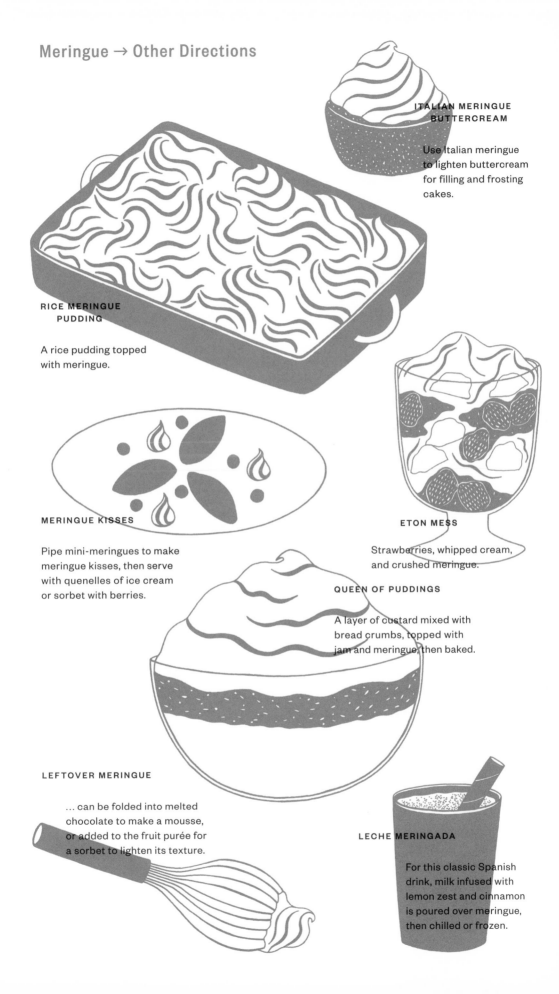

ITALIAN MERINGUE BUTTERCREAM

Use Italian meringue to lighten buttercream for filling and frosting cakes.

RICE MERINGUE PUDDING

A rice pudding topped with meringue.

MERINGUE KISSES

Pipe mini-meringues to make meringue kisses, then serve with quenelles of ice cream or sorbet with berries.

ETON MESS

Strawberries, whipped cream, and crushed meringue.

QUEEN OF PUDDINGS

A layer of custard mixed with bread crumbs, topped with jam and meringue, then baked.

LEFTOVER MERINGUE

… can be folded into melted chocolate to make a mousse, or added to the fruit purée for a sorbet to lighten its texture.

LECHE MERINGADA

For this classic Spanish drink, milk infused with lemon zest and cinnamon is poured over meringue, then chilled or frozen.

Syrup & Cordial: Simple Syrup

As the name suggests, simple syrup is a mixture of water and sugar, made to a 1:1 ratio in our starting point. To thicken the syrup, add more sugar. It's a doddle to flavor. Simple syrup can be used to flavor, sweeten, and add body to cocktails, to soak desserts like babas (page [66]) or gulab jamun, to flavor and moisten cakes (especially Genoise, page [328]), be diluted to make a soft drink, or cooked a little and added to egg whites to make Italian meringue (page [428]).

For just over 1½ cups

INGREDIENTS
1 cup sugar [A B C D]
Aromatics—optional [E F]
1 cup boiling water [G]

1   Put the sugar (and aromatics, if using) into a heatproof bowl. Pour over the boiling water and stir to dissolve.
    If you want the syrup cold and ready to use, dissolve the sugar in as little boiling water as you can get away with, then top up with ice cold water. Some prefer to heat the sugar and water in a pan, the advantage being that you can keep simmering it until you achieve the desired thickness. You'll need to remove any hard aromatics with a fine strainer or a sieve lined with cheesecloth.

2   Your plain syrup can be stored somewhere cool, in a sterilized jar or bottle, for up to a month. After a week, the flavor may start to deteriorate.
    After a month, it is likely to start clouding, which means it's time to throw it away. Add 1¼ tsp vodka (to 1½ cups syrup) to give it a few extra months' shelf life in the fridge. The more aromatics you add, the more the shelf life is compromised, so best not to make much more flavored syrup than you will use in a week.

LEEWAY

A Some cooks use two times the amount of sugar, which will obviously give thicker and sweeter results. Many cocktails are made with a 2:1 syrup, but try it to taste.

B For fruit salads, or for poaching fruit, use a 1:2 volume of sugar to water.

C Use brown sugar if you don't mind the color or more pronounced flavor. For more on brown sugar syrup, see page 434.

D Replace 1 tbsp of the sugar with the same amount of light corn syrup to prevent the syrup from crystallizing.

E Sour mix, or bar mix, is a classic syrup used for whiskey sours and collins cocktails. It's made with equal amounts of water, sugar, and lemon juice. Stir in the lemon juice once the syrup has cooled. A sour mix for margaritas is made in the same way, with lime juice in place of the lemon.

F If you're using acidic ingredients like lemon juice or tamarind, opt for a nonreactive pan—i.e. not aluminum, unlined copper, or cast iron.

G Experiment with liquids other than water, e.g. nut milks.

BROWN SUGAR

Make a simple syrup with muscovado and you'll end up with something like molasses. The Japanese make a similarly potent-tasting syrup called *kuromitsu*, using black sugar (*kurozatō,* an unrefined sugar made from cold-pressed sugarcane juice, with a molasses-like flavor). You might be presented with a miniature bottle of *kuromitsu* on the side of, say, cold arrowroot noodles, a little like soy in a sushi set. Syrup made with a lighter brown sugar like demerara will be kinder to other flavors, and is thus more suitable for cocktails. Demerara syrup abets rum and bourbon, so bear it in mind when making the syrup for your rum babas (page 66). Cocktail expert Dale DeGroff recommends it for Irish coffee, as it contains notes of butterscotch and vanilla lacking in other brown sugars. If you're out of pancake syrup, a brown sugar syrup will be a welcome stand-in—consider enhancing it with a few pinches of mixed spice and/or curry powder. A ratio of 4 parts sugar to 1 of water will give a thick pouring consistency.

CHOCOLATE

Making your own chocolate syrup will not represent much of a saving over buying a bottle in the supermarket, but it will taste good, and the list of ingredients is reassuringly short and familiar. Furthermore, because the cocoa will thicken the syrup after it's been cooked, there's no need to rely entirely on sugar for body, and you can therefore sweeten to taste—I find ¾ cup works well. Mix scant 1 cup unsweetened cocoa powder to a paste with ¾ cup sugar, 1 cup water, and ¼ tsp salt. Bring to a boil over a medium heat, whisking constantly. Simmer for 3–4 minutes, then whisk in 1 tbsp vanilla extract. Let cool, by which time it will have thickened further. Pour into a sterilized bottle; it will keep in the fridge for up to a month. Dilute it with milk for a shake, or mix a little with Irish whiskey and cream to make a liqueur. (Segnit's Irish Cream is a touch chocolatier than Bailey's, if less Irish.) Or use it to make the New York soda-fountain classic, an egg cream. Pour ice-cold whole milk into a tall glass until it's about a quarter full. Top it up, slowly, with seltzer or club soda, then add a tablespoon of your chocolate syrup and stir. Drink immediately. It's a lot nicer than it sounds. Or looks. It's brown and frothy with a head of white foam, and tastes like a chocolate milkshake spritzer. Sometimes it's served with a pretzel stick, dunked or used as a stirrer. The perfect comfort drink if your prom date has stood you up.

LEMON

Lemon "squash" (a sweetened fruit drink) was the worst thing about my childhood. Even at six I knew that it was the only drink to be actually improved by the alien note of plastic imparted by a few hours' storage in a lidded Tupperware cup. In a warm car. Lemons should sue for defamation. Never buy shop-bought lemon squash again. Making your own takes all of 10 minutes, plus the day for the lemons to infuse. For your pains you are rewarded with a drink that teleports you to the lemon groves of Sorrento, even if you're trying to break up a squabble in a playground. Thinly slice 2 unwaxed lemons and place in a bowl with 1¾ cups sugar, 1½ cups boiling water, and 1 tsp each of citric and tartaric acids. Let steep for 24 hours, then strain and funnel into sterilized bottles. It can be used immediately or kept somewhere dark and cool for up to 3 months. Once opened, the syrup will keep in the fridge for a week. Dilute to taste with still or sparkling water.

MUSCAT MARMALADE

A Spanish version of oranges in caramel, made with a syrup mixture of marmalade and Moscatel, a sweet wine from Spain with flavors of orange, tangerine, apricot jam, and honeysuckle. In a saucepan, slowly dissolve 1 cup marmalade in ½ cup Moscatel. Once the lumps have disappeared, pour the syrup into a jug, add another ½ cup Moscatel, and cool. Pour over the segments of 6 large oranges and chill before serving. Don't bother making this if you were planning to strain out the peel; marmalade without the shred is like Tarantino minus the violence. Try the same syrup on strawberries.

ORGEAT

The sweet syrup orgeat owes its name to the Latin for barley, *hordeum*. Pearl barley was one of the original ingredients, but is no longer, just as it's gone from barley sugar sweets. Old recipes vary considerably, but most include bitter almond flavoring and orange-flower water, perhaps embellished with rose or lemon essence, or a nip of brandy. Commercial versions are these days likely to be made with corn syrup and synthetic flavorings, more suited to a tarted-up coffee from a freeway service station than a highball in a tiki bar. Happily, you can make your own in a snap, using bought almond milk. Dissolve 1 cup sugar in ½ cup warm, unsweetened almond milk, then mix in another

½ cup cold almond milk, ¼ tsp good almond extract, and 1 tbsp orange-flower water. Keep in the fridge—it'll be good for 5 days. Orgeat's most popular application is in the Mai Tai, signature cocktail at Trader Vic's. Load plenty of ice into a shaker and add 2 tbsp each of dark rum, amber rum, and fresh orange juice, plus 1 tbsp each of lime juice, Cointreau, and orgeat. Shake, then strain into a highball glass full of ice. Garnish with a sprig of mint, or with a plastic monkey holding a sparkler and a rainbow-colored parasol. For something more restrained, try the curiously un-Japanese "Japanese." Shake 4 tbsp Cognac, 1 tbsp orgeat, and 2 dashes of Angostura bitters over ice and strain into a Champagne saucer with a wisp of lemon peel. Teetotallers might consider this milkshake devised by the gardener Bob Flowerdew: Mix one part orgeat with seven parts whole milk; finish with a sprinkle of nutmeg.

RASPBERRY VINEGAR

Sugar syrup plus vinegar is called a "shrub." For a simple version, make a fruit vinegar, like the raspberry kind described on page 543, and mix it with simple syrup to taste, taking care to keep it on the sharp side. Dilute with cold sparkling or still water and serve over ice. Shrub could be twinned with the French *citron pressé*, served as a tall glass of ice with freshly squeezed lemon juice and, probably, a slice or two of lemon. The sugar is served on the side, with a long spoon, so you can sweeten to your taste. In the U.S., shrubs were drunk by field workers and were sometimes known as "harvest drinks"; it was thought that their acidity made them more refreshing than plain water. Having fallen into obscurity, shrubs have in recent years staged a modest comeback, even if the new recipes tend to be far more sugary, and are often mixed with alcohol. Best drunk after you've parked the combine harvester in the barn for the night.

ROSEHIP

As drunk by the Ethiopian athlete Abebe Bikila while running the marathon at the 1964 Tokyo Olympics. Bikila was not expected to compete, having undergone an appendix operation a few weeks before the race. Not only did he decide to run, he entered the stadium alone, way ahead of his nearest competitors, winning gold and breaking the world record. Haile Selassie rewarded him with a white VW Beetle. In the U.K., during the Second World War, rosehip syrup was promoted for its high vitamin C content. At first it was used as a substitute for oranges, but as rationing increased it began to stand in for all fruit. Then, as now, rosehips were abundant in the wild. The flavor of rosehip syrup is usually, and unhelpfully, described as "fruity"; some specify notes of red-apple skin, others cranberry. The foraging writer John Wright detects a distinct note of vanilla. Apart from being watered down in a drink, rosehip syrup is also used undiluted, as you might pomegranate molasses. The Norwegian cook and writer Signe Johansen drizzles a little over goat's cheese with smoked salt, sliced radishes, and a flutter of chervil. To make the syrup, wash 2¼ lb rosehips and either roughly chop them or give them a few pulses in the food processor. Put them in a nonreactive pan with 2 quarts of boiling water and bring back to a boil. Remove from the heat and let infuse for 30 minutes before straining through a jelly bag or a sieve lined with cheesecloth. Reserve the first batch of pink liquid, then repeat the process with the strained-out rosehips, this time using just 1 quart of boiling water. The rosehips will be thoroughly depleted by now, so you can discard or compost them. Pour both batches of liquid into the same pan and reduce by half. Remove from the heat and add 5 cups sugar (or more to taste). Stir to dissolve, then return to the heat and bring to a boil for 5 minutes. Pour the cooled syrup into sterilized bottles and store somewhere cool and dark for up to 3 months. Once opened, keep in the fridge and use within a week.

TAMARIND

In countries where tamarind is popular, such as Mexico, Thailand, Jamaica, and Lebanon, it's often used as we might use citrus juices—in popsicles, nonalcoholic cordials, and cocktails, or mixed with honey and hot water to make a toddy. Give it a try, as long as you don't mind the unprepossessing shade of corduroy brown. The flavor is less neutral than lemon. Tamarind syrup has a scorched, medicinal quality, and is fruity, with maple and sherry vinegar overtones; unsweetened tamarind tastes like a prune sucking a lemon. Tamarind syrup is available in Middle Eastern groceries, but it's easy enough to make your own. Dried tamarind comes as a compacted brick. Soak 8 oz in 2 cups boiling water. Once cold, untangle the fruit and mash it into the water. Strain thoroughly, squeezing as much flavor as you can out of the tamarind, then measure the volume of the strained tamarind water. Pour it into a pan and boil for 2 minutes. Remove from the heat and stir in the same volume of sugar as you had of tamarind water. Stir until the sugar has dissolved. Mexican cooks might add a pinch of ancho chili powder to their tamarind syrup. Pour the cooled syrup into sterilized bottles and store somewhere cool and dark for up to 3 months. Once opened, keep in the fridge and use within a week.

VIOLET

According to a thirteenth-century handbook written by an Egyptian pharmacist, violet syrup is good for chest pains and coughs, rhubarb syrup strengthens the liver, and a syrup of asparagus juice and honey will crush bladder stones (and your spirit too, I'd suggest). Pour 1 quart boiling water over 2 cups of violet flowers and let steep for 8 hours (or up to twice as long if it's more convenient), then strain. Measure the resulting blue liquid, and put it, along with an equal volume of sugar, in a heatproof bowl set over a pan of just-simmering water. Stir until the sugar dissolves. According to *The Italian Confectioner* (1861), by W.A. Jarrin, this makes a syrup "more perfect than that done on the fire," by which Jarrin means the flavor is better preserved. Contemporary makers of violet syrup still favor this method. Once the sugar has dissolved, add drops of lemon juice until the syrup turns from blue to purple. Pour the cooled syrup into sterilized bottles and store somewhere cool and dark for up to 3 months. Once opened, keep the bottle in the fridge and use within a week. The petals of carnations and pinks can be treated in the same way.

Syrup & Cordial → Other Directions

JALEBI

Spirals of deep-fried dough steeped in saffron syrup.

PLÁTANOS CALADOS

Guatemalan dish of plantain cooked in cane-sugar syrup.

ESPRESSO MARTINI

Vodka, espresso, and simple syrup.

KALBURABASTI

Turkish semolina pastry stuffed with nuts and covered in syrup.

GULAB JAMUN

Deep-fried dough balls made with milk powder and soaked in rosewater syrup.

KEIRAN SOMEN

Japanese version of egg threads boiled in sugar syrup, presented in neat bundles tied with seaweed.

ICE TEA

Brewed, chilled tea sweetened with simple syrup.

LOUKOUMADES

Deep-fried bun dough soaked in honey syrup and garnished with chopped nuts.

FIOS DE OVOS

Portuguese dessert of egg threads boiled in a sugar syrup.

Sorbet & Granita: Strawberry Sorbet

Sweeten a purée, juice, or other flavored liquid and you're ready to freeze it into sorbet or granita. Whether you end up with a scoopable sorbet, a crunchy granita, or something in between will depend, in part, on the amount of sugar—granita, for instance, is less sweet—and in part on the freezing method. Use an ice-cream machine and the constant churning will aerate the mixture and minimize the crystal size. The results will be smooth verging on creamy. Use the no-churn method, whereby the sweet mixture is placed in the freezer and removed regularly to be stirred, and you'll find it difficult to achieve the same smoothness. Ultimately, I'm not sure crystal size matters as much as flavor. The vibrancy of homemade sorbet or granita is what lingers in the mind.

For a stand-alone dessert to serve 4–6

INGREDIENTS
1¼ lb strawberries A B
⅔ cup sugar B C D
⅔ cup boiling water C
Pinch of salt
1 tbsp lemon juice—optional E
1½ tsp vodka—optional F
1 beaten egg white—optional G

1 Hull and purée the strawberries. You should have about 2 cups of purée.

2 Make up a simple syrup (page 432) by dissolving the sugar in the water.
These amounts will make about 1 cup simple syrup. Note that this combination—2 cups sweet base mixed with 1 cup syrup – is also used in many of the Flavors & Variations.

3 Add the syrup to the purée, along with the salt—and the lemon juice, if using.
Bear in mind that freezing mutes flavor and sweetness.

4 Chill the mixture in the fridge.
For the smallest ice crystals possible, chill the mixture thoroughly before transferring it to the ice-cream machine or freezer.

5   If it's a sorbet you're after, churn the mixture in an ice-cream machine. With the no-churn method, you will end up with something between a sorbet and a granita, as long as you stir it enough. Pour the mixture into a plastic container, to a depth of no more than 1¼ in, and transfer to the freezer. Set a timer for 30-minute intervals and keep checking until the mix starts to ice up at the sides. When it has, break it up using a fork or blender. Repeat at least twice, until the mixture is all ice crystals. After your last stir, leave it to harden in the freezer for a few hours.

6   Remove no-churn sorbet or granita from the freezer and put in the fridge for at least 10 minutes before serving, to soften. Machine-made ices should be more readily scoopable.

LEEWAY

A   Other sweet fruit purées and juices can be substituted. Lemon, lime, and other naturally unsweet fruits need to be treated differently—see page [443].

B   Some cooks add granulated sugar directly to the fruit, rather than making a syrup, in the name of greater intensity of flavor. Conversely, if you need to stretch out the fruit, use a bit more syrup.

C   Sorbets should be about 20–30 percent sugar, granitas 10–20 percent, by weight. My rough calculation goes as follows: strawberries are about 5 percent sugar, so in 500g purée there will be 25g sugar; adding 150g sugar and 150ml (or g) water yields a mixture weighing 800g (500g + 150g + 150g) and containing 175g sugar (25g + 150g). 175/800 = a sugar content of 21.9 percent.

D   Invert syrups make a softer, more scoopable ice. Try replacing 1–2 tbsp simple syrup with golden syrup, which is sweeter than granulated sugar. Light corn syrup—less sweet than sugar—can also be used.

E   Lemon juice adds an extra taste dimension; wine vinegar can also be used—balsamic famously enhances the flavor of strawberry.

F   The finished ice can be softened by adding 1 tbsp spirits (typically 36–40% ABV) to 1 quart of the mix (i.e. twice the quantity here), or 2 tbsp if you're using a liqueur or vermouth with an ABV of around 17–22%. Vodka is often used for its neutral flavor. Once out of the freezer, sorbets containing alcohol soften more quickly.

G   The texture of sorbets can be lightened with an egg white beaten to soft peaks. Either add it toward the end of the churning or, if you're using the no-churn process, in an electric mixer at the first breaking-up, beating for at least 15 seconds. The addition of lots of egg white, or Italian meringue (page [428]), will yield something closer to a spoom—a kind of frothy sorbet.

BLOOD ORANGE

"King of the sorbets," according to a board outside the wonderful ice-cream parlor Gelupo in London's Soho. Judge for yourself, but only when blood oranges are in season, as the juice in cartons is invariably dull by comparison. Inconveniently, for the U.K. at least, blood oranges tend to be available when the year is young—not exactly prime sorbetmaking season. (That said, you won't find a better dessert to follow a hefty oxtail stew with mashed potatoes.) Use 1 cup simple syrup for every 2 cups juice. For the syrup, I like to use some or all of the sugar in cube form, rubbing the cubes over the whole citrus fruit to tease out the oil from the zest. Then add the boiling water to the pile of orange-zesty sugar and proceed as per our starting point.

CHOCOLATE & ANGOSTURA

Cocoa sorbet is chocolate in airy summer linens, the warm melt of cocoa butter swapped for soft, chilly ice crystals. Heaven, and, like the similarly bitter coffee sorbet, fabulously refreshing. It's easy to flavor it further by infusing the sugar syrup with citrus zests and spices, or simply by adding a liqueur or instant coffee. Try Angostura bitters, with its notes of nutmeg and citrus; I find the combination almost has a menthol quality. Mix 6 tbsp unsweetened cocoa powder to a paste with 5 tbsp cold water. Add boiling water to make 1 cup and stir to a smooth liquid. Add 1 tsp vanilla extract and a pinch of salt. Mix with 1 cup simple syrup. Add 1 tbsp bitters and freeze as per the starting-point method.

CIDER

Wine and Champagne are common flavorings for sorbet, but cider, being more refreshing, has the edge. Use 2 cups hard cider, 1 cup simple syrup, and 1 tbsp lemon juice as per our starting point. A dry, tannic cider will remain dry and tannic even after mixing with sugar, so you might consider a medium variety, even if you'd sooner show up in a novelty sweater than be seen ordering it in the pub. In some recipes, the apple flavor is augmented by swapping water for apple juice in the syrup, or adding a little applesauce or a shot of Calvados. Vanilla ice cream is the natural accompaniment, but you might also serve your cider sorbet with cold, thick, plain yogurt, whose malic acid content gives it the subtlest hint of green-apple flavor. At The Ethicurean restaurant in Somerset, England, they serve a scrumpy (rough, strong, hard cider) and mint sorbet with a finger of Cheddar—somewhat resembling the British "99" (soft ice cream in a cone with an antenna of flaky chocolate).

LEMON

The first book to be dedicated to the sorbet, Filippo Baldini's *De' Sorbetti*, was published in Naples in 1775. Baldini divides his flavors into the aromatic (including chocolate, cinnamon, and pistachio) and the acidic (lemon, citron, sour cherry, and strawberry). Lemon sorbet, he tells us, is good for a fever or a weak stomach. I make lemon sorbet guided by the egg test, as outlined on page 409; try making a few batches and you'll note how widely individual lemons can vary in flavor. Finely grate the zest of 3 unwaxed lemons into a bowl. Add 1 cup sugar and 1 cup boiling water and stir to dissolve. Juice the zested lemons and add the strained juice to the bowl. Let cool before slipping in a clean, uncooked egg in its shell. Pour in enough water so there's a small circle (½-in diameter) of egg showing above the liquid; mine needed about ½ cup, making the sugar content approximately 30 percent. Chill, then freeze. Lemon and fresh fennel sorbet was popular in Naples, and known as *sorbetto di caroselle*—carousel sorbet—according to Vincenzo Corrado, writing in 1778.

PASSION FRUIT

Marvel at the passion fruit. The shell is polystyrene-light, while its fragrance has the force of a cannonball. Scooping out the seeds, and tugging at the fibers, recalls the preparation of mollusks. Having scraped out two for a sorbet, with at least a dozen more to go, I found wonder giving way to boredom. Then invention. It's not cheating too egregiously to supplement a few passion fruit with orange juice. Dissolve ⅔ cup sugar in ⅔ cup warm orange juice, then add 2 cups more juice, cold. Stir in the contents of 6 passion fruit and proceed from step 3. Whether or not you include the seeds is your call. Their crunchiness is of a piece with the icy dessert, although since they're hard to detect amid the ice crystals, they don't contribute the 1980s porn-star leopard-skin effect they would in a smooth gelatin dessert.

PEACH

The cookbook of The Inn at Little Washington, in Virginia, includes a dish called Peaches Five Ways. Leaving aside the fact that we have, surely, reached peak "X Ways" (my husband recently threatened to serve "Viennetta Three Ways" for dessert), peach sorbet does sound good served with peach and vanilla ice cream, sliced peaches, peach purée, and a spritz of peach schnapps. Peach is the drupe, or stone fruit, most often made into sorbet, although I find it a bit mild and mealy. The chef and deli-owner Glynn Christian reports that the texture and sweetness of canned fruit in syrup can make it perfect for sorbets, singling out lychee for special mention. Fresh or canned, use 2 cups peach purée to

1 cup simple syrup and 1 tbsp lemon juice—you might use the syrup from the can, as long as it's sufficiently tasty and sweet—then freeze as per our starting point.

RASPBERRY & ELDERFLOWER

A combination inspired by, of all things, a premium raspberry yogurt from the supermarket. It was rich, spicy, and somehow as darkly flavored as that plump, glossy blackberry would be if you could only reach it without tearing a hole in your sweater. The list of ingredients revealed that the yogurt contained elderberry concentrate. I made a note to make elderberry syrup when the season allowed, but, in the meantime, tried raspberry with commercial elderflower cordial (cordial is a nonalcoholic concentrated syrup). Elderflower shares a heady muscat flavor with the berry it prefigures, but has a fresher, sharper character. It gives raspberries a distinct whiff of the hedgerow, as if you've picked the first crop from your garden. Elderberry, by contrast, gives them a late-summer ripeness. Follow the starting point, using 2 cups seedless raspberry purée, 1 cup simple syrup, and ¼ cup elderflower cordial/syrup. Lemon will probably be redundant, as elderflower lends its own sharp edge.

WATERMELON MOJITO

I struggled home with an enormous watermelon, squeezed into my wetsuit and snorkel mask, looked in vain for my machete, took off the mask, found the machete, and murdered the watermelon, flooding the kitchen floor in sticky red liquid. I juiced what was left, then strained the watermelon juice. All this took an hour. I made a simple syrup, stirred it into the juice with a generous squeeze of lemon, and went about freezing the mixture, setting the timer to remind me to take it out and break it up regularly. On tasting the sorbet, I realized that I had essentially dismantled a watermelon and reassembled it into a form largely indistinguishable from the watermelon I had started with, if a bit sweeter. Chilled slabs of watermelon are instant sorbet. Make a fresh mint simple syrup and add 1 cup per 2 cups watermelon juice, balance with 2 tsp lime juice and 1½ tsp white rum, and you'll have the basis of a watermelon mojito sorbet that is, on the other hand, well worth the effort.

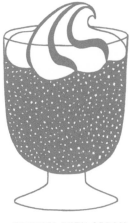

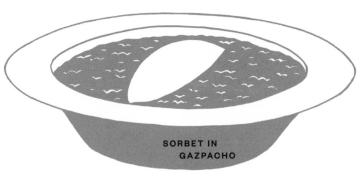

SORBET IN GAZPACHO

… or cucumber and yogurt soup (page 306).

GRANITA WITH CREAM

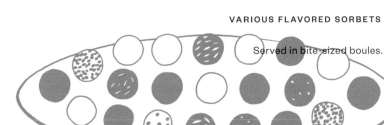

VARIOUS FLAVORED SORBETS

Served in bite-sized boules.

SGROPPINO

Vodka, lemon sorbet, and prosecco.

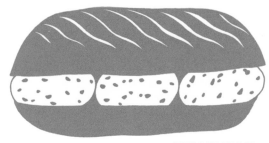

TROU NORMAND

A palate cleanser of apple sorbet in Calvados or eau-de-vie.

BRIOCHE FILLED WITH SORBET

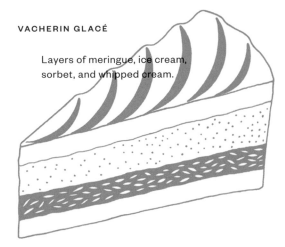

VACHERIN GLACÉ

Layers of meringue, ice cream, sorbet, and whipped cream.

SORBET "ALASKA"

A scoop of sorbet on a slice of cake, covered in Italian meringue and baked.

Gelatin Desserts: Orange Gelatin

Mix fruit juice (orange being the example here), purée, or other flavored liquids with sugar to taste, add gelatin, pour into a mold—a single large, or individual serving sizes—and let set. Alternatively, a gelatin dessert can be served in a pretty dish, in which case the set can be a bit looser, because, not being unmolded, it won't have to bear its own weight. The following quantities are for unmolded individual desserts. Improvising largely involves getting to know your chosen brand of gelatin.

For 4 individual molded desserts [A]

INGREDIENTS
4 leaves of gelatin [A B C D E F]
4 tsp sugar [C G]
2½ cups orange juice (straining is optional)
2 tsp lemon juice [C]

[1] Soak the gelatin in cold water for 5 minutes.

[2] In a nonreactive pan, over a medium heat, warm the sugar in the orange juice, stirring to dissolve, then remove from the heat.
    You may prefer to warm only the minimum amount of juice needed to dissolve the sugar, and the gelatin at step [3], say ½ cup. This way you retain a fresh rather than cooked-fruit flavor. No need to use a pan; warming the juice in a microwave will be fine.

[3] Squeeze the water from the gelatin and add the gelatin to the hot (but not boiling) juice. Stir to distribute and dissolve before stirring in the lemon juice.

[4] Strain the mix into a jug, or directly into molds or glasses.
    For colored strata, or to distribute fruit pieces evenly throughout, work in layers, letting each one set sufficiently before pouring on the next.

[5] Cool, then refrigerate to set.
    Bank on at least 4 hours for individual gelatins. More acidic mixes can take substantially longer. You can speed up the process initially by using the freezer, but it's wise to set a timer, say at 15-minute intervals, to remind you to check that ice crystals are not forming. Or see [H] under Leeway.

[6] If using molds, give them a quick dip in hot water, then invert onto a serving plate. [I]
    You may need to run a knife around them too.

LEEWAY

A If you're unsure of the size of your mold, fill it with water to the level you want, then pour the water into a measuring cup. A very large molded dessert will need proportionately more gelatin, so the set is strong enough to support the weight of the dessert when it's unmolded.

B The quantity given here of leaf (or sheet) gelatin is for the platinum-grade brand manufactured by Dr. Oetker. Use powdered gelatin or agar agar instead, but consult the instructions on the package.

C Salt and acidic ingredients can soften the set. Sugar can toughen it.

D Booze can strengthen the set, although Heston Blumenthal notes that there's a tipping point; larger amounts of alcohol can weaken it.

E The gelatin set gets stronger with time. If you're not planning to serve your molded dessert for a few days, you might risk a bit less gelatin.

F Pretty much all fruits can be used, but pineapple, kiwi, and papaya contain an enzyme that prevents gelatin from setting and needs to be denatured by simmering or steaming for 5 minutes before use. Canned pineapple or pineapple juice in a carton will already have been cooked, briefly, during the canning or pasteurization process.

G Add more sugar to taste or leave it out completely.

H Speed up the set by resting your container of warm mix in a larger vessel full of ice, and stirring to cool. When the mix starts to clot, pour it into the molds and transfer to the fridge. Even so, it will need at least a couple of hours to be unmoldable. A gelatin dessert may be fun, but it isn't fast.

I If you're not happy with the texture of your finished dessert, chop it up and gently melt it. Dilute it further if it was rubbery; add more gelatin if it was too soft. I wouldn't want to do this more than once.

BELLINI

Alcoholic gelatin—"jello shots"—might make you think of gangs of teenage boys mooning in the windows of cars in small town centers. It's a tradition that goes back a long way: Henry VIII liked his molded desserts boozy. (Not hard to picture him unconscious outside a burger joint after a bar crawl with Cardinal Wolsey.) Rescue your gelatin desserts from the frat house by avoiding vodka and lurid colors. The greater challenge lies in adjusting a well-known cocktail to the change of context: What tastes right in the glass is unlikely to be sweet enough as a dessert. The Bellini is a case in point. The combination of peach juice and prosecco will seem strikingly thin and tart in molded form. The answer is a simple syrup, used in place of the sugar in our starting point: ⅔ cup syrup added to 2½ cups peach juice and 1 tbsp lemon juice represents, in effect, the adjustment needed to keep things as they are. The results are pleasingly authentic, right down to the bubbles, trapped in the dessert as if from a celebration long ago. Dissolve 7 leaves of gelatin in ⅔ cup hot (not boiling) simple syrup (page 432) and add to the peach juice, preferably in a jug, then chill for an hour—don't let it set. To preserve the bubbles, slowly add 1¼ cups prosecco to the peach juice, pouring it against the side of the jug, just as you'd pour beer to prevent a head from forming. Stir gently, then transfer, carefully, into 8 glasses or molds and refrigerate to set.

BLACKBERRY & APPLE

Being free if they grow wild near you, blackberries are perfect for the novice gelatin-maker. Get it wrong and you can dump it and start again. Or, if you've been over-enthusiastic with the gelatin, you can always spread your over-set blackberry gelatin on toast or in a peanut butter sandwich. Purée 2 cups blackberries with 1 cup good-quality apple juice, 2 tbsp sugar, and 1 tbsp lemon juice. Strain and measure. Warm enough additional apple juice to make the blackberry mix up to 2½ cups, and use it to dissolve 4 leaves of gelatin. Add the gel-juice to the strained blackberry mix and pour into 4 molds.

COFFEE, CITRUS & CINNAMON

Coffee gelatin is a big deal in Japan. As it is in the Philippines, where chilled cubes are served in a glass dish, bathed in cream or condensed milk. The variations on coffee gelatin found in nineteenth-century

British cookbooks could be applied to any of the starting points on the sugar continuum, from caramel to panna cotta: roasted coffee beans with lemon, orange zest, and cinnamon; coffee, lemon, and vanilla; and coffee, coriander seed, and cinnamon. The last is made up with cream, which might make it an intriguing twist on coffee panna cotta.

CRÈME DE MENTHE

Culinary over-elaboration, believed Agnes Jekyll, should be discouraged: "Games of dominoes played in truffles over the chicken cream, birds' nests counterfeited round the poached eggs, jazzing jellies and castellated cakes show misdirection of energy," she writes. "Not that an occasional exception may not prove the rule—let it be made on behalf of *gelée crème de menthe,* an emerald-green pool, set in a flat glass bowl, reminiscent of Sabrina, fair in her home below translucent waves, or of Capri caverns, cool and deep; whilst the delicate aroma of peppermint will recall to Presbyterian minds those Sabbath indulgences practised by young and old at kirk in far-off Highland glens." Jekyll goes on to recommend making a quart of lemon gelatin, using a calf's foot or leaf gelatin, then, while it's warm, adding a handful of "those large green peppermint geranium leaves, thick as a fairy's blanket, soft as a vicuna robe, and to be found in most old-fashioned gardens." As an alternative, she offers 3–4 drops peppermint essence, some green coloring, and a glass of crème de menthe.

GINGER

Not a gelatin you come across too often. Nonetheless, I have my opinions. The ginger flavor should be warm, spicy, and sweet enough to stand up to the warm chocolate sauce it cries out for. The desserts should be made in individual molds, the sort that have ridges, so the sauce can form runnels. The set should be soft, but not so much that it is swiftly undone by the warmth of the sauce. Other than that, you're free to do as you please. Make a spiced ginger syrup by simmering ⅓ cup sliced fresh ginger, a few parings of lemon zest, a 2-in cinnamon stick, 2 cloves, and 1¾ cups packed light brown sugar in 1¼ cups water for 5 minutes. Let infuse for about 1 hour. Strain, add 1–2 tsp lemon juice, and dissolve 2 soaked leaves of gelatin in the warm reheated syrup. Pour into 2 molds to set. For the chocolate sauce, see page [374].

LIME

All those years I spent in the U.S., and no one offered me a Jell-O salad. They're as good as unheard of in the U.K., although the herbalist Hilda Leyel (1880–1957) gives a recipe for a grapefruit gelatin to serve with chopped eggs. Jell-O salad is less restrained. As the name suggests, it's a salad set in packaged gelatin. A classic is lime Jell-O with cottage cheese, sliced cabbage, and stuffed olives. Or there's cherry Jell-O with cranberry sauce, celery, chopped nuts, and sour cream. Jell-O salads are often set in ring molds, giving them the appearance of a colossal Murano-glass paperweight. Or something Carême might have created if he'd lived in Cleveland, Ohio, during the early 1950s. Brits should try one, for curiosity's sake, or *pour épater* some of their more straitlaced guests. Alternatively, omit the cottage cheese, cabbage, and olives and enjoy this very pale lime gelatin on its own. Combine equal volumes of strained lime juice and simple syrup (page [432]), then use 1 leaf of gelatin for every 7 tbsp of the juice-syrup mix and proceed as per the starting point (acidic bases take more gelatin to set). To make the lime flavor more complex, flavor the sugar syrup with pared lime zest. Grapefruit and lemon gelatins can also be made to these quantities.

MILK

Milk gelatin was once considered an excellent food for invalids. Nineteenth-century recipes recommend boiling a calf's foot in water for the gelatin. Once defatted and strained of sediment, the results are mixed with sugar, milk, and egg white. Today we might call it a skinny panna cotta. Junket, another wobbly dessert made with milk, is simpler to make. Add rennet to warm milk and let it set. A contributor to *Chambers's Edinburgh Journal,* in 1853, describes the preparation of junket thus: "You put some loaf sugar and nutmeg in a large glass or china bowl with perhaps a little wine or brandy. You then milk a cow, preferably an Alderney, into the bowl until three-quarters full, then add as much rennet to the warm milk as needed to curdle it." The trick, as with other molded desserts, is to ensure that the correct amount of setting agent—rennet, in this case—is used. Heston Blumenthal's junket recipe calls for 2⅔ cups whole milk and 3 tbsp sugar. Heat it to 98.6°F, then add 1 tsp vanilla extract, pour into a serving bowl, and add 1 tbsp rennet. Stir for no more than 3–5 seconds. Do not so much as move it after this, and in 10 minutes it will be softly set. In the English county of Devon, they slather this with clotted cream. Some berries would be a good accompaniment. Once cut, the junket will separate into curds and whey.

RHUBARB

Texture is often the reason cited for food aversions. The fungal squeak of mushroom, the slippery curd of cottage cheese, the ligamental stringiness of celery and rhubarb. A molded dessert will give the rhubarb-agnostic the chance to try it minus the fiber. Pairing it with apple juice enhances rhubarb's fruitier, less vegetal flavors. Gently simmer 3 heaped cups chopped rhubarb with 1¾ cups apple juice, ½ cup water, and ¼ cup simple syrup (page [432]) until the rhubarb is cooked. Strain and then measure out 2½ cups of the liquid, adding more apple juice if you're short. Stir the soaked gelatin into the warm juice until completely dissolved. The acidity of rhubarb means that more gelatin is needed to give a set that can be unmolded: I find that 5 leaves work well. Or use 4 and serve in a glass topped with a layer of vanilla panna cotta (page [456]) for a smooth, summery adaptation of the traditional British combination of rhubarb and custard.

Gelatin Desserts → Other Directions

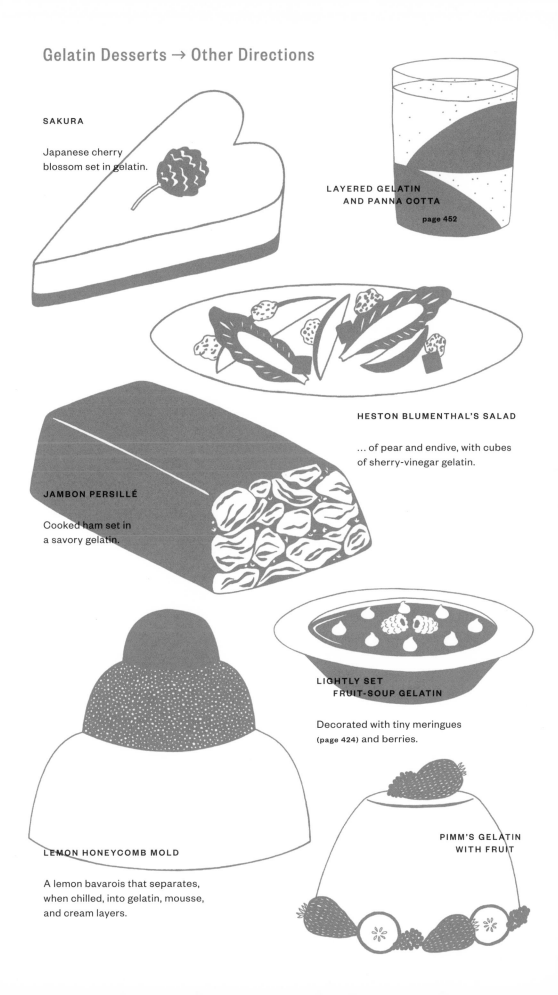

SAKURA

Japanese cherry blossom set in gelatin.

LAYERED GELATIN AND PANNA COTTA

page 452

HESTON BLUMENTHAL'S SALAD

… of pear and endive, with cubes of sherry-vinegar gelatin.

JAMBON PERSILLÉ

Cooked ham set in a savory gelatin.

LIGHTLY SET FRUIT-SOUP GELATIN

Decorated with tiny meringues (page 424) and berries.

LEMON HONEYCOMB MOLD

A lemon bavarois that separates, when chilled, into gelatin, mousse, and cream layers.

PIMM'S GELATIN WITH FRUIT

Panna Cotta: Grappa Panna Cotta

As with a gelatin dessert, the aim with panna cotta is to achieve the ideal wobble. In large part this entails getting to know the peculiarities of your chosen brand of gelatin, and learning a little about the peculiarities of gelatin *per se*. For instance, cream takes less gelatin to set it than a more watery base would. Once you've found your perfect wobble, flavoring is a relative cinch. Grappa, a classic flavor, is the example I've used here. Presenting panna cotta does have its challenges. Arguably it's easier to make it look elegant when it's presented in a glass, but then you don't get to see its shimmy.

For 6 (4-oz) or 4 (5-oz) molds or glasses

INGREDIENTS
3 leaves of gelatin [A] [B] [C] [D] [E] [F]
1¼ cups cream [F] [G]
¼ cup sugar [H]
1¼ cups milk [F] [G]
1–2 tbsp grappa [D] [I]

1 Put the gelatin to soak in cold water for 5 minutes.

2 In a pan over a medium heat, warm the cream and stir in the sugar until dissolved. Let the mix get hot, but not boil.
No need to use a pan: Heating the cream in a microwave will be fine, as long as you don't overheat it.

3 Remove the pan from the heat. Squeeze the water out of the gelatin and stir it into the hot cream until dissolved, then stir in the cold milk.

4 Stir in the grappa (or other liquid flavoring).

5 Strain into a jug, or directly into molds or glasses.

6 Cool, then refrigerate until set. Allow a minimum of 4 hours.

7 If you're unmolding them, give the molds a quick dip in hot water, then invert onto a serving plate.
You may need to run a knife between the mold and the pudding to loosen it.

LEEWAY

A   Cream needs less gelatin to set than watery fruit juice. As gelatin brands differ, however, it's tricky to give a hard-and-fast formula. The quantity given is for platinum grade, manufactured by Dr. Oetker, the most widely available leaf gelatin in the U.K. The instructions on their packaging suggest 4 leaves will set 2½ cups liquid, but I find 3 give this quantity of unmolded panna cotta the right wobble.

B   Use powdered gelatin or agar agar instead, but consult the instructions on the package.

C   Salt and acidic ingredients can soften the set. Sugar can toughen it.

D   Booze can strengthen the set, although Heston Blumenthal notes that there's a tipping point; larger amounts of alcohol can weaken it.

E   The gelatin set gets stronger with time. If you're not planning to serve your panna cotta for a few days, you might risk a bit less gelatin.

F   Use any sort of cream. Or all cream and no milk, if you like, but you may want to reduce the gelatin a fraction. Conversely, if you're using all milk, increase the quantity of gelatin.

G   Use half cream and half fruit juice (instead of the milk) for a pastel-colored, fruit-flavored panna cotta. When set and unmolded, there is likely to be a thin and rather fetching layer of juice on top.

H   Less sugar can be used—or more, but see C above.

I   Alternative flavoring options include infusing the cream and milk with a vanilla bean or other hard aromatics, such as coffee beans, citrus zest, or cinnamon sticks. Once it's achieved the desired strength of flavor, strain, then follow the method from step [1].

APPLE & MAPLE SYRUP

If you're sticking with natural ingredients, apple can be a hard flavor to sustain. The best results undoubtedly come from freshly juiced apples. The flavor is more vibrant than pasteurized store-bought juice, with a stern tannic foundation. Alternatively, farmers' markets will often sell different varieties of apple juice—you might sample a few to see which has the boldest flavor. To garnish the unmolded panna cotta, I make a sharp apple gelatin with some of the remaining juice and a squeeze of lemon, slice it into ½-in cubes, and scatter it around with pieces of candied walnut. It's a delightful autumnal dessert. Follow the starting point, using 1¼ cups heavy cream, 1¼ cups apple juice, 3 tbsp maple syrup (in place of the sugar), and 4 leaves of gelatin.

DATE

A friend came back from California raving about the date shakes. Inspired, I set to work on a panna cotta. The first indication that I had created something transcendental came when I tasted the dregs in the blender. It was caramel. Not the sugary goo from the center of a chocolate bar—not that I'm knocking it—but natural caramel, coaxed from a tree by golden sunshine. Mixed into the milk and cream for a panna cotta, it tasted like a particularly classy flavor of pudding mix, so much so that the next time I made it I couldn't resist insinuating some sliced banana into the set. It was good, in a nursery-nostalgic sort of way, but better without. I tried something more Moroccan—a side of chilled orange segments steeped in orange-flower water and a pinch of cinnamon. The orange provided a refreshing contrast to the rich, sweet pudding. For the panna cotta, remove the pits from 7 oz medjool dates and gently simmer for 15 minutes in 1¾ cups milk, 1½ cups heavy cream, 1 tsp date syrup (or brown sugar), ½ tsp vanilla extract, and a pinch of salt. Blend until smooth and stir in 4 soaked leaves of gelatin while the mixture is still warm. Pour into 8 molds or glasses. Incidentally, I like to leave this mixture unsieved, which means the panna cottas lack their usual silky texture.

GOAT'S CHEESE & MILK

Savory panna cotta: strange, but not unprecedented. One of chef Simon Rogan's signature dishes is a sous-vide squab served with a nettle panna cotta and a Sichuan pepper emulsion. Michael Wignall at Gidleigh Park hotel in England makes a dish called "umami," which combines broth, chicken cooked in a soy-laced master stock, chicken-skin crackers, and a garlic panna cotta. Goat's cheese panna cotta might seem conservative by comparison. You'll be in for a gruff surprise if you use goat's cream—it can take on a distinctly farmyard flavor if cooked a day or more in advance. But goat's cheese and milk are a deal easier to find than goat's cream, and work just as well. Less gelatin is needed on account of the thickness of cheese. Whisk 7 oz soft goat's cheese with ⅔ cup goat's milk until the cheese has dissolved. Warm another 1 cup goat's milk and add 2 soaked leaves of gelatin to it. Stir the mixtures together, then pour into 4 molds and refrigerate for at least 4 hours to set. Serve as a cheese course with sliced ripe figs and a drizzle of honey.

NESSELRODE

Carême's celebrated creation, for Russian foreign minister Count Karl von Nesselrode, is essentially a bavarois, a custard mixed with whipped cream and stiffly beaten egg whites, and set with gelatin. The custard is flavored with Maraschino and mixed with a sweet vanilla-chestnut purée. The whole thing is studded with candied fruit soaked in more alcohol. International diplomacy must have been a festive business in Imperial Russia. I adapted the Nesselrode principle for panna cotta. Which is to stretch the term, although there is panna in the custard it contains, and it is cotta. To distribute the solid ingredients throughout the pudding, you'll need to make it in layers. You might consider dispensing with the chestnut altogether, and using pieces of dried pineapple instead—texturally more appropriate, and sufficiently bright in flavor to smooth over any diplomatic crises. Roughly chop 3 tbsp raisins and steep for 1 hour in enough Madeira to cover them. Make 2½ cups crème anglaise (page 484) and, when cooled, stir in 1 tbsp Maraschino (or kirsch, which is more alcoholic, but will do). Finely slice 4–6 cooked chestnuts and cut 2 tbsp candied fruit into fine dice. Add the soaked, drained raisins, mix all the fruit and nuts together, and divide into 4 portions. Stand 4 individual molds in a container of cold water. Warm ⅔ cup of the Maraschino custard and dissolve 1 soaked leaf of gelatin in it. Mix in a portion of the fruit and nuts, then divide equally among all the molds. When the surface is fairly set, repeat three times, building up the layers. Transfer to the fridge and leave to firm up for a few hours.

PIÑA COLADA

Clearly, it was authenticity we were after. Not for us the zipline park, the Plantation Experience with working windmill, the glass-bottomed boat tour with complementary rum punch. We wanted the real Antigua. Things had got off to a promising start. The shrieks were clearly audible from our room on the second floor. The Copper & Lumber Store in Nelson's Dockyard was once a warehouse for shipbuilding materials, but is now an "Historic Inn." Despite the dismal note of heritage tourism that expression implies, it retains a genuine air of salt and creaking timbers. We ran downstairs to find the receptionist standing on a chair while a blue land crab the size of a bulldog scuttled across the floorboards. "Get a box," instructed my husband, unhelpfully. We were joined by the hotel chef. For what might have been five minutes my husband and a short man in a toque chased the crab as it pinballed from swivel chair to metal filing cabinet, until Chris, the local taxi man, walked in, picked the crab up under its armpits, and set it down on the sidewalk outside, where it clattered away to tell its crab friends about its raw yet strangely vivifying brush with humankind. Our authenticity-hunger duly satisfied, we could get on with the business of behaving like everyone else. Twenty minutes later we were sitting on the terrace of a chain hotel, watching the sun go down over an icy piña colada. Like the drink, this panna cotta must be boozy, rich, and cold. Remember to use pasteurized pineapple juice from a carton, which is cooked, and so won't inhibit setting, as fresh pineapple juice would. Follow our starting point, but dissolve the 4 soaked leaves of gelatin in 1¼ cups (not reduced-fat) coconut milk and ¼ cup heavy cream (coconut cream is a bit too powdery to use for panna cotta), warmed with 3 tbsp sugar. Stir in 1 cup chilled, pasteurized pineapple juice and 3 tbsp rum. Any rum will do, but the darker it is, the more pronounced the flavor.

VANILLA & ENHANCED VANILLA

I tried a number of different vanillas in simple shortbread cookies and failed to detect much difference between them. Panna cotta is the better vector: The mild flavor of cream withdraws, valet-like, in the presence of stronger flavors, where baked flour and butter assert themselves. Madagascan vanilla has the most familiar flavor, while Tahitian, being lower in vanillin, the bean's characteristic flavor compound, has a subtler, sweeter, fruitier, and more floral character, like a Gauguin adolescent in a wraparound skirt (or cherries and anise, to be more literal about it). Mexican vanilla is earthier and spicier. Joël Robuchon adds a single coffee bean to 2 vanilla beans to flavor 2 cups cream. Most cooks use small quantities of vanilla to enliven other flavors in sweet custard and panna cottas; Robuchon pulls off an ingenious inversion, bringing to mind those dainty variations on shades of cream sold by paint manufacturers. Vanilla with a hint of arabica. Try enhancing yours with wildflower honey, black tea, cinnamon, anise, tangerine peel, or almond extract. For vanilla *tout seul*, use a bean, not extract, whenever budget and availability allow. To flavor 2½ cups cream you'll need 1 bean *at least*. As to a maximum, it's hard to say—Wolfgang Puck serves a fifty-bean ice cream, and although it's safe to assume he's making more than half a quart, it does sound tantalizing. If using vanilla extract or paste, use 1–2 tsp.

VIN SANTO

When my twins were tiny, my social life was restricted to having people over for dinner. Days spent laundering mounds of very small onesies left neither time nor energy for much cooking, so I stuck to a handful of simple menus. One was charcuterie and olives, gathered while on a stroller-push to the nearest deli, with homemade focaccia. Then roast pork stuffed with garlic and herbs, roast potatoes, and a dark-green salad in a lively vinaigrette. To finish, a glass of *vin santo* with *cantuccini* cookies. One evening, realizing we had worked our way through a case of *vin santo* in the six months since the babies were born, I found the remnants of a bottle in the fridge. So I made a panna cotta with it, because making panna cotta requires little more effort than arranging cookies on a plate. Make as per our starting point, but replace the grappa with 2 tbsp *vin santo*. When I unmolded them, the panna cottas were as wobbly as an hour-old foal, but none the worse for it. I served them beside neat stripes of crushed *cantuccini* with a pinch of salt mixed into them. The effect was not unlike a cheesecake on a Tuscan sabbatical. The flavor of *vin santo* was unmistakable, in the deep rumor of dried fruit (in *vin santo*, the grapes are dried for months before vinification) and the oxidized quality, tempered by the cream. According to the wine expert Stephen Brook, producers "look askance" at the practice of dunking *cantuccini* in their *vin santo*, preferring we try it unaccompanied. I'm happy to comply. When I run out of *cantuccini*.

Custard

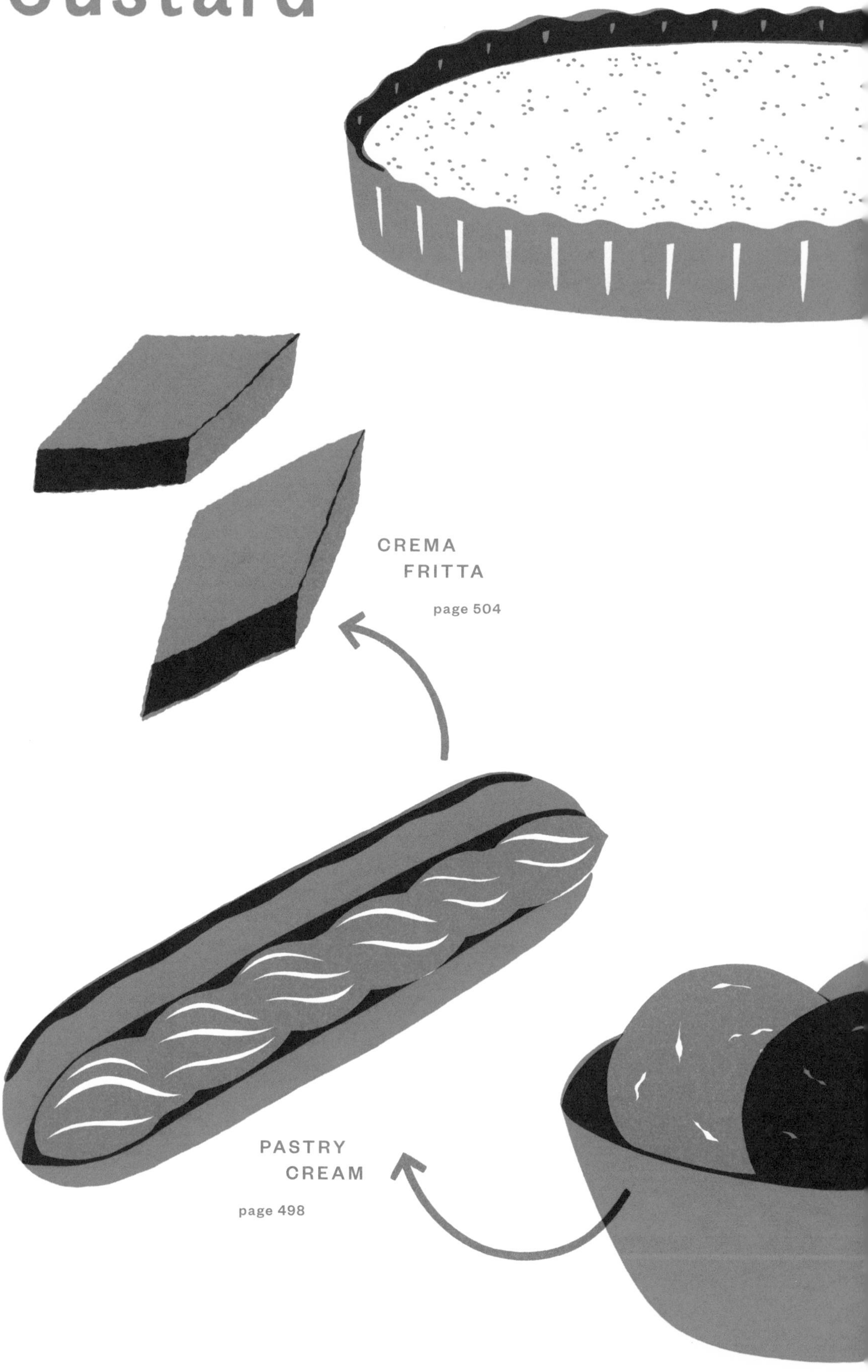

CREMA
FRITTA

page 504

PASTRY
CREAM

page 498

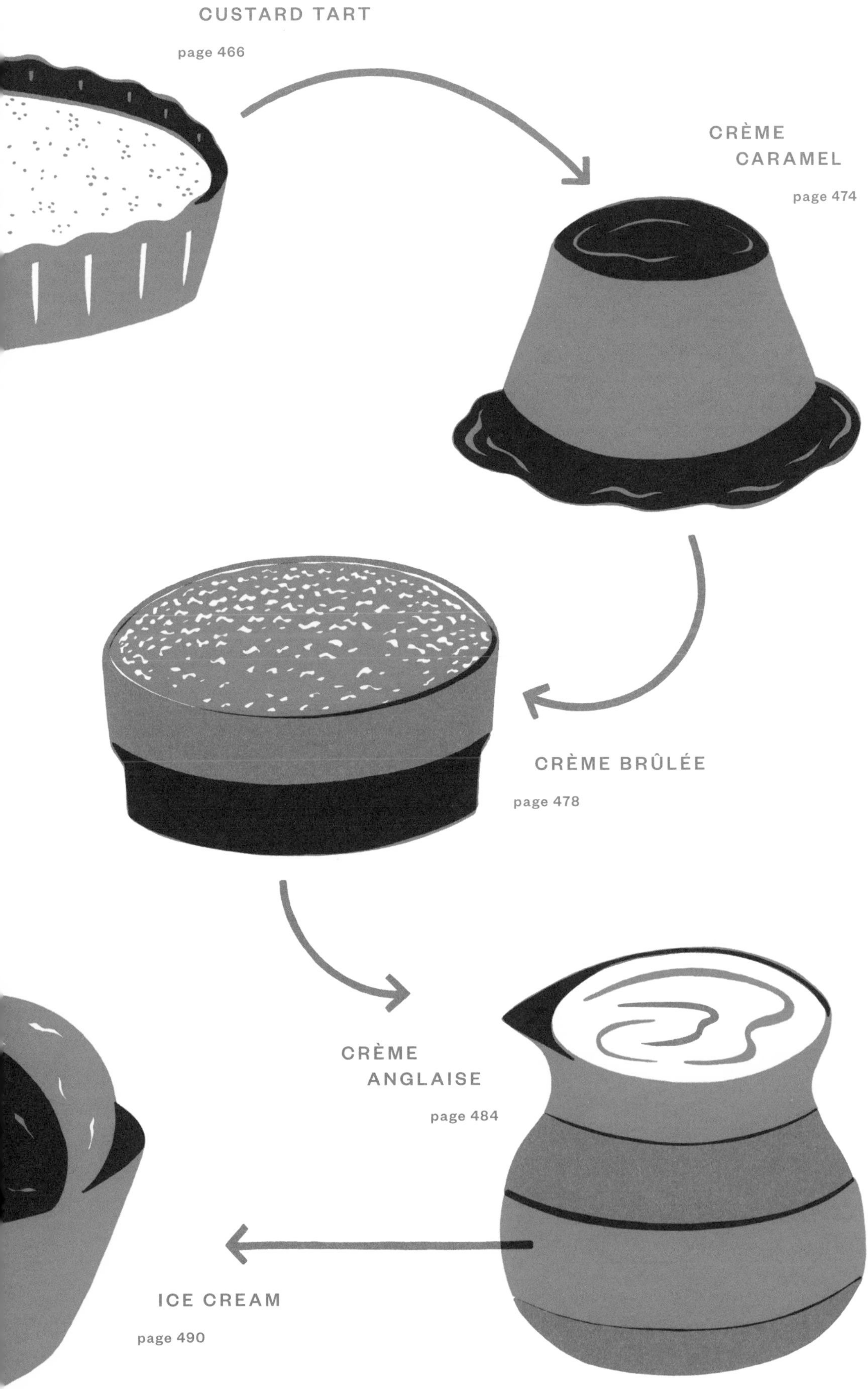

CUSTARD TART

page 466

CRÈME
CARAMEL

page 474

CRÈME BRÛLÉE

page 478

CRÈME
ANGLAISE

page 484

ICE CREAM

page 490

The practice of throwing custard pies dates back as far as 1909, when, in the film *Mr. Flip*, the great cross-eyed silent comedian Ben Turpin is believed to have been the first person ever to be "pied." Quite how the custard pie should have come by its comic reputation is open to debate. Perhaps it's because it encapsulates so much of what Anglo-Saxon culture finds funny in one easily transportable pastry case: the hint of bodily disgust in its spare-tire tremble, the inherent comedy of French words forced through the rectifying mangle of English pronunciation. "Custard" is a corruption of *croustade*, meaning "pastry shell," which makes "custard pie" something of a tautology.

It was for similar reasons that I never gave custard much thought. It was the yellow stuff poured from a dented metal jug onto school steamed puddings. However, once I began to learn how many and various its versions were worldwide, and got the hang of making it myself, I rather grew to respect it. Among other things, custard can offer an excellent neutral basis for flavor experimentation.

Custard is a pact between liquid, egg, and low-to-moderate heat. Of the three, low-to-moderate heat is the non-negotiating party. Custard is ill-suited to high temperatures; it will split, or weep, or become coarse and gritty. The liquid and egg come to the table with a more open mind. The liquid used in custard is usually milk or cream, but custardmaking principles can apply equally to fruit juice or leftover coffee, or to non-liquid ingredients like the cream cheese in cheesecake, or the butter and zest that chaperone the juice in lemon curd. Egg leaves less room for interpretation, but custard can be made with whole eggs, or the yolk or white alone. But the heat is immutable: It must stay low-to-moderate whether it's in the oven, on the stovetop, or in a steamer.

C The custard continuum starts with custard tart—baked custard in
U a pastry shell—then moves through crème caramel to crème brûlée.
S The pastry and caramel demand a moderate degree of skill. The
T custards are as simple as can be. All three are made to the same
A method. If you're new to custardmaking, it's perhaps best to start
R with an unadorned baked custard. To serve 4, beat 3 eggs with 5 tbsp
D sugar in a jug. Stir in 3 cups warm milk and pour the mixture through
  a strainer into a buttered baking dish. Other than keeping the heat
T low, the single most useful thing for the custardmaker to remember
A is the following rule of thumb: 1 egg will set 1 cup milk. Stick to this
R ratio and you'll be all but guaranteed a soft, wobbly custard. Grate
T some nutmeg over the top and bake in a water bath at 275°F until
just set. (By "water bath," I mean a roasting pan or similar, large enough to contain the custard dish, with hot water poured in until it reaches halfway up the outside of the custard dish.) Start checking after about 30 minutes. The custard is ready when it's set but for the slightest wobble in the middle. Baked custard used to be a popular dessert, but is considered a little ordinary these days. Perhaps because it's in contrast to other flavors and textures that custard really comes

into its own: Crème brûlée is made by its cracked hat of burnt sugar; Portuguese *pastéis de nata* would be *nada* without their espresso-sized cups of flaky pastry. In the same vein, you might consider a large baked custard as the centerpiece of a pick-and-mix dessert—*grand-aïoli*-style. Place the custard dish on a plinth with a big silver spoon and encircle it with a tureen of plum compote, a bowl of salted chocolate crumbs, a plate of lemon-scented madeleines and another stacked high with snappy ginger cookies, a bouquet of small paper cones filled with grated white chocolate, and a small handful of whole nutmegs and their tiny grater. Let your guests dip and scoop and grate as they please.

Or just roll up your sleeves and make a custard tart. The pastry shell of custard tarts does more, incidentally, than provide a crisp contrast to the soft filling—it also protects the heat-sensitive custard from the direct heat of the oven, which means the water bath can be dispensed with. Even so, the cooking temperature for most custard tarts is kept low—between 250°F and 300°F (as this is too low for the pastry to cook, the case is baked before the custard goes into it). There are recipes that stipulate higher temperatures—as much as 400°F—but this will generally be because the tarts have been filled with a cold custard mixture. The high heat is solely to warm the custard, and is reduced after 10 minutes or so. Fritz Blank argues that the quiche Lorraine made by the late Hungarian-American chef Louis Szathmáry owed its excellence and authenticity to the hot blast he gave it initially, followed by a relatively cool 325°F for 15–20 minutes. With typical eccentricity, Chef Louis, as Szathmáry was better known in his adoptive Chicago, also called for cooled beurre noisette to be vigorously stirred into the custard before cooking.

CRÈME CARAMEL From custard tart to crème caramel: The only difference in the custard used for these two classic dishes is the ratio of egg to milk. For the crème caramel, or indeed any custard that you can upend on a plate without it collapsing, you'll need 2 eggs per 1 cup milk. The firmness of an upendable custard will not only be apparent in the mouth; it's audibly different to the sort made with 1 egg per cup, making a delightful gulping sound when you scoop out a spoonful.

An egg sets 1 cup milk in a container; 2 eggs set the same amount of milk for a firm, unmoldable custard. Once you've committed this rule to memory, you're free to start improvising. Furthermore, you can work on the basis that each white or yolk counts as half an egg. If, for example, you want to make a custard that sets in its dish, you could use 2 egg whites for 1 cup milk (remembering that, if you beat them, whites will soufflé up when cooked). By the same logic, 4 egg yolks per cup of milk will make a rich, unmoldable crème caramel with a velvety texture. Desserts like this are popular in Portugal and Spain, where they were historically associated with nunneries. Some say that egg yolks were donated to religious foundations by local vintners, who used the albumen to clarify their wines; others that the nuns stiffened their wimples with egg whites. Either way, the holy sisters mixed the yolks with sugar syrup, rather than milk, to make such delicacies as *tocino de cielo* and *ovos-moles*.

I ate something similar at a restaurant in Lisbon called Tasca da Esquina. It was as yellow and shiny as a fresh egg yolk itself: a crème that had no need for caramel. It had the texture of a warm candle, and tasted like the sort of bland, bleary happiness that descends on the threshold of sleep. If bland happiness isn't your bag, you can always flavor the syrup, as in the Portuguese *pudim abade de Priscos*, made with lemon, cinnamon, bacon fat, and port. Or use cream, in which case you'll be making something more akin to a crème brûlée.

C R È M E   Try a crème brûlée and a crème caramel side by side and
B   you'll understand the respective differences egg yolks and whites,
R   or combinations therein, make to a cooked custard. Crème brûlée,
Û   made with yolks only (2 yolks per cup of cream is standard), has
L   none of the resistance to the teeth that whites lend to crème caramel,
É   which is usually made with whole eggs (2 per cup of milk). Whites
E   make for quite a rubbery set, yolks something softer—the reason
why eating a crème brûlée pings the same bell in your pleasure
center as closing the door of a Mercedes, when the car you drive is
a Toyota Yaris.

By the same token, chefs often primp everyday custard-based dishes, like tarts and bread pudding, by replacing the whole eggs with oodles of luxurious yolks. Marcus Wareing's famous custard tart uses 9 egg yolks for 2 cups cream, making it, in effect, a crème brûlée set in a pastry shell. Princess Diana's favorite dessert, according to her former chef Darren McGrady, was a bread pudding made—like Wareing's custard tart—with a crème-brûlée custard in place of the normal stuff, poured over buttered bread and Amaretto-plumped raisins. No wonder she fell for a heart surgeon. A less extravagant option than using yolks only is just to up the yolk-to-white ratio. Nigel Slater makes a crème caramel with 3 whole eggs and 2 yolks in place of the standard 4 eggs. You get the picture.

It's worth noting that all the custard recipes on the continuum call for the milk or cream to be heated before it is added to the yolks. You'll find recipes elsewhere that don't stipulate this, but the technique applies in *Lateral Cooking*—firstly because warming the dairy allows you to infuse it with hard aromatics like vanilla beans, cinnamon sticks, or citrus zest, and secondly because it helps the custard to reach its thickening temperature faster. This is the reason why crème anglaise is invariably made with warm milk; a shorter cooking time is a boon when you're craned over the stovetop, stirring vigilantly, tapping your foot as you wait for the magic to happen. Straining is nearly always called for at some point. It makes for a smoother custard, partly by intercepting any stringy bits, aromatic debris from infusing the milk, or flecks of hardened yolk. The last have a tendency to form if you let your yolks and sugar sit together for too long without whisking. Strain any custard that can be easily strained. Not every recipe for pastry cream calls for it to be pushed through a sieve, but tiny lumps form in it so readily that it's worth the effort. Some cooks even do this to the cream cheese and egg mix for cheesecake. (I tried it once, for some reason expecting it to be fun. It wasn't. It was like sieving cream cheese, whose only benefit was in providing a fresh synonym for swimming in molasses. Don't bother: It isn't necessary.)

You'll note that the methods are indeterminate, tending to vague, when it comes to cooking times. Frankly, custard is ready when it's ready. Custard couldn't give a hoot if you're glued to the radio or TV, rapt at the heartrending climax of the afternoon drama, or poised to nab a bargain on eBay. Its cooking time will depend on the quantity of custard, the material your dish is made of, the material your water bath is made of, the caprice of your oven, and the temperature of the custard mixture when you put it in the oven. The only answer is to start checking it as early as it *might* be ready, remain vigilant thereafter, and be prepared to spring it from the oven the moment you think it is. To earn your stripes as a custardmaker means learning to judge by eye. In the case of baked custards, I find this falls somewhere between "unsure" and "unsure I'm unsure." Custards will continue to cook after their removal from the heat, so it's best to err on the side of impatience. If you're sure it's cooked, it's probably overcooked.

C Crème anglaise is ready when it reaches 176°F. If you don't have a
R thermometer to hand, take it off the heat when it's just become thick
E enough to coat the back of a spoon and hold the line when you run
M a finger through it. The same rule applies to the custard for crème
E brûlée, which can be made on the stovetop rather than in the oven.
  Delia Smith's recipe for "proper custard" is, in fact, a stirred crème
A brûlée custard, because it's made entirely with cream. Most crème
N anglaise recipes are rather less rich, calling for whole milk, or milk
G mixed with a *little* cream, and relying on a little more egg yolk—
L 2 per 1 cup—for richness. A small quantity of flour is optional for
A crème anglaise, with yolks alone making for a silkier texture. Flour
I bolsters the thickening effect of the yolks, but the main reason it's
S added is for heat protection. Cautious cooks might prefer to use
E a double boiler to the same end, but if you use a heavy-based pan
and are able to keep the heat low, you can make your anglaise directly
on the stovetop and it won't be as painfully slow.

Nowadays, crème anglaise is almost exclusively considered a sauce, but in the nineteenth century it was often served as a dessert in its own right, chilled, and flavored with bitter almond, chocolate, liqueur, or lemon zest. Ferran Adrià gives a recipe that should, in my opinion, revive the custom: a white-chocolate custard served in a soup bowl and topped with toasted pistachios. You can make something similar by following our starting point for crème anglaise, but halving the quantities, omitting the vanilla (as the white chocolate will furnish that flavor), and replacing the milk with heavy cream. When the custard reaches 176°F, or is thick enough to trace a line through on the back of the spoon, pour it over 1½ cups finely chopped white chocolate and leave for a few minutes before whisking until smooth. Divide among 6 dishes and sprinkle with the toasted nuts. Devour it by the ladleful and kid yourself you could have worked at El Bulli.

I make *petits pots au chocolat* the same way; the oven-baked sort is too apt to disappoint. Stir hot, slightly creamy custard into chopped dark chocolate, as you would for ganache, and it turns into a perfectly smooth, luxurious chocolate goo. Crème anglaise is also the starting point for bavarois. Bavarois is otherwise known as Bavarian cream, but it's far foxier to lift one eyebrow and purr *bav-arrr-WAH*. It's a stirred custard, essentially, containing gelatin, and with whipped cream and/or stiffly beaten egg whites folded into it. Bavarois sets into a light mousse: smooth and melt-in-the-mouth, yet firm enough to unmold or be cut into slices.

I C E C R E A M
A third reason you might want to make more custard than you need: Freeze any leftover crème anglaise and you'll have gelato. Don't worry if your custard is only milk-based: Many gelati are made this way. The results will be denser, as milk doesn't retain air whipped into it like cream does. Texture's loss, however, is flavor's gain— the advantage of the extra density will be a greater intensity on the palate. If it's ice cream you had actually set out to make, our starting point here is just a few tweaks away from crème anglaise, calling for a mixture of cream and milk, and more sugar. In most custards, the quantity of sugar can be increased or decreased to taste, but in ice cream it has structural implications. The higher sugar content helps create smaller ice crystals, resulting in a smoother texture. Reduce the sugar too much and your ice cream will be crunchy. The method for making custard for ice cream is the same as for crème anglaise, but once the desired thickness is achieved, the custard is cooled, chilled, then frozen. The finished (but as yet unfrozen) custard can be augmented with whipped cream (adding more air), fruit purée, or any number of flavorings: The suggestions on pages 492-6 are only there to stimulate the infinite gelateria of your imagination.

PASTRY CREAM Pastry cream, the next starting point on the continuum, is similarly sweet to ice cream, but is always made with milk, rather than cream, as the thickening is supplied by flour. Flour gives crème pâtissière the heft to support layers of pastry or fruit. As with so many custards, it's usually worth making a double batch. Most sweet soufflés have a pastry-cream base. Flavor the custard as you fancy, whisk in some French meringue (page 424), transfer it to prepared soufflé dishes, and bake in the oven. The recipe for pastry cream given here can also be used to make "pudding," the thick, soft, dense or light American dessert, although admittedly a version on the modestly sweetened side. The few puddings I've tried in the U.S. have been enough to lift me from my dining chair on a wave of hyperglycemic euphoria.

C
R
E
M
A

F
R
I
T
T
A

With *crema fritta* we reach continuum's end. It's made with even more flour than pastry cream, meaning that the quantity of egg can be reduced. *Crema fritta*—literally, "fried cream"—is a custard robust enough to cut into slices when cold. It's then coated with bread crumbs and deep-fried. In Venice, *crema fritta* is sold as a street snack during *celebrazioni*. The custard is often flavored with lemon, either on its own or in combination with vanilla, or *rosolio*, a local liqueur derived from rose petals. Traditionally it's cut into diamond shapes, rolled in ground nuts, then fried and served with a fruit compote. And it's not limited to Venice: Served as a dessert course, *crema fritta* was all the rage in San Francisco in the 1950s. Elsewhere in Italy, *crema fritta* is just as likely to be served as part of a savory course. Anna Del Conte recalls a meal in the Marche region where she ate slices of it alongside salami and prosciutto. Some sources maintain it's an essential part of a traditional Bolognese *fritto misto*. Hard to imagine, I know. I once made a custard flavored with lemon and vanilla and fried the pieces in olive oil. The first thing to note is that cutting custard into diamonds is a very pleasant culinary experience—up there with peeling the skin from an avocado half in one go. Fried and left to cool, the pieces of *crema fritta* were reminiscent—unsurprisingly, given what goes into them—of both pancakes and béchamel, which serves to suggest how well they might go with hot or cold meats.

A Chinese variant on the theme of fried custard, *chi ma kuo cha*, is made with eggs, flour, water, and a little milk. The golden slices are sprinkled while still hot with a mixture of crushed, toasted sesame seeds and sugar. Making *chi ma kuo cha* I was reminded of churros. As you'll know if you've ever breakfasted in Spain, churros (page [150]) consist of a stiff batter of flour and water, extruded into ridged lengths, deep-fried, and dusted with a shake of sugar. They're usually served with a dipping cup of thick hot chocolate—which would, come to think of it, make an inauthentic and utterly irresistible accompaniment to a few warm slices of sesame-sprinkled, fried Chinese custard.

Custard Tart

This starting point makes an ordinary custard tart: 2 eggs will give a just-set texture to 2 cups milk, 3 something more definitely sliceable. Variations on the basic custard tart include pumpkin pie, quiche, and cheesecake. You'll find that a fair few of them skip the heating stage. It's fine to put cold custard in the oven: It just might take a little longer to cook. If you prefer a baked custard without the pastry, see ᶜ under Leeway.

For a deep 8-in tart to serve 8 ᴬ

INGREDIENTS
1 deep 8-in tart shell made with shortcrust pastry (page 566) ᴮ ᶜ
2 cups milk ᴰ ᴱ
1 vanilla bean ᶠ
3 eggs ᴳ
¼ cup sugar ᴴ
Freshly grated nutmeg—optional ᴵ

1 Make the pastry shell and bake it blind (page 567).

2 Pour the milk into a saucepan. Slice open the vanilla bean and scrape the seeds into the milk. Put the bean in too, then bring the milk just up to a boil over a medium heat. Remove from the heat and let infuse for 10 minutes to 1 hour before removing the bean.

3 Reheat the milk until it's just beginning to bubble.
   Or heat it, if you have skipped step 2.

4 In a heatproof bowl, whisk the eggs and sugar together.
   Don't leave the eggs and sugar together unwhisked for too long, or solid specks of yolk will begin to form.

5 Gradually stir the warm milk into the egg mixture.
   This process is called tempering.

6 Strain the custard through a sieve into the blind-baked pastry shell and bake at 275°F for 30–50 minutes. ᴶ
   Judge if it's ready by gently agitating the pan, starting at the shortest possible cooking time. When the custard is set, but still a bit wobbly in the middle, remove from the oven.

7 Grate over a little nutmeg, if you like. Serve warm or at room temperature.

LEEWAY

A For a deep 10-in tart, make twice the quantity of the custard filling.

B The pastry used for custard tarts can vary considerably. Delia Smith opts for a basic dough with lard and butter; others use yolk-enriched sweet pastry (page 567) with flavorings, rough puff (page 574), or phyllo.

C Omit the pastry for a small, plain baked custard. Simply strain the mixture into a buttered baking dish, place in a water bath, and bake as opposite. If you want to unmold it, follow the proportions for crème caramel by adding an extra egg.

D Cream—any sort—can be used in place of some or all of the milk. Skim milk or 1% or 2% milk make too thin a custard, although they are fine mixed with some cream.

E Crème fraîche or sour cream can be used in place of all or some of the milk to give a refreshing lactic tang.

F Other hard aromatics like cinnamon sticks or star anise can be infused in the same way. If using vanilla *extract* (or any other liquid flavoring), skip step 2, then add to taste at the end of step 5, starting with 1 tsp. At this stage the custard will still be warm enough for a bit more sugar to be dissolved in it, if necessary.

G You can get away with 2 eggs (1 will set 1 cup milk), but 3 is pretty standard. As with most custards, yolks can be substituted for whole eggs—use 2 yolks in place of each egg. For his award-winning custard tart, Marcus Wareing uses 9 yolks for 2 cups heavy cream and 6 tbsp sugar.

H The ¼ cup given here is a modest quantity of sugar; some recipes double it.

I Nutmeg can also be grated into the custard at step 5.

J The Flavors & Variations section includes custard tarts cooked at 350°F or higher, but these have a little flour added, which stabilizes the custard at this heat.

CORIANDER SEED

You don't need to toast the seeds, but you do need to crush them. Don't use store-bought ground coriander, as it's unlikely to have the more feminine quality of the freshly crushed seeds. Pellegrino Artusi's recipe for custard tart gives the option of flavoring it with vanilla *or* with crushed coriander seeds. I'd suggest combining the two. Crush 1 tbsp coriander seeds and add to the milk with the split vanilla bean at step 2.

ELDERFLOWER

Not quite custard as we know it, but a fourteenth-century recipe collection called *The Forme of Cury* (from *cuire*, the French for "to cook") includes a recipe for a tart called *sambocade*, made with curds, bread crumbs, sugar, egg whites, and washed elderflower blossoms. For a simpler, silkier custard, use elderflower cordial (a concentrated nonalcoholic syrup). It's always worth making your own, but on the assumption you lack the time and/or elderflowers, here's a version based on the cordial you can buy. For 2 cups milk, add 3 tbsp elderflower cordial and ¼ tsp vanilla extract at the end of step 5. Check for sweetness and intensity of flavor and adjust accordingly.

LEMON

Tarte au citron was the first posh dessert I learned to make. At roughly the same time I also got the knack of a neat little zucchini timbale to serve as an appetizer. Did I ever get some mileage out of those two recipes. I cooked them for all of my friends, and when I ran out of them, I made more friends, rather than add any new dishes to my repertoire. Years later, when I moved from the tiny flat in West London where I'd learned to cook, I dismantled my dining table and found a large piece of petrified lemon tart jammed to its underside. The list of suspects ran to many pages. There's no need to heat the cream for this custard. For a shallow 8-in tart, use 2 eggs, 2 egg yolks, the juice and finely grated zest of 2 lemons, ¾ cup sugar, and ½ cup cream. Mix everything together except the zest. Strain the mixture, then stir in the zest and pour into your blind-baked tart shell. Bake it in a 275°F oven for 25–30 minutes. Once cool, sift over a fine veil of confectioners' sugar.

NEW YORK CHEESECAKE

A proper New York cheesecake should be deep enough to need its own psychoanalyst. Its European forebears were made with strained cottage cheese, but with the invention of Philadelphia cream cheese in the 1880s, Americans devised a bigger, better cheesecake of their own. Originally made in a pastry shell, then on zwieback crumbs (zwiebacks are the sweet, almost weightless crackers that for some reason are called "French Toast" in U.K. supermarkets), these days the base of a New York cheesecake is usually crushed graham crackers, which are a *bit* like British digestive biscuits (i.e. cookies). The filling is a sort of custard, but the thickness of the cream cheese means that fewer eggs are needed to set it. For a cheesecake to serve 12, press your chosen base evenly into the bottom of a 9-in springform pan encased in foil. (For a graham-cracker base, judge how many crackers you need by paving them unbroken over the bottom of the pan, before crushing them into a fine crumb and mixing with about a third of their volume in melted butter.) Mix 2¼ lb room-temperature, full-fat cream cheese with 1½ cups sugar, ⅔ cup sour cream, 1 tbsp vanilla extract, the zest of 2 lemons, ¼ cup flour, and 3 extra large eggs for only as long as it takes to combine everything. Scoop the mixture onto whatever base you've chosen, then bake in a water bath at 325°F for 1¼ hours. Remove the finished cheesecake from its water bath and foil and let it cool before leaving in the fridge to chill and firm up for at least 4 hours or, better, overnight. You don't have to eat it all at once. Well wrapped, it can be frozen for a month, although the texture when thawed will not be quite as good. For a smaller cheesecake, halve the quantities, use a 6-in springform pan, and reduce the baking time to 50 minutes.

PANETTONE BREAD PUDDING

Think of a bread pudding as custard tart with the crust on the inside. Slice 10 oz panettone and let it dry out. Buttering the slices is optional. Arrange them in a greased baking dish. How you like your pudding will determine the size of the dish and the position of the panettone: If you're partial to the soggy part, you'll want more of the slices immersed in the custard; if you prefer the crispy bit, ensure there's plenty sitting proud. Pour over a custard made by beating together ⅔ cup heavy cream, 1 cup warm whole milk, 2 eggs, and 2 tbsp sugar, then bake at 275°F. Start checking for a wobbly set from 25 minutes. When it's cooled slightly, sprinkle with confectioners' sugar. Finely grated citrus zest and/or a tot of Marsala, Amaretto, or vanilla extract can be added, but the panettone's own flavor infiltrates the custard and is pretty glorious without enhancement. In place of panettone, try buttered bread, brioche, or croissants—or challah (page 56), which is said to make an outstanding variation. You may want to add a handful of two of dried fruit soaked in rum, brandy, or fruit juice.

POOR KNIGHTS OF WINDSOR

Synonymous with French toast or *pain perdu*. The connection with the Poor Knights, military pensioners put up at Windsor Castle following the Battle of Crécy in 1346, is unclear, but you might read a certain poorhouse dignity into the pudding's enterprising use of humble ingredients. My dad called the same thing eggy bread or gypsy toast.

Whatever you call it, you might think it a bit of a stretch as a variation on custard tart—but, as with the panettone pudding on the previous page, it calls for the same kind of simple custard, with the bread standing in for the pie crust. Beat the milk and egg together (1–3 tbsp milk per egg) and add a pinch of salt before pouring the mixture into a wide, shallow dish. Soak slices of bread in the custard, then shallow-fry in clarified butter or oil: How thick you slice the bread, and how long you soak it in the custard, are as much a matter of taste as the depth of browning you give it. Some add a little sugar, vanilla, or cinnamon (or all three) to the custard, as you might to crème anglaise. There are recipes that call for a tot of sherry or brandy, and some cooks like to drizzle maple syrup, or sprinkle confectioners' sugar, over the finished pudding. In Portugal and Brazil, an eggy bread called *rabanada* is eaten at Christmas with a festive port- or wine-flavored syrup.

PUMPKIN

Classic American pumpkin pie is only a variation on a standard custard tart. But can the British ever learn to love its peculiar taste? You can add enough spice and sugar to sink a clipper, and yet still—that weird migrainous headiness, like a vegetarian lobster bisque. The thanks *I'd* be giving were that I only had to eat it once a year. Still, it's not only Americans who go for pumpkin-flavored custards. In Thailand, a sugary version is baked in scooped-out pumpkins and served in slices. In Japan, Beard Papa, the Osaka-based bakery that specializes in pastry-cream-filled choux puffs, includes pumpkin in its range of flavors. For American pumpkin pie, mix a 14-oz can of condensed milk with a 15-oz can of unsweetened pumpkin purée, 2 extra large eggs, 2 tsp pumpkin-pie spice (or 1 tsp ground cinnamon, ½ tsp each of ground ginger and nutmeg, and ¼ tsp each of ground allspice and cloves), and a pinch of salt. Pour into a deep 9-in unbaked tart shell and bake at 400°F for 10 minutes, then reduce the oven temperature to 325°F. Start checking after 40 minutes and remove when the filling is just set. Serve at room temperature. Note, incidentally, that this pie goes into the oven with the pastry unbaked, and that the oven temperature is at the very upper limit for dishes involving custard.

QUICHE LORRAINE

Clucking at the distinctly low practice of using grated cheese in quiche Lorraine, Elizabeth David speculates that it might be a corruption of the older tradition, endemic to that part of France, of adding fresh white cheese (*fromage blanc*) to the cream used in tarts. I have to admit I prefer my quiche made as follows. Assuming you have blind-baked your deep 8-in tart shell (page 567), fry about 5 oz bacon lardons until they're beginning to turn golden, then remove with a slotted spoon and drain on paper towels. Coarsely grate ¾ cup Gruyère. Scatter the cooked lardons over the tart base. Briefly mix scant 1 cup each of crème fraîche and heavy cream with 3 eggs, ½ tsp salt, and two-thirds of the cheese. Pour this custard over the lardons, sprinkle with the rest of the cheese, and bake at 300°F until the custard has golden-brown patches and the center is almost set: about 35–40 minutes.

SAFFRON

Flavor your custard with saffron and it will turn an ocher of such richness it will look as if you've used two dozen egg yolks. Moreover, saffron has a depth and peculiarity of flavor to match its color. Its intensity seems to egg certain chefs on to excess: It's the J.P. Morgan Palladium Card of haute cuisine. At his restaurant in Santa Fe, James Campbell Caruso serves a baked saffron custard filled with morcilla (the rich Spanish blood sausage), roasted bell peppers, and fried sage. Mark Hix gives a recipe for individual all-butter puff-pastry tarts deep-filled with saffron custard. He uses light cream, which will be rich—but why not max out the saffron card and make it heavy? Or clotted? Clotted cream and saffron is as classic a Cornish combination as cider and amphetamines. Or there's *om ali*, an Egyptian baked custard embedded with shards of baked phyllo or puff pastry, toasted nuts, and dried fruit. Some mix saffron into the custard, others might use rosewater or orange-flower water. A sort of moneyed bread pudding. To flavor 2 cups milk/cream, use a generous pinch of saffron strands—let's say 15, although, to paraphrase Leona Helmsley, counting saffron stigmas is for the little people.

STOCK

Chawanmushi is a popular Japanese savory custard, usually made with dashi, but other homemade stocks can be put to similar ends. Like many Asian custards, it's steamed until set. I would categorize it as a baked custard, but in Japan it's considered more of a soup, partly because it's one of the few dishes eaten with a spoon as well as chopsticks. The inventive cook, suggests Shizuo Tsuji in *Japanese Cooking*, will be brimming with variations. Slices of fish paste, slivers of lemon zest, parboiled bamboo shoots, gingko nuts, or lily root might be set into the soy- and mirin-flavored, egg-enriched stock, aside from more familiar ingredients like mushroom and carrot. Nobu opts for warm scallop and tops it off with a spoonful of caviar and a little pared lime zest. *Chawanmushi* means "teacup," which is what it's served in.

Refreshing cold versions are offered during the summer. Typically, for each tea cup allow scant 1 cup stock and 1 egg for each cup.

TARRAGON, LEEK & SOUR CREAM

Tarragon and sour cream make a terrific summer pairing in a savory tart. Like Nancy and Peggy, the Amazon half of Arthur Ransome's *Swallows and Amazons*, they're a cool twosome with enough character to offset the sweet goody-goodiness of pea, leek, asparagus, or crab. If you don't have sour cream or crème fraîche, or if you're intolerant of cow's milk, goat's cream is another great match for tarragon. Next time it's sunny, and you'd rather be picnicking than wrangling pastry in a warm kitchen, do without the tart shell. Once cool, the crustless quiche will be firm enough to divide into pieces. Slice 2 leeks and soften them in a little butter. Meanwhile, beat 2 eggs, 1 cup sour cream, 2 tsp finely chopped tarragon, and a pinch of salt in a jug (no need to heat the mixture). Scatter the soft leeks and a handful of fresh peas in a watertight 8-in tart pan. Pour the custard over the vegetables (through a strainer if you like) and bake at 275°F until just set—it'll take about 35 minutes. Rush to your riverbank to eat your quiche while it's still warm, maybe with a cool salad of baby romaine leaves and radishes, tossed in a lemony dressing.

YOGURT

Fine to replace some, or all, of the dairy in your custard with yogurt, but beware of super-lowfat varieties, which are too watery to give a good result. You can make a baked custard using plain Greek yogurt in place of the milk; flavored with a little vanilla and lemon zest, the effect is very similar to a cheesecake without its crumb crust. This is a mildly adapted version of Sam and Sam Clark's recipe. No need to scald the yogurt: Just whisk 1½ cups Greek yogurt (not lowfat) with 3 egg yolks, ¼ cup sugar, 1 tbsp flour, 1 tsp vanilla paste, and the finely grated zest of 1 lemon and 1 orange. In a separate bowl, beat 3 egg whites to stiff peaks, then beat in 2 tbsp sugar, continuing to beat until the mixture is glossy. Fold into the yogurt mix and pour into a watertight 10-in round pan resting in a water bath. Bake at 350°F for 20 minutes, then remove and sprinkle over a handful of roughly chopped pistachios. Return to the oven to bake for a further 20 minutes, until the top is golden. Lift from the water bath immediately, then cool and refrigerate. Serve with seasonal fruit.

Custard Tart → Other Directions

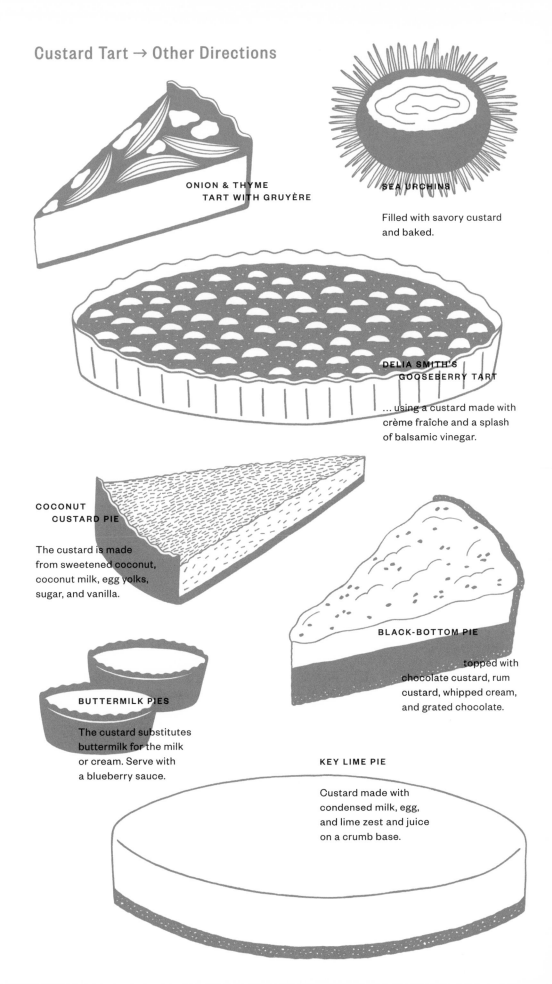

ONION & THYME TART WITH GRUYÈRE

SEA URCHINS

Filled with savory custard and baked.

DELIA SMITH'S GOOSEBERRY TART

... using a custard made with crème fraîche and a splash of balsamic vinegar.

COCONUT CUSTARD PIE

The custard is made from sweetened coconut, coconut milk, egg yolks, sugar, and vanilla.

BLACK-BOTTOM PIE

topped with chocolate custard, rum custard, whipped cream, and grated chocolate.

BUTTERMILK PIES

The custard substitutes buttermilk for the milk or cream. Serve with a blueberry sauce.

KEY LIME PIE

Custard made with condensed milk, egg, and lime zest and juice on a crumb base.

Crème Caramel

There is negligible difference between the custard in a crème caramel and a custard tart. Both are made with whole eggs and milk—but for our crème caramel, we use 4 (rather than 3) eggs per 2 cups milk, to make sure the custard is strong enough to support its own weight when unmolded. In some contemporary recipes, a more luxurious texture is achieved by replacing some of the milk with cream, and some of the whole eggs with yolks.

For 6 crème caramels made in 5- to 6-oz ramekins or darioles [A]

INGREDIENTS
2 cups milk [B]
1 vanilla bean [C]
4 eggs [D]
4 tbsp sugar [E]

FOR THE CARAMEL
⅔ cup sugar
2 tbsp boiling water

1 To make the caramel, put the sugar and boiling water in a heavy-based pan over a medium heat. Keep a beady eye on it, stirring intermittently as it starts to color.

2 When it's turned brick-red, immediately pour into the ramekins and swirl around to coat the bases evenly. Transfer to a large roasting pan or similar and set aside.
   Don't be tempted to pour in too much caramel; it will only stick to the bottom of the dishes. Better to stir a few tablespoons of warm water into any remaining caramel and serve it on the side.

3 Pour the milk into a saucepan. Slice open the vanilla bean and scrape the seeds into the milk. Put the bean in too, then bring the milk just up to a boil over a medium heat. Remove from the heat and let infuse for 10 minutes to 1 hour before removing the vanilla bean.

4 Reheat the milk until it's just beginning to bubble.

5 In a heatproof bowl, whisk the eggs and sugar together.
   Don't leave the eggs and sugar together unwhisked for too long, or solid specks of yolk will begin to form.

6   Gradually stir the warm milk into the egg mixture.

7   Strain the custard through a sieve into a jug, then divide among the dishes. Set them in a roasting pan.

8   Pour enough tap-hot water into the pan to come halfway up the sides of the ramekins. Cover the pan with a loose tent of foil.
    The foil will prevent the top of the custard from becoming overly brown and thick.

9   Bake at 275°F. After 30 minutes, remove the foil and check the set of the crèmes. Keep checking until they are almost set, with a slight wobble in the center.

10 Remove from the oven and carefully lift the ramekins out of the water bath. Cool, on a rack if possible, then chill.

11 To serve, run a sharp-pointed knife around the edge and unmold onto plates.
    If the caramel seems stuck, place the dishes in a roasting pan, add ⅛ in or so of boiling water, and leave for 1 minute to loosen.

LEEWAY

A   For a large crème caramel, cook this quantity in a 1-quart dish: Try to find one wide enough for the custard not to be much deeper than 2 in. Bake for about 1 hour, checking to see if it's ready from 50 minutes.

B   Some use 50/50 milk and cream for additional richness. You can use coconut milk rather than cow's, but it will tint your crèmes a melancholy gray.

C   Other hard aromatics like cinnamon sticks or star anise can be infused in the same way. If using vanilla *extract* (or any other liquid flavoring), skip step 3. Add them to taste at the end of step 6, starting with 1 tsp. Grated nutmeg can also be added here. At this stage the custard will still be warm enough for a bit more sugar to be dissolved in it, if necessary.

D   Whole eggs can be replaced with 2 yolks for a more unctuous texture.

E   The 4 tbsp given here is a modest quantity of sugar. Many recipes—especially more recent ones—double it.

BAY LEAF

In recent years bay leaf has been restored, to some extent, to its former status as a standard flavoring for custards. Elizabeth David thought that bay tasted like vanilla and nutmeg—which are the standard custard flavorings—so the suggestion in a 1929 edition of *Homes & Gardens* to mix a small amount of bay with brandy should by rights give your custard an eggnog-like quality. Traditionally bay was used in mixtures with lemon or orange zest. With a potato peeler, pare off 3 strips of lemon or orange zest (well scrubbed, if not from unwaxed fruit). Put in a pan with 3 fresh bay leaves (or 5 dried) and 2 cups milk. Scald and let infuse for about 30 minutes. Other classic combinations with bay include bitter almond and brown sugar, or cinnamon. If the latter appeals, seek out some *tejpat*, also called Indian bay leaf. It's a similar color and shape to the European laurel, if unrelated, and has a notably cinnamon-like flavor. When I opened a package and breathed in, I instantly thought of toasted hot cross buns.

COFFEE

Cult burgeristas Shake Shack sometimes sell a coffee custard with doughnut pieces in it. Too rich for me, but it's a fun idea. To my mind the bitterness and complexity of coffee make it one of the most satisfying, which is to say least monotonous, flavorings for custards. Instant coffee works very well, even if you disdain it in a cup. Add 1 tbsp to the hot milk at the end of step 3 and check for strength and sweetness. On the other hand, Richard Olney makes the custard for his crème caramel using "very strong, freshly made drip coffee." Mix it 50/50 with milk and follow our starting point, using either ½ vanilla bean or ½ tsp vanilla extract to round out the flavor.

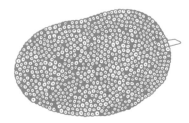

JACKFRUIT

In Southeast Asia, jackfruit, like mango and papaya, is used in savory dishes when unripe. Given the chance to mature, it has an insistently chewy texture, a whiff of old-fashioned, powdered Parmesan from a plastic shaker, and a flavor like slivers of mango wrapped in Bayonne ham. It's often cooked with coconut milk, then puréed, which restrains its ruder side and makes it a popular flavoring for custards. Chef David Thompson has been known to garnish his unmolded jackfruit custard not with caramel but with the seeds of the fruit, boiled and sliced, along with grated fresh coconut and a banana fritter.

ORANGE

In France and Spain, it's not uncommon to make a baked custard cup with orange juice in place of milk or cream. Follow the crème caramel method, leaving out the vanilla and doubling the sugar. Aside from sweetening the juice, the sugar adds some body, too. For all its ease of preparation the combination of caramel and orange yields a satisfyingly complex blend of bitter, sharp, and sweet. More unusually, chef Simon Hopkinson makes the custard for his orange crème caramels by whizzing the carefully pared zest of 4 large oranges with 5 tbsp sugar in a food processor, then scalds it with the milk and lets it infuse for 1 hour. The zest releases an abundance of essential oils, so this way you'll get a bold, true orange flavor.

ORANGE-FLOWER WATER

Gertrude Stein's lover, Alice B. Toklas, had a voice "like a viola at dusk," according to the poet James Merrill. She also made a mean crème renversée: crème caramel by another name. The Toklas method was to use evaporated milk for the custard, flavored with orange-flower water. It was said to be particularly good with chocolate sauce. A century earlier, Eliza Acton did away with all the crème nonsense and called the dish French custard, infusing the milk with a few petals of orange blossom—"very superior," she notes, "to that derived from the distilled water." I'd have liked to see her say *that* to Gertrude's face. In the absence of blossoms, use 2 tsp orange-flower water for 2 cups milk.

PANDAN

Pandan, or screwpine, is a commonly used flavoring for steamed custards in Southeast Asia. Raw pandan smells somewhat alarmingly of ammonia, but when heated it releases the same flavor compound as cooked basmati rice. Fresh leaves are less widely available than the kind of bottled essence that's the color of a dragon's underbelly and is found in Asian markets. Pandan is often paired with coconut; the combination tastes like freshly baked coconut cake. For 2 cups full-fat, unsweetened coconut milk, use 4 leaves, raked with a fork to bring out their oils. The pandan flavor works very well with the caramel, but for an authentic approach, pour the plain custard into cups or ramekins and steam, covered, checking from 20 minutes to see if set.

SAUTERNES

Nigella Lawson singles out a Sauternes custard she ate at Quaglino's as one of the best things she tasted in her twelve years as a restaurant critic. It was served in the manner of a crème caramel, with Armagnac-soaked prunes. To make something like it, adapt our starting point by replacing the milk with ⅔ cup Sauternes and 1½ cups heavy cream, and 2 of the eggs with 4 yolks, also adding 1 extra tbsp sugar. You'll need to warm the Sauternes separately from the cream, and whisk it into the eggs before the cream is added. For another layer of flavor, consider the entry in the *International Dictionary of Food and Cooking* on "crème bachique": a custard flavored with Sauternes and cinnamon.

Crème Brûlée

King of custards. Crème brûlée owes its fabulous texture to a mixture of egg yolks and cream. Only 4 yolks are used for 2 cups cream, so the set is loose—you couldn't turn it out of a dish. The custard is made to the same method as crème caramel, although unlike crème caramel it can also be cooked on the stovetop, using the same ingredients as below, but following the directions for crème anglaise (page 484). I tend to favor the oven method, which is less prone to overheating or overcooking. Without its brûlée roof, the dessert becomes *petits pots de crème*, often served, at least in restaurants, in dinky porcelain "churns."

For 4 individual crèmes made in shallow crème brûlée dishes or 5- to 6-oz ramekins [A]

INGREDIENTS
2 cups heavy cream [B]
1 vanilla bean [C]
4 egg yolks
4 tbsp sugar [D]
Pinch of salt
Sugar for the brûlée top

1   Pour the cream into a saucepan. Slice open the vanilla bean and scrape the seeds into the cream. Put the bean in too, then bring the cream just up to a boil over a medium heat. Remove from the heat and let infuse for 10 minutes to 1 hour before removing the vanilla bean.

2   Reheat the cream until it's just beginning to bubble.

3   In a heatproof bowl, whisk the egg yolks with the sugar and salt. Don't leave the eggs and sugar together unwhisked for too long, or solid specks of yolk will begin to form.

4   Gradually stir the warm cream into the egg mixture.

5   Sit your crème brûlée dishes or ramekins in a large roasting pan or similar. Strain the custard mixture through a sieve into a jug, then divide among the dishes. Pour enough hot water into the roasting pan to come halfway up the sides of the dishes. [E]

6 Bake at 275°F, checking for set after 20 minutes for shallow crème brûlée dishes, 30 minutes for ramekins.
The crèmes are done when they are almost set, with a slight wobble in the center. Remove immediately from their water bath and let cool, preferably on a rack.

7 Once cool, chill the crèmes.
They can be kept, covered, in the fridge for a few days.

8 Sprinkle each crème with a thin layer of sugar and apply a blowtorch. Or put them under a hot broiler, close to the heat, and keep watch. Refrigerate until ready to serve.

LEEWAY

A A simple rule of thumb: 1 egg yolk and 1 tbsp sugar per ½ cup cream. If you're making a large crème brûlée, note that the quantity here, made in a 1-quart dish, can take up to 40 minutes to cook.

B Some of the cream can be replaced with milk: 50/50 is common and works well. Watch it, though: skimp too much on the cream and the custard will lack the proper luxuriousness.

C Replace the vanilla bean with other hard aromatics. If you're using vanilla extract (1–2 tsp) or any other liquid flavorings, stir them in at the end of step 4. Beware of adding too much liquid—it will jeopardize the gentle set.

D Use more or less sugar. I find between 2 tsp and 1 tbsp per crème ideal.

E Joël Robuchon dispenses with the water bath, baking his crèmes at 225°F for 45 minutes. He also cold-infuses sweetened heavy cream and milk with 4 vanilla beans in the fridge overnight—great if you *really* hate cleaning milk pans.

BANANA

Bananas *and* custard is an English nursery classic. Using banana to flavor a silken crème brûlée, on the other hand, is to give it an elocution lesson. It works so well because the banana's tropical, spicy, floral notes have much in common with vanilla, which is itself strongly associated with custard in all its variants, but particularly with crème brûlée. You'll get the best result from ripe, even overripe bananas, which will have developed sufficient richness and complexity of flavor. Remember that some of their sweetness will also leach into the cream, so you might want to keep any additional sugar in check. Follow the starting point, omitting the vanilla. Treat the sliced banana like a hard aromatic by adding it to the cream at step 1, tasting to check how the flavor is developing: 1 banana can flavor up to 4 cups of milk; 2 will give a deeper, faster result. When it tastes good and banana-y, strain and continue.

BRANDY ALEXANDER

Brandy Alexander, the sweet, viscous cocktail of Cognac, crème de cacao, and cream, was the chief agent of loss in John Lennon and Harry Nilsson's notorious eighteen-month "lost weekend" of 1973–75. (How on earth did Lennon stay so thin? I'd look like Mama Cass after a week on the stuff.) Midway through Lennon and Nilsson's binge, Gilbeys of Ireland launched Baileys Irish Cream, which is the same sort of thing, except with Irish whiskey instead of brandy. Crème de cacao, incidentally, tastes a bit like Tia Maria with the coffee taken out. Crème brûlée is suitable for all sorts of cocktail flavorings where a fair amount of cream is used; milk-only would be to profane the memory of John and Harry's nights at the Rainbow Bar and Grill. Add 2 tbsp Cognac, 1 tbsp crème de cacao, and ½ tsp freshly grated nutmeg to the custard mixture at the end of step 4.

CHAI SPICE

The sine qua nons of chai spice are cinnamon, cardamom, and clove, but you might also add star anise, aniseed, black pepper, and/or saffron to your blend. Whole spices will give a more complex, pleasing result. A chai-spice custard is ideal for un-brûléed *petits pots de crème*, which look all the more delightful primped with little silver- or gold-leaf decorations, as found on kheer and other milk puddings served at Indian celebrations. Condensed milk can be substituted for some of the cream or milk, but check the sweetness before reaching for additional sugar. Infuse 2 cups cream/milk with a 4-in cinnamon stick, 2 cracked cardamom pods, and 3 cloves to the required strength. Strain the mixture and proceed from step [2].

CINNAMON

Before vanilla became easily available, the British enjoyed their custard flavored with cinnamon. The Spanish and Portuguese still do. Most of their custard tarts are cinnamon-flavored, with or without the addition of citrus zest. Portugal's famous *pastéis de nata* are flavored with cinnamon and lemon, as is Spanish *crema catalana*, although the latter comes in a cinnamon and orange version too. *Crema catalana* is often considered interchangeable with crème brûlée. This might be true of modern versions, but not of many older recipes, like the one from the Fundació Institut Català de la Cucina passed on by Claudia Roden, which calls for milk, rather than cream, and adds cornstarch. The Iberian mix of spice and citrus looks a bit basic compared to the recipe given by Hannah Glasse, the eighteenth-century English cookery writer, for an all-cream baked custard flavored with cinnamon, mace, nutmeg, orange-flower water, rosewater, and the sherry-like tipple, sack. In her *New System of Domestic Cookery*, published in 1806, Mrs. Rundell adds bay to a cinnamon-nutmeg base and finishes it with peach-water and either brandy or ratafia, the almond-flavored liqueur. For a straight cinnamon custard, infuse 2 cups cream/milk with 2 (4-in) cinnamon sticks or 1 tsp ground cinnamon at step [1].

GINGER

A mixture of gingers can give a layered result. Fresh ginger (the only kind, incidentally, used by Wolfgang Puck in his ginger crème brûlée) has a clean, citrusy character. Puck warms 2 slices of fresh ginger in 2 cups cream and lets it steep for 15 minutes. Candied ginger lends a confectionery sweetness, thanks to its sugar content, and a very slightly soapy edge. Use 2–3 nuggets, sliced—bash them a bit to release the flavor faster. On its own, ground ginger makes for an unpleasantly dry, peppery custard, but ¼–½ tsp added to a crème brûlée flavored with fresh or candied enhances the gingeriness of the other. Alternatively, a few pinches of apple-pie spice will give a flavor more reminiscent of gingerbread. Chef Philip Johnson serves a chilled ginger custard with pumpkin cheesecake and maple ice cream: a festival of custards. Consider using brown sugar for ginger crèmes, adding it to taste—it might take a little more than you would use for, say, vanilla.

RUM

There's a German cake called *Rahmapfelkuchen* in which a simple rum-flavored custard is baked over a cake batter mixed with raisins and apple slices. Sounds good to me, bar the raisins, which are to rum custard what midges are to the Scottish Highlands. (I got so fed up, as a kid, picking raisins out of rum-and-raisin ice cream, that I took to something no child should ever have to contemplate: turning down ice cream.) Swirl a tot of dark rum around your palate and you'll understand how natural a companion it is for custard, with its notes of vanilla, roasted coffee, orange zest, banana, nutmeg, and caramel. I had been looking forward to making a rum crème brûlée, and had all the cream and yolks at the ready, but my bottle of Gosling's Black Seal— a Bermudan black rum with a deep, dark sweetness like the fudge sold in hell's gift shop—had become mysteriously depleted. All I had in any useable quantity was a half-bottle of Mount Gay, the golden Barbadian rum that smells like apricots steeped in a smoky single malt. Heaven mixed with ice-cold club soda and a spritz of lime, sipped at dusk on the maple-burl sundeck of one's 85-foot sailing yacht. But how would it register in a custard? I decided to enhance the Mount Gay with a measure of black rum's dark spiciness by infusing the custard with half a vanilla bean and a thick twig of cassia. Under its caramel roof the crème tasted like a rum-and-coke float. Pleasantly disconcerting how the paleness of the custard belied the deep, dark flavor: a nun with a piratical heart. Use 3 tbsp rum for 2 cups cream.

STRAWBERRY

Custards, when combined with red-berry purées, can turn a rather disheartening shade. Anyone expecting a Barbie-pink custard, or the pastel prettiness of cheap ice cream, will be in for a shock. The color will be closer to what upmarket paint manufacturers might call Dengue Flush. Or Gravestone Rose. A few drops of cochineal or red food coloring will make things easier on the eye. If you can't bear to fake it, take heart that the flavor will still be intensely pink, especially when the custard has been made with cream. Make a crème brûlée with it and it'll taste like a strawberry yogurt that's been to finishing school. Start by puréeing and straining 8 oz fresh, hulled strawberries, and measure out just under 1 cup. Whisk 3 tbsp sugar with 4 egg yolks. Stir 1¼ cups heavy cream into the yolk mixture, followed by the strawberry purée. Divide among 4 ramekins and continue from step 5 of the starting point. Your custards should be just about set with a slight wobble in the center. Cool and chill, then brûlée or top with a little whipped cream.

TRIPLE CRÈME

Vanilla is apt to barge in and dominate the room. I wanted to make something that tasted of cream, rather as *fior di latte* ice cream lets the milk do the talking. The primrose-yellow clotted cream I remembered from childhood vacations in Cornwall, in the southwest of England, would be just right for my *petits pots de crème*: rich, with an almost savory more-ishness. Strangely, however, this was almost entirely absent from the clotted cream I picked up in the supermarket, possibly because it had been pasteurized in a way that the recklessly microbial cream of childhood memory didn't have to be. Still, it had a pleasantly nutty and mild cooked flavor that I thought I could enhance with the tang of crème fraîche. Made by adding bacteria to cow's-milk cream with a fat content of at least 30 percent, crème fraîche is then left at a warm-ish temperature for about 12–16 hours to allow it to thicken and develop its characteristic flavor. Just as yogurt can be made by adding a small amount of live yogurt to milk, so you can make crème fraîche by adding a small amount of live yogurt to either light whipping cream or heavy cream. This mixture of two creams is then added to a third type of cream—a good organic heavy cream. Follow the starting point, using ¼ cup clotted cream, ½ cup crème fraîche, and 1¼ cups heavy cream gently warmed with ¼ cup sugar. The result is an almost idealized cream flavor: Cadgwith Cove tea rooms, circa 1982.

Crème Anglaise

A.k.a. custard sauce or stirred custard. I use the French term to distinguish it from the other custards on the continuum. Compared to crème brûlée, this crème anglaise contains more egg yolk and sugar—5 yolks and 5 tbsp sugar per 2 cups of milk/cream. Whole eggs can be used, but they make for a frothier—i.e. not particularly custardy—sauce. The same can be said of the addition of flour or cornstarch; you lose the silkiness. Adding starch means that you don't have to be so vigilant with the heat: Leave out 1 egg yolk and whisk in 2 tsp cornstarch at step [3].

For 2⅓ cups, enough for a sauce to serve 4–6 [A]

INGREDIENTS
2 cups milk [B]
1 vanilla bean [C]
5 egg yolks [D] [E]
5 tbsp sugar [F]
Pinch of salt

[1] Pour the milk into a saucepan. Slice open the vanilla bean and scrape the seeds into the milk. Put the bean in too, then bring the milk just up to a boil over a medium heat. Remove from the heat and let infuse for 10 minutes to 1 hour before removing the vanilla bean.

[2] Reheat the milk until it's just beginning to bubble.

[3] In a heatproof bowl, whisk together the egg yolks, sugar, and pinch of salt.
Don't leave the eggs and sugar together unwhisked for too long, or solid specks of yolk will begin to form.

[4] Gradually stir the warm milk into the egg mixture, then pour into a clean pan.

[5] Cook the custard over a low to medium heat, stirring constantly and taking care not to let it boil, until it's thick enough to coat the back of a spoon.
Use a double boiler or diffuser if your stovetop is too fierce. The time your crème anglaise takes to thicken will depend on the pan you're using, and the heat of the burner. Bank on around 10 minutes for this quantity. Be as patient and watchful as a cat.

6   Strain through a sieve into a jug. Serve warm or cold.
Cover the surface of the custard with plastic wrap or parchment paper
to prevent a skin from forming.

LEEWAY

A   Leftover custard can be used as the base for ice creams, *petits pots au chocolat*, bavarois, and fruit fools, so err on the side of excess and expand your custard repertoire. You can scale up the recipe easily—1 egg yolk and 1 tbsp sugar for every scant ½ cup milk.

B   For richness, substitute cream for some or all of the milk. Remember, though, that richer is not always better. Many chefs use a 50/50 mix of milk and cream. Note that vanilla, especially if you're using a bean, will itself create an impression of richness.

C   If you're using vanilla extract (1–2 tsp) or any other liquid flavorings, stir them into the custard at step 6. after straining. You can skip step 1.

D   Add a few extra yolks for a fuller texture and a deeper shade of yellow.

E   If you're short of eggs, use 1 whole in place of 2 yolks, but remember that the results will be frothier. Egg-free custard is made using cornstarch in place of the eggs— British custard powder consists of cornstarch, coloring, and vanilla flavoring.

F   Sweetness is a matter of taste: I've encountered everything from 2 to 12 tbsp sugar per 2 cups milk.

BONE MARROW

A restaurateurs' favorite. At Dell'anima in New York's West Village, they spread bone-marrow custard sauce on bruschetta and top it with gremolata, the garnish of lemon, garlic, and parsley usually served with the better-known bone-with-a-hole dish, osso buco. While the flavor of bone marrow is mildly meaty, some chefs use it to enrich their desserts, for instance adding a little to vanilla-flavored baked custards. Whether for sweet or savory ends, put 2¼ lb clean sliced veal or beef shank bones to soak in cold, salted water for half a day. Transfer to a pan and cover with fresh water, then bring to a boil and simmer for about 20 minutes, or roast them at 450°F for 15–25 minutes. When they are cool enough to handle, remove the marrow from the bones. This should yield enough to flavor or enrich a crème anglaise made with 2 cups milk. Whisk it into the custard while it's still hot. Any remainder can be frozen.

CALVADOS

The hints of apple and dried fruit in Calvados are the clinchers in the custard sauce served at The Delaunay, in London, with their apple *Scheiterhaufen*, a Germano-Austrian bread pudding whose name roughly translates as the sort of pyre or stake-like structure reserved for condemned women. Anyone who balks at a third course that sounds excremental and celebrates the burning of innocent homeopaths will, I'm afraid, be missing out. Order it in Vienna and you'll receive something pretty similar to a regular bread pudding, usually with the addition of fresh fruit—apple slices are common. Calvados custard sauce is also good with mince pies and Christmas plum pudding, or made into an ice cream to serve alongside Normandy buckwheat crêpes (page 124) and apple slices fried in butter. Stir 2 tbsp Calvados into a finished crème anglaise made with 2 cups milk or cream.

CARAMEL

Tapped from their molds, the crème caramels of my childhood quivered primrose on their plates, their tops a glossy, semi-translucent amber. I fell every time for their fragrance of hot caramel, only to put a spoonful in my mouth and discover the texture was not to my liking. I've come around to it since, but reserve a special place in my repertoire for custard *flavored*, as opposed to topped, with caramel; it doesn't look as enticing, but tastes terrific. Caramel used to be a pretty popular flavoring, probably because it was cheap. It's now back in vogue, mainly thanks to the wild popularity of the salted variety. Boil 4 tbsp sugar and 2 tbsp water together. When the mixture turns a golden, toffee-ish color, carefully—it will splatter—pour into 2 cups *hot* milk and stir until dissolved. Follow the starting point from step 3, adding 1 tsp vanilla extract at step 6. For salted caramel custard sauce, stir in about ½ tsp salt flakes, also at step 6, then add pinch by pinch to taste;

salinophiles may like to keep going to a full teaspoon. A simpler (if slightly inferior) toffee-ish flavor can be achieved by using brown sugar in place of white, rather than making a caramel—as for the butterscotch pudding on page 500.

CHICKEN STOCK & LEMON

Egg plus lemon and a light stock equals avgolemono, a Greek sauce, or, further diluted, soup. The egg thickens the chicken stock. The lemon keeps things interesting. To what extent is debatable. As a soup, it's okay, if a little unexciting—avgolemonotonous. It's far better as a sauce, especially when served with globe artichoke, asparagus, stuffed grape leaves, or meatballs. Its sweet-and-sour taste and silky texture make it a lowfat alternative to mayonnaise, or even hollandaise if it's made thick with a tasty, unctuous stock. Whisk the finely grated zest and juice of 1 lemon into the egg yolks (instead of the sugar in the starting point) and slowly add the warm stock. Pour into a pan and simmer over a low heat until the mixture thickens. As with any custard, you can play faster and looser with the heat if the mixture has been stabilized with a little starch: flour and cornstarch are sometimes used, and for the soup version, a small quantity of semolina, rice, vermicelli, or tiny pasta shapes, like orzo, will do the same job. Similar egg and lemon mixtures are found across Europe and the Middle East—for example, Spanish *agristada*, Turkish *terbiyali*, and Syrian *beddah b'lemuneh*. If you've been to Greece, or a Greek restaurant, you've probably been served avgolemono in one form or other. Visitors to Rome, on the other hand, are likely to have tasted pretty much everything the city has to offer before they get around to ordering *tagliatelle alla bagna brusca*, an obscure pasta dish that incorporates an avgolemono-like sauce. The name translates as "noodles in a brutal bath," which sounds like a caption penned by a photographer specializing in mafia crime scenes. It is, in fact, a Jewish dish, cooked, in order to preserve the rules of the Sabbath, on a Friday and served the next day at room temperature. Some sources identify *bagna brusca* as the precursor of the cold pasta salad—the sort of gluey, impacted fusilli sold in supermarket salad bars. The brutal bath begat the clammy tub.

CHOCOLATE

What do chocolate cheesecake, chocolate crème brûlée, and chocolate ice cream have in common? They're guaranteed to disappoint. Ooh, you think. Cheesecake and chocolate! Twice as good as just cheesecake. And then it turns out to be half as good. You're on safer ground with *petits pots au chocolat:* so chocolaty and so *petit* you'll be left wanting more. Pour a warm crème anglaise made as per our starting point, using 50/50 milk and cream, over 1 cup chopped good dark chocolate. Leave for 1 minute, then stir until it turns a uniform, glossy brown. Pour into pots and, when cool, top each with a dollop of whipped cream. Some pâtissiers call this mixture chocolate *cremeux.* Stick to the vanilla stipulated in the starting point, or substitute the appropriate hard aromatics, extracts, or liqueurs to make mocha, chocolate-orange, chocolate-mint, or chocolate-cinnamon versions. My favorite chocolate custard confection, however, has to be the plain chocolate cake with chocolate custard sauce that was served in my school cafeteria. No monstrous theme-restaurant portion of Death by Chocolate or Double Chocolate Mental Cake has ever given me as much satisfaction. The cake was dry, slightly salty, and as square as a geography teacher. The custard sauce, poured, or rather dislodged, from a dinged aluminum jug, was a shade of brown that said institutional way before it said chocolate. It should have been called "sensible chocolate dessert." And yet this was its secret. Against the plainness of the cake, the chocolate flavor had a job to do—that is, to make it a treat. Relive my youth by making the chocolate cake on page [339], baking all of the batter in an 8-in square pan for 25 minutes. Don't bother to frost it. Make the custard sauce by whisking 3 tbsp sifted unsweetened cocoa powder into the egg yolks and sugar at step [3].

COCONUT

Hugely popular in Thailand, where coconut custards are typically steamed. They're usually made with coconut milk, lots of sugar, and some freshly grated coconut. In Brazil, a similarly sweet coconut custard sauce is made with 6 egg yolks, 2 cups sugar, 1 cup coconut milk, and ½ cup water. They call it *baba de moca*—baby's dribble. Toasted coconut is an excellent variation, made by toasting ½ cup dried shredded coconut, adding it to the 2 cups milk at step [1], and heating it gently, then giving it about an hour to infuse. Remember to strain it. You want your custard sauce to be silky.

EGGNOG

A bavarois is a crème anglaise lightened by stiffly beaten egg whites, whipped cream, or both, and set with gelatin. I make an eggnog-flavored bavarois and pour it into a prebaked, sweet-pastry tart shell for a suitably festive-tasting alternative to Christmas plum pudding. The first time I made it, both my father-in-law and my husband complained that it wasn't boozy enough. A year later I doubled my initial 3 tbsp rum, but have a suspicion that they were still sneaking into the kitchen and pouring an extra capful over their slices. If 6 tbsp makes my loved ones sound like closet tipplers, take note that *Good Housekeeping* magazine recommends 10 tbsp for the same quantity of cream, a proportion that might not sit so easily with the tricky bit of crochet on the following page. Maybe best to start low, and add incrementally to taste. Note that bavarois also contains raw egg, so all in all it's pretty much off-limits to anyone who's very young, very old, frail, pregnant, who can't drink, won't drink, is avoiding carbs, or hasn't got room for a dessert. It might just be you, in your lopsided paper hat, alone with your booze pie and a party popper. Make a custard sauce to the crème anglaise method, using the yolks of 3 eggs (save the whites for later), 1¼ cups heavy cream, 5 tbsp sugar, and 1 tsp vanilla extract (or a bean, if you prefer). While the custard is still warm, stir in 3 soaked and squeezed leaves of gelatin. Then add 3 tbsp each of brandy and dark rum and ¼ nutmeg, grated. Beat the reserved egg whites to firm peaks and fold into the cooled custard mixture. Whip ⅔ cup heavy cream and fold that in, too. Pour into little glasses, or into a deep 8-in blind-baked tart shell (page 566), or over a gingersnap-cookie crumb base of the same size. Grate more nutmeg over the top. You can omit the brandy and use twice the rum, or vice versa—pretty much anything goes.

HONEY

The American National Honey Board suggests making a honey custard for French toast, fried in butter and served with a scattering of pecans. As a rule, stirred custard is usually a yolks-only affair, but *Pleyn Delit*, a modern collection of medieval recipes, includes a dish that might have been named by Edmund Blackadder: *strawberyes with crème bastard.* Use 4 egg whites per 2 cups milk, flavor with 4 tbsp honey, 4 tsp sugar, and a pinch of salt, and pour over rinsed, hulled, slightly sweetened strawberries. I made my *bastard* with a mild honey and the result was ghostly white and blandly sweet—like custard sauce stripped of its essential custardiness, or one of those obsolete canned milks with carefully vague names like Magic Topping.

Ice Cream

The previous point on the custard continuum, crème anglaise, can be frozen to make ice cream, but you may find it a little lacking in sweetness. The only difference, in fact, between the starting points for crème anglaise and ice cream is the higher sugar content in the latter, plus the addition of some cream mixed in with the milk. (Make this with milk only and you'll have an Italian gelato.) You may also prefer to double the quantity of vanilla, as flavors become muted in the freezing process.

For about the same amount as a premium 16-oz tub

INGREDIENTS
1⅓ cups milk ᴬ ᴮ
⅔ cup cream ᴬ ᴮ
1–2 vanilla beans ᶜ ᴰ
5 egg yolks ᴮ ᴱ ꟳ
½ cup sugar ᴳ
Pinch of salt

1 Pour the milk and cream into a saucepan. Slice open the vanilla bean(s) and scrape the seeds into the pan. Put the bean(s) in too, then bring the milk and cream just up to a boil over a medium heat. Remove from the heat and let infuse for 10 minutes to 1 hour before removing the bean(s).

2 Reheat the milk/cream mix until it's just beginning to bubble.

3 In a heatproof bowl, whisk the egg yolks with the sugar and salt. Don't leave the eggs and sugar together unwhisked for too long, or solid specks of yolk will begin to form.

4 Gradually stir the warm milk/cream mix into the egg mixture, then pour into a clean pan.

5 Cook the custard over a low to medium heat, stirring constantly and taking care not to let it boil, until it's thick enough to coat the back of a spoon.
Use a double boiler or diffuser if your burner is too fierce. The time your custard takes to thicken will depend on the pan you're using, and the heat of your stovetop. Bank on around 10 minutes for this quantity.

6 Cool as quickly as possible, straining the custard through a sieve into a bowl set in a larger bowl or sink full of iced or cold water. Stir regularly to encourage cooling and prevent a skin from forming. Transfer the custard to the fridge as soon as it's no longer warm, placing a circle of parchment paper on the surface—again, to prevent a skin from forming.
Chilling before freezing will help to create smaller ice crystals, and therefore a softer texture, in the finished ice cream.

7 The chilled custard can be frozen in an ice-cream machine. Alternatively, freeze the custard by pouring it into a plastic container (8-in square or thereabouts will be ideal for this quantity). Cover the surface with plastic wrap, apply the lid, and freeze for about 1½ hours, or until the ice cream is frozen around the edges. Remove and mash/whip with a fork, or use an electric mixer, to break up the ice crystals. Replace the lid and return to the freezer, repeating the process two or three times at hourly intervals until an ice-cream consistency is achieved. Add any solid flavorings when the custard is well into its churn in a machine, but still soft enough for them to distribute easily, or, if you're using the no-churn process, on the final stir.
No-churn ice cream should be removed from the freezer and left at room temperature for 20–30 minutes to soften before serving (maybe less if it contains alcohol). Precisely how long it needs will depend on the ingredients and the respective temperatures of your freezer and room.

LEEWAY

A All milk or all cream is fine.

B For richness, use extra egg yolks, or more cream than milk.

C If you're using vanilla extract (1 tbsp) or any other liquid flavorings, stir them in at the end of step 5 when the custard has cooled a bit.

D If you're using alcohol rather than vanilla as a flavoring, 2 tbsp spirit or 3 tbsp fortified wine (or liqueur of around 20% ABV) are the suggested maximums for the quantity here. The more you add, the more you compromise the ice cream's ability to freeze.

E Some cooks would use 6 egg yolks, others fewer. The more yolks, the richer and more egg-flavored the ice cream will be.

F Egg-free ice cream can be made with a cornstarch-based custard. Alternatively, seek out recipes for Philadelphia-style ice cream. That's Philadelphia the city, by the way, not the brand.

G Some might add another 2 tbsp sugar. Reduce the sugar too much and the ice cream will lose its smoothness, as sugar promotes smaller ice crystals. Replace 2 tbsp of the sugar with 1 tbsp golden syrup for an even softer set.

ALMOND

Bitter almond is a particularly good flavoring for an ice cream to accompany a fruit dessert like plum crisp or to fill choux puffs topped with sliced almonds and a shake of confectioners' sugar. Add 1 tsp almond essence or 2 tbsp Amaretto at the end of step 5. Burnt almond is a variation that used to be very popular for ice cream. *That'll* be a good recipe for my book, I thought—anyone can burn stuff. It turned out to a bit more complicated than that. Indeed, it was considered fancy enough to serve at Abraham Lincoln's second inauguration ball in 1865. In early versions, blanched, chopped almonds were added to melted sugar, and the mixture caramelized. Once cooled and set, it was ground, mixed into a vanilla-laced custard, and frozen. These days we'd probably call this praline ice cream: Add at least ½ cup praline powder (page 416) at step 7. Another old recipe suggests layering it with orange sorbet in an ice-cream mold, and serving in slices with bitter-almond angel food cake. By the time Fannie Merritt Farmer's classic *Boston Cooking-School Cook Book* was published, in 1896, the recipe had become a deal simpler—Farmer just adds blanched almonds to a caramel custard. Not really burnt almond at all. Boiled almond. Which has a less than presidential ring.

BROWN BREAD

Brown-bread ice cream dates back to at least 1768, when M. Emy included a recipe in his *L'Art de bien faire les glaces d'office*, and it remains very popular in Ireland. But best not make this for anyone who goes white-lipped at the sight of toast crumbs in the butter. Spread 5 de-crusted slices of brown bread with 3–4 tbsp butter. Sprinkle over ½ cup sugar (white or brown) and, if you like, 1 tsp apple-pie spice or cinnamon, or both. Cut the sugary, buttered bread into pieces, place on a baking sheet, and toast in a 350°F oven until crisp, dry, and ready to be blitzed into bread crumbs. Fold the duly blitzed crumbs into the custard toward the end of step 7. Historically, the custard for the ice cream was enhanced with noyau, an almond-flavored liqueur, or a cherry-flavored kiss of Maraschino, but these days it's more likely to be flavored with vanilla, with the optional addition of a jigger of rum. A more unusual recipe calls for lemon juice and a large quantity of sugar to be mixed in with the cream-soaked crumbs, recalling the filling for traditional British treacle tart.

CREAM CHEESE

Alain Ducasse serves a cream-cheese ice cream with a berry compote and crunchy topping, but it's so glorious you might want to serve it with nothing else. It is to vanilla ice cream what d'Isigny is to butter. Follow the starting point, using 50/50 milk and cream, 3 egg yolks, ¾ cup sugar, and no vanilla. Once the custard is thick, and while it's still warm, thoroughly whisk in ½ cup soft cream cheese and 1 tsp lemon juice; chill, then freeze in the usual way. To make the crunchy topping, rub 5 tbsp unsalted butter into ¾ cup flour, then stir in ¾ cup sugar and ½ cup ground almonds. Spread out the mixture on a greased baking sheet and bake at 350°F for about 15–20 minutes until crisp and golden brown. Let cool. Spoon some berry compote into 4 serving glasses and top each with a scoop of the ice cream, along with a scattering of the crunchy topping.

LEMON

In her "Very Good Old Fashioned Boiled Custard," the Victorian food writer Eliza Acton infuses milk with lemon zest for 30 minutes and stirs in a wineglass of good brandy at the end. When Acton was writing, lemon vied with vanilla as the most popular flavor for ice cream. In the modern gelateria, sadly, lemon is relegated to the sorbet section. Revive the tradition at home by making the wonderful, and wonderfully simple, lemon ice cream I came across in John Thorne's *The Outlaw Cook*. Thorne attributes the recipe to several writers, but makes his own adjustment, meaning the ice cream doesn't require regular stirring as it freezes. I have made another adjustment, changing the cream to the whipping variety. Stir the juice and finely grated zest of 1 unwaxed lemon with ⅓ cup superfine sugar until the sugar dissolves. Stir in ⅔ cup whipping cream, transfer to a container so the mixture is an inch deep, and place in the freezer. That's it: 3–4 hours later it should be ready. The ice cream will need 5–10 minutes at room temperature to soften before serving. I can't think of another dish that lays the components of lemon flavor so bare—with the simple lemon, herbal, and floral notes successively revealing themselves as the ice cream starts to melt in your mouth. Then the sourness rises and your palate is refreshed for another hit. Other excellent recipes for basic fruit, sugar, and cream (i.e. custard-free) ices include strawberry and balsamic in *Ices*, by Caroline Liddell and Robin Weir, and red currant in *Lola's Ice Creams and Sundaes*, by Morfudd Richards. Note, however, that these versions are frozen in the usual way, rather than simply being placed in the freezer and left alone.

MASTIC

Popular in Greece and Turkey, where it's used to flavor ice cream and milk puddings, mastic comes from the *Pistacia lentiscus* tree. It's a relative of the cashew but has more in common, flavorwise, with the pine nut, or the note of resin in retsina, reminiscent of the evergreen smells that waft onto Corfu's pine-fringed beaches in summer. (Lawrence Durrell couldn't get enough of retsina, insisting that you could drink gallons of the stuff without fear of a hangover. Also that it made you "high-spirited" rather than drunk. I love retsina too, but not enough to test his theory properly.) Crystals of mastic resin are easily available online. Freeze 2 pea-size crystals for 20 minutes, then grind with 1 tsp sugar using a pestle and mortar. Stir into the custard at the end of step 5, then chill and freeze the ice cream as per our starting point. Mastic ice cream is often served with fruit compotes, but as its pine note is so evocative of Christmas trees, try serving it with mince pies or plum pudding.

MINT

In the U.S., the mint-choc combination crops up in a "grasshopper," a cocktail of crème de menthe, white crème de cacao, and cream just as likely to appear on the dessert as the drinks menu. Grasshopper pie has a chocolate-cookie crust and a bavarois filling flavored with crème de menthe. Anything grasshopper-flavored will, in color, probably be the shocking green we Brits associate with mint, which makes it all the more surprising to discover that peppermint ice cream is often colored reddish-pink, or red and white, Stateside. If you're curious to try this sort, add about 6 tbsp crushed red-colored, mint-flavored boiled candies toward the end of churning, or, in the case of no-churn freezing, on the last whisking. If the candies alone don't furnish enough peppermint flavor, gradually add ¼ tsp peppermint oil to the chilled custard at step 6 until it acquires the right intensity (peppermint flavors vary widely in strength). Use garden mint for a less punchy, more nuanced flavor: Add 1½ cups chopped leaves and stalks to the 2 cups milk and cream once warmed, then let infuse for 10 minutes. Strain and continue from step 2.

OLIVE OIL

In a hotel on the outskirts of Ronda, in Spain, next to an old Arab bathhouse at the foot of the gorge, I sat in the garden, fanned by the breeze through the palm trees, nibbling on cubes of manchego and sipping a watermelon juice the color of the inside of my eyelids. Time passed, slowly, in the Spanish fashion. A clock tower, somewhere, tolled its assent to a sundowner. I ordered some fino. It came in a frosted glass with a dish of self-satisfied olives. I watched the shadow of a horse elongate in a parched field. And then my husband said, come on. We're going to dinner. What's wrong with eating here? I said. We're on vacation, he said. We've got to *try* places. Our respective positions, vis-à-vis *trying places on vacation,* constitute the sort of impassable philosophical gorge without which our marriage would, no doubt, be unpleasantly cloying and consensual. Said positions being a) accepting the foreclosure of possibility involved in making any sort of decision, in favor of actually maybe just sitting still for a second and enjoying yourself (mine) vs. b) caving in to the neurotic guidebook-fueled fear of missing out and quite possibly ruining the evening for everybody (his). I relented. Resentfully. The thing about staying at the foot of the Ronda gorge is: Going out to dinner involves *scaling a cliff-face*. There are steps—but about five hundred of them. Fine, I thought. If you're going to unseat me from paradise and make me walk a vertical mile for a dinner of uncertain quality, that dinner better be damn good. We arrived at my husband's chosen restaurant. The walls were covered with bullfighting posters and flea-market oil paintings of flamenco dancers straining out of their boleros. We were the only diners. The Spanish eat late, said my husband. It's a quarter to ten, I said. A plate of *pata negra* arrived. It was dark as a blood clot and pinstriped with fat. Not bad. Next, an unseasonal oxtail stew, excused by my hoof uphill. Not bad either. And then dessert arrived. A rectangular palette of four ice creams: one flavored with yogurt, one with cream cheese, another with something I've forgotten, and a fourth with an olive oil that made each spoonful taste of fruit and grass and pepper, like a picnic suspended in cream and frozen in time. When I eventually put down my spoon I realized that the restaurant was full to the very last table, as if the empty room had been a desolate dream. Whisk 5 tbsp olive oil into the cooled custard before you chill it. You may need to whisk it again before you freeze it. Clearly, you need an oil with a particularly pronounced, complex flavor—if, when trying a drop on your index finger, you're thinking more "oil" than "olive," choose again.

PARMESAN

The Parmesan ice-cream sandwich is one of Ferran Adrià's most celebrated ideas. The ice cream, which is savory, contains no sugar or egg, just cream and cheese, and is served between two Parmesan tuiles with a dab of lemon marmalade. Conversely, an eighteenth-century cookbook, *The Complete Confectioner,* by Frederick Nutt, gives a recipe for a *sweet* Parmesan ice cream, calling for 6 eggs, scant 1¼ cups sugar syrup, scant 2½ cups heavy cream, and ¾ cup grated Parmesan. The finished custard is strained before being cooled, then frozen. What better friend for an overripe fig?

PASTIS

I use pastis to make ice cream and serve it as a coupe with a sharp black-currant sorbet. Not for the fainthearted: as strident a pair as rival madames in a magistrate's court. Add 1–2 tbsp pastis at step 6, tasting after the first tablespoon and then adding more to taste. Naturally, any aniseed spirit will do. If you have several to hand, try them one by one and see if you have a preference. The differences will be subtle, but more distinct when tried side-by-side than you might imagine; like gin, the various brands of pastis, ouzo, and arak each rely on proprietary blends of spices, flowers, and aromatics. Note, however, that sambuca is a liqueur, and so will be much sweeter—it's made with the essential oil of fennel, meaning it retains a natural fragrance of the herb, according to the legendary London-based bartender Salvatore Calabrese.

PISTACHIO

The test of a good gelateria. If the pistachio ice cream is no good, go elsewhere. If you're self-sufficient in your ice-cream needs, consider buying a jar of pistachio paste: It will cost more than the equivalent amount of raw nuts, but the hard work of roasting (essential for intensifying the flavor) and pounding is done for you—you'll need about 4 oz. If the paste proves tricky to find, try grinding ¾ cup shelled, skinned, roasted unsalted nuts with a few pinches of salt. Place in a pan with 1⅓ cups milk and bring up to boiling point, then let infuse for an hour. Add the ⅔ cup cream and 2 tsp mild honey to the pistachio milk and scald again, then proceed from step 2. At the end of step 6, stir in more cream—1 cup light whipping or heavy—then chill and freeze as per the starting point. Note that in commercially produced ice cream, pistachio flavor is almost always supplemented with vanilla or almond essence, which is like dabbing Eau de Guerlain behind your ears and then spraying yourself with Right Guard. A far better and more natural enhancement is a little freshly grated nutmeg.

SESAME

At Roka, in London, I ate an astounding cherry blossom and black sesame dessert. It arrived on a gray ceramic half-pipe like a prop from a miniature skate park. Under a roof of gelatin the color of old Scotch tape sat a narrow block of black-sesame ice cream, surrounded by chippings of smoke-colored marshmallow and sheets of shattered sugar. Amid this peculiarly Japanese scene of dereliction lay four pink cherry blossom macaroons, two of which were topped with scarlet domes of cherry gelatin that looked like red egg yolks and were just as runny as yolks when you cut into them. It was without doubt the oddest dessert I'd ever seen. But the flavor wasn't entirely unfamiliar: The nutty sesame and sharp cherry recalled the classic childhood combination of peanut butter and jelly, but with greater subtlety. Toast 6 tbsp black sesame seeds in a dry skillet for a few minutes, taking care not to let them burn. Let cool, then grind them using a pestle and mortar. Make up a vanilla ice cream as per our starting point, adding the ground sesame seeds at the end of step 6. Chill and freeze as normal. Alternatively, ready-toasted sesame seeds are available in Japanese and Chinese groceries, or you could try your luck with ground-up Sesame Snaps for a golden sesame praline.

SWEET CORN

There are offbeat ice-cream flavors, like asparagus or garlic, that must be eaten to be believed. Not so sweet corn. Anyone who's gnawed on a hot, sugary ear slathered in creamy butter will see the potential. Leave out the vanilla for this one if you like. Cook 1½ cups fresh or frozen kernels in 2 cups milk for 15 minutes. (Don't use canned corn if it's a sweet custard you're after—the sulfurousness imparted by the canning process is incontestably savory.) Check the milk for depth of flavor, then proceed from step 2, straining the milk through a sieve onto the egg mixture; taste for sweetness. Retaining the kernels and stirring them into the finished ice cream is an option. Or, if you don't fancy that, add them to cornbread (page 78), or mix them with a thick batter to make fritters (page 144).

Ice Cream → Other Directions

ON A WARM WAFFLE

page 139

ICE-CREAM CAKE

Softened ice cream mixed with candied fruit, nuts, and/or chocolate, layered on a cake base and frozen, then decorated.

ICE-CREAM LOTI

Singaporean ice-cream sandwich, made with multicolored sweet bread.

COKE FLOAT

Add a scoop of ice cream to a fizzy drink, milkshake, or cocktail.

ICE-CREAM SANDWICH

ICE-CREAM BOMBE

Three layers of different-flavored ice cream surrounding a grated-chocolate center.

ICE-CREAM TRUFFLES

Roll small scoops of ice cream into balls and dust with cocoa powder.

Pastry Cream

Add a little flour to the custard for ice cream and it becomes pastry cream, otherwise known as crème pâtissière (or "creme pat" if you're in the restaurant trade). It's used for millefeuille or napoleons, Boston cream pie, choux pastries, fruit tarts, and Danish pastries. In the U.S., it's eaten by the spoonful as a dessert called "pudding." Fold whipped cream into pastry cream to make crème diplomat, which has a lighter texture, although it will dilute any added flavorings unless the cream is flavored too.

For about 2½ cups—enough to fill 12 (6-in) éclairs, 24 profiteroles, 8 choux puffs, or a 7- to 9-in layer cake

INGREDIENTS
2 cups milk ᴬ
1 vanilla bean ᴮ
½ cup sugar ᶜ
5 egg yolks ᴰ ᴱ
3 tbsp cornstarch ᶠ
2½ tbsp flour ᶠ
Pinch of salt
2 tbsp unsalted butter—optional ᴳ

1 Pour the milk into a saucepan. Slice open the vanilla bean and scrape the seeds into the milk. Put the bean in too, then bring the milk just up to a boil over a medium heat. Remove from the heat and let the flavor develop for 10 minutes to 1 hour before removing the bean.

2 Add half the sugar to the milk and heat until it's just beginning to bubble.

3 In a heatproof bowl, whisk together the egg yolks, the rest of the sugar, the cornstarch, flour, and salt.

4 Gradually stir the warm milk into the egg mixture, then pour into a clean pan.

5 Cook over a low to medium heat, stirring constantly, until the mixture comes to a boil, then simmer, stirring frequently, until thick and firm—about 2 minutes.

6 Pass through a sieve if you think it needs it.

7   Let cool a little, stir in the butter or any liquid flavorings, then cover the surface with plastic wrap or a light dusting of sugar to prevent a skin from forming. Pastry cream will keep in the fridge for up to 3 days.

LEEWAY

A   1% or 2% milk is acceptable. Skim milk is too thin.

B   If you're using vanilla extract (2 tsp) or any other liquid flavoring, rather than a vanilla bean, skip step 1 and stir it in gradually at the end of step 5.

C   The ½ cup given here is a standard quantity of sugar. Increase or decrease it to taste.

D   Make a less unctuous pastry cream using whole eggs in place of some of the yolks—say 2 eggs and 2 yolks per 2 cups milk.

E   Some cooks use only 4 yolks for this quantity of milk, others as many as 6.

F   Some recipes call for only cornstarch, others only flour.

G   There are chefs who add anything from 2 tbsp to 5 tbsp whipped, unsalted butter to the warm pastry cream to lend it a very soft texture. With 1 cup butter added to this quantity of crème patissière, it becomes crème mousseline.

ANISEED

Licorice ice cream is fit for the gods, but the spectacle of my husband's mouth suddenly blackening reminded me of poor Wikus in *District 9*, after he's vomited his first gobbet of alien plasma. Unless you're doing the catering for Comic-Con International, probably best to use aniseed or pastis rather than actual licorice to flavor custards. And don't take any nonsense from self-proclaimed aniseed-o-phobes. Just spring it on them by using it as a pastry-cream filling for profiteroles, retaining the classic chocolate sauce, as suggested by David Lebovitz. Add 1 heaped tsp lightly toasted aniseed in place of the vanilla at step [1], and let infuse for at least 30 minutes. Then strain and continue from step [2].

BUTTERSCOTCH

I have a rigorously unresearched feeling that butterscotch is a less popular flavoring than it was when I was a kid. In any case, if you make it from scratch, for a pastry cream "pudding," ice cream, or crème anglaise, you'll be reminded just how permanent a place it deserves in our affections. Like vanilla and chocolate, it's a flavor that it takes some effort of contrariness to dislike. In the U.S., it's still a big deal, especially in the South, where butterscotch custard pie is a traditional favorite. It's not uncommon to augment the butterscotch with vanilla, whiskey, or a little bit of both. The "scotch" in "butterscotch" has nothing to do with whiskey, incidentally: It's thought to be etymologically related to "scorched." The "butter" in "butterscotch," on the other hand, has everything to do with the butter traditionally used in butterscotch confectionery, and butter is often added to pastry cream after its final sieving (but while it's still warm). The characteristic butterscotch flavor comes from the type of sugar used. Simply substitute dark brown sugar for the standard white stuff, and add ½ tsp vanilla extract at the end of step [5]. Don't forget a pinch of salt—in fact, make it two pinches.

CHESTNUT

Go ahead and boil, peel, and purée fresh chestnuts yourself, but the precooked, vacuum-packed sort are almost as good. Or, if you have a deli nearby that sells imported French food, simply open a can of *crème de marrons*, which is not only precooked and pre-puréed but pre-sugared to boot. In Japan, chestnut is a popular flavoring for sweets. A manufacturer called Kobe-Fugetsudo makes a custard-filled waffle that to Western eyes looks like a suntanned monkfish suffering from a particularly nasty attack of gastric reflux. There's a choice of vanilla, green tea, or chestnut pastry cream, the latter including a whole chestnut, which pokes out like a lolling tongue. The Italian-American chef Mario Batali gives a recipe for *sformato di castagne*, a savory custard made with puréed, cooked dried chestnuts, fontina, Parmesan, and nutmeg. For a more classic, sweet pastry cream, gradually whisk in ½ cup chestnut purée toward the end of step [5].

HAZELNUT

The Spanish make a simple dessert, similar to pastry cream, called *natillas de avellanas*—*natillas* being the diminutive of the Spanish word for cream, *nata*, and thus roughly translating as "little cream." (*Avellanas* are hazelnuts.) It's essentially a pastry cream with brandy, vanilla, and finely ground, blanched hazelnuts added at the end. *Salsa di nocciole* is a similar Italian dish described in *The Silver Spoon*: 1 cup toasted, skinned, ground hazelnuts are folded into 2 cups pastry cream with 3 tbsp brandy. Imagine *that* as a cake filling. As a shortcut, and for smoother results, you could replace the hazelnuts and brandy with 2 tbsp Frangelico liqueur.

MALTED MILK

Momofuku, David Chang's restaurant chain, has moved to trademark Cereal Milk™, made with a mixture of toasted cornflakes, milk, brown sugar, and salt. Brown-bread ice cream works on a similar principle, with the baked sugared bread crumbs lending a more-ish flavor of toasted cereal. It's a firm favorite in Boston, where the bread crumbs are sometimes omitted in favor of the breakfast cereal Grape Nuts, those tiny nuggets of wholegrain wheat and malted barley that look like gravel in a model-railroad siding and make the leftover milk in the bowl taste like cold Horlicks (a malted-barley drink sold in powdered form and mixed with hot milk). Which takes us back to intellectual property law. A century ago, Horlicks had a go at its own language-grab, objecting to a product called "Hedley's Malted Milk" in a landmark case (*Horlicks v. Summerskill*, 1917). The judge ruled that, as Horlicks never referred to "malted milk" without appending the brand name, it was merely a descriptive term, and not a trademark—which is, in turn, perhaps a reason why the brand has taken on the status of proprietary eponym, like Coke or Viagra. Feel free, in that case, to call your malted-milk pastry cream malted-milk pastry cream. It's a mighty flavor in its own right, but is often added as a secondary flavor to shakes—banana, strawberry, chocolate, peanut, and (less commonly these days) orange, ginger, or eggnog. Like vanilla, it lends strength to other flavors' arms, but it also has nutritional value, and is less limited to pairings with sweet stuff. *The Practical Druggist New Dispensatory* of 1908, for example, includes the recipe for a Hot Oyster Malt, a mixture of Horlicks, oyster bouillon, and celery salt, with an optional topping of whipped cream. No danger of anyone trying to trademark that. For a malted-milk pastry cream or pudding, whisk about 3 tbsp of Horlicks into the yolks, flour, and sugar at step [3].

TEA

Green tea is a common flavoring for pastry cream in Japan. It might seem novel to Western palates, but in the early nineteenth century cookbooks like *The Italian Confectioner* by W.A. Jarrin included recipes for both green- and black-tea ice creams. In *The Art of Cookery*, from 1836, John Mollard suggests infusing a pint (about 2½ cups) of cream with coriander, cinnamon, and lemon zest for 10 minutes, before adding about ⅔ cup strong green tea and sugar. The mixture is then strained onto 6 egg whites and returned to the stovetop until thickened. Mollard serves this cold, pudding-style, with ratafia cookies, but amaretti, being similarly almond-flavored, would make a fine substitution.

For a pastry cream flavored with matcha green tea, use 4–5 tsp powder. Skip step [1]. Instead, make a paste with the tea and a little of the scalded milk at step [4], then thoroughly stir in the remainder of the warm milk and add to the yolks, flour, and sugar. For an Earl Grey custard, treat ¼–½ cup loose leaves as you would a vanilla bean—add them to the pan of milk and scald. Let infuse for a few minutes, tasting for depth of flavor. Beware of leaving it too long, for fear of imparting a tannic quality. You don't want your custard tasting of old nails.

TOASTED WHITE CHOCOLATE

Gourmands turn their noses up at white chocolate on the basis that it isn't really chocolate at all—just a cloying confection of cocoa butter, milk solids, and sugar. But it comes into its own in custard, primarily because it tastes overwhelmingly of vanilla. Follow our starting point, stirring in ⅔ cup chopped good-quality white chocolate at the end of step [5], while the pastry cream is still hot. Or try the version of Ferran Adrià's dessert on pages [463-4]. In recent years, several recipes for toasted white chocolate have been doing the rounds. Its fake-tan complexion gives it the look of Caramac, Nestlé's caramel-flavored condensed-milk bar, but it tastes far more refined. You're essentially making toffee with highly luxurious cocoa butter. Ideally, use a white chocolate with a minimum 30% cocoa-butter content; 20% cocoa butter will work, but the result will be a bit chalky. Break 4 oz into fragments, scatter over a parchment-lined baking sheet, and toast in a low oven (225°F), pushing the pieces around from time to time to make sure they melt and brown evenly—this will take about 35–45 minutes. Stir the soft toasted chocolate into the hot pastry cream at step [5] and pipe into puff-pastry horns.

Pastry Cream → Other Directions

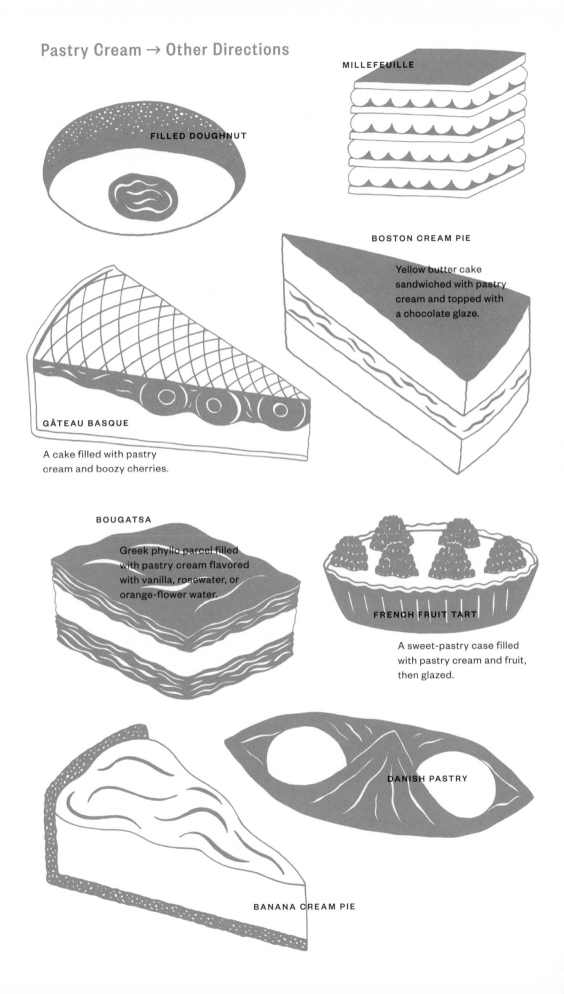

MILLEFEUILLE

FILLED DOUGHNUT

BOSTON CREAM PIE

Yellow butter cake sandwiched with pastry cream and topped with a chocolate glaze.

GÂTEAU BASQUE

A cake filled with pastry cream and boozy cherries.

BOUGATSA

Greek phyllo parcel filled with pastry cream flavored with vanilla, rosewater, or orange-flower water.

FRENCH FRUIT TART

A sweet-pastry case filled with pastry cream and fruit, then glazed.

DANISH PASTRY

BANANA CREAM PIE

Crema Fritta

The custard for *crema fritta* contains more flour and a little less egg than pastry cream. When it cools, it achieves a firm-enough set to be cut into shapes and deep-fried; in more elaborate versions, grated marzipan (page [280]) and crushed macaroons (page [288]) are mixed into the custard before it is left to set. The unfried custard recalls the thick roux used to make croquettes, or the thick mixture of cooked milk and semolina used to make gnocchi alla Romana. In Italy, *crema fritta* is sometimes eaten as part of a *fritto misto*. The French call it *crème frite*, the Spanish *leche frita*, and *The Oxford Companion to Food* an "ice-cream fritter."

For an 8-in square dish, to serve 4–6

INGREDIENTS
Flavorings, such as vanilla, citrus zest, liqueurs—optional [A] [B]
2 cups milk
2 eggs [C]
¼ cup sugar [D]
¾ cup all-purpose flour
Pinch of salt
Beaten egg [C] and bread crumbs [E] for coating
Vegetable oil for frying [F]
Confectioners' sugar for dusting

1   If using a vanilla bean, citrus zest, other hard aromatics, or ground spices, pour 1¾ cups of the milk into a pan, add the flavorings, and warm to just below boiling point over a medium heat. Remove from the heat and let infuse for 10 minutes to 1 hour. Then discard or strain out flavorings. Any liquid flavorings are added later, at step [5].

2   Heat the milk until it's just beginning to bubble.

3   In a heatproof bowl, whisk together the eggs, sugar, flour, salt, and the remaining milk to make a paste.

4   Gradually stir the warm milk into the egg mixture, then pour into a clean pan.

5   Cook over a low to medium heat, stirring constantly, until it comes to a boil. Simmer, stirring frequently, for 5 minutes until very thick and firm. Remove from the heat. Gradually stir in liquid flavorings, if using.

6   Pour into a greased 8-in square dish. Let cool and set at room temperature.
    Give it at least 2 hours. Once cool, it can be kept in the fridge for up to 2 days.

7   When ready to cook, cut into batons or diamonds and dip in beaten egg, then bread crumbs. Heat the oil in a deep fryer or large pan to 350°F and deep-fry in batches until golden and crisp. Serve as they are, or dust with confectioners' sugar.
    If you are new to deep-frying, see page [17].

LEEWAY

A   Limit any liquid flavorings to 1 tbsp. You don't want to jeopardize the set.

B   In Spain, the typical flavoring is cinnamon, with either orange or lemon zest.

C   Some recipes call for egg yolks only. Use 4 yolks per 2 cups milk and dip the batons in the beaten whites (instead of whole egg) before crumbing and frying them.

D   The quantity of sugar in some variants can be double the amount here. Pellegrino Artusi's recipe, on the other hand, calls for as little as 1½ tbsp sugar for 2 cups milk. If, like Artusi, you're serving your *crema fritta* in a savory context, it's a good idea to keep the sweetness down.

E   Ground almonds can be used for coating, instead of bread crumbs.

F   The typical Venetian method is to fry the pieces in lard before giving them a shake of confectioners' sugar and orange-flower water. Marcel Boulestin uses a vanilla bean for flavoring, fries the cut pieces in clarified butter, and serves them with a chocolate sauce.

Sauce

SABAYON

page 514

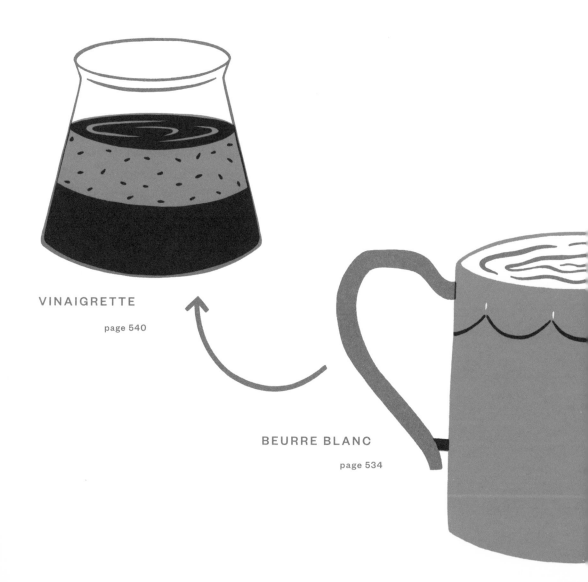

VINAIGRETTE

page 540

BEURRE BLANC

page 534

HOLLANDAISE

page 520

MAYONNAISE

page 526

SABAYON Sabayon sits at a junction of the custard and sauce continuums. Heat is applied with the same caution as for crème anglaise or brûlée, but sabayon differs in being whisked rather than stirred, and using substantially less liquid to egg. Hence its home among the sauces.

Something else that sets sabayon apart from other custards is that, being made with alcohol, it once had a reputation as a pick-me-up. It was said to be good for a cold, quite the thing to restore a flagging lady at the end of a ball or gird the loins of a groom on his wedding night and, in stark contrast to current advice, excellent for pregnant women. In Italy, schoolkids and *paesani* would stop by the *caffeteria* on their way to school or the fields, and set themselves up for the day with a shot of froth. In the classic recipe, egg yolks are whisked with sugar and wine in a double boiler until the mixture thickens into a foamy mass. Left for too long, a sabayon will eventually return to its liquid state, which is why it's usually made to order in restaurants, and was historically prepared tableside, whipped up by a red-faced waiter. It takes some effort; there will never be a ready-made version. Sabayon is inconvenience food, which is part of its charm.

Bear this in mind if you're making it at home for guests. If you have an eat-in kitchen, and your stove sits against the wall, they will have a view of your back for a full eight minutes. An electric mixer takes the strain off your forearm but presents its own challenges. First, the noise is liable to put a damper on free-and-easy dinner conversation. Second, my mixer has a cord only just long enough to reach one of the burners on my stove—the most ferocious one—which means interposing a rather rickety diffuser between the pan and the flame, added to which the metal bowl resting over the pan of simmering water can't help but rotate as I beat the mixture. It's precarious. Invariably I resemble the cover of a cookbook illustrated by Ralph Steadman: *Fear and Loathing in the Preparation of Dessert*.

If you're worried about maintaining a steady low temperature, you can always add a bit of flour to stabilize the mix, as you would with other custards. This makes the double boiler unnecessary, even if Delia Smith does both, whisking a teaspoon of cornstarch into her four-egg-yolk zabaglione before cooking it over a pan of simmering water. The notion of a floury sabayon is not new. In a learned mid-nineteenth-century Italian journal, I came across a *sambajon casalingo*, "housewife's sabayon," made with chestnut flour.

A make-ahead option, if you're happy to eat your sabayon cold, is to carry on whisking over chilled or iced water after your sabayon has been optimally frothed over heat. This will make it more robust. Folding the results into whipped cream will add more texture, as well as tamping the sweetness (in a good way) and lending the flavor greater length. Sabayon's shortcoming can be its abruptness.

The cream sabayon is a versatile mixture used in professional kitchens to make a number of classic desserts. It can be flavored and frozen to make a parfait, or poured over macerated fruit and then brûléed. When combined with fruit purée, it makes a mousse, whose bubbles can be preserved with a touch of gelatin.

That's not to say that the more conventional cream-free sabayon lacks versatility. It may be served as a dessert, a sauce, or a short drink. I use the French term for its elasticity—ask for zabaglione and you can expect to be served a dessert made with Marsala. Sabayon, on the other hand, can be made with any alcoholic drink you fancy, as well as fruit juice, flavored milk, chicken stock, and so on. Sabayon made with melted butter, on the other hand, is essentially hollandaise.

H Like sabayon, hollandaise is classically made in a double boiler,
O but instead of sugar and booze, you whisk the egg yolks with lemon
L juice or a vinegar reduction before adding the butter slowly as you
L continue to whisk. Hollandaise sauce has a reputation for being
A difficult, but it needn't be. As long as you watch the heat, just as you
N would a custard, and don't try to rush things, you'll be fine. Even
D though it pays to treat it like one, hollandaise isn't a custard, but an
A emulsion of fat and water, as are all the sauces on this continuum.
I Emulsions are temporary pacts between molecules who prefer their
S own company. Agitation—by stirring, whisking, or shaking—forces
E the molecules together, but shortly after the agitation stops, they
will separate again. This can be forestalled by a mediating ingredient like egg yolk, whose protein molecules have hydrophilic "heads," which form bonds with water, and hydrophobic "tails," which repel it in favor of oil—thus forming a stable molecular bridge between the two otherwise immiscible substances. Other ingredients can be used as the emulsifier, but egg yolk is particularly effective.

As with sabayon, an electric mixer will make quicker work of emulsifying your hollandaise, and will save your arm. A blender or food processor makes it almost foolproof. I say almost, as in my experience the tricky thing with hollandaise is serving it warm. It is strikingly resistant to reheating, and is therefore best made immediately before serving. It can be kept warm in a double boiler, for a short while at least, and I've read of some cooks using a Thermos, but by far the safest bet is to use the blender method a few minutes before you're ready to serve. For example, you might lay some cod loins on foil, season them, scribble them with mild olive oil, wrap the foil, and cook them in a 350°F oven for 12 minutes. Slide a tray of lightly oiled asparagus spears into the oven at the same time as the fish, then melt the butter for the sauce. About 3 minutes before the fish will be ready, use the warm butter to make your hollandaise in the blender. Stir in some chopped herbs and serve everything together. When they're in season, I might also put some Jersey Royal potatoes on to simmer before preparing the fish. The sauce elevates the simple meal to a level of luxury that seems indecent, given that the whole thing is done in a quarter of an hour. Hollandaise is named after a country famed for its dairy products, just as its oily cousin, mayonnaise, is said to owe its name to Mahon, the capital of olive-rich Menorca. But it was the French, not the Spanish, who made mayonnaise a fixture of the chef's repertoire, and the Americans who made it a pantry staple. Its admission into the mainstream came with the late-nineteenth-century drop in the price of edible oils, caused by the increased cultivation of oil-producing crops in California and Florida. Around the same time, advances in fresh-produce distribution systems encouraged a new fashion for salads. By 1907, Edward Schlorer, a Philadelphia grocer, had discovered how to make his wife Amelia's homemade mayonnaise shelf-stable; by 1920, Mrs. Schlorer's Mayonnaise was successful enough to warrant an ad campaign and recipe booklet. Hellmann's was trademarked in 1926. The versatility and convenience of the bottled sauce were a great draw, and not only for salads. Being easier to spread than cold butter, it soon became the natural choice for the sandwichmaker. And in 1837, the wife of Hellmann's salesman Paul Price invented chocolate mayonnaise cake. It contained no eggs or fat other than the amounts included in the mayo, and it was thickened with dates and walnuts. Like all oil-based cakes, the result was agreeably moist, and versions of the recipe are still popular today.

MAYONNAISE Homemade mayonnaise is a world apart from the sort that comes in a jar. It is oilier, shinier, more flavorful, and more indicative of its origins. It tastes of oil and eggs. Hellmann's tastes of Hellmann's. Many manufacturers use deodorized oil to achieve the desired blandness. Novice mayomakers might start out with similarly recessive sunflower or canola oil. Whichever you choose, taste a little of the oil on a teaspoon first, as its flavor will be amplified by the emulsion. As little as 10 percent strong olive oil, in combination with something less characterful, can remind you of the days when you didn't care for olives much. Go as far as 30 percent and the bitterness can catch the back of your throat. Color is another factor. A richly verdant extra virgin olive oil might look appetizing in a white-china dipping bowl, but it will give your mayo a distinctly queasy complexion.

Before you start whisking (or flick the switch of your blender) you might consider whether it's worth making your mayonnaise from scratch at all. Certainly, if you plan to add strong flavors—say for a Thousand Island dressing—it might be just as well to use the jar variety. Homemade mayo can be exquisite, but its subtleties can be hard to detect once you've mixed in tomato-chili sauce and finely chopped bell pepper, onion, and so on.

For at least my first eighteen years I'm not sure I ate mayonnaise other than as a constituent of a salad dressing. My introduction to mayonnaise in unadulterated form came when I moved to London and started buying my lunch from a café in a precinct of totalitarian drabness just off Shepherd's Bush Green. The café was run by a man who had longness covered—long face, long limbs, faraway look in his eyes. He resembled a greyhound, all the more so on cold days, when he wore a woolen vest. I would order an egg sandwich and with somber scrupulousness he would apply mayonnaise to two slices of processed white bread, covering every last millimeter without, somehow, wasting a speck. Next he would guillotine a peeled boiled egg in a stainless-steel slicer, which may or may not have had a few extra wires strung across it to make the rounds even thinner, then lay them neatly over the bread in one layer with no overlap. A sprinkle of salt from pinched fingers. The top slice of bread overlaid and pressed lightly. The whole cut on the diagonal and wrapped in a paper bag with the corners twisted like a hanky on a bald man's head at the seaside. They were always exquisite, Mr. Greyhound's egg sandwiches.

Eventually I got a better job in a ritzier part of town and had to put up with premixed, chopped egg salad piled to such depths that the slices of (seeded, brown, *high-quality*) bread stood no hope of touching unless you pressed down so hard that all the filling oozed out the sides. It wasn't right. I missed Mr. Greyhound. I like to think he graduated from Shepherd's Bush to a Japanese prefecture, where he won fame for the precision of his egg sandwiches, married a poetess, and lived out his days in a wooden house by a river lined with cherry trees.

B E U R R E As I've said, all the starting points on the sauce continuum
    are emulsions, but note that the next, beurre blanc, contains no egg.
B   You might even think of beurre blanc as eggless hollandaise. And
L   to lose egg is to lose the domestic kitchen's star emulsifier—the main
A   reason beurre blanc is that much harder to prepare. Why not stick
N   with simple hollandaise? The answer is texture. Both sauces taste as
C   good as their butter content suggests, but beurre blanc is silkier.

To make a classic beurre blanc, you start with a reduction of shallots, wine, and vinegar, then add cold butter, cube by cube, while whisking constantly over a low heat. Some recipes call for the wine or vinegar to be reduced to almost nothing before the butter is added, but in our starting point a fair bit of reduced wine is retained—I think it makes for a more interesting flavor, and suspect it helps the sauce emulsify. Beurre blanc originated in the Loire, and is classically made with white wines from the region, but the flavor can be varied by changing the reduction, either by using a different liquid or adding aromatics to it. Dry white vermouth lends a heavily aromatic quality without departing too far from the original, while a survey of restaurant menus will yield a rainbow of beurres beyond blanc—Chartreuse, Pernod, Tabasco, and, a long way from the Loire, the combination of ginger and soy. Cream is another common addition: A little added to the reduction, and then reduced a bit further, also aids emulsification, and helps prevent the sauce from separating too easily. Many restaurants prepare their beurre blanc this way, to keep it ready for use throughout service.

VINAIGRETTE As hollandaise is to mayonnaise—a hot buttery version of the cold oil-based sauce—beurre blanc is to vinaigrette. Hollandaise and mayonnaise stay emulsified, but in beurre blanc and vinaigrette the alliance is temporary: When left to sit, they separate. In bottles of premixed dressing the oil lies imperiously atop the vinegar, like it knows it's the more expensive of the two. A determined shake and they're recombined.

A simple vinaigrette can be made with just oil and vinegar: three or four parts oil to one of vinegar. Place an oil and vinegar dressing next to an otherwise identical version with mustard added and you'll notice the droplets of oil are considerably bigger in the two-ingredient version, which will split much faster. A minced garlic clove can help stabilize matters, but few ingredients create as strong an emulsion as egg yolk. Use mustard, garlic, *and* yolk and your emulsion becomes a thick, creamy dressing, as you'll know if you've ever combined these ingredients to make a proper Caesar salad from scratch. Tomato paste, cream, and silken tofu are less common emulsifiers that can, nonetheless, take a dressing in an interesting direction.

Vinaigrettes are often mixed up as a bit of an afterthought, but a good one will pay dividends. In my experience, a little sweetness nearly always gives an everyday vinaigrette a leg up to memorability. A grated shallot adds a quality that's just about worth grating a shallot for— and some say onion juice works wonders. It's also worth trying sherry vinegar where you might normally use balsamic or red wine vinegar, or a combination of vinegar and lemon juice, rather than one or other. Small quantities of Marmite (yeast extract) or anchovy, that secret ingredient in so many delicious sauces, will contribute a note of umami.

The one thing worth remembering about leafy salads is that to dress them properly with vinaigrette they must be tossed using your hands. Start by adding less dressing than you think you'll need, then add more in increments until every leaf has a fine coating. You may find you need to include a nail brush in your *batterie de cuisine*, but quite apart from perfectly dressed salads, you'll find this technique furnishes exquisitely oil-softened skin. It's certainly the closest I'll ever get to a manicure.

Practice—seasoned with judicious experimentation—makes perfect. The aim, as with all sauces, is to create something rich *and* sharp, with some body to it. An emulsion of oil and vinegar is the usual way to go, but you might alternatively cut a dollop of nutty tahini paste with lemon juice. Puréed avocado, silken tofu, or fruit juices reduced to a syrupy consistency can also take the oil's part. Remember to taste your dressing on whatever you're serving it with—dip a leaf in it, or try it on a spoonful of your warm lentil salad. Knowing your dressing tastes good on its own is about as useful as being able to line dance in front of the bedroom mirror.

I've been making vinaigrettes since childhood. It's one of the first jobs my mother was prepared to delegate. In recent years I have taken to making my own mayonnaise and hollandaise with reasonable frequency. Following the principles laid out in the sauce continuum, however, has introduced sabayon and beurre blanc to my repertoire too. Restaurant culture has taught us to associate classic sauces with pricey ingredients and elaborate preparations—and yet homely dishes like fishcakes and spinach, salmon and broccoli, or lamb chops with a baked potato can benefit enormously from a saucier's flourish. And the satisfaction-to-effort ratio is high. As Charles Senn puts it in his *Book of Sauces* (1915), "The skill and knowledge of a cook is shown in no other part of the culinary art so prominently than in the way in which his or her sauces are prepared. To be able to make a perfect sauce is indeed the height of the art of cooking."

Sabayon

A sabayon can be served as a sauce—sweet or savory—or in larger portions as a dessert, the most famous example being Italian zabaglione. Sabayon is a custard, meaning it must either be cooked over a low heat, say in a double boiler, or have a little starch added to protect the mixture from the heat—just ½ tsp cornstarch will suffice for the quantity below, added to the yolks from the get-go. To enrich the sabayon, remove from the heat at the end of step ² and whisk in 2–4 tbsp cubed, cold, unsalted butter, one piece at a time. The mixture may appear to loosen initially, but it will thicken up as you add the fat.

For 4 servings of sauce or zabaglione

INGREDIENTS
4 egg yolks
4 tbsp sugar ᴬ
Pinch of salt
4 tbsp sweet white wine for the sauce, or ½ cup Marsala for the dessert ᴮ

¹ Place all the ingredients in a large heatproof bowl and whisk for 1 minute—the mix will expand in volume and become pale.
If you're using an electric mixer, the bowl will need fairly high sides, so the sabayon doesn't spatter your apron and the kitchen walls.

² Place the bowl over—but not touching—barely simmering water and whisk its contents to the ribbon stage.
Ribbon stage is when the mixture that drops from the whisk holds its shape for a few seconds. For the quantity here, this will take 5–7 minutes using an electric mixer, a bit longer—about 10 minutes—if you're braving it by hand.

³ Serve immediately, while still warm, or remove the bowl and keep whisking until the mixture cools—a process you can expedite by resting your bowl of sabayon in a larger bowl of cold or iced water.

LEEWAY

A Use less sugar—1 tsp per yolk will still work. In fact, sugar isn't essential, and can be skipped altogether to make savory versions.

B While Marsala is the wine used for zabaglione, you can try the dessert with any sweet wine you fancy: Madeira, port, sweet sherry, Moscato, Sauternes, etc. For the sauce, the sweet wine can be replaced with all sorts of liquids, sweet or savory—see Flavors & Variations.

CHAMPAGNE

Next time you're serving Champagne and there's a fairweather drinker among your guests—the type who accepts a glass so as not to appear ungrateful, then restricts their intake to a hamsterish sip—whip it away before they feel obliged to knock back the rest. You now have the key to one of the most delicious sabayons known to humanity. What elevates it is the yeastiness yielded by Champagne in the company of whisked egg yolks. The results are reminiscent of brioche dipped in a lightly mulled Muscadet. Best to keep the sugar low—1 tsp per egg yolk. Champagne sabayon often serves as an eiderdown for strawberries, but poached apricots can kick them out of bed, and the ensemble looks darling in a Champagne saucer sprinkled with Angostura bitters, served with a cigarette wafer and a store of Dorothy-Parkeresque wisecracks. Savory Champagne sabayon (omitting the sugar entirely) is a classic seafood dressing. Try it spooned onto oysters broiled on the half-shell: Add some of the salty oyster liquor to the Champagne, and whisk a little butter into the sauce at the end. In the absence of Champagne, cava has the right biscuity yeastiness. At Cinc Sentits in Barcelona, they serve a cava sabayon layered in a shot glass with warm maple syrup, chilled cream, and a pinch of Majorcan salt, which had me springing in the air like the tiny live shrimp sold from wooden boxes by old ladies outside the Boqueria market.

CHERRY BEER

Trebor used to make the most terrific sour-cherry boiled candies. They must have had a pH of about 1.5. One suck and your eyes were slits; three candies and you were in the E.R. with a perforated palate. Like so much in life, they're just not the same now. I get some of the same kick from *kriek*. A decent Belgian *kriek*, or cherry beer, is made by flavoring lambic beer with *Schaarbeekse krieken*, a local variety of Morello cherry. Lambic differs from other kinds of beer in being the product of spontaneous fermentation. It's made in large vessels in the open air, allowing, in place of cultivated brewer's yeasts, naturally occurring yeasts in the atmosphere and on the ingredients to do the work. The cherries (or raspberries) are added to the beer for a second fermentation, as much as a pound of fruit per two quarts of beer, so the flavor is pingingly intense. If you're expecting anything along the lines of a beer alcopop, advises writer Pete Brown, you're a long way off. Alcopops are predominantly sweet, and their flavors closer to the toy-town fruitiness of confectionery. A lambic beer is both sour and bitter, with naturally fruity flavors. Beware, however, that the popularity of *kriek* among the hordes of beer fans that flock to Brussels means you'll have to watch out for cheap, sweetened, ersatz varieties. The combination of pronounced fruit and sourness in the real thing makes for a sabayon that's full of flavor without being too sweet. A treat on dark-chocolate ice cream.

COFFEE

The molecular gastronomist Hervé This divides sabayons into two categories—the sumptuously flavored and the gentle. Coffee and lobster are filed under the first category. Sauternes, rum, and vanilla under the second. Like Delia Smith, the not-so-molecular gastronomist, This likes to add "a dash of starch" to the ingredients, to prevent lumps. For a simple coffee sabayon, use 1 tbsp instant coffee dissolved in ¼ cup hot water and then cooled in place of the wine in our starting point. Raymond Blanc's version is more elaborate. He creates a faux *café crème* by filling a chocolate espresso cup (complete with chocolate saucer) with coffee sabayon and finishing it with a *crema*-style froth of kirsch sabayon. The base for both flavors is prepared using 2 egg yolks, 2 tbsp sugar, 1½ tsp lemon juice, and ¼ cup Muscat or other sweet wine, taken off the heat once it's ready and whisked until cold. Then ⅓ cup cream, whipped to soft peaks, is folded in. For the coffee sabayon, fold 3 tbsp *ristretto* coffee into 1 cup of the finished sabayon, then fold 1 tsp kirsch into the remainder for the *crema* topping.

MARSALA

On an island in the Tiber I ate a zabaglione to make the Visigoths spare Rome. It had been folded into cream, frozen, spooned onto cubed pandoro, and sprinkled with tiny wild strawberries. The dish was finished with a few drops of a balsamic vinegar that tasted so deep I imagined the chef wearing a vial of it on a chain around his neck. Zabaglione is usually made with Marsala, the fortified Sicilian wine. Typical tasting notes for Marsala include toasted almond, citrus, vanilla, caramel, and honey. Over the centuries, other wines have been used to make similar preparations. The sixteenth-century cook Bartolomeo Scappi called for the sweet Madeira known as malmsey, in a butt of which poor Clarence, according to Shakespeare, was drowned on the orders of his brother, King Richard III. Worth bearing in mind if you have any left over, and some very small rivals to bump off. In malmsey you may detect notes of chocolate, candy apples, toasted nuts, and marmalade; Scappi supplements this with cinnamon, and suggests adding butter at the end of whisking. Pellegrino Artusi opts for sherry, and suggests further fortifying your fortified wine with a dash of rum. Mario Batali uses *vin santo* and no sugar, but does add butter, cream, salt, and pepper, serving it with grilled asparagus. Essentially, all sweet wines seem to be viable for zabaglione, but if you're using a non-sweet variety, it's safer to call the result a sabayon. Wolfgang Puck makes a version with Merlot and serves it with berries tossed in sugar and lemon.

MILK & HONEY

And the Lord spake unto Moses, saying, "Depart… Unto a land flowing with milk and honey." And Moses was like, well, okay, Lord. But, hello, cholesterol? Is the milk, like, skim? Biblical scholarship suggests that the "milk" probably represented a generic promise of fatty things, and the "honey," sweet stuff like pomegranates, dates, and grapes. Still, literalists might like to make James Martin's sabayon of almond milk and honey: Use 3 egg yolks, ¼ cup packed light brown sugar, ¼ cup honey, and ⅓ cup almond milk, whisking them all together in a double boiler until thick and moussey. Then add 2 tbsp Amaretto and continue to whisk for 2 minutes. Martin spoons the slightly cooled sauce over room-temperature berries, then puts the dishes under a hot broiler for a further couple of minutes until lightly golden.

MUSTARD

Mustard and fish is less common a combination than you might think. In Sweden, gravadlax is served with mustard sauce, and mustard seeds bob about in tubs of rollmops, while in Bengal, fish is cooked with both mustard oil and seeds, but otherwise it's rare. Rosamond Man and Robin Weir maintain that fish has the greatest potential of all the mustard pairings they tried for *The Mustard Book*. For the record, they include recipes for chocolate cookies made with mustard, mango and dill mustard iced fool, and a banana, apple, and mustard chutney, so the fish claim is not made lightly. Marco Pierre White makes a savory sabayon flavored with coarse grain mustard, which he serves with fish. First, he reduces 1¾ cups fish velouté (page [174]) by half and lets it cool; meanwhile, he makes a sabayon with 4 egg yolks, a few drops of water, and 4 tbsp clarified butter. The sabayon is then mixed with the velouté, 4 tbsp whipped cream, and 2 tsp coarse grain mustard to a pouring consistency.

ORANGE

Buy four large oranges at the time of year they're supposedly at their best. Peel one and find that its membranes could be used to surface the nose cones of reentry capsules. Remove the other oranges from the fruit bowl, isolate them like disobedient children, and ignore them for three days. On the fourth day, throw them away. Realizing that you have nothing for dessert that night, retrieve them from the trash and rinse off the coffee grounds. Juice 1 orange and add 1 tbsp each of Cointreau and water (the water helps prevent the eggs from curdling). Using a sharp knife, fillet the segments from the other 2 oranges. Make it a point of pride to remove the white pith and as much of the membrane as possible while wasting the minimum of flesh. Divide your filleted orange supremes between two small plates. Proceed as per the starting point, making a sabayon with the juice mixture, 2 egg yolks, and 1 tbsp sugar. Spoon it over the segments, followed by the lightest dusting of apple-pie spice. Don't skip the Cointreau; it provides the bitter-marmalade, supercharged oranginess I think the dish needs.

AS A BASE FOR PARFAIT

Whisk the sabayon until cool. Whip cream to soft peaks and fold in, along with a purée or liquid flavoring, then freeze.

THOMAS KELLER'S LEMON SABAYON TART

Made using a sabayon enriched with butter and flavored with lemon juice, poured into a tart shell, and baked.

SABAYON ICE CREAM

Fold whipped cream into sabayon and freeze.

POUR OVER BERRIES AND BRÛLÉE

EGG-YOLK CHOCOLATE MOUSSE

Whisk the sabayon until cool. Fold it and some softly whipped cream into melted chocolate, then chill until set.

AS A SOUFFLÉ BASE

Fold in egg whites beaten to soft peaks and bake.

Hollandaise

Turning melted butter into hollandaise miraculously banishes its greasiness. Mixing up the following quantity by hand isn't too painful, but I would nearly always choose the machine method over the stovetop. There are those who consider this cheating and call the results "butter mayonnaise." I've never had any complaints. Fold in whipped cream before serving to create a sauce mousseline: Use half the butter quantity in light whipping or heavy cream—½ cup for the quantities below. Alternatively, fold in 2 egg whites beaten to stiff peaks for a frothy, lighter sauce.

For 4–6 servings

INGREDIENTS
4 egg yolks [A]
Pinch of salt
4 tsp lemon juice, warmed [B]
1 cup unsalted butter, melted and still warm (but not hot) [C] [D]
White pepper

STOVETOP METHOD

1 In a heatproof bowl set over, but not touching, barely simmering water, whisk the yolks and salt with 2 tbsp warm water for 30 seconds. Still whisking, add the warmed lemon juice.

2 With the heat on very low, add a small quantity of the warm butter and whisk in thoroughly to make a nice thick emulsion, then continue to add butter in increments, avoiding adding the solids at the bottom of the butter pan as best you can.
I add butter by the tablespoon for the first 4 tbsp, then the rest in thirds. Whisk after each addition of butter until the mixture is rethickened. If the sauce splits, try adding a little water or an ice cube and giving it a good whisk before continuing. If that doesn't work, start again with a new egg yolk and incorporate the split sauce as if it were just butter.

3 Taste and adjust the seasoning, adding more lemon juice, salt, and/or pepper as required. [E]
A little water can be added if the sauce is too thick.

4 Use immediately, or keep warm in a covered dish over barely simmering water or in a Thermos for up to 1 hour.

MACHINE METHOD

1 Blitz the yolks, salt, 1 tsp warm water, and warm lemon juice in a blender or food processor for a few seconds.
Note that if you're making a smaller quantity than this, you'll need a small bowl in the processor so the blades can reach the ingredients.

2 With the machine running, drizzle in the warm butter through the tube, or hole in the pusher, slowly to start with, avoiding adding the solids at the bottom of the butter as best you can.

3 Check for seasoning, adding more lemon juice, salt, and/or pepper as required. If necessary, thin by blending in a little warm water in small increments.

4 Use immediately, or keep warm in a covered dish over barely simmering water or in a Thermos for up to 1 hour.

LEEWAY

A A hollandaise made with a higher ratio of egg yolks to butter is less likely to separate, but may taste a little eggy.

B A vinegar reduction is sometimes used in place of the lemon juice. Put 2 tbsp each of white wine vinegar and water, 1 bay leaf, and 4 black peppercorns in a nonreactive pan and simmer until reduced by about two-thirds (leaving about 4 tsp liquid). Strain and let cool slightly. If you make hollandaise (or beurre blanc) frequently, make a larger batch of this reduction and store it in a labeled jar in the fridge, where it should keep for a few months. Some cooks add further flavor to the reduction with mace, tarragon, or shallots.

C Use clarified butter if you like, but with the dairy solids and water removed, the hollandaise will be thicker and, ironically, less buttery-tasting. To thin a hollandaise made with clarified butter, whisk in a splash of water at the end.

D If the butter is hot rather than warm, the finished sauce risks being too thin.

E Some cooks also like to add a pinch of cayenne or a dash of Tabasco.

BLOOD ORANGE

Sauce maltaise, the variation on hollandaise classically served with asparagus, calls for blood oranges. According to Jane Grigson, it's even better made with Sevilles. The advantage of blood oranges, however, is that they stick around a little later in the year than Sevilles, and so might just still be available at the beginning of the asparagus season. Try your maltaise à la Grigson with a piece of fine white fish, or alongside Sevilles' seasonal coevals like purple sprouting broccoli. Whether or not to include the zest is a matter for debate; some find the bittiness, not to mention the bitterness, incongruous in the lusciously textured sauce. New Orleans chef John Besh serves crab cakes with a variation on hollandaise, flavored with an aromatic reduction of the juice of locally grown satsumas, white wine vinegar, fresh ginger, shallots, peppercorns, coriander seeds, thyme, and bay. Maltaise sounds relatively simple by comparison. Add the finely grated zest of 1 orange to the egg yolks at step [1]. Juice the bald orange and set 2 tsp aside; warm the rest of the juice with 1 tbsp water and pour onto the yolks while whisking in a double boiler, before proceeding from step [2]. Once made, check the sauce for seasoning, and add the set-aside juice.

BROWN BUTTER

Sauce noisette is a hollandaise in a serious mood. Some of the butter is browned first, contributing a caramelized flavor quite distinct from the tang of the standard sauce. This makes it unsuitable for brunch dishes—not, I hasten to add, for gustatorial, but moral reasons. Eat bacon, brioche, and beurre noisette before noon and where will the day end? Deep-fried popcorn foie gras, three bottles of Château d'Yquem, and a fistfight. There are straightforward ways of preparing noisette, but consider for a moment sauce Kientzheim, which Hervé This serves on poached fish or grilled meat: You won't find a better sauce named after a village on the D28 in Alsace. Brown your butter, intermittently adding small splashes of orange juice, milk, or water to prevent it from burning (an idea This credits to Pierre Gagnaire). Let cool, then whisk it into a mixture of egg yolk, lemon juice, mustard, and salt. You'll note that the method is more akin to making mayonnaise than hollandaise, in that the egg is not heated. Alice B. Toklas uses the same technique for her "hollandaise au beurre noisette," although in her case the "noisette" refers to hazelnuts, not browned butter. She finishes the sauce with vinegar, rather than lemon juice, and serves it with salmon. The typical method for beurre noisette hollandaise is to brown about 15 percent of the butter, make the sauce with the other 85 percent, and then whisk or blend in the warm, liquid beurre noisette at the end.

CHILI

The British partiality to chili might seem recent, but as far back as 1860, Eliza Acton was advocating cayenne as an addition to all sorts of preparations, including the hollandaise-like Dutch sauce. Acton's sauce mixes egg yolks, lemon, butter, water, salt, cayenne, and nutmeg, but unlike most hollandaise recipes, all the ingredients are placed in the pan at the same time—although she does note that it might be safer to use a double boiler and stir constantly. Dutch sauce was the suggested accompaniment to boiled eels or boiled calf's head. Cayenne has recently lost ground to chipotle as the variety of chili most commonly specified for hollandaise, perhaps because the latter's smokiness is so apt to pep up classic brunch dishes; chipotle hollandaise is pretty terrific on a hot corn-on-the-cob too. Use ¼ tsp cayenne for a 4-yolk hollandaise. Or add 2–3 tsp chipotle paste with the yolks at step [1] and substitute lime juice for lemon.

COURT BOUILLON

Returning to New York from a business trip to Paris, "Diamond" Jim Brady, the nineteenth-century railroad magnate and gourmand, told Charles Rector, the proprietor of a restaurant he frequented, about an exquisite dish he had eaten at a place called Au Petit Marguery. So unforgettable was this Sole Marguery, draped in a hollandaise made with the light fish stock called court bouillon, that Brady was moved to an ultimatum: Unless Rector learned how to reproduce the dish, he would take his business elsewhere. And Brady's was not the sort of business you could afford to lose. Once he had digested his breakfast of bread, eggs, muffins, grits, pancakes, fried potatoes, chops, and steaks washed down with orange juice, he would stave off any mid-morning hunger pangs with a few dozen clams or oysters. Diamond Jim, the Mr. Creosote of the Gilded Age. Rector duly took his son out of Cornell University—or so the story goes—and dispatched him to Paris in pursuit of the recipe. Poor Rector Jr. took a job in the Au Petit Marguery kitchens, where he slaved for fifteen hours a day until he got the hang of the sauce. He then booked himself onto a ship home, and was met at the docks by Diamond Jim himself, who drove the kid back to Rector's and stayed to polish off no less than nine helpings. It's said that when Brady's body was examined, after his death from a heart attack in 1917, he had a stomach six times the size of an average adult's. Ironically, the version of sauce Marguery recorded in *The Rector Cookbook* (1928) is considerably lighter than the classic hollandaise, being less reliant on butter. Rector uses 4 tbsp white wine and 1 cup reduced fish stock, whisking in 3 egg yolks, then adding ½ cup butter over a gentle heat, as you would for hollandaise. The sauce is then seasoned, strained, and finished with 1 tsp chopped parsley. More elaborate versions of sauce Marguery involve shrimp, oyster, and mussel essences.

DILL

I was lying in bed, stroking the fur cuffs of my peignoir, dictating my brunch. Potato rösti, made to a depth such that the surface would be crisp and golden brown, the inside soft and white. On top of that, a layer of dark orange, dry-smoked salmon, a perfectly poached egg, and finally a ladleful of thick yellow hollandaise flecked with dill. Then came the bombshell. *Someone* had forgotten to buy the smoked salmon. I flounced to the kitchen, rejecting all offers of bacon, and made the dill hollandaise anyway. We had it on poached eggs with homemade, skin-on fries. In my opinion, dill is the ideal herb for hollandaise: Its evergreen briskness lifts the warm fug of butter. Add 2–4 tbsp finely chopped dill to the sauce. Some cooks infuse a vinegar reduction (as at ᴮ under Leeway) with the dill, although this way you miss out on the flecks, indispensable to my eye.

MINT

Sauce *paloise* is a well-known, if seldom seen, variant of béarnaise (itself a variation of hollandaise) in which the tarragon is replaced with fresh mint: a shoo-in with *entrecôte frites*, or lamb chops and sauté potatoes. Diana Henry serves it with roast lamb, and I like it with a hearty casserole of lamb and beans. Vegetarians might try serving it with pea or fava bean fritters. Make a reduction of white wine vinegar (as described at ᴮ under Leeway), adding 1 tbsp finely chopped mint with the other aromatics, then follow the starting point for hollandaise, stirring 2–4 tbsp freshly chopped mint into the finished sauce.

OLIVE OIL

A good variation—just don't call it hot mayonnaise. Choose a mild olive oil, more golden-colored than forest green; 3 egg yolks to scant 1 cup warm olive oil. Make as per our starting point, adding the olive oil in increments, in the same way as you would butter.

PASSION FRUIT

Passion fruit is such a tart. The overpowering perfume, the leopard-skin pulp. Dilute the flavor and its tutti-fruttiness gives way to a beautiful balance of floral and sulfurous notes, while its acidity does the job that lemon (or a vinegar reduction) normally does in hollandaise. In Hawaii, where the fruit is popular (albeit in its yellow form, as opposed to the purple-skinned variety commonly available in the rest of the U.S. and the U.K.), passion-fruit hollandaise is a favorite. It's an edible lei for crab cakes, poached or roasted white fish or wild salmon, and seared tuna. Use strained passion-fruit pulp in place of the lemon juice—each purple fruit should yield 1–2 tsp.

TARRAGON & SHALLOT

Restricting béarnaise to *steak-frites* is to cramp its style. Robert Carrier drapes it on deep-fried breaded mussels. Simon Hopkinson reminds us that béarnaise works wonders on lamb, turbot, and even baked potato. In the novelization of *The Prisoner*, Number Six rustles up a béarnaise to serve with *oeufs à la Beaugency*—poached eggs on artichoke hearts—complaining as he does so about the poorly equipped kitchen. No garlic press, no mouli. Jarred spices. Anyone would have thought he was in rural Wales in the late 1960s. Reduce 2 tbsp minced shallots, 3 tbsp tarragon vinegar, and 1 tbsp water to about 1 tbsp liquid. Strain, cool a little, and add to the yolks in place of the lemon juice, then follow the starting point. Once all the butter has been incorporated, stir in 2–3 tbsp finely chopped tarragon leaves. Sauce Choron is the blushing bride of béarnaise. Many recipes call for a skinned, deseeded, and diced tomato to be folded in at the same time as the chopped tarragon.

Mayonnaise

A semi-solid emulsion of egg and oil flavored with mustard and
lemon juice or vinegar. Homemade mayonnaise is creamier
and less gelatinous than store-bought. You should also find it less
vinegary and sweet, and the flavor of egg will be more apparent.
It's particularly delightful fridge-chilled on freshly fried *frites*,
the sort sold in paper cones in Belgium and the Netherlands.
Whip ½–⅔ cup heavy or light whipping cream and fold it in
for a mayonnaise Chantilly, a lighter, airier version traditionally
served with, say, poached salmon, rather than in an egg salad
sandwich. Mayonnaise is very stable, and thus welcomes the
addition of all sorts of ingredients once made.

For 1 ½ cups

INGREDIENTS
2 egg yolks ᴬ
1–3 tsp Dijon mustard ᴮ
A few pinches of salt
1¼ cups oil ᶜ ᴰ
1–3 tsp lemon juice or wine vinegar ᴱ
A few pinches of pepper—optional ᶠ

HAND METHOD

1 Whisk the yolks with the mustard and a few pinches of salt.
   The yolks need to be at room temperature. If your eggs have been in
   the fridge, sit them in warm water for 5 minutes before cracking and
   separating them. Be moderate with your seasoning. You can always
   adjust it later.

2 Add the oil slowly, the first teaspoon or two drop by drop,
   whisking constantly. Once the emulsion is established, begin
   adding the oil a teaspoon at a time, then a tablespoon at a time,
   and finally in a slow, steady stream. When all the oil has been
   added, give the mixture a good 30-second whisk.

3 Whisk in the lemon juice or vinegar and seasoning to taste.

4 Store, covered or in a lidded jar, in the fridge for up to a week.

MACHINE METHOD

1 Put the yolks, mustard, and salt in the bowl of a small blender or food processor, then pulse.

2 With the machine running, drizzle in the oil through the tube or hole in the pusher, starting slowly.

3 Once all the oil is in and the mayo is emulsified, remove the lid, add the lemon juice or vinegar and seasoning to taste, then reseal and blitz again.

4 Store, covered or in a lidded jar, in the fridge for up to a week.

LEEWAY

A Famously, 1 egg yolk can turn a great deal of oil into mayonnaise, but a more typical quantity is ⅔–1 cup oil per yolk. No need to add all of the oil; stop when you have as much mayo as you need, or it's as thick as you like it.

B The mustard is for flavor—it's fine to leave it out.

C The more oil you use, the thicker the mayo will be. Thin it, once made, by whisking in a little water.

D Oil-wise, use sunflower, canola, peanut, or a very mild olive oil. Be cautious of using too much characterful olive, walnut, or hazelnut oils—most cooks dilute these with something blander and cheaper.

E Some cooks add the vinegar or lemon juice to the yolk mixture at the start, but it's better for the stability of the emulsion to add them at the end.

F Some recipes include a little white pepper; others suggest black pepper.

BACON

Given how easy it is to accumulate bacon fat, it seems foolish not to try it in place of oil in a mayonnaise. It's become commonplace—either out of sheer contrariness, or the immunity of youthful waistlines to saturated fat and carbohydrate—to pile one unashamedly rich ingredient on another. Deep-fried double blue-cheese burger. In a clotted-cream brioche. With bacon mayo! Avoid such Babylonian gluttony and set off your bacon mayo with something bracingly bitter. The combination of bitter leaves and salty pork fat recalls a Lyonnais-style *frisée aux lardons,* the classic French salad of curly endive, bacon bits, and poached egg, or the old Italian habit of dressing radicchio with hot lard and cheese shavings. I like bacon mayonnaise on a salad of Belgian endive, toasted hazelnuts, and apple. It's also good spread on a toasted panino, stuffed with a mixture of grilled and raw radicchio, and very thin slices of chili pecorino. You can use all bacon fat in your mayo, but if you haven't been hoarding it, 1 tbsp mixed with ½ cup bland oil will give a definite bacon flavor. Obviously the fat will need to be in liquid form, and strained. Taste the mayo before adding any extra salt: it may not need it. Finish with 1 tsp sweet paprika and a splash of red wine vinegar at step [3].

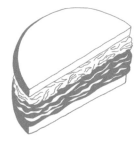

CHEESE

We know things won't work out between Annie Hall and Alvy Singer when she orders pastrami on white with mayonnaise. Alvy looks like he's swallowed a dill pickle sideways. It's the ultimate solecism, on a par with asking for your entrecôte *bien cuite.* Not only will Annie's sandwich be hopelessly stodgy without the wry astringency of mustard, but it will probably be non-kosher too, since mayonnaise is not *kashrut* unless the egg yolks have been checked for blood spots. She would have been no better off ordering a Reuben sandwich, involving as it does the proscribed combination of meat and cheese. If all this makes no odds to you, I recommend getting wise to the blue Reuben, which substitutes tangy blue-cheese mayo for the Russian dressing. In the U.K.,the inevitable surfeit of Stilton at Christmas makes it a good time to experiment with blue-cheese mayo—try it in a sandwich with plenty of thinly sliced turkey. One Boxing Day (the day after Christmas), for want of sauerkraut, I used a coleslaw instead, made with thinly sliced, raw Brussels sprouts. Classically, blue-cheese mayonnaise is served with Buffalo wings, or thinned and poured over a bacon and spinach salad. Add about 2–4 oz flavorful cheese to your finished mayonnaise, blending or mashing depending on whether you want a smooth or more textured dressing.

CURRY

For all their insouciance toward Indian food, the French do like their curry flavor. Curry mayonnaise is a mainstay of the *supermarché* aisle. Danes are partial too, according to Jane Grigson, who notes that curry mayo is often served with pickled herring, meat, and salads, *grand-aïoli*-style. If you're making it from scratch, she advises, use peanut or corn oil. Brits consume most of their curry mayonnaise in the form of coronation chicken, a recipe as tenacious as the monarchy itself. Rosemary Hume's original version, created for the Queen's coronation lunch in 1953, has a remarkable depth of flavor. Chopped onion is softened in a little oil with curry powder, then simmered with red wine, tomato paste, a bay leaf, slices of lemon, seasoning, and water to create an aromatic paste, which is strained before being mixed with mayonnaise and apricot purée. It's finished with lemon juice and a little whipped cream. Danish curry mayo is quicker to rustle up: 1 tbsp curry powder and 4 tbsp heavy cream are added to 1½ cups mayonnaise, along with lemon juice, salt, and pepper to taste.

GARLIC

If only the Spanish had snuck a spoonful of allioli onto every plate of sausages and fries, Benidorm might still be a cute little fishing village. Your average 1960s Costa-del-Sol-bound British vacationer was not fond of garlic and oil, and nothing is garlickier or oilier than allioli. The sauce originated in Catalonia, where the garlic alone emulsifies the olive oil. These days most allioli is made with eggs in the (less tricky) mayonnaise fashion—as is its Provençal equivalent, aïoli, revered enough in France to earn a superlative and a place at the center of a meal—*le grand aïoli*. My first encounter with a *grand aïoli* was not, sad to say, at a hundred-foot table in the village square, attended by dapper farmers with moustaches like broom-ends, but at a swanky French restaurant in London. My friend had disappeared behind the sort of multilevel stand normally used for *fruits de mer*. Here it held bowls of blanched green beans, new potatoes half-hatched from their skins, hard-cooked eggs, their yolks stippled and minutely fissured like cold butter, whip-slim carrots with bushy green tops, radishes, a rag-tag militia of rough-cut bread "soldiers," and, at the top, a whole globe artichoke. In France, *le grand aïoli*—or *l'aïoli monstre*, as it's sometimes called—is traditional for a summer lunch or on Christmas Eve. It's also a perfect appetizer for a weekend dinner, as so much of it can be prepared ahead. I'd follow it with a slow-roasted leg of lamb, partly because the next day you can pile thick slices of cold meat and vegetables with a dollop of aïoli into a sandwich as a handheld memento of the night before. Some recipes stipulate mincing the garlic and whisking it with the egg yolks before adding the oil, but as garlic varies so much, I tend to crush it into a paste and then add this in increments to the finished mayonnaise, tasting as I go. For an aïoli made with 1¼ cups oil, use somewhere between 2 and 6 cloves, depending on their size and intensity. Also consider smoked, roasted, or black garlic. Wild garlic is an option too, as long as you blanch and dry it before blending it with the oil, which you then strain through a fine sieve and use as you would any other oil.

GREEN GODDESS

Green goddess dressing is a mixture of mayonnaise, tarragon vinegar, onion, anchovy, chives, parsley, and tarragon, thought to have been invented at the Palace Hotel in San Francisco. It's very vinegary, and modern versions tend to replace much of the vinegar with sour cream. Avocado is another recent addition, which at least ensures the dressing ends up being the right color. The story goes that sometime around 1920, the chef at the Palace, Philip Roemer, created the sauce for the great English actor George Arliss, a guest at the hotel while he was appearing in a play called *The Green Goddess* (hopefully Arliss stayed somewhere less eager to please when he appeared in *The Seagull*). For the original, wince-inducing version, mix the following into 1½ cups mayonnaise: ½ cup tarragon vinegar, 1 scallion, minced with 10–12 anchovy fillets, ¼ cup finely chopped parsley, 2 tbsp finely chopped tarragon, and ½ cup snipped chives. For the milder version, replace the vinegar with sour cream and 2 tbsp lemon juice.

GRIBICHE, RÉMOULADE & TARTAR

Gribiche sounds like a toadying courtier in a Molière play. It is, in fact, one of a family of piquant, bitty, mayonnaise-based sauces that includes rémoulade and tartar, and that might contain chopped cornichons or sour gherkins, capers, shallots, hard-cooked egg white, and *fines herbes* (chervil, chives, parsley, and tarragon). *Gribiche* is made by emulsifying cooked, sieved egg yolks with mustard, oil, and lemon juice or vinegar, but the proportions and method are the same as for our mayonnaise starting point. It won't stiffen as much as raw-egg mayonnaise, and is more liable to split, but can easily be stirred back together. *Gribiche* was classically served with boiled tongue or *tête de veau*, but it is excellent with cold roast beef, boiled eggs, and fried fish, as you might expect of a sauce so similar to tartar. Hard-cook 2 eggs, remove the yolks (saving the whites for later), and sieve them, then whisk into the mustard, season, and proceed as per the starting point. When the mayonnaise is finished, add the reserved egg whites, finely chopped, along with 1 tbsp each of finely chopped capers and shallots, and

1–2 tbsp finely chopped *fines herbes*. For rémoulade, mix 2 tsp Dijon mustard and 1 tsp anchovy paste into 2 raw egg yolks at step 1, then add 1 tbsp each chopped capers, cornichons, parsley, tarragon, and chervil to the finished mayonnnaise. (This is a more elaborate rémoulade than the version outlined under mustard below.) Tartar is essentially the same as rémoulade, minus the anchovy and with the juice of half a lemon added with the green bits.

MISO

Henry Adaniya quit his upscale restaurant in Chicago to sell hot dogs in Hawaii. Not any old hot dogs. The menu at Hank's Haute Dogs includes a seafood dog with daikon relish and miso mayo. The chef Masaharu Morimoto makes an intriguing miso mayo for shrimp tempura, flavoring a store-bought sauce with lemon juice, white miso, orange zest, chili paste, and orange liqueur. There are as many types of miso as there are blossoms under the cherry tree, but for uses like this the lightness of white miso recommends itself. Mix 1 tbsp white miso paste with 2 tsp wasabi paste, 2 tbsp lime juice, 2 tbsp water, and 1 tsp light brown sugar until smooth. Add to 1½ cups mayonnaise.

MUSTARD

Rémoulade, the classic dressing for shredded celeriac (a.k.a. celery root), is also a mustard mayonnaise, although the same term can refer to one of the piquant, bitty mayos listed under *gribiche* opposite. Add 3–5 tbsp Dijon mustard to 1½ cups mayonnaise. I like to use a mix of smooth and grainy mustard, for visual interest as much as anything.

PRAWN COCKTAIL

Prawn (or shrimp) cocktail has almost shaken off its naff reputation in the U.K. Chefs need no longer seek refuge in euphemisms like sauce bagnarotte. Or sauce Marie Rose, which evokes all the sumptuousness of something that's been rotting on the seabed for five hundred years. (The Mary Rose was a Tudor warship that sank in 1545.) Of course, the reason for all the rebranding in the first place was that so many prawn cocktails would only have been improved by burial at sea. I had forgotten why I loved prawn cocktail so much until I visited Gothenburg: It's not so much the sauce as the prawn. There they were sweet, mildly briny, and as chewy as a mermaid's upturned nose. I asked the waiter where they were from, expecting him to frown in gentle bemusement and say, why, Gothenburg Bay, as if the very idea of importing seafood was unthinkable in Sweden. "Greenland," he said. Still, the Swedes clearly know where to buy their prawns *from*, as did the Brits, before warmwater prawn farming flooded the market with disgusting, squelchy sea-bugs with a chemical base note that makes them taste as if they've been double-dipped in a verruca bath. If a weekend in Gothenburg is out of the question, find a good fish market, or use crab instead. For my seafood sauce, use two parts mayonnaise to one part tomato ketchup, adding dashes of Worcestershire sauce and lemon juice to taste. Season with salt, pepper, and cayenne. A dram of brandy or vodka will perk it up. Related dressings include Louie, Thousand Island, and Russian, all three of which include the same finely chopped additions—tomato, pickles, and shallots.

QUINCE & GARLIC

Allioli de Codony is garlic mayonnaise enhanced with quince purée. Claudia Roden cites it in *The Food of Spain*, along with an allioli flavored with apple or pear. Typically, both are served with grilled or roasted meats and boiled potatoes. Poach or roast 8 oz quinces (or 2 small apples, such as Granny Smith, or pears) in their skins until very soft. Peel, core, and mash the cooked flesh into a purée. Whisk it into 1½ cups mayonnaise, together with 3–4 minced garlic cloves and ¼ cup extra virgin olive oil.

RED PEPPER

Rouille ("rust") is a mayonnaise-style sauce made with garlic, red chili, and maybe some saffron too. It's popular on the French Mediterranean coast, where it's served with bouillabaisse, grilled fish, or boiled eggs. In its most famous incarnation, *rouille* is spread over large croutons of garlic-rubbed French bread and lowered, along with pinches of grated Gruyère, into a similarly rust-colored *soupe de poissons*. If you are unlucky, you'll be served the sort of sissy *rouille*—mild metal fatigue, rather than rust—in which the chili has been replaced with benign red bell pepper. Some recipes stipulate a basic mayonnaise-style approach, adding 1 deseeded red chili and 2–4 garlic cloves, pounded to a paste, with 1 tbsp tomato paste for flavor (instead of the usual mustard), and red wine vinegar and lemon juice to lend the sauce some backbone. Other recipes replace the egg yolk with mashed potato or bread crumbs, as in Greek *skordalia*.

SEA URCHIN

Long before umami was on everyone's tongue, anchovy was used to add a savory quality to all manner of sauces. For example, fish sauce, which in Southeast Asia is made predominantly with anchovies, can be stirred into bought mayo to furnish one of the many layers of flavor in Vietnamese *bánh mì* sandwiches. Rather more glamorously, Michel Roux makes a sea-urchin mayonnaise to accompany shellfish by adding the sieved coral of a dozen sea urchins to a mayonnaise made with 2 egg yolks, 1 tbsp Dijon mustard, 1 cup peanut oil, and 2 tbsp lemon juice. Whip ½ cup light whipping cream to soft peaks, then carefully fold it in, along with 1 tbsp Grand Marnier and a few drops of Tabasco. Serve with cold crustaceans.

SEAWEED & WASABI

Japan may not be the first country you associate with mayonnaise, but makimakers will have piped a combination of wasabi and mayo onto their nori before rolling it up. At The Hand and Flowers pub, in Marlow, England, Tom Kerridge adds seaweed to wasabi mayo and serves it with oyster fritters. Seaweed and wasabi mayo is a treat with fish *fritto misto*, served with plenty of lemon wedges, so you can flit between salty, hot, and sour seasonings. The type of seaweed Kerridge stipulates is gutweed, *Ulva intestinalis*, so-called because it resembles Shrek's entrails. In Japan, the stuff is specially cultivated. In the U.K., you can collect it on your wellies if you go for a walk along the beach. The forager John Wright notes that sampled direct from the rockpools it tastes of nothing but salt. Dried in the oven or by the sun, crumbled into nori-like flakes or deep-fried in shreds, it takes on more typical green-vegetable flavors. Kerridge gives 2 oz raw gutweed a thorough rinse and then blends it in a food processor with ½ cup rice vinegar, 2 egg yolks, and 1 tsp wasabi paste, then slowly adds 1 cup vegetable oil until the mixture emulsifies. Kerridge suggests heightening the flavor of the mayo by adding the oyster liquor to it at the end.

TUNA

Vitello tonnato has a face for radio. Even on the most exquisite Milanese dinnerware, the pallid combination of veal and tuna mayo will still look like a faded color photograph from a 1950s cookbook. Capers, the typical garnish, are hardly red currants in the looks department. Who cares, though? It's so delicious it won't be around long enough to offend anyone's aesthetic sensibilities. The veal is sometimes replaced with pork or chicken; some cooks prefer to roast the meat, while others poach it. Either way, the dish is usually served at room temperature, or better still, chilled on a sweltering day. In the absence of a chi-chi beach club, or deck of a yacht, find the nicest spot in the garden and set yourself up with a glass of something pink. The following should be enough for 2 pounds or so of meat. In a blender or food processor, mix 1 cup mayonnaise with a 6-oz can or jar of good-quality tuna (including the oil), 4 anchovy fillets, rinsed, and 1–2 tbsp lemon juice. When the mixture is smooth and creamy, stir in 2–3 tbsp rinsed and dried capers. Some like to loosen the sauce with a bit of the cooking liquid, if the meat was poached. Slice the cooked meat very thinly, arrange on a plate, and evenly pour the sauce over it. Alternatively, Marcella Hazan recommends assembling *vitello tonnato* in lasagne-like layers of meat and sauce. She advises that the finished dish can be kept in the fridge for up to a week.

Beurre Blanc

An eggless hollandaise, in essence—meaning that, minus the thickening effect of egg yolk, a beurre blanc will be thinner than a hollandaise made with the same quantity of butter. Nonetheless, it'll still be thick enough to hold its shape on the plate, assuming it hasn't been sitting around for too long. Beurre blanc usually accompanies fish, but vegetarians should not miss out. I would happily eat it on nothing more complicated than steamed broccoli rabe on fluffy white basmati rice. Here the ratio of reduction to butter is 5 tbsp to 1 cup—not unlike that for vinaigrette.

For 6–8 servings

INGREDIENTS
1 large shallot (or 2 small ones) [A]
1 cup chilled unsalted butter [B] [C]
¼ cup white wine vinegar [A] [D]
⅔ cup dry white wine [A] [D]
Salt
Squeeze of lemon juice—optional

1   Finely chop the shallot. Cut a third of the butter into ½-in cubes and the rest into ¾-in cubes.

2   Place the shallot and vinegar in a small, nonreactive saucepan and reduce, simmering until there is almost no liquid left. Add the wine and reduce by half. [E]

3   Over a low heat, start adding the butter, small cubes first, one at a time, while whisking the reduction constantly. When each cube has *almost* melted, add the next until all the butter is used. This process is called "mounting." Lift the pan off the heat every now and then to keep the temperature down. The sauce should thicken as you add more butter. If it starts to look like melted butter, keep whisking, but take it off the heat and add more cold butter. If that doesn't save it, one option is to melt the rest of the butter and use your split sauce to make hollandaise (page 520).

4   Season and strain.
    If you opt not to strain, leaving the shallot in situ, make sure you mince it and that it's soft before serving the sauce. This may mean starting with a little more liquid for the reduction and simmering it for a little longer.

5 Stir in the lemon juice, if using, and serve warm.

Ideally, beurre blanc should be served immediately. It can be kept for a short time in a double boiler, but is prone to splitting. Others recommend keeping it in a Thermos. You'd be wise to warm your dinner plates, to help retain the heat when served.

LEEWAY

A Treat the reduction as an opportunity to flavor the sauce. Besides wine and vinegar, stock, cream, and fruit juices can be used, enhanced by other aromatics alongside or in place of the shallot.

B Most recipe books recommend unsalted butter, but, according to Richard Olney, Breton salt butter is the authentic choice. Paul Gayler claims that lightly salted will give slightly thicker results. If you do use salted butter, avoid adding any extra salt until you've tasted the sauce.

C Add as much unclarified butter as you like, since it contains what it needs to self-emulsify. Clarified butter won't do the job.

D There is wide variation in recipes for the syrupy reduction. It can be made with wine only, or vinegar only, or a combination of the two. Some cooks dilute it with water. In this version, the butter is added to a relatively large amount of liquid in the pan; in other versions, there is virtually no liquid.

E To help prevent the sauce from splitting, add 2 tbsp heavy cream to the reduction at the end of step 2 and warm it before the butter goes in. Or add some cream when the butter is fully incorporated and then gently heat through.

Beurre Blanc → Flavors & Variations

APPLE

Fish have a sour tooth. Lemon is an obvious favorite, but mackerel loves gooseberries, and shrimp dream of assignations with unripe mango. An apple beurre blanc is paired with halibut, salmon, and scallops; it will be safe with most fish, or you could make the leap from surf to turf and try it with slices of stuffed pork loin. Make a reduction with ¼ cup cider vinegar and ⅔ cup apple juice, then follow the starting point, garnishing with some neat matchsticks of a tangy, crisp apple at the end. The cellular, snow-crunch texture of apple is particularly pleasing next to the softness of the fish and has an enlivening, condiment-like effect on most vegetables.

CHIVE

Newcomers to beurre blanc might like to practice on their wives. With the addition of a few tablespoons of finely chopped chives, it can elevate a weekend breakfast of poached eggs on toast into something approaching brunch. As noted at E under Leeway, the most foolproof way to make the sauce is to add a tablespoon or two of cream to the reduction, and reduce the mixture a little further before adding the butter. Considered heretical, according to the cooking teacher James Peterson, but also "virtually impossible to detect." It'll be between you and your maker. There are, in fact, recipes that call for 1 cup cream, with a couple of tablespoons of reduction and 1 cup butter—but with as much cream as butter, is it still a beurre blanc?

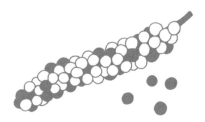

GREEN PEPPERCORN

According to Anne Willan, until the mid-twentieth century, beurre blanc was hardly known outside of the northern Loire and southern Brittany. It owes its fame to the celebrated Parisian chef Mère Michel, who whisked it up in prodigious quantities, night after night, to accompany the typical Loire dish of poached pike. Green peppercorns—that is, fresh, undried black peppercorns—were similarly unfamiliar in Europe until the 1960s, when the Malaysians began preserving and exporting them. On arrival in Paris, they caused a sensation, especially in a sauce to accompany steak, or cooked with duck. In Asia, green peppercorns are popular additions to stir-fries and curries. They're not quite as fiery as black peppercorns, but share their fruitiness, albeit with a whisper of bay leaf. Their notable absence nowadays is perhaps down to their overexposure on the rectangular black plates of the 1980s; they are therefore ripe, in their unripeness, for a revival. Try 2 tbsp brined peppercorns, drained and stirred into the sauce after the last of the butter has been added. You can also buy dried green peppercorns: They look like the petrified peas that roll out when you clean underneath the fridge. Use 3 tbsp, very coarsely cracked, again added just after the last of the butter. Steak is the obvious partner, but green peppercorns are very good with fish, especially a piece of wild salmon.

LAVENDER & ROSEWATER

You'd be hard-pressed to think of a flavoring for beurre blanc that hasn't been tried already. Robert and Molly Krause's combination of lavender and rosewater is one of the most unusual I've encountered. It comes from their *Cook's Book of Intense Flavors*. It's served with glazed, charcoal-grilled portobello mushrooms. A reduction is made of dry white wine and shallots, dried lavender buds, and black peppercorns, which is then mixed with the butter and plenty of rosewater. The Krauses advise adding the rosewater in increments, until a clear but not overwhelming rose flavor is achieved.

LEMONGRASS & LIME LEAF

Asian ingredients in a beurre blanc? As incongruous as shadow puppetry at the *Comédie Française*. But try it, and I defy you to demur. Some substitute rice vinegar for the white wine; others flavor their reduction with typically Eastern aromatics, like lemongrass and lime leaf. Finishing these beurres blancs with a splash of soy sauce is not unheard of.

MUSCADET & OTHER WHITE WINES

Most recipes for beurre blanc call for white wine, but Champagne can't hurt. Sake is excellent. Chef Jean-Paul Moulie goes so far as to suggest using *sweet* white wine for a sauce to pair with sole or scallops. But to be strictly authentic, it's probably safest to use one of the Loire region's dry white wines to make the reduction. There are plenty to choose from, such as flinty Muscadet, Vouvray, or Sancerre—made with Melon de Bourgogne, Chenin Blanc, and Sauvignon Blanc grapes, respectively. You can use just white wine for the reduction and no vinegar, if that's more to your taste. The classic Loire Valley partner for the sauce is poached pike. Rarely seen on British menus nowadays, pike was so prized in medieval England that it cost ten times as much as turbot. Consumption declined in the Victorian era, however, when the improvement of transport networks helped to make sea fish more readily available.

RED MULLET LIVER

Jane Grigson gives a "can't fail" recipe for a beurre blanc to serve with red mullet, which calls for the liver, a well-known delicacy, to be left intact in the whole, scaled fish while it's grilled. When the fish is done, the liver is removed, chopped, and added to the freshly made sauce. To make enough for 4 servings, reduce 4 chopped shallots and ⅔ cup dry white wine until the liquid has almost gone and the shallots are soft. Add 3 tbsp heavy cream to the pan and bring to a vigorous boil. Whisk in ½ cup lightly salted butter, bit by bit, until you have a rich amalgamation. (Grigson advises that if the beurre blanc looks like it's splitting, remove it from the heat and thoroughly whisk in 1 tbsp cold water.) Once all the butter has been incorporated, season, add a squeeze of lemon juice, and stir in the chopped liver.

RED WINE

The definition of a gloomy Monday is a snaplock container full of red-meat leftovers, but no gravy. In such situations, a beurre rouge is your friend. Instead of the white wine in a standard beurre blanc, red wine, or a mixture of red wine and red wine vinegar, can be used for the reduction. Anne Willan recommends a Pinot Noir or Gamay. If the resulting sauce is too sharp, smooth its edges with a teaspoon or two of red-currant jelly. Arthur Potts-Dawson makes a beurre rouge for a dish of smoked eel, beet, and celery leaves, starting the sauce by adding cubed beet to the shallot, followed by black peppercorns, red wine, and red wine vinegar. Once his reduction is syrupy, he adds a little cream and then the butter. Note that he strains the sauce before serving.

SNAIL

When Miss Piggy orders escargots, she asks the waiter to "hold the snails." I might sympathize, were it not for the charming way the rubbery little gastropods are served, in their special recessed dishes, each snail bathing in its pungent, emerald measure of butter, ready to be prized out with a deft choreography of snail fork and tongs. The ritual was enough to get me over my aversion to its problematic part, i.e., eating the snail. The aromatics from classic snail butter might be borrowed for a beurre blanc to serve with grilled lobster on the half-shell. It's a comparable experience, even down to the accompanying claw crackers and picks. The sauce is also excellent with the earthy tones of trout. Add 3 minced garlic cloves with the shallot for the reduction, then proceed as per the starting point, adding 4–6 tbsp finely chopped parsley at the end.

WHITE CURRANT

It's fitting that the Dutch should have been the first to grow currants as a common garden plant during their Golden Age of painting—hold a stem to the light and the berry has the soft translucence of a pearl earring. These days, sadly, you're more likely to come across white currants in art galleries than food markets. They are generally sweeter than red currants, which is not to say they aren't tart, but it's a little easier to appreciate their flavor. Historically, fresh currants were used more as an herb than a fruit. At Ravintola Aino, a traditional Finnish restaurant in Helsinki, roasted Arctic char is served with a white-currant beurre blanc, in keeping with the fundamental principles of berry combination: red currants with lamb, white currants with fish.

Vinaigrette

The simple salad dressing usually made with one part vinegar to three or four parts oil. Jane Grigson would sometimes go as high as a 1:5 ratio; conversely, you'll find the occasional recipe that calls for 1:2, in which case the sharpness is often offset with sugar or honey.

For about ⅔ cup

INGREDIENTS
2 tbsp wine vinegar [A] [B] [C]
1 tsp mustard [D] [E]
Salt and pepper
1–2 tsp honey or sugar—optional
1 garlic clove, minced—optional
½ cup oil, such as sunflower or olive [F]

SHAKING METHOD

1 Put everything but the oil in a securely lidded container and shake to combine.
   The oil is left out so the salt (and sugar, if using) can be easily dissolved in the vinegar.

2 Add the oil, replace the lid, and shake vigorously.
   Check for seasoning and flavor: A vinaigrette is better tasted on whatever you'll be using it for, rather than on a spoon.

3 Ideally, make your dressing at least an hour ahead so the flavors have a chance to mingle.
   Shake or whisk to recombine, if necessary.

WHISKING METHOD

1 Combine the vinegar, mustard, and seasoning—plus the honey or sugar and the garlic, if using—with a whisk or fork.

2 Gradually whisk in the oil until the dressing is thick.
   Check for seasoning and flavor: A vinaigrette is better tasted on whatever you'll be using it for, rather than on a spoon.

3 Ideally, make your dressing at least an hour ahead so the flavors have a chance to mingle.
   Whisk to recombine if necessary.

SAUCE ↓ Sabayon ↓ Hollandaise ↓ Mayonnaise ↓ Beurre Blanc ↓ Vinaigrette

LEEWAY

A Choose from the following vinegars (listed in order of increasing acidity): rice, cider, Champagne, white wine, red wine, sherry.

B Lemon juice is a common alternative to vinegar. It is more acidic but tends to be used in much the same proportions. You might add some finely grated zest too. Very delicious on warm broccoli served with roast pork.

C Experiment with several acids and oils in one dressing. A mix of lemon juice and wine vinegar makes a particularly good dressing.

D Mustard will help thicken the dressing, but if you don't fancy that tang, sieved boiled egg yolk, a raw egg yolk, some cream, silken tofu, mayonnaise, or tomato paste will help the emulsion form.

E Most vinaigrette recipes call for Dijon, but other mustards can be used—coarse grain, a few pinches of strident English powder, Creole, or your own homemade flavored mustard.

F Olive, sunflower, peanut, corn, canola, avocado, or grapeseed oils all work well. If you're using walnut or hazelnut oil, you might want to cut it with a milder-flavored oil.

BALSAMIC

You're about as safe buying an inexpensive bottle of balsamic vinegar as you are a Rolex from the guy with the watches hung inside his overcoat. There is a lot of deceptive labeling abroad. Price is often—but not always—the best guarantor of quality. Considering the effort involved in reducing grape must to a syrup, then allowing it to ferment, oxidize, and slowly evaporate, as, over a minimum of twelve years, it's transferred to ever-smaller casks made of different woods, if the vinegar seems cheap then it's probably a fake. A quart of dark, viscous balsamic will have started out as no less than 200 pounds of must. Vinegar aged for twelve years will be labeled *balsamico tradizionale*; twenty-five years or longer, *tradizionale extra vecchio*. The latter will set you back about the same as a bottle of good vintage Champagne, and you'd be as wise to make a vinaigrette with it as a mimosa with Krug. If the price tag is more in keeping with, say, a bottle of hard cider, you're probably looking at a very ordinary vinegar that's been boiled down, then sweetened and colored with caramel in an industrial vat the size of the medieval hilltop village it's pretending to be from. Somewhere between the extremes of artisanal and industrial balsamic lies "balsamic vinegar of Modena," a blend of wine vinegar, cooked must, and (sometimes) caramel, nothing special on its own but decent in a vinaigrette. Use more of it than you would wine vinegar in our starting point: one part balsamic to two to three parts oil, and hold off adding any sweetness until you've tasted the vinaigrette, as the balsamic will contribute its own.

BEEF DRIPPINGS

In colonial America, when salads were the privilege of those with kitchen gardens, melted butter alone was considered enough of a dressing. Similarly, as mentioned under bacon on page [528], bitter leaves were once commonly dressed with melted lard in Italy. For the most part, with the growing popularity of oils and demonization of saturated fats, the practice has died out. Tom Kerridge bucks the trend by making a dressing of ¾ cup slowly melted beef drippings, 3 tbsp Cabernet Sauvignon vinegar, and ¼ cup each snipped chives and finely chopped scallion greens, poured onto a salad of tomato, red onion, and sourdough croutons that have been tossed in drippings before being toasted. The salad is finished with lemon thyme leaves and toasted nigella seeds.

PEANUT & LIME

For about fifteen years, until I moved house and finally replaced my fridge, I kept my perishables in a salad crisper held together with duct tape: less of a storage compartment for fresh produce than the space under the culinary carpet into which hearts of romaine and softening quarters of tomato were swept. Once in a while I would either tip the whole thing into the composter or, if the contents were edible, make a cheerfully inauthentic *gado-gado*. This wonderful Indonesian dish usually includes cooked potato, green beans, hard-cooked eggs, sliced tomato and cucumber, shredded Napa cabbage, bean sprouts, and shrimp crackers—a distant cousin to salade Niçoise. Quite how distant might be measured in teaspoons of *bumbu kacang*, or peanut dressing. Replace the oil in vinaigrette with peanut butter and cut it with the standard quantity of acid—a 50/50 mixture of lime juice and rice vinegar is ideal. Use soy sauce for the salt element and sweeten with brown or palm sugar, which you'll need to dissolve first in the acid. As the resulting dressing will be too thick to pour, *bumbu* should be thinned with water or coconut milk. As with tahini sauce—tahini, lemon juice, garlic, salt, and water—the sweet spot is elusive. It can take a fair bit of water to achieve pouring consistency, and yet it's easy to overshoot and end up with something too runny. Augment the *bumbu* dressing with one or more of the following: shrimp paste, sliced scallions, chopped peanuts, minced garlic, fresh chili pounded to a paste, or chili sauce.

RASPBERRY & HAZELNUT

Is it because salads are the food of the fashionable that they date so quickly? I assert my right to drizzle raspberry vinegar and hazelnut oil on my warm goat's cheese salad without fear of the flared nostril. Good-quality fruit vinegars are harder to find than they are to make. In a glass jar, steep 1 quart raspberries, cranberries, or blackberries (patted dry) in just enough white wine vinegar to cover the fruit (about 2 cups). Or you might try pineapple with cider vinegar. Cover and leave somewhere cool for 3–10 days, tasting intermittently for strength. When you're happy with the flavor, strain the vinegar through a jelly bag, or strainer lined with cheesecloth, into a nonreactive pan, letting it drip through overnight, then boil for 10 minutes, pour into a sterilized bottle, and seal. To sweeten the vinegar, if desired, measure it, and, as it comes to a boil, add a quarter to a half of its volume in sugar, then skim off any scum as it simmers. Store in a cool, dark place and use within a year. Once opened, keep in the fridge. If you're short of vinegarmaking time, try adding a little fruit liqueur to a dressing; crème de cassis, mûre, or framboise will lend a little sweetness too. Cassis vinaigrette is a revelation on an avocado, mozzarella, pink grapefruit, and quinoa salad.

SALSA VERDE

There are many variations on salsa verde. Its typical aromatics affiliate it to the extended *gribiche*, rémoulade, and tartar family (page 530), except that its base is always a vinaigrette. Salsa verde is served with warm poached meats (classically *bollito misto*), cold roasts, fried fish, or with smoked salmon and scrambled eggs. Make it thick and knobbly and spread it on a sandwich made with fried sweet potatoes and good white bread. You can blitz the ingredients in a blender, especially if, contra the sandwich idea, you want the sauce quite smooth. Or pound it in a pestle and mortar, if you have one large enough; or simply go at it on a chopping board with a big knife. To make enough for 4 servings, mash 1 hard-cooked egg yolk and scrape it into a small bowl with ¼ cup red wine vinegar, a grinding of pepper, and some salt. Mince 1 small shallot and 6 rinsed, salted anchovy fillets and add to the yolk mixture. Roughly chop 2 tbsp rinsed salted capers and add those too, then slowly whisk in ½ cup extra virgin olive oil. To finish, very finely chop a large handful of parsley and stir it in. Check for seasoning. Consider adding other herbs, like mint, tarragon, thyme, and basil; or using anchovy paste instead of fillets, lemon juice rather than vinegar, and garlic instead of the shallot. Some cooks thicken their salsa verde with mashed potato or soaked bread crumbs, but if you're aiming for piquant freshness, stick with the heaps of parsley.

SESAME & SOY

Sesame and soy dressing is the reason Chinese chicken salad is an American classic. The saltiness makes everything taste juicy, the sesame lends a pervasive muskiness, and fresh ginger adds zing. The dressing is typically used on Napa cabbage, carrots, red cabbage, scallions, and cooked chicken, all shredded. The garnish consists of cold deep-fried noodles, roasted peanuts, and cilantro. As the flavor of sesame oil goes a long way, the usual vinaigrette proportions can be altered to 1 tbsp each toasted sesame oil and peanut oil, 2 tbsp each rice vinegar and light soy sauce, 2 tsp English mustard, 1–2 tsp grated fresh ginger, and 1 minced garlic clove. Add sugar (or honey) and chili to taste.

STOCK

Let's have lunch, said my husband. It was Sunday. We had just walked past the Zuni Cafe, the late Judy Rodgers's legendary restaurant in San Francisco. With no reservation, I was expecting the same reaction as Patrick Bateman gets in *American Psycho*, when he calls the most happening place in Manhattan and requests a table that night at 8:30. Hysterical laughter. As luck would have it, Zuni had a table. Rodgers's signature dish was chicken salad. Chicken salad? How good could that be? Very good, it turned out. The bird itself was wood-roasted and had the oddly dry moistness and deep umami that separate the epic chicken from the everyday. What elevated it to ineffable was the bread salad the bird was sitting on. Rodgers described it as "a scrappy extramural stuffing," which is a modest way of describing something that makes life that little bit more worth living. In *The Zuni Cafe Cookbook*, the instructions run to four and a half pages, so here's an approximation for 2–4 people. While your chicken is roasting, put 1 tbsp dried currants to soak in 1 tsp red wine vinegar and 1 tbsp water. Turn 8 oz stale, white, open-crumbed, decrusted bread into large croutons by tearing it into large pieces, brushing with olive oil, and then toasting it under the broiler, turning now and then, until lightly golden and crisp on both sides. Transfer to a baking dish and drizzle with a Champagne or white wine vinaigrette, made to a 3:8 ratio with mild olive oil. Do this unevenly, so the degree of dressing will vary from bite to bite—and save some of the dressing for later. In the oven or a dry skillet, toast 2 tbsp pine nuts. Soften 2–3 thinly sliced garlic cloves and 4 finely sliced scallions (including some of the green) in a little olive oil, then add to the croutons, along with the drained currants, pine nuts, garlic, and scallions. Unevenly drizzle over 2 tbsp homemade chicken stock—just enough to imbue the salad with the rich, unctuous meatiness that gives the dish its defining depth of flavor—then put the croutons into the oven with the chicken for its final 5–10 minutes. Turn off the oven and remove the chicken, leaving the salad in for another 5 minutes before transferring it to a salad bowl. Sprinkle over some of the juices from the chicken's roasting pan, add several handfuls of washed and dried salad leaves (arugula, red mustard, and frisée are recommended) and more vinaigrette, then serve on a warm platter with the cut-up chicken. It's a warmer-weather alternative to roast chicken with the trimmings, although you may find yourself hankering after it year-round.

WALNUT & ROQUEFORT

In a French restaurant in London, not so long ago, I ordered a Belgian endive, pear, and Roquefort salad. I peered under an endive leaf. And another. No Roquefort. I made a mental note never to revisit the place and set about my unintentionally vegan lunch. And discovered where the Roquefort was: in the dressing, and all the better for its modesty. Roquefort can be like the party guest you only gradually realize is a bit of a bully. Too much and by the end of the meal your mouth will taste like the interior of the Combalou caves. Bitter endive can take Roquefort down a peg, but I'm all for keeping it subtle from the outset. For a dressing, you'll need to recalibrate the typical proportions of a vinaigrette (1:2 vinegar to oil) to allow for the cheese's fattiness and saltiness. For 2 servings, I recommend 4 oz cheese, 2 tbsp white wine vinegar, ¼ cup walnut oil, and a grinding of pepper.

YOLK

Raw egg yolks make a wonderfully creamy dressing that will hold its emulsification. This is a maximalist dressing: thick, full of flavor, and best used on robust leaves that can take its weight—radicchio, frisée, and spinach. Mix 1 yolk with 3 tbsp white wine vinegar, 2 tbsp water, 2 tsp sugar, 1 tsp salt, 1 tsp mustard powder, 1 tsp treacle or molasses, and ½ tsp each of Worcestershire sauce, dried oregano, garlic granules, and chili powder. Once all is combined, slowly add ½ cup mild olive oil and shake or whisk to emulsify.

Pastry

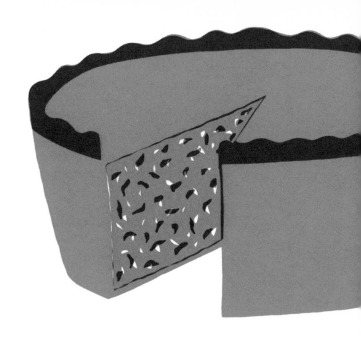

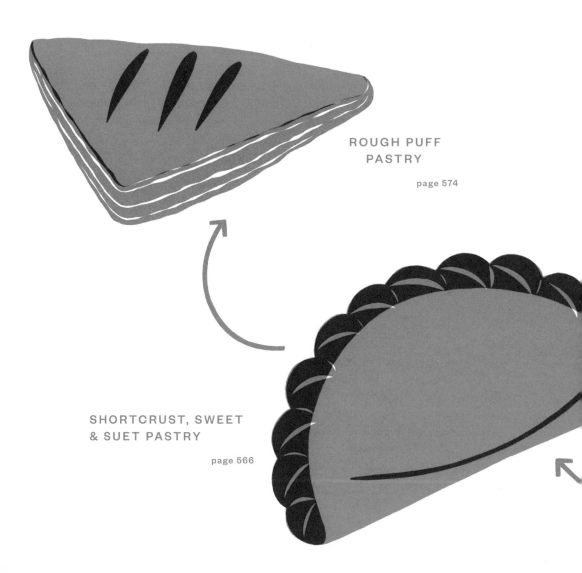

ROUGH PUFF
PASTRY

page 574

SHORTCRUST, SWEET
& SUET PASTRY

page 566

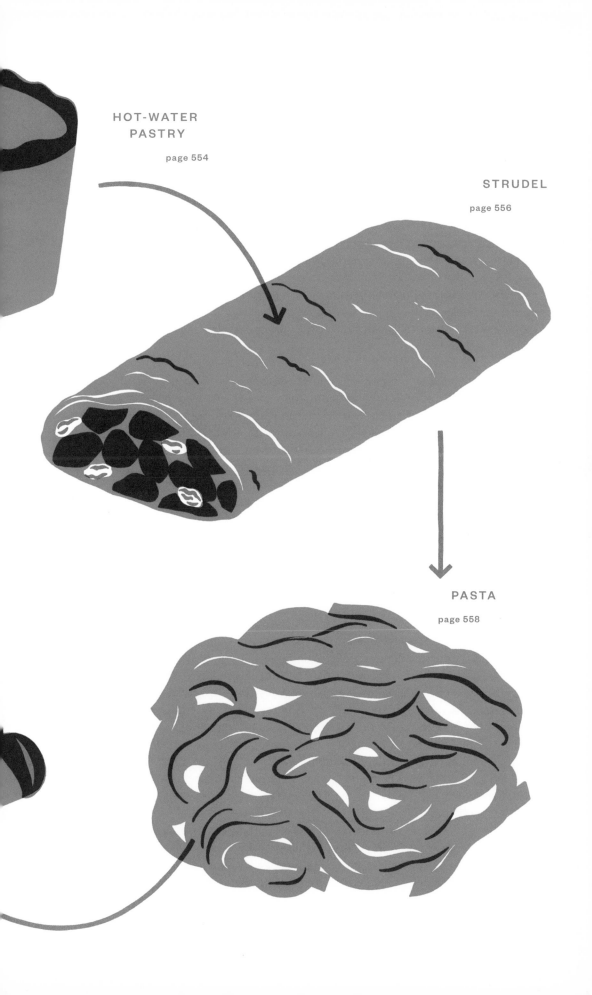

HOT-WATER
PASTRY

page 554

STRUDEL

page 556

PASTA

page 558

If you're good with your hands and you've never made hot-water crust pastry, put down this book immediately and rectify matters. Its combination of pliancy and firmness means you can work this dough, like clay, into a deep, free-standing piecrust—hence its disarmingly archaic alias "hand-raised pastry." Although I have taken to calling it "vacation-home pastry," the kind you make when you discover that the kitchen in your adorable wisteria-smothered cottage in Nether Whateversop contains three dozen takeout menus but no cooking pots. To make a batch of hot-water pastry, you mix hot water, melted lard, and flour; as the water and fat are absorbed, they react with the flour to yield a strong, slightly sticky texture, as happens when you prepare polenta or semolina halva. The hot water stretches the gluten strands, so the dough you end up with is the opposite of tender shortcrust. Longcrust. It's an incredibly satisfying pastry to make, in part because handling the warm, pliable dough is such a tactile pleasure, and in part because it's among the most impeccably behaved pastry doughs in the repertoire—easy both to roll and to mold.

Working freehand is by no means obligatory. You can achieve a greater regularity of shape by molding the dough to the inside of a muffin or springform pan. I've gone with this for the starting point. Or you can do as they do in Melton Mowbray, England, and use a "pork pie dolly," a wooden implement a bit like a large, minimalist chess piece around (as opposed to inside) which the dough is formed. A glass jar will serve much the same purpose, but lacks the benefit of a handle to help ease the dough from the mold. Once your dough vessel is constructed, filled, and lidded, you can turn your thoughts to decoration. At the very least you'll want an evenly crimped perimeter with a pair of steam-emitting central nostrils. If there's dough left over, you might want to add a few leaves, or anything from heraldic escutcheons to species-identifiable songbirds. Get in the habit and you may find yourself wandering around museums with pie-tinted spectacles.

The robustness of hot-water pastry demands a similar heft from its fillings. Pork pies are as stout as John Bull, with their chewy mixture of chopped and ground pork and bacon that conceals, in the case of gala pie, a mysteriously elongated cross-section of boiled egg. Scotch pie, which is individual-sized and usually filled with ground mutton or beef, comes into its own in the manner of its construction. The roof of hot-water pastry is laid a little lower than the high point of its sides, creating a kind of parapet where mashed potato, baked beans, or thick gravy can be held without spillage—thus obviating, with a typically Scots mixture of ingenuity and thrift, the need for a plate.

S T R U D E L Delicate strudel might not seem the obvious next step on the pastry continuum, but it's also made by adding warm water to flour (in weight, 1:2). A little fat (oil or butter), egg yolk, and lemon juice are added before it's given a good knead. Minor as these tweaks may look on paper, they're enough to create a daintiness that derives, paradoxically, from the dough's strength: It can be rolled and pulled so thinly without breaking precisely because of its cohesiveness. As with hot-water pastry, its strength comes from the effect of heated water on flour. Bread or 00 flours are sometimes recommended for strudel, because they contain more gluten than all-purpose flour, which can also be used. Strudel dough is kneaded, like bread, which stretches the strands of gluten even further. Recipes invariably call for a little lemon juice, wine, or vinegar, all of which will relax the gluten and make the dough easier to shape. I once tried a batch without the acid. Every time I rolled it out, it pinged back to its smaller self. The Sisyphean strudel.

Like hot-water pastry, strudel pastry dough demands moderately skilled handiwork, but of quite a different sort. Most recipe writers— even those who don't pander to their readers by making a religion out of convenience—will tell you to forget making strudel pastry from scratch and buy a box of phyllo instead. Even Claudia Roden says there's no reason to make it, before letting on to the best reason of all: Homemade strudel is better. If you're up for the challenge, bear in mind that the skill in strudelmaking lies not in the preparation of the dough, which is straightforward, but in coaxing a modest amount of it into an enormous semi-transparent dough tablecloth. You'll need a table or kitchen island to work on, so you can coax the dough toward and then gently over the edges. A Hungarian grandmother will prowl her strudel-in-progress like a championship pool player, assessing the dough and the best angle to approach it. Some work their strudel on parchment paper taped to the table, but a floured cloth is traditional, and easier to wrangle when it comes to the rolling stage. For, once you've made your diaphanous sheet, more hurdles await you. The strudel must still be rolled around its filling and transferred to its baking sheet, like a patient from gurney to hospital bed. You make strudel for the same reason you play the wire-loop game at the church fair: because you can't resist the challenge.

If you don't have great form as a pastrymaker, take heart. Strudel, unlike most other pastries, enjoys being handled, so you can take your time. Shortcrust favors reptilian levels of cold-bloodedness. With strudel, warm hands are not a problem. Rings, knuckledusters, and press-on fingernails are. To stretch the dough, you must slide your fists underneath without ripping it (I find a wooden spoon is a useful substitute for fists). Quite how cooperative you find the dough will differ from batch to batch: Sometimes it feels so resilient you can almost pick it up by one edge and flap it thinner, as if shaking out a bedsheet. By tradition, the final product should be thin enough to read through. If a few tears and holes develop as you pull, don't worry; they won't matter when the strudel is rolled up. Nor should you be overly concerned about the aesthetics of the finished pastry. *Strudel* means "whirlpool" in German, so let it be wild and whirly, not all neat and buttoned up. It's not a Swiss roll.

Apple, cherry, apricot, and ground poppy seeds are classic fillings, although beyond its heartland—essentially, the countries of the former Austro-Hungarian Empire, especially Austria, Hungary, and the Czech Republic—few of us will have tried anything other than the apple variety. For Nora Ephron, cabbage strudel, which she regularly bought from Mrs. Herbst's Hungarian Bakery on Manhattan's Third Avenue until it closed in 1982, held such Proustian significance that she insisted she could remember little else about her first marriage. You feel for her ex-husband—until you try the strudel in question. I attempt to recreate it by shredding a whole, medium-sized white cabbage and an onion, mixing in a few pinches each of salt, caraway seeds, and white pepper, dotting with 4 tbsp butter, and covering the dish with foil. Bake, giving the mixture the occasional stir, for an hour at 350°F. Let it cool before rolling it in strudel pastry (made to our starting point) and bake for a further 30–40 minutes at 375°F, until the strudel is golden brown. As Ephron points out, cabbage strudel is traditionally served with soup or roast pheasant, but I would happily eat it on its own with a cold glass of Grüner Veltliner and *The Good Soldier Švejk*.

If you're short of space, or would like to practice your dough-stretching technique across more modest expanses than the full tablecloth, strudel dough can be put to similar uses as phyllo. Fashion your dough into squares, lightly dust them with flour, and work with one at a time, keeping the others at room temperature, wrapped in plastic wrap. It's a time-consuming process, for sure, but you'll eventually have enough for something along the lines of baklava, or the Greek spinach and cheese pie spanakopita, or a multilayered dish of your own invention. The pastry won't be as thin as store-bought phyllo, but it will be good. Be sure to be generous with the butter between each sheet—it helps ease the praise from your guests' mouths.

Neither strudel nor phyllo dough are more than a gluten strand away from the dough used to make cannoli, the Italian dessert made from a circle of dough, folded around a mold to make a tube, and, once fried, filled with sweetened ricotta and candied fruit. Cannoli dough might be made using Marsala or white wine in place of water, and I've seen recipes where a little cocoa is added. Meanwhile, in South America, there are empanadas and pasteles made with a cannoli-like dough laced with cachaça. Like cannoli, they are deep-fried and emerge from the hot oil with a shiny, pimply surface that looks positively teenaged.

Unlike pasta, which should be as smooth as a baby's skin. Complexions aside, strudel pastry and pasta dough have much in common. See, for example, Jane Grigson's tip, to chill trimmings of strudel dough and grate them into soup "as a pasta." In one of Jacob Kenedy's lasagne recipes, apple, raisins, and sugar take the place of the classic ragù and béchamel, to make a kind of layered strudel. In Hungarian cuisine, similar desserts might include sweetened cottage cheese and egg noodles between the layers.

Pasta sits between strudel and shortcrust on the pastry continuum. The dough can be made like strudel, using water and flour with optional additions of oil or egg, but the more common method, and our starting point for pasta, is simply to combine flour and egg. The dough is made—that is, kneaded, rested, and then fashioned into thin sheets—pretty much as it is for strudel, but the weight ratio of egg to flour is the same as the fat-to-flour ratio for shortcrust pastry, i.e., 1:2. In the U.S., where weighing ingredients is less common, an egg or 2 yolks per ¾ cup of 00 flour is a good rule of thumb.

Once your dough is rested, you can roll it out by hand, especially if you're only making a few portions. A pasta machine will give you a thinner, finer result, and is certainly welcome when you have large amounts to make, but it's worth bearing in mind that machines and fine artisan flours are not what make great pasta; making lots of pasta makes great pasta. Pastamaking is fun and inexpensive, and yields a texture that's much better than most of the pasta you can buy. Furthermore, it's tweakable in all sorts of exciting directions. The same dough can be used to make Chinese egg noodles and dumpling wrappers, and there are potentially unlimited variations in flavor.

Flavored pasta does have its detractors. I declare myself a mild skeptic, but novelty, in my view, is a self-regulating condition. You might buy the ludicrous tagliatelle striped like a banker's suspenders, or linguine flavored with blood/shrimp roe/rosewater, but at suppertime, you're naturally drawn to plain old Barilla instead. In many cases, it has to be said, the flavoring is more detectable to the eye than the tongue. Squid ink is a case in point. Spinach pasta makes mild metallic reference to the cooked leaf, sometimes with a hint of nutmeg if enough is added, but the effort involved in puréeing the spinach and then incorporating it into the dough is more at the service of color and texture than flavor.

If you're tempted to flavor pasta, first ask yourself—is it worth it? Are your saffron or basil or flecks of diced gumdrops likely to be masked by the sauce? Might it not be easier, and more effective, to flavor your pasta after cooking, as the Hungarians do by tossing noodles in butter and caraway seeds? If you're determined to put your flavor into, rather than onto, your pasta, I'd advise you to do a practice run with a small batch, using ⅓ cup flour and 1 egg yolk. There's a Jean-Georges Vongerichten recipe for curry tagliatelle that goes well with mussels, but I think it's the exception. The most interesting pasta variations are made with grains other than white wheat, rather than flavorings.

SHORTCRUST   Shortcrust pastry can be flavored, but you have to be careful that any additions don't detract from the texture. Ground nuts, or gluten-free grains like corn, can work percussive wonders in the mouth, but will make the dough much harder to handle. Citrus zest and spices are a safer bet—used in modest amounts, their flavor won't come at the expense of the lovely shortness you want.

Shortcrust pastry is made with half a stick of butter for every cup of flour, plus the minimum amount of water, or egg, needed to bring these together into a dough. The less water used, the less unwanted gluten will develop. The more you prevent gluten from developing, the crumblier and more melt-in-the-mouth your pastry will be. Thoroughly rubbing or cutting the fat into the flour is another way to restrict gluten formation, effectively by waterproofing the grains. Delegating rubbing-in duties to your food processor will make for a finer texture, and therefore more waterproofing. Tip your finely crumbed mix into another bowl and spritz with just enough cold water to make a dough—add the water while the mixture is still in the food processor and it's all too easy to over-wet it.

S
U
E
T

P
A
S
T
R
Y

Pastry can be made shorter still by swapping butter for lard, which contains no water. Use a 50/50 butter and lard mix for an optimal balance of flavor and texture. Suet, another fat that can be substituted for the butter, makes for a delicious if unfashionable pastry—one that's equally effective in sweet and savory recipes, and is as comforting as a pair of moccasins with integral socks. Fresh beef suet is best, if you're lucky enough to have a butcher that sells it. Elizabeth Nash, writing in 1926, claimed that suet pastry was good for children, being "wholesome, nourishing and easy to digest," and best mixed with self-rising or whole wheat flour. It used to be common in British steak and kidney pudding, as well as jam roly poly, and was also often fashioned into dumplings that were tossed into stews for the last 20 minutes of cooking. I find suet pastry ideal for pasties, or topping pot pies, when I don't have time to make rough puff. The chef Jesse Dunford Wood uses it to top his Cow Pie, out of which pokes a stub of marrow bone, in lieu of an open-throated pie bird. The marrow melts and stays warm and irresistibly scoopable in the pie-coddled bone. It's so rich that even Desperate Dan would be slumped cross-eyed in the corner were he desperate enough to eat it all up.

S
W
E
E
T

P
A
S
T
R
Y

Pâte sablée is another variation on shortcrust pastry, with most recipes calling for much more butter than the standard shortcrust, a fair amount of sugar, and egg, or just a yolk, to bring the dough together. It's often flavored with vanilla or lemon zest. *Sablée* is used for fruit tarts, *petits fours,* and cookies. While nothing can outclass it in a strawberry tart, for most other sweet pastries it's fine to supplement a standard shortcrust with confectioners' sugar, stirred into the bread-crumb-like mix before the water or egg is added. I usually make more pastry dough than I need, as any surplus can be shaped and baked as cookies: The ingredients and method sit between cookies (page [350]) and shortbread (page [356]). *Larousse's pâte sablée* recipe, by the way, is identical to the starting point for cookies—that is, pretty restrained. Rich isn't always better. My grandmother made her apple pies with plain unsweetened shortcrust, and they were unimprovable.

ROUGH PUFF You might think of rough puff pastry as a shortcrust where you got bored before you'd properly rubbed in the butter. Puff pastry gobbles up a lot of butter—between ¾ and a whole stick of butter per cup of flour. John Henry Walsh notes that puff pastry appeals to "those who consult only their palates, without attending to the interests of their bodies or purses." A pure-butter puff, he reckons, can only be bettered by including a little lard in it.

To make the classic, French, un-rough puff, you need to start with a *détrempe*—an envelope of pastry with little or no butter in it—then roll out cold butter into a sheet called a *beurrage*, lay it over the *détrempe*, and fold it up. Between rests in the fridge, the rectangle of dough is subjected to multiple folds, turns, and rollings-out, a process known in cooking school as "lamination." Croissants (page 49) are made roughly the same way, except that in their case the *détrempe* is a bread dough.

In a pâtisserie course, I was taught to make proper puff pastry by the *détrempe-beurrage* method and use it in a millefeuille, the classic multistory confection of pastry and whipped cream. As I swept away a surfeit of confectioners' sugar, it was no longer so easy to conceal that my millefeuille was roughly 985 feuilles short. Casting a stern eye over the class's efforts, chef clapped his hands and said, "Now you need never make puff paste again. What you can buy in the supermarket is far superior." Which may be true, but I urge you to have a go at least once, on the off chance you discover a hidden talent for this odd combination of pâtisserie and origami.

With characteristic hauteur, chef didn't teach us rough puff, which avoids the effort involved in making two separate components in favor of one shaggy dough, brought together with a fair amount of cold water and a little coaxing. Once chilled, rough puff is rolled, folded, and turned just like standard puff. Four turns might do for a pot-pie topping or turnovers, but six will yield *palmiers* or *vols* that look like they have a bit of *vent* in them. Make a few batches of sausage rolls, and you may find a good rough puff easier to pull off than a good shortcrust—and by good I suppose I mean impressive, as the loveliness of puff's texture is so much more apparent. I've only given the method for rough puff pastry, with notes under Leeway for anyone who fancies trying their hand at the haute version.

A last word on the absence of choux from the pastry continuum. The choux technique has much more in common with those on the cornbread, polenta, and gnocchi continuum, especially gnocchi— indeed, little nuggets of choux dough are piped into boiling water to make gnocchi Parisienne. If you've never made choux but have prepared polenta, or made semolina halva or gnocchi alla Romana, the process will be familiar: You'll find the starting point for choux on page 100.

Hot-Water Pastry

Used for hearty, lidded pies with dense fillings like pork or game. The pastry can be fitted into a pan, around a mold, or shaped by hand (hence its other name, hand-raised pastry). It has a chewy, slightly flaky texture. Flavored versions aren't entirely unknown—grated nutmeg or mace might be added—but they are very rare, which means there's no Flavors & Variations section here. It is common, however, to sweeten hot-water pastry dough: Sift in a tablespoon or two of confectioners' sugar with the flour.

For 6 individual, decorated pies made in a 6-cup muffin pan [A] [B]

INGREDIENTS
3 cups all-purpose flour [C]
¾ tsp salt
½ cup lard, diced [D] [E] [F]
½ cup hot water [F] [G]
Beaten egg to glaze

1 Sift the flour into a bowl and mix in the salt. Make a well in the center.

2 Put the lard in a small pan with the hot water and melt over a medium heat.

3 Pour the hot lard and water mixture into the well in the flour and quickly stir together with a wooden spoon, then knead the hot dough lightly for a minute—no longer, or it will become greasy.

4 Shape the dough while it's still warm. If you're not quite ready, cover the bowl with plastic wrap to keep the dough pliable.

5 Apportion the dough to base/lid/decoration (two-thirds for the bottoms, and the remaining third for the tops and some decoration), then roll it out to a thickness of about ⅛ in. Cut out 6 circles for the bases of your pies and press into your greased muffin cups.
   Alternatively, you can create the pie shapes freehand, or use a pie dolly or empty jelly jar as a mold.

6 Fill with whatever robust ingredients you fancy. [H] [I]

7 Cover with the dough lids and make a hole in their centers to emit steam. Brush with egg. Bake at 350°F, being guided by the filling for the cooking time.

Small pork (or vegetable) pies will take about 50–60 minutes.

LEEWAY

A Double the quantities to make a large pie with a lid and decorations (pull off a third of the dough for these). Grease an 8-in round springform pan well before lining it with the dough. It's common to remove the springform ring, gently, some way into the baking time, and egg-glaze the pie all over before returning it to the oven to brown. It's not essential, but if you do plan to do this, make sure the crust sits within the springform ring, so the springform can be removed without decapitating the pie. If the top is in danger of burning, tent loosely with foil.

B Hot-water pastry dough can be used for tart cases, but it will have a flaky, chewy texture.

C Use white bread flour or 00 flour.

D Drippings, vegetable shortening, or butter can be used in place of lard. Unless it has been clarified, butter contains some water, so if you're making a large batch of dough, use approximately 10 percent extra butter and 10 percent less water.

E Some modern recipes call for more fat, say ¾ cup for 3 cups of flour.

F Others call for less lard, water, or both, but add an egg or two.

G The recipe in *Larousse* calls for milk rather than water: hot-milk pastry.

H For pork pies, put 12 oz none-too-lean pork shoulder and 5 oz slab bacon in a food processor with 1 tsp sage and 1 tsp thyme—both finely chopped—½ tsp ground mace, 1 tsp salt, and ½ tsp white pepper. Blitz until coarsely chopped; remove about half and blitz the rest until ground, then combine the two halves. Divide the filling among the pies, cover with the dough lids, and bake as outlined at step **7**, removing the pies from the pan about 30 minutes into their baking time and placing them on a baking sheet. Give them an all-over egg wash and return to the oven for 25–30 minutes.

I For a vegetarian alternative, use butter in place of the lard in the pastry and fill the pies with a samosa-like mix of diced cooked potato and carrot, shredded cabbage, and peas, flavored with spices and chili. These pies will only need about 35–45 minutes in the oven.

Strudel

Pulled and stretched until it's about 40-denier, then rolled around a filling. There are no Flavors & Variations for strudel pastry, as all the modifications apply to what goes inside. Apple, cherry, or apricot are the classics, often mixed with a little dried fruit or chopped nuts and some bread or cake crumbs to soak up stray fruit juices. Common savory fillings include cooked cabbage or ragù. Once the dough is stretched, it should be filled and rolled immediately, so consider preparing the filling before you start, if it will take longer than the dough's 30-minute resting time. And if your dough-pulling is going badly, take Egon Ronay's advice. Screw it up and start again.

For a strudel to serve 6–8 [A]

INGREDIENTS
2 cups bread flour or 00 flour [B]
A few pinches of salt
½ cup warm water
1 tbsp bland oil [C]
1 tsp lemon juice [D]
1 egg yolk [E]
Melted butter for brushing

1   Sift the flour into a bowl and mix in the salt. Make a well in the center.

2   Mix the water, oil, lemon juice, and egg yolk together, then pour into the well. Bring together to make a slightly sticky dough, adding more water in small increments if needed.

3   Knead well, until the sticky dough becomes unsticky but soft. You should be able to do this without flouring your work surface, but it's okay to use a little flour early on if necessary.

4   Brush the dough lightly with oil and leave under a warm, upturned bowl for 30 minutes.

5   Cover a large area (a kitchen island or table where the edges of the dough can hang over at least three of the sides is ideal) with a clean cloth or parchment paper, lightly floured. Roll out the dough on the cloth or parchment until it's fairly thin, then carefully start to stretch from the inside outward, using the backs of your hands (remove any jewelry if you can).

Keep going until the dough is paper-thin and evenly stretched. Trim off any thick edges. Paint with melted butter.

6 To assemble your strudel, you can either dot the filling all over the dough sheet, or fashion the filling into a plump ridge along one of the long edges of the sheet, leaving a margin of an inch or so, to be flipped over the filling before you roll. [F G]

7 Use the cloth or paper to help you roll up the strudel. Carefully transfer it to a lightly greased pan—in a horseshoe shape if you like, or if the size of the pan compels it—and brush with more melted butter. Make sure the short ends are neatly tucked under.

8 Bake for about 30–40 minutes at 375°F until golden and crisp. Brush the strudel with butter once more when it's baked, and dust with confectioners' sugar if the filling is sweet.

LEEWAY

A   For a good practice quantity, use 1 cup flour, a pinch of salt, 4 tbsp water, 1 tsp oil, ½ tsp lemon juice, and 1 egg yolk. It'll stretch out to the size of a dish towel, and make enough for a side dish, lunch, or dessert for 4.

B   All-purpose flour will do.

C   Melted butter can be used in the dough instead of oil.

D   Vinegar—wine, cider, or white—can be used instead of lemon juice.

E   The egg yolk (or whole egg, as called for by some recipes) will make the dough softer, but also richer, crisper, and browner when cooked. Nonetheless, it can be omitted.

F   For a classic apple strudel, peel and core about 1½ lb sharp-tasting apples and slice them into wedges. Cut the wedges into small pieces and mix with the finely grated zest and juice of 1 lemon, ¼–½ cup sugar, ¼ cup bread crumbs, and 1 tsp ground cinnamon. Some cooks add finely chopped nuts, additional spices, or mincemeat.

G   A savory filling (white cabbage) is given on page [550].

Pasta

Our starting point for egg pasta is pretty standard and uses only egg and flour. The weight ratio is 1:2, the same as it is for butter and flour in shortcrust pastry. An egg-free option is given at ᴳ under Leeway. The previous starting point, for strudel (page ⁵⁵⁶), can also be used to make pasta.

For 2 as a main course where pasta is the primary constituent ᴬ

INGREDIENTS
1½ cups 00 flour ᴮ
A few pinches of salt ᶜ
2 extra-large eggs or 4 egg yolks ᴰ ᴱ ᶠ ᴳ ᴴ

1   Sift the flour onto a pastry board or into a large bowl and mix in the salt. Make a well in the center and add the egg. Work into a dough using the tips of your fingers, then knead for 5–10 minutes until smooth.

2   Cover with plastic wrap or a clean dish towel and let rest at room temperature for at least 30 minutes, or in the fridge if you're not going to use it for a while.

3   Roll out the dough using a pasta machine or a rolling pin on a floured surface, aiming for a thickness of under ⅛ in, then cut as desired.
    John Wright recommends scattering flour liberally, as if someone else is doing the clearing up. Ideally the rolling surface should be dusted with a gluten-free flour like semolina or cornstarch, as they're less likely to turn sticky or make your pasta tough.

4   Bring a large pan of salted water to a boil. Add the pasta. Ribbons and sheets will take 2–3 minutes, but test a piece in advance of the rest if you're unsure.
    For lasagne, some cooks precook the pasta sheets for a few minutes before layering them in the baking dish, but you needn't if the sauce between the sheets is moderately wet, and the lasagne is going to be baked for at least 30 minutes.

5   Dry any excess pasta at room temperature, allowing air to flow around it (a clothes-drying rack is ideal for ribbons).
    It can take as long as a couple of days to dry thoroughly. Once it has, store in an airtight container and use within 6 months (this applies to plain egg pasta—variations involving other ingredients may need to be used sooner).

LEEWAY

A A dough made with ¾ cup flour and 1 extra-large egg will roll out to about a 12-in square, using a rolling pin.

B Although 00 flour is usually specified, pasta can be made with bread or all-purpose flour. See the Flavors & Variations section for notes on other types of flour.

C Salting the dough: Giorgio Locatelli and the authors of *The Silver Spoon* do it. Marcella Hazan and Valentina Harris don't. Pick your team. Note that salted cooking water will effectively salt the pasta.

D For a yellower, richer dough, use 4 yolks rather than 2 eggs per 1½ cups 00 flour.

E Some cooks supplement the eggs with a little oil: about 1 tsp for the starting point quantities.

F You can use as many as 8 egg yolks to 1½ cups flour. According to Jacob Kenedy, this will make "a decadent pasta." It's not right for stuffed pasta, however, since more yolks make for reduced elasticity and a "crisper" pasta.

G If you're out of eggs, make eggless pasta: 2 cups 00 flour, ⅔ cup warm water, and 2 tsp olive oil. Make a well in the center of the sifted flour and add the water and oil. Knead for 10 minutes and then continue from step 2. Egg shortage or not, I think this is the better option for whole wheat flour.

H Elizabeth David's version of ravioli Caprese calls for butter rather than eggs, which she says makes the dough easier to roll out than egg pasta. Rub 3½ tbsp butter into 2 cups 00 flour and a pinch of salt, then gradually add enough boiling water to bring the dough together. Knead, then roll.

BUCKWHEAT

In Valtellina, northern Italy, and over the border in the Swiss canton of Graubünden, buckwheat is traditionally used to make *pizzoccheri,* short pasta ribbons often served with a dish of the same name that comprises potato, cabbage, cheese, and sage. To make the pasta, follow our starting point, but use one part buckwheat flour to two parts wheat flour (00, if you have it), and for every 1 egg or 2 yolks add 1 tbsp warm water, beating them together before adding to the flour. Once rolled out, cut the dough into ribbons about 3 in long and ½ in wide. Cook wide strips of savoy cabbage and ½-in slices of potato in salted water for 5 minutes, then add the *pizzoccheri* and continue to simmer until the pasta is al dente. When everything is cooked through, drain and layer with grated cheese in a preheated baking dish, finishing with a drizzle of garlic butter, some finely chopped sage, and a bit more grated cheese. Cook in a 350°F oven for 20 minutes. The authentic cheese to use in *pizzoccheri* is Valtellina Casera DOP, but fontina mixed with some Grana Padano or Parmesan is a good nonlocal substitute. Not all recipes call for egg in the pasta—in some a simple dough is made with water, like the buckwheat noodles on page [30].

CHESTNUT

Anna Del Conte recommends chestnut pasta alongside rabbit in a *dolceforte* (sweet and sour) sauce. She uses 1 cup 00 flour to 1 cup chestnut flour and 2 extra-large eggs—but add the egg gradually because chestnut flour isn't as thirsty as wheat. Giorgio Locatelli's milder-flavored version calls for 1⅔ cups 00 flour and only ½ cup chestnut flour, plus 1 tsp olive oil and the yolks of 7 eggs; he serves it with wild mushrooms. If you could eat your words, this would taste like a Robert Frost poem.

CHOCOLATE

Chocolate pasta is perfect for the person who prefers making food to eating it. The dough is lovely to handle, silky, and easy to cut into tagliatelle; the trim, mahogany-colored noodles look very classy coiled on a white plate. But the pleasure stops there. The flavor is vague, until the bitterness of cocoa asserts itself like a parting insult. Take the hint. There are so many nicer things to do with flour, eggs, and cocoa. My husband, ever the optimist, gave the chocolate noodles a second chance and tried another helping with some sugar sprinkled on it. "That's much better," he said. And it was, just as something unpleasant plus sugar is nicer than something horrid without it. Add 3½ tbsp unsweetened cocoa powder to our starting point.

CORN

A dough can be made with fine cornmeal, wheat flour, egg, and a little warm water. Not that I've ever seen an Italian recipe for *egg* pasta that calls for corn. Don't let that put you off. Replace ½ cup of the 00 flour in our starting point with ½ cup fine cornmeal. As is often the case with egg pasta involving gluten-free flour, a splash of water added with the egg will help to create a bit of stickiness, the better to bring the dough together. I cut the rolled-out dough into strips and then into 1-in squares with a fluted pastry wheel. (If you don't have one in your kitchen drawer, check your kids' dough-cutter set.) After a brief boil in salted water, it was clear that the sweet and chunky little stamps would flatter a hearty, salty sauce. And there's nothing heartier or saltier than *cacio e pepe*, the Roman pasta dish that makes carbonara look like a tossed salad. For 1 serving, coarsely crush 1 tsp black peppercorns with a pestle and mortar and set aside. Cook enough corn pasta for a single serving for 2 minutes and drain it (retaining 3–4 tbsp of the cooking water), then set aside. In the pasta pan, melt a pat of butter over a medium heat and toss in the crushed pepper. After 30 seconds, add the reserved pasta-cooking water and bring to a simmer. Add the pasta, stir, then add 2 tbsp finely grated Parmesan. Remove from the heat and stir in about 4 tbsp finely grated pecorino, a tablespoon at a time, stirring gently after each spoonful has melted. The result should be a cheese sauce that is midway between thick and runny. Grind over a little more black pepper and serve.

CURRY

There's a recipe for curry-flavored pasta in *Simple to Spectacular* by chef Jean-Georges Vongerichten and food writer Mark Bittman. Curry is one of the few pasta flavorings that really seem to work. Vongerichten and Bittman keep their accompaniments simple; with curry fettuccine, for example, they recommend a light tomato sauce, some shrimp, or a little rich brown chicken stock. I toss curry fettuccine in a little salted butter and serve it in a tangled pile with a poached egg on top, scattered with a few toasted cumin seeds. Use 2 tbsp curry powder for our starting point quantities.

GRANO ARSO

When did you last look at a field of smoldering wheat stubble and think: supper? In Puglia, they make a flour from it, the char lending color and a deep, smoky flavor. *Grano arso* is enjoying something of a resurgence in Italy. You might find it fashioned into *cajubi*, twisted pasta shapes served with a dried-pea sauce; *cecatelli*, "little blind ones" (so-called for their resemblance to tiny, empty eye sockets); or *orecchiette*, the ear-shaped pasta traditionally served with *cime di rapa* or turnip tops. *Strascinati*, which look a little like pumpkin seeds, are also often made with *grano arso*, and served with cherry tomatoes, squash blossoms, and ricotta. In the absence of *grano arso*, try toasting some of the flour you use in your homemade pasta, as in the toasted rye variation on page 564.

NETTLE

Add a pinch of Sichuan pepper to your nettle pasta dough to make people think they've been stung. Nettle pasta is comparable to the spinach variety and is made the same way. A shopping bag full of young nettles will suffice for 4 cups 00 flour. John Wright, forager extraordinaire, claims that the plastic shopping bag is the accepted standard measure for nettles. Sticklers for precision may prefer to weigh out 4 oz leaves. Start with 3 rather than 4 eggs, to allow for the water you won't be able to squeeze out of the nettles. Mix ½ tsp salt into the flour. Wash the nettle leaves, then simmer them for 10 minutes. Squeeze out as much water as possible, then mince them. Add to the dough as you work in the egg. Wright uses nettle pasta for ravioli, filled with a mix of chopped cooked nettles, sautéed chopped pignuts (the tuber of a wild herb) or pine nuts, and wild garlic, bound with egg.

PARMESAN & PARSLEY

Oretta Zanini de Vita describes a Puglian specialty called *semola battuta* ("beaten flour") in which grated Parmesan and finely chopped parsley are added to durum-wheat semolina and eggs, then kneaded together to form a dough. Chickpea-sized pieces are pinched out, rolled, and simmered in a clear broth. At Easter, the broth would have traditionally been made with turkey. De Vita notes that a similar, if softer, dough is put through a potato ricer to make a *stracciatella*.

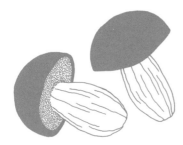

PORCINI

Code di topo ("mouse tails") pasta is made in Lazio with powdered porcini mushrooms—which, I suppose, makes for an authentically murine shade. Porcini powder is widely available to buy, but if you have a coffee/spice grinder, you can mill your own from dried porcini pieces. With your own store of powder you can dress as a fairy and prance around the kitchen, sprinkling magical mushroom dust on everything. Use your porcini dust as a steak rub, in cobbler dough (page 36), or for a savory custard tart (page 466), or mix it with bread crumbs and Parmesan for an umami-rich crust. For porcini pasta, add about 4–5 tsp powder to our starting point.

SAFFRON

In far-off days when it was more plentiful than fresh eggs, chefs added saffron to their pasta to replicate the sunset-orange of egg yolks. Sardinian *malloreddus*, the small shell-like gnocchi, and *ciciones* ("little chickpeas") are created from a dough made of warm, saffron-infused water and semolina flour. Saffron pasta is not to everyone's taste. In the mid-1800s, Francesco Chapusot, chef to the English ambassador to Turin, complained that saffron gave Neapolitan pasta "a detestable odor." Tentative cooks can always add a few strands to the cooking water for plain pasta. Some people do a similar thing with red wine to make their pasta pink. Great if you can't think of anything better to do with red wine. For each 1½ cups 00 flour, grind about 20 saffron strands to a powder. Soak in 1 tsp warm water for 30 minutes before beating into the egg. This will be enough to give your pasta a rich yellow color, but for a detectable saffron flavor, you'll need to use double the number of strands.

SPELT

Compared to wheat, spelt tastes richer, is higher in protein, and more fibrous. Its tough hull protects the grain from pollutants and insects, meaning fewer chemicals and pesticides need be used in its cultivation. Whereas the hull of modern wheat is discarded in the field during harvest, the hull of spelt is left on until the grain is milled, keeping it fresher and more nutritious. Those who find it hard to digest wheat can often tolerate spelt. Which is not to say that spelt is gluten-free— its gluten content, while lower than wheat's, is the reason it makes such excellent pasta and bread. (Spelt also rises faster than wheat, making it good for a one-rise loaf.) In other words, spelt is teacher's pet. It comes in white and whole wheat forms, both of which can be substituted for the 00 flour in our starting point, although the whole wheat type will benefit from more moisture—add 1 tsp bland oil or a little water along with the egg.

SPINACH

Why, I used to wonder, go to the trouble of making regular pasta look less attractive, for no noticeable improvement in flavor? Then I made some of my own, and saw how the subtle variation in flavor is really rather lovely when the pasta is freshly made. Once you've mastered puréeing the spinach and mixing it into the dough, try the same with different leaves. Arugula is a reliable variant. Fancy Italian pastamakers L'Origine use radicchio. Or have a go at resolutely unfancy nettle pasta (opposite). Aliza Green advises that any vegetable, cooked until soft and then puréed, should work. Try artichoke, asparagus, or even a combination of butternut squash, apple, and prune if you like, with the proviso that outlandish variants may at some point overlap with off-the-shelf baby food. Start with 2 tbsp puréed spinach to ¾ cup flour, plus 1 egg. Or ¼ cup spinach purée works well if you want a stronger color and flavor. Add a little extra flour to make the dough kneadable if it seems too wet.

SQUID INK

Some serious people take a dark view of squid-ink pasta. Peter Kaminsky says it's the sort of cliché Italian kitchens resort to when their skill falls short of their ambition. Marcella Hazan considers it "deplorable." On the other hand, Tarquin Winot, sulfurous narrator of *The Debt to Pleasure* by John Lanchester, hosts entirely black meals in his entirely black room at Cambridge University. The menu includes squid-ink pasta with grated truffles, *boudin noir* on black radicchio, black-dyed crème brûlée for dessert, and Black Velvet (Guinness and sparkling white wine) to drink. Almost without exception, cephalopods release ink as a defense against predators, clouding their view and, as has been recently discovered, anesthetizing the olfactory nerves of crabs and eels. You may think your olfactory nerves have been anesthetized eating squid-ink pasta. Its flavor is often entirely undetectable. The food writer Colman Andrews reckons that cuttlefish ink is richer in flavor than squid. It is deeper in color too. If you want to make the direct comparison yourself, you can buy cuttlefish ink and squid ink online and in some upscale grocers. Make ink pasta as per the eggless version given at ᴳ under Leeway, using only 6 tbsp water and 2 tbsp ink.

TOASTED RYE

Ivan Orkin, proprietor of Ivan Ramen in New York, became something of a celebrity in Japan after opening his ramen shop in Tokyo. His ramen are made with a mixture of toasted rye flour, all-purpose flour, and bread flour; the toasted rye element accounts for 10 percent of the total flour weight. The same proportion makes a very good egg pasta. It'll be surprisingly dark, considering the small amount of rye, with a mildly toasted flavor. Pasta made entirely from rye is the color of milk chocolate and tastes like pumpernickel bread. Accordingly, it's often served with the kinds of ingredients you'd expect between two slices of rye. The innovative chef Wylie Dufresne grates pastrami over his.

WHOLE WHEAT

In the Veneto, a whole wheat pasta called *bigoli*, similar to *bucatini* in that it resembles lengths of electrical cabling, is traditionally made using a contraption that resembles a wooden goat designed by Oliver Postgate. Twist its horns and pasta is extruded through its nose. A superior talking point for your kitchen now that everyone has a bright-red retro stand mixer. *Bigoli* are usually served with a sauce of slow-cooked onion, anchovies, and sardines that wouldn't taste half so good with white pasta. *Lane pelose* ("hairy wool") is, as the name suggests, a similarly fibrous variety of fettuccine, made with whole wheat flour and bran. Whole wheat pasta comes into its own with strong, rustic flavors, like garlic, chorizo, coarse Italian sausage, or purple sprouting broccoli. As noted at ᴳ under Leeway, I think this pasta is better made with warm water and oil than with egg. Either way, you may need a little more egg or water than with white flour.

Pasta → Other Directions

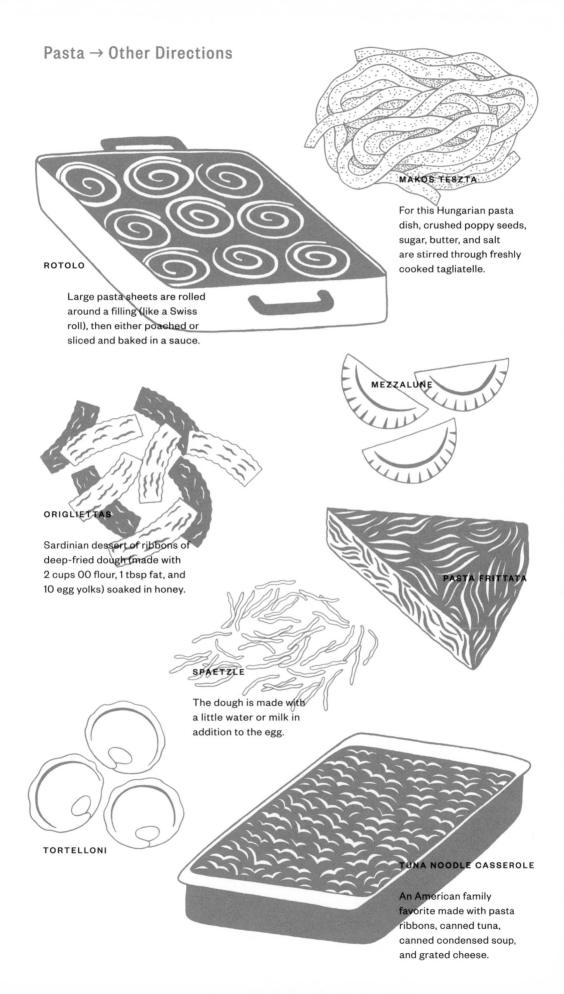

MAKOS TESZTA

For this Hungarian pasta dish, crushed poppy seeds, sugar, butter, and salt are stirred through freshly cooked tagliatelle.

ROTOLO

Large pasta sheets are rolled around a filling (like a Swiss roll), then either poached or sliced and baked in a sauce.

MEZZALUNE

ORIGLIETTAS

Sardinian dessert of ribbons of deep-fried dough (made with 2 cups 00 flour, 1 tbsp fat, and 10 egg yolks) soaked in honey.

PASTA FRITTATA

SPAETZLE

The dough is made with a little water or milk in addition to the egg.

TORTELLONI

TUNA NOODLE CASSEROLE

An American family favorite made with pasta ribbons, canned tuna, canned condensed soup, and grated cheese.

Shortcrust, Sweet & Suet Pastry

Rich and crumbly shortcrust, a basic piecrust pastry, is made with a simple weight ratio of 1:2 fat to flour and a minimal amount of liquid (water or egg). For suet pastry, see ᴰ under Leeway, and for sweet pastry, see under ᴵ.

For 12 oz, enough to line a 10-in tart pan ᴬ ᴮ

INGREDIENTS
2 cups all-purpose flour ᶜ ᴰ ᴱ
¼ tsp salt
1 stick cold unsalted butter, diced ᴰ ᴱ ᶠ ᴳ
Cold water ᴴ
Egg—optional ᴴ

1 Sift the flour into a large bowl and mix in the salt.

2 Add the fat and cut it in with a knife or pastry blender, or rub lightly through your fingertips, until the mixture resembles bread crumbs.
This "waterproofs" the flour, suppressing gluten formation.
A food processor will make a better job of it, if you have one.

3 Using as little as possible, gradually add cold water (or egg, or a mixture) to bring the crumbs together.

4 Form the dough into a disk, smoothing out any cracks that appear at the edges, wrap in plastic wrap, and leave in the fridge for at least 30 minutes or up to 3 days. Or wrap well and freeze for up to 3 months.
If you're not lining a round pan, form the dough into a square or rectangle or whatever shape suits your end.

5 Roll out the disk of dough a few times, then make a quarter turn and do the same until the dough is the ideal thickness (⅛–¼ in) and width. You may need a fine veil of flour to prevent the rolling pin from sticking to the dough. Some cooks prefer to roll out pastry dough between two sheets of plastic wrap. For tarts, ease the dough into the prepared pan, letting the edges hang over the rim rather than trimming them to fit. Prick the base all over with a fork, and chill in the fridge for at least 30 minutes.
The chilling helps to prevent shrinkage. Pasties and double-crust pies can be filled and baked without a second spell in the fridge.

6 To bake blind, cover the dough with foil or parchment paper, weigh down with pie weights (or rice or dried beans), and bake at 375°F for 20 minutes. Remove the foil or parchment and the weights and return the tart shell to the oven for 5–8 minutes, then carefully trim off the overhanging pastry.

If your filling is particularly wet, egg-wash the tart shell before returning it to the oven for a few minutes to seal. Once the shell has cooled, it's ready to be filled and baked again—or just pour in a filling that needs no further cooking, like chocolate ganache (page [380]) or a bavarois (page [488]).

LEEWAY

A For a tart 6 in across, use ¾ cup flour and ¼ stick butter; 1⅔ cups flour and 7 tbsp butter is enough for a 9-in tart.

B The quantities here will make 4 pasties.

C All-purpose flour is best. Self-rising can be used, but the pastry is likely to have a softer, crumblier texture.

D Suet pastry is made with the same proportions of ingredients, and by the same method, but using pure beef suet as the fat and adding enough water to bring fat and flour together into a soft dough. It's best to use self-rising flour (or add 1 tsp baking powder per ¾ cup all-purpose flour), to stop the pastry being too dense.

E You can reduce the fat by as much as a quarter: 1 tbsp fat per ⅓ cup flour is about as low as you can go. Elizabeth Nash recommends self-rising flour for low-fat pastry.

F Conversely, you can increase the fat by up to 50 percent. *Larousse* gives a recipe for an enriched shortcrust calling for three-quarters of the flour weight in butter.

G Most recipes favor butter, although many chefs recommend a 50/50 combination of butter and lard, the former for flavor, the latter for texture. Vegetable shortening and duck or goose fat can also be used.

H Use the minimum amount of cold water needed to bring the dough together; you can use egg instead, or a mixture of the two.

I There are many variations on sweet pastry. The following is only a tweak away from our starting point. Stir in about ⅔ cup confectioners' sugar at the end of step 2. Make a well in the center, add 1 extra large egg, and bring the dough together, adding a little cream, milk, or water, if necessary. Chill the dough for at least an hour before rolling it out and blind-baking as above.

ALMOND

Never work with animals, children, or almond pastry, they say. Even with a good amount of gluten-rich wheat flour mixed in with the ground almonds, lining a pan with it is a slog, as it's so coarse and crumbly. It's fairly common to add some ground almonds to sweet pastry, even if the amount is so small it doesn't get any specific mention in the recipe title. The resulting dough can be made easier to handle by freezing it and then grating and pressing it into its pan. Or simply chill it, roll it out, and accept that a little paving and patching may be necessary. Next time you linger at a pâtisserie window, admiring the Linzertorte within, check if its apparently immaculate lattice roof conceals a multitude of joins and imperfections. Linzertorte is an Austrian jam tart made with a spiced almond or hazelnut sweet pastry. Some recipes call for 50/50 ground almonds and flour by weight, but I find this difficult to work with, and prefer something more like 30/70; note that the pastry shell is not blind-baked. For an 8-in tart, I use 1 cup ground almonds, 1 cup all-purpose flour, 1 stick unsalted butter, ¼ cup sugar, ½ tsp ground cinnamon, and ¼ tsp ground cloves. Bring the dough together with a beaten egg rather than water. Once chilled, use what you need to line a shallow tart pan, leaving the rest in the fridge. Prick the dough in the pan, then chill while you roll out the remaining dough and cut it into ribbons for the lattice. Fill the tart with jam—you'll need the entire contents of a 1-lb jar—and set about your latticework. Chill the dough any time it starts to get tacky and difficult. Transfer the Linzertorte to a preheated baking sheet and bake in a 350°F oven for 30–35 minutes. Use any leftover dough for a bonus of rough jam tarts.

ANISEED & SESAME

Every October, *El Señor de los Milagros* ("The Lord of Miracles"), an image of Christ weighing almost a ton, is paraded through the streets of Lima, Peru, by devotees in purple habits, accompanied by vast crowds sustained by an elaborate confection called *turrón de Doña Pepa*. Doña Pepa was a freed, seventeenth-century Angolan slave, said to have created her *turrón* after joining the procession and being cured of paralysis in her arms. Eating a slice is liable to paralyze your pancreas. *Turrón de Doña Pepa* is a stack of egg-yolk-heavy sticks of shortcrust pastry, flavored with aniseed and sesame, drenched in sugar syrup, and then decorated with multicolored sprinkles like one of those pits of plastic balls in children's play centers. The recipe is said to have come to Doña Pepa in a dream. If aniseed gives you nightmares, you can always leave it out. In more recent versions, the syrup flavorings vary widely: They might include molasses, quince, orange zest, and clove; or apple, lime, prune, cinnamon, clove, and allspice. Add 1 tbsp sesame seeds and 2 tsp aniseed to our starting point.

BUDGIE FEED

That is, your own mix of fragrant seeds—too good for Joey. Works with both savory and sweet dishes. Smooth, simple fillings like custard are best, giving the flavors of the seeds their due, and maximizing the textural contrast. For dough made to our starting point, try a mix of 2 tbsp each poppy and mustard seeds and 1 tsp nigella seeds; 2 tsp celery seeds in place of the nigella is great for poultry (celery seeds were once a standard pastry seasoning for chicken pot pie).

CARAWAY

Caraway develops hints of citrus zest when cooked. It can lift the heaviness of all types of pastry, but is particularly welcome in rich and robust varieties like suet. Try a little in a steamed marmalade pudding. One of caraway's classic pairings is pork, which is perhaps why it tastes so good in a hot-water pastry (page 554) made with lard. Both Jeremy Round and Hugh Fearnley-Whittingstall use it in a shortcrust dough, the latter for an onion and Gruyère tart. Stay your hand, however: You want about 1 tsp for a batch of dough made to our starting point.

CHEESE

Easy-cheesy. Roll out shortcrust dough, sprinkle it with grated cheese, fold, and re-roll. For cheese straws, cut into strips, sprinkle with more grated cheese, and bake on a lightly greased baking sheet at 375°F for 12–15 minutes. Aside from its savory uses, cheese pastry is traditional in apple (and, less commonly, pear) tarts and pies. I use it for jam tarts—the salt-sweet combination is irresistible. Delia Smith makes red onion and goat's cheese tarts with cheese pastry, supplementing grated Cheddar with mustard powder and paprika. (Mustard will enhance the cheesiness of pastry as much it does béchamel.) Dried thyme is another good addition—1–2 tsp per 2 cups of flour. The nimble-fingered can use cheese pastry dough to encase large, stuffed green olives. Press out circles, form each into a cup in your palm, and swaddle each olive as if it were a baby pink from its bath. Bake at 375°F for 10–15 minutes. Make as per the starting point, but add about ½ cup freshly grated Parmesan, or Parmesan mixed with Gruyère or mature Cheddar, and stir it in once the butter has been rubbed in.

CHOCOLATE

Recently I was flicking through the yellowing newsprint in my recipe scrapbooks when I realized I had never once tried to make the dish that I most wanted to eat, a chocolate-pastry tart filled with vanilla custard and pears. The main reason for this was the spiritual torment of rolling out chocolate pastry. Reading Dan Lepard's *Short and Sweet* finally shed some light on what to do about it: As powdered flavorings soften the gluten in the flour, the higher gluten content of bread flour makes it better able to withstand them. I tried a batch and made the pear tart, which wasn't half as nice as the scrapbook picture had led me to imagine. Most recipes substitute 15–20 percent of the flour weight with cocoa; you'll also need to add some sugar to counter the bitterness. Mix 2 cups white bread flour with a rounded ½ cup unsweetened cocoa powder, ½ cup confectioners' sugar, 1¼ sticks unsalted butter, a pinch of salt, 1 egg yolk, and just enough ice-cold water to bring it together. It's still a soft dough, so likely to need extra chilling before rolling out.

CINNAMON

Cinnamon pastry encases apple pie as naturally as a tweed jacket does a farmer's check shirt. Sara Paston-Williams takes it in a more unusual direction; she makes her cinnamon pastry with lard and uses it for black-currant tart. Cinnamon pastry works in savory contexts, or in cuisines where the sweet-savory borders are less rigorously policed. Try it with Moorish ingredients like squab and almond. Replacing ½ cup of the flour with ½ cup ground nuts can lend extra bite and flavor: 1½ tsp ground cinnamon will flavor a batch of pastry made with our starting point quantities—consider adding a little sugar too.

CORN

To sweeten pastry slightly without adding sugar, substitute ¼ cup fine cornmeal for the same volume of wheat flour. It lends a crisper, pleasantly gritty texture, too, reminiscent of shortbread made with rice flour. In Italy, this kind of pastry is popular in *crostate*, which can be roughly translated as "open tarts." For some Italians a *crostata* is a smart confection of glossy jam imprisoned in neat lattice pastry; for others it's a rough round of pastry with fruit plonked in the middle and the outer edge hoisted up over it, pleated along the way—a tart for want of a tart dish. The neatly criss-crossed variety, you imagine, would take a dim view of its rustic namesake. Sloppy *crostate* are equally suited to savory fillings, even if they're less common than sweet. Try a thick ratatouille with Gruyère, or butternut squash, spinach, and blue cheese. Whatever you fill it with, guard against excessive wetness.

CREAM CHEESE

Cream cheese gives pastry a pleasing tang and a texture that's flaky without being puffy. The fat-to-flour ratio in many recipes is high, so you'll need a cool room to roll it in, and a fridge shelf on standby for a possible mid-roll chill. I find it easier to roll this between two sheets of plastic wrap. Turnovers are a good place to start if you're unfamiliar with the flavor of cream-cheese pastry. Apricot jam is hard to beat as a filling and is also a standard for *rugelach*, the Jewish cream-cheese pastries that are perfectly at home in the company of croissants and Danish pastries, but considerably simpler to make. Start by creaming 8 tbsp each butter and full-fat cream cheese with 2 tbsp confectioners' sugar and ½ tsp vanilla extract. Beat in 1½ cups flour and bring the mixture together to make a dough. Divide in half and flatten each half into a disk, then wrap in plastic wrap and leave in the fridge for a few hours or up to a couple of days. Roll out each disk to a 9-in round, then spread *thinly* with jam up to half an inch shy of the edge, leaving a circle of about 2-in diameter uncovered in the center. Scatter a mixture of sugar, ground cinnamon, and finely chopped walnuts over the top. Cut into 12 wedge-shaped slices, as you would a pizza, then roll up each triangle from the wide end to the tip and transfer to a nonstick baking sheet, with the tips tucked underneath. Paint with egg wash, sprinkle with sugar, and bake at 350°F for 20–25 minutes. Cream-cheese pastry is put to daintier use in tassies: bijou tartlets usually deep-filled with sweetened chopped pecans, but also ideal receptacles for savory fillings like crab mayonnaise (leave out the confectioners' sugar).

HAZELNUT

The Irish chef Denis Cotter uses a hazelnut shortcrust for his chanterelle and sea spinach tart. With the addition of a little sugar, the same pastry can be used for sweet tarts. Try it with whatever jam you have to hand for a variation on Linzertorte (page 568), or with a chocolate ganache filling (page 380). Replace ½ cup of the flour with ½ cup ground roasted hazelnuts; the proportion is lower than for almonds because hazelnuts are stronger in flavor.

LEMON

Go ahead and match your shoes and handbag. Lemon pastry is lovely in a lemon tart. If that's a shade too obvious, follow Heston Blumenthal and mix the zest with vanilla seeds. The resulting pastry is fit for the most luxurious lemon tart, with a filling the shiny yellow of a drenched sou'wester. Lemon pastry is also great for Italian-style sweetened ricotta pies, baked cheesecakes, and crab tart. The finely grated zest of 1 lemon will flavor enough pastry for an 8-in tart shell, although double that amount if you want the lemon to zing. Some chefs add a few drops of lemon juice to bind the pastry, as the acidity is believed to reduce shrinkage.

OLIVE OIL

The sweet Swiss-chard tart *tourte aux blettes* is a classic of Niçoise cuisine. The dish begs plenty of questions: about the advisability of mixing greens with sugar, whether Parmesan ever has a place in a dessert, and how many sackfuls of chard leaves are needed to fill an entire pie. That the pastry is made with oil, as opposed to a hard fat, might also strike you as peculiar. Diana Farr Louis explains that olive oil pastry, while used occasionally in Spain, Provence, and Italy, is a much bigger deal in Crete. The method bears close comparison with strudel dough (page 556). Flour is kneaded with oil, wine, and warm water, then rested at room temperature before being rolled out thinly. At the 1986 Oxford Symposium on Food & Cookery, Janet Laurence presented the results of a test using various cooking oils to make pastry. She reported that oil pastry is less given to shrinking but, unlike a pastry made with hard fat, is best used immediately after it has been made, as the longer the dough rests, the greasier it becomes.

ROSE
Popular throughout the Middle East and Maghreb, *ma'moul,* crumbly cookies stuffed with dried fruit and nut pastes, are indispensable nighttime sustenance during Ramadan. In some versions, the pastry is made with yeast, *mahleb* (an almond-like flavoring extracted from cherry pits), and mastic (a resin used to flavor gum and alcoholic drinks, particularly in Greece). This simple version is essentially a shortcrust made with semolina, wheat, and sheep's butter, flavored with rosewater. Use a higher proportion of fine semolina than wheat flour if possible, but all flour will do. As a rule, round *ma'moul* are filled with dates, oblong with pistachio, and domed with walnut. Use 1 cup fine semolina, ½ cup flour, 7 tbsp butter, 2–3 tbsp milk, and 1 tbsp rosewater, following the same method as for shortcrust (some like to add a little sugar too). Divide the pastry into 20 pieces and roll into walnut-sized balls. Authentic *ma'moul* are made with a special mold, like a very deep wooden spoon with a star-shape or spiral design carved into the cavity. Press the pastry into the mold and tap sharply to eject. In the unlikely event that you don't have a *ma'moul* mold, indent each ball with your thumb to form a cup. Fill with a thick purée of dried fruit. Work the pastry over the fruit to enclose it completely and place your uncooked *ma'moul,* seam-side down, on a lightly greased baking sheet, gently pressing each one with the tines of a fork. Bake at 325°F for 20 minutes. Sprinkle with confectioners' sugar when cooled.

TURMERIC
The Jamaican patty is a Cornish pasty with a perma-tan. The record is uncertain, but it's thought that English settlers brought pasties with them to the Caribbean, where they absorbed African and Indian influences, including the ground turmeric that lends them their sunny complexion. Authentic patty pastry is neither puff nor flaky, as is sometimes assumed, but a form of shortcrust made with suet, lard, butter, or a mixture. The confusion may arise from the small amount of baking powder, unusual in a pastry recipe, which is often added to provide a little lift and promote browning. Stir ½ tsp each baking powder, ground turmeric, and curry powder into the flour in our starting point. The patty filling is usually ground beef with bread crumbs, onion, and an aromatic combination of hot chilies, thyme, scallions, garlic, and curry powder, plus perhaps some nutmeg and paprika. To deprive a patty of its prebaking egg glaze would be like venturing onto a beach without a basting of Ambre Solaire. *Not* advised.

VANILLA
A simple way to make lightly sweetened pastry taste sweeter. To flavor a dough made with 2 cups flour, use the seeds scraped from 1 split vanilla bean, 1½ tsp vanilla extract, or 1 tsp vanilla paste.

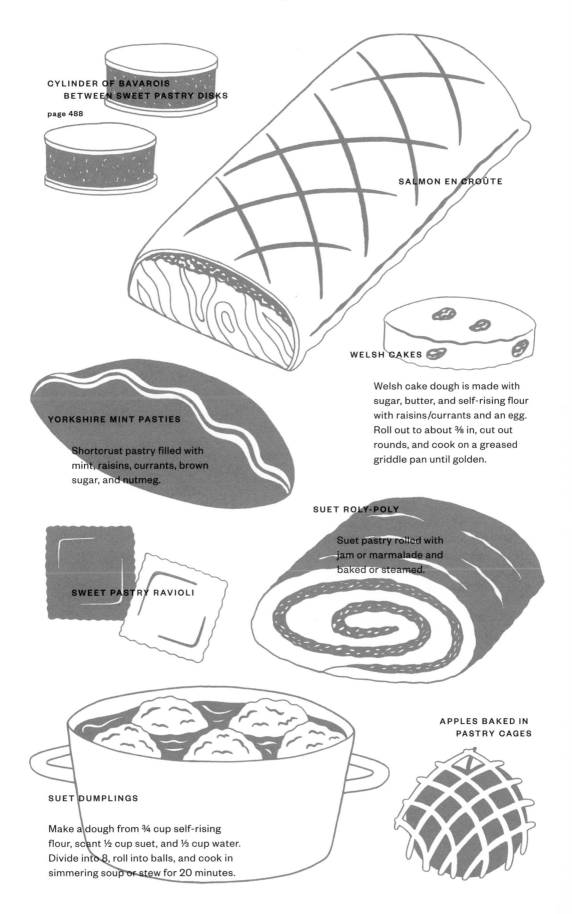

CYLINDER OF BAVAROIS BETWEEN SWEET PASTRY DISKS

page 488

SALMON EN CROÛTE

WELSH CAKES

Welsh cake dough is made with sugar, butter, and self-rising flour with raisins/currants and an egg. Roll out to about ⅜ in, cut out rounds, and cook on a greased griddle pan until golden.

YORKSHIRE MINT PASTIES

Shortcrust pastry filled with mint, raisins, currants, brown sugar, and nutmeg.

SUET ROLY-POLY

Suet pastry rolled with jam or marmalade and baked or steamed.

SWEET PASTRY RAVIOLI

APPLES BAKED IN PASTRY CAGES

SUET DUMPLINGS

Make a dough from ¾ cup self-rising flour, scant ½ cup suet, and ⅓ cup water. Divide into 8, roll into balls, and cook in simmering soup or stew for 20 minutes.

Rough Puff Pastry

This quick version of puff pastry involves a higher ratio of butter to flour than shortcrust's, and, some would say, more work, although not if you count all the shaping and blind-baking shortcrust can require. There are no Flavors & Variations here, although I have seen recipes for chocolate rough puff, and a version calling for oil in place of the butter. Notes on making highfalutin puff can be found on page 553.

For a rectangle about 12 x 8 in—enough for a large pie lid [A] [B]

INGREDIENTS
2 cups all-purpose flour [C]
A few pinches of salt
1½ sticks cold unsalted butter, diced [D] [E]
6+ tbsp ice-cold water [F]

1 Sift the flour into a large bowl and mix in the salt.

2 Add the fat and cut it in with a knife or pastry blender, or rub lightly through your fingertips, stopping some way short of a bread-crumb texture, while the dough is still shaggy and has visible strands of butter in it.

3 Pour the water evenly over the shaggy dough, then tip out the dough onto a cold surface and compact it with a rolling pin or your hands, aiming to fashion it into a rectangle about three times longer than it is wide, and ½ in thick.
   Forming it into a cohesive block might take a bit more water and a light kneading. If you find that the dough is sticking, you may want to lightly flour the surface, dough, and rolling pin.

4 Take the short ends and bring them almost together in the middle, leaving a small gap which, when you fold these over once more, effectively becomes the inside spine of your "book" of dough. Wrap and chill for at least 20 minutes. [G]

5 Repeat the rolling and folding process (called a "turn") between three and five more times, always starting with the shorter ends as top and bottom, and being careful not to press so hard that the layers compact. Chill the dough for at least 20 minutes between each turn. Dough that's been chilled for more than a few hours may need some time out of the fridge to soften before it can be rolled into the desired shape.

It's advisable to keep a record of how many turns you've done. If time is not on my side (and the kitchen is cool), I will do two turns and then chill the pastry.

6 When the lamination is complete, thoroughly wrap the dough in plastic wrap and chill for at least 30 minutes or up to 3 days. Or it can be frozen for up to 6 weeks.

7 For a pie lid, roll out the dough to a diameter slightly larger than your pan or dish. If there is a rim, it can be brushed with egg and the lid fitted on directly. If not, you can fashion a rim from dampened strips of dough fitted onto the dampened edge of the pan or dish. Egg-wash this rim and fit the lid on top.

8 Bake at 400°F, making sure you wait for the oven to heat properly—too cool an oven will cause the butter to melt before the rising starts.
A piecrust will need about 30 minutes to rise and turn golden brown.

LEEWAY
A If you're adapting a recipe that calls for store-bought puff, note that these quantities make 1 lb 2 oz pastry.
B This makes enough rough puff for 6 jam turnovers.
C All-purpose flour is recommended, or a 50/50 mix of all-purpose and bread flour.
D As with shortcrust, butter or a mixture of butter and lard is almost universally recommended.
E Rough puff can be made with a 1:2 butter to flour weight ratio, e.g. about 1 stick butter to 2 cups of flour. Other recipes call for a very buttery 2 sticks of butter to 2 cups flour.
F 1 tsp lemon juice added to the water will make the dough easier to work with.
G Delia Smith makes a rough puff without any folding. She freezes the butter before grating it into the flour and mixing to achieve the shagginess, then brings it together with cold water.

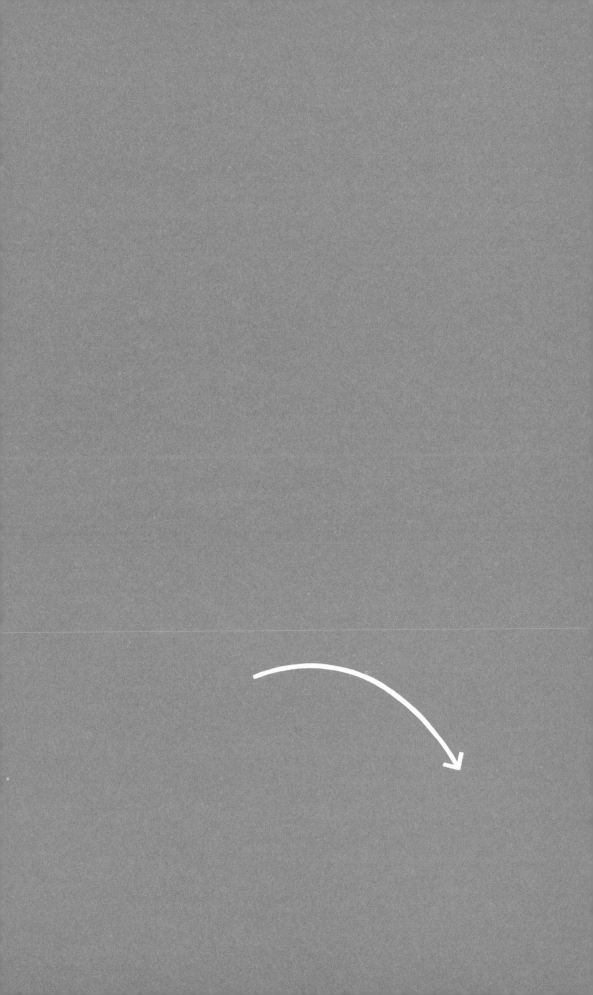

Bibliography

We live in a golden age of food writing. Researching this book has been a reminder of the astonishing richness and variety of source material at the cook's disposal. I am immensely grateful to the many chefs and cookery writers whose work I have drawn on in this book. Where I have referred to someone else's recipe, I have summarized it. Readers wishing to consult the recipes in full should refer to the original sources, given below.

A

Acton, Eliza. *Modern Cookery for Private Families*. Longmans, 1845.
Adrià, Ferran. *The Family Meal*. Phaidon, 2011.
Albala, Ken. *Beans: A History*. Bloomsbury, 2007.
Albala, Ken. *Cooking in Europe 1250–1650*. Greenwood, 2006.
Albala, Ken. *Nuts: A Global History*. Reaktion Books, 2014.
Amis, Kingsley. *Everyday Drinking*. Bloomsbury, 2009.
Anderson, Robert. *The Miscellaneous Works of Tobias Smollett*. Mundell, 1796.
Anderson, Tim. *Nanban: Japanese Soul Food*. Square Peg, 2015.
Andrews, Colman. *Catalan Cuisine*. Macmillan, 1988.
Ansel, David. *The Soup Peddler's Slow and Difficult Soups*. Ten Speed Press, 2005.
Arndt, Alice. *Seasoning Savvy*. Routledge, 2008.
Artusi, Pellegrino. *The Art of Eating Well*. Translated by Kyle M. Phillips III.
    Random House, 1996.
Auslander, Shalom. *Hope: A Tragedy*. Picador, 2012.

B

Baker, Jenny. *Simple French Cuisine*. Faber & Faber, 1990.
Baldini, Filippo. *De' Sorbetti*. 1775.
Balzac, Honoré de. *Eugénie Grandet*. Caxton, 1897.
Bareham, Lindsey. *A Celebration of Soup*. Penguin, 2001.
Bareham, Lindsey. *In Praise of the Potato*. Michael Joseph, 1989.
Basan, Ghillie. *The Complete Book of Turkish Cooking*. Hermes House, 2013.
Beard, James. *Love and Kisses and a Halo of Truffles*. Arcade, 1995.
Beard, James. *The Theory and Practice of Good Cooking*. Random House, 1977.
Beckett, Fiona, & Beckett, Will. *An Appetite for Ale*. Camra, 2007.
Beeton, Isabella. *Mrs Beeton's Book of Household Management*. S. O. Beeton, 1861.
Behr, Edward. *The Art of Eating Cookbook*. University of California Press, 2011.
Bender, Aimee. *The Particular Sadness of Lemon Cake*. Windmill, 2011.
Berry, Sophie. *The A–Z of Marzipan Sweets*. Two Magpies, 2013.
Bertinet, Richard. *Dough*. Kyle Books, 2008.
Bertuzzi, Barbera. *Bolognese Cooking Heritage*. Pendragon, 2006.
Besh, John. *My Family Table*. Andrews McMeel, 2011.
Besh, John. *My New Orleans*. Andrews McMeel, 2009.
Blanc, Raymond. *Kitchen Secrets*. Bloomsbury, 2011.
Blumenthal, Heston. *The Fat Duck Cookbook*. Bloomsbury, 2009.
Blumenthal, Heston. *Heston Blumenthal at Home*. Bloomsbury, 2011.
Blumenthal, Heston. *Historic Heston*. Bloomsbury, 2014.
Blythman, Joanna. *What to Eat*. Fourth Estate, 2013.
Bompas, Sam, & Parr, Harry. *Jelly with Bompas & Parr*. Pavilion, 2010.
Boulestin, Marcel. *Boulestin's Round-the-Year Cookbook*. Second edition. Dover, 1975.
Boulud, Daniel, & Greenspan, Dorie. *Daniel Boulud's Café Boulud Cookbook*.
    Simon & Schuster, 1999.
Boulud, Daniel, & Bigar, Sylvie. *Daniel: My French Cuisine*. Grand Central Publishing, 2013.
Bourdain, Anthony. *The Nasty Bits*. Bloomsbury, 2006.
Boxer, Arabella, & Traegar, Tessa. *A Visual Feast*. Ebury, 1991.
Boyd, Alexandra (ed). *Favorite Food from Ambrose Heath*. Faber & Faber, 1979.
Branston, Thomas F. *The Pharmacist's and Druggist's Practical Receipt Book*.
    Lindsay & Blakiston, 1865.

Brantt, W.T., & Wahl, W.H. *The Techno-Chemical Receipt Book*. H.C. Baird, 1887.

Bremzen, Anya von, & Welchman, John. *Please to the Table*. Workman, 1990.

Brillat-Savarin, Jean Anthelme. *The Physiology of Taste*. Translated by M.F.K. Fisher. Knopf, 1949.

Brown, Catherine. *Classic Scots Cookery*. Angel's Share, 2006.

Brown, Pete. *Three Sheets to the Wind*. Pan Macmillan, 2006.

Buford, Bill. *Heat*. Jonathan Cape, 2006.

Bull, Stephen. *Classic Bull: An Accidental Restaurateur's Cookbook*. Macmillan, 2001.

Burdock, George A. *Fenaroli's Handbook of Flavor Ingredients*. CRC Press, 1971.

Butcher, Sally. *Veggiestan*. Pavilion, 2011.

c

Calabrese, Salvatore. *The Complete Home Bartender's Guide*. Revised edition. Sterling, 2012.

Calvel, Raymond. *The Taste of Bread*. Translated by Ronald L. Wurtz. Springer, 2001.

Camorra, Frank, & Cornish, Richard. *MoVida*. Murdoch Books, 2007.

Campion, Charles. *Fifty Recipes to Stake Your Life On*. Timewell Press, 2004.

Cappatti, Alberto, & Montinari, Massimo. *Italian Cuisine: A Cultural History*. Columbia University Press, 2003.

Carême, Marie-Antoine. *L'Art de la Cuisine*. 1883.

Carrier, Robert. *Great Dishes of the World*. Nelson, 1963.

Chang, David, & Meehan, Peter. *Momofuku*. Clarkson Potter, 2009.

Chapman, Pat. *India: Food & Cooking*. New Holland, 2007.

Chave, Anna C. *Mark Rothko: Subjects in Abstraction*. Yale University Press, 1989.

Chiffers, Martin, & Marsden, Emma. *Crème de la Crème*. Hodder & Stoughton, 2017.

Christian, Glynn. *Glynn Christian's Contemporary Home Cooking*. Hamlyn, 1986.

Ciesla, William M. *Non-Wood Forest Products From Temperate Broad-Leaved Trees*. Food & Agriculture Organization of the United Nations, 2002.

Claibourne, Craig. *Craig Claibourne's Kitchen Primer*. Random House, 1969.

Clark, Sam & Sam. *Morito*. Ebury, 2014.

Clark, Sam & Sam. *The Moro Cookbook*. Ebury, 2001.

Clermont, B. *The Professed Cook*. 1769.

Coady, Chantal. *Rococo: Mastering the Art of Chocolate*. Weidenfeld & Nicolson, 2012.

Contaldo, Gennaro. *Gennaro: Slow Cook Italian*. Pavilion, 2015.

Corrado, Vicenzo. *Il Credenziere di Buon Gusto*. Saverio Giordano, 1820.

Corrigan, Richard. *The Clatter of Forks and Spoons*. Fourth Estate, 2008.

Cotter, Denis. *Café Paradiso Cookbook*. Atrium Press, 1999.

Curley, William. *Couture Chocolate*. Jacqui Small, 2011.

D

David, Elizabeth. *English Bread and Yeast Cookery*. Allen Lane, 1977.

David, Elizabeth. *French Provincial Cooking*. Michael Joseph, 1960.

David, Elizabeth. *Italian Food*. MacDonald, 1954.

David, Elizabeth. *Spice, Salt and Aromatics in the English Kitchen*. Penguin, 1970.

Davidson, Alan. *The Oxford Companion to Food*. OUP, 1999.

Davidson, Alan & Jane. *Dumas on Food*. Folio Society, 1978.

DeGroff, Dale. *The Essential Cocktail*. Clarkson Potter, 2009.

Del Conte, Anna. *Amaretto, Apple Cake and Artichokes*. Vintage, 2006.

Del Conte, Anna. *The Classic Food of Northern Italy*. Pavilion, 1995.

Dhillon, Kris. *The Curry Secret*. Right Way, 2008.

Deutsch, Jonathan. *They Eat That?: A Cultural Encyclopedia of Weird and Exotic Food from around the World*. ABC-CLIO, 2012.

Dickie, John. *Delizia! The Epic History of the Italians and Their Food*. Free Press, 2007.

Disch, Thomas M. *The Prisoner*. Penguin, 2010.

Ducasse, Alain. *Ducasse Made Simple*. Stewart Tabori Chang, 2008.

Dunford Wood, Jesse. *Modern British Food*. Absolute Press, 2017.

Dunlop, Fuchsia. *Every Grain of Rice*. Bloomsbury, 2012.

E

Early, Eleanor. *New England Sampler*. Waverly House, 1940.

Ellis, Bret Easton. *American Psycho*. Vintage, 1991.

Emy, M. *L'Art de bien faire les glaces d'office*. Chez Le Clerc, 1768.

Ephron, Nora. *I Feel Bad About My Neck*. Knopf, 2006.

Escoffier, Auguste. *Le guide culinaire*. Translated by H.L. Cracknell & R.J. Kaufmann. Second edition. Routledge, 2011.

The Ethicurean. *The Ethicurean Cookbook*. Ebury, 2013.

F

Farmer, Fannie Merritt. *The Boston Cooking-School Cookbook*. Little, Brown, 1896.

Farmer, Fannie Merritt. *Chafing Dish Possibilities*. Little, Brown, 1898.

Farr Louise, Diana. *Feasting and Fasting in Crete*. Kedros, 2001.

Fear, Annette, & Brierty, Helen. *Spirit House: Thai Cooking*. New Holland, 2004.

Fearnley-Whittingstall, Hugh. *Hugh Fearlessly Eats It All*. Bloomsbury, 2006.

Fearnley-Whittingstall, Hugh. *The River Cottage Meat Book*. Hodder & Stoughton, 2004.

Fermor, Patrick Leigh. *Between the Woods and the Water*. John Murray, 1986.

Field, Carol. *The Italian Baker*. Revised edition. Ten Speed Press, 2011.

Fisher, M.F.K. *How to Cook a Wolf*. Duall, Sloan & Pearce, 1942.

Fisher, M.F.K. *With Bold Knife & Fork*. Pimlico, 1993.

Flay, Bobby. *Bobby Flay's Mesa Grill Cookbook*. Clarkson Potter, 2007.

Flottum, Kim. *The Backyard Beekeeper's Honey Handbook*. Crestline, 2009.

Floyd, Keith. *Floyd's American Pie*. BBC Books, 1989.

Forster, E.M. *A Room with a View*. Edward Arnold, 1908.

Foss, Richard. *Rum: A Global History*. Reaktion Books, 2012.

Frederick, J. George. *The Long Island Seafood Cookbook*. The Business Bourse, 1939.

Freud, Clement. *Grimble*. Collins, 1968.

Fussell, Betty Harper. *The Story of Corn*. University of New Mexico Press, 1992.

G

Gilette, F.L., & Zieman, Hugo. *The White House Cookbook*. L. P. Miller, 1887.

Gill, A.A. *Breakfast at the Wolseley*. Quadrille, 2008.

Gill, A.A. *The Ivy: The Restaurant and Its Recipes*. Hodder Headline, 1999.

Glasse, Hannah. *The Art of Cookery Made Plain and Easy*. L. Wangford, 1747.

Goldstein, Darra. *Baking Boot Camp*. John Wiley & Sons, 2007.

Goldstein, Darra. *The Oxford Companion to Sugar and Sweets*. OUP, 2015.

Gordon, Peter. *Fusion: A Culinary Journey*. Jacqui Small, 2010.

Gray, Rose, & Rogers, Ruth. *River Cafe Cookbook Green*. Ebury, 1996.

Gray, Rose, & Rogers, Ruth. *River Cafe Cookbook Two*. Ebury, 1997.

Gray, Rose, & Rogers, Ruth. *River Cafe Two Easy*. Ebury, 2005.

Green, Aliza. *Making Fresh Pasta*. Apple Press, 2012.

Greenspan, Dorrie. *Baking Chez Moi*. Houghton Mifflin Harcourt, 2014.

Grigson, Jane. *English Food*. Penguin, 1992.

Grigson, Jane. *Fish Cookery*. Penguin, 1975.

Grigson, Jane. *Jane Grigson's Fruit Book*. Michael Joseph, 1982.

Grigson, Jane. *Jane Grigson's Vegetable Book*. Michael Joseph, 1978.

Groom, Nigel. *The Perfume Handbook*. Chapman & Hall, 1992.

H

Haroutunian, Arto der. *The Yogurt Cookbook*, Grub Street, 2010.

Harris, Valentina. *The Italian Regional Cookbook*. Lorenz, 2017.

Hazan, Marcella. *Essentials of Classic Italian Cooking*. Knopf, 1992.

Helmuth, Chalene. *Culture and Customs of Costa Rica*. Greenwood, 2000.

Hemingway, Ernest. *Men Without Women*. Charles Scribner's Sons, 1927.

Henderson, Fergus. *The Complete Nose to Tail*. Bloomsbury, 2012.

Hieatt, Constance, & Hosington, Brenda. *Pleyn Delit: Medieval Cookery for Modern Cooks*. University of Toronto, 1996.

Hopkinson, Simon. *Roast Chicken and Other Stories*. Ebury, 1996.

Hopkinson, Simon. *Second Helpings of Roast Chicken*. Ebury, 2006.

Hosking, Richard (ed). *Eggs in Cookery: Proceedings of the Oxford Symposium on Food and Cookery 2006*. Prospect Books, 2007.

Howard, Philip. *The Square, The Cookbook, Volume 2: Sweet*. Absolute Press, 2013.

Howe, Robin. *German Cooking*. André Deutsch, 1953.

Hudler, George W. *Magical Mushrooms, Mischievous Molds*. Princeton University Press, 2000.

Hughes, Robert. *Barcelona*. Vintage, 1992.

Hutton, Wendy. *Green Mangoes and Lemon Grass*. Kogan Page, 2003.

J

Jack, Albert. *What Caesar Did for My Salad*. Penguin, 2012

Janick, Jules, & Moore, James. *Fruit Breeding*. John Wiley, 1996.

Jarrin, W.A. *The Italian Confectioner*. Routledge, 1861.

Jekyll, Agnes. *Kitchen Essays* (1922). Persephone Books, 2008.

Johansen, Signe. *Scandilicious*. Saltyard Books, 2011.

K

Kaneva-Johnson, Maria. *The Melting Pot: Balkan Food and Cookery*. Prospect Books, 1995.

Kaplan, David, Fouchald, Nick, & Day, Alex. *Death & Co*. Ten Speed Press, 2014.

Karmel, Elizabeth. *Soaked, Slathered, and Seasoned*. John Wiley, 2009.

Katz, Sandor Ellix. *The Art of Fermentation*. Chelsea Green, 2012.

Keillor, Garrison. *Leaving Home*. Viking Press, 1987.

Keller, Thomas. *The French Laundry Cookbook*. Workman, 1999.

Kenedy, Jacob. *Bocca: Cookbook*. Bloomsbury, 2011.

Kenedy, Jacob. *The Geometry of Pasta*. Boxtree, 2010.

Kennedy, Diana. *Nothing Fancy*. Second edition. University of Texas Press, 2016.

Kerridge, Tom. *Proper Pub Food*. Absolute Press, 2013.

Khoo, Rachel. *The Little Paris Kitchen*. Michael Joseph, 2012.

Kijac, Maria Baez. *The South American Table*. Harvard Common Press, 2003.

Kitchen, Leanne. *Turkey*. Murdoch Books, 2011.

Kochilas, Diane. *The Greek Vegetarian*. St Martin's Press, 1999.

Krause, Robert & Molly. *The Cook's Book of Intense Flavors*. Fair Winds Press, 2010.

Krondl, Michael. *Sweet Invention: A History of Dessert*. Chicago Review Press, 2011.

L

Lanchester, John. *The Debt to Pleasure*. Picador, 1996.

Lane, Frank Walter. *Kingdom of the Octopus*. Sheridan House, 1957.

Lawson, Nigella. *How to be a Domestic Goddess*. Chatto & Windus, 2000.

Lawson, Nigella. *How to Eat*. Chatto & Windus, 2002.

Lawson, Nigella. *Nigellissima*. Chatto & Windus, 2012.

Lean, Lucy. *Made in America*. Welcome Enterprises, 2011.

Lebovitz, David. *The Perfect Scoop*. Ten Speed Press, 2007.

Leiths School of Food and Wine. *Leiths How to Cook*. Quadrille, 2013.

Lepard, Dan. *Short and Sweet*. Fourth Estate, 2011.

Leyel, Mrs. C.F. (Hilda) & Hartley, Miss Olga. *The Gentle Art of Cookery* (1925). Quadrille, 2011.

Liddell, Caroline, & Weir, Robin. *Ices*. Grub Street, 1995.

Locatelli, Giorgio. *Made in Italy*. Fourth Estate, 2006.

Locatelli, Giorgio. *Made in Sicily*. Fourth Estate, 2011.

M

Mabey, Richard. *The Full English Cassoulet*. Chatto & Windus, 2008.

Madison, Deborah. *Vegetarian Cooking for Everyone*. Broadway Books, 1997.

Majumdar, Simon. *Eating for Britain*. John Murray, 2010.

Man, Rosamond, & Weir, Robin. *The Mustard Book*. Grub Street, 2010.

Manzano, Nacho (www.ibericarestaurants.com).

Mariani, John F. *Encyclopedia of American Food*. Bloomsbury, 1983.

Marks, Gil. *Encyclopedia of Jewish Food*. John Wiley, 2010.

Martin, James. *Sweet*. Quadrille, 2015.

Martinelli, Candida (ed). *The Anonymous Andalusian Cookbook*. Translated by Charles Perry. CreateSpace, 2012.

Mason, Laura. *Sugar-plums and Sherbet*. Prospect Books, 1998.

Masters, Alexander. *The Genius in my Basement*. Fourth Estate, 2011.

Master-cooks of King Richard II. *The Forme of Cury*, 1390.

Mathiot, Ginette, & Dusoulier, Clotilde. *The Art of French Baking*. Phaidon, 2011.

Maze, Andrée (La Mazille). *La Bonne Cuisine de Périgord*. Flammarion, 1929.

McConnell, Andrew. *Cumulus Inc*. Lantern, 2011.

McGee, Harold. *McGee on Food and Cooking*. Hodder & Stoughton, 2004.

McGrady, Darren. *Eating Royally: Recipes and Remembrances from a Palace Kitchen*. Rutledge Hill Press, 2007.

McLintock, Mrs. *Mrs McLintock's Receipts for Cookery*. 1736.

McWilliams, Mark. *The Story Behind the Dish*. Greenwood, 2012.

Melville, Herman. *Moby-Dick*. Harper & Brothers, 1851.

Mendel, Janet. *My Kitchen in Spain*. William Morrow, 2002.

Merle, Gibbons, & Reich, John. *The Domestic Dictionary and Housekeeper's Manual*. William Strange, 1842.

Mollard, John. *The Art of Cookery*. Whittaker, 1836.

Molokhovets, Elena. *Classic Russian Cooking*. Indiana University Press, 1992.

Montage, Prosper. *Larousse Gastronomique* (1938). Hamlyn, 2009.

Moore, Victoria. *How to Drink*. Granta Books, 2009.

Morales, Martin. *Ceviche*. Weidenfeld & Nicolson, 2013.

Muir, John. *My First Summer in the Sierra*. Houghton Mifflin, 1911.

N

Nash, S. Elizabeth. *Cooking Craft*. Sir Isaac Pitman & Sons Ltd, 1926.

Nobu Matsuhisa, & Edwards, Mark. *Nobu West*. Quadrille, 2006.

Norman, Jill (ed). *The Cook's Book*. Dorling Kindersley, 2005.

Norrington-Davies, Tom. *Cupboard Love*. Hodder & Stoughton, 2005.

Nutt, Frederick. *The Complete Confectioner*. 1819.

O

Oliver, Garrett. *The Oxford Companion to Beer*. OUP USA, 2011.

Oliver, Jamie. *Jamie at Home*. Michael Joseph, 2007.

Oliver, Jamie. *Jamie's Italy*. Michael Joseph, 2005.

Olney, Richard. *The French Menu Cookbook*. Simon & Schuster, 1970.

O'Neill, Molly. *The New York Cookbook*. Workman, 1993.

O'Neill, Molly. *One Big Table*. Simon & Schuster, 2010.

Ono, Tadashi, & Salat, Harris. *Japanese Soul Cooking*. Jacqui Small, 2014.

Orkin, Ivan. *Ivan Ramen*. Ten Speed Press, 2013.

Ottolenghi, Yotam. *Plenty*. Ebury, 2010.

Ottolenghi, Yotam, & Tamimi, Sami. *Jerusalem*. Ebury, 2012.

Ottolenghi, Yotam, & Tamimi, Sami. *Ottolenghi: The Cookbook*. Ebury, 2008.

P

Paston-Williams, Sara. *Good Old-fashioned Puddings*. National Trust Books, 2007.

Pedroso, Celia, & Pepper, Lucy. *Eat Portugal*. Leya, 2011.

Pellacio, Zakary. *Eat With Your Hands*. Ecco Press, 2012.

Peril, Lynn. *College Girls*. W.W. Norton, 2006.

Perkins, John. *Every Woman her own Housekeeper, or The Ladies' Library*. 1796.

Peter, K.V. *Underutilized and Underexploited Horticultural Crops*. NIPA, 2007.

Peterson, James. *Sauces, Salsas & Chutneys*. Ten Speed Press, 2012.

Philp, Robert Kemp. *The Family Save-all*. 1861.

Pieroni, Andrea, & Price, Lisa Leimar. *Eating and Healing: Traditional Food as Medicine*. Routledge, 2006.

Pintabona, Don. *The Tribeca Grill Cookbook*. Villard, 2000.

Plath, Sylvia. *Collected Poems*. Faber & Faber, 1981.

Potts-Dawson, Arthur. *Eat Your Veg*. Mitchell Beazley, 2012.

Proust, Marcel. *À La Recherche du Temps Perdu*. Grasset & Gillimard, 1913–27.

Puck, Wolfgang. *Wolfgang Puck Makes it Easy*. Thomas Nelson, 2004.

Q

Quinzio, Jeri. *Of Sugar and Snow: A History of Ice Cream Making*. University of California Press, 2009.

R

Ransome, Arthur. *Swallows and Amazons*. Jonathan Cape, 1930.

Rector, George. *The Rector Cookbook*. Rector, 1928.

Reichl, Ruth (ed). *The Gourmet Cookbook*. Houghton Mifflin, 2004.

Reinhart, Peter. *Peter Reinhart's Artisan Breads Every Day*. Ten Speed Press, 2009.

Rhodes, Gary. *New British Classics*. BBC Books, 2001.

Richards, Morfudd. *Lola's Ice Creams & Sundaes*. Ebury, 2009.

Riley, Gillian. *The Oxford Companion to Italian Food*. OUP, 2007.

Roahen, Sara. *Gumbo Tales: Finding My Place at the New Orleans Table*. W.W. Norton, 2008.

Robertson, Chad. *Tartine Book No. 3*. Chronicle, 2013.

Robertson, Chad. *Tartine Bread*. Chronicle, 2010.

Robertson, Robin. *Fresh from the Vegetarian Slow Cooker*. Harvard Common Press, 2012.

Robuchon, Joël. *The Complete Robuchon*. Grub Street, 2008.

Roden, Claudia. *A New Book of Middle Eastern Food*. Penguin, 1985.

Roden, Claudia. *The Food of Italy*. Chatto & Windus, 1989.

Roden, Claudia. *The Food of Spain*. Michael Joseph, 2012.

Rodgers, Judy. *The Zuni Cafe Cookbook*. W.W. Norton, 2003.

Rombauer, Irma S. *The Joy of Cooking*. Bobbs-Merrill, 1936.

Ronay, Egon. *The Unforgettable Dishes of My Life*. Gollancz, 1989.

Root, Waverley. *Food*. Simon & Schuster, 1981.

Root, Waverley. *The Food of France*. Cassell, 1958.

Root, Waverley. *The Food of Italy*. Scribner, 1971.

Roscoe, Thomas. *The Tourist in Spain: Andalusia*. Robert Jennings, 1836.

Rose, Evelyn. *The New Complete International Jewish Cookbook*. Pavilion, 2011.

Rosengarten, Frederic. *The Book of Edible Nuts*. Walker, 1984.

Round, Jeremy. *The Independent Cook*. Barrie & Jenkins, 1989.

Roux, Michel. *Eggs*. Quadrille, 2007.

Roux, Michel. *Sauces*. Quadrille, 2009.

Roux, Michel, Jr. *Cooking with the Masterchef*. Weidenfeld & Nicolson, 2010.

Rudner, Rita. *I Still Have It... I Just Can't Remember Where I Put It*. Random House, 2008.

Ruhlman, Michael. *Ruhlman's Twenty*. Chronicle, 2011.

Ruhlman, Michael. *The Elements of Cooking*. Scribner, 2007.

Rumble, Victoria R. *Soup Through The Ages*. McFarland, 2009.

Rumpolt, Marx. *Ein new Kochbuch*. 1851.

Rundell, Mrs. *New System of Domestic Cookery*. John Murray, 1806.

S

Savage, Brent. *Bentley Contemporary Cuisine*. Murdoch Books, 2010.

Scappi, Bartolomeo. *Opéra dell'arte del cucinare*. 1570.

Schwabe, Calvin W. *Unmentionable Cuisine*. University of Virginia Press, 1995.

Scotter, Jane, & Astley, Harry. *Fern Verrow*. Quadrille, 2015.

Scully, Terrence, & Scully, D. Eleanor. *Early French Cookery*. University of Michigan Press, 1995.

Senn, Charles. *The Book of Sauces*. The Hotel Monthly Press, 1915.

Serventi, Silvano, & Saban, Françoise. *Pasta: The Story of a Universal Food*. Translated by Anthony Shugaar. Columbia University Press, 2002.

Shakespeare, Margaret M. *The Meringue Cookbook*. Van Nostrand Reinhold, 1982.

Sheraton, Mimi. *1,000 Foods to Eat Before You Die*. Workman, 2015.

Shopsin, Kenny. *Eat Me: The Food and Philosophy of Kenny Shopsin*. Knopf, 2008.

The Silver Spoon. Phaidon, 2005.

Simmons, Marie. *Taste of Honey*. Andrews McMeel, 2013.

Simon, André. *Guide to Good Food and Wines*. Collins, 1952.

Sinclair, Charles G. *International Dictionary of Food & Cooking*. Routledge, 1998.

Smith, Andrew F. *Food and Drink in American History*. ABC-CLIO, 2013.

Smith, Andrew F. *New York City: A Food Biography*. Rowman & Littlefield, 2013.

Smith, Andrew F. *The Oxford Companion to American Food and Drink*. OUP US, 2009.

Smith, Delia (www.deliaonline.com).

Smith, Delia. *Delia Smith's Complete Illustrated Cookery Course*. BBC Books, 1989.

Smith, Delia. *Delia Smith's Christmas*. BBC Books, 1994.

Smith, Delia. *Delia's Complete How to Cook*. BBC Books, 2009.

Smith, Michael. *Fine English Cookery*. Faber & Faber, 1973.

Speck, Maria. *Ancient Grains for Modern Meals*. Ten Speed Press, 2011.

Spring, Justin. *The Gourmands' Way*. Farrar, Straus & Giroux, 2017.

Spry, Constance, & Hume, Rosemary. *The Constance Spry Cookery Book*. Second edition. Grub Street, 2011.

Staib, Walter. *The City Tavern Cookbook*. Running Press, 2009.

Stein, Rick. *Rick Stein's Far Eastern Odyssey*. BBC Books, 2009.

Stein, Rick. *Rick Stein's Spain*. BBC Books, 2011.

Stevens, David. *Bread: River Cottage Handbook No. 3*. Bloomsbury, 2008.

T

This, Hervé. *Molecular Gastronomy*. Columbia University Press, 2002.

Thompson, David. *Thai Food*. Pavilion, 2002.

Thoreau, Henry David. *Walden*. Ticknor & Fields, 1854.

Thorne, John, *The Outlaw Cook*. Prospect Books, 1998.

Todhunter, Andrew. *A Meal Observed*. Knopf, 2004.

Toklas, Alice B. *The Alice B. Toklas Cookbook*. Michael Joseph, 1954.

Toussaint-Samat, Maguelonne. *A History of Food*. Blackwell, 1992.

Tsuji, Shizuo. *Japanese Cooking: A Simple Art*. Kodansha, 1980.

Tucker, Susan. *New Orleans Cuisine*. University Press of Mississippi, 2009.

Tyree, Marion Cabell. *Housekeeping in Old Virginia*. 1879.

U

Ude, Louis Eustache. *The French Cook*. 1815.

Uhlemann, Karl. *Chef's Companion*. Eyre & Spottiswoode, 1953.

V

Villas, James. *Biscuit Bliss*. Harvard Common Press, 2003.

Vongerichten, Jean-Georges, & Bittman, Mark. *Simple to Spectacular*. Broadway Books, 2000.

W

Walker, Harlan. *The Fat of the Land: Proceedings of the Oxford Symposium on Food and Cookery 2002*. Footwork, 2003.

Wallace, David Foster. *Consider the Lobster and Other Essays*. Little, Brown, 2005.

Walsh, John Henry. *The English Cookery Book*. G. Routledge & Co, 1858.

Wareing, Marcus. *Nutmeg & Custard*. Bantam Press, 2009.

Warner, Valentine. *What to Eat Now*. Mitchell Beazley, 2008.

Waugh, Evelyn. *Brideshead Revisited*. Chapman & Hall, 1945.

Wells, Robert. *The Modern Practical Bread Baker*. Simpkin, Marshall, Hamilton, Kent & Co, 1939.

White, Marco Pierre. *Marco Pierre White in Hell's Kitchen*. Ebury, 2007.

Whitley, Andrew. *Bread Matters*. Fourth Estate, 2009.

Willan, Anne. *Reader's Digest Complete Guide to Cookery*. Dorling Kindersley, 1989.

Willan, Anne. *La Varenne Pratique*. Crown, 1989.

Wolfert, Paula. *Paula Wolfert's World of Food*. HarperCollins, 1988.

Wright, Clifford A. *The Best Soups in the World*. John Wiley, 2009.

Wright, Clifford A. *Little Foods of the Mediterranean*. Harvard Common Press, 2003.

Wright, John. *Hedgerow: River Cottage Handbook No. 7*. Bloomsbury, 2010.

Wright, John. *Seashore: River Cottage Handbook No. 5*. Bloomsbury, 2009.

Y

Young, Kay. *Wild Seasons*. University of Nebraska Press, 1993.

Z

Zanini de Vita, Oretta. *Encyclopedia of Pasta*. University of California, 2009.

OTHER SOURCES

Blank, Fritz. "Cackleberries and Henfruit: A French Perspective" in *Eggs in Cookery: Proceedings of the Oxford Symposium on Food and Cookery 2006*. Prospect Books, 2007.

Brook, Stephen. "Vin Santo." *Decanter*, 1 May 2001.

Child, Julia. "'La Nouvelle Cuisine': A Skeptic's View." *New York* magazine, 4 July 1977.

Cooper, Derek. *The Listener*. Volume 94, 1975.

The Farmer's Bulletin No. 1236: Corn and Its Uses as Food. US Department of Agriculture, 1923.

The Food Journal. Volume 4, 1874.

Giornale dell'Imperiale Regio Istituto lombardo di scienze, Volumes 15–16, 1846.

Graff, Vincent. "Squirrel Salad... You must be nuts!" *Daily Mail*, 2 August 2010.

Leith, Sam. "Notebook." *Daily Telegraph*, 13 February 2004.

Myhrvold, Nathan, & Gibbs, W. Wayt, "Beer Batter is Better." *Scientific American*, 1 February 2011.

Prairie Farmer Magazine, Volume 84, 1912.

Root, Waverley. "The Pistachio—Color It Green." *The Washington Post*, 6 September 1979.

Skinner, Thomas, M.D. "The Granulation of Medicines." *Pharmaceutical Journal: A Weekly Record of Pharmacy and Allied Sciences*. Second series, Volume III, 1862, pages 572–6.

www.bbc.com/food

www.bbcgoodfoodshow.com

www.cheflovers.com

www.finedininglovers.com

www.foodandwine.com

www.greatbritishchefs.com

www.theguardian.com/lifeandstyle/food-and-drink

www.independent.co.uk/life-style/food-and-drink

www.nola.com

www.sbs.com.au/food

www.southernfoodways.com

www.telegraph.co.uk/foodanddrink

Index

Credits

Page 5 *Breakfast at the Wolseley*, by A.A. Gill. Quadrille, 2008.

Page 5 *My First Summer in the Sierra*, by John Muir. Houghton Mifflin, 1911.

Page 12 *Grimble*, by Clement Freud. Collins, 1968.

Pages 39–40 *Classic Bull: An Accidental Restaurateur's Cookbook*, by Stephen Bull. Macmillan, 2001.

Page 47 *Brideshead Revisited*, by Evelyn Waugh. Chapman & Hall, 1945.

Page 49 *English Bread and Yeast Cookery*, by Elizabeth David. Allen Lane, 1977.

Page 52 *Kitchen Essays* (1922), by Agnes Jekyll. Persephone Books, 2008.

Page 59 *English Bread and Yeast Cookery*, by Elizabeth David. Allen Lane, 1977.

Page 75 *Heat*, by Bill Buford. Jonathan Cape, 2006.

Page 75 *Between the Woods and the Water*, by Patrick Leigh Fermor. John Murray, 1986.

Page 83 *Walden*, by Henry David Thoreau. Ticknor & Fields, 1854.

Page 119 *Japanese Cooking: A Simple Art*, by Shizuo Tsuji. Kodansha, 1980.

Page 127 *Green Mangoes and Lemon Grass*, by Wendy Hutton. Kogan Page, 2003.

Page 134 *Eating for Britain*, by Simon Majumdar. John Murray, 2010.

Page 141 *Leaving Home*, by Garrison Keillor. Viking Press, 1987.

Page 146 *An Appetite for Ale*, by Fiona Beckett & Will Beckett. Camra, 2007.

Page 155 *Roast Chicken & Other Stories*, by Simon Hopkinson. Ebury, 1996.

Page 155 *The Best Soups in the World*, by Clifford A. Wright. John Wiley, 2009.

Page 155 *The Elements of Cooking*, by Michael Ruhlman. Scribner, 2007.

Page 158 *La Varenne Pratique*, by Anne Willan. Crown, 1989.

Page 162 *Floyd's American Pie*, by Keith Floyd. BBC Books, 1989.

Page 166 "Squirrel Salad… You must be nuts!' by Vincent Graff. *Daily Mail,* 2 August 2010.

Page 166 *Guide to Good Food and Wines*, by André Simon. Collins, 1952.

Page 170 *Hedgerow: River Cottage Handbook No. 7*, by John Wright. Bloomsbury, 2010.

Page 183 *The Independent Cook*, by Jeremy Round. Barrie & Jenkins, 1989.

Page 189 *Love and Kisses and a Halo of Truffles*, by James Beard. Arcade, 1995.

Page 190 *Hugh Fearlessly Eats It All*, by Hugh Fearnley-Whittingstall. Bloomsbury, 2006.

Page 190 *The Square, The Cookbook, Volume 2: Sweet*, by Philip Howard. Absolute Press, 2013.

Page 195 *Mark Rothko: Subjects in Abstraction*, by Anna C. Chave. Yale University Press, 1989.

Page 197 *Guide to Good Food and Wines*, by André Simon. Collins, 1952.

Page 202 *The Oxford Companion to Food*, by Alan Davidson. OUP, 1999.

Page 212 *The River Cottage Meat Book*, by Hugh Fearnley-Whittingstall. Hodder & Stoughton, 2004.

Page 212 *Italian Food*, by Elizabeth David. MacDonald, 1954.

Page 218 *Daniel: My French Cuisine*, by Daniel Boulud & Sylvie Bigar. Grand Central Publishing, 2013.

Page 222 *The Clatter of Forks and Spoons*, by Richard Corrigan. Fourth Estate, 2008.

Page 223 *The Unforgettable Dishes of My Life*, by Egon Ronay. Gollancz, 1989.

Page 234 *Moby-Dick*, by Herman Melville. Harper & Brothers, 1851.

Page 237 *New England Sampler*, by Eleanor Early. Waverly House, 1940.

Page 240 *Eat Portugal*, by Celia Pedroso & Lucy Pepper. Leya, 2011.

Page 242 *The Food of France*, by Waverley Root. Cassell, 1958.

Page 278 *Paula Wolfert's World of Food*, by Paula Wolfert. HarperCollins, 1988.

Page 282 *Men Without Women*, by Ernest Hemingway. Charles Scribner's Sons, 1927.

Page 283 *The Backyard Beekeeper's Honey Handbook*, by Kim Flottum. Crestline, 2009.

Page 284 *Food*, by Waverley Root. Simon & Schuster, 1981.

Page 285 *Barcelona*, by Robert Hughes. Vintage, 1992.

Page 322 *Short and Sweet*, by Dan Lepard. Fourth Estate, 2011.

Page 327 *Sugar-plums and Sherbet*, by Laura Mason. Prospect Books, 1998.

Pages 348–9 *Taste of Honey*, by Marie Simmons. Andrews McMeel, 2013.

Page 369 *I Still Have It… I Just Can't Remember Where I Put It*, by Rita Rudner. Random House, 2008.

Page 376 *Love and Kisses and a Halo of Truffles*, by James Beard. Arcade, 1995.

Page 377 *Moby-Dick*, by Herman Melville. Harper & Brothers, 1851.

Page 388 *How to Drink*, by Victoria Moore. Granta Books, 2009.

Page 406 *College Girls*, by Lynn Peril. W.W. Norton, 2006.

Page 420 *Beans: A History*, by Ken Albala. Bloomsbury, 2007.

Page 449 *Kitchen Essays* (1922), by Agnes Jekyll. Persephone Books, 2008.

Page 476 *The French Menu Cookbook*, by Richard Olney. Simon & Schuster, 1970.

Page 477 *The Gourmands' Way*, by Justin Spring. Farrar, Straus & Giroux, 2017.

Page 477 *Modern Cookery for Private Families*, by Eliza Acton. Longman, Brown, Green & Longans, 1845.

Page 513 *The Book of Sauces*, by Charles Senn. The Hotel Monthly Press, 1915.

Page 517 *Molecular Gastronomy*, by Hervé This. Columbia University Press, 2002.

Page 550 *Jane Grigson's Fruit Book*, by Jane Grigson. Michael Joseph, 1982.

Page 552 *Cooking Craft*, by S. Elizabeth Nash. Sir Isaac Pitman & Sons Ltd, 1926.

Page 553 *The English Cookery Book*, by John Henry Walsh. G. Routledge & Co, 1858.

Page 564 *Essentials of Classic Italian Cooking*, by Marcella Hazan. Knopf, 1992.

Extracts from *Breakfast at the Wolseley* by A.A. Gill reprinted by permission of Quadrille. ©2008 A.A. Gill. Extracts from *Brideshead Revisited: The Sacred and Profane Memories of Captain Charles Ryder* by Evelyn Waugh, reprinted by permission (first published by Chapman & Hall 1945, Penguin Classics 1999). ©1945 by Evelyn Waugh. Extracts from *Classic Bull: An Accidental Restaurateur's Cookbook* by Stephen Bull reproduced with permission of Pan Macmillan through PLSclear. ©2001 Stephen Bull. Extracts from *The Complete Short Stories* by Ernest Hemingway published by Jonathan Cape. Reprinted by permission of The Random House Group Ltd. ©1992. Reprinted by permission of Scribner, a division of Simon & Schuster, Inc. from *Men Without Women* by Ernest Hemingway. Copyright ©1927 by Charles Scribner's Sons. Copyright renewed 1955 by Ernest Hemingway. All rights reserved. Recipe on page 245 from *Rick Stein's Far Eastern Odyssey* by Rick Stein published by BBC Books. Reprinted by permission of The Random House Group Limited. ©2009. Recipe on page 300 from *Nigellissima* by Nigella Lawson published by Chatto & Windus. Reprinted by permission of The Random House Group Limited. ©2012. "Olive Oil & Chocolate Cake" from *Nigellissima: Easy Italian-Inspired Recipes* by Nigella Lawson, Pabulum Productions Limited. Used by permission of Clarkson Potter/Publishers, an imprint of Crown Publishing Group, a division of Penguin Random House LLC. All rights reserved. Recipe on page 358 from *How To Be A Domestic Goddess* by Nigella Lawson published by Chatto & Windus. Reprinted by permission of The Random House Group Limited. ©2000.

Acknowledgments

Thank you to my husband, Nat, who has given a vast amount of time and thought to this book. Not only do I benefit from the brilliance of his mind but the resilience of his digestive system. Comfort food can be quite threatening in large quantities: Sixteen consecutive nights of panna cotta is more of an ordeal than it sounds. I am also massively indebted to my agent, Zoë Waldie, who has been so supportive of my work over the last ten years, and somehow manages to combine wild enthusiasm with an indispensable sense of perspective. It has been as great a pleasure to work with Richard Atkinson, my commissioning editor at Bloomsbury, as it was the first time around: He has that rare ambidexterity, an equal feeling for the big picture and small detail. This book would not have been possible without his commitment to getting things just-so. Alison Cowan edited the text and recipes, an enormous task she approached with patience, deep knowledge, and a unique enthusiasm for testing anything involving lentils or beans. Also at Bloomsbury, Alexandra Pringle, Natalie Bellos, Lisa Pendreigh, Lena Hall, and Kitty Stogdon have all been an invaluable help in turning a big idea into a big book. Thanks also to Amanda Shipp, Thi Dinh, Jen Hampson, and Arlene Alexander for ushering it into the world so skillfully and stylishly.

A Practice for Everyday Life designed *Lateral Cooking* and put so much thought and craft into making an unusual book both beautiful and easy to use. I don't think I ever left their offices without a smile on my face.

As one of his many thousands of fans, I asked Yotam Ottolenghi to write the foreword because there's no one who better encapsulates the pleasures of creativity in the kitchen, and the part food writing might play in the process. I get a little ping of happiness every time I see his name on the cover.

Deiniol Pritchard at The Fat Duck and Lucy Thomas at Tastemakers were generous enough to help me with a number of food-science questions. And I must thank all the cooks, chefs, authors, and bloggers I've read and consulted, for their tips, hints, and explanations. Out of a combined sense of paranoia and control freakery I have for the past seven and a half years refused to tell anyone, other than the select band of collaborators who needed to know, what this book was about. I must now offer my apologies to the friends who still bothered to ask me, year in, year out, how it was going, and put up with answers as nonspecific as they were long-winded: Dudi Appleton, Polly Astor, Alexei Boltho, Emma Booty, Pete Brown, David Foy, James Lever, John Lowery, Kerry Millet, Antonia Quirke, Clare Reihill, and Liz Vater. Thanks to you all for the support, late nights, and long lunches. In the latter half of the long haul, Bruna Dos Reis and Eleanor Hardy helped make the writing possible by keeping two small children (and often their mother) entertained.

Thank you to Norma MacMillan, who took on the unenviable task of helping to translate the book for the American audience. And to Laura Phillips and Lea Beresford at Bloomsbury USA, who helped prepare and launch this edition with great patience and enthusiasm. I'm also much indebted to my brother-in-law, Seymour Segnit, and to Toni Bodonji, who did such a great job upgrading my website.

Finally, this book is dedicated to my very special friend Sarah-Jane Ingram. It was SJ and her friend Beverley, on a holiday in the South of France many years ago, who made me want to learn to cook. Admittedly the motivation was more attracting boys than perfecting my cheese soufflé, but in time the secondary benefit displaced the first, and furnished a hobby that has given me daily pleasure and the privilege of having written two books.

About the author

Niki Segnit's first book, *The Flavor Thesaurus*, won the André Simon Award for best food book, the UK Guild of Food Writers Award for best first book, and was shortlisted for the Galaxy National Book Awards. It has been translated into thirteen languages. On BBC Radio 4, she has contributed to *The Food Programme*, *Woman's Hour,* and *Word of Mouth*, and her columns, features, and reviews have appeared in the *Guardian*, the *Observer*, the *Times*, the *Times Literary Supplement*, the *Sunday Times,* and *Prospect* magazine. She lives in London with her husband and two children.

BLOOMSBURY PUBLISHING
Bloomsbury Publishing Plc
1385 Broadway, New York, New York, 11218

BLOOMSBURY, **BLOOMSBURY PUBLISHING** and the Diana logo are trademarks
of Bloomsbury Publishing Plc

First published in Great Britain in 2018
This edition published in the United States in 2019
Text © Niki Segnit, 2018 and 2019
Foreword © Yotam Ottolenghi, 2018
Illustrations © A Practice for Everyday Life, 2018

Library of Congress Cataloging-in-Publication info is available.

ISBN: HB: 978-1-63557-264-3
eBook: 978-1-63557-441-8

2 4 6 8 10 9 7 5 3 1

PROJECT EDITOR Alison Cowan
DESIGNER A Practice for Everyday Life
ILLUSTRATOR A Practice for Everyday Life
INDEXER Vicki Robinson
PRINTED AND BOUND in China

To find out more about our authors and books visit www.bloomsbury.com and sign up
for our newsletters.